ENCYCLOPEDIA OF
POLITICAL THOUGHT

ENCYCLOPEDIA OF POLITICAL THOUGHT

GARRETT WARD SHELDON

® Facts On File, Inc.

Encyclopedia of Political Thought

Facts On File, Inc.
132 West 31st Street
New York NY 10001

Library of Congress Cataloging-in-Publication Data
Encyclopedia of political thought / [edited] by Garrett Ward Sheldon.
p. cm.
Includes bibliographical references and index.
ISBN 0-8160-4351-5
1. Political science—Encyclopedias. 2. Political science—History—Encyclopedias.
3. World politics—Encyclopedias. I. Sheldon, Garrett Ward, 1954–
JA61.E52 2001
320'.03—dc21   2001023590

Facts On File books are available at special discounts when purchased in bulk quantities for businesses, associations, institutions or sales promotions. Please call our Special Sales Department in New York at 212/967-8800 or 800/322-8755.

You can find Facts On File on the World Wide Web at
http://www.factsonfile.com

Text and cover design by Cathy Rincon

Printed in the United States of America.

VB FOF 10 9 8 7 6 5 4 3 2 1

This book is printed on acid-free paper.

CONTENTS

LIST OF
CONTRIBUTORS

PATRICK HAYDEN is an assistant professor of philosophy at New England College, New Hampshire.

TOM LANSFORD is an assistant professor of political science at New England College, New Hampshire.

WAYNE LESPERANCE is an assistant professor of political science at New England College, New Hampshire.

PAUL VOICE is an assistant professor of philosophy at Bennington College, Vermont.

PREFACE

This *Encyclopedia of Political Thought* is intended to present, in clear and concise form, the many ideas, concepts, persons, and movements in the world's political history. It covers everything from abstract ideals (like *freedom* and *justice*) to major thinkers (Aristotle, St. Thomas Aquinas, Locke, Marx) and contemporary movements (feminism, environmentalism, pacifism) from around the world (Western, Indian, Islamic, Chinese).

Political ideas and theories have always informed practical political change, and it is my hope that this encyclopedia leads to greater understanding of political concepts what will contribute to a more just and peaceful world. In many ways, it is a more detailed treatment of my book *The History of Political Theory.*

I am grateful to the several scholars who contributed some of the articles in this volume. My editor at Facts On File, Owen Lancer, has been a great help in this endeavor, and the excellent manuscript preparation by Linda Meade is very appreciated.

"veritas vos liberabit"

—Garrett Ward Sheldon
Editor

A

abolition

The movement to abolish SLAVERY, while most notable in the United States, can trace its origins to other countries such as the United Kingdom. Although most abolitionist activity occurred in these two countries, antislavery efforts were under way throughout most of Europe. In Britain, for example, abolitionists worked to end the international slave trade and to free slaves in the British colonies. Unlike the United States, slavery had never flourished in the United Kingdom. Many English did, however, prosper as a result of the slave trade to the colonies. William Wilberforce, a statesman and orator, headed the antislavery movement in England. In 1807, he helped persuade Parliament to pass a bill outlawing the slave trade. In 1833, another bill abolished slavery throughout the British Empire.

Between the 15th and the 19th centuries, an estimated total of 15 million Africans were forcibly transported to the Americas. U.S. antislavery efforts may be traced back to its early settlements. Among some colonials, slavery was viewed with considerable disdain. In the 1680s, for example, Quakers in Pennsylvania condemned slavery on moral grounds. In the late 1700s, several prominent founding fathers of the American Revolution, including Thomas Jefferson and Patrick Henry, not only spoke out against slavery but suggested the emancipation of slaves as part of the new Republic's CONSTITUTION.

Serious antislavery efforts, however, did not emerge until the formation of the American Colonization Society in 1816. This organization led antislavery protests during the early 1800s. It sought to repatriate freed slaves back to Liberia. The first periodicals dedicated to the abolition movement were published by Elihu Embree in 1819. This Jonesboro, Tennessee, based weekly newspaper called for the immediate emancipation of Africans living in the United States. Embree also established *The Emancipator* in 1820. Eleven years later, in 1831, William Lloyd Garrison, one of the best known abolitionists, published another newspaper, *The Liberator.* Garrison's demand for the immediate FREEDOM of slaves was well received and supported by the American Anti-Slavery Society, which was founded in 1833. Despite bitter opposition by southern slave states, the abolition movement spread throughout the northeastern United States. Violent opposition to the movement surfaced with the murder, in 1837, of Elijah P. Lovejoy by an angry mob. Lovejoy, a newspaper editor in Illinois, had published antislavery editorials.

The situation in the United States was complex because the social and economic base of the 11 southern states was agrarian and labor intensive. Furthermore, in the era of "Cotton is King," southern slave owners were reluctant to do away with the extremely lucrative cotton-based agriculture. Finally, in response to growing abolitionist attacks, the South intensified its system of slave control, particularly after the Nat Turner revolt of 1831. By that time, U.S. abolitionists realized the failure of gradualism and persuasion, and they subsequently turned to a more militant policy, demanding immediate abolition by LAW.

By the late 1830s and early 1840s, abolition efforts took on a new form. In addition to the traditional activism, which was the hallmark of the movement, abolitionists took more direct action such as seeking public offices and establishing new political parties such as the Liberty Party and the Free-Soil Party. After 1854, most abolitionists supported the party of Lincoln, the Republican Party, because of its northern roots and antislavery platform.

With the onset of the American Civil War in 1861, abolitionists urged the North to make abolition one of its wartime goals. Their efforts were rewarded in 1863 when President Abraham Lincoln issued the Emancipation Proclamation. Although not comprehensive, the proclamation declared slaves freed in most of the Southern states. It was not until 1865 with the passage of the Thirteenth Amendment to the Constitution that slavery was abolished throughout the United States.

Further Reading
Jones, Howard. *All On Fire: William Lloyd Garrison and the Abolition of Slavery.* New York: St. Martin's Press, 1998.

abortion

The ending of a pregnancy by surgical or chemical removal of the fetus from the woman. The intense political debate caused in the United States by the Supreme Court's decision in the case of *Roe v. Wade* (1973), which decriminalized abortion but placed restrictions on when during pregnancy the procedure could be performed, has been compared to that over abolition of slavery in the early 1800s. Positions on the abortion issue revolve around the pro-choice view that a fetus is part of the woman's body, not a separate human being, and that, therefore, government laws should not prevent her from aborting or disposing of it; and the pro-life view that the preborn fetus is a human being in development with rights to continued life and that, therefore, abortion is the murder of inno-

cent human life, requiring legal protection. Both sides agree that abortion is a moral issue but dispute whether the individual woman or society at large should make the decision whether or not abortion is allowed. Liberal Democrats, women's rights groups, and mainline PROTESTANT churches in the United States (Presbyterian, Episcopal, Lutheran) have tended to be "pro-choice"; conservative Republicans, the CATHOLIC Church, and EVANGELICAL Christians have tended to be "pro-life." As the U.S. SUPREME COURT became increasingly conservative in the 1980s and 1990s, its rulings on abortion allowed greater restrictions on abortions by state legislatures. The social debate over abortion continues to be intense.

Further Reading
Hunter, James Davison. *Before the Shooting Begins.* New York: Free Press, 1994.

absolutism

The idea that a ruler or government has absolute or total power. This implies that no other persons, groups, or institutions have power. Examples of absolutism include absolute monarchs like King Louis XIV of France, Nazi leader Adolf HITLER of Germany, and Soviet communist dictator Joseph STALIN. In each case, the absolutist leader is not limited or restrained by any other individual or power. Limits on an absolutist ruler or government might come from (1) other people with power who counteract the ruler's authority; (2) legal or constitutional limits on a ruler's power; (3) other institutions or groups (political parties, the church, labor unions) who challenge the absolute power of the state. This is why most absolutist leaders and governments make all other people and institutions dependent on them. So in Nazi Germany, the Boy Scouts became The Hitler Youth; in Communist Russia, the Boy Scouts became the Communist Youth League. All private social organizations (clubs, fraternities, churches) become attached to the state and under its control. A main writer on absolutism, Thomas HOBBES, argues that the state must have absolute control of individuals, property, information, and police to prevent ANARCHY and chaos. Other arguments in favor of an absolutist state include DIVINE RIGHT OF KINGS (which says that God has placed a certain person or family in power as his representative on earth); the COMMUNIST dictatorship of the proletariat (in which the working class or its representative party rules with absolute power to accomplish economic socialism); FASCIST nationalism (as in NAZI Germany where racial purity is achieved by a certain "pure" [Aryan] leader). In each of these cases, the absolute ruler is not restrained by law, other rulers, custom, or God. In actual fact, most of these absolute governments were limited by some other social groups or forces (the social elite, businesses, the church, or, ultimately, military defeat by other nations).

Historically, the concept of an absolutist state occurs in the early Modern period (1600–1700s) in reaction to the monarchs in France, Germany, Russia, and Britain. These monarchies of the Middle Ages asserted their absolute authority as their actual power was declining with the rise of industrialism, republican government, and the middle class. Sir Robert FILMER in England and Bishop Bossuet in France argued that kings were God's vice regents—to be given absolute respect and obedience. The rule of these divine kings was considered always just and good for the whole society. During the Middle Ages (A.D. 500–1500) the Roman CATHOLIC Church in Europe and the Eastern Orthodox Church in Russia tended to support this view of absolute authority of the king (or czar) under the ultimate authority of God. With the rise of modern REPUBLICANISM (in Parliament in England and the Estates General in France), absolutism was challenged with the ideals of popular SOVEREIGNTY of the governed and the rule of law.

The U.S. Constitution with its system of CHECKS AND BALANCES, which deliberately divides power among different branches and levels of government, is a direct response to absolutist government. From PURITAN thinkers John LOCKE and John CALVIN, whose teachings influenced the founding of the U.S. Constitution, came a suspicion of human nature as inherently sinful and domineering. Therefore, the source of absolutist government was really in human nature itself—a universal desire of every person to be in control and to dominate others. The solution for this human tendency to want all power was to separate and divide power constitutionally (such as between legislative, executive, and judicial branches of the state) and, in the words of James MADISON, to "pit ambition against ambition," or counteract power with other power in society. This institutional solution to absolutism relies less on human virtue and more on formal rules and procedures to prevent concentration of absolutist political power.

Further Readings
Barnes, Thomas Garden. *Renaissance, Reformation, and Absolutism.* Lanham, Md.: University Press of America, 1979.
Daly, J. *The Idea of Absolute Monarchy in Seventeenth-Century England.* 1978.
Durand, G. *What is Absolutism?* In *Louis XIV and Absolutism,* R. Hutton, ed. Columbus: Ohio State University Press, 1976.
Franklin, J. *Jean Bodin and the Rise of Absolutist Theory in France.* Cambridge, Eng.: Cambridge University Press, 1973.
Harris, R. W. *Absolutism and Enlightenment.* London: Blandford Press, 1964.
Jones, Richard H. *The Royal Policy of Richard II: Absolutism in the later Middle Ages.* New York: Barnes & Noble, 1968.
Slavin, Arthur Joseph. *The New Monarchies and Representative Assemblies: Medieval Constitutionalism or Modern Absolutism?* Boston: Heath, 1964.

activism/activist

The involvement of a citizen in a social cause or political movement. A person who engages in social activism is often called an activist. Such social involvement, which ranges from public demonstrations and marches, to publishing tracts and newsletters, to lobbying public officials and news media, has become common in Western democratic countries in the 20th century. Some common movements associated with activism include the civil rights movement, the women's movement, environmentalism or the Green movement, and the gay and lesbian rights movement. Activists are often portrayed as liberal or even radical, and activism as usually critical of the existing social order or morals. Although activism had more positive connotations during the liberal 1960–70s era, it has acquired generally more negative images among conservatives during the 1980–90s. Activists are sometimes portrayed as heroic, at other times as fanatical.

activism, judicial

The practice of courts, especially federal courts in the United States, to use legal conflicts to determine social policy. Rather than seeing the judicial process as limited to criminal or civil disputes between individuals, judicial activism sees the courts as applying law (or the CONSTITUTION) to social issues, such as racial or gender equality, education, prison conditions, and environmental quality. The classic example of judicial activism was the U.S. Supreme Court decision in the case of *Brown v. Board of Education* in 1954, in which all public schools in the United States were ordered to integrate black and white students, ending racial segregation. Since then, U.S. federal courts have used legal issues to legislate policy over voting districts, job safety, prison conditions, and environmental matters. Critics of judicial activism (which is often associated with the Supreme Court under Chief Justice Earl Warren, or "the Warren Court") argue that it exceeds the proper role and authority of the courts and takes power from the legislature. Judicial activism, therefore, raises fundamental questions about the distribution of power among the various branches of government (legislative, executive, and judicial) and the roles of each branch of government relative to the others. U.S. FEDERALISM involves a system of CHECKS AND BALANCES that cause the different functions of the various branches of government to impinge on each other and, to a certain extent, to overlap each other, which makes it difficult to define exact limits of authority in each branch. Arguments over the extent of the courts' role and authority are consequently highlighted by judicial activism.

Acton, John Emerich Dalbery (Lord) (1834–1902)   *British historian and politician*

Commonly referred to as Lord Acton, he is best known for the phrase "Power tends to corrupt; absolute power tends to corrupt absolutely." This famous statement, often quoted by critics of concentrated political authority, expresses Acton's basic philosophy. As an English Catholic, he expressed a belief in the sinful nature of people, of the tendency of all humans to want power and to use it to dominate and oppress others; therefore, he believed it good to limit the authority of any state or person, as holding power tends to "corrupt" an individual or to bring out their worst qualities (pride, arrogance, vanity, tyranny). Like Edmund BURKE, he was critical of the ROUSSEAU idea of powerful central government and of the brutal use of state power in the French Revolution. He appreciated the American and PURITAN ideals of liberty of thought and freedom of conscience; Acton saw the British and American ideals of divided power, mixed governance, and pluralism as preventing tyranny and abuse of authority. Like James MADISON's conception of countervailing forces and CHECKS AND BALANCES in both society and the state, Lord Acton approved of wide distribution of power to preserve individual liberty. These lib-

eral ideals made Acton a popular resource against 20th-century TOTALITARIAN regimes (FASCISM and COMMUNISM).

Acton grew up in a Catholic English family of minor nobility and attended a university in Munich, Germany. In 1895, he became the regius professor of history at Cambridge University. He was familiar with leading British public figures, including Foreign Secretary Granville, Prime Minister Gladstone, and Queen Victoria. He saw the church as a check on state power and attended the Vatican Council in Rome, where he opposed the doctrine of papal infallibility in 1870. He edited the Catholic magazine, *The Rambler.* Through his students at Cambridge, Lord Acton greatly influenced ideas of liberty and pluralism in the 20th century.

Further Readings

Acton, Lord, ed. *Essays on Freedom and Power.* New York: World Publishing, 1948.
———. *Essays on Church and State,* ed. D. Woodruff. New York: Viking Press, 1952.
Fothergill, Brian, ed. *Essays by Diverse Hands: Being the Transactions of the Royal Society of Literature,* New Series, vol. XLI. London: Royal Society of Literature, 1980.
Himmelfarb, G. *Lord Acton: A Study in Conscience and Politics.* Chicago: University of Chicago Press, 1952.
Matthew, D. *Lord Acton and His Times.* Tuscaloosa: University of Alabama Press, 1968.

Adams, John (1735–1826)   *U.S. president and political thinker*

Born in then British colony Massachusetts of an English PURITAN family and educated at Harvard College, Adams was actively involved in the American Revolution, he served in the Continental Congress, contributed to the DECLARATION OF INDEPENDENCE, negotiated the peace treaty with Great Britain, and was the first U.S. ambassador to the United Kingdom. Adams was vice president to the first U.S. president, George Washington, and succeeded him as the second president of the United States (1797–1800). He lost a second term as president to his political rival, Thomas JEFFERSON. Both Adams and Jefferson died on the 50th anniversary of the Declaration of Independence, July 4, 1826. Adams was a leader in the early FEDERALIST Party, which included George Washington and Alexander HAMILTON and advocated the U.S. CONSTITUTION, a strong national government (as opposed to states rights) and a strong executive branch or presidency (as opposed to legislative or congressional power). As president, his initiation of the Alien and Sedition Acts, which suppressed freedom of speech and press that were critical of his administration, proved unpopular and helped Thomas Jefferson and the Democratic–Republican Party supplant the Federalists as the leading political party in America in the early 1800s (Presidents Jefferson, MADISON, and Monroe). Adams is also the father of a kind of political dynasty that included his son John Quincy Adams (sixth president of the United States), Charles Francis Adams (U.S. diplomat), and Henry Adams (U.S. historian), a distinguished American family in the public and business life of the United States.

John Adams wrote two books on political theory: *Defence of the Constitutions of the Government of the United States* (1787) and *Discourses of Davila* (1791), along with political pamphlets and numerous letters (including an extended, late-in-life correspondence with his political rival Thomas Jefferson.

Inheriting a view of human nature from his Puritan ancestors and John CALVIN as sinful and vain, Adams maintained that people are motivated by "the passion for distinction" or social prominence. Human selfishness and pride, in the traditional CHRISTIAN sense, lead people to seek honors, distinctions, and the adulation of others; this causes rivalries, ambitions, and conflicts. Society and government should be organized to control sinful ambitions (particularly of the poor's resentment of the rich, the ignorant's envy of the well educated, and the obscure's hatred of the famous). He admired the conservative British constitution with its mix of monarchy, aristocracy, and democracy and wanted the U.S. government to imitate that regime (through the president, the Senate, and the House of Representatives). This aristocratic approach to U.S. politics offended many common people who preferred the more equalitarian system of Jefferson's DEMOCRATIC PARTY. But Adams regarded the common run of citizens as poor, ignorant, and fickle; envious of the rich and educated; and willing to use the government to redistribute wealth and power to themselves. Pure democracy for Adams, then, was destructive and anarchic. A system that elevated a "natural ARISTOCRACY" to positions of government was necessary for the United States to be a just and prosperous country. For Adams, this natural aristocracy was the talented and virtuous in society, who were qualified to rule by dint of their prominent family background, education, and wealth. In Adams's ideal U.S. Constitution, these aristocratic

John Adams, second president of the United States of America.
(PAINTED BY E. SAVAGE IN 1800, LIBRARY OF CONGRESS)

rulers would occupy the Senate, the presidency, and the judiciary, providing a check and healthy restraint on the popular assembly (House of Representatives) and state governments. This was necessary for a stable, honest society because if the majority of people (who are poor) controlled the state, they would use it to redistribute wealth to themselves through taxes and bankruptcy laws, thereby injuring the thrifty, wise, and hardworking citizens and causing the "idle, the vicious, the intemperate" to "rush into the utmost extravagance of debauchery," and greed. For Adams, redistributing wealth would only encourage sloth, and soon the clever and thrifty would become wealthy again and the lazy become poor, requiring another redistribution of wealth by the state. He maintained that the right to private property was as sacred as "the laws of God" and, after British thinker John LOCKE, regarded a state that did not protect property as unjust.

Adams's proud and haughty behavior as president alienated many of his Federalist supporters as well as the common people.

Further Readings

Howe, J. R. Jr., *The Changing Political Thought of John Adams.* Princeton, N.J.: Princeton University Press, 1966.
Paynter, J. *John Adams: On the Principles of Political Science.* 1976.

Wood, G. S. *The Creation of the American Republic.* New York: Norton, 1969.

Zvesper, J. *Political Philosophy and Rhetoric: a Study of the Origins of American Party Politics.* New York: Cambridge University Press, 1977.

African American

The term *African American* is a relatively modern one. Put simply, it describes Americans of African origin. However, the term is incomplete in several regards. First, it does not include nonblack African Americans of Semitic origin. Second, it does not reflect the significant diversity within the group it seeks to describe: African Americans in Mississippi may have little in common with their counterparts in New York or Portland, for example.

The term is better understood as a symbol of empowerment among black Americans. Historically, blacks in America referred to themselves as African. Throughout the 18th and 19th centuries, the term *African American* did not exist. This group was referred to themselves simply as Africans. For example, the African Methodist Episcopal Church, formed in the late 18th century, used the term *African* to describe black people.

Names or labels for former slaves have always been mutable. As a result of the historic and contemporary influences of RACISM, African Americans sought their own label or identity. Instead of having a variety of names such as *colored, negro, black,* or the extremely derogatory term *nigger* forced on them, this community in the early 1900s sought the label of either *Afro* or *African American* in an effort to take ownership of their collective identity. This new term would not only refer to the descendants of slaves brought to the "New World" in chains, but would also include their contemporary immigrants brought to the Americas in search of economic and political opportunity.

Like many other ethnic Americans, African Americans use this label as an organizing reference for general notions of culture, language, religion, values, and identity that has served to influence American history. Indeed, in the realm of politics, economics, religion, culture, music, dance, and theater, the impact of African Americans is significant. One notable scholar argued that the 20th century, often termed the American century, would be better described as the African-American century because of the impact of that particular community.

Contemporary African-American thought centers around the enduring issue of equality. A broad debate within the community is taking place concerning the issues of middle-class African Americans, the continued breakdown of families, and notions of empowerment and identity. Chief among the debaters are prominent African-American thinkers such as Cornell West, Jesse JACKSON, Henry Louis Gates, and Kweisi Mfume.

Further Reading
West, Cornell. *Race Matters.* Auburn, Calif.: Audio Partners, 1994.

Albertus Magnus, St. (1200–1280) *Medieval theologian and philosopher*

Albertus entered the Dominican Order at Padua in 1223. He taught at several Catholic schools (including at Cologne, where St. Thomas AQUINAS was his student). Like Aquinas, Magnus drew from a vast store of theology and philosophy (Arabic, Jewish, Greek, and Augustinian). This synthesis of philosophy and CHRISTIAN theology greatly affected the changing views of political thought in the West in the Middle Ages. Particularly, his use of ARISTOTLE's political ideals within the context of the church of the Middle Ages changed the outlook of Western Christianity. St. Thomas Aquinas fully developed this synthesis in his *Summa Theologica.* In 1260, Magnus was elected bishop of Ratisbon, but he resigned from this administrative work to devote his life to writing and scholarship. He was canonized and proclaimed a doctor of the church by Pope Pius XI in 1931.

alienation

The idea of being an alien or stranger in one's own world—of feeling lonely, strange, or of not belonging in one's surroundings. This concept of alienation is present in much of Western political thought, but especially in MARXIST communist sociology theory. The earliest representation of this concept in the West is found in Judeo-CHRISTIAN religion where individual persons are separated from God by their willful sin and rebellion against God's law (the Ten Commandments, etc.). Because human happiness and fulfillment requires being close to God, one's creator, the alienation from God through sin and selfishness produces misery and destruction. The Jewish people overcame this separation from God by sacrifices and rituals designed to restore the proper, loving relationship between God and humanity. For Christians, the sin of humanity demands a punishment, which Jesus Christ, the Son of God, provides through his death by crucifixion on the cross. Through faith in that death and restoration to life through the Resurrection of Christ, the believer receives forgiveness from God and restoration of a right relationship with the Lord. Through realization of the love of God through Christ and the indwelling of the Holy Spirit in believers, the alienation between God and humans is eliminated, and people can have the joy of heaven even on earth. More recent sociological concepts of alienation are not that optimistic or spiritual.

Roman law, and later, European and English law, viewed alienation in terms of the holding or selling ("separating") of property or persons. The Latin term *alienare* means, "to remove or take away." So, to separate legally a person's possessions or rights to property (or liberty, in the case of slaves) becomes a kind of alienation, and because some kinds of property or rights could not be taken away, they came to be known as inalienable, as in Thomas JEFFERSON's phrase in the DECLARATION OF INDEPENDENCE of "inalienable rights" to life, liberty, and the pursuit of happiness. Having other legal rights or possessions taken away has been described as being alienated, such as the term in civil law *alienation of affection* when, for example, one woman sues another woman for stealing her husband.

Philosophy and sociology in the 19th and 20th centuries use alienation more in economic, social, and psychological ways. For the German philosopher HEGEL, humanity goes through continual separations in history, much as a child does from parents and schools. Karl MARX, the father of communism, saw alienation primarily in social and economic terms. People in industrial society are alienated in four ways. Because Marxism sees humanity as an economic producer, our alienation in CAPITALIST society is estrangement from (1) the product of our work because our labor is not performed freely and creatively so that we do not recognize or understand it; (2) the human nature, which is meant to produce freely but is in bondage to forced work; (3) nature itself, which humanity is supposed to subdue and control but which enslaves humans; and (4) other humans because capitalism forces individuals to compete and fight with each other while they are supposed to cooperate in fulfilling everyone's needs and control nature and society. COMMUNIST society is sup-

posed to overcome all of these forms of alienation, producing happy, creative, and fulfilled people. The historical experience of communist countries did not confirm this theory, but it continued in much of sociological and CRITICAL ideas.

In the 20th century, EXISTENTIAL philosophy extended the concept of alienation to the human condition, regardless of historical or social situation. By nature, humans are lonely and incomplete, separated and estranged. This existentialist view sees no hope in God, faith, psychology, economics, or politics. It recommends the acceptance of a depressing aloneness, an inevitable emptiness in human life. It claims that any belief to the contrary (hope in God, community, or economics) is unrealistic and "bad faith." Jean-Paul SARTRE's books *Roads to Freedom,* Albert CAMUS's *The Stranger,* and Colin Wilson's *The Outsider* all reflect this pessimistic, hopelessness of existentialism that claims to be "courageous" rather than foolishness or self-pity.

Further Readings
Feuer, L. *What Is Alienation? The Career of a Concept.* Spring 1962.
Fromm, E. *The Sane Society.* New York: Fawcett, New York: Holt, Rinehart and Winston, 1955.
Lichtheim, G. "Alienation." In *International Encyclopedia of the Social Sciences,* vol. I. David L. Sills, ed.. New York: Macmillan, 1968, 264–68.
Lukes, Steven. "Alienation and anomie." In *Philosophy, Politics and Society,* 3rd ser., P. Laslett and W. G. Runciman, eds. New York: Barnes & Noble, 1967.
Marx, K. "Estranged labour." In *The Economic and Philosophic Manuscripts of 1844.* New York: International Publishers, 1964.
Ollman, B. *Alienation: Marx's Conception of Man in Capitalist Society.* New York: Cambridge University Press, 1970.
Schacht, R. *Alienation,* 1st ed. London: Allen & Unwin, 1970.
Schwalbe, Michael L. *The Psychosocial Consequences of Natural and Alienated Labor.* New York: State University of New York Press, 1986.
Weisskopf, Walter A. *Alienation and Economics.* New York: Dutton, 1971.
Wright, James D. *The Dissent of the Governed: Alienation and Democracy in America.* San Diego, Calif.: Academic Press, 1976.

Althusser, Louis (1918–1990) *French philosopher and political theorist*

Born in Birmandreïs, Algeria, Althusser later served in the French military during World War II and spent five years in a German prisoner-of-war camp. Following the war, Althusser studied philosophy at the prestigious École Normale Supérieure in Paris, where he later also taught as a professor. He joined the French Communist Party in 1948 and became widely known for his contributions to the theoretical debates concerning MARXISM during the 1960s and 1970s. His major works include *For Marx* (1965) and *Reading Capital* (1968). Althusser's popularity declined in the early 1980s when he was confined to a psychiatric institution for three years after strangling his wife in 1980.

Althusser's Marxist theory was influenced by structuralism, which views social and cultural structures as complex systems of differentially related elements organized according to their own specific rules. For Althusser, structuralist Marxism differs from traditional Marxism in two significant respects: It is antihumanist and antieconomist. First, according to Althusser, HUMANISM privileges the notion of an individual subject or consciousness that precedes social experience and action. However, Marx's work demonstrated that consciousness is determined primarily by class location and social conflicts associated with the prevailing mode of production. Thus, Althusser insists that social structures should not be considered as the intentional products of subjects who possess a pregiven human nature, but that human subjects are produced by existing social conditions. In particular, IDEOLOGY plays a fundamental role as a determining force shaping consciousness. The dominant capitalist mode of production reproduces itself, for example, by forming individuals with an ideological consciousness appropriate to the social division of labor and to the desires and habits of material consumption and accumulation. In other words, individual human behavior becomes an effect rather than a simple cause of the existing social structure in which it is located, even though the ideological framework leads individuals to consider themselves as self-determining agents.

Second, Althusser rejected economic determinism, or "economism," the conventional Marxist doctrine of the economic system being the most important driving force in determining the organization of society and its political, legal, and cultural components. Althusser argued instead that the structure of society consists of relatively autonomous levels (the ideological, political, cultural, and so forth) that can function and can be analyzed, independent of the economic system. Each level functions as a mode of production whose fundamental characteristics distinguish it from other levels. One consequence of Althusser's argument was a challenge to the Marxist theory of HISTORICAL

MATERIALISM, according to which, historical progress is necessarily determined by economic conflict between the ruling class and the oppressed classes of each form of society. Such a straightforward account of historical progress is surely misleading, Althusser suggested, given the "interpellation" of ideology and the relative autonomy of science, religion, law, education, and other ideological state apparatuses. Nevertheless, Althusser's critique was tempered by his claims that the "effectivity" of the relatively autonomous levels of society is, in the end, determined by the economy and that the later Marx himself recognized the complexity of historical change following a radical "epistemological break" with his early humanistic theory.

Further Reading
Smith, S. *Reading Althusser: An Essay on Structural Marxism.* Ithaca, N.Y.: Cornell University Press, 1984.

American political thought

The political ideas dominant during the almost 400 years since Europeans settled on the North American continent and what became the United States of America. American political thought is diverse in origin and historical development, but certain dominant themes of DEMOCRACY, EQUALITY, INDIVIDUALISM, religion, and progress characterize uniquely "American" political theory when compared with European, Asian, or African.

The earliest American political thought was simply an extension of the prevailing British government: an absolute MONARCHY, limited representative Parliament, FEUDALISM, and an official Protestant state church. The British colonies in North America were ruled with royal governors under royal charters, beginning with those of Queen Elizabeth I. All land and authority was granted by the Crown and protected by the British military.

The first uniquely American political thought came with the PURITAN English settlements in Massachusetts. Their governing document, the MAYFLOWER COMPACT is considered the first written CONSTITUTION in America. The Puritans were English Calvinists who worked to achieve a pure, uncorrupted CHRISTIAN church and Christian community. The Mayflower Compact declared the Puritan intent to create the colony "for the glory of God, and the advancement of the Christian faith" and to frame "just and equal laws, ordinances, acts, Constitutions and offices" which would further that end and to which they promised "all due submission and obedience." From the beginning, this Puritan political thought was more democratic than the British monarchy, from the Calvinist Christian theology that held all individuals equal before God as creatures of God. An early governor of Massachusetts, John WINTHROP, described this Puritan ideal of a Christian commonwealth in his writings and speeches. He saw the community as in a covenant with God, as those covenants in the Bible between the Lord and his people. As in the Old Testament covenants, the people promise to live according to God's law, and God, in return, promises to bless and protect them. Governors, then, covenant or contract with the people to rule them justly, and citizens agree to obey and respect them. Thus, Winthrop makes a distinction between "natural LIBERTY," which is the sinful human's freedom to do whatever he wants, and "moral liberty" which is the individual's freedom to follow God's law and will and be blessed. The government, for Puritans, must only preserve that "moral liberty" because it leads to peace, order and happiness; the natural liberty of sinful humans leads to selfishness, crime, and destruction. For the Puritans, the devil is continually tempting individuals to sin and trying to destroy the Christian commonwealth, so vigilance and prayer are continually necessary.

Puritan political thought dominated New England through the 1600s and early 1700s, but by the time of the American Revolution in 1776, it had been supplemented there and in other American colonies by other political ideologies.

Scholars still debate the exact origins and ideals of early American political thought, but general agreement has settled on three main sources of that theory: (1) Calvinist CHRISTIANITY; (2) the British liberalism of John LOCKE; and (3) REPUBLICANISM that is CLASSICAL. Calvinist Christianity, like the New England Puritans, also dominated the Presbyterian and Reformed churches in the middle and southern American colonies with its covenant theology, individualism, and resistance to monarchy. The philosophical liberalism of John Locke, with its belief that individuals possess natural rights (to life, liberty, and property) and form a government through a SOCIAL CONTRACT, which is limited to protecting those rights, was popular in the American colonies. Classical Republican ideas came from ancient Greek and Roman philosophers (such as ARISTOTLE and CICERO) and emphasized the virtue of small democratic communities in which all citizens

helped in governing. All of these ideas contributed to the case for the American Revolution against the British Empire and national independence for the new United States. Calvinist Christians feared the established Church of England and Roman CATHOLIC Church, Lockean liberalism portrayed the British Parliament and king as violating the rights of the American colonists, and classical Republican ideals saw the empire as corrupt and immoral. The combination of these ideologies united most Americans against Great Britain (as, for example, expressed in Thomas JEFFERSON's famous DECLARATION OF INDEPENDENCE.)

After America won its independence from Great Britain, the idea of the Revolutionary era found expression in conflicting views of the new U.S. government. Two main parties emerged at this time, each with a distinct theory of democracy: The FEDERALISTS (such as George Washington, James MADISON, and Alexander HAMILTON) favored a strong national government over the states to protect individual rights to private property and to promote commercial development and military power; the ANTIFEDERALISTS (such as Patrick HENRY, Thomas Jefferson, and Samuel Adams) favored a weaker central government, more politics at the state level, and a continued agrarian economy. The Federalists drew more from Calvinist ideas (with an emphasis on human sin, requiring a federal system of limited, divided power through constitutional CHECKS AND BALANCES) and the liberalism of John Locke, with its insistence on central government's role in protecting individual rights against community encroachment. Antifederalists drew more on classical Republican ideals of small-scale democracies (STATES RIGHTS), community control over the individual, and suspicion of strong central government. Both parties ended up compromising to a certain extent, and American federalism became a kind of blending of the two theories, though Federalists continued somewhat in the probusiness end of the later REPUBLICAN PARTY and the Antifederalists were concerned with social equality and community in the modern DEMOCRATIC PARTY.

The next great impetus for political thought in the United States was the Civil War or War Between the States (1861–65), which was seen by Northern ABOLITIONISTS as over the issue of black slavery but by Southerners as over states rights. Black ex-slave Frederick DOUGLASS argued that the federal government had a constitutional right (and duty) to end slavery in the South legally; John C. CALHOUN insisted, however, that states held the ultimate authority over the matter and could even nullify national legislation. Abraham LIN-COLN began by respecting the institution of slavery in the South but restricting its expansion westward. Then Lincoln proposed ending slavery gradually and financially compensating slave owners. Finally, with the outbreak of war and citing Thomas Jefferson's phrase in the Declaration of Independence that "all men are created equal," Lincoln (in his Gettysburg Address) proclaimed slavery abolished and all slaves emancipated.

Following the Civil War, the U.S. economy rapidly industrialized, prompting changes in political thought. A philosophy favorable to unrestricted free-market CAPITALISM came to be called SOCIAL DARWINISM. William Graham SUMNER argued that free competition among businesses and among individuals allowed the bright and hardworking to succeed and the foolish and lazy to die out. So, for Sumner, government taxes on the rich to assist the poor harmed the good citizens while encouraging laziness and perpetuation of the impoverished class. Only free, voluntary charity to the poor is socially acceptable. This became the philosophical basis of laissez-faire or CONSERVATIVE, probusiness ideology in American political thought, which continued right up through Ronald REAGAN and the conservative Republican Party in contemporary United States. The LIBERAL response to industrial capitalism in the United States was the WELFARE STATE, which used the federal government to regulate business for the common good and to tax the wealthy at a higher rate to fund social programs for the poor (education, health care, public housing, etc.). This liberal use of the national government to control business for the common people was expressed in writing by Woodrow WILSON in the early 1900s, Franklin Delano ROOSEVELT in the 1930s, and John F. KENNEDY in the 1960s (the "New Freedom," the "New Deal," and the "New Frontier" respectively).

This Conservative (RIGHT)–Liberal (LEFT) debate over the proper role and extent of government has dominated American political thought throughout the 20th century and into the 21st century. The most recent philosophical writings on this controversy include John RAWLS's *A Theory of Justice,* which provided a sophisticated case for welfare liberalism called the "maximum strategy." According to Rawls, a perfectly rational human being would choose a social system which "maximized the minimum," or made living in the most disadvantaged conditioned preferable in that society than in any other. Because people don't

know where they will land in the economy (rich or poor) or society (prominent or obscure), they would want a system that takes care of them if they become sick, poor, or lowly. Rawls allows for variations of wealth so long as the rich become richer by benefiting the whole society (e.g., by inventing something that benefits society, manages resources more efficiently, etc.), and pay more in taxes to help the disadvantaged (in education, public health and housing, etc.). An equally sophisticated philosophy of the Conservative Right appeared in Robert NOZICK's book *Anarchy, State and Utopia,* which argued for "The minimalist State"— low taxes, free enterprise, no social services or welfare, and unrestrained business activity. Despite these ideological differences of conservative/liberal and Republican Party/Democratic Party, the variations in U.S. politics and political thought are mild compared with most Western democracies (which have parties ranging from FASCIST nationalism to COMMUNISM). A general consensus exists in the United States for a "mixed economy" with extensive free-market capitalism but wide-ranging social services, equalizing the population and providing relative equality of opportunity.

Greater social conflicts occur over ideological CULTURE WARS, as described by James Davison HUNTER in his classic sociological study *Culture Wars* (1991). The book suggests that the issues in U.S. politics are no longer over Left and Right, liberal or conservative economic policies, but over views of reality and morality. Hunter argues that these cut across economic class, political party, race, gender, or religion. As the Democratic Party's policies helped the social downtrodden, it increasingly reached out to other social outcasts (minorities, blacks, women's liberation groups, gays and lesbians, animal rights, etc.) and the Republican Party became the defender of traditional Judeo-Christian morality. Hunter argues that political ideology in the United States now divides between "orthodox" people who adhere to some absolute standard of ethics (God, church, the Bible, etc.) and "progressive" citizens who make judgments according to relative standards, personal preference, and historical trends.

The future trends of American political thought are difficult to predict, but with the Internet and greater internationalism, it is likely to be more cosmopolitan and multicultural. A great commentator on American political culture, Frenchman Alexis de TOCQUEVILLE, in his book *Democracy in America* (1835, 1840), stated that the constants in American culture are equality, democracy, and a basic Christian ethic. Despite social and technological changes in America, these principles seem to persist in American political theory.

Further Reading
Dolbeare, Kenneth. *American Political Thought.* New York: Chatham House, 1981.

anarchism/anarchy

The political philosophy that holds that all state AUTHORITY or POWER is oppressive and unjust, that the abolishing of government will produce the greatest individual and collective freedom and prosperity and that it is governmental authority that imposes unfair rules on people, steals their money, and keeps them in slavery. Therefore, to eliminate the state will result in JUSTICE and an end to poverty, violence, bondage, and war. Ironically, many anarchists have used violence and terrorism to try to destroy the existing government. Underlying the anarchist's political theory is a view that human beings are naturally peaceful, loving, and cooperative and that only the state system makes them selfish and cruel; so ending the government will unleash humanity's positive qualities. This optimistic view of human beings goes back to French philosopher Jean-Jacques ROUSSEAU and his idea that people are naturally virtuous but corrupted by society. This is contrary to most of Western political thought, which regards humanity as naturally selfish and bigoted who can only be made cooperative through education, political participation, religious ethics and spiritual development, and the threat of legal punishment. So anarchism is the very opposite of most Western knowledge in that it identifies individual and social problems with both the state and all other forms of authority (in business, the military, the church, and the family). So the ideal in anarchism is a kind of unrestrained, free child, with no controls or directing, and the belief that this would produce a perfect social harmony of self-directed, self-controlled individuals freely relating to one another in a purely voluntary, happy way.

Other than this basic idealism over natural human kindness and peace and rejection of all authority, anarchists vary tremendously over how to achieve this utopia of perfection. Some anarchists believe in free-market, laissez-faire CAPITALISM to achieve all-perfect, authority-free happiness; others want a COMMUNIST economy to achieve the same result; still others seek a religious community to accomplish anarchy. In each case, it is not believed that an anarchic social system

Reproduction of anarchist handbill in article "The Chicago Anarchists of 1886." (LIBRARY OF CONGRESS)

would produce chaos and disorder (as it is often accused) because the free individuals will be self-regulating and respectful of others' RIGHTS. The idea is that people can control themselves *internally* and individually best, without *external* control (by law, government, parents, teachers, church or God). Most of all, anarchists hate all authority. The fact that an anarchist society has never succeeded does not prove to anarchists that it is unrealistic, just that the evils of authority and power keep creeping back into life.

The main philosophers of anarchism wrote in the 19th and early 20th centuries in Europe and Russia. The first was Frenchman Pierre-Joseph PROUDHON whose maxim "property is theft" attacked power associated with wealth and advocated a socialist or communal anarchism without private property. The German thinker Max Stirner developed a more individualistic anarchy that allowed absolute private freedom which later developed into LIBERTARIANISM. Peter KROPOTKIN, a Russian anarchist, advocated a communist anarchism in which peasants and workers would cooperate. Some anarchists blended MARXISM with anarchism, conceiving of a highly organized technological society without any coercive qualities, preserving absolute individual liberty. In Spain and Italy, anarcho-syndicalist movements tried to combine trade unions with anarchist ideals. How the anarchist freedom was to occur was not clear. Some anarchists (especially Marxists) wanted an armed violent revolution (like the Russian Revolution of 1917); others expected a spontaneous revolt of the masses of people, overthrowing existing authority in the state, the church, the family, and the economy. Some anarchists thought violent acts (assassinating political leaders or bombing government buildings) would set off this sudden revolt and usher in the total freedom of anarchism. Such acts of terrorism and violence by anarchists gave them the popular image of a crazed idealist with a bomb under his (or her) coat.

Anarchism also seeded other movements, like FEMINISM (women's revolt against male authority), PACIFISM (peace activists against military organizations and war), ENVIRONMENTALISM (against corporate power and pollution), ANIMAL RIGHTS (against human dominance over other animals), and atheism (against the authority of God, church, and religion). Each shares hostility toward authority.

Anarchism is viewed as unrealistic in the Western tradition of political thought and as having an inaccurate view of human nature (as naturally cooperative) and society (as capable of functioning without authority). Anarchists are seen by their critics as self-deceived and self-righteous, denying the egoism and desire for power in their own hearts while criticizing it in others, and identifying all evil with established authority, rather than with inherent human weakness.

Further Readings

Bakunin, M. *Bakunin on Anarchy,* S. Dolgoff, ed. New York: Knopf, 1972.
Carter, A. *The Political Theory of Anarchism.* New York: Harper & Row, 1971.
De Leon, David. *The American as Anarchist: Reflections on Indigenous Radicalism.* Baltimore: Johns Hopkins University Press, 1978.
Hoffman, Robert Louis, ed. *Anarchism,* 1st ed. New York: Atherton Press, 1970.
Joll, J. *The Anarchists,* 2nd ed. Cambridge, Mass.: Harvard University Press, 1979.
Krimerman, L. I., and Perry, L., eds. *Patterns of Anarchy.* Garden City, N.Y.: Doubleday, 1966.
Miller, D. *Anarchism.* London and Toronto: J.M. Dent & Sons Ltd., 1984.
Rocker, R. *Anarcho-syndicalism.* Gordon Press, 1938. Reprint, with a preface by Noam Chomsky, Boulder, Colo.: Westview Press, 1989.
Sonn, Richard David. *Anarchism.* New York: Macmillan Library Reference, 1992.
Taylor, M. *Community, Anarchy and Liberty.* New York: Cambridge University Press, 1982.
Woodcock, G. *Anarchism.* Cleveland: World Pub., 1963.

ancient constitution

A concept in 17th-century English legal and political thought that claimed that Saxon England, prior to the Norman Conquest of 1066, had a constitution guaranteeing individual LIBERTY, political participation, and RIGHTS to private property. The Norman (French) kings then imposed MONARCHY and FEUDALISM on Britain, robbing the English of their "ancient liberties." The restoration of this ancient constitution by Parliament in the revolution of 1688 then was seen as a return to ancient VIRTUE and DEMOCRACY against monarchy, decadence, and slavery.

The existence of an ancient constitution representing a golden age of English liberty was seen by royalist historians as mythical, and the contemporary historian J. G. A. POCOCK confirms their view. Developed by Parliamentary lawyers in the 1600s to justify the deposing of the king of England, this ancient constitution distorted English political and legal history. Sir Edward COKE and William BLACKSTONE interpreted English common law to invent this ancient constitution to undercut the authority of the English monarchy and to transfer political power to the republican Parliament. By situating liberal English rights to political participation and property in an ancient constitution that existed *before* the English monarchy (which justified its sovereignty on past heredity), the Parliamentary lawyers justified overthrowing (or at least limiting) the monarch. The lack of historical validity of this ancient constitution did not prevent others, notably American colonists like Thomas JEFFERSON, from employing it to justify American independence from the British government in the 1770s, claiming the right to self-government and liberty from the ancient constitution. So this idea, developed by the English Parliament, was eventually used against that same Parliament by the British colonists who learned it studying English law in America.

The reality is that British liberal ideals of natural rights to life, liberty, and property, developed by philosophers such as John LOCKE, were projected back into history as an ancient constitution to support a political struggle in the 1600s in England and the 1700s in America. It is an example of using (or inventing) the past to affect contemporary politics.

Further Reading
Pocock, J. G. A. *The Ancient Constitution and the Feudal Law.* New York: Cambridge University Press, 1957.

animal rights

A political movement, primarily in the 20th century, that argues for rights of nonhuman animals (dogs, cats, foxes, chickens, whales, etc.) against domination or use by human beings. This ranges from opposition to experimentation on animals (for medical or cosmetic research) to prevention of cruel or neglectful treatment of farm or domestic animals, to vegetarianism, or the noneating of meat. Animal rights organizations (such as P. E.T.A.: People for the Ethical Treatment of Animals) use a variety of means to assert their cause—from lobbying legislatures to pass laws protecting animals to public demonstrations around animal laboratories, to destroying animal experimentation facilities and attacking scientists.

The philosophic foundation of most animal rights groups grows from a view that all living species are equal and equally worthy of dignity and FREEDOM. Opposition to this view comes from biologists who note that most animal species kill other species for food, from economic businesses that find markets for animals, and from the Judeo-CHRISTIAN perspective that God gave animals to humanity for its use and so humans properly have "dominion" over other creatures (Genesis 10). Still, all of these arguments for humans' superiority to other animals concede that humankind should take care of other creatures (Adam is to "dress and keep" the Garden of Eden, Jesus is described as "the good shepherd" who loves and cares for the sheep, John 10:14–15). So, even in the Christian tradition, though animals are given by God to humankind for use, humans are commended to be kind to all living things, as gifts from God. As St. Peter wrote of the prophet Balaam, "a dumb ass speaking with a man's voice forbad the madness of the prophet" (2 Peter 2:16).

Ancient Greek philosophy (the Platonist Porphyry) held that human excellence forbids inflicting pain on any living creature and (Plutarch's *Moralia*) that vegetarianism respects the moral worth of animals.

Enlightenment rationalism in philosophers KANT and Descartes is less sympathetic to animals' moral dignity because it claims that they do not have reasoning capabilities. Critics of this view fear that it can be easily extended to humans who are devoid of reason (mentally disabled, fetuses, the senile, etc.), so protecting animal life helps to protect helpless human life.

The key to the modern animal liberation movement is the prevention of *suffering* of animals, whether inflicted by hunting, experimentation, or confinement.

The first law against cruelty to animals was passed by the PURITANS in Massachusetts, North America, in 1641. Other advocates of kindness to animals include British philosopher Jeremy BENTHAM, Henry Salt, George Bernard Shaw, and GANDHI. Early proponents of animal rights, especially in England, were known as Anti-Vivisection Leagues. Contemporary leaders include Peter Singer and Tom Regan.

An important distinction in the animal rights movement is whether the motivation for noncruelty to animals is primarily from the elevation of nonhuman animals equal to that of humans or as the promotion of human kindness and love generally and how best to achieve that. It is a highly emotional issue that promises to remain a part of political theory and action in the world.

Further Readings
Frey, R. G. *Interests and Rights: The Case against Animals.* Oxford, Eng.: Clarendon Press, 1980.
Magel, C. R. *A Bibliography on Animal Matters and Related Matters.* Lanham, Md.: University Press of America, 1981.
Mason, J., and Singer, P. *Animal Factories.* New York: Crown, 1980.
Midgley, M. *Animals and Why They Matter.* Athens: University of Georgia Press, 1983.
Morris, Richard Knowles, and Fox, Michael W., eds. *On the Fifth Day: Animal Rights & Human Ethics.* Washington, D.C.: Acropolis Books, 1978.
Regan, T. *The Case for Animal Rights.* Berkeley: University of California Press, 1983.
Regan, Tom. *All That Dwell Therein: Animal Rights and Environmental Ethics.* Berkeley: University of California Press, 1982.
Singer, P. *Animal Liberation: A New Ethics for our Treatment of Animals.* New York: New York Review of Books, 1965.
Turner, J. *Reckoning with the Beast: Animals, Pain, and Humanity in the Victorian Mind.* Baltimore: Johns Hopkins University Press, 1980.
Williams, Jeanne, ed. *Animal Rights.* New York: H. W. Wilson, 1991.

anthropology

Anthropology is the study of human beings, with an emphasis on their evolution. The academic discipline is generally divided into two broad fields: physical anthropology, which is the study of human physical traits and evolution; and cultural anthropology, which involves the examination of human culture, society, and interpersonal relationships. Physical anthropology, especially the early debate over evolution, influenced the development of 19th-century sociology and political theory. Meanwhile, cultural anthropology has had a major impact on the development of political thought, both in terms of the development of civilizations, as well as the role and impact of societal relationships. A subset of cultural anthropology, philosophical anthropology, examines humans as both products of their environments and as the creators of the values that shape environments.

Contacts between the Europeans and various indigenous peoples in the 1600s and 1700s spurred the eventual development of anthropology. European intellectuals sought to develop explanations for the technological differences between themselves and native peoples, whom they deemed as "savages." Initially, anthropology was dominated by a linear concept of history that held that human societies passed through stages of development. They evolved from a primitive state through phases to become "civilized." The work of Charles Darwin on evolution influenced this line of thought and led to the development of SOCIAL DARWINISM, which contended that those societies that were more technologically advanced were so because they were more evolved or more fit. Such ideas were used to justify the acquisition of territories and colonies during the age of imperialism in the 19th century. Social Darwinists also asserted that the developed world, including the Western European nations and the United States, had a duty to take care of the lesser-developed peoples by governing for them and civilizing them through Christianity and political education. This sentiment was especially strong among nations such as Great Britain, France, and Germany. In the United States, these theories would be used to justify the western continental expansion known as MANIFEST DESTINY and the U.S. conquests of territory such as the Philippines.

By the 20th century, many questioned these assumptions, and the strong ethnocentric and cultural biases of the earlier anthropologists were abandoned for a more pluralistic approach that viewed each cul-

ture as the product of unique environmental and societal factors. This relativism eliminated many of the earlier prejudices and led to an emphasis on fieldwork and the collection of empirical data. Much of the new methodology of the science was related to the work of Marx and his materialist view of scientific inquiry, which stressed empirical observation. The functionalism of the new approach was rooted in the efforts to find common cultural foundations for a variety of activities within a given society.

One 20th-century political phenomenon studied by anthropologists has been the rise of the "cult of personality" in certain nations. The effort to raise political leaders to an almost deitylike status has occurred in a variety of nations and cultures, including Germany, the Soviet Union, China, and various states in the Middle East. Anthropology provides one manner of examining the fusion of political, religious, and societal ideals in a political leader and the means by which dictatorial rulers are able to use culture to augment or ensure their power.

Further Reading
Shore, C., and Wright, S., eds. *Anthropology of Policy: Critical Perspectives on Governance and Power.* New York: Routledge, 1997.

anticlericalism

A political attitude and movement that is hostile to CHRISTIAN ministers or clergy ("clerics"), especially CATHOLIC priests. The main attack of anticlericalism is those churches or clergy that have political power or are closely associated with the STATE. For example, this negative attitude toward church officials began in Europe in the 18th century, especially in France, where the REPUBLICAN forces resented the political power of the Roman Catholic Church and its support of the French MONARCHY. So, after the French Revolution of 1789, the Catholic Church and clergy lost its privileges.

In general, anticlericalism has been a response to the church and clergy being too close to political power, becoming wealthy and powerful in a worldly sense, supporting the CONSERVATIVE power structure rather than representing Christ to the world and being meek, humble, and spiritual.

In other countries, anticlericalism attacked the official church and sought to strip it of its worldly wealth and power. In Spain and Portugal, between 1830 and

1870, attempts were made to limit the power of the Catholic Church in politics. In Latin America, national independence movements often coincided with attacks on the Catholic Church, which was seen as defending the Spanish Empire. So, in Mexico, for example, the revolution for independence went hand-in-hand with abolishing church control of government, though the social and cultural influence of Catholicism continued.

In the United States of America, anticlericalism has never been strong, partly because legal separation of CHURCH AND STATE prevented the clergy from having formal political power. Even in those states that had official churches (e.g., Connecticut, Virginia, and Massachusetts), the ministers seldom ruled directly and were at the forefront of popular, democratic movements (such as the Revolutionary War). Consequently, freedom of religion in America has produced a generally positive image of clergy, respect for religious institutions, and pervasive social and cultural influence by the church. Criticism of particular denominations or church leaders (especially when they get too involved in politics, like Marion "Pat" ROBERTSON running for president) is common in the United States, but public opinion polls consistently reveal a high regard for ministers in general. The closest thing to anticlericalism in the United States is some radical Protestant church's belief in the "priesthood of all believers" and resistance to a full-time, professional clergy. Quakers, Mormons, some Baptists, and Disciples fear the sharp distinction between ordained clergy and laity (ordinary church members) because it introduces an unhealthy hierarchy in the church and authority in the clergy. Most U.S. churches avoid this by democratically appointing their ministers.

Further Reading
Sanchez, J. M. *Anticlericalism.* Notre Dame, Ind.: University of Notre Dame Press, 1972.

Antifederalists

A group of political leaders, who, after the American Revolution, opposed the ratification of the new U.S. CONSTITUTION. Several prominent American leaders were Antifederalists, including Patrick HENRY, Samuel Adams, and George Mason. Thomas JEFFERSON was not a member of this group because he supported the Constitution, but he sympathized with their view. The Antifederalists opposed the new Constitution because they felt that it gave too much power to the central federal government (and away from the state governments) and it gave too much authority to the executive (president) and judicial (Supreme Court) branches of the national government at the expense of the legislature (Congress).

The Antifederalists wished to keep the loose confederacy of the government during the American Revolution (under the Articles of Confederation) with a weak central government and most power in the individual states. The supporters of the U.S. Constitution, or FEDERALISTS, such as James MADISON, George Washington, and Alexander HAMILTON, found the decentralized politics of the Articles of Confederation too weak, chaotic, and ineffective. The Federalists believed that without the strong central government of the U.S. Constitution, the United States would be threatened by foreign countries and troubled by conflict between the states. The Antifederalists felt that the VIRTUE and DEMOCRACY of a decentralized confederacy was worth having less military strength and national commerce. They feared that the strong central regime of the U.S. Constitution's federal government would lead to financial corruption, political oppression, and IMPERIALISM.

With the ratification of the U.S. Constitution, in 1787, the Antifederalists were defeated, but their views favoring STATES RIGHTS and a limited federal government continued. The secession of Southern states during the American Civil War and establishment of the Confederate States of America is an expression of this Antifederalist sentiment. Even after the defeat of the South, the imposition of national supremacy over domestic affairs continues into the 20th century (e.g., during the presidency of Ronald REAGAN 1980–89).

Further Reading
Main, J. T. *The Anti-Federalists.* Chapel Hill: University of North Carolina Press, 1961.

Aquinas, St. Thomas (1225–1274) *Theologian and philosopher*

The leading CATHOLIC thinker of the Middle Ages, author of the enormous book *Summa Theologica,* which discusses all topics of ethics, religion, politics, economics, and metaphysics. This worldview, which came to be known as THOMIST theology, is now the official perspective of the Roman Catholic Church.

Aquinas was born in Naples, Italy, of a prominent family. He entered the Dominican religious order against the wishes of his parents and studied at the University of Paris under ALBERTUS MAGNUS; at the university, he imbibed the newly translated writings of the ancient Greek philosopher, ARISTOTLE. St. Thomas Aquinas is best known for combining CHRISTIAN doctrine with CLASSICAL philosophy, drawing on the wisdom and insights of the Greek thinkers, but putting their ideas within a Christian context.

The first way Aquinas integrates Aristotelian philosophy into Christian thought is through his emphasis on human Reason, or intellectual ability. Like the Greeks, Aquinas believes that humans can know and understand reality through their reasoning intellects; the fall of Adam does not totally corrupt the human mind, only the will, so learning and education are good and can serve God. This gives medieval Christianity its intellectual quality, its careful, often detailed reasoning as developed in scholasticism. The Protestant REFORMATION was partly a rejection of the "overintellectualization" of Christianity and an attempt to return to the simple biblical faith of the early church. Interestingly, St. Thomas Aquinas (known by the nickname "The Dumb Ox" for his large, dull appearance) was one of the most intellectual of Christians, but after having a direct spiritual encounter with God late in life, he never wrote again and said that his massive writings reminded him of "straw."

Like Aristotle, Aquinas considered humans as naturally social and political by virtue of reason, speech, and moral virtue. He saw the government as just part of the universal empire of which God is the maker and ultimate ruler. Aquinas adopts Aristotle's "teleological" approach to reality, which sees things in terms of their purpose or goal—their ultimate complete development. So, for example, an acorn has an end, or *telos*, of becoming a full-grown tall oak tree. A human being has a purpose or end, designed by God to be fully developed in his or her divinely given talents and abilities and to love and serve God. The church is to teach the truth of God and to assist the faithful in fulfilling their God-given *telos*, individually and collectively.

Consequently, like Aristotle, St. Thomas Aquinas sees things in terms of their development or "completeness." Something is "superior" to another only by its being more complete or comprehensive. Hence, the family is superior or more important than the individual because it is more self-sufficient. The society is more comprehensive than the family and so is more important; politics is superior to economics because it encompasses property. God is most superior and excellent because he created the universe and is all-encompassing.

This way, Aquinas discusses politics in terms of greater and lesser laws: (1) divine or eternal law; (2) natural law; and (3) human or positive law. Divine law is the order that governs the universe, the only perfect and unchanging law, ordained by God. In its totality, it is beyond the comprehension of humans with their limited minds. But the Almighty reveals portions of this eternal law to humankind, such as in the Ten Commandments and the Bible generally.

A part of the divine law governing nature is natural law: This defines the limits of nature and their qualities, including the planets, wildlife, physics, biology, psychology, the seasons, and so on, what today we would call science. But natural law is subordinated to God and divine law—it can be superseded by the Lord (through miracles) and is inferior to God and his law. Humans participate in divine law partly by understanding natural law through Reason.

Human or positive law consists of specific expressions of natural law in particular places and times in history (what we think of as governmental laws); it changes most frequently. Natural law, however, changes very slowly, and divine law changes not at all. Human law is ordained for the common good of society (not for a special interest or single group). Like Aristotle, St. Thomas Aquinas admits that several types of government can be good if they serve the interest of the whole society and not just the rulers' interest. The rule of one (monarchy), the rule of a few (aristocracy), or the rule of the many (democracy) can all be just. Like Aristotle, he saw the "mixed regime" of kingship, ARISTOCRACY, and polity most stable.

Because human law is part of, and subordinate to, natural law and divine law, it must conform to those higher laws to be valuable and just. A law or statute that is contrary to natural or divine law will not work but will bring social disorder and injustice. The church advises the state so that political laws will line up with natural and divine law to the good of society. The Catholic Church's stands on abortion, nuclear weapons, and economic policy reflect this Thomist belief. For example, the Catholic position against abortion follows from abortion's violation of divine law (against murder) and natural law (against terminating the natural development or telos of the fetus, or unborn child). So the human laws allowing abortion are contrary to the higher laws, will produce social trouble and chaos, and so should be changed. Similarly, the church's position against homosexuality flows from that practice's deviation from divine law (against sodomy) and natural law (that sex is designed to occur between male and female and that its goal is reproduction). Civil laws that violate natural and divine law will not work in the long run but will create more problems.

Another example of the interaction of laws is property law. Aquinas adheres to Aristotle's reasons in favor of private-property ownership (society is more orderly and prosperous if individuals can own property rather than having everything in common), but the laws that define and protect private property must be subordinate to natural law and divine law. The ultimate purpose of property is to sustain human life. God and nature require, therefore, that the wealthy hold their property in stewardship (not as their own, but God's, to be used for his purposes, in charity, etc.). So, if the human law against theft prevents starving people from living, St. Thomas says that they can take what others have in superabundance, obeying a higher law.

The sources of knowledge for St. Thomas Aquinas are four: (1) Scripture (the Bible); (2) reason; (3) tradition; and (4) experience. These are called the four legs of the stool of knowledge. The church in St. Thomas's time was the source of most of these sources of knowledge and perpetuated them in the church's teachings and universities. Aquinas later was named the patron saint of all Catholic universities.

Monarchy was the prevalent form of government in the Middle Ages. Aquinas supported the monarchical state with this logic: God is one; the common good is one; the monarch is one ruler.

Because of its emphasis on order and hierarchy, Thomist theology is often seen as conservative.

Further Readings
Aquinas, Thomas. *Summa theologiae,* ed. T. Gilby. 60 vols. Garden City, N.Y.: Image Books, 1963–81.
———. *The Political Ideas of St. Thomas Aquinas: Representative Selection.* Ed. and introd. by Dino Bigongiari. New York: Hafner Pub. Co., 1953.
Chesterton, G. K. (Gilbert Keith). *Saint Thomas Aquinas.* Garden City, N.Y.: Image Books, 1956.
D'Entreves, A. P., ed. *Aquinas: Selected Political Writings.* Oxford, Eng.: Basil Blackwell, 1948.
Donohue, John W. *St. Thomas Aquinas & Education.* New York: Random House, 1968.
Kenny, Anthony John Patrick. *Aquinas: A Collection of Critical Essays.* Anthony Kenny, ed. New Yirk: Macmillan, 1976.
O'Connor, D. J. *Aquinas and Natural Law.* London: Macmillan, 1967.
Weisheipl, J. *Friar Thomas D'Aquino: His Life, Thought and Works.* Garden City, N.Y.: Doubleday, 1974.

Arendt, Hannah (1906–1975) *German-born U.S. political theorist*

Arendt was born in Hanover and raised in Königsberg, studied philosophy at the University of Marburg, where she had an affair with Martin HEIDEGGER, and received her doctorate in 1929 for a study of St. AUGUSTINE. With the NAZI rise to power, Arendt was forced to flee to Paris in 1933, had to escape to the United States in 1941 after the Nazis occupied France, and became a United States citizen in 1951. Arendt was a lecturer at Princeton University and the University of Chicago and a professor for many years at the New School for Social Research in New York City, where she also held key positions in several Jewish organizations.

Arendt established her reputation as a keen analyst of politics and society in the MODERN age on the basis of her penetrating studies of totalitarianism and the horror of genocide in the 20th century. In 1963, Arendt observed the trial of Adolf Eichmann, the Nazi official responsible for the deaths of millions of Jews during the HOLOCAUST, which provided the material for her book, *Eichmann in Jerusalem.* Arendt coined the famous phrase *the banality of evil* to describe the unexceptional character of Eichmann, who employed the most common features of the modern bureaucratic and technological state for the purpose of systematically and efficiently exterminating millions of human beings. Some commentators sought to demonize Eichmann as an inhuman monster, but Arendt made the more important point that the Nazi enterprise was horrific precisely because it was planned and executed by ordinary individuals with an unquestioning obedience to authority. Arendt argued that the motive of expediency had become a central feature of the modern state, at the expense of moral judgment and the ability to think from the point of view of others.

Arendt's effort to demystify the Nazi regime can be traced back to her monumental *The Origins of Totalitarianism,* published in 1951. After detailing the historical precedents to the TOTALITARIAN political system, in particular the administrative structure of imperialism, Arendt focused her analysis on Nazism

Hannah Arendt studying a paper with a reporter. (Library of Congress)

and Stalinism. For Arendt, the prevalence of totalitarianism in the 20th century and its success in eradicating political freedom through IDEOLOGY and terror makes it "the burden of our time." According to Arendt, perhaps the most striking feature of totalitarianism is the way it intentionally deprives whole communities of their humanity. Unlike despotism, which creates enemies of the state who are then made to conform to the power of the ruler, totalitarianism creates victims who are eliminated from the state by being deprived of identity, community, and legal status. The victims of totalitarianism are rendered anonymous through the comprehensive eradication of their human rights and sense of personhood by means of propaganda and the arbitrary use of legal and political power. Against these victims, the totalitarian state organizes the masses around myths of common national identity and the willing submission to a single authority.

Beyond these concerns, Arendt also developed a theory of politics based on the classical Greek idea that political action is the sphere of human freedom. In *The Human Condition*, Arendt explained that what is distinctive about the classical conception of politics is its emphasis on the meaningfulness or value of political action as such. The Greek conception that political action is the most meaningful form of human activity

thus stands in opposition to the modern conception of politics and its narrow focus on political action as a mere means to some efficient end. In Arendt's estimation, modern politics is dominated by UTILITARIANISM, with the result that conformity rather than creativity has become its guiding principle. She suggested that the 20th century has been marked by a gradual loss of the right to public action and opinion, a right that serves as a cornerstone of the social sphere where individuals ought to be able to act in association with others as equals. Consequently, Arendt concluded that an essential dimension of "the human condition," our freedom to interact creatively with others, has been gradually restricted.

Further Reading
Young-Bruehl, E. *Hannah Arendt: For Love of the World.* New Haven: Yale University Press, 1982.

aristocracy
A form of government in which "the best" rule. From the Greek terms *aristoi* (or "best") and *cracy* ("rule of"). Many political thinkers and regimes have advanced this form of government but disagree over what, or who, the best people are and how they should govern. For the Greek philosopher PLATO, in *The Republic* the aristocracy consists of the wise who know VIRTUE. His ideal regime is governed by "PHILOSOPHER-KINGS" who set up a truly just society, including economic, educational, and military systems. For ARISTOTLE, the aristocracy is the rule in the ancient Greek polis of the most civilized, reasonable, prosperous, and educated elite. For CHRISTIAN political thought (St. AUGUSTINE, the PURITANS, etc.), there is no pure aristocracy on earth because all people are sinful, but a government with truly Christian rulers or saints will be the best possible government.

All aristocratic governments imply an elite which excludes many (inferior) people from political power. Questions, then, of who is the aristocracy and how they are recognized arise. Aristotle, for example, excludes non-Greeks (or barbarians), women, slaves, the poor, ignorant and young people from governance. Since reason and leisure are required for just, wise rule only adult, Greek, male, wealthy citizens should have positions of authority. During the European Middle Ages most states had a ruling aristocracy based on family heredity; the monarchy and nobility descended through certain families who had "blue blood." Modern, republican regimes rejected this hereditary idea of "the best" but retained an idea that some people make better rulers than others. American Thomas JEFFERSON held that a "natural aristocracy" of virtue (morals) and talents (ability) existed in society and that it should occupy positions of political leadership. This Jeffersonian aristocracy was democratic in two senses, however: (1) It was born into all classes, families, and nationalities, and (2) it was to be elected to office by the people generally. The cultivating of this natural aristocracy, for Jefferson, required a public education system, economic opportunity, and political DEMOCRACY. It is in the interest of the whole society to recognize the good and talented young people even from poor and humble backgrounds and to elevate them through education to positions of leadership. A healthy democracy will select this natural aristocracy in popular elections. Jefferson contrasted this natural aristocracy of "wisdom and virtue" with those of birth (heredity) and wealth (riches) and felt that if the "pseudo-aristocracies" of money or family ruled, the American republic would be corrupted. John ADAMS, another early American thinker, also conceived of a natural aristocracy but identified it with the socially prominent and financially prosperous. Adams felt that someone with a good educational, economic, and social background would handle authority well. These Jeffersonian and Adams definitions of aristocracy are basically those held by the modern DEMOCRATIC and REPUBLICAN Parties in the United States.

COMMUNIST and other radical political thinkers deny any idea of an aristocracy except a reverse one of the downtrodden, oppressed, exploited, and miserable. This radical antiaristocratic view says that those least prepared and accepted by society (impoverished, criminal, minorities, uneducated) should govern. So in the early Soviet Union, social outcasts such as STALIN were elevated to positions of power, with brutal results.

Even though a legal aristocracy has been eliminated in most modern countries, the idea of a "best" kind of people in society who should govern continues, though the definition of it varies.

Further Reading

Cannadine, David. *Aspects of Aristocracy: Grandeur and Decline in Modern Britain.* New Haven, Conn.: Yale University Press, 1994.

Aristotle (384–322 B.C.)   *Ancient Greek philosopher*

Born in northern Greece of a wealthy family, his father was the physician to the king of Macedon. In 367 B.C., Aristotle moved to Athens and studied at PLATO's academy. He later became the tutor of young Alexander the Great. At Alexander's death in 322, much anti-Macedonian sentiment gripped Athenian society, so Aristotle left to avoid persecution. Aristotle is considered one of the most brilliant, possibly the greatest, philosopher in the Western heritage. His investigations and writings cover the entire range of liberal arts studies, from physics and biology to ethics, logic, politics, theater, art, poetry, and music. Widely regarded as a genius, his ideas have influenced all future scholarship on ethics, aesthetics, science, philosophy, religion, and politics. Aristotle's views on government inform CLASSICAL political theory (Greek and Roman—as CICERO); Medieval theology (St. Thomas AQUINAS); Modern republican thought (James HARRINGTON); and contemporary democratic theory (Benjamin BARBER).

Aristotle conceived of humans as naturally social and political by virtue of two human faculties: reasoned speech and moral choice. These uniquely human abilities make society and politics humanity's home, and apart from his or her community, a person is not fully human. These traits of reason, speech, and ethics are innate in humanity but require cultivation and education to become fully developed. Aristotle takes a TELEOLOGICAL approach to reality that looks at everything in terms of its development to completion. A frequent example of this is an acorn, whose *telos* or potential is a fully grown, healthy oak tree. But that full development, while inside the acorn, requires specific environmental encouragement—the best soil, rain, sunlight, surrounding plants, and so on—and most acorns do not reach their full potential or "perfection." So Aristotelian teleology looks at the ultimate end or goal or purpose of a thing when judging its excellence. Humans are potentially the greatest creatures, but without "law and morals" they can fall *below* the beasts in depravity and cruelty. So it is everyone's concern to have each person in the society receive an education and moral cultivation, or the whole country will suffer. Humankind exists between the gods and the beasts.

Aristotle idealizes the ancient Greek POLIS, the small democratic community in Athens. The ideal citizen is one who is properly prepared (educationally, economically, and politically) to participate in governance—ruling as a judge, administrator, and so on; this idea of everyone knowing how to "rule and be ruled" becomes the classical definition of CITIZENSHIP and the standard for all future REPUBLICAN governments.

The state itself emerges out of a teleological development for Aristotle. First, the individual is born into a family or household; then various families live together in a village or society; finally, the state encompasses various villages. Politics is thus an organic development, for Aristotle. The telos, or goal, of politics strives toward self-sufficiency or perfection, which is completeness or having everything it needs to live and live well. Thus, the family encompasses the individual, society encompasses families, and politics encompasses society. Hence, politics, for Aristotle is the "master science" and is superior to the individual (psychology) or property (economics). Family and society provide for humans' material, animal needs or "mere life," but politics, through rational deliberation and governing, achieves the "good life" by employing humanity's highest, godlike faculties (reason, speech, morals). So for Aristotle, ruling is nobler than commerce or moneymaking. His ideal civilized person is prosperous enough to be freed from work to serve in public life or ruling. For Aristotle, a wealthy person who continues to make money and care only about possessions is a slave to lower nature. This became the basis of much Western aristocratic views of the "gentleman" who does not deal with trade and money but with the higher intellectual, moral, and political matters, using higher human faculties. From this, Aristotle claims certain preconditions for real citizenship: education, wealth, and experience; this is why he excludes those who are irrational (slaves, workers) or have limited reasoning ability (women and children).

Aristotle categorizes regimes by the number of rulers and their character. Kingship is the rule of one; aristocracy is the rule of a few; polity is the rule of the many. All of these regimes are just because they rule not for their own interest but for the good of the whole society. So, justice in a government is not determined by the number of rulers, but by the quality of their ruling. Each form of state can be corrupted when those in government rule for their own interest rather than the common good. The corrupt form of kingship is tyranny; the corruption of aristocracy is oligarchy; and the corrupt form of polity is democracy.

Aristotle discusses what causes political change or REVOLUTIONS. Generally, they are the fault of the government or rulers especially being unfaithful to the principles of the CONSTITUTION (e.g., introducing monarchy into a polity or the rule of the many into a kingship). Most radical changes in politics come from varying notions of EQUALITY. The worst government, for Aristotle, is tyranny, the single ruler governing for his own passions. The tyrant kills the best people, destroys social organizations, spies on citizens, causes internal rivalries and strife, keeps the populace impoverished and busy, discourages schools and learning, makes war with his neighbors, and harasses intelligent, serious people. A just ruler, seeking to preserve order and stability, will act in a different way: selecting leaders of skill and morals, remaining loyal to the constitution and laws, and promoting virtue.

Most of Aristotle's political writings occur in his published lectures, *The Politics*. Some discussion of society also occurs in his *Nicomachean Ethics*. Here he develops the ethics of moderation, or the "Golden Mean." This says that virtuous behavior is that between the extremes of excess and deficiency. For example, in matters of money, the best is the Golden Mean of "generosity" between the excess of "extravagance" and the deficiency of "stinginess." The mean or moderate with respect to military conduct is "courage"; the deficiency of this virtue is "cowardess," and the excess is "recklessness." So the good or moral action is moderation, which resides between two extremes. This Golden Mean ethics produces the Greek maxim "Moderation in all Things" and the Western moral view that extreme action is necessarily evil. In this view, the good person is one who has a character that habitually (without having to think about it) chooses the Golden Mean in every situation. It is knowing what is the right thing to do with the right persons. It measures virtue by what is "appropriate" or proper. The person who knows this has been trained and cultivated in the Golden Mean.

One of the social relationships that helps to cultivate ethics in the individual is friendship. Human friendship, for Aristotle, can be based on (1) use, (2) pleasure, or (3) goodness. Relationships based on use involve someone being useful to you; those based on pleasure involve someone being pleasant (attractive, wealthy, etc.); those based on goodness concern the goodness or character of the other person. Only the friendship based on the mutual regard for the other's character are stable and permanent; those based on use and pleasure (which are transient) often end in quarrels and separation.

Because the character of citizens is affected by their environment, Aristotle sees the society as regulating much of life to ensure JUSTICE. For example, he finds that different kinds of music greatly affect character and actions, so the society has an interest in preventing hostile or destructive music, especially among the young. Fine and sacred music brings out the best in people; harsh and obscene music can lead to destructive behavior and social chaos, so it is properly regulated by society.

Further Readings

Aristotle. *The Complete Works,* J. Barnes, ed.; includes *The Politics,* B. Jowett, transl. Princeton, N.J.: Princeton University Press, 1984.

———. *The Politics,* 2nd ed., E. Barker, ed. Oxford: Clarendon Press, 1948.

———. *Articles on Aristotle: 3—Ethics and Politics,* M. Schofield and R. Sorabji, eds. London: Duckworth, 1977.

Carnes, Lord, and O'Connor, David K., eds. *Essays on the Foundations of Aristotelian Political Science,* Richard Bodeus et al., contributors. Berkeley: University of California Press, 1991.

Fritz, K. von, and Kapp, E. *Aristotle's Constitution of Athens.* 1950.

Gadamer, Hans Georg. *The Idea of the Good in Platonic–Aristotelian Philosophy,* transl. by and with an intro. and anno. by P. Christopher Smith. New Haven, Conn.: Yale University Press, 1986.

Lear, Jonathan. *Aristotle: The Desire to Understand.* New York: Cambridge University Press, 1988.

MacIntyre, Alasdair D. *Three Rival Versions of Moral Enquiry: Encyclopedia, Genealogy, and Tradition.* Gifford lectures delivered in the University of Edinburgh in 1988. Notre Dame, Ind.: University of Notre Dame Press, 1990.

Mulgan, R. G., *Aristotle's Political Theory.* Toronto: Clarendon, 1977.

Schollmeier, Paul, *Other Selves: Aristotle on Personal and Political Friendship.* Albany: State University of New York Press, ca. 1994.

Swanson, Judith A., *The Public and the Private in Aristotle's Political Philosophy.* Ithaca, N.Y.: Cornell University Press, 1992.

Atatürk, Kemal (1881–1938) *Turkish soldier, political leader and reformer, and founder and president of modern Turkey*

Kemal assumed the name *Atatürk,* or "father of the turks," in 1934 in place of his original name Mustafa Kemal. He grew up in the decaying Ottoman Empire, attending a military academy and rising quickly in the Imperial Army because of his courage and intelligence. In 1908, Kemal became involved in the Young Turk movement's attempt to overthrow the waning Ottoman regime and establish a modern REPUBLIC in Turkey.

During World War I, he commanded a victorious force in the Dardenelles, gaining great prestige as a heroic military leader. For Americans, he might be seen as similar in character and fame to Gen. George Washington, the leader of the Continental army and first president of the United States.

After Turkey's defeat in WWI, the Allies divided the Ottoman Empire among the victors, with the sultan ruler in Constantinople cooperating. Kemal and other Turkish patriots saw this as treasonous. In May 1919, Atatürk helped form the Turkish National Party and an independent army. Later that year, a new government was formed by nationalist congresses in Erzerum and Sivas. When the British occupied Constantinople, Atatürk set up a new government in the city of Ankara. A fierce civil war ensued, and the Turkish forces defeated the allies, expelled the Greeks and the Armenians, and abolished the sultanate. Modern Turkey established a European constitutional republic with a parliament and elected Atatürk president in 1923, 1927, 1931, and 1935. Very rapidly, Atatürk reformed Turkish society from a feudal ISLAMIC MONARCHY to a MODERN, SECULAR, Western republic. He abol-

Kemal Atatürk, 1924. (LIBRARY OF CONGRESS)

ished the religious/political rule of the Islamic caliphate and instituted Western standards of LAW, economics, and education. French, German, and Swiss models were employed. Atatürk's reforms in Turkey, collectively known as Kemalism, constituted the modernization of a traditional Islamic state. Kemalist political philosophy consists of six principles: (1) republicanism; (2) nationalism; (3) populism; (4) statism; (5) secularism; and (6) reformism. Republicanism implies a Western, parliamentary system of government (with regular elections, RIGHTS that are CONSTITUTIONAL, and multiple political parties). Nationalism means a country independent of foreign domination and distinct in history, geography, and culture. Populism means a DEMOCRATIC culture and self-government. Statism refers to the mixed economy of Turkey, allowing private PROPERTY and entrepreneurship but with some state industries and public regulation of economics for the common good. Secularism means the formal, legal separation of CHURCH AND STATE, ending the state domination of Islamic clerics, and FREEDOM of individual conscience in matters of faith and religion. Turkey is one of a few Islamic countries that provides constitutionally guaranteed freedom of religion. The individual in Turkey is allowed to investigate and believe any religion one chooses, without civil penalty or social punishment. This rests on the view that only freely chosen, informed religious belief is pleasing to God. Reformism is the series of radical social reforms that Atatürk instituted to transform Turkey from a MEDIEVAL, Middle Eastern monarchy into a modern Western civilization. Turks embrace Western science and progress, including equal rights for women, the European legal system, secular public education, the Latin (rather than Arabic) alphabet, the Western calendar, and European dress styles.

Together, Atatürk's reforms transformed a weak, isolated, impoverished country into a strong, prosperous, advanced nation that is integrated into the Western world.

Although sometimes criticized for his methods, Atatürk is recognized internationally as a great political leader and thinker who transformed an important part of the 20th-century world. He is revered in Turkey as the nation's Founding Father and an inspiration to contemporary Turkish leaders. Although his nation is still developing to achieve fully the goals of his 1930s reforms, it has advanced impressively. Perhaps because of Atatürk's military and political background, the army in Turkey enjoys an unusual

respect and is seen as the preserver of Atatürk's republic and vision. As a combination soldier, statesman, ruler, and reformer, Atatürk is unrivaled in the twentieth century.

Further Readings
Kazancigil, Ali and Ozbudun, Ergin, eds. *Atatürk, Founder of a Modern State*. Hamden, Conn.: Archer Books, 1981.
Kinross, Patrick Balfour, Baron. *Atatürk, the Rebirth of a Nation*. London: Weidenfeld & Nicolson, 1995, 1964.
Sheldon, G. W. *Jefferson and Atatürk*. New York: Peter Lang, 2000.
Volkan, Vamik D. *The Immortal Atatürk: A Psychobiography*. Chicago: University of Chicago Press, 1986, 1984.

Augustine, St. (354–430)   *Christian theologian, political thinker, and bishop*

Born in Northern Africa (what is now Algeria), which was largely CHRISTIAN at that time, Augustine's father was a lawyer, his mother (St. Monica) a Christian. He received a classical education in Greek philosophy, ROMAN LAW, rhetoric, and literature with the intent of becoming a lawyer. Attracted by philosophy, he began a long journey for truth, eventually becoming a professor in Rome. There he met St. Ambrose, bishop of Milan, and was converted to Christianity under his inspiring preaching. In 391, he was seized by a church crowd after delivering a talk and was ordained as a priest on the spot. Four years later, he was made bishop of Hippo, North Africa.

Augustine is probably the most influential thinker in the Western Christian church, both CATHOLIC and Protestant. This "Augustinian" Christianity remains the basis of most Catholic and Reformed theology. He is revered by both St. Thomas AQUINAS and John CALVIN. Augustine wrote an enormous amount of religious literature, sermons, letters, and books, the most famous of which are his *Confessions* and *The City of God*. The latter contains his political philosophy, the first systematic Christian political theory in the West. Augustine lived during the end of the Roman Empire (the destruction of Rome by barbarians led by Alaric the Goth in 410). Many Romans blamed the fall of their empire to the rise of Christianity and decline of pagan Roman religions. In his book *The City of God*, Augustine argued that it was actually the sins of those pagan beliefs that led to the moral decay and social and military weakness of the Roman Empire. In the process of defending the faith, St. Augustine developed a unique Christian political thought.

Augustinian political theory revolves around The Two Cities: the City of God—or transcendent heavenly kingdom—and the City of Man—or all earthly governments (regardless of kind). The City of God is that eternal realm ruled directly by God of perfect JUSTICE, perfect peace, and perfect love. The City of Man is all earthly states characterized by imperfect justice, imperfect peace, and incomplete love. Because of humanity's sinful nature, worldly governments will always be marked by corruption, greed, and lust for power; its values are ever wealth, domination, and prestige— emerging from human sin and pride. The city of God is marked by humility, poverty, lowliness, and love, as exemplified by Christ. Sometimes, Augustine refers to the City of Man as Babylon or Rome, and The City of God as Jerusalem. Another way of defining these two realms is by their respective loves: the love of humankind (or HUMANISM) versus the love of God.

So Augustinian Christian political theory breaks with classical Greek and Roman thought in refusing to have confidence in *any* earthy regime, party, leader, or cause. All worldly attempts at reform are doomed by human self-righteousness and pride; only faith in God through Jesus Christ is satisfying. Because Jesus said "the kingdom of God is within you"—indwelling believers through the Holy Spirit—Christians reside in both Kingdoms or Cities. Since the Resurrection of Christ, the faithful live in the City of God, even on earth, spiritually, while still living in the City of Man temporarily. This "dual citizenship" of Christians requires them to be obedient to rulers but to regard God as their only true king and to see life on earth as a transient pilgrimage preparing them for eternal life in heaven.

The church connects the Two Cities and resides in each: It has buildings and ministers and schools on earth, but its true home is with God in heaven. It represents God on earth as the Holy Spirit lives within the church and proclaims the truth of God's love and forgiveness through Christ to the world. The church, "the body of Christ," like Jesus when he walked the earth, is "in, but not of" the world: It resides and works in the world but adheres to heavenly values of humility, meekness, love, and forgiveness. For Augustine, the church must avoid the two temptations of (1) being totally *in* the world and corrupted by worldly power, wealth, and prestige; and (2) being wholly *outside* the world in purely mystical, spiritual contemplation. The church is to urge the government to grow closer to God's perfect justice and peace without ever expecting

it to succeed by worldly reforms. Only when Christ returns to rule directly will perfect justice and peace reign in the world. Earthly political programs or movements that promise perfection (like COMMUNISM) are a deception because sinful humans can never completely overcome their greed, selfishness, and oppression. Like the slogan on U.S. coins, Augustine believed only "In God We Trust." Christians should work on their internal, spiritual perfection more than external, social perfection.

In his life as a bishop of the Catholic Church, St. Augustine practiced what he preached. Although no earthly government could ever be perfect, he encouraged Christians to serve in the government to achieve the best possible state. Although such a Christian state would never be the City of God, it would receive the church's counsel and become better. Bishop Augustine frequently wrote to secular Roman rulers imploring them to rule more justly and mercifully, seeing their political careers as divine callings to be required as given by God, in God's service, and accountable to God on Judgment Day. John Calvin got his idea of the magistracy being a divine calling and "ministry" from St. Augustine.

For example, Augustine as a bishop once wrote to a Roman governor asking for leniency for some convicted murderers who had killed some Catholic priests, appealing to Christ's dictum of "not returning evil for evil." The Western church has continued this role of advising, rebuking, and encouraging the state, as in the American Catholic Bishops Pastoral Letters on nuclear war or economic policy. In the PURITAN tradition in America, this took an even more direct form, as the meeting house served for both public worship and public meetings, and ministers often advised the government.

From this perspective, St. Augustine developed a theory of the hierarchy of authority. The most basic authority, ordained of God, is parents, then local officials, then regional officials then national officials, then the church, and finally God. If a person receives conflicting orders from two authorities, that person, for Augustine, should obey the higher authority. So, if the government orders a citizen to do something contrary to God's law and will (such as mass murder), he should disobey the state and be obedient to God. This may cause Christians to be persecuted by the government (as they were in pagan Rome when they refused to worship emperors), but martyrdom guarantees heavenly glory. This idea of a higher law above the government forms the basis of future CIVIL DISOBEDI-ENCE. It limits the power of earthly states.

Augustine also wrote on international politics, proclaiming that in a sinful world, war would not be eliminated and so Christians may participate in just wars where one country is defending itself or has a claim to justice greater than its opponent. Still, it is the church's duty to encourage peaceful resolutions of political conflicts.

St. Augustine remains the premier Christian political thinker in the West, influencing most churches and church–state relations ever since.

Further Readings

Augustine, St. *The City of God,* D. Knowles, ed. H. Bettenson, transl. Harmondsworth, Eng.: Penguin, 1972.
———. *The Political Writings of St. Augustine,* Intro. by Henry Paoluci, ed., including an interpretative analysis by Dino Bigongiari. South Bend, Ind.: Gateway Editions, 1962.
———. *De Libero Arbitrio Voluntatis.* (St. Augustine on free will), Carroll Mason Sparrow, transl. Charlottesville: University of Virginia Press, 1947.
Brown, P. *Augustine of Hippo: A Biography.* London: Faber & Faber, 1967.
Markus, R. A. *Saeculum: History and Society in the Theology of St. Augustine.* Cambridge, Eng.: Cambridge University Press, 1970.
Marrou, H. I. *St. Augustine and His Influence through the Ages.* New York: Harper Torch, 1957.
Martin, R. "The two cities of Augustine's political philosophy." *Journal of the History of Ideas* 33 (1972).

authority

In political thought, authority is the power to rule, control, or set standards. It may exist in a person(s); in a position; within a political structure or social system; or in a law, document, or dogma. Authority implies that this rule or preeminence is accepted or legitimate, recognized, obeyed, and respected. All polities and political theory have some standard of accepted authority, except for radical LIBERTARIAN theories or theories of ANARCHISM, which place all authority solely within each individual. Authority is often contrasted with LIBERTY or FREEDOM, and most great thinkers have tried to reconcile individual and social liberty with just authority. Radical DEMOCRATIC movements, which often correspond with claims to universal EQUALITY, are often hostile to all authority. Frequently, revolutions (such as the French of 1789 and the Russian of 1917) begin by attacking established authority (king, church, private PROPERTY) but ended up establishing more authoritarian governments and reducing social liberty even more than in the past. The question then is: What constitutes a good, just authority?

In PLATO's *Republic,* just authority is rule by the PHILOSOPHER-KINGS, exercising wisdom and VIRTUE in governance. He contrasts this with the increasingly less just authority of other regimes (the rule of the military, the wealthy, the common people, and the tyrant). ARISTOTLE's *Politics* views the best authority as that of the collective deliberation of the Greek POLIS made up of well-educated, virtuous, civic-minded citizens. This ultimately places good authority in Reason or the best intellectual part of humanity. ROMAN LAW, for CICERO, embodies this best Reason, so it enjoys respectable authority over the whole Roman Empire. The Judeo-CHRISTIAN political tradition sees all authority as emanating from God and channeled through his anointed rulers (Moses, King David, Jesus Christ, etc.). Even cruel rulers can be used by God to punish human sin, and the condemned Jesus tells the Roman governor Pontius Pilate that earthly rulers would not have power unless God gave it to them, so they are responsible to God for how they use it. After his Resurrection, Jesus proclaimed (in Matthew 28:18), "All authority in heaven and earth has been given to me." Believing this, the MEDIEVAL church claimed that European kings were God's servants and accountable to God for their actions. If the ruler was not faithful, the church could remove his authority. Similarly, the American PURITANS believed their legitimate authority and prosperity rested on designing and maintaining a society in conformity to God's law. Moral authority and political authority are linked in this view.

MODERN views of authority tend to be more formal or legalistic. Max WEBER described three kinds of authority: (1) charismatic (based on the leader's personality); (2) traditional (based on the leader's past or hereditary rule); and (3) legal–rational. The last characteristic of modern BUREAUCRACY places authority in *positions* rather people. So, for example, the authority in U.S. national government resides in offices (the presidency, Congress, courts) with specific powers and prestige, not in individuals (who come and go). So, in the modern world, authority tends to rest in the official position a person occupies, and when he or she leaves that office, the authority ends except for any personal or moral authority the person retains. For example, President Jimmy CARTER continued in political life (as a peace negotiator, etc.) after leaving office on the basis of his personal moral authority.

In the British liberal tradition of HOBBES and LOCKE, legitimate political authority comes from a SOCIAL CONTRACT among the people who submit to authority by the "CONSENT of the governed." Unjust authority then becomes that which we did not make ourselves or consent to, only voluntary, informed submission to authority being legitimate and democratic.

In COMMUNIST or MARXIST theory, political authority comes from economics and history; the social class that controls economic production also commands political authority, and in turn is controlled by technology. So the "DICTATORSHIP of the proletariat (working class)" is just during the socialist stage of history. For FASCIST (e.g., NAZI) theory, authority is rooted in the race and nation and concentrated in the leader who uses power with no restraints. The STATE becomes the ultimate authority and is almost worshiped as a god. Various radical theories want to place authority in the outcasts of society and in those least prepared to rule (educationally, economically, politically) to diminish the preponderance of authority.

Most political thinkers see authority as necessary to social order, peace, and prosperity. The problem is how to establish good, just, respected authority. Education, ethics, and healthy family and economic life are seen as contributing to this.

Further Readings
Arendt, J. *What Is Authority? In Between Past and Future.* Cleveland and New York: Viking, 1968.
Flathman, R. *The Practice of Political Authority: Authority and the Authoritative.* Chicago: University of Chicago Press, 1980.
Friedrich, C. J., ed. *Nomos I: Authority.* Cambridge, Mass.: Harvard University Press, 1958.
Raz, J. *The Authority of Law.* Oxford: Clarendon Press, 1979.
Watt, E. D. *Authority.* London: Croom Helm, 1982.
Weber, M. *The Theory of Social and Economic Organization* (1922), A. R. Henderson and T. Parsons, transl. New York: Macmillan, 1947.
Wolff, R. P. *In Defense of Anarchism.* New York: Harper & Row, 1970.

autonomy/autonomous

The idea that a person or group or nation is independent, separate, and self-sufficient. For ARISTOTLE, this involved a rich variety of relationships: in family, society, friendship, active CITIZENSHIP, and religious contemplation. Only someone connected in all these ways has everything a rational human being needs and so is self-sufficient. For most of Western political thought, the idea of individual autonomy is seen as a deceptive fiction, as individuals are actually dependent on so many others (economically, educationally, emotionally, spiritually).

A group's autonomy implies its independence from others, especially from its perceived antagonists. So, black Muslims claim autonomy from the white American power structure; FEMINIST and lesbian movements assert autonomy from men. National autonomy, or a country's SOVEREIGNTY, argues for a nation's FREEDOM and independence from other countries' control over their economic or political affairs. As the world becomes more interdependent technologically, economically, and politically, national autonomy becomes less prevalent or realistic.

According to the NATURAL LAW view of St. Thomas AQUINAS, individuals and groups are inevitably related (to nature, society, God) whether they recognize it or not. Such an objective view of our condition differs from the autonomy perspective that regards individuals as self-determining. The question for much of political theory, then, is how much independence (personal or national) is possible within an interdependent reality. The United States has tried to reconcile this by allowing considerable private space (such as freedom of belief, movement, choice) while recognizing the complex interdependence of modern society.

Awakening

A religious revival that brings social and political effects. For example, THE GREAT AWAKENING that occurred in America from 1740 to 1770 democratized Christianity in the colonies and prepared the way for the American Revolution. This occurred by the rise of EVANGELICAL ministers (often ordinary Christians) who attracted more public attention than the established clergy. This broke down the hierarchy and AUTHORITY of the church, increased democratic self-government of the congregations, and prepared the American mind for political DEMOCRACY. Whether attributed to divine inspiration or social change, the massive religious conversions, deepened morality, and individual responsibility of such revivals always have social and political consequences.

After the American Revolution (1776) and ratification of the United States CONSTITUTION (1787), another religious revival occurred, commonly called the Second Great Awakening. Lasting from 1790 to 1830, this move of the Holy Spirit spread across the western frontier (e.g., Kentucky, Tennessee, Ohio) where Americans were moving to new farmland. Like its predecessor, this Awakening caused massive conversions to Christianity, a strong democratic movement in the churches, and an increase in personal morality and piety. It saved the country from a social and moral breakdown that followed the disappearance of the old British imperial social structure and allowed a social economic FREEDOM based in individual ethical conduct. This fueled various social reform movements, such as the prohibition of alcohol and the abolition of slavery. While the Great Awakening of the mid 1700s occurred primarily in the existing churches (PRESBYTERIAN, Anglican, Congregational), the Second Great Awakening spawned new evangelical denominations (BAPTIST, Methodist), which soon became the largest churches in the United States. Relying more on ordinary Christians, emphasizing "the priesthood of all believers," these religious awakenings diminished the monopoly of ordained clergy on church leadership and increased the democratic culture in U.S. religion. This, in turn, spread an EGALITARIAN and democratic worldview in other aspects of society, especially politics, business, and the family.

Similar religious revivals or awakenings have occurred throughout the West (e.g., Savonarola in 15th-century Florence, Italy; the Moravians in 18th-century Germany; Methodists in 18th-century Britain) with political ramifications. Usually, they are aimed at attacking individual immorality and political corruption, causing personal and social transformations.

Further Reading
Miller, P., and Heimert, A. *The Great Awakening*. Indianapolis: Bobbs-Merrill, 1967.

B

Bacon, Sir Francis (1561–1626) *British statesman and philosopher*

Bacon's most important contribution to political thought was his integration of science and government. Living at a time when scientific knowledge was suspect, Bacon designed an ideal state (in his book *New Atlantis*) that relied on a "College of Science" or "Solomon's House" to advise and guide government. The phrase "Knowledge is Power" comes from this Baconian idea that science and technology lead to political, economic, and military power and prestige. This makes Bacon one of the first MODERN political thinkers who believe that humans should control nature for their own purposes through enlightened, scientific knowledge. Much of his writings concern empiricism, or the scientific method for searching for truth (for example, his book *Proficience and Advancement of Learning,* 1605). This affected his views of politics and religion. His "New Philosophy" encouraged a more machinelike REPUBLICAN state than the prevailing personal MONARCHY of his time, and he encouraged a critical, skeptical approach to religious faith.

Born to a noble English family, Bacon was educated at Trinity College, Cambridge University, studied law at Gray's Inn in London, and served in Parliament. Under King James I, Bacon served the British monarchy in several administrative positions, including attorney general and lord chancellor. Later in his life, he was accused of bribery and corruption and retired, disgraced, to private life.

Bacon is seen as a transitional figure between the CHRISTIAN MIDDLE AGES and the modern scientific world.

Further Readings

Bacon, Francis. *The essayes or counsels, civill and morall.,* ed. with intro. and commentary by Michael Kiernan. Cambridge, Mass.: Harvard University Press, 1985.

Bacon, F. *The Advancement of Learning and New Atlantis,* A. Johnston, ed. Oxford, Eng.: Clarendon Press, 1974.

———. *Essays,* J. Pitcher, ed. Harmondsworth, Eng.: Penguin Books, 1985.

Bozeman, Theodore Dwight. *Protestants in an Age of Science: The Baconian Ideal and Ante-Bellum American Religious Thought.* Chapel Hill: University of North Carolina Press, 1977.

Du Maurier, Daphne, Dame. *The Winding Stair: Francis Bacon, His Rise and Fall,* 1st ed. Garden City, N.Y.: Doubleday, 1977, 1976.

Peppiatt, Michael. *Francis Bacon: Anatomy of an Enigma,* 1st American ed. New York: Farrar, Straus & Giroux, 1997.

Bakunin, Mikhail Aleksandrovich (1814–1876)
Russian revolutionary and anarchist

Bakunin was the eldest son of a small landowner whose estate was near Moscow. He was educated at a military school in St. Petersburg and later served as an officer in the emperor's army stationed on the Polish frontier. He resigned his commission in 1835 and spent the next five years in Moscow studying philosophy, literature, and politics. In 1840, Bakunin traveled to Berlin to continue his education and there became engaged with the YOUNG HEGELIANS. After brief visits to Belgium and Switzerland, Bakunin settled in Paris and became involved with a network of French, German, and Polish socialists, including Karl MARX and Pierre-Joseph PROUDHON. Inspired by the movement for national liberation in central and Eastern Europe, Bakunin participated in the revolutions of 1848. Arrested for his role in the Dresden insurrection of May 1849, Bakunin was returned to Russia, where he remained imprisoned until 1857 when he was exiled to Siberia. He managed to escape in 1861, traveling first to London, then to Italy, and finally to Geneva in 1864.

At this time, Bakunin began to articulate his particular version of ANARCHISM, the main points of which drew him into a conflict with Marx while both were members of the International Workingmen's Association, or "First International," an organization of working-class parties seeking to transform the capitalist societies into socialist commonwealths and to oversee their eventual unification in a world federation. Although for Marx the first goal of the revolution was the dictatorship of the proletariat, Bakunin believed that the centralization of power had to be abolished in all its forms. For Bakunin, the centralization of authority signifies the delegation of power from one individual or group to another, which raises the risk of EXPLOITATION by the individual or group to whom power has been ceded. The state must be the primary object of criticism because it is the ultimate form of centralized authority that will invariably use its enormous power to subject and exploit the people. Bakunin argued that for liberation to occur, individuals and groups must retain their power in terms of their ability to determine political matters for themselves. This position contrasted sharply with the Marxist notion of a single revolutionary class (proletariat) that was to be represented by a unitary vanguard party established to assume control of the state.

Bakunin's contention was that political power must be kept at the local level through the utilization of small administrative bodies. For him, FEDERALISM was to be the key to building new forms of EGALITARIAN social arrangements committed to the freedom of all individuals, who were seen by Bakunin as naturally social. The destruction of the old society and the creation of the new must begin with the abolition of the right of inheritance and the subversion of private property, which is the key to the capitalist exploitation of the working class. To promote his anarchist ideas, Bakunin formed the semisecret Social Democratic Alliance in 1869, which he conceived as a revolutionary avant-garde within the First International. This brought to a head the dispute between Marx and Bakunin, and in the ensuing power struggle at a congress of the First International at The Hague in 1872, Marx secured the expulsion of Bakunin and his followers from the International. Bakunin's followers, called the autonomists, were active in Spain and Italy for some time thereafter. Bakunin himself spent the last years of his life impoverished in Switzerland.

Further Reading
Saltman, R. B. *The Social and Political Thought of Michael Bakunin.* Westport, Conn.: Greenwood Press, 1983.

Baptist

A CHRISTIAN church denomination noted for emphasizing the separation of CHURCH AND STATE, a highly DEMOCRATIC form of church government, and an individual, personal relationship to God. English and American Baptists derive from European "Anabaptist" Protestant Christians, and their ideals of religious FREEDOM and LIBERTY of conscience greatly affected political and religious life in Britain and America. JEFFERSON's Virginia statute for religious freedom and later U.S. constitutional freedom of religious belief embodied Baptist ideals for liberty of individual conscience and church independence from STATE control.

Baptists now constitute the largest Protestant church in the United States of America. Each Baptist church is independent but usually is a voluntarily part of an association. The individual church is run democratically, with each member having a vote, and ministers are elected by the congregation. This democratic kind of church government helped the Baptists grow rapidly in America. During the Second Great AWAKENING (1790–1830), a Christian revival that spread across the new Western frontier, the Baptist church grew to be the largest denomination in America. Its democratic church structure and reliance on uneducated lay ministers allowed it to spread rapidly. With a simple Christianity based in the Bible (rather than creeds), Baptists historically have been theological and political CONSERVATIVES. As an EVANGELICAL church, Baptists have emphasized spreading Christianity through foreign missionaries.

Prominent Baptists include the Englishman John BUNYAN (author of the classic book *Pilgrim's Progress*); colonial American Roger WILLIAMS (who built the first Baptist church in Providence, Rhode Island); the first president of Harvard University, Henry Dunster; London preacher Charles Spurgeon; and U.S. evangelist Billy Graham.

The theological roots of Baptists rest on the belief that only adult Christians (who can make a personal confession of faith in Christ) should be baptized. They reject the baptism of infants on that basis. This caused persecution of Baptists in Europe by both CATHOLIC and Calvinist Protestant churches. Only in the United States did the Baptist view enjoy widespread acceptance and influence. American Baptists are almost evenly divided between white and African-American believers, though most churches are not racially integrated. Baptists now exist in almost every nation in the world; in Russian and Eastern European countries, most Protestants are Baptists. Latin America and China have increasing Baptist populations. Often associated with political democracy and economic CAPITALISM, this church often flourishes in areas experiencing those developments.

Although still theologically distant from the Catholic Church, Baptists in the United States have shared positions on many political issues (such as opposing ABORTION, HOMOSEXUALITY, divorce, etc.) and have been united in being strongly anti-COMMUNIST.

Further Reading
Carroll, B. H. *Baptists and Their Doctrines.* Nashville: Broadman & Holman, 2000.

Barber, Benjamin (1939–) *Academic, political philosopher, and democratic activist*

A leading U.S. DEMOCRATIC theorist of the 20th century, Barber is best known for his book *Strong Democracy,* considered a classic text on COMMUNITARIAN democracy. Heavily influenced by ROUSSEAU and HEGEL, Barber's work critiques the INDIVIDUALISM of British LIBERALISM and argues for political participation, direct democracy, and citizen involvement in collective social choices. He believes that democracy is a way of life as well as a form of government, that power should flow from the bottom up, and that individual RIGHTS should be balanced by social responsibility. Barber celebrates individual membership in family, communities of all kinds, and political participation at all levels.

In his principal work on political theory, *Strong Democracy,* Barber argues, after ARISTOTLE, that humans are naturally social by virtue of their capacities for reason, speech, and political deliberation. The fulfillment of human nature as well as social justice, therefore, requires direct individual involvement in collective governance. Humans are not independent, but interdependent, and the only real freedom each can enjoy is participating in making the laws under which we live. Barber's emphasis on "participatory" democracy distinguishes his DIALECTICAL politics. Thought must be connected to action as real praxis. For Barber, no moral absolutes exist, only those created by the democratic community; JUSTICE, FREEDOM, EQUALITY, RIGHTS, and LIBERTY all receive their substantive definition through concrete political action. In *Strong Democracy,* Barber advances several specific reforms to help implement his ideas, including interactive public television, the multichoice format of referendum, universal citizen service, and political control over economics. As such, Barber's ideas greatly influenced the participatory and communitarian democratic movements (though he eschewed the latter term in his self-definition).

Educated at Harvard, the London School of Economics, and Grinnell College, Barber spent most of his academic career teaching at Rutgers University. Since 1988, he served as the founding director of the Walt Whitman Center for the Culture and Politics of Democracy at Rutgers, which strives to encourage civic participation through numerous programs and internships. Barber served as consultant to President Bill Clinton, the European Parliament, and numerous political leaders and civic organizations.

In addition to 14 books, Barber has written for television, the theater, and opera. He served as the founding editor of the scholarly journal, *Political Theory.*

A prolific thinker and activist in politics and the arts, Barber influenced democratic theory and practice in the United States and the world.

Further Reading

Barber, Benjamin R. *Strong Democracy*. Berkeley: University of California Press, 1984.

Bayle, Pierre (1647–1706)   *French philosopher and critic*

The son of a CALVINIST minister, Bayle was born and raised in France during the reign of Louis XIV, whose revocation of the Edict of Nantes outlawed PROTESTANTISM in 1685. Educated at the Jesuit College in Toulouse, Bayle converted to CATHOLICISM, but several years later he adopted Calvinism. Bayle moved to Geneva in 1670 and continued his education in philosophy and theology until returning to France in 1674. In 1675, he was appointed professor of philosophy at the Protestant academy in Sedan, where he remained until taking up a position as professor of philosophy and history in Rotterdam, the Netherlands, in 1681. Bayle was dismissed from this position in 1693 after a heated dispute with a Calvinist colleague concerning the latter's extreme orthodoxy. He then spent the last years of his life completing what is probably his most famous work, the *Dictionnaire historique et critique (Historical and Critical Dictionary)*.

In the *Dictionary*, Bayle employed his critical and skeptical approach in compiling a series of biographical articles on mostly obscure historical figures, which were then supplemented by digressive analyses of controversial factual, theological, and philosophical problems. Bayle's skepticism toward all ideological and religious orthodoxy had a great influence on many of the major ENLIGHTENMENT thinkers, even though the *Dictionary* was condemned by the French Reformed Church of Rotterdam and banned by the French Roman Catholic Church soon after its publication.

Although the *Dictionary* was a massive work consisting of numerous entries and annotations, the underlying theme of the text was that of Bayle's longstanding plea for broad political TOLERATION of divergent opinions on religion. In 1686, Bayle had published his *Commentaire philosophique sur ces paroles de Jésus-Christ "Constrains-les d'entrer" (Philosophical Commentary on the Words of Jesus Christ "Compel them to come in")*, in which he attacked religious intolerance and defended the claim that the intolerant should not be allowed to persecute others. Bayle even went so far as to suggest protecting the "rights of the erring conscience" against persecution by authorities who dogmatically assert knowledge of absolute truth with respect to religious matters. According to Bayle, religion and morality are independent of one another because religion can be based only on faith and not on reason. Therefore, contrary to the beliefs of many of his contemporaries, Bayle argued that theist and atheist alike are able to act morally. Toleration, in Bayle's uncompromising defense, is a necessary political remedy to the disease of sectarian violence and state repression.

Further Reading

Lennon, T. M. *Reading Bayle*. Toronto: University of Toronto Press, 1999.

Beccaria, Cesare Bonesana (1738–1794)   *Italian criminologist and economist*

Born in Milan to an aristocratic family, Beccaria was educated at a Jesuit school in Parma and received a law degree from the University of Pavia in 1758. Beccaria then returned to Milan and became involved in literary and intellectual societies associated with the ENLIGHTENMENT. After publishing a small pamphlet on monetary reform in 1762, Beccaria began to write a critical study of criminal law at the suggestion of Count Pietro Verri. This work, *Dei delitti e delle pene (On Crimes and Punishment)*, was published anonymously in 1764 and met with immediate success, appearing in English, French, German, Spanish, Dutch, and American editions during the next decade. In 1768, Beccaria was appointed professor of economics and commerce at the Palatine School in Milan, and in 1771 he assumed a position on the Supreme Economic Council of Milan. He remained a public official for the remainder of his life.

On Crimes and Punishment advanced the first systematic treatment of criminology and criminal PUNISHMENT based on several fundamental concepts of MODERN political theory. First, Beccaria employed the idea of a SOCIAL CONTRACT to account for the origin of political authority. According to Beccaria, each person sacrifices a limited amount of liberty for the purpose of establishing civil government. Laws are created under the terms of the social contract to maintain social order and to protect the liberty of the members of the community. However, Beccaria stressed that while the government is authorized to punish those who transgress the laws, the only legitimate use of punishment is to defend the liberty of society as a whole against individual transgressors. Employing punishment to coerce confessions, intimidate opponents, and consolidate political power is illegitimate and unjust.

Second, Beccaria also adopted the principle, popularized in UTILITARIANISM, that "the greatest happiness of the greatest number" is the only criterion to be used for evaluating laws and social policy. Beccaria's commitment to social reform motivated his critique of barbaric and inhumane punishment. Because the primary purpose of punishment is to ensure the continued existence of society, laws and punishments carried out through the arbitrary use of power must be eliminated because they threaten the happiness of individual members of society. Consequently, Beccaria argued that torture and capital punishment, especially when used in response to minor offenses, undermine respect for legitimate authority.

In addition, Beccaria held that deterrence rather than retribution should be the aim of punishment. Mere retribution is neither useful nor necessary for the protection of society. The chief problem that Beccaria identified in the administration of justice was the inconsistency and inequality of sentencing, due primarily to the extensive discretionary powers of judges. Beccaria suggested that laws should clearly define crimes and that judges should be restricted to determining only whether a person has or has not violated the law. Once a person has been found guilty, Beccaria believed that punishment should be applied quickly as it is the swift certainty of its application that best deters others. Finally, Beccaria argued that punishment should be proportional to the gravity of the offense, excluding such severe punishments as torture and capital punishment. Even the most serious of criminal offenses, Beccaria insisted, ought to be punished by long-term imprisonment rather than by death. Ultimately, Beccaria's goal of penal reform was an expression of his desire to protect "the rights of man."

Further Reading
Maestro, M. *Cesare Beccaria and the Origins of Penal Reform.* Philadelphia: Temple University Press, 1973.

Becket, Sir Thomas (1118–1170) *English chancellor and archbishop of Canterbury*

As an English churchman involved in politics, Becket represents the check on royal power by the church. In 1163, King Henry II coerced English bishops to approve laws that transferred power from ecclesiastical to secular (royal) courts. Becket, as archbishop of Canterbury (the highest authority in the English church), refused the king's order. King Henry II convened a council of his loyal barons and bishops to punish Becket, forcing the archbishop to escape to France. After extensive negotiations between the king, Becket, and the pope, during which two bishops loyal to the king were excommunicated and Henry II threatened to expel from England all clergy associated with Becket, a reconciliation was realized. Becket returned to England triumphantly. His resistance to royal encroachment was popularly seen as a valuable check on the government and limitation on arbitrary royal power. When he refused to absolve the excommunicated English bishops unless they swore allegiance to the pope, the king shouted words in a fit of rage, which four knights took as orders to kill Becket. The archbishop was murdered in the cathedral on December 29, 1170. The European response to this assassination of a church leader by the state was shock and horror. Pope Alexander III named Becket a saint of the church on February 21, 1173, and King Henry had to do public penance.

Becket's resistance to the government and martyrdom stands as a historical example of opposing state power by appealing to a law higher than worldly power and forms a basis for CIVIL DISOBEDIENCE on moral grounds.

behaviorism/behaviorist

An approach to the study of individuals and society that relies on data or information observed and measured by the senses of perception (sight, hearing, etc.). MODERN social science relies heavily on behaviorism. It is essentially the application of the scientific method of EMPIRICAL observation to human psychology and society. This involves looking at behavior, or human actions, rather than motives, reason, or other aspects of human life, claiming that this method of study yields greater knowledge of human nature and society than traditional philosophical rational or spiritual approaches. Behaviorism claims only to "describe" the facts, not to evaluate or to judge them. It claims to be "value-free" science, as opposed to imposing some interpretation or standard (from ethics, culture, religion) from outside the observed phenomenon. So, for example, a behaviorist political scientist studies the voting behavior of different social groups (e.g., women, CATHOLICS, southerners) but does not evaluate or judge their wisdom or "rightness"; just the "facts" are reported. Critics of behaviorism assert that this ethical neutrality is itself a value judgement. Most Western social sciences (psychology, sociology, POLITICAL SCIENCE) rely at least in part on behaviorism.

The philosophical foundation of behaviorism is found in Thomas HOBBES, especially his book *Leviathan*, in which it is posited that humans are governed by sensory stimulation (pleasure and pain) and that the movements prompted by those sensations explain human activity. This contrasts with the CLASSICAL (ARISTOTLE) view that humans are governed by reason and the religious view (e.g., St. Thomas AQUINAS) that people are at least potentially governed by faith and morals. Hobbes's perspective produces a hedonism and ethical relativism contrary to much of the Western political tradition. His emphasis on POWER, wealth, and other worldly qualities renders behaviorism one of the aspects of modern political REALISM.

Further Reading
Baum, W. M. *Understanding Behaviorism*. New York: HarperCollins College Publishers, 1994.

Bellamy, Edward (1850–1898)   *U.S. writer, journalist, and socialist utopian*

Born in Massachusetts, Bellamy is best known for his UTOPIAN novel, *Looking Backward* (1889), which was one of the most popular utopian SOCIALIST books critical of U.S. CAPITALISM, INDUSTRIALISM, and late 19th-century society. In this book, Bellamy's main character (who awakens from a hypnotic 100-year sleep in the year 2000) sees how the United States has solved the problems of capitalism and competition in his own time. He is told that economic competition in the 20th century caused the ruin of many businesses and the consolidation of all firms into one big monopoly. Then the American people, democratically, nationalized this economic monopoly, creating a SOCIALIST system of cooperation, harmony and prosperity in the United States. Poverty and competition are eliminated by the state-operated economy. Socialism is thus portrayed as "economic democracy."

Bellamy's novel sold widely in the 1890s and spawned 150 "New Nationalist" clubs that worked to implement his reforms. His ideas of government regulation of the economy for the common good later found expression in the PROGRESSIVE and LIBERAL DEMOCRATIC PARTY. The ideas of using the central government to end unemployment, poverty, and misery continue as major theme in AMERICAN POLITICAL THOUGHT.

Several of Bellamy's predictions of latter 20th-century American life were startlingly prophetic. For example, he predicted that the economy would rely on credit cards. In his utopian scheme, each citizen would be allotted an annual salary on their credit card, and they would simply charge things at the state stores that they need. Money would be eliminated. Because everyone would feel secure from want, greed and savings would end. The state would provide for each "from cradle to grave." Socialism would rely solely on humans' higher impulses of dedication and honor, each recognizing his or her duty to work hard for the common good. Like many other utopians and socialists, Bellamy believed that humans are naturally good, corrupted only by society to become mean, selfish, and materialistic. Contrary to the REALISM of the CHRISTIAN tradition in America which situates evil inside the human heart and will (see St. AUGUSTINE, James MADISON) utopians like Bellamy thought that simply changing social institutions and public education would produce decent, unselfish, hardworking human beings. The only incentive people need, for Bellamy, is others' gratitude and a sense of patriotism to the nation. This socialist utopian optimism over the naturally noble qualities in humanity was largely disappointed in the 100 years that followed the publication of Bellamy's book, but it represents a utopian socialist thread in AMERICAN POLITICAL THOUGHT.

Further Readings
Aaron, Daniel. *Edward Bellamy, Novelist and Reformer.* Schenectady, N.Y.: Union College, 1968.
Bellamy, Edward. *Equality.* New York, London: D. Appleton-Century Incorporated, 1933.
———. *Looking Backward, 1000–1887,* with an intro. by Paul Bellamy and decorations by George Salter. Cleveland, New York: World Publishing, 1945, 1888.
Looking Backward, 1988–1888: Essays on Edward Bellamy, Patai, Daphne, ed. Amherst: University of Massachusetts Press, 1988.

Bennett, William J. (1943–)   *U.S. conservative political thinker*

William Bennett is the codirector and cofounder of Empower America, a fellow with the Heritage Foundation, a conservative think tank, and the author of 11 books. Notable among his writings are *The Book of Virtues, The Children's Book of Virtues,* and *The Death of Outrage: Bill Clinton and the Assault on American Ideals,* which reached number one on the *New York Times* best-seller list. His latest book, *The Educated Child: A Parent's Guide,* reflects his emphasis on the issues of educational reform and the decline of morality in U.S. society. Dr. Bennett served as President Reagan's chairman of the National Endowment for the Humanities and secretary of education and as President G. H. W. Bush's drug czar. Dr. Bennett emerged as a leading conservative political figure in the 1980s, serving under Presidents Reagan and Bush. After leaving government, he has continued to speak out strongly and controversially about social issues, U.S. education, national character, and the values that strengthen and preserve society.

Empower America reflects the values most commonly associated with the writing and philosophy of Bennett. Specifically, the organization and its cofounder/codirector are devoted to ensuring that government actions foster growth, economic well-being, FREEDOM, and individual responsibility. To this end, Bennett has continued his high-profile efforts against government BUREAUCRACY and monopolies since leaving government in 1990. He has identified several areas, such as educational reform, tax reform, internet and technology, social security reform, and national security, on which he wishes to have an impact. To each of these fields, he brings a conservative perspective, encouraging self-sufficiency and personal responsibility.

Bennett's efforts to improve the U.S. system of education are thematically driven by what he calls the Three C's: choice, content, and character. The current education system, according to Bennett, is failing American children, and much of the federal government's involvement in education during the past several decades has been intrusive and misguided: That's why attempts to return control to parents and communities are so important. Such a view led Bennett to conclude, like many of his conservative counterparts, that the Department of Education should be dramatically reduced or eliminated in favor of STATE-led initiatives and control.

In addition to his work with Empower America, Bennett leads several organizations dedicated to restoring social conscience. Although he is a well-known Republican, Bennett has consistently reached across party lines to pursue important common purposes. He works closely with Senator Joseph Lieberman, a Democrat, on the issues of popular culture and worldwide religious persecution. Bennett and former Democratic senator Sam Nunn are cochairs of the National Commission on Civic Renewal. Most recently, Bennett and former Democratic governor Mario Cuomo were named cochairs of the Partnership for a Drug-Free America.

Further Reading
Bennett, William J. *The Death of Outrage: Bill Clinton and the Assault on American Ideals.* New York: Free Press, 1998.

Bentham, Jeremy (1748–1832)   *British philosopher, jurist, and political reformer*

As a UTILITARIAN philosopher, Bentham related goodness or ethics to sensory happiness (pleasure and pain) in the tradition of Thomas HOBBES. He believed that social good was "the greatest happiness for the greatest number." This philosophy has DEMOCRATIC, even SOCIALIST, tendencies because it measures JUSTICE by the majority's material condition. In its time, it was considered very radical, as justice in 18th-century England was seen as defined by an ARISTOCRACY of superior knowledge and wealth. Bentham's materialist utilitarian thought defines *good* in terms of economic goods rather than cultural, intellectual, or spiritual values.

The practical reforms emerging from Bentham's philosophy included more humane penal institutions, parliamentary reform (universal suffrage, secret ballots, annual elections), and criminal procedure. Bentham was critical of the traditional English legal system of William BLACKSTONE and of John LOCKE's NATURAL RIGHTS philosophy. He called individual natural rights "simple nonsense" and imprescriptible right "nonsense upon stilts." By this, he attacked individual rights from God or Nature because for him democratic government was necessary to secure these rights. This follows the British tradition that individual rights are dependent on and limited by society, not contrary to or against society. Unlike Locke or the American view of "inalienable rights" from God, Bentham's emphasis on the community basis of rights leads to WELFARE STATE and socialist conceptions of individual rights granted by society (and potentially taken away by society).

For this reason, Bentham supported the French Revolution of 1789 (contrary to Edmund BURKE), though he later criticized its excesses. Because of his endorsement of government-promoted equality, security, and economic welfare, Bentham is influential in the later concept of the welfare state, LIBERALISM, and SOCIALISM.

Further Readings
Harrison, R. *Bentham*. London: Routledge & Kegan Paul, 1983.
Hart, H. L. A. (Herbert Lionel Adolphus). *Essays on Bentham: Studies in Jurisprudence and Political Theory*. Oxford, Eng.: Clarendon Press; New York: Oxford University Press, 1982.
Hume, L. J. *Bentham and Bureaucracy*. Cambridge: Cambridge University Press, 1981.
Rosen, F. *Jeremy Bentham and Representative Democracy: A Study of the Constitutional Code*. Oxford, Eng.: Clarendon Press, 1983.
Steintrager, James. *Bentham*. Ithaca, N.Y.: Cornell University Press, 1977.

Blackstone, Sir William (1723–1780)   *English legal philosopher, jurist, and politician*

Best known for his writing on the English common law, Blackstone penned the four-volume *Commentaries on the Laws of England* (1765–69), which greatly influenced views of British government and law throughout the world. This legal scholarship came out of his lectures at All Souls College, Oxford University.

Blackstone interprets the English common-law tradition through the parliamentary supremacy view of the glorious revolution of 1688. This posits an ANCIENT CONSTITUTION of English rights and liberties in Pre-Norman (1066) England that was corrupted by Norman monarchy, feudalism, and CATHOLIC Christianity. In this Whig view, the modern revolution of 1688, which gave supreme power to the REPUBLICAN Parliament, strictly limited the power of the monarchy, established the Protestant Christian faith, and allowed extensive private PROPERTY and commerce, was simply a restoration of the ancient liberties in England. This views MEDIEVAL English common law through the modern LIBERALISM of John LOCKE. Blackstone discusses English law through the categories of Persons (volume I); Property (volume II); Private Wrongs or torts—civil law (volume III); and Public Wrongs or criminal law (volume IV). The last book also discusses penal law with humane recommendations for reforming the barbaric punishments in England at the time.

Blackstone's writings effectively codified the modern British liberal, NATURAL RIGHTS view of English law.

He greatly influenced subsequent British politics and law throughout the empire. In the North American colonies, most lawyers read Blackstone and used his ideas on individual rights, republican government, and the ancient constitution in their arguments for American independence during the American Revolution. Thomas JEFFERSON, author of the DECLARATION OF INDEPENDENCE and other Revolutionary pamphlets, especially employed Blackstone against the British imperial system and policies. Blackstone is still regarded as a classic on English common law.

He was educated at Pembroke College, Oxford, and after teaching at All Souls, Oxford, Blackstone served as a Tory member of Parliament and ended his distinguished career as a British judge. Blackstone's legal philosophy is considered representative of Whig natural-rights liberalism and CONSERVATIVE British constitutionalism.

Further Readings
Blackstone, W. *Commentaries on the Laws of England*, facsimile ed. Chicago: Chicago University Press, 1979.
Boorstin, D. *The Mysterious Science of the Law*. Cambridge, Mass.: Harvard University Press, 1941.
Jones, G. *The Sovereignty of the Law: Selections from Blackstone's Commentaries*. London: Macmillan, 1973.

Bloch, Ernst (1885–1977)   *German Marxist and theorist of utopia*

Ernst Bloch was one of a group of 20th-century MARXISTS who challenged the reductive materialism and dogmatic determinism of classical Marxism. He is best known for his UTOPIANISM. Bloch argued that reality (nature and persons) is "unfinished," characterized by potential and possibility (the "not-yet"). Nature is thus dynamic, and persons are desiring. His utopianism thus consists of the possibility of "reuniting" nature (the object) and persons (the subject). Bloch's work pays little attention to the economic substructure and focuses instead on the superstructural categories of language and culture. Here, the idea of possibility is expressed in his notion of Hope. Hope is the anticipation of utopic possibilities: It brings into consciousness the "not-yet thought" and thus makes a utopian future realizable. Bloch's major work, *The Principle of Hope* (1959), is an encyclopedic survey and analysis of hope and anticipation in the realms of both the mundane (for example, in daydreams and popular literature) and in philosophy, art, and religion. Bloch distinguishes between concrete and abstract utopias, the former being those utopic visions that are grounded in the social and economic reality of the historical age. Marx's own utopia in which EXPLOITATION is ended is just one, albeit the most important one, of the possible concrete utopias. In this way, Bloch retains his Marxist identity by insisting on the necessity for grounding, although not reducing, thought and ideals in the real circumstance of society and by characterizing history as a TELEOLOGICAL process that ends beyond capitalism. Bloch's brand of Marxism is made distinct by his insistence on the dynamic nature of reality, history, and human thought and by his explicit rendering of the utopian aspects of Marxist theory. His drawing attention to the role of the subjective and his deep analysis of the subjective are perhaps his most important contribution to Marxist scholarship in the 20th century.

Bloch was born to Jewish parents in Ludwigshfen in Germany. His father was a railway official. He studied philosophy, physics, and music at the University of Munich, completed his doctorate in 1909, and moved to Heidelburg, where he met and worked with the aesthetician and Marxist Georg Lukacs. Lukacs was the most important influence on Bloch's own work. In 1933, Bloch left Germany because of the rise of Nazism and made his way to the United States, where he lived until after World War II. In 1948, he took a professorship at the University of Leipzig in what was then East Germany. His relations with the officials of the communist government grew steadily worse (he was prevented from publishing, and his work was condemned), and in 1961 he defected to West Germany. There he was appointed professor of philosophy at Tubingen. He died in 1977.

Further Reading
Hudson, W. *The Marxist Philosophy of Ernst Bloch*. New York: St. Martin's Press, 1982.

Bodin, Jean (1529–1596) *French political philosopher*

Bodin represents and encapsulates THOMIST political theory of the late MIDDLE AGES in Europe. He is best known for his writings on SOVEREIGNTY, which contributed to the absolutist authority of French kings (as Louis XIV). But his identification of absolute political power with the state ruler does not preclude the distribution of social influence in different groups. So, while Bodin says that the MONARCHY has absolute sovereignty or power to make or overrule any law, the monarchy exists within a "commonweal" of society, different classes and interests. The wise and good ruler respects the common good and representatives of other orders (estates, corporations, colleges, the church). After ARISTOTLE, Bodin acknowledges different forms of government (monarchy, ARISTOCRACY, polity) and their corruption (TYRANNY, oligarchy, DEMOCRACY) and insists that a "just" government of any form can be popular in serving the common good. A king has great authority but is limited by divine law and God. An awesome responsibility rests on rulers because abuse of power produces fear, hatred, dissension, and destruction. The chief end of the commonwealth, exemplified by the governors, should be religious piety, JUSTICE, valor, honor, VIRTUE, and goodness. Suspicious of the common peoples' greed and vanity, Bodin opposed democratic government. Humans, as St. Thomas AQUINAS asserted, are between the beasts and the angels and only reach goodness through careful education and moral development. After PLATO, he saw the commonwealth reflecting human nature with "understanding"—the highest virtue—followed by reason, the anger desiring power and revenge, and—the lowest—brutish desire and lust. If the higher faculties do not rule the lower instincts, chaos ensues.

A devout and mystical CHRISTIAN, Bodin viewed this world within a larger cosmic context of spiritual beings and warfare. A wholesome society must be aware of dark, demonic spirits who are opposed to Christ. Bodin's last published work dealt with witchcraft and its effect on politics and society. Although the government should take care that the economic needs of its people are satisfied, this should be followed by concern for their ethical and religious needs, as the Commonwealth's ultimate goal is to bring people to "divine contemplation of the fairest and most excellent object that can be thought or imagined" [Christ]. A CONSERVATIVE French CATHOLIC, Bodin nevertheless encouraged tolerance for French Protestant Christians and opposed King Henry III's persecution of the HUGUENOTS.

Bodin is recognized as a brilliant, eclectic political thinker. He studied widely in law, history, mathematics, metaphysical philosophy, several languages, and astronomy before entering French political and religious life. His major work, *The Six Books of a Common-*

weal (1576), influenced Western political thought for 200 years after its publication. His idea that humans are part of a "great chain of being" who are connected to all other beings in the universe contributed to MODERN (e.g., Madisonian) notions of balancing different elements and groups through moderation and CHECKS AND BALANCES.

Further Readings

Bodin, J. *Method for the Easy Comprehension of History* (1566), B. Reynolds, transl. New York: Columbia University Press, 1945.

———. *The Six Books of a Commonweal,* R. Knolles, transl., K. D. McRae, ed. Cambridge, Mass.: Harvard University Press, 1962.

———. *Colloquium of the Seven about Secrets of the Sublime* (1841), M. L. D. Kuntz, transl. Princeton, N.J.: Princeton University Press, 1975.

Denzer, H., ed. *Jean Bodin.* Munich: C. H. Beck, 1954.

Franklin, J. *Jean Bodin and the Rise of Absolutist Theory.* Cambridge, Eng.: Cambridge University Press, 1973.

King, P. *The Ideology of Order: a Comparative Analysis of Jean Bodin and Thomas Hobbes.* London: Allen & Unwin, 1974.

Lewis, J. U. "Jean Bodin's 'logic of sovereignty'," *Political Studies* 16 (1968): 202–22.

Parker, D. "Law, society and the state in the thought of Jean Bodin," *History of Political Thought* 2 (1981): 253–85.

Rose, P. L. *Bodin and the Great God of Nature. The Moral and Religious Universe of a Judaiser.* Geneva: Droz, 1980.

Bolingbroke, Henry St. John, first viscount
(1678–1751)   *British statesman, historian, philosopher, and writer*

Lord Bolingbroke is best known for his development of the classic British REPUBLICAN theory. In this theory, a healthy, virtuous English republic is dependent on a sturdy, independent citizenry, especially yeoman "County" gentry tied to the land, agriculture, and rural values and traditions. The British Parliament and the king should reflect this virtue of farmers and patriots. Corruption of this republic comes from a highly centralized government that is tied to business, commerce, paper money, the stock market, banks, and appointed administrators. Bolingbroke saw the long ministry of Robert Walpole as embodying such antirepublican corrupt government with its high taxes, public debt, standing army, and imperial pretensions. Much of Bolingbroke's "civic republicanism" influenced the American Revolutionaries Thomas JEFFERSON and James MADISON. The American resistance to the British Empire was seen as preserving the "virtuous republic" of yeoman farmers against the corrupt financial and military "Court" of Great Britain under King George III. This "republican ideology" continued in the United States under the Jeffersonian Republicans and agrarians who opposed the political centralization, patronage, and financial manipulation of Alexander HAMILTON and the FEDERALISTS. Bolingbroke's ideas differed from the Americans in their faith in a "Patriot King" preserving traditional British values and in a socially CONSERVATIVE "gentleman's" republic that is opposed to social EQUALITY. Bolingbroke's republicanism is more aristocratic than its American derivative: It opposes banking and commerce from a nostalgic "rural gentry" perspective; this becomes a romantic English Tory outlook later that is associated with Edmund BURKE.

Adopting the CLASSICAL republican ideas of ancient Greek and ROMAN POLITICAL THOUGHT, Bolingbroke's republicanism sees history in terms of the cycles of birth, growth, decline, and death of a republic. The healthy "adult" republic emphasizes civic VIRTUE, the common good, self-sacrifice, and so on, while creeping corruption tempts with private interest, economic gain, and personal immoral conduct. Once a state is corrupted by financial intrigue and power politics, it can only be revived by a return to original republican principles of public virtue, devotion to the common good, patriotism, and duty.

Further Readings

Bolingbroke, H. St J. *Political Writings,* I. Kramnick, ed. Arlington Heights, Ill.: Harlan Davidson, 1970.

———. *Historical Writings,* I. Kramnick, ed. Chicago: University of Chicago Press, 1972.

———. *The Idea of a Patriot King,* S. W. Jackman, ed. Indianapolis: Bobbs-Merrill, 1965.

Dickinson, H. T. *Bolingbroke: Tory Humanist.* London: Constable, 1970.

Hart, J. *Viscount Bolingbroke: Tory Humanist.* Toronto: University of Toronto Press, 1965.

Kramnick, I. *Bolingbroke and His Circle.* Cambridge, Mass.: Harvard University Press, 1968.

Bolshevik

The Marxist COMMUNIST Party formed in Russia in 1903, led by V. I. LENIN, and gaining political power in the October 1917 Russian revolution that established the SOVIET UNION. It is contrasted with the MENSHEVIK Party by advocating a small, minority, revolutionary, "vanguard," communist, working-class party that would guide the proletariat in overthrowing the existing government and establish SOCIALISM. This tightly knit elite revolutionary party was very authoritarian but claimed to represent the interests and goals of the revolutionary working class. Lenin described its philosophy as "democratic centralism"—democratic formulation of political goals but centralized administration of those policies. It is sometimes blamed for the autocratic and TOTALITARIAN form that Soviet communism later took, especially under Joseph STALIN.

Further Reading
Shapiro, L. *The Communist Party of the Soviet Union.* New York: Random House, 1960.

Bonhoeffer, Dietrich (1906–1945) *German theologian, political philosopher, and anti-Nazi activist*

A Lutheran minister, Bonhoeffer adopted a view of religion and politics more akin to that of John CALVIN. He insisted that the church uphold CHRISTIAN moral standards and hold the government accountable to them (to "call sin by its name"). This led him to criticize the NAZI regime from the pulpit, which led to his arrest in 1943 and execution in 1945. He was a leader in The Confessing Church in Germany, which resisted HITLER's government.

In his book, *Ethics,* Bonhoeffer asserts that CHURCH AND STATE are related by being both under the authority of Christ but with different, if complimentary, roles in the world. The STATE's function is to punish evil (crime) and promote good (virtue). It does this through the legal system and moral public education. But to do this, the government must know what morality is, which it can only learn from religion, or the church. Hence, the church (or "spiritual office") is distinct from the state but is necessary to it. In the sense of St. AUGUSTINE, the church advises the government. The state should respect and support the church but leave it alone in matters of faith. The government oversteps its legitimate role when it interferes with the church's spiritual and doctrinal autonomy. This is where Bonhoeffer's church ran afoul of the German Nazi state. Hitler tried to impose "Aryan Christianity" on the German Christian church, which subordinated traditional theology to FASCIST political ideology. Bonhoeffer and The Confessing Church resisted this and attacked the Nazi Party for its crimes. This he saw was as a duty of the church of Christ. "It is part of the Church's office of guardianship that she call sin by its name and that she shall warn men against sin; for

'righteousness exalteth a nation,' both in time and in eternity, 'but sin is perdition for the people,' both temporal and eternal perdition (Proverbs 14:34). If the Church did not do this, she would be incurring part of the guilt for the blood of the wicked (Ezekiel 3:17). This warning against sin is delivered to the congregation openly and publically . . . not to improve the world, but to summon it to believe in Jesus Christ and to bear witness to the reconciliation which has been accomplished through Him and to His dominion." During a time when Nazi propaganda was deceiving many in Germany (calling mass murder ethnic cleansing, and military aggression national liberation) Bonhoeffer insisted that the church "call sin by its name" (murder is murder, theft is theft, etc.), even if it leads to persecution. This view of Christianity as a moral witness in the political world affected much later LIBERAL and EVANGELICAL church activity in the public arena (especially in the United States) after World War II. So, besides being a prominent martyr, Dietrich Bonhoeffer developed an important perspective on religion and politics in the MODERN world. Educated in Germany at the universities of Tubingen and Berlin, he attended Union Theological Seminary in New York.

Further Readings
Bethge, E. *Dietrich Bonhoeffer.* New York: Harper & Row, 1970.
de Gruchy, John W., ed. *The Cambridge Companion to Dietrich Bonhoeffer.* Cambridge, Eng.: Cambridge University Press, 1999.
Green, Clifford, J. *Bonhoeffer: A Theology of Sociality.* Grand Rapids, Mich.: Wm. B. Eerdmans Publishing Co., 1999.

Bracton, Henry de (1210–1268) *British jurist*

Henry de Bracton (Henry of Bracton) was a long-serving British judge who wrote the seminal work on MEDIEVAL English common law. Bracton's treatise, *On the Laws and Customs of England,* remained the main interpretation of British law until the mid-1700s. He also served as a clergyman and ended his career as chancellor of Exeter Cathedral.

Bracton was born in Devon, and his family name is alternately Bratton or Bradtone. He studied law at Oxford and became a judge under Henry III. By the time he entered the legal profession, the curia regis, or king's court, had evolved into a distinct legal forum. By 1245, Bracton had become a justice in Devon. He served on the court that became known as the King's Bench from 1247–50 and from 1253–57. During his tenure, he gained renown for his legal acumen and received a number of royal favors. In spite of the struggles between the MONARCHY and the nobility, Bracton emerged as a nonpartisan jurist who was respected by both sides. He served as an early model for the nonbiased judiciary. He collected some 2,000 decisions in a casebook, or law report, that pioneered the use of precedents and *stare decis* ("let the decision stand" of lower courts). Bracton's casebook would be emulated from 1291 to 1535 in the publication of an annual legal yearbook. After his retirement from the court, Bracton continued to serve on judicial commissions and as a legal advisor to the monarchy.

Bracton's opus *On the Laws and Customs of England* was the first systemic attempt to codify the common law of Great Britain. Although it is now accepted that much of the work was done previously and that Bracton's main contribution was to edit these early pieces, many of the later sections were authored by the jurist. Bracton sought to provide guidance for lesser judges because English common law was not codified or written down; instead, common law was based on accepted customs and traditions. Judges needed guidance because customs and traditions varied from locality to locality. In addition, Bracton understood that justices often misapplied the law as a result of their own ignorance or inexperience or applied the law according to their own purposes.

The work contends that justice comes from God and that laws are accepted restraints on offenses against the community or individuals. Bracton asserted that the English legal system was a combination of accepted traditional law and church law, thereby merging justice and law. Nonetheless, Bracton argues for the existence of both judges and the church. Judges or magistrates are needed to interpret and administer the law, and priests to interpret and administer the will of God. *On the Customs and Laws of England* further reaffirms the supremacy of the monarch but maintains that the monarch must be subject to God and law. Without the supremacy of law, Bracton proclaims that the monarch's rule would be based solely on personal will. Leaders of the anti-Royalist faction in the English civil war used Bracton's arguments on the supremacy of law to support their rebellion against Charles I.

In 1264, Bracton was appointed to be the archdeacon of Barnestable. This appointment was followed within the year by his selection as chancellor of Exeter Cathedral. The bishop of Exeter also named Bracton to honorary posts at both Exeter and Bosham. He died in 1264 and was buried in Exeter Cathedral.

Further Reading

Van Caenegem, R. C. *The Birth of the English Common Law.* Cambridge, Eng.: Cambridge University Press, 1988.

Buber, Martin (1878–1965)   *German philosopher, Jewish theologian, and Zionist activist*

In 1898, Buber joined the Zionist movement that strove to establish a Jewish homeland in Israel. Connected with his vision of an ideal Jewish nation was his book *Paths in Utopia* (1949), which examined the COMMUNITARIAN, decentralized aspects of the SOCIALIST theoretical tradition and partly implemented in the modern Israeli society.

Most of Buber's writings were on religion, and they influenced both Judaism and Protestant Christianity, especially his book *I and Thou* (1937). From 1916 to 1924, he edited a German Jewish journal *Der Jüde.* He taught theology and ethics at Frankfurt University. With the rise of HITLER and the NAZI Party in Germany in the 1930s, systematic persecution of Jews began, forcing Buber to leave the country. He assumed a professorship at the University of Jerusalem.

Buber's political thought, representative of some leftist Israeli ideology, grows out of his activist mysticism that strives to infuse spiritual values into daily life.

Further Readings

Diamond, Malcolm Luria. *Martin Buber, Jewish Existentialist.* New York: Harper & Row, 1968.
Friedman, Maurice S. *Martin Buber's Life and Work: The Early Years, 1878–1923.* New York: Dutton, 1981.
Manheim, Werner. *Martin Buber.* New York: Twayne Publishers, 1974.
Susser, Bernard. *Existence and Utopia: The Social and Political Thought of Martin Buber.* Rutherford, N.J.: Fairleigh Dickinson University Press, 1981.

Buckley, William F., Jr. (1925–)   *American political commentator and libertarian thinker*

William F. Buckley, Jr., describes himself as a LIBERTARIAN journalist. This title, reflected on his most recent book cover, describes a fusion between the ideological underpinnings of conservatism and libertarianism, combined with the trappings of journalism. More specifically, the goals of such a school of thought are to point out to the straight libertarians and to the conservatives how much they have had in common and how effective the symbiosis would be between them. Ever present in his thinking and writing, Buckley seeks to answer the question: Does this augment or diminish human LIBERTY? In many ways, Buckley's views are neither conservative nor liberal. His view, for example, on the legalization of drugs in the United States runs contrary to other political conservatives such as William BENNETT. Conversely, Buckley's pro-life stance along with his preference for small government puts him at odds with liberals.

Wearing several hats, Buckley is an editor, author, and lecturer who was born in the United States, raised in Europe, and is a 1946 graduate of Yale University. Buckley is a popular, eloquent, and witty spokesman for the conservative point of view. Early in his career, Buckley was an editor for *The American Mercury*. In 1955 he founded the *National Review*, which soon became the leading journal of conservativism in the United States. Currently, he serves as its editor-at-large. He ran unsuccessfully for mayor of New York in 1965 on the Conservative Party ballot, hosted the television show *Firing Line* from 1966 to 1999, and writes a syndicated newspaper column for United Press Syndicate that reaches more than 300 newspapers. Among the nonfiction books he has written are *God and Man at Yale* (1951) and *The Unmaking of a Mayor* (1966). Literary success for Buckley has come with his fictitious novelistic accounts of the adventures of an American spy during the cold war and include *Saving the Queen* (1976) and *A Very Private Plot* (1994). More recently, he completed *The Redhunter* (1999), a largely favorable fictional presentation of Sen. Joseph McCarthy's activities.

Buckley has been outspoken politically against the WELFARE STATE, New Deal Democrats, such programs as affirmative action, and, generally, the negative consequences of government excess. Perhaps most notable of his opinions has been his position on the drug war. Buckley in several speeches and articles has declared the American war on drugs over and lost. He has advocated the legalization of drugs, albeit regulated to prevent access to minors. This position is a departure from many of his political cohorts, who consistently advocate in favor of stronger penalties and tougher measures to reduce the trade and use of illegal narcotics in the United States.

William F. Buckley, Jr., ca. 1967. (LIBRARY OF CONGRESS)

William F. Buckley, Jr., has become among the most prominent conservative political theorists and commentators of the 20th century. All told, he has authored 42 published books. Among the many honors Buckley has won is the Presidential Medal of Freedom, awarded to him in 1991.

Further Reading
Buckley, Jr., William F. *Let Us Talk of Many Things: The Collected Speeches with New Commentary by the Author.* Roseville, Calif.: Forum, 2000.

Bukharin, Nikolai Ivanovich (1888–1938)
Marxist economic theorist and politician

Bukharin combined with his theoretical work a life of political engagement in the BOLSHEVIK revolution and the establishment of the COMMUNIST SOVIET UNION. After falling from favor with Stalin, he was executed.

It is difficult to disentangle Bukharin's writings and their reception from the intrigues, distortions, and ambitions of the Russian political ELITE, among whom Bukharin moved. After being arrested by the czar's police and later escaping Russia to Western Europe, he joined Lenin in Poland. He worked on the Bolshevik newspaper *Pravda* and later on a similar project in the United States. Following the Russian revolution in 1917, Bukharin returned to Russia, became a member of the Communist Party Central Committee, and was appointed editor of *Pravda*. After the death of Lenin, Bukharin was appointed to the Politburo and became closely involved in the intrigues and disagreements concerning economic policy, which pitted those who believed in the "gradualism" of allowing the economy to develop in accord with materialist Marxist predictions against those who wanted to intervene and initiate a quick industrialization. Bukharin took the former view, but when STALIN changed his opinion in 1928, Bukharin's position became precarious. He was expelled from the party in 1929, reinstated later after recanting his views. In January 1937, he was arrested, expelled again from the party, accused by being a counterrevolutionary, put on trial, and executed.

Bukharin's most famous work is *Historical Materialism*. Its purpose is to give an accessible account of the principles and ideas of Marx's theory of HISTORICAL MATERIALISM. In this sense it is textbook; however, Bukharin also wanted to offer some new thoughts and interpretations in defense of Marx's account of history. This work displays the influence of Western sociology on Bukharin's thought in the attention he gives to the possible independence of the superstructure from the material base of society and his moving away from the strict determinism of the classical Marxist model. However, Bukharin's awareness of the real political consequences of subscribing to this "Western" view is evident in his insistence that he remains true to strictly Marxist premises.

After his execution, Bukharin was officially written out of Russian history as part of the Bukharin-Trotsky gang of spies, wreckers, and traitors. This Stalinist-imposed silence has lifted, and the important role he played in Russian politics in the 1920s has been recognized. He has become associated with a "humanist SOCIALISM," a specifically anti-Stalinist possibility for communism. However, little of this reputation rests on his writings or ideas but rests rather on his political activities and the memory of his fate at the hands of Stalin.

Further Reading

Cohen, S. *Bukharin and the Bolshevik Revolution*. New York: Knopf, 1973.

Bunyan, John (1628–1688) *English Puritan writer and activist*

Most famous for his book *Pilgrim's Progress,* a CHRISTIAN allegory of the individual soul's travel from sin to salvation, Bunyan influenced Puritan theology in Britain and America. The themes of INDIVIDUALISM, LIBERTY of conscience, and EQUALITY complemented the REPUBLICAN parliamentary cause in England and the Puritan settlements in North America. Seeing a person's life as a journey involving a series of moral choices conformed nicely with MODERN PROTESTANT POLITICAL THOUGHT and DEMOCRATIC politics.

Born to a poor family in Bedfordshire, England, Bunyan read only the Bible in his youth. He served in the parliamentary army during the English civil war (1644–46), married a pious Christian woman who introduced him to EVANGELICAL thought, joined an independent (congregational) church in 1653, and was ordained a minister in 1657. After the restoration of the monarchy in 1660 and general persecution of Christian "dissenters" occurred, causing Bunyan to be imprisoned for preaching the Gospel, he spent much of the time between 1660 and 1672 in prison. There he wrote his famous autobiography, *Grace Abounding to the Chief of Sinners* (1666). In it and in *Pilgrim's Progress* Bunyan ties the individual's moral development with spiritual warfare and social turmoil.

The Puritan themes emphasize that "worldly" society—like the corrupt, luxurious, and decadent ARISTOCRACY in England—presents temptations that lead to the soul's destruction and damnation and advocate a simple, godly lifestyle that must appeal to poor, simple folks. The hope for a decent, wholesome Christian society that would obey God's laws and prevent God's wrath from destroying the City of Destruction fed into American Puritan society. Puritans fleeing to Massachusetts and Connecticut saw this as leaving "Sodom and Gomorrah" and entering the Promised Land, establishing a city on a hill as a beacon to the lost of the world. Such New Jerusalem theology influenced America's view of itself, including the presidency of Ronald REAGAN, who employed Puritan rhetoric in his speeches. Bunyan's Puritan theology underlies many PROTESTANT countries' views of their COVENANT obligations to God and their destiny.

Further Reading
Southey, R. *John Bunyan*. 1830.

bureaucracy/bureaucratic

Although this concept has several meanings, it is technically "rule by bureau" or government by official agency. In the 20th century, it often has negative connotations of inefficiency, complexity, unresponsiveness, undemocratic and elitist governmental, or private organizations. So to call someone or some state "bureaucratic" usually is a criticism of "red tape," complex regulations, uncooperative officials, and general ineffectiveness.

Bureaucracy is a fairly recent development in Western governments, though Eastern regimes such as the Ottoman Empire and China had a highly bureaucratic STATE for centuries. Generally, the larger and more complex a country or agency, the more bureaucratic it becomes. So, for example, the Roman CATHOLIC Church (or at least its administrative center, the Vatican) is often seen as characterized by bureaucracy because of its large, worldwide organization.

Max WEBER, the leading modern thinker on bureaucracy, claimed that as most organizations (states, businesses, political parties, universities, labor unions, hospitals, etc.) became more complex and large, they would inevitably become more bureaucratic. Weber, a German sociologist, identified several traits in the ideal bureaucracy: (1) hierarchy (ranks of authority); (2) impersonality (treatment of people is uniform regardless of who the clients is); (3) continuity (officials work as full-time, professional, salaried experts); and (4) merit (employment and advancement are according to established standards such as education, experience, and performance, not personal connections or arbitrary favoritism). The professional, competent, fair administrators produced by such a bureaucracy were seen by many in the 19th-century European and American worlds as an improvement over the arbitrary, incompetent, dictatorial rule of hereditary princes or party bosses. The development of the civil service in those countries was seen as creating a clean, honest, efficient public service out of the incompetent, corrupt, and ineffective rule of ordinary citizens. This contempt for nonexperts often makes the bureaucracy a target for public scorn and periodic attacks by politicians and common people. In the United States, government bureaucracy is often contrasted with the efficiency of the private, business sector, and conservatives often try to "cut back" the bureaucracy through budget cuts and public personnel reductions. Attempts at "privatization" of public programs (welfare, prisons, education, housing) are often appealed to as less bureaucratic than government programs. In general, American DEMOCRATS and LIBERALS, who favor more federal government regulation, are less critical of the STATE bureaucracy, while REPUBLICANS often attack the bureaucracy and the taxes required to operate them.

Recent organization theory challenges the claims of bureaucracy by asserting that smaller organizations (and individuals) are more efficient than large organizations, that HIERARCHY can reduce the flow of information and creative innovations, that specialization can foster inflexibility, and that impersonal, uniform rules can be inhumane.

Democratic criticism of bureaucracy usually centers around the loss of popular control of government to administrative experts and the relative impotence of short-term, elected representatives when compared to permanent career civil servants. Attempts to control the bureaucracy range from such open access laws as the Freedom of Information Act (allowing ordinary citizens access to government records) and legal procedures guaranteeing individual private RIGHTS against bureaucratic fiat.

Further Readings
Albrow, M. *Bureaucracy*. New York: Praeger Publishers, 1970.
Blau, P. M., and Meyer, M. W. *Bureaucracy in Modern Society*. New York: Random House, 1971.
Kamenka, E., and Krygier, M. *Bureaucracy*. New York: St. Martin's Press, 1979.
Kellner, P., and Crowther-Hunt, N. *The Civil Servants*. London: Macdonald, Raven Books, 1980.
Page, E. C. *Political Authority and Bureaucratic Power*. Knoxville: University of Tennessee Press, 1985.
Rizzi, B. *The Bureaucratization of the World*. New York: Free Press, 1985.

Burke, Edmund (1729–1797) *British statesman and political philosopher*

Born in Ireland, educated at Trinity College, Dublin, Burke migrated to London to study law. Through a long political career including terms in Parliament, Burke came to represent the traditional British CONSERVATIVE thought. Burkean conservatism values the past traditions, manners, education, and culture. It rejects sudden change, radical innovation, and newness in fashion. For Burke, the ideas, practices, and traditions (including in art, music, religion, and economics) that have endured for many years embody the best in Western civilization and have a civilizing effect on later generations. New ideas and techniques are unproven until they have stood "the test of time," so a healthy society will pass down (through education and culture) the best of the historical past through training of the young in CLASSICAL philosophy, art, music, and literature. Humans are not born good but require careful nurturing and training to develop into good, moral, civilized beings. If proper training of the young is neglected or radical innovations in education and the family interjected, chaos and misery will follow. For Burke, humanity is distinguished from other species by its "taste" or aesthetic, artistic appreciation of beauty. If that human capacity to produce and love beauty is cultivated, it will create an ethical, civilized populace. This requires exposure to the most beautiful art, music, landscapes, architecture, and manners at a young age. Much of Burke's objection to radical reform movements comes from their rejection of the past, which he sees as the source of civility.

Burke's mature conservatism is developed in response to the French Revolution of 1789 in his book, *Reflections on the French Revolution*. The French revolutionaries' claim that they could remake and improve society according to DEMOCRATIC theories was repulsive to Burke. Such "speculative" philosophy for him ignored the slow, organic progress of political change. A SOCIAL CONTRACT for Burke was not (as it is in ROUSSEAU) something you could quickly define in your mind and apply to society; the true social contract is a long-term, cultural phenomenon between the past, the present, and the future. Sudden political change, without respect for past traditions and other cultural aspects (family, property, religion, education) will produce a nightmare of violence and disorder rather than improvement and progress. Burke claims that the British revolutions (1640, 1688) did not discard the past wholesale but preserved the valuable traditions of English law and civilization, only improving upon major problems (and those gradually). The American Revolution of 1776 was in this British tradition of *preserving* English liberties and rights, so Burke approved of it. What troubled him about the French Revolution (as would the later Russian and Chinese revolutions) was the sudden and radical changes made in government and society. The violence and oppression that

follows such "idealistic," utopian revolutions would not have surprised Burke.

Radical revolutionaries tend to come from the ranks of the poor, rejected, and dissatisfied in society. When they gain power, they use it ruthlessly to destroy the traditional institutions and people who rejected them. Consequently, for Burke, most postrevolutionary governments are cruel and vindictive, and their leaders mean and angry. Burke contrasts these mad revolutionaries with the mild, civilized authority of established rulers.

A Burkean conservative values those institutions and people who preserve the best of the past. These consist of the wealthy, the church, the military, the family, and the well educated. Private PROPERTY, religion, and traditional education form the cultural foundations for LAW, stability, and good order. Change should occur gradually and thoughtfully, careful not to disturb any valuable aspect of the past. Respect for AUTHORITY, ancestors, and tradition preserves the good society. This explains why Burke regards old ideas or "prejudices" as good—they knit together society.

Edmund Burke also argued for the independence of the British Parliament and the "representative" role of the parliamentary member (as opposed to the "delegate" role). A representative uses independent wisdom and judgment, while a delegate simply expresses the direct will of constituents.

Burke's philosophy influences later conservative political thought in the West. His love of the past and respect for tradition arises during every conservative period, including during the REAGAN era in the United States and Thatcher era in Great Britain.

Further Readings

Burke, E. *Reflections on the Revolution in France*, C. C. O'Brien, ed. Harmondsworth: Penguin, 1968.

———. *Edmund Burke on Government, Politics and Society*, selected by B. W. Hill, ed. London: Fontana, 1975.

———. *The Political Philosophy of Edmund Burke*, London: Longman, 1986.

———. *Writings and Speeches of Edmund Burke*, P. Langford, ed. Oxford, Eng.: Clarendon Press, 1981.

Dreyer, F. A. *Burke's Politics: A Study in Whig Orthodoxy*. Waterloo, Ont.: Wilfrid Laurier University Press, 1979.

Freeman, M. *Burke and the Critique of Political Radicalism*. Chicago: University of Chicago Press, 1980.

Kramnick, Isaac. *The Rage of Edmund Burke: Portrait of an Ambivalent Conservative*. Boulder, Colo.: Basic Books, 1977.

Macpherson, C. B. *Burke*. Oxford, Eng.: Oxford University Press, 1982.

O'Gorman, F. *Edmund Burke: His Political Philosophy*. Bloomington: Indiana University Press, 1973.

Pocock, J. G. A. *Burke and the Ancient Constitution: A Problem in the History of Ideas.* 1960.

Stanlis, P. J. *Edmund Burke and the Natural Law.* Ann Arbor: University of Michigan Press, 1965.

byzantine

In a political system or environment, *byzantine* refers to a great deal of secrecy, intrigue, conspiracy, trickery, and complexity. Named after the political atmosphere of the Byzantine, or Eastern Roman, Empire, which ruled a vast area (from A.D. 330 to 1453) from the city of Constantinople (now Istanbul). Because of the complexities and corruption of the Byzantine Empire, its politics were extremely intricate, devious, and violent. The governing of many different nationalities around the Balkans, the frequent invasion from foreign armies, and the close ties between the state and the Eastern Orthodox Church led to mysterious and difficult politics. Corrupt and violent struggles over power, often masked by high ideals, complex diplomacy, and eccentric personalities, made Western governments seem open, logical, and orderly by contrast. So, when a MODERN regime or government (such as Stalinist Russia, Maoist China, or the U.S. presidency of Bill Clinton) is described as byzantine, it means that the power relationships within it are complex, intense, and difficult to understand. This difficulty to comprehend such "byzantine" governments makes it hard to negotiate with them or change them, so, for example, Western states found it challenging to negotiate nuclear arms treaties with the Soviet Union for its byzantine qualities.

Further Reading
Angold, Michael. *The Byzantine Empire 1025–1204: A Political History.* London: Oxford University Press, 1997.

Caesar

An imperial Roman title for the emperor or DICTATOR over the Roman Empire. Originally named after the emperor of Rome, Julius Caesar (102 B.C.–44 A.D.), the term *Caesar* came to mean the leader of the Roman Empire. Because the imperial Caesars assumed more and more dictatorial power, the term *Caesar* came to be associated with undemocratic, tyrannical government. This image of ABSOLUTE ruling AUTHORITY in one person was transferred to the German imperial title *kaiser* and the Russian term *czar.*

Further Reading

Walter, Gerard. *Caesar, a Biography,* transl. from the French by Emma Craufurd, Therese Pol, ed. New York: Scribner's, 1952.

Calhoun, John C. (1782–1850) *American statesman and political theorist*

Calhoun is best known for his defense of a STATES RIGHTS view of the U.S. CONSTITUTION. His theories of states' nullification of federal laws and the right of individual states to secede from the union greatly influenced the South in the U.S. Civil War. His argument for "concurrent (state) majorities" is seen as an attempt to preserve the institution of black slavery in the Southern states.

In Calhoun's theory, earlier associated with the ANTIFEDERALISTS, he conceived of the United States of America as a compact among sovereign independent states. In this view, the central, national government in Washington, D.C., was limited to foreign affairs, the states retaining control over internal domestic policy, so the majority in the federal government (CONGRESS) had to have the concurrence of the majorities of state governments for a law to be truly national. If the federal government passed a law that was obnoxious to a state, that state could vote to nullify or invalidate it within its borders, and if the national government consistently opposed the interests of a STATE, that state or any group of states could withdraw from the union and establish its own nation (as the Confederate States of America did in the South prior to the Civil War).

Calhoun's ideas had an appeal in the slave-owning southern states in the early 1800s, when they felt threatened by encroachments of the federal government, but his theory of concurrent majorities was rejected by the leading founder of the U.S. Constitution, James MADISON, and in practice it made national law and coherent public policy inefficient and unworkable. They fueled the southern tendency toward states rights and secession, especially in South Carolina, Calhoun's home state.

John Calhoun was born in rural South Carolina. He graduated from Yale University in 1804. Before going into national politics, he served in the state legislature, later went on to represent South Carolina in Congress, and ultimately served as secretary of war under President James Monroe and as vice president under President John Quincy Adams. Calhoun's major political philosophy writings were not published until after his death, but his books, *Disquisition on Government* and *Discourse on the Constitution and Government of the United States,* greatly influenced southern political thought prior to the Civil War. His large plantation became the foundation of Clemson University.

Further Readings

Calhoun, J. C. *A Disquisition on Government,* with selections from the *Discourse,* C. Gordon Post, ed. Indianapolis: Bobbs-Merrill, 1953.

Hartz, L. *The Liberal Tradition in America.* New York: Harcourt, Brace & World, 1955.

Jenkins, W. S. *Pro-Slavery Thought in the Old South.* Gloucester, Mass.: P. Smith, 1935.

Parrington, V. L. *Main Currents in American Thought,* vol. II. New York: Harcourt, Brace & World, 1958: 69–82.

Wiltse, C. *A Life of John C. Calhoun,* 3 vols. Indianapolis: Bobbs-Merrill, 1944–51.

Calvin, John (1509–1564)/Calvinist *Protestant Christian theologian, reformer, and governor*

John Calvin is probably the most important, influential thinker of the Protestant REFORMATION of the CHRISTIAN church in Europe in the 16th century. Calvinist or Reformed churches appeared in Germany, the Netherlands, England (PURITAN), Scotland, France (HUGUENOTS), parts of Eastern Europe, and North America. Calvinism especially characterized the churches of the United States of America (New England Puritans, Scots PRESBYTERIANS, Dutch Reformed, and many BAPTISTS). Most founders of the U.S. CONSTITUTION were Calvinist Protestant Christians (for example, James MADISON). The Calvinist theology of INDIVIDUALISM, salvation by grace through faith, divine election, occupational calling and work ethic, and REPUBLICAN church polity permeates American culture and society.

In his political thought, Calvin conceived of CHURCH AND STATE as both under the authority of Christ. Both ecclesiastical and civil government are called to serve God, although in different capacities. The church teaches the people Christian truth and advises the government. If civil laws do not reflect the truth of God, they will not succeed. In Calvin's city of Geneva, Switzerland (where he ruled for 20 years), as well as in other Calvinist cities (Edinburgh, Scotland; Boston, Massachusetts), the Bible was the standard for public education and civil law. A Christian commonwealth rested on the strong cultural influence of the church as well as Christian magistrates.

For Calvin, the job of government or "magistracy" was as sacred a calling as the church ministry. State officials were accountable to God for their actions and carried an awesome responsibility for carrying out just laws and displaying an honest, virtuous life. Knowing that people in high positions of authority would be an example to the young, government rulers must be above reproach in duty and integrity. As God's servants, church ministers and civil magistrates deserve the honor and respect of the people. America Puritan John WINTHROP reflected this understanding of the proper role of the Christian ruler.

In the MEDIEVAL Europe of ARISTOCRACY and MONARCHY, Calvin's thought introduced REPUBLICAN principles of EQUALITY and elected government in both church and state. Instead of priests appointed by bishops, most Calvinist ministers were elected by church congregations and shared power with elders and deacons. Instead of hereditary princes, most Calvinist states elected their rulers for limited terms. Then, church and state were to cooperate in establishing and maintaining a Christian commonwealth. The civil state primarily punishes crime but also promotes Christian virtue by education, rewards, honors, and so on. The church primarily preaches the gospel of Christ but also punishes by excommunication of notorious, unrepentant sinners. With sinful, fallen human nature, no society will ever reach perfection, for Calvin, but the combined rule of Christian churches and Christian governors will produce the most healthy, moral society possible.

John Calvin's own life reflected his synthesis of religion and politics. He was a scholar, theologian, and political ruler. He governed the city of Geneva as chief magistrate with assistance from four ranks of officials: pastors, doctors, elders, and deacons. Additionally, a "consistory" of ministers and laypeople served as a tribunal of social morals. Geneva under Calvin became a city known for great piety, strict morals, cleanliness, order, and economic prosperity. His chief theological book, *Institutes of the Christian Religion,* has greatly influenced most Protestant Christian churches.

Further Readings

Calvin, J. *Institutes of the Christian Religion,* vols. XX and XXI, J. T. McNeill, ed., F. L. Battles, transl., Library of Christian Classics. Philadelphia: Westminster Press, 1960.

Dillenberger, J., ed. *John Calvin: Selections from His Writings.* Oxford, Eng.: Oxford University Press, 1975.

Höpfl, H. *The Christian Polity of John Calvin.* Cambridge, Eng.: Cambridge University Press, 1982.

Monter, E. W. *Calvin's Geneva.* New York: Wiley, 1967.

Parker, T. H. L. *John Calvin: A Biography.* Philadelphia: Westminster Press, 1975.

Wendel, F. *Calvin: The Origins and Development of His Religious Thoughts.* New York: Collins, 1963.

Camus, Albert (1913–1960)   *French essayist, novelist, and playwright*

Camus was born into impoverished conditions in Mondovi, Algeria. His father was killed in World War I, and his mother worked as a charwoman to support the family. Camus won a scholarship to attend the Algiers *lycée* in 1923 and later studied philosophy at the University of Algiers, where he obtained a *diplôme d'études supérieures* in 1936 for a thesis on the works of Plotinus and St. Augustine. During this period, Camus began to write and produce plays for the Théâtre du Travail (Workers' Theatre), which sought to expose working-class audiences to the theater, and he also briefly belonged to the Algerian Communist Party (1934–35). Camus then began a career as a journalist, producing book reviews and a series of articles detailing the injustices of life in Algeria under the colonial rule of the French. In 1940, he moved to Paris and became active in the resistance movement during the German occupation of France. For two years after the war, Camus served as editor of the Parisian daily *Combat,* a position that allowed him to deepen his engagement with political activism but which ultimately left him disillusioned at the absence of moral integrity in politics.

During the 1940s and 1950s, Camus wrote the major publications that established his reputation, including *The Stranger* (1942), *The Myth of Sisyphus* (1942), *The Plague* (1947), *The Rebel* (1951), *Exile and the Kingdom* (1952), and *The Fall* (1956). In 1957, he received the Nobel Prize for literature. Camus was killed in a car accident near Sens, France, on January 4, 1960.

Camus is generally, though sometimes controversially, associated with the movement of French EXISTENTIALISM. Although he was closely associated for a time with Jean-Paul SARTRE, their relationship ended in a bitter dispute, and Camus often expressed reservations about existentialist philosophy. Nevertheless, Camus's reflections on the human condition and his focus on the moral dimensions of human life have important affinities with the existentialist tradition. Two notions in particular can be seen as forming the nucleus of Camus's thought: the notion of absurdity and the notion of revolt.

In his early writings, Camus struggled with the apparent contradiction of human existence, namely, that human beings desire to find a meaningful world and instead find a world without meaning. This contradiction underlies the notion of the absurdity of life because there are no guarantees for the validity of values used to guide human existence. In a striking analogy, Camus compares life to the myth of Sisyphus, suggesting that human actions are akin to the labors of Sisyphus, who was condemned by the gods to roll a stone up a mountain, watch it roll back down, and repeat the process endlessly. Given the absurdity of existence, Camus examined the question of whether our lives are worth living in a meaningless world. His response was that the indifference of the world to the fate of humanity provides the very motivation for human action, in terms of rebellion against that indifference.

Camus's later writings thus focused on the notion of revolt. According to Camus, the individual's only defensible response to the absurdity of existence is revolt, in particular against both the passive nihilism of meaninglessness and the prevalence of social and political injustice. He viewed revolt as a means to the creation of human solidarity by prompting moral action that helps to cultivate a sense of humanity while resisting any form of religious or political absolutism. In Camus's words, "I revolt, therefore we are." In the end, Camus articulated an ethics of revolt that sought to expose the extent of our responsibility for the conditions of human existence. Hope and courage rather than despair and fear are the positive qualities of revolt, whose aim should be to overcome human isolation and to promote mutual respect for the basic RIGHTS of all persons.

Further Reading

Bronner, S. E. *Camus: Portrait of a Moralist.* Minneapolis: University of Minnesota Press, 1999.

canon law

The formal rules and laws of the Christian church primarily developed during the European MIDDLE AGES and greatly influencing Western LAW, jurisprudence, ETHICS, and political thought. Canon law is developed in the CATHOLIC Church heavily from A.D. 1100 to 1500 and deals primarily with personal morals, church discipline, administration of holy sacraments, and the respective powers of clergy and secular rulers.

Eastern Orthodox and Protestant Christian churches, partly because they relied less on ancient Roman legal codes, developed canon law less fully than the Roman Catholic Church.

Canon law began with the codification of religious doctrine and rules at representative church councils, such as the councils at Nicaea (A.D. 325) and Chalcedon (A.D. 451), which also developed major church creeds. Other sources of canon law were decreed from bishops (especially the bishop of Rome, the pope), influential theologians and other church leaders (e.g., St. Dionysius of Alexandria, St. Gregory, and St. Basil of Caesarea). As the Catholic Church became more centralized in authority and organization, these various sources were collected, arranged, clarified, and widely disseminated throughout the Western Christian church in Gratian's *Decretum* (A.D. 1140). Increased power of the papacy in Rome led to a further collection of canon law in 1234 (*The Book of Decretals*), which continues down to the present day through papal decrees.

At first, canon law affected only clergy and other religious institutions, but with the increased worldly power of the Catholic Church, it came to dominate much of civil law and government also. Corporate law began as canon law, as *corporations* originally meant towns, churches, monastic communities, "colleges" (craft GUILDS, schools, societies), and diocesan organizations rather than businesses. The idea of a corporate body was that the group or community had RIGHTS, duties, PROPERTY, and possessions that did not belong to any individual. Canon law, then, defined the terms of the association, offices and responsibilities of members, distribution of authority, and so on. Most church bodies were ruled by the community, electing leaders and making policy decisions collectively. The modern political idea of common CONSENT actually began in these church communities governed by canon law.

So the greatest influence of canon law on MODERN secular political thought was the example it gave of a universal, systematic code of principles and procedures—a rational, orderly, legalistic state.

During the Middle Ages, Catholic canon law also prescribed relations between CHURCH AND STATE, clergy, and secular rulers. Generally, it held church authority superior to civil government, pope over king, and the rights of clergy to separate courts and legal privileges. As the Roman Catholic Church exercised more detailed rule of civil government and social life (feast days, fasting, religious rituals and habits, commerce, etc.), it caused resistance in the form of ANTICLERICALISM and the Protestant REFORMATION, which strove to limit the church primarily to spiritual matters.

Still, much of modern political theory derived from church canon law. BODIN acknowledged his debt to the canonists' ideas on SOVEREIGNTY and John LOCKE's NATURAL RIGHTS philosophy is beholden to St. Thomas AQUINAS's systematic theology.

Debates over the relative power of pope and bishops, councils and local churches occur within canon law development and the modern conception of parliamentary constitutionalism derives from the conciliar movement in the church, which sought to balance the authority of the pope with that of bishops, councils, and corporations.

Further Readings

Berman, J. H. *Law and Revolution: the Formation of the Western Legal Tradition.* Cambridge, Mass.: Harvard University Press, 1983.

Muldoon, James. *Popes, Lawyers, and Infidels: The Church and the Non-Christian World, 1250–1550.* Philadelphia: University of Pennsylvania Press, 1979.

Tierney, B. *Foundations of Conciliar Theory: The Contribution of the Medieval Canonists from Gratian to the Great Schism.* Cambridge, Eng.: Cambridge University Press, 1955.

———. *Religion, Law and the Growth of Constitutional Thought 1150–1650.* Cambridge, Eng.: Cambridge University Press, 1982.

Ullmann, W. *Medieval Papalism: The Political Theories of the Medieval Canonists.* London: Methuen, 1949.

———. *Law and Politics in the Middle Ages: Introduction to the Sources of Medieval Political Ideas.* Ithaca, N. Y.: Cornell University Press, 1975.

capital punishment

The issue of capital PUNISHMENT and advocates for its abolition predate the modern era. Widely used in ancient times, examples of capital punishment can be found in 1750 B.C. in the Code of Hammurabi. From the fall of Rome to the beginnings of the modern era, capital punishment was practiced throughout Western Europe. The modern movement for the abolition of capital punishment began in the 18th century with the writings of MONTESQUIEU and VOLTAIRE, as well as Cesare BECCARIA's *Essay on Crimes and Punishments*. In the United Kingdom, Jeremy BENTHAM was influential in having the number of capital crimes reduced in the 18th and 19th centuries. Some of the first countries to abolish capital punishment included Venezuela (1863), San Marino (1865), and Costa Rica (1877). As of early 1999, 65 countries had abolished the death penalty, including all of the members of the European Union. In some other countries, capital punishment was retained only in the cases of treason and war crimes. In fewer instances, death remained a penalty under the LAW, though, in practice, executions were not carried out.

Of those countries that did utilize the death penalty as part and parcel of their legal system, most can be found in the Caribbean, Africa, and Asia. The United States and China are believed to impose capital punishment most frequently. In the United States, since the 1970s, almost all capital sentences were imposed for homicide. It is important to note that sentencing by federal courts in the United States are the exception. In criminal cases, states and localities almost always retain jurisdiction and legal AUTHORITY to execute convicted criminals. Today, 38 states and the federal government have reinstituted the death penalty.

There has been intense debate regarding the constitutionality, effect, and humanity of capital punishment: Critics charge that executions are carried out inconsistently, or, more broadly, that they violate the "cruel and unusual punishment" provision of the Eighth Amendment of the U.S. CONSTITUTION. Supporters of the death penalty counter that this clause was not intended to prohibit executions.

In the 1972 case of *Furman v. Georgia,* the U.S. Supreme Court ruled that capital punishment as then practiced was unconstitutional because it was applied disproportionately to certain classes of defendants, notably those who were black or poor. This ruling voided the federal and STATE death penalty laws then in effect but left the way open for CONGRESS or state legislatures to enact new capital punishment laws, a process that began almost immediately. In *Gregg v. Georgia* (1976), the court allowed capital punishment to resume in certain states. A separate penalty phase of the trial, during which the jury reviews mitigating cir-

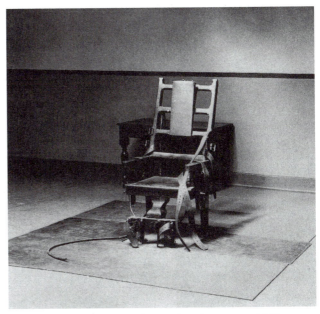

Death chamber and electric chair at Sing Sing prison, 1965. (LIBRARY OF CONGRESS)

cumstances and weighs the need for capital punishment, is now required for some capital cases.

In 1982, Texas became the first state to execute a prisoner using lethal injection; some 75 percent of executions now employ this method. The gas chamber, hanging, the firing squad, and, most commonly, the electric chair are still used in some states. Florida's electrocutions, however, have been heavily criticized following several grisly malfunctions. Texas easily leads all other states in the number of executions carried out. In recent years, the Supreme Court has made it more difficult for death-row prisoners to file appeals; at the same time, studies continue to show striking disparities in the imposition of capital punishment.

Further Reading
Bedau, Hugo Adam. *The Death Penalty in America: Current Controversies.* New York: Oxford University Press, 1982.

capitalism/capitalist

An economic system characterized by private ownership of PROPERTY, wage labor, investment, competition, and free markets. Both advocates of capitalism (e.g., Adam SMITH, John LOCKE) and critics of a capitalist economy (e.g., Karl MARX) agree that capitalism is a unique economic system, distinct from both agrarian FEUDALISM in the MIDDLE AGES in Europe and 20th-

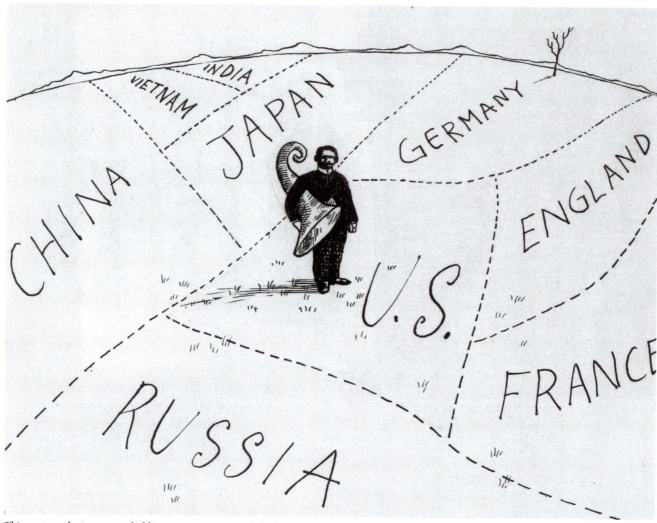

This cartoon depicts a man holding a cornucopia, symbol of prosperity, standing in U.S. territory, bordered by other countries.
(LIBRARY OF CONGRESS)

century SOCIALISM. The special quality of money or "capital" in capitalism, where it is saved and invested to create *more* wealth, is a unique economic phenomenon. British LIBERAL philosopher John Locke described its origins in his *Second Treatise of Government* (1690). In Locke's theory, private property comes from a person mixing his labor or work with the common unowned earth or nature (granted to humankind by God) and producing new value. Then money is invented to represent that labor-produced value and property. If enough money is saved and used to buy other people's labor, which produces more value or profit, the money "earns" more wealth or "interest" for the owner. Money that produces more wealth is "capital." So capitalism is an economy dominated by invested capital, wage labor, banks and interest, pro-

duction of commodities (goods produced for exchange or sale), and material incentives.

Capitalism has dominated Western economics since the 17th century and the world economy since the 20th century. It tends to be very efficient in exploiting natural resources, workforces, and markets. Capitalism generates enormous wealth and material prosperity, but critics claim it causes wide divisions of wealth and poverty. Karl Marx, the father of COMMUNISM, claimed that capitalism exploits all workers, is just a certain stage of human history, and inevitably leads to socialism. Socialism in Marx's view generates "capital" but uses it for general social needs rather than private profit. The historical experience of socialism has not justified Marx's claim that it would be more productive and fair than capitalism. Instead, socialist economics (the SOVIET UNION, Cuba, Maoist China and the like) have stagnated and declined.

Most contemporary Western economies are not purely capitalist, however. They mix capitalism and socialism (or WELFARE-STATE Liberalism), allowing private enterprise but having extensive governmental regulation of business, social programs for the poor, public education, health care, and retirement systems.

Further Reading

Amin, Samir. *Specters of Capitalism: A Critique of Current Intellectual Fashions*, Shane Henry Mage, transl. New York: Monthly Review Press, 1998.

Carlyle, Thomas (1795–1881) *Victorian essayist and social critic*

Carlyle championed a romanticist vision of literature, society, and politics against the enlightenment, scientific, and prudential view that gradually came to dominate Victorian England. His early work introduced to a British audience German idealist and romantic philosophers and writers such as Goethe and Schiller. It is this combination of ROMANTICISM and idealism that informs his critique of society and his interpretation of literature. Carlyle's major works range over a wide number of topics: His first book is a work of philosophy (*Sartor Resartus*); he wrote numerous essays and commentaries, an important work of historical interpretation (*The French Revolution*), and a collection of lectures on the place of the heroic in society (*On Heroes, Hero-Worship, and the Heroic in History*).

In *Sartor Resartus*, Carlyle sets out his understanding of reality as essentially spiritual rather than material and his diagnosis of society's moral misfortunes as coming from a combination of unbelief and mechanism. These messages are clothed in the literary device of a fictional German professor, "Teufelsdrockh," whose character and pronouncements capture not only Carlyle's opinion but also his sense of humor and satirical tone. Carlyle's deep misgivings concerning the calculating, pleasure-based, prudential morality of his time is best exemplified in his opposition to the doctrine of UTILITARIANISM formulated by his one-time friend John Stuart MILL. He described Mill's utilitarian morality as "pig philosophy."

Carlyle's contribution to political theory is contained in his work on the French Revolution and in his theory of the heroic. The former contains his view of history as an essentially moral and spiritual progress, expressed in an account of the French Revolution from the execution of Louis XV to the rise of Napoleon. Here, as in the latter, Carlyle argues that history is biographical, a story about the decisions and actions of great individuals. It is not the social and economic circumstances of a people that drives history forward, but the spiritual as exemplified by heroic figures such as Napoleon and Cromwell. Toward the end of his life he argued for an elitist politics and against democracy, "which means despair of finding any Heroes to govern you." This understanding of great individuals as both moral and historical ideals prefigures NIETZSCHE's fuller and more sophisticated philosophy.

Carlyle was born in Ecclefechan in Scotland and attended Edinburgh University. He had an important influence on Victorian society, in particular in the areas of literature and politics. His antidemocratic views, his biographical view of history, and the rhetorical rather than argumentative character of much of his writings has diminished his attraction for contemporary scholars. Nevertheless, Carlyle remains a persuasive and articulate antienlightenment advocate.

Further Reading

Heffer, S. *Moral Desperado: A Life of Thomas Carlyle*. London: Weidenfeld & Nicolson, 1995.

Carter, James ("Jimmy") Earl, Jr. (1924–) *U.S. president, international statesman, businessman, evangelical Christian*

Jimmy Carter is best known for his U.S. presidency (1977–81) and his extensive public and charitable service after retiring from the presidency. His political thought combined moderate DEMOCRATIC PARTY policy with a strong EVANGELICAL Christian faith.

Born on a farm in Georgia, Carter was known for his disciplined, intellectual life. His high performance as a student led to his entering the prestigious U.S. Naval Academy in 1942. After serving as an officer in the navy, Carter returned to his home to run the family farm and business in Georgia. In 1962, his political career began in the state senate, followed by election as governor of Georgia in 1970.

Carter's sudden rise to national politics followed the political scandals of Watergate and the resignation

Jimmy Carter, 39th president of the United States. (LIBRARY OF CONGRESS)

of President Richard Nixon. America felt a shame and disillusionment with politics, and Jimmy Carter's honesty, decency, CHRISTIAN ethics, and morality won him wide support. Despite his popularity, his presidency was plagued with economic and international problems: a long business recession marked by both high unemployment and inflation, and the national disgrace of Iran taking Americans hostage in the embassy in Teheran. Still, President Carter's administration is remembered as successful in achieving the first Israeli-Arab peace treaty (between Israel and Egypt)—personally negotiated by Carter—and full diplomatic relations with China. Domestically, Carter accomplished civil-service reform, environmental legislation, and energy policy. Carter's tenure as president was marked by high standards of morals and idealism growing from his evangelical faith. An active BAPTIST, he infused his political activities with religious values and saw his public service as a calling from God.

As such, Jimmy Carter's political philosophy drew from a CONSERVATIVE, evangelical Christianity, theologically drawn from St. AUGUSTINE, John CALVIN, and Reinhold NIEBUHR. As a Baptist he believed in the strict separation of CHURCH AND STATE refusing to allow worship services in the White House. His evangelical Christianity believes in a personal, individual relationship to God that would lead to noble social work and dedication. This Reformed Protestant worldview also believed in REALISM: that humans are naturally sinful and selfish and the world always dominated by love of money and power. Quoting Niebuhr, Carter said, "The sad duty of politics is to establish justice in a sinful world." Like St. Augustine, Carter never expected politics to create a perfect humanity or society, but he believed that Christians are obliged to strive to improve the world with greater JUSTICE, FREEDOM, EQUALITY and charity. Internationally, this led Carter to work for HUMAN RIGHTS around the world, especially in the SOVIET UNION. Domestically, this was expressed in his famous "national malaise" speech of July 1979, which criticized American materialism and consumerism from a Christian viewpoint. Despite his enjoying the admiration of most Americans, the economic crisis in the late 1970s caused Carter to lose the presidential election to Ronald REAGAN in 1980.

However, Jimmy Carter had even greater political influence after retiring from the presidency through his international diplomacy, various political and economic assistance programs out of his Carter Center, and his personal church and charitable activities. Carter negotiated peace accords in Haiti, Korea, and Sudan, preventing bloody wars. The Carter Center in Atlanta sponsors programs promoting worldwide DEMOCRACY, economic development, health care, and urban revitalization (such as the African Governance Program; the Human Rights Program; Interfaith Health Program; the Commission on Radio and Television Policy; and the Task Force on Child Survival). Carter explained that after being president, he could effectively raise millions of dollars for such programs to improve the world. He also worked personally through Habitat For Humanity, a private organization dedicated to building houses for the poor. As a teacher, writer, poet, and lay religious leader, Jimmy Carter represented a Renaissance man to the 20th century and continued to influence the world greatly after the end of his official political career.

Further Reading

Ariail, Dan, and Heckler-Feltz, Cheryl. *The Carpenter's Apprentice: The Spiritual Biography of Jimmy Carter.* Grand Rapids, Mich.: Zondervan, 1996.

Catholic

The social and political philosophy of the Roman Catholic Church, the largest CHRISTIAN church in the Western world. The general Catholic view of society and politics derives from the writings of its great theologians St. AUGUSTINE and St. Thomas AQUINAS. St. Augustine provided the first systematic Christian political theory in his book *The City of God,* in which he develops the idea of the The Two Cities (The City of Man or all worldly governments and The City of God or the eternal heavenly realm). St. Thomas Aquinas's *Summa Theologica* looks at politics through three levels of LAW: (1) divine law; (2) NATURAL LAW; and (3) human law. Both Augustinian and Thomist political thought informs Catholic teaching on politics, society, economics, the family, international relations, and Christians' relations to the secular world.

A dominant theme in Catholic political thought is its universality, its claim to apply to all the world's peoples at all times in history. The term *catholic* means "universal" and means that the Christian church transcends nationalities, languages, and regions. Christians are united by the spirit of Christ, regardless of national, ethnic, or language difference. This idea of a catholic church contrasts with both pagan tribal religions and the Christian churches identified with a specific region or country (such as Greek Orthodox, Russian Orthodox, or the Church of England).

During the MIDDLE AGES, Catholic political thought became closely associated with European monarchies (in France, Spain, England, etc.) through CANON LAW. So, when REPUBLICAN political revolutions occurred in those countries, Catholic political theory was often rejected along with the MONARCHY. But the Catholic Church, primarily through papal encyclicals or political documents by the pope, applied Catholic teachings to MODERN politics. Pope Leo XIII, in the encyclical *Inscrutabili* (1878), affirmed the relevance of traditional Catholic political truth in the Modern DEMOCRATIC, industrial world. In the encyclical *Libertas* (1888), he established basic Catholic doctrine on the family, relations between CHURCH AND STATE, and economics in the West. In these and other encyclicals, the pope affirmed the family as the basic unit of society, the sin of racism, the need for world peace, the morality of allowing religious pluralism, and the legitimacy of democracy. In 1931, Pope Pius XI's encyclical *Quadragesimo anno* advanced the need for SOCIAL JUSTICE and social charity and that the government should promote the common good of the society, including ensuring the economic well being of all segments of society. In 1963, Pope John XXIII affirmed the Catholic doctrine of the dignity of human individuals, "for men are redeemed by the blood of Jesus Christ, they are by grace the children and friends of God and heirs of eternal glory" (*Pacem in terris*). The last pope of the 20th century, John Paul II, has written extensively on Catholic social and political thought. With the collapse of COMMUNISM in Russia and Eastern Europe, John Paul II has emphasized that neither SOCIALISM nor CAPITALISM are ideal systems but should be subordinated to God's truth. In the United States of America, the Catholic bishops have published several pastoral letters on political matters from opposition to nuclear war and abortion to favoring social programs for the poor.

So Catholic political thought is an evolving, progressive doctrine that grows out of the traditional religious teachings of the church.

Further Reading
Hanson, Eric O. *The Catholic Church in World Politics.* Princeton, N.J.: Princeton University Press, 1990.

Charlemagne (742–814)   *Emperor of the Holy Roman Empire, political and religious leader in the European Middle Ages*

Charlemagne, or "Charles the Great" is chiefly known for uniting the Western European empire, coordinating his kingdom with the Roman CATHOLIC church, and developing administrative and educational institutions in the West. His advancement of governmental unity and ecclesiastical and educational reform caused the Carolingian RENAISSANCE of learning, Christian civilization, and political stability. He ruled over Europe from the Mediterranean to Britain and sponsored the palace school, church-state councils, clarification of CHRISTIAN doctrine and discipline, and uniformity of law across Europe. As a soldier, statesman, and church leader, Charlemagne represents one of the greatest leaders of the Western tradition. He was crowned Holy Roman Emperor by Pope Leo III on Christmas Day, A.D. 800.

Further Reading
Fichtenau, Heinrich. *The Carolingian Empire.* 1957.

checks and balances

The theory that government TYRANNY is prevented by dividing social and political power through distinct, separate branches or offices of state. The idea is that by distributing political functions among different institutions of society and government, FREEDOM and JUSTICE are preserved and maintained. No one person or group can hold all POWER.

This idea of separating and spreading out power to promote justice appears in the writings of Frenchman MONTESQUIEU, English writers BOLINGBROKE and BLACKSTONE, and American founder James MADISON. In Britain, the division of state into monarch, House of Lords, and House of Commons is seen as accomplishing checks and balances—each institution of government limiting, or checking, the power of the others. In the U.S. CONSTITUTION, the division of the national or federal government into executive (president), legislative (CONGRESS), and judicial (courts) branches achieves the same purpose of widely distributing AUTHORITY and protecting the people from arbitrary or dictatorial rule. Also, the U.S. separation of power between centralized and decentralized governments (national vs. STATE) is also seen as a check on absolutist political power.

The origin of this idea is the political thought of ARISTOTLE and his idea that the most stable regime or state is a "mixed" form of government with the rule of one (king), the rule of a few (ARISTOCRACY), and rule of the many (DEMOCRACY) is combined in one state, balancing social interests. In James Madison's U.S. constitutional thought, this derives also from his Calvinist CHRISTIAN religion, which holds that all humans are selfish and sinful and will use political power to control and oppress others, so state authority must be divided to ensure social peace, justice, and stability.

Further Readings

Barker, E. *Essays on Government,* chap. 5. Oxford, Eng.: Oxford University Press, 1946.
McIlwain, C. H. *Constitutionalism and the Changing World.* Cambridge, Eng.: Cambridge University Press, 1939.

Chinese political thought

The political thought of China from the Shang and Chou dynasties to the present time. The dominant philosophies of Chinese philosophy are: (1) Confucianism; (2) legalism; and (3) Taoism. Although 20th-century China drew from many Western ideas (LIBERALISM, COMMUNISM, CAPITALISM, DEMOCRACY), the thought and culture of ancient China continues to influence modern China.

The dominant political thought (and religion) of China is Confucianism, from the Chinese thinker Confucius (551–479 B.C.) and his book, *The Analects.* According to this collection of classic Chinese wisdom and sayings, the ideal government has the rule of VIRTUE and moral example rather than military might or hereditary privilege. Confucius's emphasis on restoring the religious ceremonies of the Chou dynasty reflected his belief that goodness consisted of dignified order, calm, wisdom, and devotion to the common good. A wise, moral, self-controlled ruler will govern by the strength of his character and noble example rather than by worldly power or clever deals. A good government will earn the respect of others, and subjects will want to be under their AUTHORITY. A truly Confucian emperor will have people of similar high character and virtue (civilized gentlemen) in other positions of public trust. Well-educated, refined persons will display the cardinal virtue of human nature: "benevolence," which will inspire the common people to strive for higher, noble things. Brute force or crass self-interest are signs of corrupt human nature and statecraft.

Strongly patriarchal, Confucian thought sees the state as an extension of the father-ruled family. In both, women and children and subjects are to be obedient to the father-ruler. But the man rules gently and graciously; his authority is not harsh or cruel. The orderly HIERARCHY of virtue and knowledge (as in PLATO's *Republic*) creates "heaven"—an earthly, not a spiritual, paradise. The rule of the wise and good over the ignorant and evil reflects a divine order and symmetry. Hence, Chinese politics often elevates the scholar and sage over the worker and peasant.

Confucian political theory was developed by Mencius (372–289 B.C.). He followed Confucian philosophy by seeing four embryonic virtues in the hearts of humans, but almost in Augustinian CHRISTIAN terms, saw human desire and selfishness ("sin" for Christians) as predominant in uncultivated humans, which is the source of all violence, crime, and evil, hence the need to revive ancient ceremonies and customs to "civilize" humans and prevent chaos and disorder.

Legalism provided an alternative school of thought to Confucianism in China. A collection of thinkers and politicians dating from the third century B.C., legalists emphasize legal rules and administrative procedures as the source of order and justice. Similar to the Western tendency to rely on universal (ROMAN) LAW and bureaucracy, the legalists depended less on the character of the rulers and more on the system of government, codes, regulations, and laws.

Taoist political theory rests on the view that the world is vain and absurd, incapable of order or goodness, and plagued by foolishness and dysfunction. The wise person, therefore, cultivates a detachment from the world and achieves an otherworldly calm and peace. Because the world and politics are ridiculous and useless, the best ruler is one who does not take it too seriously but admires rural simplicity and detachment, only ruling out of a sense of duty and resignation.

Another strain of Chinese political thought emphasizes military discipline and the need for aggressive warfare. Mo Tzu (470–391 B.C.) regarded Confucian ceremony and ancestor worship as foolish and exclusive. His military government regarded the common people as equal and fighting as the highest activity. This part of Chinese ideology continues throughout its history in violent nationalist warfare.

Throughout Chinese history, these philosophical perspectives are interwoven and blended, resulting in policy often confusing to Westerners. High-minded ETHICS combined with brutal authoritarian warfare seems inconsistent to many Western minds, but they reflect the blending of ancient Chinese traditions. Twentieth-century adoptions of LIBERAL DEMOCRACY, MARXISM, communism, and capitalism (for example, in MAO TSE-TUNG) reflect these ancient Chinese schools of thought.

The communist revolution in 1949 blended MARXIST–LENINIST theories of economic class struggle and capitalist IMPERIALISM with traditional Chinese political philosophy and nationalist sentiments. Its leader Mao Tse-Tung employed a communist view of China's economic problems (capitalist exploitation and imperialism from European powers) with a nationalist defense against Japanese invaders drawing on Chinese peasant masses. Hence, in later 20th-century political thought, China's dominant ideology is summarized as "Marxist–Leninist–Mao Tse-tung Thought." In it, unlike orthodox (Stalinist) Marxism (which saw peasants as economically backward and politically reactionary), Chinese communist theory emphasized the revolutionary SOCIALIST "masses" (including industrial workers or "proletariat" and agrarian peasants) because the vast majority of people in China were poor rural farmers.

Mao's communism also drew on traditional Confucian ideas through his emphasis on "correct thinking or consciousness" and "self-criticism" as the basis of POLITICAL CORRECTNESS and social progress. His "let a hundred flowers bloom, a hundred schools of thought contend" during the cultural revolution of the late 1950s reflects political thought of the Chou dynasty (700 B.C.). Maoism's warning that even a communist revolution could be ruined by an oppressive BUREAUCRATIC state (as in the Soviet Union) derives from traditional Eastern wisdom. The Chinese government's reaction to his anarchic cultural revolution, in favor of order, respect for authority, and peace, reflects traditional Chinese legalistic philosophy.

Further Reading
Ames, R. T. *The Art of Rulership.* Honolulu: University of Hawaii Press, 1983.

Christian/Christianity

The political thought of the historical Christian Church and Christian people. Historically, this means the major thinkers of the CATHOLIC (see St. AUGUSTINE and St. Thomas AQUINAS), Protestant (see John CALVIN and Martin LUTHER), and Eastern Orthodox (see BYZANTINE) churches. Each group of Christians has formulated various ideas on the proper view of politics and religion, CHURCH AND STATE, the role of the Christian in the world, JUST-WAR DOCTRINE, and so on. Generally, Roman Catholic political thought has viewed the church as having authority over the state. Generally, Protestant (e.g., BAPTIST) thought has allowed state control over the church in worldly matters or the formal "separation" of church and state. Eastern Orthodox Christian thought (e.g., Greek Orthodox, Russian Orthodox churches) has tended to combine church and state authority sometimes with religious officials ruling the state or, in Russia, declaring the secular king (czar) "Christ on Earth."

In contemporary American politics, Christian political thought takes many forms. The LIBERAL "mainline" churches (Episcopal, Presbyterian, United Church of Christ, Lutheran) tend to be on the political LEFT, advocating federal government welfare programs, women's rights, CIVIL RIGHTS, gay and lesbian rights, and ABORTION rights. The Catholic Church tends to be liberal on economic policy (aid to the poor, etc.) but CONSERVATIVE on social policy (antiabortion, antidivorce, anti-HOMOSEXUALITY). The EVANGELICAL Protestant churches (Baptist, charismatic) tend to be conservative on both economic and moral issues.

Further Reading
Troeltsch, E. *The Social Teaching of the Christian Churches*. London: Allen & Unwin, 1931.

Christian Right

A political group and movement in the United States of America beginning in the 1970s. Associated with Rev. Jerry Falwell, Marion "Pat" ROBERTSON, the Moral Majority, the Christian Coalition, and the presidency of Ronald REAGAN, the "Christian Right" is really a loose coalition of conservative Protestants in the United States. Rejecting the moral laxity of the liberal churches and fiscal liberalism of the DEMOCRATIC PARTY, the Christian Right claimed to be "pro-family, pro-defense and pro-morality." They work for legislation against welfare programs, ABORTION, pornography, and HOMOSEXUAL rights. Fervently anti-COMMUNIST, they support a strong military defense. In the Middle Eastern policy of the United States, they tend to be strongly pro-Israel, seeing the Jews of the Bible as God's chosen people.

In practical politics, the Christian Right has tended to be aligned with the REPUBLICAN PARTY. The group enjoyed considerable influence in the presidential administration of Ronald Reagan (1981–89) and to a lesser extent during President George Bush's administration (1989–93), as reflected in the federal government's support for reduced social welfare programs, restored PRAYER IN SCHOOLS, increased defense spending, and favorable treatment of EVANGELICAL Christian television media. Conservative evangelical Christians supported George W. Bush's election in 2000. The Christian Right also campaigns for conservative state officials and programs that influence education, welfare, and criminal justice policies in many states (e.g., laws restricting abortion, divorce, and welfare; toughening criminal penalties; and introducing religious instruction, prayer, and "traditional values" in public schools).

Demographically, members of the Christian Right tend to be white, middle- or lower-middle-class, evangelical or charismatic Christians. They often take a providential COVENANT view of U.S. history, seeing the United States as uniquely blessed of God and needing to be obedient and faithful to God's laws and ordinances.

The Christian Right is often criticized by the media, the Democratic Party, university academics, and the liberal churches (as well as non-Christian groups) as being intolerant, reactionary, and dangerous. Despite this opposition, the Christian Right's activity does not seem to be diminishing. Founding many Christian schools and colleges (or home schooling) since the 1970s, these conservative Christian activists now bring a new generation of believers to politics in America.

Further Reading
Rozell, Mark J., and Wilcox, Clyde, ed. *God at the Grass Roots: The Christian Right in the 1996 Elections*. Lanham, Md.: Rowman & Littlefield, 1997.

church and state

Ideas on the proper relationship of "religion and politics" or relations between church and government.

Prior to the Judeo-CHRISTIAN religious tradition, and still in many Eastern countries, no distinction was made between worldly or secular authority and religious or spiritual authority. In the pagan Roman Empire, rulers (or CAESARS) were considered gods, so the state was worshiped as both an earthly and heavenly power. Both Jews and early Christians refused to worship the king as they considered him a false god, and they were persecuted as a consequence. Church members in the Roman Empire were often forced to light candles and bow down to government officials and if they refused, were put to death. The emperor Nero killed thousands of Christians who refused to worship him.

With Emperor CONSTANTINE, Christianity became first a legal, accepted religion and then the official religion of the Roman Empire (A.D. 330). The correct relationship of religion and government was addressed by several prominent Christian theologians, including St. AUGUSTINE, St. Thomas AQUINAS, Martin LUTHER, and John CALVIN.

In the CATHOLIC teaching (Augustine and Aquinas), the church and state are separate but related, the former primarily concerned with spiritual teaching and worship and the latter with police functions and military defense. Because just laws require moral knowledge and religion is the source of morality, the church must advise the government on secular legal matters. Ultimately, if the society and the church have a conflict over a public issue, the church should prevail because it is closer to God. This led to the Roman Catholic Church and its leader, the pope, dictating laws to European monarchs.

Emperor CHARLEMAGNE (800–814) challenged this church supremacy in politics when he began to appoint bishops himself. This culminated in Pope Gregory VII's ban on such "lay investiture" of Catholic bishops in 1073.

The Protestant REFORMATION modified the Catholic view of church-state relations. Martin Luther claimed that the government had supreme authority in social matters and that the church should be primarily concerned with spiritual matters and the individual's "inner life." John Calvin saw a shared rule of society by government and religious leaders. This caused German Protestant princes to assume legal authority over the church, an idea later adopted by King HENRY VIII in England.

With the proliferation of separate, DISSENTING Protestant churches in England and America, the idea of toleration of various sects and freedom of religious belief expanded. This reached its height in the United States, where individual religious belief and freedom is protected by the CONSTITUTION. This reflects the idea of separation of church and state. The U.S. Supreme Court decides the relationship of religion and politics, including prayer in public schools, rights of religious expression and employment, and spiritual education. Constitutional law is complex, but it tries to steer a line between the two FIRST AMENDMENT clauses that govern church-state relations in the United States. The "establishment clause" states that the federal government shall not make laws respecting an establishment of religion, that is, an official state church (as the Church of England); the "free exercise" clause says that CONGRESS shall not make a law violating the free exercise (belief, expression, etc.) of an individual's religion. Protecting one of the clauses (such as avoiding public support of religion by permitting prayer in schools) may harm the other clause rights (punishing those who want to express their religion by praying in school). The Supreme Court has tried to strike a balance between these two, avoiding entanglement with government in religion and not persecuting religious people. So, for example, in various rulings it has held that students may not pray (led by a school official) during regular school hours in the school building but may pray together as a group or club in the building before or after regular school hours.

The primary motivation of religious FREEDOM in America was to keep the government out of regulating church affairs (doctrine, liturgy, worship, polity, etc.).

Early American BAPTISTS, especially in Virginia, fought for noninterference of the state in church matters, resulting in Thomas JEFFERSON's statute for religious freedom. But American Christians continued to believe that state laws required moral knowledge to be just, and moral knowledge required religious influence in the government. The hope of EVANGELICAL Christians was that religious liberty would create widespread conversions to Christianity and that a generally Christian culture would make Godly laws and policy.

As the United States became more pluralistic (with non-Western, non-Christian inhabitants) as well as more LIBERAL politically, this evangelical expectation of a Christian America was disappointed. By the 1950s, U.S. society became less and less recognizably Christian in culture. An attempt to restore the earlier religious atmosphere in the United States was made by the CHRISTIAN RIGHT in passing laws conforming to religious sensibilities (limited divorce, restricting ABORTION, allowing PRAYER IN SCHOOL, etc.). The dynamic between church and state promises to continue to be an active feature of U.S. culture in the future.

Further Readings
Brownlie, I., ed. *Basic Documents on Human Rights.* Oxford, Eng.: Clarendon Press, 1971.
Figgis, J. N. *Churches in the Modern State.* London: Longmans, Green & Co., 1913.
———. *Political Thought from Gerson to Grotius 1414–1625.* New York: Harper & Row, 1960.
Hardy, A. *The Spiritual Nature of Man.* Oxford, Eng.: Clarendon Press, 1979.
Jordan, W. K. *The Development of Religious Toleration in England,* 4 vols. London: George Allen & Unwin, 1932–40.
Malinowski, B. *The Foundation of Faith and Morals.* Norwood, Pa.: Norwood Editions, 1936.
Moyser, G., ed. *Church and Politics Today.* Edinburgh: T & T Clark, 1985.
Nicholls, D. *The Pluralist State.* New York: St. Martin's Press, 1975.
Sturzo, L. *Church and State,* 2 vols. Notre Dame, Ind.: University of Notre Dame Press, 1962.
Troeltsch, E. *The Social Teaching of the Christian Churches,* 2 vols. London: George Allen & Unwin, 1931.

Cicero, Marcus Tullius (106–43 B.C.)   *Roman lawyer, statesman, and political philosopher*

Born into a prominent public family in Rome, Cicero received a CLASSICAL education emphasizing the Greek classics of philosophy (especially PLATO and ARISTOTLE). Living during a time when the Roman Empire was expanding, causing a strain on the old Roman REPUBLIC and increasing the power of the imperial MONARCHY (CAESAR), Cicero adapted Greek REPUBLICAN theory to a large EMPIRE. He emphasized military VIRTUE or patriotism and the rule of universal LAW and is seen as a traditional, nostalgic Roman citizen. He valued the stoic Roman soldier who had a strong sense of duty and love of country. Cicero lamented the decline of this faithful, CONSERVATIVE Roman lifestyle and the rise of luxury, immorality, and decadence. He saw the decline of traditional Roman civilization (loyalty to family, STATE, and virtue) as leading to first moral decline, then economic weakness, then military defeat. His criticism of the immorality of Rome and creeping DICTATORSHIP led to his assassination by Mark Anthony's henchmen in 43 B.C., one year after the murder of Julius Caesar.

Cicero, unlike Aristotle, identifies man's "social nature" with public-spirited duty and patriotism, shared love of country, and a willingness to sacrifice for the common good. Instead of Aristotle's small Greek polis of reasonable citizens interacting personally, Cicero sees reason encoded in Roman law, which can be applied by judges across the vast Roman Empire. He said that "no principle enunciated by the philosophers . . . has not been discovered and established by those who have drawn up codes of law for States." He adopted Aristotle's idea of a "mixed CONSTITUTION" of kingship (rule of one), ARISTOCRACY (rule of a few), and DEMOCRACY (rule of the many), so Cicero supported the Roman senate but saw the need for executive (emperor) authority, especially during social breakdown. The best leader would be a combination soldier, orator, and statesman, for Cicero.

Cicero is remembered as a kind of heroic prophet: warning Rome to return to its glorious, disciplined past and seeing the decline of virtue as leading to destruction. Although the Roman Empire declined and fell during a period of hundreds of years, Cicero was correct in identifying the sources of its ruin in economic luxury, moral decadence, and individual indulgence. His advice for maintaining a healthy, virtuous republic influenced later republican thought, especially in England and America (see James HARRINGTON and Thomas JEFFERSON).

Further Readings

Douglas, A. E. *Cicero*. Oxford, Eng.: Clarendon Press, 1968.

Millar, F. G. B. "State and subject: the impact of monarchy." In *Caesar Augustus: Seven Aspects*, F. G. B. Millar and C. Segal, eds. Oxford, Eng.: Clarendon Press, 1984.

citizen/citizenship

The way we define who is a citizen, or a member of a nation or society. It deals with the qualities or activities of a citizen of a country. This ranges from the CLASSICAL Greek definition of someone who actually rules or participates in governance to the modern limited idea that a citizen is simply a person born and living in a certain country. Citizenship implies a more important, active life than just being a subject of a ruler (or slave of a master); being a citizen implies having some kind of power to make or influence laws or determine public policy that affects oneself.

The most complete or rich concept of citizenship comes in ARISTOTLE's idea of a person who rules, governs, participates in making laws, or serves as a judge or administrator in government. The Aristotelian ideal of active citizenship then involves "participation" in public life. This has influenced all later DEMOCRATIC ideas of citizenships, which regard a passive, uninvolved, or apathetic person as not really a citizen. Aristotle said that such active citizens must be qualified and prepared—educationally, economically, and politically—to govern well, but with the right preparation, active citizenship can be the most satisfying human life because it uses the highest human faculties of reason, speech, and ethics. This classical democracy, however, can only exist in a small community where everyone can know fellow citizens. In a large country then, classical citizenship is either impossible or requires dissecting jurisdictions into smaller units (such as states, countries, wards, etc.). Thomas JEFFERSON admired this Aristotelian ideal of citizenship and tried to replicate it in a large country (the U.S.) through division of government locally, regionally, and nationally. Jefferson also hoped that public education, economic EQUALITY, and political participation (as well as CHRISTIAN ethics) would prepare Americans for full citizenship.

Roman citizenship began with the Greek ideal of political qualification and participation through the Roman senate, but with its expanding EMPIRE, it had to rely more and more on formal, legal definitions of citizenship. Legal citizenship is based here on where you are born or whether you bought your citizenship. Then citizenship granted certain legal rights (as when St. Paul complained that as a Roman citizen he could not be beaten publicly without a trial [Acts 22:25]).

During the MIDDLE AGES, in Europe, citizenship tended to be limited to associates with membership in a class, GUILD, corporation, or royally sanctioned

Department of Labor training service. Italian class receiving instruction in English and citizenship, Newark, N.J. Y.M.C.A. (LIBRARY OF CONGRESS)

organization (church, college, town, etc.). Christianity placed the individual's citizenship both on earth (The City of Man) and in heaven (The City of God); St. AUGUSTINE believe Christians have a duty to serve in government to promote the common good, but no worldly regime is perfect, and our true citizenship is in heaven through Christ. Protestant thinker John CALVIN emphasized that people are equal through universal sinfulness, which commended a democratic form of government in both church and state. Many Christian churches diminish the importance of political citizenship by focusing on spiritual development and "the inner life" and by regarding all worldly governments as dominated by pride, vanity, power, and prestige.

The MODERN, LIBERAL idea of citizenship revolves around "representative" democracy. In this view, citizens are those who are either born or naturalized in the country and have the right to *vote* for rulers who make the laws. This once-removed citizenship allows the person to participate directly (if elected to governmental office) or indirectly (by choosing those in positions of power) or to not be involved in politics at all. The tendency of Western democracies to have fewer and fewer people vote in elections causes concern that a small ELITE really runs the country and that society is becoming more undemocratic. Benjamin Barber's *Strong Democracy* addresses this concern. Also, as more people in the world become increasingly interested in their private economic lives, the concern with the public good diminishes. Consumerism, selfish hedonism, and complex interest groups all decrease full, national citizenship.

An alternative in some societies is to identify citizenship with an ethnic or religious character (as being Jewish in Israel, Muslim in Arab countries, Chinese, African, etc.) rather than with human reason or governance. This extends the citizenship to many but makes it superficial and tribal (see FASCISM). The United States, because of its multiethnic quality, cannot base citizenship on religion, race, or even language. Consequently, citizenship in the United States and the Western world generally is a fluid, changing phenomenon.

Further Readings

Holmes, S. *Benjamin Constant and the Making of Modern Liberal-ism.* New Haven, Conn.: Yale University Press, 1984.

Machiavelli, N. *The Discourses,* B. Crick, ed. Harmondsworth, Eng.: Penguin Books, 1970.

Marshall, T. H. "Citizenship and social class." In *Sociology at the Crossroads, and Other Essays.* London: Heinemann, 1963.

Pocock, J. G. A. *Virtue, Commerce and History.* Cambridge, Eng.: Cambridge University Press, 1985.

Rousseau, J. J. *The Social Contract,* M. Cranston, transl. Harmondsworth, Eng.: Penguin Books, 1968.

civil disobedience

The disobeying or breaking of a law for moral, religious, or other reasons, either by an individual or an organized group. Examples of civil disobedience include refusing to pay taxes, blocking roads or government offices, striking or refusing to work in the offending government, and marching in demonstrations without state permission. The act may be designed to pressure the government to change laws or policies or just to voice opposition and present a "moral witness." Civil disobedience became popular in the United States in the 1960s to protest the Vietnam War, racial discrimination, and environmental policy.

A leading writer on civil disobedience was American Henry David THOREAU who coined the term in an essay ("Civil Disobedience") in 1848. Thoreau explained that he broke the law by not paying taxes to the state of Massachusetts to protest the U.S. policy in the Mexican War and the institution of slavery in the South. The failure to protest unjust state laws was effectively contributing to that injustice, in Thoreau's view. He saw civil disobedience as a matter of individual conscience and actually spent time in jail as a consequence.

A leading activist in 20th-century civil disobedience was Mohandas GANDHI in India. Resisting what he saw as unjust British colonial policy, Gandhi organized marches, sit-ins, and hunger strikes. He insisted on the nonviolent quality of civil disobedience, always accepting abuse without returning it. Passive resistance became a part of Gandhi's highly successful civil disobedience in India against the British. He insisted that his nonviolent approach to reforming public policy involved basic respect for law and the social system.

This nonviolent approach to civil disobedience was adopted in the CIVIL RIGHTS movement in the United

Civil rights march on Washington, D.C., August 28, 1963. (NATIONAL ARCHIVES)

States in the 1950s and 1960s, especially by black leader Martin Luther KING, Jr., who used marches, boycotts, and demonstrations in an attempt to achieve racial justice in the United States. He, like Gandhi, shamed his opponents by using peaceful means of protest, while they responded with police clubs and attack dogs. Organized civil disobedience, then, won social sympathy for the civil rights cause.

The philosophical origin of civil disobedience to state laws goes back to CHRISTIAN conceptions of God's "higher law," which the faithful must obey even if means breaking civil law. The early Christian refusal to worship Roman rulers led many to be jailed or executed. St. AUGUSTINE says that at times the church should advise believers to disobey the state when it violates God's law. Suffering the consequences of government persecution, personal martyrdom is better than disgracing Christ and possibly being sent to Hell for eternity. St. Thomas AQUINAS wrote in *Summa Theologica* that if a human law violated a higher natural law or divine law, the Christian may disobey the lower law. For example, because divine law defines food as created to sustain life, if a starving man steals bread to stay alive, he is not breaking the law. In NAZI Germany, Dietrich BONHOEFFER and other Christians resisted the FASCISTS on religious grounds and were executed by the state.

In all theories of civil disobedience, the perpetrator is expected to accept whatever punishment might result from the action.

Further Readings

Bedau, Hugo Adam, ed. *Civil Disobedience: Theory and Practice.* New York: Pegasus, 1969.

Gandhi, M. K. *Non-Violent Resistance.* New York: Schocken Books, 1961.

Rawls, J. *A Theory of Justice,* chap. 6. Cambridge, Mass.: Belknap Press of Harvard University Press, 1971.

Singer, P. *Democracy and Disobedience.* Oxford, Eng.: Clarendon Press, 1973.

Thoreau, Henry D. "Civil disobedience." In Bedau, Walzer M., ed., *Obligations: Essays on Disobedience, War and Citizenship.* Cambridge, Mass.: Harvard University Press, 1970.

civil liberty/civil liberties

The fundamental RIGHTS and FREEDOMS necessary to full human life and political activity, especially liberty of thought, belief, speech, expression, and association. In United States CONSTITUTIONAL LAW, it is the body of Supreme Court rulings (or decisions) relating to the FIRST AMENDMENT rights to free speech, free press, freedom of religion, and free association or political assembly to influence or criticize the government. The idea is that these basic human rights and liberties are given by God and nature and cannot be legitimately taken away by a government; rather, part of a just state is protecting those individual freedoms. A government that violates those rights and liberties, for John LOCKE's British LIBERALISM, is TYRANNICAL, and the people can overthrow it. If a STATE punishes free speech or writing with prison or fines or execution, if it persecutes religious groups or forbids citizens' associations, it is breaking the SOCIAL CONTRACT and violating God-given NATURAL RIGHTS. Protection of civil liberties is most valued and prominent in Britain, the United States, and other Western democracies. The right to own private PROPERTY and engage in free-market business is often included in these liberties, so they often accompany

CAPITALISM. Civil rights are seen as a prerequisite to a political democracy.

Further Reading

Gellner, Ernest. *Conditions of Liberty: Civil Society and Its Rivals.* New York: Allen Lane/Penguin Press, 1994.

civil religion

A religion that worships the STATE or those things that support the society and government. The value of the religion is seen in terms of how it helps the nation function in an orderly way—a religion that reinforces a community's social and cultural mores or ways. This is contrasted with transcendent religions like CHRISTIANITY that worship a God apart from the nation and above any particular society (see St. AUGUSTINE, CATHOLIC).

Most ancient religions were tied to a particular region and community, the Greek city-states each had their own gods and dogmas that defined their region as divinely made and directed, and this was reinforced by regular celebrations and festivals that linked the community with these deities. The idea that a transcendent God created and loved all humanity and had values above any particular culture was foreign to these civil religions. From a Christian perspective, such civil religion worships the state and is idolatry (worshiping a false god). But even Christianity has at times been captured by a particular country or government, as in the Russian Orthodox Church.

The clearest expression of MODERN civil religion is given by French philosopher Jean-Jacques ROUSSEAU, who coined the phrase *civil religion* in his book *The Social Contract* (1762). In Rousseau's definition, which greatly influenced the deism of the French Revolution, the key elements of a civil religion (which he favored) were (1) that it will make citizens love their duty to the state; (2) a concentration on teaching ethical behavior; (3) the conception of one mighty, intelligent, and beneficent deity possessed of foresight and providence; (4) the reality of life-after-death and the reward of the virtuous and punishment of the wicked in that afterlife; (5) the tolerance of all religions that do not challenge the civil religion or undermine the state. So, the value of civil religion is to produce moral, orderly, dutiful citizens who will sacrifice for the community. Any other religion is measured by that standard of social usefulness. For Rousseau, this civil religion was needed to keep a REPUBLIC virtuous and orderly. Thomas JEFFERSON's appreciation of Christian ethics (or "the ethics of Jesus") as a support for the American democratic system follows this viewpoint. The standard for religious truth is how *useful* it is to society. A creed that makes people mystical or withdrawn from the world (or critical of the government) is to be suppressed. Hence, the Rousseauian French revolutionaries persecuted Christians, especially CATHOLICS who objected to the new French government and supported the French MONARCHY and ARISTOCRACY.

In the 20th century, FASCISM is noted for its use of civil religion. NAZI Germany extolled "The State" and "The Leader" (Führer) to a godlike status. Many German Protestants endorsed "Aryan Christianity," which viewed Hitler's regime and the modern German nation as God's instrument. This corruption of the church discredited the Christian faith.

In the United States of America, a kind of "civil religion" exists when Christianity is mixed with national patriotism and the line between God and country is blurred. The quasi-religious tones of certain national holidays, such as the Fourth of July, Memorial Day, Thanksgiving Day, and Martin Luther King, Jr., Day, afford a semblance of civil religion that identifies Americans as a "chosen people" of God, under his spcial providence and care, receiving unique blessings and protection so long as his people follow and obey his laws. Early American PURITAN theology, with its COVENANT view of Christianity, its belief that they were to create "a city on a hill," a godly civilization as a beacon of hope to the world and work under special responsibilities to be faithful to God, became interwoven with America's civil religion. President Ronald REAGAN skillfully employed rhetoric expressing this religious foundation of America in explaining contemporary REPUBLICAN PARTY policy. The diversity and EVANGELICAL character of most of American religion has limited this use of Christianity as a civil religion, and it retains its transcendent, universal quality among most American believers. So, for example, when a church or minister (as Marion "Pat" ROBERTSON running for U.S. president) identifies religion too closely with politics, the American tradition of separation of CHURCH AND STATE rejects that attempt to co-opt religion for purely political purposes.

A true civil religion has to be vague enough to gather broad support, so the traditional faiths (Judaism, Christianity, Islam) are less serviceable for that purpose. A general ethical, monotheism empha-

sizing social morality, is more likely to become a civil religion. With the U.S. CONSTITUTIONAL guarantee of religious freedom and pluralism, such a uniform civil religion is less likely to exist.

Further Reading
Bellah, R. N., and Hammond, P. E. *Variety of Civil Religions.* New York: Harper & Row, 1980.

civil society

A society advanced enough to have organized groups and activities, such as businesses, markets, schools, clubs, professional associations, and governmental institutions. In the MODERN, LIBERAL thought of Thomas HOBBES and John LOCKE, civil society is contrasted with the pre-political state of nature where isolated individuals roam around, compete with one another, and injure each other. Civil society "civilizes" the natural human, who through reason, creates the SOCIAL CONTRACT that establishes organized society and delegated government. For Hobbes and Locke, this secures social peace, allowing safe development of trade, commerce, education, arts, and prosperity. The STATE is limited to protecting individual RIGHTS, including those of associations in civil society (such as clubs, businesses, religious groups, etc.). When the state (as in COMMUNISM) takes over all human rights and associations under the government, it destroys civil society. So one of the challenges for former communist countries (such as the SOVIET UNION) has been to *establish* the institutions of civil society. If under a TOTALITARIAN regime no private associations were allowed (like the Boy Scouts or professional groups) apart from the state, the state takes time to set up the independent groups necessary to civil society. So although the United States enjoys an extensive nongovernmental civil society, whenever the state or large corporations seem to be taking over smaller associations, it is feared the civil society may be lost and TYRANNY will emerge. James MADISON insisted that a large variety of groups in civil society (PLURALISM) was needed to secure FREEDOM.

Political thinkers, who favored a strong, centralized state (MARX, HEGEL, ROUSSEAU) tended to be critical of civil society with its many independent groups and associations. Rousseau viewed civil society as full of vanity, pomp, inequality, and elitist authority, so his unified state under the GENERAL WILL destroyed much of civil society. Marxist communism viewed civil society as CAPITALIST materialism, brutal competition, and anarchic inefficiency, so Marx's workers' state (or "dictatorship of the proletariat") annihilated most of civil society's independent organizations.

Today, civil society refers to that private realm of individuals and nongovernmental associations that perform much of the economic, social, and religious activity in the West. Current Western thinking holds that a healthy, diverse civil society is necessary to stable PROGRESS in the economy and responsive, REPUBLICAN government. The tendency to have the central state run more and more of private life has diminished in most Western democracies.

Further Readings

Black, A. *Guilds and Civil Society in European Political Thought from the Twelfth Century to the Present.* Ithaca, N.Y.: Cornell University Press, 1984.
Ferguson, A. *An Essay on the History of Civil Society,* D. Forbes, ed. Edinburgh: Edinburgh University Press, 1966.
Keane, John. *Civil Society: Old Images, New Visions.* Stanford: Stanford University Press, 1998.
Rosmini, Antonio. *Rights in Civil Society,* Denis Cleary and Terence Watson, transl. Durham, N.C.: Rosmini House, 1996.

class

A term used by many political thinkers to denote an economic, social, or political group. ARISTOTLE talks about the class of CITIZENS made up of adult, Greek men with a certain level of economic independence, educational attainment, and political experience, and he contrasts this with classes of "noncitizens" (women, children, slaves). PLATO's *Republic* divides society into three natural classes conforming to individuals' natural dispositions: (1) rulers; (2) soldiers; and (3) workers. The rulers, for Plato, are distinguished by the VIRTUE of wisdom (PHILOSOPHER-KINGS); the soldiers have the virtue of courage; and the workers or business people have the virtue of moderation. For Plato, these social classes are inevitable and good—they reflect differences in human beings and, if organized properly, create social harmony and JUSTICE. St. Thomas AQUINAS's conception of classes reflects the social structure of the European MIDDLE AGES: MONARCHY (royalty), ARISTOCRACY, peasants, and churchmen or priests. In this Thomist view, each class is important to the functioning of the whole society, but each is different and requires distinct sets of laws to govern it. The British CONSTITUTION of monarchy, Lords, and Commons reflects this MEDIEVAL conception. Western democracies, like the United States of America, claim to have no legal or official classes (the U.S. constitution forbids titles of nobility or aristocracy), but social, economic, and religious classes continue in those countries.

Marxist COMMUNIST theory emphasizes economic class throughout history, especially owners of property and workers. In MARXISM, technology produces different economic classes at various historical stages. During the earliest human communities (primitive communism of tribal society), no classes exist because production is very low level—just hunting and gathering with no fixed wealth. In CLASSICAL antiquity (ancient Greece and Rome) a slightly more-advanced agricultural economy divides society into master and slave classes. In the Middle Ages (A.D. 500–1500), Marxism says that the economic classes are landlords and peasants. During industrial capitalism, classes are bourgeoisie (capitalists) and proletariat (workers). In SOCIALISM, Marx maintained that the working class takes over political power and that this eventually leads to communism (a classless society based on highly advanced production, common ownership of PROPERTY, extreme abundance, and the elimination of work). Absolute FREEDOM, prosperity, and the end of war characterize future communist society, according to Marx. The failure of this system has caused a reexamination of its premises, but Marxism's tendency to look at society in terms of antagonistic classes, EXPLOITATION, oppression, and conflict greatly influenced the sociological view of race, gender, and class relations. Elaborate development of views of classes in society, by education, economic, power, consciousness, and gender has defined much of secular social science.

Communist thinker and Russian revolutionary V. I. LENIN extended Marxist class theory to world IMPERIALISM, with advanced CAPITALIST nations being "bourgeois" (even their working classes) and with poor Third World new colonies being exploited "proletariat" countries. This Marxist–Leninist perspective affected much of African and Latin American politics in the latter half of the 20th century. Such class theory declined in influence in the early 21st century with the growth of Third World democracies and the fall of communism.

Other thinkers on social class include Max WEBER, who focuses more on official power, and Karl MANNHEIM, who emphasized noneconomic class groups. In general class analysis has come to be seen as too simplistic to be valuable in political thought; individual character transcends class identification, and placing individuals in race, gender, economic, and educational groupings seems to be oppressive rather than liberating. The American credo to judge people by their individual personality and accomplishments eschews class perspectives.

Further Reading
Roemer, J. *A General Theory of Exploitation and Class*. Cambridge, Mass.: Harvard University Press, 1982.

classical

Political thought of the CLASSICAL or ancient Western world. This usually means the Golden Age of Greece (Athens) 400–300 B.C. and Rome (200 B.C.–A.D. 200). Among the major classical Greek political philosophers are SOCRATES, PLATO, and ARISTOTLE. The leading Roman or Latin political thinkers are Cato, Posidonius, CICERO, TACITUS, and MARCUS AURELIUS.

Although important differences exist among different classical thinkers, they are considered similar in their concerns for JUSTICE, VIRTUE, devotion to the common good, and citizen participation in rule through rational deliberation. Aristotle is the fullest expression of classical political thought. His belief that people are naturally "social and political animals" who require training and experience in governing to be fully human forms the basis of much classical thought. This active citizenship requires educational, economic, and cultural preparation to form the independent, reasonable, ethical, just citizen. Politics is a high occupation to the gentleman who is freed from economic concerns by wealth and is happy to exercise his reason and ethics in rule. Consequently, those social conditions that harm such personal and political fulfillment are dangerous. The main threat to civic virtue and the just REPUBLIC is TYRANNY, or the concentration of political and economic power in the hands of a few people who use government to further their own interests. This is the classical definition of *corruption*: rulers who govern for their own interest rather than for the common good. Provisions should be made in the just republic to prevent the concentration of power and wealth and corruption.

This "classical REPUBLICANISM" affects Western political thought through the RENAISSANCE, the MIDDLE AGES (St. Thomas AQUINAS), and MODERN Anglo-American thinking (James HARRINGTON, Thomas JEFFERSON).

Further Reading
Finley, M. I. *The Legacy of Greece*. Oxford, Eng.: Clarendon Press, 1981.

Coke, Sir Edward (1552–1634) *English jurisprudence scholar, judge, and writer*

Coke (pronounced "Cook") greatly influenced the British and American view of English common law and government. He held that common law (or the body of court rulings in English history) provided a foundation for individual RIGHTS, PROPERTY, and CITIZENSHIP, along with parliamentary legislation and royal power. Such historical precedent of judges' decisions, along with major legal documents such as the MAGNA CARTA, embodied a collective wisdom superior to any one individual's reason. This conclusion effectively put the RULE OF LAW above the king. This displeased King James I, who dismissed Coke as chief justice in 1616. But Coke's analysis of the limits on MONARCHY by Parliament and the common-law tradition were invoked by British parliamentarians against the Crown in the 1640s and 1680s, and by American revolutionaries such as Thomas JEFFERSON in the 1770s. Coke's respect for the past in English common law became the basis for American CONSTITUTIONAL LAW, which consults past court decisions when making rulings on new cases.

Coke's primary writings appear in his books *The Institutes of the Laws of England* and *Reports*.

Further Readings
Bowen, Catherine Drinker. *The Lion and the Throne: The Life and Times of Sir Edward Coke (1552–1634)*, 1st ed. Boston: Little, Brown, 1957.
Coke, Sir Edward. *Institutes of the Laws of England*, 4 vols. 1797.
———. *Reports*, 13 vols. 1777.
Hill, C. *Intellectual Origins of the English Revolution*. Oxford, Eng.: Clarendon Press, 1972.
Hobbes, T. *Dialogue Between a Philosopher and a Student of the Common Laws of Emgland*, J. Cropsey, ed. Chicago: University of Chicago Press, 1969.

Coleridge, Samuel Taylor (1772–1834) *Poet, philosopher, and political theorist*

Coleridge was born in Devonshire, England, the son of a clergyman. He is known most widely as a romantic poet, but he was also an influential and important political theorist and philosopher. As a philosopher, he was an idealist who was influenced by the German thinkers KANT and Schelling and the British idealist Berkeley. As a political critic and theorist, Coleridge wrote extensively on the foundations of political theory, on the connections between CHURCH AND STATE, against UTILITARIANISM, and on the role of the intelligentsia, as well as contributing to the major political debates of his time.

Coleridge's philosophy is theological. It is premised on the idea that our access to reality and our knowledge of the world are connected to and mediated through God. The fundamental role of religion in his thought is made clear in the Kantian distinction he draws between reason and understanding. The latter is the category in which he places all knowledge and awareness based on our senses. This is the knowledge of empirical sciences. Reason is a higher category of knowledge containing not only the a-priori truths of logic and mathematics, but also religious, aesthetic, and poetic truths and ideals. In this way, Coleridge intends to secure the epistemological and metaphysical status of religious belief by reserving a faculty for its apprehension and arguing for its superiority as a mode of knowing. With these premises in place Coleridge goes on to provide innovative accounts of the will, self-consciousness, and the mind-body problem. Most particularly, Coleridge brings into philosophical focus the metaphysical and epistemological role of language and the imagination.

Coleridge's contribution to political philosophy and social criticism is contained in a number of essays in the periodicals the *Watchman* and the *Friends,* his *Lay Sermons,* and his only book on political matters, *The Constitution of the Church and State.* Coleridge was also a frequent contributor to newspapers on issues of contemporary importance, such as the Reform Bill of 1832. In *On The Principles of Political Philosophy,* Coleridge argues against two systems of political justice. In the first, fear is the foundation of legitimate authority. He rejects this Hobbesian view as "baseless" in either history or our own experience. He also rejects a second view in which justice is based on the calculation of what is expedient. This approach is a view "under which the human being may be considered, namely, as an animal gifted with understanding, or the faculty of suiting measures to circumstances." Coleridge sets out his own understanding of political justice by arguing that it must be based on the proper application of the laws of reason rather than the faculty of understanding.

In *The Constitution of the Church and State,* Coleridge argues toward two important conclusions: first, that a system of land ownership and aristocracy is crucial for the moral well-being of the state—he claimed that commercialism, while important for the progress of the state, nonetheless would undermine it without the restraint and moral foundation provided by the aristocracy; second, that a national church and the establishment of a clerisy would attend to the moral welfare and advancement of citizens. He makes a distinction between civilization and cultivation, where the latter signifies the development of individual moral self-understanding, and the former the material and political progress of society. He says that first we must become men and only then citizens. It is the task of the clerisy and the national church to attend to and promote the cultivation of individuals.

Coleridge's work taken as a whole, including his poetic work, marks him alongside BENTHAM as one of the leading intellectual influences of 19th-century England. He contested the prevailing empiricist framework by bringing forward idealist and romantic arguments and insights to the debate on human knowledge and political justice.

Further Reading
Morrow, J. *Coleridge's Political Thought.* New York: Macmillan, 1990.

commandments

The Ten Commandments given by God to Moses (as described in the Bible's book of Exodus), and form the basis of Judeo-CHRISTIAN law and morals. These commandments form the fundamental law of the Western world. Sometimes called the Decalogue, they include God's commandments against idolatry, murder, stealing, adultery, coveting, and lying. They also enjoin honoring one's parents and respecting the Sabbath (rest day). The West's social laws punishing murder, theft, perjury (lying), adultery, and regulating business on the Lord's day reflect these biblical commandments. Christians' view that no one can completely fulfill the requirements of the "Law" leads to God's grace in forgiving them through Jesus Christ taking the punishment for our sins in his death on the cross. Then "faith" in Jesus as the Son of God and "dying for our sins" gives believers eternal life in heaven through his Resurrection. This commends repentance of individual sins against these commandments and reliance on God's holy spirit to strengthen and improve us. Jesus states that he did not come to "abolish" the law (or the Ten Commandments) but to "fulfill" them means both this divine forgiveness for breaking the law and divine renewing to help believers follow the law. In the Sermon on the Mount, (Matthew 5–7), Jesus explains that his ETHICS deepen the Ten Commandments by applying them to thoughts and intentions as well as actions (so lust becomes a kind of adultery, anger a kind of murder). In Western political and legal thought, usually only the actual breaking of a commandment is punished in earthly courts, while sins of the mind are judged in heavenly realms. See CHURCH AND STATE.

Further Reading

Davidman, Joy. *Smoke on the Mountain: An Interpretation of the Ten Commandments*. Philadelphia: Westminster Press, 1954.

communism/communist

A political theory and system that believes that greater EQUALITY and JUSTICE will exist in a society where no private ownership of productive PROPERTY (land, factories, stores) is allowed. Communist society places ownership of "the means of production" (property) in the state or community. The assumption is that private ownership of property somehow corrupts humans, making them greedy, selfish, arrogant, and uncooperative. This view, that it is the social environment that causes immoral behavior, contrasts with the CLASSICAL, CHRISTIAN and British LIBERAL perspective that evil exists *within* human nature. Communism believes that human nature is determined by external social and economic relations, so if the community is more fair and equal, persons will automatically be more kind, virtuous, and unselfish. This contrasts with Christ's words "Seek ye first the Kingdom of God and His righteousness and all these [economic] things shall be added" (Luke 12:31), which puts morality first and economic justice following. Whether human nature determines society or social conditions affect nature has been a constant debate in political thought. Most thinkers, after ARISTOTLE, acknowledge the interaction of "nature and nurture," but the debate continues.

Western political thought has advanced communist ideas in various forms for more than 2000 years. In PLATO's *Republic,* the "Guardians," or military, practice communism (owning no big property but only necessities for soldiers—clothes, weapons—and those provided by the STATE), as appropriate to their role in society. Wealth and luxury would corrupt military personnel because their job of fighting and defending the country in war requires toughness and hardship. If the

soldiers become used to an easy, luxurious lifestyle, they will be ineffective as warriors, so communism is the best economic system for them. Plato does not advocate public ownership of property for the business class, however.

In the early CHRISTIAN church, believers "held all things in common," sharing property according to need. Those Christians who had more wealth gave some to those who had nothing, usually through the leaders of the church (Acts 4:32). This was not communism because private ownership was still practiced, but it was rather a form of Christian charity. St. Thomas AQUINAS articulated the CATHOLIC perspective on private property, drawing on both the Bible and Aristotle's philosophy. Worldly goods are given by God for the sustenance of human life. Private ownership aids that end or the purpose of earthly property by making people more careful of their goods, providing incentives for work, and causing a more orderly society. However, St. Thomas insists that private ownership is limited by the needs of the poor and the necessity of Christian charity. If a rich person knows of a person in need, he should convey some property to the poor, acknowledging that his wealth is a gift from God.

Other Christian thinkers, notably Sir Thomas MORE's *Utopia* (1516) and the English Levellers, advanced more radical common ownership of property. Throughout European and American history, small religious communities have established communes where property is shared in common. American writer Nathaniel Hawthorne described such a 19th-century SOCIALIST commune in New England in his novel *The Blithedale Romance.* PURITAN John LOCKE, however, in his *Second Treatise of Government,* said that private ownership of property is a God-given NATURAL RIGHT along with life and LIBERTY. God may have given the earth to humanity in common to sustain human life, but individuals must appropriate and possess private property for it to serve its divine purpose. For this Calvinist "work ethic," private-property accumulation teaches diligence and discipline and that the communist tendency to "share" property is just a clever excuse for stealing the property of others.

Modern socialist communism emerges in Europe just prior to the French Revolution of 1789. ROUSSEAU blames all vanity, greed, and inequality on private property and advocates government control of wealth for the common good. PROUDHON declares that "property is theft" and attacks CAPITALISM as the source of all poverty and misery." Babeuf's *Manifesto of the Equals* (1796) argues for community ownership of land and the same education and diet for everybody.

Twentieth-century communism (as practiced in the SOVIET UNION, China, and other countries) came from the ideas of Karl MARX. In Marxism, or "scientific socialism," communism is the final stage of history, which ends economic classes, EXPLOITATION, and oppression. Like other socialist theories in the 1800s, Marx saw socialism and communism as solving the problems of poverty and misery brought on by the Industrial Revolution. Capitalism would inevitably lead to socialism (public ownership of large property and economic planning by the STATE), and technological advances would finally lead to communism (a heavenly society of FREEDOM and prosperity with no economic classes, no need to work, and no exploitation, poverty, misery, or war). These bright promises of Marxist communism, along with his view that history was moving inevitably toward socialism, caused many people to work for its realization. Many a Communist political Party formed in Europe, and Marxist revolutions occurred in Russia and China. The promised abundance and freedom of communism was disappointed. A society and economy completely controlled by the state for the sake of equality became oppressive and inefficient. After a 70-year experiment with communism, the Soviet Union abandoned the system for a more market-oriented economy. Other socialist countries modified the state-planned system with greater private property ownership and individual economic freedom. Socialism and communism did not deliver on their promise to end human egoism and competition by community means. Instead, they caused worse poverty and misery than the system they overthrew. However, the ideas in communism to provide universal education and a basic level of economic abundance were adopted by capitalist countries through social welfare programs and a "mixed economy" of private business and government assistance to the poor and disabled.

Further Readings
Babeuf, G. "Manifesto of the Equals," S. Lukes, transl. A. Arblaster and S. Lukes, eds. In *The Good Society*. New York: Random House, 1991.
Beer, M. *A History of British Socialism*, vol. I. London: G. Bell & Sons, 1923.
Corcoran, P. ed. *Before Marx: Socialism and Communism in France, 1830–48*. London: Macmillan, 1983.

communitarian

A political theory that emphasizes the RIGHTS, INTERESTS, and good of the whole community or nation over the individual. For example, ROUSSEAU held that the community, through the GENERAL WILL of society, could control the individual citizen (or his activities or property) for the benefit of the larger good. Because the individual person as *part of* the whole community is beholden to the society for his or her existence, this is not an infringement of his or her rights, and if the individual participates in making the community laws under which he lives, this total control is not oppressive.

Critics of "communitarian DEMOCRACY," following the British LIBERALISM of John LOCKE, claim that no rights or interests exist above the individual and that government is designed only to protect individual person's rights. Much of Western liberalism sees the "whole" interest of communitarian thought as a fiction that is simply used by a part of society to impose its will on others. They fear that communitarian theories lead to FASCISM (absolute obedience to the state) and COMMUNISM (state control of the economy).

In contemporary AMERICAN POLITICAL THOUGHT, Benjamin BARBER's *Strong Democracy* shows communitarian tendencies, though he eschews the title *communitarian*.

Further Reading
Plant, R. *Community and Ideology*. London: Routledge, 1974.

Comte, Isidore Auguste Marie François Xavier (1798–1857) *French philosopher*

Isidore Auguste Comte was the leader of the positivist school in France. He was one of the founders of sociology. Comte developed a HUMANIST religion that called for the replacement of God with a supreme being who was centered on the essence of humanity. Although he was overshadowed by figures such as MARX, Comte influenced diverse thinkers including George Eliot and John Stuart MILL.

Comte was born in Montpellier, France, to a staunch Royalist and Roman CATHOLIC family who rejected the REPUBLICANISM of the French Revolution. He entered the École Polytechnique at age 16, but he rejected the royalism of his family. After being expelled from the Polytechnique, Comte settled in Paris where he became the secretary to the reformer and SOCIALIST Claude-Henri de SAINT-SIMON. While with Saint-Simon,

Comte worked with his mentor to develop a science of human behavior. Comte broke with Saint-Simon in 1824 and gained his own fame after he delivered a series of lectures on POSITIVISM.

These lectures provided the basis for Comte's greatest work, *Cours de philosophie positive* (*Course of Positive Philosophy*). The six-volume work was written between 1830 and 1842. In his opus, Comte asserted that each science needed its own methodology and that each science is dependent on its antecedents. Hence, philosophy is dependent on history, physics dependent on astronomy, and so forth. He contended that each science goes through three distinct phases: theological (where humans view nature and natural law as dependent on the will of a deity); metaphysical (cause and effect begin to replace divine will); and positive (the quest for absolute knowledge of an area). Comte's positivism manifested itself in the belief that progress was both irreversible and inevitable. However, he did not believe that humans could obtain perfect knowledge.

Comte helped develop the modern discipline of sociology (and he coined the term *sociology*). He contended that sociology had not yet entered the positive stage but that it ultimately would clarify the other sciences. Sociology would be able to provide a framework by which social customs and traits could be quantified into laws. He envisioned the modern division of sociology into two distinct branches: social statics, or the comparative study of different social systems; and social dynamics, or the study of social change. Comte also differentiated between order and PROGRESS. Order was marked by consensus on the fundamental principles of a society, while progress was marked by change in the underlying principles as had been the case in Europe from the REFORMATION through the French Revolution. Comte asserted that a synthesis of order and progress could produce a global society that would not fight over religious or political differences. Comte's later works included the 1848 book *Discours sur l'Ensemble du positivisme* (*A General View of Positivism*), and the 1851 piece, *Système de politique positive* (*System of Positive Polity*).

In Comte's estimation, the events of the French Revolution had been negative in that they had broken down the old order but had not produced a new one. He advocated a new religion of humanity that would be led by an industrial-elite priesthood and that would have as its highest deity a supreme being who combined the essence of existence with the harmony of

nature. Scientific principles would guide everyday life, and Comte devised a new calendar based on honoring 13 great thinkers, including ARISTOTLE, DANTE, and Shakespeare.

Further Readings

Harp, G. *Positivist Republic: Auguste Comte and the Reconstruction of American Liberalism, 1865–1920.* University Park: Pennsylvania State Press, 1995.
Standley, A. *Auguste Comte.* Boston: Twayne Publishers, 1981.

conciliarism

A 15th-century movement in the CATHOLIC Church that strove to have councils or representative assemblies of the church determine policy. This is contrasted with the prevailing power of the bishop of Rome, or pope. It was a DEMOCRATIC, REPUBLICAN movement in the Roman Catholic Church that emerged during the great schism when three separate bishops claimed to be pope. A solution was seen in reforming church governance through periodic councils, like CONGRESSES, in which the representatives of the whole church were considered a greater authority than the official hierarchy of church administrators. In terms of political or governmental theory, it represented a battle between legislative and executive authority. The idea of a more representative church governance emerged during the Councils of Constance (1414–18) and Basle (1431–49). It reflected developments in CANON LAW in the 12th and 13th centuries, in which the early church practice of ruling synods and reliance on scripture for church rules and discipline prevailed. The rise of church and civil CORPORATIONS (colleges, guilds, towns) that were self-governing influenced conciliarism. This democratic impulse in the church affected modern CONSTITUTION republican political thought, eventually supplanting monarchies in Europe with representative parliaments. The conciliarist movement ended with the assertion of papal supremacy in the late 15th century and the pope's reinforcement of his supreme authority through agreements with various European monarchies. The Protestant REFORMATION of the 16th century was partly a result of the failure of the conciliar movement. For three centuries after this, republican church government was not associated with the Catholic Church. The Vatican II Roman Catholic council (1962–65) is seen as democraticizing the church with some of the conciliarist ideals.

Further Readings

Baker, D., ed. "Councils and Assemblies," vol. VII of *Studies in Church History.* Cambridge, Eng.: Cambridge University Press, 1971.

Black, A. *Monarchy and Community: Political Ideas in the Later Conciliar Controversy, 1430–1450.* Cambridge, Eng.: Cambridge University Press, 1970.

———. *Council and Commune: The Conciliar Movement and the Council of Basle.* London: Burns & Oates, 1979.

Cate, James Lea. *Medieval and Historiographical Essays in Honor of James Westfall Thompson,* James Lea Cate and Eugene N. Anderson, eds. Chicago: University of Chicago Press, 1966.

Condorcet, Marie-Jean-Antoine-Nicolas de Caritat, marquis de (1743–1794) *French philosopher, mathematician, and political theorist*

Once of the major figures of the FRENCH ENLIGHTENMENT, Condorcet was born in Ribemont, Picardy. From the age of 11, he was educated at the Jesuit College in Reims and then at the College of Navarre in Paris, where he studied mathematics and philosophy. Condorcet devoted the next several years to serious mathematical investigations, which resulted in his admission to the Académie des Sciences in 1769. Condorcet's mathematical skills provided the foundation for his later notions of social reform based on probability theory. Condorcet argued that the social sciences can approach the physical sciences in terms of their ability to generate mathematical estimates of the probabilities of human action within social institutions. He believed that the calculus of probabilities was particularly relevant when it came to understanding individual and collective choices in democratic politics. One problem he addressed, in his *Essai sur l'application de l'analyse à la probabilité des décisions rendues à la pluralité des voix* (*Essay on the Application of Analysis to the Probability of Majority Decisions*), is that of how individuals' preferences can be aggregated into some determinate collective choice through the mechanism of majority rule in a DEMOCRACY. Condorcet suggested that, if individuals are motivated to vote according to their ideas of the common good, it is almost certain that majority voting will lead to collective results responsive to their individual preferences.

Condorcet's advocacy of a probabilistic framework for social choice reveals his belief that the success of moral and social progress depends on the elimination of instinctive or habitual calculations of interest in favor of rational deliberation and calculation. Condorcet's faith in the power of reason was, of course,

typical of ENLIGHTENMENT thinkers, and he expressed his ideas for a rational social order on his election to the Académie Française in 1782. Indeed, Condorcet's notions of the perfectability of human beings and the possibility of rational social progress came to define his intellectual and political activities for the remainder of his life.

Condorcet became deeply involved in the debates and events surrounding the French Revolution of 1789. That same year, he secured a seat as a member of the municipal council of Paris and drafted his own version of the Declaration of the Rights of Man. Soon after, Condorcet published essays that called for equal rights for women, educational reform, and the abolition of torture and SLAVERY. In 1791 he was elected to the Legislative Assembly. However, Condorcet aligned himself politically with the moderate Girondin and against the radical JACOBIN wing at the National Convention called to establish the new French republic in 1792. Condorcet composed the draft Girondin constitution of 1793, which was grounded in parliamentarian principles and a liberal commitment to NATURAL RIGHTS and universal suffrage. However, the convention instead adopted the Jacobin version of the constitution. With the rise of the Jacobin to power, Condorcet was forced to go into hiding in Paris. While in hiding from July 1793 to March 1794, Condorcet wrote his famous *Esquisse d'un tableau historique des progrès de l'esprit humain* (*Sketch for a Historical Picture of the Progress of the Human Mind*), in which he formally presented his account of the various stages of humanity's progression and probable emancipation from domination. Condorcet also described what he believed would be the three characteristic features of the future historical epoch of humanity: (1) the destruction of inequality between nations; (2) the destruction of inequality between classes; and (3) the indefinite intellectual, moral, and physical perfectibility of human nature itself.

After leaving his asylum in Paris, Condorcet was arrested on March 27, 1794 and died in prison two days later.

Further Reading

Goodell, E. *The Noble Philosopher: Condorcet and the Enlightenment.* Buffalo, N.Y.: Prometheus Books, 1994.

congress

A DEMOCRATIC representative institution of a government or organization (such as the Congress of the

United States of America or the Congress of Industrial Organizations). Usually a congress has elected members for limited terms and is governed in its procedures and powers by a CONSTITUTION and/or bylaws. At times, a congress (like the Continental congresses of the revolutionary American colonies in the 1770s–80s or the Turkish congresses of the 1920s) is a revolutionary government alternative to the established regime (such as the British Crown and Parliament or Ottoman sultanate). Most governmental congresses are bound by limited, delegated powers (such as printing currency and establishing a postal system in the U.S. Constitution). The U.S. Congress is bicameral (two chambers), consisting of the upper house (Senate) and the lower house (House of Representatives) and performing the legislative function of federal government between the executive (president) and the judicial (courts) branches of government.

Further Reading
Griffith, E. S. *Congress*. New York: New York University Press, 1961.

conscientious objection

When a person objects to serving in the military or warfare because of deeply held philosophic or religious beliefs against war. Certain pacifist groups, such as the Quakers, oppose all war, and their members refuse to serve in the army. In some countries (such as the United States of America), such conscientious objection to military service is respected, and the government allows this as an exemption to compulsory (draft) army participation. Most nations do not respect the individual's moral conscience in this way and either compel military duty or punish (with prison or death) such conscientious objections to war. The issue is one of obeying a "higher law" than the state and of whether a society regards it as legitimate (see CIVIL DISOBEDIENCE). In the United States, the exemption to military service on conscientious objection grounds must involve a deeply held ethical or theological objection to *all* war or violence, not simply opposition to a particular war or government policy. This became a major public issue during the 1960s and 1970s when many recruits did not want to serve in the Vietnam War but were not against all war. If a person believes in war to defend one's country but does not wish to serve in a specific war policy, conscientious objection exemption is not allowed.

consent

In MODERN Western political thought, *consent* means an individual agreeing to or accepting the government or laws under which he or she lives and that the only LEGITIMATE state is such "government by the consent of the governed." This idea that the only just state is one the people have chosen (or popular SOVEREIGNTY) rejects governments that are unpopular or forced on people (such as absolute MONARCHY, COMMUNIST, and FASCIST). Democratic REPUBLICS claim to be established by consent both in their constitutional formation (or SOCIAL CONTRACT) and in periodic elections when the people choose their leaders by voting. Such political activities forming and maintaining the government are expressed consent, while living under the established state and elected rulers (and the laws they make) is tacit consent.

The idea of political consent emerges in the British LIBERAL thinkers of the 17th century, especially Thomas HOBBES and John LOCKE. They saw the creation of the state out of a STATE OF NATURE through a social contract involving common consent. Different thinkers view how this consent occurs, what is agreed to, and how much power the government receives by consent differently. For Hobbes's *Leviathan,* individuals surrender all their rights (to PROPERTY, expression, belief, commerce) to the STATE in exchange for social peace, and they consent to obey the ruler in all things. For Locke's *Second Treatise,* individuals consent to give up to the government only their executive social function (to punish criminals), but they retain their rights to life, LIBERTY, and property. The social contract in Locke's theory (and American government) is for the state to *protect* the NATURAL RIGHTS of the individual, and each person only consents to obey only that much governmental AUTHORITY. As social relations become more complex, the terms of consent—what individuals agree to obey—become more complicated. But once the system is established by consent, a person living in the society must accept the laws (tacit consent) or be punished for lawbreaking. If someone is totally unwilling to agree to the consensual social system, they reserve the right to migrate to another country, where they can accept the terms of law and government.

Further Readings
Pitkin, H. "Obligation and consent." In *Philosophy, Politics and Society,* 4th ser., P. Laslett, W. G. Runciman, and Q. Skinner, eds. New York: Barnes & Noble, 1972.
Plamenatz, J. *Consent, Freedom and Political Obligation*. London: Oxford University Press, 1968.

Simmons, A. J. *Tacit Consent and Political Obligations*. 1976.
Weale, A. "Consent," *Political Studies 26* (1978).

conservative

A political viewpoint that sees value in conserving past TRADITIONS, especially the timeless truths about human nature and society in the Judeo-CHRISTIAN religion. The leading modern conservative was Edmund BURKE, an English philosopher and statesman, who believed that the perennial truths of Western civilization (from ancient Greek and Roman philosophy and law, Western Christianity, CLASSICAL literature such as that of Shakespeare, high art, architecture, and music) reflect the best things in the world and must be taught to young people to produce civilized, decent, and moral human beings and a healthy, orderly society. Burke and other conservatives do not believe that humans are naturally good, noble, and perfectible, but rather, from a Judeo-Christian perspective, see people as fallen, sinful, selfish, and rebellious. So to become as good as possible, economically and morally, people must be shaped and disciplined by the best of the past (education, art, family, patriotism, LAW, religion, PROPERTY). This requires AUTHORITY in the family, the church, the school, and government. So, conservatives want to "conserve" those aspects of society and culture that civilize and improve human beings. Like ARISTOTLE and Christ, they assert that only through virtue can man be happy.

From this conservative attitude, Burke criticized LIBERAL and RADICAL social movements, beginning with the French Revolution of 1789. These "PROGRESSIVE" social movements are in error in two ways: (1) They assume that humans are good by nature and only made bad by their environment, so (2) the way to improve humanity is to change society radically, throwing out the past and creating an entirely new social order. For conservatives, this radical dream of creating a perfect society (through DEMOCRACY, EQUALITY, COMMUNISM, FEMINISM, etc.) will end in nightmare and disaster. The arrogance of any group or generation to think it knows more than the wisdom of the past ages will doom it to destruction and misery.

So, all utopian schemes or idealistic reforms, for conservatives, will lead to chaos and unhappiness. They are, therefore, to be resisted as a cruel and deceptive trick. Any reform group that promises to solve all human problems is suspect, for conservatives. It is much better to preserve the best of the past, to be patient with the world's wrongs, and to change or improve social conditions slowly. Stability, order, dignity, respect, authority, religion, property, classical education, traditional family, and patriotism are the conservative values.

This "organic" British conservatism sees the SOCIAL CONTRACT with the past and the future—revering the past traditions and caring for the future world that we leave our children. Burkean conservatives hate innovation, disrespect ,and change for the sake of change. They even identify a restless desire for radical change with mental illness. Most of all, they fear the seductive quality of radical reformers' promises of LIBERTY and prosperity for all because they deceive the ignorant and destroy the good. Twentieth-century revolutions (communism in Russia and China) show the disaster of such radical change; the new regimes are more oppressive than the ones they overthrow. The American Revolution of 1776 Burke saw as acceptable because it *preserved* traditional British values of mixed government, property rights, and law. Like the British Revolution of 1688, the U.S. CONSTITUTION preserved the past rather than discarding it. For conservatives, civilized society (art, industry, education, order, stable family, religious traditions) is a fragile structure that takes generations to build up but that is easily and quickly ruined by radical reform.

This backward-looking stance of conservatives gives them a reputation for being reactionary, dull, and against progress. Burke felt that given human limitations, progress and improvement can occur only very slowly and gradually; any sudden change for good is an illusion. So a conservative places importance on private life: family, church, neighborhood, friendship, work, where people have close relationships and can really make a difference in others' lives. Grand social movements, for conservatives, do not really touch people for good, which require personal contacts.

Contemporary expressions of conservative thought occur in the U.S. REPUBLICAN PARTY's probusiness stance (encouraging private property wealth), Christian conservative morality (upholding traditional religious values), and strong military policies (protecting national power and independence). Some conservatives split over Reagan's free-market economic policy, claiming that unregulated CAPITALISM is a radical force for change that upsets traditional standards.

In Western political thought, conservatism, or "RIGHT wing," politics take various forms. In France,

Joseph de Maistre advocated an ideal MEDIEVAL, French, CATHOLIC society. In Germany, a secular order unified by the nation characterized conservative thought (in its extreme form NAZISM). In Britain, Michael OAKESHOTT continued the Burkean conservative tradition. In the United States, William F. BUCKLEY, Daniel Bell, George F. WILL, and Irving Kristol expressed a traditional conservatism. Economists F. A. Hayek and Milton Friedman represent conservative fiscal outlooks, especially in their criticism of liberal economic policies.

Most modern societies have a balance between conservative and liberal attitudes, causing a moderate overall policy.

Further Reading
Hunter, James Davison. *Culture Wars.* New York: Basic Books, 1991.

Constantine (A.D. 274–337) *Roman Emperor and church/state leader*

Emperor Constantine consolidated authority over the Roman Empire by claiming absolute sovereignty over the Roman principate. After having a vision of the cross before an important military battle, Constantine adopted the letters symbolizing Christ on his standard and granted toleration to previously persecuted Christians. He soon showed imperial favor on the church, and Christianity became the official religion of the Roman Empire in A.D. 330. His linking of Christianity and government led to the emperor presiding over church councils (such as Nicaea in A.D. 315) and leading to the Eastern Orthodox idea that emperors (and czars) are supreme authorities over both CHURCH AND STATE. The unifying of secular and sacred power in the Orthodox churches contributed to their separation from the Western Catholic Church, which acknowledge separation of church and state.

Constantine built his imperial center in the Eastern city of Byzantium, subsequently called Constantinople (now Istanbul, Turkey). He reformed many laws along CHRISTIAN ethical lines, including humanizing criminal law, improving the conditions of slaves, establishing charitable institutions for poor children, and proclaiming the Lord's Day (Sunday) a holiday. His benefits to clergy and churches tied Christianity to the state, causing, for some, the worldliness and corruption of church leaders.

Further Reading
Jones, A. H. M. *Constantine and the Conversion of Europe.* London: English Universities Press, 1948.

constitution/constitutional

Usually, a written document that describes the structure of a government and the fundamental RIGHTS of citizens. For example, the U.S. Constitution describes the structure of the American federal government; it defines the functions and limits of each branch of state (executive, legislative, judicial) and the relation of the centralized national government with the decentralized state governments. It also contains a Bill of Rights in the first ten amendments (such as individual FREEDOM of speech, press, religion, and assembly). Most written constitutions also include a preamble, or statement of the purpose of government, and amendment procedures, or how the constitution can be legally changed.

Because the Constitution of a government establishes the institutions that make laws, it is considered prior to and the foundation of those laws, so if a legislature passes a law contrary to the Constitution (such as restricting freedom of speech or religion), that law is considered invalid or "unconstitutional." Usually a court (such as the U.S. Supreme Court) decides if a statute violates a constitutional provision. The historical body of these court decisions are called constitutional law, and, like the English common law, it relies on past cases or "precedent" in deciding new cases. This makes constitutional law, at least in theory, CONSERVATIVE and past bound, as Edmund BURKE would say. When the court relies on social, economic, or contemporary political movements rather than strictly past legal decisions, it is known as judicial activism. Constitutional law is an evolving doctrine, providing stable, gradual change.

Another less common definition of *constitution* is the way a government and society are constituted, or made up. The British constitution is of this kind; it is not a written document but a tradition of institutions and practices (such as the mixed government of monarchy, Lords, and Commons; the English common-law tradition; land tenure, etc.). This is a more cultural definition of CONSTITUTION. Most MODERN democratic republics have a written constitution, but not all countries are faithful to their nation's constitutional principles.

Further Reading
McIlwain, C. H. *Constitutionalism*. Cambridge, Eng.: Cambridge University Press, 1939.

corporatism

A social theory and practice, especially in FASCIST Italy in the 1930s, that divides society into corporations, or groups according to economic functions (such as unions, professional associations, business interests, etc.). The corporations regulate member activities and represent their interests to the state. The state coordinates the whole society through balancing of corporate needs and contributing to the entire nation. A modification of the MEDIEVAL CATHOLIC view of society with recognized corporations in CANON LAW (church orders, trade GUILDS, colleges, towns, etc.). Fascist Italy under Benito Mussolini tried to adapt this social system of the Middle Ages to modern CAPITALIST, industrial society. Fascist corporatism hoped to avoid both MARXIST COMMUNISM and capitalist LIBERAL DEMOCRACY through this "middle-way" system. HEGEL's political philosophy influenced corporatist fascism by viewing the state as reconciling groups in national unity. Within this system, corporations have an exclusive monopoly over a certain economic activity. So, unlike capitalist economics in which businesses compete, a corporatist economy composed of, say, several steel companies would have a single steel monopoly run by that steel manufacturing corporation under the general management of the state. Such corporatism seemed more orderly than competitive market capitalism and secured greater employment security for workers. The New Deal in the United States in the 1930s under President Franklin ROOSEVELT allowed some corporate monopolies in major industries and large labor unions (earning it the label *fascist* by some CONSERVATIVES), but the U.S. economy remained overall capitalist. The disadvantage of corporatism was its less innovative, less productive, and more inflexible qualities, compared with free-market capitalism.

In the political sphere, corporatism relied on greater management of the corporate monopolies by the central state. This is contrasted with the PLURALISM politics of liberal democracies in which many interest groups lobby the government and the state serves as a "referee" among competing interest groups. Again, the corporatist fascist state claimed to be more secure, orderly, and just (representing the interests of the *whole* society) than either liberal, capitalist democracies or class-based Marxist SOCIALIST or COMMUNIST societies. Liberal democracies (such as the United States and Britain) criticized fascist corporatism for being too AUTHORITARIAN and monopolistic; communists criticized it for subjecting labor unions to the state and preventing working class revolution.

Several contemporary nations retain elements of corporatism, usually through strong labor unions and business associations that negotiate with the government for legal and economic benefits. Sweden and Austria, as well as some Latin American nations, exhibit considerable social corporatism. The United States and Great Britain are the least corporatist countries on Earth; the INDIVIDUALISM and market-oriented economics of these countries make them less likely to be corporatist. The European community shows increasing signs of corporatist structures. Most modern corporatist systems rely on high levels of state taxation and extensive social welfare services.

Further Reading
Malloy, James M., ed. *Authoritarianism and Corporatism in Latin America*. Pittsburgh: University of Pittsburgh Press, 1977.

covenant

An agreement or compact or contract between at least two beings. In political thought, this comes primarily from the Bible view of the covenant between God and his people, or Israel. In several places in scripture, God declares, "I will be your God and you will be my People" (for example, Exodus 19:5: ". . . if ye will obey my voice . . . and keep my covenant, then ye shall be a peculiar treasure unto me above all people . . ."). This covenant involves God giving his people blessings, protection, prosperity, and love in return for them obeying his laws, commandments, and guidance. A divinely "covenanted people" are chosen by God, for special favor but also special obligations: to live moral, holy, reverent, godly lives, individually and socially. When the people with whom God has made a covenant and whom he has blessed disobey his laws, God brings curses and punishments upon them. The Jewish Bible, or Old Testament, is the story of God's chosen people, the Jews, alternately being faithful to their covenant with God (and prospering) and breaking their covenant with God (and suffering defeat and destruction). See Deuteronomy 28–30. This covenant view is taken up by several Protestant Christian churches, especially John CALVIN's, and later English and American PURITANS. Besides the Old Testament covenant, they added the covenant of grace (or forgiveness through Jesus Christ), church covenants, and governmental covenants. The covenant between God and his people was to be enlivened and represented in the church among Christian believers (who pledged to help each other live a godly life) and the Christian commonwealth (who pledged to serve God, obey his laws, and spread his gospel).

When the English Puritans arrived in America, they wrote and signed the MAYFLOWER COMPACT, a covenant among themselves, God, the church, and their government. America saw itself as a New Israel, God's people under special divine blessing and protection as long as they followed God's laws, but who were able to lose God's provision if they sinned. Early Massachusetts governor John WINTHROP said, "Thus stands the cause between God and us; we are entered into Covenant with him for this work. . . . We shall be as a City on a Hill." Such a view of Christian America's unique calling and responsibility to build a godly society continues in U.S. culture down to Ronald REAGAN's presidency. The fear of U.S. CONSERVATIVE Christians that their country has broken its covenant with God through immorality, greed, and secularism fuels the political movement of the Religious RIGHT.

Covenant theology also known as "federal" theology influences modern political theories of social compact, SOCIAL CONTRACT, and FEDERALISM, as well as a providential view of U.S. history.

Further Reading
Stoever, William K. B. *A Faire and Easie Way to Heaven: Covenant Theology and Antinomianism in Early Massachusetts.* Middletown, Conn.: Wesleyan University Press, 1978.

creationism

A theory of the creation of the world that follows literally the biblical account (Genesis 1–2) that God created the earth and all living things in seven (24-hour) days. This is a direct religious response to Charles Darwin's scientific evolution theory that asserts that humans were formed over millions of years and that they evolved from lower species rather than being made by God. The creationist CHRISTIAN view is associated in America with the CONSERVATIVE, FUNDAMENTALIST PROTESTANT churches (see CHRISTIAN RIGHT). Creationism, then is one part of the Religious Right political movement, which regards the atheism of Darwinian evolution as

degrading humanity to the level of beasts and contribution to the breakdown of American Christian civilization. Social problems such as depreciation of human life (through ABORTION and EUTHANASIA), secular INDIVIDUALISM (breakdown of family and church), and ethical relativism (loss of Judeo-Christian standards in society) are all linked to the scientific view of human's creation. If humans were not created by God with specific divine purposes and responsibilities, Creationists assert, the social order would be meaningless, and the social and moral fabric will become torn.

Creationism (or creation science) became prominent in the United States in the 1920s with George Price's book *The New Geology* which challenged the scientific explanation of the origins of the world and humanity and termed Darwin's theory of evolution "a gigantic hoax." U.S. Democrat William Jennings Bryan led a campaign against the teaching of biological evolution in the schools, culminating in the famous Scopes Trial or the "Monkey Trial" that upheld state laws prohibiting the teaching of Darwinism.

Biological evolution continues to be taught in U.S. schools and universities, however, and has become a kind of orthodoxy in the mainline scientific community. In 1981, Arkansas passed a law requiring the instruction of "Creation Science" alongside the teaching of scientific evolution in the public schools. The U.S. Supreme Court declared the law unconstitutional as imposing religion on the scientific curriculum, but controversy continues between this biblical religious view of creation and the secular scientific theory, which represents a larger split in political and social thought in the modern United States. (See CULTURE WARS.)

Further Reading
Ashton, John. *In Six Days.* El Cajon, Calif.: Master Books, 2000.

critical theory

A school of thought associated with 20th-century MARXISM leading to the "New LEFT" political movement that applied COMMUNIST theory to culture, psychology, and society, as well as to economics. Developed in the "Frankfurt School" in Germany in the 1920s, it claimed to be an interdisciplinary application of Karl MARX's DIALECTIC to all aspects of modern life. It was inherently atheistic and radical, hence its own self-identification as "critical" of everything in existing society. Its attack on all structures of order and authority (in the traditional family, community, church, government, and business) led to the radical FEMINIST, student, workers, gay/lesbian/transsexual, and modern art and theater movements of the 20th century. Sometimes call Humanist Marxism, it was equally critical of Soviet or "orthodox" communism for its overemphasis on economics and its AUTHORITARIAN politics. Critical theory appealed to intellectuals rather than proletarian workers and influenced many Western academics, giving the European and American university its radical character after World War II.

Associated with the philosophers Max Horkheimer, Theodor Adorno, Herbert MARCUSE, and Walter Benjamin, the critical theory school came to the United States in the 1930s when the Frankfurt Institute for Social Research was closed in 1935.

Critical theory focused on the "domination" of all societies (LIBERAL CAPITALIST, communist, and FASCIST) and claimed to have a program of "liberation" through dialectical reason, sexual experimentation, and alternative economics. The "new morality" of sexual liberation, challenging traditional gender roles and the CHRISTIAN family, led relatively quickly into ABORTION on demand and gay/ lesbian/transsexual movements. The rejection of historical Western religions led to such alternative spiritual movements as New Age, occult, and Zen Buddhism in Europe and America.

Although critical theory was not a large-scale political movement (except possibly for the radical counterculture student movements in France and America in the 1960s), it influenced various Leftist and liberal wings of major political parties (such as the Labour Party in Britain, the Green Party in Germany, and the DEMOCRATIC PARTY in the United States).

Further Readings
Bottomore, T. B. *The Frankfurt School.* London: Tavistock, 1984.
Held, D. *Introduction to Critical Theory.* Berkeley: University of California Press, 1980.
Horkheimer, M., "Traditional and critical theory" (1927). In *Critical Theory.* 1972.
———and Adorno, T. *Dialectic of Enlightenment.* New York: Herder & Herder, 1972.

Croce, Benedetto (1866–1952)   *Italian philosopher*

Croce was a Hegelian idealist who applied this view to aesthetics, history, politics, and ETHICS. His philosophy of art has had the most influence outside his native Italy, although he makes important contributions to both historical understanding and the political and ethical. Croce distinguishes four aspects, or distinct moments, of human understanding: the True, the Beautiful, the Useful, and the Good. These moments are analogous to the Hegelian idea of Spirit and like HEGEL's Spirit, they are manifest in history. They are also pure concepts in that they have no content independently of human history, thought, and actions. We read their content and arrive at understanding by attending to our present and past circumstances.

Croce's aesthetics begins with the idea that the aesthetic experience is cognitive. Its form of cognition is intuition, which Croce understands in the KANTian sense of preconceptual perception. Art, particularly poetry, aims at eliciting emotion, and our appreciation of art consists in our intuitive understanding and comprehension of these emotions. What is important for Croce is not to intellectualize the aesthetic experience and not to reduce it to mere sensations. "Cosmic intuitions" are the awareness of the universal character of art (the Beautiful), provoked by a particular manifestation of it. Finally, for Croce, art aims only at the Beautiful, and so art properly understood is never concerned with the True, the Useful, or the Good. Work that aims to be instructive, pleasurable, or moralistic is not art.

Croce's work on history, politics and ethics is contained in a number of works beginning early in his career with work on MARX (*Historical Materialism and the Economics of Karl Marx*) and Hegel (*What is Living and What is Dead in the Philosophy of Hegel*) and moving through publications on history (*Theory and History of Historiography*) and VICO (*The Philosophy of Giambattista Vico*) and the ethicopolitical text, *History as the Story of Liberty,* which was published toward the end of his life. Croce's political philosophy was heavily influenced early in his career by his friend and collaborator Giovanni GENTILE and later by the advent of fascism in Italy. Following his Hegelian inclinations, Croce makes no distinction between philosophy and history and between theory and practice, arguing that the philosophical comes to us through our encounters with the historical. This identification of the normative with the actual allowed Croce's views to oscillate between a form of historical inevitability and, later, during and after FASCISM, an account allowing for LIBERAL forms of political agency. This tension in Croce's work is also apparent in his discussions of the relations between the political and the ethical. Here, Croce wants to keep distinct the pure concepts of the Useful and the Good, assigning the political to the former and the ethical to the later. It is on this basis that he criticizes utilitarianism for confusing and mixing these concepts. However, if politics is merely the art of the Useful, then the political and its institutions are beyond the call of the ethical. The rise of fascism encouraged Croce to make clear the need for an ethical dimension within the political. Whether this is, in the end, compatible with the starting point of his project is the subject of debate.

Croce was born in Pescasseroli in southern Italy to a wealthy family. Orphaned as a child, he spent much of his life in the Italian city of Naples. He became a life member of the Italian senate in 1910 and was deeply involved in liberal politics following the defeat of fascism in World War II. He died at the age of 86.

Further Reading
Bellamy, R. P. "Liberalism and historicism: Benedetto Croce and the political role of idealism in modern Italy 1890–1952." In Moulakis, A., *The Promise of History: Essays in Political Philosophy*. Berlin: De Gruyter, 1986.

Cromwell, Oliver (1599–1658)   *English soldier, statesman, and Puritan religious leader*

Most remembered as lord protector of the English commonwealth period (1653–58) Cromwell espoused democratic parliamentary ideals but ruled as a virtual dictator. Living during the English civil wars (1640–60) between CATHOLIC royalty and Protestant Parliament, Cromwell was a military leader of the PURITAN army that defeated King Charles I. He led the movement to declare the monarch a traitor and signed the warrant leading to the execution of Charles I. Parliament named Cromwell lord protector. He ruled England through a series of constitutional experiments reflecting his Puritan theology and REPUBLICAN ideology. The "barebones" Parliament was an example of this; it consisted of 140 "saints" nominated by the church congregations and appointed by the lord protector. At other times he ruled through the major generals of the new model army, but most of Cromwell's government was via his powerful personal and spiritual magnetism. He refused to be crowned king. He saw English history at a perilous point between the true church and the forces of the anti-Christ. His government reformed church-governing structures as well as the country's morals and customs, along Puritan CHRISTIAN lines. Education and laws were modeled upon the Christian Bible, and many decadent social amusements (e.g., theater) and witchcraft were prosecuted.

Cromwell's experiment in a Christian commonwealth was not entirely successful, but it influenced the later parliamentary "glorious revolution" of 1688, which did establish parliamentary supremacy and Protestant Christianity in Britain. He said of his political career "I have not sought these things; truly I have been called unto them by the Lord."

Educated at Cambridge University, Cromwell served in Parliament and represented the independent (Congregational) church interests before commencing his famous military and political service. Known to combine great humility (describing himself as "a worm") with great fierceness (as in the invasion of Ireland), Cromwell's character was complex and mysterious.

Further Reading
Ashley, Maurice. *Oliver Cromwell*. London: John Cape, 1937.

cultism

A cult is a social group that is usually associated with a dominant, forceful leader. Cults often have religious and political overtones. For example, in the United States, several religious cults have formed around charismatic leaders who claimed to be the Christ or God. The cult leader usually demands total submission to himself or herself, claiming absolute authority over the members of the cult. Often, religious cults will revolve around a belief in the imminent end of the world and preparation for the destruction of Earth. Frequently, cults separate themselves from the larger society and prepare for the end by stockpiling food, weapons, and computers. The cult leader often claims to be in direct communication with God and directs the cult accordingly. Often fearful of outside interference, cults in recent times commit mass suicide (for example the Jim Jones cult, the Hale-Bopp Comet cult, and the Branch Davidian cult). Their stockpiling of weapons often brings a cult under investigation by the government.

Politically, some regimes have been accused of cult leader worship (as the SOVIET UNION's leaders after Joseph STALIN's death complained of his "cult of personality") when a dictator assumes godlike status.

The sociological definition of a religious cult is a group whose beliefs or practices lie way outside the established religious institutions. So, often, state churches accuse (and outlaw) minority churches of being cults, when in fact they are only different sects, or denominations, of the same religion. In American Christianity, the churches that derive from the predominant beliefs of the Bible (such as Mormons, Scientology, the Unification Church, and Hare Krishnas) are regarded as cults (especially if they revere a human "founder" above Christ).

The political concern with cults surrounds their exclusive and often destructive social behavior. Random acts of violence or terrorism, "mind control" over members, and immoral practices by leaders draw social criticism of cults. This causes some dominant religious and political groups to use the term *cult* to criticize and harass their enemies. So, for example, the Russian Orthodox Church led the Russian parliament to pass a law persecuting cults that included many western CHRISTIAN churches and missionaries. The Muslim (ISLAMIC) world sometimes accuses Christianity of being a cult for worshiping Jesus as the Son of God.

Western freedom of religion allows the existence of cults as long as they do not commit illegal acts and do not violate the NATURAL RIGHTS of their members (especially the right to leave the cult when the individual chooses). Religious LIBERTY allows voluntary membership in cults that are not engaged in illegal activities or enslavement of members.

Further Reading
Enroth, R. *A Guide to Cults*. Downers Grove, Ill.: Intervarsity Press, 1983.

culture wars

A way of viewing social conflict, especially in the United States, which does not rest on class, race, gender, or political party identification. The term became popular after the publication of James Davison HUNTER's book *Culture Wars* in which Hunter, a sociologist at the University of Virginia, studied the social conflicts in the United States (over the media, welfare, ABORTION, HOMOSEXUALITY, education policy, the family,

etc.) and found that groups on different sides of the issues were formed by moral attitudes rather than by economic class, race, gender, or political-party membership. Hunter divides cultural attitudes into orthodox and progressive groups: The orthodox people adhere to some transcendent standard of moral authority (the church, the Bible, the Torah or Koran, the classics, the pope, etc.) to which they subordinate their own preferences in moral and political judgment; the progressive viewpoint regards morals as relative to historical change and individual preference. So, for example, orthodox culture regards homosexuality as wrong because they obey a higher law. The progressive culture regards homosexuality as acceptable because some people want to engage in it and because they place human preferences above any religious teaching.

Hunter applies this "culture-wars" division in society to many political issues, including battles over the media, the military, arts, education, and religion. He finds that Roman CATHOLICS, EVANGELICAL CHRISTIANS, CONSERVATIVE humanists, Jews, and Muslims (ISLAMIC) tend to be orthodox in their moral perspectives; secularists, Liberal mainline Christians (Episcopal, Presbyterian, U.C.C., Unitarian-Universalists), and atheists, however, tend to be of the progressive mindset. In general conservatives and REPUBLICANS are orthodox, and liberals and DEMOCRATS are progressive, but each group tends to be mixed.

The main contribution of Hunter's thesis was the transcending of the simplistic MARXIST sociological view of social divisions by class, race, and gender. Hunter's research showed that the conservative orthodox includes the poor, workers, blacks, women, and other minorities. The liberal progressives include middle-class whites, men, and many well-educated people. This offers a more complex, sophisticated way of looking at social issues based on beliefs rather than on social condition. It has caused both political parties in the United States to view social policy in moral and ethical terms, rather than purely economic terms.

Further Reading
Hunter, James Davison. *Culture Wars*. New York: Basic Books, 1991.

D

Dante Alighieri (1265–1321) *Italian poet, theologian, and political philosopher*

Best known for his epic CHRISTIAN poem *The Divine Comedy,* Dante expresses a profound understanding of the political and religious problems of MEDIEVAL Europe. Active in the government of Florence, Italy, Dante saw both the political and ecclesiastical corruption of the Middle Ages. His literary depictions of Hell (*Inferno*) and Purgatory (*Purgatorio*) represent the social and church evils of his day. Specifically, Florence, the wealthiest and most cultured of the Italian cities, is shown as corrupted by greed, materialism, vanity, and jealousy among leading families. The church of Rome is suffering from excessive worldly power and prestige, which weakens and discredits its spiritual leadership. The rise of political prominence of the papacy is presented as the decline of the CATHOLIC Church from its primary role to reflect the humility and love of God through Christ. This leads Dante to reassert the Augustinian insistence on the separation of CHURCH AND STATE, each serving a distinct function under divine providence. Dante advocates "two suns" to lighten the human path—the religious and the political realms serving distinct purposes but cooperating in a common love of God and humanity.

In his book *On Monarchy* (*De Monarchia*), Dante argues for the solution to the world's problems in a "one world government," or universal MONARCHY, that could overcome the struggles among competing states. He also sees the HOLY ROMAN EMPIRE as the center of the world empire. The secular emperor was to have direct commission from God to rule, not mediated through the Catholic Church or the pope. In this way, Dante foreshadows the REFORMATION ideas of Martin LUTHER and John CALVIN, seeing government officials as directly responsible to God and not under the total jurisdiction of the church. Still, Dante respects the Catholic Church leadership and insists that it continue to exercise an informal, advisory role vis-à-vis the state; he says that the king should show the reverence of an "eldest son to his father" to the bishop of Rome.

Dante fell out of favor with Pope Boniface VIII and the new rulers of Florence, forcing him to leave his home city and wander from town to town in Italy. He was accused of corruption and had his PROPERTY confiscated.

Further Readings

D'Entrèves, A. P. *Dante as a Political Thinker.* Oxford, Eng.: Clarendon Press, 1952.
Holmes, G. *Dante.* New York: Hill & Wang, 1980.

Declaration of Independence (1776)

A document written by Thomas JEFFERSON declaring the North American colonies (now the United States of America) politically independent from the British Empire (Crown and Parliament). It is considered a "founding" document of American government (along with the later CONSTITUTION of 1789) because it presents the dominant political theory of the United States.

The philosophy of the Declaration of Independence is the NATURAL RIGHT, SOCIAL CONTRACT view of John LOCKE. It presents a British LIBERAL view of HUMAN NATURE, society, and government. Individuals are seen as "free, equal and independent," possessed of reason and the natural rights of "life, LIBERTY and the pursuit of happiness," which form a government to protect those rights. When a STATE violates those natural human rights (to own private PROPERTY and to enjoy liberty of movement, thought, and religion) the people can replace the rulers with a government that properly secures those HUMAN RIGHTS. The American Revolution (1776–83) was justified on these ideas originating in John Locke's *Second Treatise of Government*. The Declaration of Independence listed numerous violations of the American colonists' rights, including unfair taxes ("taxation without representation" in Parliament), military rule over civilian government, restriction on free trade, interference with religious liberty, and suspension of trial by jury. All led to oppression and TYRANNY.

Great Britain regarded American independence as treasonous and sent the British army and navy to force the colonies to remain loyal to king and Parliament. The American Revolution concluded with the colonies winning their political independence and nationhood. Consequently, the principles of national independence in this declaration have been adopted by many colonies and oppressed peoples (such as Mexico, African countries, Vietnam, and the democratic Chinese students' movement). The ideals of consentual, representative government in the Declaration of Independence continued in the foundation document of the American republic: the U.S. Constitution.

Jefferson's statement in the declaration that "all men are created equal" was employed by President Abraham LINCOLN in arguments for the emancipation of slaves in the United States and the Confederacy during the Civil War.

Further Reading

Boyd, Julian P. *The Declaration of Independence; the evolution of the text as shown in facsimiles of various drafts by its author. Issued in conjunction with an exhibit of these drafts at the Library of Congress on the 200th anniversary of the birth of Thomas Jefferson. 1945.

democracy/democratic

A society or government ruled by the people or by popular SOVEREIGNTY. The idea of popular government originated in the ancient Greek political thought of Athens. The word *democracy* derives from the Greek words *demos* ("people" or "many") and *cracy* ("ruled by" or "regime of"). Democratic government is the favored type of government in the MODERN period, and other forms of rule (such as MONARCHY—rule of one—or ARISTOCRACY—rule of a few) are considered illegitimate or inherently unjust. Almost all states in the 20th-century world (even COMMUNIST and FASCIST) claimed to be democratic or a "REPUBLIC." All nondemocratic states are considered dictatorial in this modern view.

Historically, however, Western political thought has not favored democratic styles of government. PLATO and ARISTOTLE often associated the rule of the many with the ignorant, impoverished masses, producing unjust, foolish government. For CLASSICAL political theory, virtuous governing required qualified citizens, and most people would not be intellectually, morally, economically, and culturally prepared to rule wisely. So, a more elitist governing group was preferred (usually adult, male, wealthy, educated, experienced persons) by the ancient Greek and Roman philosophers. During the Middle Ages in Europe, St. Thomas AQUINAS adopted this classical view that just government ruled for the "common good" but did not have to be democratic to do so.

The modern preference for democratic, REPUBLICAN government came from the British LIBERALISM, which conceived of just government from the "CONSENT of the governed." Any human possessed of reason and having an interest in social law should be allowed to participate in governing. John Locke's SOCIAL CONTRACT view of the state is automatically democratic because every member of society has equal natural rights requiring state protection, is taxed to support that STATE, and therefore has a right to have a say in the laws governing him or her. From this modern liberal logic, the franchise, or right, to participate in governing through voting is properly extended to more and more individuals. The experience in the West has been to gradually expand the SUFFRAGE (voting) right to more citizens (women, the poor, minorities, the young, etc.).

Questions arise then over "who" is "the people" and "how" do they rule in a democracy. In the United States of America, a typical modern republic, citizenship has few requirements (basically being born or naturalized in the country, being at least 18 years old, and not being mentally ill or in prison). The purpose or mode of governing in a democracy includes: (1) to prevent dictatorship or TYRANNY; (2) to promote social and moral well-being; (3) to advance economic wealth and military power. All of these rationales for democracy have been used to support it.

The Protestant CHRISTIAN political thinkers (Martin LUTHER, John CALVIN) based their arguments for democracy (in CHURCH AND STATE) on the universal sinfulness of humans, recommending limited political power in any single ruler or group. James MADISON, the leading founder of the U.S. CONSTITUTION, adhered to this Christian view that democratic PLURALISM was necessary to prevent sinful people from allowing political power to lead to social oppression. The system of CHECKS AND BALANCES in the U.S. government was designed to pit "ambition against ambition" and prevent tyranny. Democracy is seen as a necessary evil for imperfect humans.

Early in the MODERN period, arguments occurred over how representative a democracy could become. MONTESQUIEU held that a true democracy required a small country like the Greek polis, where every citizen knew everyone else. Given the larger, more complex nations in modern times such classical or "direct" democracy was impractical and representative "republics" were formed, in which not everyone would govern but could *choose* those who did govern, through voting in elections. Thomas JEFFERSON tried to combine the classical, participatory democracy with the large U.S. republic through a system of local, state, and national republics, or FEDERALISM. The fear among classical or COMMUNITARIAN democratic thinkers (such as Benjamin BARBER) is that the larger a representative democracy (or REPUBLIC) becomes and the more distant the central government from most citizens, the greater danger there is for an unresponsive, corrupt, dictatorial state. Alexis de TOCQUEVILLE argued that the less personal contact each citizen had with the government, the more likely a "tyranny of the majority" led by a demagogue could occur in large democracies. This is why he saw the U.S. jury system as preserving democratic culture—it involves small groups of citizens engaging in serious political discourse and public decision making. Where modern society makes government more complex and distant from average citizens, concerns for election reform, voter participation, political parties, and media portrayal of politics become topics for study in political science.

With the rise of COMMUNIST and SOCIALIST ideology in the 19th century (see Karl MARX), democracy took on economic dimensions. The view that public ownership of property and a state-planned economy (socialism) was "economic democracy" led to many "social democratic" movements and political parties. This Leftist argument that political equality and democracy could not be realized where great inequalities of wealth existed challenged Western or CAPITALIST democracies. Because state operation of economics (as in the SOVIET UNION) usually required centralization of political power, this "peoples" or "socialist democracy" usually resulted in less democratic governments, but the concern with matching economic and social equality with political equality contributed to the mixed or WELFARE-STATE democracies of the West.

Most study of democracy now has to do with how "truly democratic" modern republics are or to what extent formal democratic systems mask the true power of ELITES in business, professions, unions, or other interest groups. As democratic theorist Benjamin Barber summarizes it: "The democratic ideal remains one of the most cherished and at the same moment most contested of political ideals." He sees current threats to democracy more from mass society (consumerism, privatism, commercialism, and the trivialization of popular culture) than from power-hungry rulers.

Further Readings

Arrow, K. *Social Choice and Individual Values.* New Haven, Conn.: Yale University Press, 1951.
Bachrach, P. *The Theory of Democratic Elitism.* Boston: Little, Brown, 1967.
Barber, B. *Strong Democracy.* Berkeley: University of California Press, 1984.
Dahl, R. *Preface to Democratic Theory.* Chicago: University of Chicago Press, 1956.

Democratic Party

Unlike that of other countries, the U.S. CONSTITUTION does not mention political parties. Nevertheless, despite opposition by prominent leaders such as George Washington, the American political system developed around a two-party system. The modern-day Democratic Party, founded by Thomas JEFFERSON as the Democratic– Republicans, is the oldest party still in existence in the United States. Originally, the party was created to oppose Alexander HAMILTON's Federalist Party. The Democrats emphasized personal LIBERTY, the limitation of federal government, and STATES RIGHTS.

By 1828 the party's name was shortened to the Democratic Party. It enjoyed diverse support ranging from a coalition of southern farmers to northern city dwellers. The Democrats demonstrated success early on as well. From Thomas Jefferson, who was elected president in 1800, until 1825, the Democrats retained the presidency.

A RADICAL group of Democrats led by Andrew Jackson won the elections of 1828 and 1832, but arguments over SLAVERY created or deepened splits within the party, and the Civil War nearly destroyed it. The party revived after the disputed election of 1876, and the end of Reconstruction brought the Solid South into the Democratic fold. During this period emerged the term *yellow dog Democrat*, which referred to southern voter's preference for a yellow dog over a Republican.

In 1913, the Democrats again regained the presidency under Woodrow WILSON. Again during the Depression they took office with Franklin D. ROOSEVELT, who initiated the NEW DEAL programs. Roosevelt's liberal New Deal programs, which ranged from the Civilian Conservation Corp to the Works Progress Administration, changed the relationship between the federal government and the citizen. Previously, citizen interaction with government took place primarily at the local level. In some cases, the regional or state government would provide services. The federal government was, historically, the remedy of last resort because it had neither the institutions nor capital to field large-scale social service programs. The New Deal program changed the nature of the Democratic Party and, subsequently, the federal government, emphasizing a greater role for Washington in the social and economic lives of the citizenry. In the ensuing years, the modern Democratic Party had by then become an uneasy alliance of labor, minorities, middle-class reformers, and southern Democrats. The latter group became disaffected by the growing civil-rights movements and reforms ushered in by Democratic administrations such as John KENNEDY's and Lyndon Johnson's. Southern defection materialized in the failed campaigns of Hubert H. Humphrey and George McGovern in 1968 and 1972 respectively.

This alliance reflected the progressive values of a party working for change and reform. The REPUBLICAN PARTY, on the other hand, was known for its aversion to change and its traditional roots. In many ways, this philosophical division explains the defection of southern Democrats. Known for their conservative views on civil rights, the role of government, and labor, they found themselves often at odds with the national platform of the Democratic Party, which was considerably more liberal.

Following the Watergate affair, the Democrats nominated and elected in 1976 a relatively unknown governor from Georgia, Jimmy CARTER, to the presidency. Carter's inability to cope with economic problems and to free U.S. hostages in Iran led to his defeat in 1980 by Republican Ronald REAGAN. Reagan's election was particularly troubling for the Democrats because many of his supporters came from traditional Democratic strongholds. Middle-class voters, women, and southerners defected from their long held positions in the Democratic Party to elect Reagan.

Although the party did not win the presidency again until the 1992 election of Bill Clinton, it remained a POWER in CONGRESS and at the STATE level throughout the 1980s. In 1994, however, the Democrats lost their majorities in both houses of Congress.

Throughout its history, the Democratic Party has called itself "the party of the people," a title that was justified by its traditional support, which tended to be less prosperous, less skilled occupationally, and less educated than Republicans. Nevertheless, the party learned in 1980 that it could no longer take for granted the votes of groups that had been traditionally ranked among the Democrats. Disaffection with Carter's economic policies sent many union members, AFRICAN AMERICANS, and other minority groups over to the Republican side, and the once solidly Democratic South now became increasingly Republican.

Although the Democrats reclaimed some of the so-called Reagan Democrats for their presidential candidate in 1992, by 1994 the party, according to polls, had fewer loyalists than the Republicans. The ebb and flow of Bill Clinton's popularity as president may in large part be attributed to his particularly liberal initiatives once taking office. Indeed, when the Clinton administration established a national health-care plan as one of its top priorities, voters expressed their concern at the ballot box. After a considerable national debate carried out largely by special interest groups and members of the administration, voters dealt Clinton a significant blow in the 1994 election, returning control of the House of Representatives to the opposition Republican Party for the first time in 44 years.

Further Reading
Fish, Bruce, and Fish, Becky Durost. *The History of the Democratic Party.* New York: Chelsea House, 2000.

despot/despotic/despotism

A government or ruler that has absolute authority, leaving others as totally subservient slaves. Often related to DICTATORSHIPS, TYRANNY, or TOTALITARIAN regimes, despotism has a long history in Western political thought. Throughout, it is contrasted with DEMOCRACY, REPUBLICAN government, the RULE OF LAW, and EQUALITY.

ARISTOTLE described despotic governments in contrast to civilized Greek republics. The Asian and Middle Eastern "barbarians" lived under absolute despots whose personal tyrannical rule turned everyone else into a virtual slave. Absolute submission to the authority of the despotic ruler characterized non-Greek societies in Aristotle's view. By contrast, the Greek POLIS encouraged shared governance, widespread citizen participation, and free individuals. From Aristotle's Hellenistic view of "civilized," democratic societies and "barbaric," despotic societies, he concluded that some peoples were "natural slaves." This also justified taking such peoples as slaves once they were conquered in war. Similarly, although Aristotle's polis is the shared rule of free people, he allows "despotic" rule in the Greek household (husband over wife, parent over child, master over slave), but in the public realm, free citizens engage in collective deliberation and governance.

The MIDDLE AGES used despotism to describe a tyrannical monarch in Europe. MODERN international theory in GROTIUS and PUFENDORF permitted European domination of colonial peoples on the ground that they were slaves by nature who were used to despotic rule and were incapable of self-governance. Thomas HOBBES saw the right of despotic enslavement from CONSENT following conquest.

In the 16th and 17th centuries, REFORMATION Christians often referred to the pope's absolute power over the church as despotic, the faithful being reduced to unthinking slavery. Frenchman MONTESQUIEU argued that European monarchies that adopted oriental codes of absolute power became despots (such as Louis XIV). The Turkish, ISLAMIC Ottoman Empire served as an example of despotic ABSOLUTIST power (under the sultan) to 18th-century Westerners. The Chinese emperor was often regarded as an archetypical despot, and Oriental subservience as reflecting natural slavish nature. The Russian czar appeared to be oriental in this sense, with ignorant oppressed Russian serfs only capable of following a strong absolutist dictator. ROUSSEAU charged that Czar Peter the Great tried to liberalize Russian society too quickly, as those centuries of despotic government made the Russian people incapable of self-government. Thomas JEFFERSON hesitated to extend full democratic rights to the people in the newly acquired Louisiana Territory on the grounds that, being used to the despotism of French monarchy, feudalism, and Catholicism, they were incapable of self-rule.

Karl MARX saw Asiatic societies (e.g., India) as despotic and economically stagnant, brought into modern world economics by British colonialism and capitalism. Contemporary military dictatorships in Africa and Latin America are sometimes described as despotic. Totalitarian communist regimes such as Cuba and North Korea are often characterized as despotic.

Further Reading
Anderson, P. *Lineages of the Absolute State.* London: N.L.B., 1974.

Dewey, John (1859–1952)   *U.S. philosopher and educator*

Dewey was one of the most influential U.S. philosophers of the 20th century. Born in Burlington, Vermont, Dewey received his bachelor's degree from the University of Vermont in 1879. After teaching high school for two years following graduation, Dewey began graduate studies in philosophy at Johns Hopkins University. He received his doctorate in 1884 and then taught for 10 years at the University of Michigan. In 1894, Dewey left for the University of Chicago where he became head of the department of philosophy, psychology, and pedagogy. While at Chicago, Dewey founded and directed the famous laboratory school, or "Dewey School," which allowed him to develop and test his pedagogical theories on the need to design education that was sensitive to the active and creative dimensions of learning. Dewey's books *School and Society* (1900) and *The Child and the Cur-*

riculum (1902) were important works from this period.

Dewey next joined the department of philosophy at Columbia University in 1904, where he taught until his retirement in 1930. During his tenure at Columbia, Dewey became deeply involved in social issues and political affairs. He traveled and lectured extensively and published widely in both popular and academic journals. Dewey's basic philosophical enterprise became associated with the American school of PRAGMATISM. Dewey was critical of metaphysical idealism, stressing instead a naturalistic analysis of experience. According to Dewey, there is no such thing as a fixed human essence that is somehow independent of larger natural processes. Rather, human beings are fully immersed in diverse natural and cultural environments, and human life consists of a plurality of interrelated experiences and situations that possess unique, qualitative characteristics. Experience as a whole is defined by the "transactions" that occur in nature between organism and environment.

Dewey also developed comprehensive theories of ETHICS and DEMOCRACY. In his ethical theory, Dewey adopted an experimental approach that he viewed as being similar to the methodology of the natural sciences. Rejecting traditional metaphysical accounts of divine or cosmic sources of absolute values, Dewey insisted on the plurality of moral criteria that can be generated as functional principles of social action. According to Dewey's theory of "instrumentalism," concepts are formed and used as tools for testing hypotheses and solving problems. In a similar fashion, values are created in response to the obtaining of satisfactory results in our choices of actions and objects. In other words, the activity of valuation refers to value judgments about actions and objects that yield satisfaction and therefore are considered desirable in terms of how we think we should live. Considerations of moral action can then be addressed by positing experimental hypotheses about the consequences of prescribed behavior under certain conditions. Those plans of action that lead to the preferred situation can be used to modify and resolve problematic circumstances. Dewey was clear, however, that the search for solutions to moral dilemmas must be carried out through a social process, a public exchange of concerns, alternatives, and analyses. Moral deliberation necessarily involves social communication if consensus is to be reached. In this way, Dewey appealed to what he called "democracy as a way of life."

For Dewey's social and political philosophy, it was vitally important to take seriously the role of the community in the lives of individuals. If individual and group conflict is to be resolved, communication and consensus must replace dogmatism and ABSOLUTISM. For this reason, Dewey emphasized the role of education in DEMOCRACY. As mentioned above, Dewey considered democracy to be much more than the presence of certain political procedures and institutions; it is a way of life. In *The Public and its Problems* (1927) and in other works, Dewey noted that a successfully functioning democracy requires that its citizens develop habits that enable them to communicate, to learn, to compromise, to respect others, and to tolerate the variety of norms and interests that exist in a shared social life. Social cooperation rather than extreme individualism is a fundamental component of a democracy that is able to liberate the capacities of each person. Against the SOCIAL-CONTRACT tradition of HOBBES and LOCKE, Dewey argued that the human individual is a social being from the start and that individual achievement can only be realized through the collective means of social institutions and practices.

Further Reading
Westbrook, R. B. *John Dewey and American Democracy.* Ithaca, N.Y.: Cornell University Press, 1991.

dialectic/dialectical

A philosophical view that knowledge derives from knowing reality as a whole that encompasses opposites or contradictions. Originally developed in Eastern mystical religion and philosophy as the "yin/yang" perspective, this dialectical approach most affected Western political thought in HEGEL, MARXISM, COMMUNISM, and FASCISM.

The dialectical view or logic claims that reality or things include opposites. A single day, for example, includes daytime and nighttime, light and dark. So the whole consists of two different elements, which give definition to each other—man/woman; husband/wife; child/parent; student/teacher; and so on. No single thing can be completely known except by reference to its "other," or opposite. It is simply understanding the way things relate to other things within a comprehensive universe.

The German philosopher Hegel applied this Eastern religion to history, claiming that the clashing of opposites propelled civilization forward and that by understanding current "contradictions," we could see what was "becoming." This then becomes a kind of philosophical fortune telling or prophesy.

Karl MARX adapted this Hegelian dialectic to economic classes (master/slave; landlord/peasant; capitalist/worker) and claimed that social and political history is propelled by this conflict of economic classes that represent forces and relations of production. For Marxism, this "dialectical materialism" led history through various stages from FEUDALISM to CAPITALISM to SOCIALISM to communism. The process was an inevitable evolution, so the idea was to attach oneself to the "progressive" social class (in capitalism the proletariat or industrial workers). Finally, history would end in communism, a classless society of economic abundance and political liberation.

Fascist political theory (as in Benito Mussolini in Italy and Adolf HITLER in Germany in the 1930s) adopted the Hegelian dialectic in a different way. For fascist philosopher Giovanni GENTILE, each individual has the opposites of a "particular will" and a "universal will" within them. The particular will is one's personal interests, desires, and talents; the universal will is one's culture, race, nationality, heritage, and language within one. Growing in "self-consciousness" is coming to know that universal (Germaness, Italianness) will that is embodied in the STATE (and the powerful state leader). So, Fascist countries subordinated individual citizens to the will of the state, claiming that dialectically this was fulfilling or "realizing" the individual. Dialectical fascist theory also justified aggressive warfare on the grounds that the dominating nations (such as NAZI Germany) dialectically "overcame" the "opposition" of the dominated nations (such as Poland). This rationalized brutal dictatorship and military aggression. Fascist countries claimed that they were only asserting their "RIGHTS" and that other (conquered) countries were in their way. The dialectic became more diabolical as the communist and fascist systems used it to justify all kinds of cruel and inhuman policies (such as attempted extermination of the Jews, oppression of foreign peoples, forced labor camps, etc.)

In later praxis-school Marxism (see CRITICAL THEORY), the dialectic was used to explain all social causes in terms of the "ideal" criticizing the "real" and leading to progressive human liberation and "self-realization." Seeing all social relations (as between classes, races, genders) in terms of conflict, the praxis Marxist "overcomes" oppression between men and women,

blacks and whites, rich and poor, through revolutionary criticism of any group or individual who has power and "transforming" the dialectical conflict into "unity." This New LEFT perspective informs much of sociology and neo-Marxist political philosophy.

In a different, purely logical Western perspective, the dialectic can also mean the use of opposing arguments in discussion (such as the Greek philosopher SOCRATES arriving at truth through a method of asking questions and revealing the internal contradictions in an opponent's opinions). The adversarial legal system in Anglo-American jurisprudence and clashing "free-marketplace-of-ideas" liberalism of John Stuart MILL are dialectical in this sense (as is free-market competition).

Further Reading
Jordan, Z. A. *The Evolution of Dialectical Materialism*. New York: St. Martin's Press, 1967.

dictator/dictatorship

A government or state ruled by one person with absolute AUTHORITY (dictator). That is a single ruler who can dictate: all laws, policies, and personnel in the state. *Dictatorship* another term for DESPOTISM or TYRANNY. The word *dictator* usually carries the negative meaning of a "brutal dictator" who governs by whim, cruelty, and violence. In the 20th century, the COMMUNIST leaders Castro (in Cuba) and STALIN (Soviet Union) were often described as dictators because they ruled with absolute power. NAZI leader Adolf HITLER established a personal dictatorship in Germany in the 1930s. Often, African and Middle Eastern countries have dictatorships after the military takes over the government. The dictator is not limited in power by laws, other rulers or independent groups, CIVIL SOCIETY, or political institutions. Karl MARX applied this concept to the "dictatorship of the proletariat"—the working-class dictatorship set up after a proletarian or communist revolution to create a socialist economy and state. In this Marxist sense, dictatorship is not necessarily evil because he claimed that all governments were class dictatorships of some sort.

Further Reading
Ehrenberg, John. *The Dictatorship of the Proletariat: Marxism's Theory of Socialist Democracy*. New York: Routledge, 1992.

German Nazi dictator Adolf Hitler, Russian dictator Joseph Stalin, Italian dictator Benito Mussolini, and Louisiana politician Huey Long are dressed as Napoleon Bonaparte. Painting by Miguel Covarrubias, 1933. (LIBRARY OF CONGRESS)

Diderot, Denis (1713–1784)   *French philosopher, novelist, and critic*

Diderot was born in Langres and received his master's degree from the University of Paris in 1732. He spent the next 10 years engaged in assorted occupations, including teaching and writing sermons for a fee. He also immersed himself in the study of mathematics, literature, and languages and translated a number of English works into French. In 1746 Diderot published his *Pensées philosophiques* (*Philosophical Thoughts*), which contained a bold critique of Christianity. That same year, at the request of his friend, the mathematician Jean Le Rond d'Alembert, Diderot became a contributing editor to the monumental *Encyclopédie,* a multivolume review of the arts and sciences of the day whose guiding perspective was a faith in the progress of the human mind inspired by RATIONALISM. Other contributors included the most prominent philosophers of the period, such as VOLTAIRE, ROUSSEAU, d'Holbach, and Turgot.

Diderot's own philosophical orientation was rationalist. He was an advocate of the scientific method and developed a version of materialism that held the universe to be a purely physical system composed of ele-

mentary material particles containing energy. Moreover, in the *Lettre sur les aveugles* (*Letter on the Blind*) of 1749, Diderot presented an evolutionary theory for the development of organisms, including the influence of hereditary factors. Because this treatise contained a passage that questioned the notion of a divine purpose in nature and the existence of an intelligent God, Diderot was arrested by the authorities and imprisoned at Vincennes for three months.

Diderot's materialism led him to conceive of morality as a product of both physiology and culture. Human beings are decidedly natural animals, possessed of basic biological needs and driven by emotions and sensations. But they also possess imagination, memory, and intelligence and are able to adapt to different environments and modify their beliefs and habits. Through an appropriate education, it is possible to cultivate our national capacities and to live a life of virtue and JUSTICE that may bring happiness.

Diderot was also a prominent critic of the social and political institutions of the day, believing them to be unnecessarily restrictive and conservative. In a number of writings, including articles in the *Encyclopédie,* Diderot strongly supported the ideals of modern DEMOCRACY against the traditional authority of royalty. He asserted that "the people" are the true source of SOVEREIGNTY, and therefore they should choose representatives and determine legislation and the operation of government. To prevent tyranny, church and state must be separated. In addition, Diderot actively campaigned for the elimination of capital punishment and other forms of inhumane punishment. Overall, Diderot's contribution to the intellectual development of the ENLIGHTENMENT is significant, primarily due to the publicity his work on the *Encyclopédie,* brought to the philosophical and political ideas of the period.

Further Reading
Furbank, P. N. *Diderot: A Critical Biography.* New York: Knopf, 1992.

discrimination

A concept prevalent in the 20th century, held especially by American LIBERALS, that claims an injustice is done by society when individuals of equal ability are treated unequally. This assumes that differences in race, gender, disability, or sexual orientation do not have an effect on a person's behavior or functioning. In other words, liberal views of discrimination regard all humans as basically equal, despite their individual differences, and therefore deserving of equal treatment by the law and society.

An older view of humanity, in ARISTOTLE, also premises discrimination on EQUALITY. Aristotle held that it is as unjust to treat people who are different (unequal) the same as it is to treat people who are the same differently. Human distinctions that should be respected include culture, age, gender, and nationality. To treat individuals of unequal ability (say a C student and an A student) as equals would be as unfair as treating two persons of equal ability unequally. The Greek philosopher PLATO asserted that humans could be divided into three distinct categories: (1) the intellectual, (2) the spirited, and (3) the economic. Each group, in Plato's Republic, should receive a distinct education suited to their abilities and a position in society using their talents. To treat all equally would be an injustice, for Plato.

In the MIDDLE AGES, St. Thomas AQUINAS combined Aristotelian philosophy with CHRISTIANITY and held that three groups in society (priests, soldiers, and rulers) are different by nature and deserve different treatment and laws.

The MODERN idea of discrimination as a purely negative or unjust action comes from the liberalism of John LOCKE, which viewed humans as by nature equal as members of the same species. Locke held that the state should treat individuals equally before the law because of that shared humanity. But the law treating individuals equally was to be limited to protecting their individual liberty and property. Twentieth-century American liberalism expanded this to use the state to impose equality on private organizations and relationships. Now, discrimination came to mean excluding anyone from something they desire (schooling, jobs, status) on the basis of race, gender, religion, sexual orientation, age, or disability. Such discrimination implies an absolute equality and any denial of that sameness as unjust. The social effect of this doctrine has been the racial and sex integration of schools, businesses, the military, professions, and government. In the United States, such equalizing policies have been associated with affirmative action or diversity, which actively recruited minorities and women who had previously been excluded from positions and institutions. The resistance to perceived reverse discrimination and revised opinions on the positive aspects of

cultural, ethnic, gender, and racial uniqueness has caused a reappraisal of the concept of discrimination. The value of programs for the "gifted" and artistic programs for certain talented children, the apparently innate but complementary differences between the ways men and women think and communicate, and the preservation of distinctive cultural and religious heritages have balanced the current definition of social discrimination.

Further Readings
Babcock, B., Freedman, A., Norton, E., and Ross, S. *Sex Discrimination and the Law: Causes and Remedies.* 1975.
Fullinwider, R. K. *The Reverse Discrimination Controversy.* Totowa, N.J.: Rowman and Littlefield, 1980.
Goldman, A. H. *Justice and Reverse Discrimination.* Princeton, N.J.: Princeton University Press, 1979.

dissent/dissenter

The act of not accepting a political, social, or religious authority. An individual who refuses to agree to or assent to such power is often called a dissenter. Like CIVIL DISOBEDIENCE, dissent may involve disagreement with one government policy, ruler, or law or with the entire social system. Often, *dissenter* or *nonconformist* was the term used to describe the Christians (such as BAPTISTS) who would not conform to the established state church (CATHOLIC in Europe, Orthodox in Russian, Anglican in Britain). Another prominent example of dissenters were the intellectuals (like Andrey Sokaroff and Aleksandr Solzhenitsyn) who protested the restrictions on individual freedom and political rights in the SOVIET UNION. Dissenters stand up for their principles against the state and often are persecuted, jailed, and killed.

divine right of kings

The doctrine that European monarchs (such as French king Louis XIV) have their authority directly from God and that it is not limited by other people, LAWS, or CONSTITUTIONS. The theory of divine right of kings, largely refined by Frenchman Jean BODIN, emerged in the 16th century in response to popular challenges to royal authority. Often associated with ABSOLUTISM, such ideas tied the European monarchies closely to the Roman CATHOLIC Church and made resistance to the monarch also rebellion to God almighty. Consequently, when antimonarchy revolutions in Europe occurred, they tended also to be anti-Catholic (in France, HUGUENOT or deist, in England, Protestant).

St. Thomas AQUINAS implied a divine-right doctrine in his discussion of kingship, but he emphasized that even absolute monarchs are bound and limited by God's law.

Further Reading

Milton, John. *Political Writings*, Martin Dzelzainis, ed., Claire Gruzelier, transl. Cambridge, Eng.: Cambridge University Press, 1991.

Douglass, Frederick (1817–1895)   *U.S. slave and antislavery activist*

A leading black ABOLITIONIST, Douglass was born a slave in eastern Maryland. At the age of 20, he escaped to the northern United States and freedom. In New York, Douglass started a newspaper (*The North Star*) devoted to the abolitionist (antislavery) cause. A dramatic and colorful speaker and writer, he riveted audiences with horrifying depictions of the cruelty and injustice of southern slave life. He ridiculed U.S. society and morals that would permit ownership of human beings. He played on the guilt, shame, and national humiliation caused by the institution of enslavement. Douglass ridiculed northern, free states as much as southern slave society for allowing the continuance of black (African-American) slavery and often employed CHRISTIAN imagery and arguments against the hypocrisy and self-righteousness of U.S. slave owners and their supporters. Well versed in the Bible, Douglass appealed to the common humanity of blacks and whites and the unchristian spirit of U.S. slavery. He avowed a faith in Christ and the ultimate will of God in the freedom of slaves.

His political theory claimed that the U.S. CONSTITUTION justified the forcible emancipation of southern slaves, without compensation to their owners. He denied that STATES RIGHTS protected the rights of southerners against federal-government encroachment of the tradition of black slavery. Douglass ridiculed the moderate abolitionists who advocated respecting the PROPERTY rights of southern slave owners and merely worked for the restricting of the expansion of slavery into new Western states.

After the American Civil War and liberation of African-American slaves, Douglass supported the FEMINIST movement to apply legal and political EQUALITY to

Frederick Douglass, ca. 1870. (LIBRARY OF CONGRESS)

female Americans. For these reasons, Frederick Douglass is greatly admired by LIBERAL civil rights advocates, African Americans, and American feminists, who see him as a hero.

Further Reading

Foner, P. S. *The Life and Writings of Frederick Douglass.* 5 vols. New York: International Publishers, 1950–1955.

Duns Scotus, Johannes (1264–1308)   *English Medieval philosopher*

Educated at Oxford and the University of Paris, Duns Scotus is chiefly known, as is St. Thomas AQUINAS, for combining the ideas of ARISTOTLE with CHRISTIANITY. Unlike Aquinas, however, he places NATURAL LAW on the "will" of God rather than on his mind, thereby moderating the Aristotelian (and Thomist) emphasis on human reason. Hence, the primary Christian act (including that of Christian rulers) is an act of the love of God rather than a purely intellectual knowledge of church doctrine. His theology became the foundation of the Franciscan Order of the Western Church. There it served as a moderating influence of the rationalism of the Thomist CATHOLIC doctrine. His teaching that the state naturally arises from the common CONSENT of the people provided an early SOCIAL-CONTRACT view of politics and government.

Further Reading
Harris, C. R. S. *Duns Scotus*. Oxford, Eng.: Clarendon Press, 1927.

Durkheim, Émile (1858–1917) *Philosopher of science and founder of sociology*

Durkheim founded sociology as a distinct discipline within the social sciences. He achieved this by identifying a new object of study, social facts, and by applying to this object the methods of a POSITIVISTIC science. Durkheim's work can be divided into two categories: those works attending to the foundations and methods of sociology, and those works in which he applies these methods to particular social facts.

Durkheim was not the first to attempt to study society in a scientific manner. His own acknowledged intellectual predecessors, Auguste COMTE, Charles de Montesquieu, and Herbert Spencer, studied some aspect of social organization and cohesion without generalizing their method and extending the scope of their analysis. Durkheim was, however, the first to resist systematically the idea that social phenomena were to be explained and accounted for by their reduction to other phenomena. For example, he rejected the notions that economic activity was *nothing more* than transactions between individual agents; that religious custom could be explained as *nothing more* than psychological events taking place inside people's heads; that the state or nation is *nothing more* than the aggregate of its INDIVIDUAL members. In these and other cases, Durkheim insisted that there was a distinct social fact to be examined and explained in the same way that there were distinct psychological, economic, and biological facts. Thus the subject matter of sociology is the objectively existing social facts of such phenomena as trade, suicide, religious practice, and so on. What makes all these facts *social* is their connection within the social organism, the social solidarity that institutions and practices confer, and the external coercive power that they exercise over the lives of individuals and groups. There is, therefore, for Durkheim, a nonreducible connectedness between social facts and a normativeness to them. With this idea of society in hand, Durkheim categorized and explained differences between tribal, traditional, and modern societies, most notably referring to social solidarity of traditional societies as mechanical.

Durkheim's understanding of scientific method was standardly positivistic. What is important is how he applied these methods to society and how he drew significant conclusions from the results.

First, he argued that sociological explanation is functional rather than causal. By this he meant that to understand a social fact, one must understand it in relation to the social whole—one must know how it functions within the web of social relations. Social facts are thus explained by reference to other social facts rather than being explained by nonsocial, say biological or economic, facts. This idea of functional explanation goes together with a regard for the importance and significance of empirical data. For example, by collecting empirical data on suicide rates in different countries and between kinds of individuals, Durkheim drew conclusions about the social and moral character of different forms of society.

Second, by employing the notion of functional explanation, Durkheim introduces the idea of normal and pathological social facts. In this regard, Durkheim's notion of "Anomie" identified a pathological characteristic of modern societies where the division of labor so isolates individuals from the organic social network that society loses its capacity to check and influence their perspective and desires.

Durkheim was born in Épinal, France. He studied philosophy at the École Normale Supérieure and later in his career became the first professor of sociology at the Sorbonne. He died at the age of 59.

Further Reading
Lukes, S. *Émile Durkheim*. New York: Harper & Row, 1973.

E

Eastwood, David (1959–) *British historian, political philosopher, and academic*

Educated at Sandbach School, Cheshire, and St. Peter's College, Oxford, Eastwood distinguished himself early as an astute historian of 18th-century British political culture and thought. His book, *Governing Rural England, 1780–1840* (1994) is a perceptive treatment of local governance in traditional British society. Eastwood applies his vast knowledge of British political history and culture to contemporary British politics (for example, he was the founder of the National Centre for Public Policy in Swansea). He rose quickly in an academic career at Oxford University (Senior Tutor, Pembroke College) and the University of Wales (professor of history and head of department, dean of faculty, and pro-vice chancellor), as well as fellow of the Royal Historical Society (literary director since 1994). In the year 2000, Eastwood became the chief executive of the Arts and Humanities Research Board, a British government agency concerned with research in higher education throughout the United Kingdom. Eastwood has lectured internationally, and his prolific writings reflect both a keen appreciation of British political traditions and a progressive view of the future British and Western European state.

Further Readings
Eastwood, David. *Governing Rural England.* London: Oxford University Press, 1994.
———. *Government and Community in the English Provinces 1700–1870.* New York: St. Martin's Press, 1997.

ecclesiology/ecclesiastic

The term used to describe the ideas and practices of church government, especially in the Western, CATHOLIC Church. In Protestant Christian churches, this is sometimes referred to as "church polity." It describes the governing structure of the church, whether Episcopal (bishop-led), Presbyterian, congregational, or papal (pope). Developed largely by MEDIEVAL CANON-LAW writers, ecclesiology determined the respective power of the pope, bishops, priests, religious orders, church councils, and other church organizations. As the administration of the church is always developing, this discipline of ecclesiology is a growing, changing field.

egalitarian/egalitarianism

An ideal or practice advocating human equality. In the history of Western political thought, several bases have provided the foundation for believing that all people are fundamentally equal: (1) that every human being is created by God "in God's own image" (Genesis 1:27) and have equal dignity from that divine creation; (2) each person has fallen away from God through sin ("for all have sinned and fallen short of the glory of God" [Romans 3:23]); (3) every human being has reason; (4) as physical beings of the same species, humans have biological EQUALITY, as evidenced by their ability to reproduce with each other. This last argument for human equality forms the basis of the MODERN scientific, British LIBERAL view or egalitarianism in Thomas HOBBES and John LOCKE. It was this physiological definition of equality that JEFFERSON referred to in his famous phrase in the DECLARATION OF INDEPENDENCE, that all "are created equal." This biological basis for equality leaves many aspects of society characterized by inequality (wealth, status, income, occupation, power, prestige), but it commends equal legal rights appropriate to that physical existence ("life, LIBERTY, and property").

Alexis de TOCQUEVILLE regarded the United States of America as the most egalitarian society, where every individual is regarded as equal to any other because of the Modern liberal philosophy and the predominant Protestant CHRISTIANITY in the United States. No *legal* differences of status are allowed in the United States; the CONSTITUTION forbids government-granted titles of nobility and distinction. But U.S. society allows great inequality of wealth, social status, occupational prestige, and so on; however, these "private" inequalities are not supported to undermine the basic political equality of "one person, one vote."

During the 20th century, this basic legal equality has been extended to more and more groups and social circumstances not envisioned by liberal philosophers. SOCIALISM and COMMUNISM argued for economic equality; FEMINISM strove for gender equality; the CIVIL RIGHTS movement, for racial, religious, and ethnic equality. ANIMAL RIGHTS and HOMOSEXUAL rights activists attempt to extend social equality to creatures and practices that were not included in the original scientific definition of human equality.

Extensions of the concept of human equality challenge other social values (*freedom*, distinction, TRADITION, religious and moral precepts, biological families, etc.). A HIERARCHICAL view is the opposite of egalitarianism because it claims that some persons, social structure, ideas, and values are better than others; not all are equally valid. So, egalitarianism promotes continued debate and public discussion. ARISTOTLE recommended a justice that treats true equals the same and unequals differently. The challenge in political thought and practice has been to determine how people are similar and different and to treat them accordingly.

Further Reading
Nielsen, Kai. *Equality and Liberty: A Defense of Radical Egalitarianism.* Totowa, N.J.: Rowman and Littlefield, 1984.

elite/elitism/elitist

A member of a small superior minority or ruling group. Similar to the CLASSICAL idea of ARISTOCRACY, *elite* originally meant the best people at the top of organizations (governmental, religious, social, and economic). For example, a prince or an executive might be considered an elite. The leaders of the church, social clubs, or big business have been portrayed as elite leadership. Any profession (law, medicine, and academic) has its elite members who have distinguished themselves by great accomplishments, honors, and fame. In the early CHRISTIAN political thought of St. AUGUSTINE, such an elite was most susceptible to corrupting pride, vanity, and evil. A worldly elite was almost always wicked and selfish. In MODERN political thought, this criticism of elites shifts to their undemocratic characteristics. REPUBLICAN revolutions (17th-century England, 18th-century France, 19th-century Germany, 20th-century Russia and China) tended to attack some ruling elite, which was portrayed as elitist and corrupt.

Even after democracy was established in most countries, elite theory asserted that a small social elite still controlled the government (the rich, certain families, government officials, etc.). Leaders in the COMMUNIST countries, such as the Soviet Union, were seen as a party elite that received privileges and power that most citizens did not enjoy. Elite rule is portrayed as using manipulation and coercion to maintain its powerful position in society. The control of the media, education, and election campaigns allegedly keep the elite in power while giving the majority the illusion that the popular will prevails. A close-knit network of elites with rapid, secret communication supposedly thwarts any effective challenge to their power. Often, conspiracy theories emerge around elite views of power: that some small group (the CIA, banks, graduates of Yale, the oil industry, etc.) secretly controls every aspect of life. Often, elites are identified with certain races (e.g., white or Asian), gender (males), religion (Christians or Jews), or regions (the northeast or Hollywood).

An alternative to elite theory in political thought is PLURALISM, which says that many groups compete for influence in society and government. In this view, no elite group has permanent power, but all must compete in the "political marketplace" for control. Out of this rival competition of groups, James MADISON felt, society would remain under democratic control, and individual freedom would be preserved. Such multiple interests make elites unstable and unpredictable.

The concept of elite is ambiguous in contemporary political thought. It is viewed favorably (such as in an elite university) or unfavorably (as an academic elite or liberal elite), depending on the context in which it is used. But generally, in Modern DEMOCRATIC culture, *elite* is a negative term, and much political activity is devoted to "opening up" elite strongholds (in the state, the military, social, and religious organizations). Affirmative action is largely a policy to accomplish the destruction of perceived racial and gender elites.

Further Readings

Bachrach, P. *The Theory of Democratic Elitism.* Boston: Little, Brown, 1967.
Bottomore, T. *Elites and Society.* London: Routledge, 1966.
Field, G. L., and Higley, J. *Elitism.* London: Routledge, 1980.

empire/imperial

A large geographical area ruled by a central political power. For example, the Roman Empire, the Chinese Empire, the British Empire, or the Ottoman Empire. Usually, an empire includes rule over a variety of national and ethnic groups, and its political unity enhances economic development and trade. A military component that keeps subjected people under control is always a feature of an empire. Before the 20th century, an empire was considered a sign of superior culture, law, and military power. Since the emergence of MARXISM, empires have been portrayed as inevitably exploitative and hegemonic. National-liberation movements going back to ancient Israel's rebellion against Roman domination and continuing in America's Revolutionary War against the British Empire have marked MODERN history. Mexico's breaking from the Spanish Empire, Vietnam against French imperialism, and Afghanistan against the SOVIET UNION reveal the prevalence of resistance to imperial rule.

Politically, an empire is the most centralized system of the state. A vast area ruled by a single state is the least democratic or local kind of government. When the French Revolution of 1789 turned from a republic to the French Empire under Emperor Napoleon, it was seen as betraying its ideals. In the 20th century, V.I. LENIN asserted that neo-colonialism allowed formal, technical, political independence, but economic imperialism really controlled the world through London, New York, or Berlin. Many developing countries (Africa, Asia, Latin America) perceive themselves as part of the economic empires of the United States and Europe, under the World Bank.

The benefits of empire have included expansion of civilization, religion, and economic development. The Roman philosopher CICERO gave the CLASSICAL rationale for empire as the extension of universal LAW and (military and commercial) order. In the MIDDLE AGES, DANTE advocated a one-world empire under the CATHOLIC Church to end all war and social conflict. The contemporary one-world-government movement is essentially advocating a world empire for the same purposes.

Further Reading

Pagden, Anthony. *Lords of All the World: Ideologies of Empire in Spain, Britain and France c. 1500–c. 1800.* New Haven, Conn.: Yale University Press, 1995.

Engels, Friedrich (1820–1895)   *German communist thinker and collaborator of Karl Marx*

Born into a wealthy capitalist family, Engels became a critic of INDUSTRIALISM, especially of the poor condition of the factory workers. Engels wrote several articles and books describing the squalid housing, poor health, and overworked condition of the industrial mill workers in Germany and England in the mid-1800s. He attacked the hypocrisy of the respectable middle-class CHRISTIANS who exploited the working poor and pretended that they were better than the impoverished masses.

Engels moved to northern England in 1842 to manage a family business. He became involved in SOCIALIST politics and investigated the living conditions of Manchester clothing-mill workers. At this time, he began to develop theories about the problems of CAPITALIST economics ("Outlines of a Critique of Political Economy") and solutions through socialism. In 1844, he collaborated with Karl MARX on the satirical essay *The*

Holy Family, ridiculing the ruling establishment in Germany. This began a lifelong partnership between Marx and Engels, in which they co-authored many of the classic texts of COMMUNIST theory (including *The Communist Manifesto,* 1848; *The German Ideology,* 1846; and *Capital,* 1867, 1885, 1994). Engels supported Marx financially, as Karl was unemployed and living in London. Engels would cut a money note in half and mail the separate halves to Marx to avoid their being stolen.

Engels wrote several books on economic history and theory, the most famous being *The Condition of the Working Class in England* (1845), which depicted the wretched living and working conditions of factory laborers in Manchester. The unfairness and cruelty of this early industrial system led Engels to advocate a collectivist, planned, socialist economy, owned and operated by the workers themselves. Such was the only way to have a humane society, in his view.

Engels developed the philosophy of DIALECTICAL materialism, which was implicit in MARXISM and stated that history is impelled by economic forces. Even nature and science (e.g., Darwinism) follow this dialectical process of clashing opposites, destruction, and progress. Conflict and opposition, then, become the inevitable sources of advancement in the world and society. In *The Origin of the Family, Private Property and the State* (1884) Engels provides an anthropological treatment of human development, extolling primitive tribal communism and identifying all social evils with the emergence of private PROPERTY. Here, he critiques "the bourgeois family" of Western CHRISTIAN society and advocates women's liberation and "open" relationships. They provide the basis for LEFTIST attacks on the traditional family and culture by assigning them to a particular historical/economic era, rather than a perennial nature or God-given values. With this approach, socialist theory often dismisses the traditional Judeo-Christian family and allows easy divorce and "free love."

Scholars argue over how similar Marx's and Engels's ideas were, some Marxists claiming that Engels lacked the philosophical subtlety and sophistication of Karl Marx. For example, Engels's insistence of a strict determination of the "superstructure" of society (law, government, education, art, etc.) by the economic "structure" is seen by CRITICAL-THEORY Marxists as mechanical and false. This formality of Engels's materialism is sometimes blamed for the rigid, brutal communism of the SOVIET UNION and other communist countries.

Engels served as the literary executor of Karl Marx after the latter's death in 1883. He edited the last two volumes of *Das Kapital* and many shorter works of Marx. Through the spread of socialist and communist ideas in the 19th and 20th centuries, Marx and Engels became the two most prominent founders of that movement.

Further Readings
Carver, T. *Engels.* New York: Hill and Wang, 1981.
———. *Marx and Engels: The Intellectual Relationship.* Bloomington: Indiana University Press, 1983.
Engels, F. *The Condition of the Working Class in England.* Henderson, W. O. and Chaloner, W. H., transls. and eds. Stanford, Calif.: Stanford University Press, 1971.
Henderson, W. O. *The Life of Friedrich Engels,* 2 vols. London: F. Cass, 1976.
Lichtheim, G. *Marxism.* London: Routledge, 1964.
Marcus, S. *Engels, Manchester and the Working Class.* New York: Random House, 1974.
McLellan, D. *Engels.* Sussex, Eng.: Harvester Press, 1977.

Enlightenment, The

An intellectual and political movement in Europe and the United States in the 18th century that optimistically believed that human reason and goodness could create a peaceful, prosperous society and perfect people. Thinkers associated with the Enlightenment are Frenchmen Jean-Jacques ROUSSEAU, François-Marie VOLTAIRE, and Charles de MONTESQUIEU (the *philosophes*); Englishmen John LOCKE and Jeremy BENTHAM; German philosopher Immanuel KANT; Scots David HUME and Adam SMITH; and Americans Thomas JEFFERSON, Benjamin FRANKLIN, and Thomas PAINE. Enlightenment thinkers were critical of TRADITION, the past, religion, HIERARCHY, and CONSERVATISM. They believed in progress—that humans and society can progress and improve (economically, morally, politically) by using their reason. Hence, the Enlightenment emphasized education as important to social and individual progress. They saw shaping the political (along REPUBLICAN lines) and economic (with technology and INDUSTRIALISM) environment as vital to progressive improvement of humanity. Consequently, they rejected past institutions: agrarian FEUDALISM, ARISTOCRATIC and monarchical government, traditional CHRISTIAN religion (especially CATHOLIC), and the patriarchal family. Often, Enlightenment thinkers were atheists or deists, rejecting all religion and spiritual matters as "superstition" or "metaphysical." This reflected their faith in science, empiricism, and materialism. For many Enlightenment thinkers, humans are naturally good and ethical, so democracy makes the best regime. This rejects the traditional Judeo-Christian view that humans are sinful and only good by God's spirit.

Enlightenment ideas influenced the DEMOCRATIC revolutions in Europe and America in the 1700s. They were carried on by the socialist and communist ideas of Karl MARX, Friedrich ENGELS, and V. I. LENIN. These Enlightenment views were criticized by many conservative thinkers (such as Edmund BURKE), the Catholic Church, and other traditional philosophers. By the mid-20th century, the failed social revolutions in France, Russia, and China; two world wars; and the brutality of fascism challenged the Enlightenment optimism over the goodness of humans, social progress, and human reason. POST-MODERNISM is partly a response to this disappointment with Enlightenment Modernism, as are revivals of conservative, Christian, and other pre-Enlightenment ideas.

Further Reading
Hampson, N. *The Enlightenment.* New York: Pelican, 1968.

environmentalism/environmental

A social and political movement that seeks to promote laws and policy that protect the natural earth environment, conserve natural resources and wildlife, prevent harm from pollution and toxic industrial wastes, and restore healthy natural living and working environments in the world. Early environmentalists John Muir and Aldo Leopold in the 19th century emphasized preserving unspoiled natural environments in the United States through national parks and preserves. Such approaches to environmentalism continued in the 20th century through such groups as the Audubon Society and the Sierra Club. These groups lobby the government to have legislation passed promoting preservation of nature areas from commercial development. This led in the 1960s to environmentalists working to regulate businesses (such as factories, chemical companies, the automobile industry) that pollute the natural environ-ment (air, rivers, lakes, oceans, land). The American Clean Air and Water Act legislated much of the environmentalist cause. Laws concerning toxic waste disposal, workers' environmental safety, animal population control, and food labeling also emerged from the environmental movement. Because much of

its focus is on economic sources of environmental damage, this environmentalist agenda is often seen as in conflict with business activity and interests.

A recent development in the political thought of environmentalism is the environmental-justice movement. Emerging in the 1980s in the United States, this section of environmentalism blends MARXISM, COMMUNISM, FEMINISM, and racial awareness with concern for the natural environment. Using Marxist economic class analysis, it identifies attacks on the environment with CAPITALIST imperialist exploitation of workers, the poor, women, people of color, and the developing world. For example, it argues that most dangerous toxic waste dumps are placed near African-American neighborhoods in the United States or near "people of color" in the developing world (Africa, Latin America, Asia). So, environmental protection cannot be accomplished without attacking racism, sexism, classism, and capitalism. A recent statement by an environmental group stated: "Environmental racism is seen by the environmental-justice movement as an extension of institutional racism in housing, education, employment, and so on." In its National People of Color Environmental Leadership Summit in 1991 a statement was issued that included "Environmental justice affirms the sacredness of Mother Earth, ecological unity and . . . the right to be free from ecological destruction." The radical environmental movement is often very critical of the earlier "white middle class" environmentalism as mere collaborators with the business establishment that is exploiting and destroying Earth and its peoples. So, the environmental movement is really several different movements that often disagree with each other as much as with the polluters.

Activities of environmentalists range from lobbying the government to peaceful demonstrations and campaigns, to CIVIL DISOBEDIENCE and unlawful blocking of nuclear power plants, waste sites, etc. Criticized by some conservatives as fanatical extremists, worshipers of "Mother Earth" or "tree huggers," the environmental movement nevertheless has been effective in influencing U.S. public policy, especially in the DEMOCRATIC PARTY. Albert Gore has been a prominent representative of this movement and its concerns.

Further Reading
Jagtenberg, Tom. *Eco-Impacts and the Greening of Postmodernity: New Maps for Communication Studies, Cultural Studies, and Sociology.* Berkeley, Calif.: Sage, 1997.

equality

In political thought, equality usually refers to how humans are equal, the same, and deserving, therefore, of equal treatment by the society and government or equal conditions in life. The basis for this MODERN notion of human equality is found in John LOCKE's materialist philosophy that emphasizes equal rights to members of the same species. This egalitarian theory emphasizes "humanness" over individual differences in race, color, sex, religion, nationality, disability, education, culture, talents, abilities, accomplishments, or interests. From this biological basis of equality, the concept of *equality before the law*, or governmental treatment of all on an equal basis (rather than DISCRIMINATION) is advanced. The Fourteenth Amendment to the U.S. CONSTITUTION's "equal protection" clause is a codification of this principle. Similarly, the CIVIL RIGHTS acts that prohibit discrimination in employment or government services and benefits on the basis of race, sex, age, religion, national origin, or disability reflect this species approach to defining equality.

Older bases for defining human equality include (1) the Judeo-CHRISTIAN view that all people are "created in God's image" (Genesis 1:27) or, as Thomas JEFFERSON put it in the DECLARATION OF INDEPENDENCE, "all men are created equal"; (2) the Christian view that all humans are sinful and evil ("all have sinned and fallen short of the glory of God" [Romans 3:23]) and in need of redemption and forgiveness through Jesus Christ; (3) the CLASSICAL Greek view in ARISTOTLE that rational citizens are equal members of the state; (4) the MARXIST COMMUNIST theory that all humans are equal as workers or producers. Each of these foundations of human equality commend different social consequences: from total inequality in society but "equal in the sight of God" to equality before the law but social and personal inequality; to state guaranteed "equal opportunity" but unequal wealth, to absolute equality of condition (income, status, privileges).

In the United States, the equal dignity of all human beings combines with formal "equality before the law" to form the most egalitarian culture in the world, while permitting great difference of wealth, social status, prestige, and so on. This ideal is expressed in John RAWLS's *Theory of Justice,* which argues that social and economic inequalities are acceptable if (1) greater wealth is secured in such a way as to benefit the least advantaged (as through invention and sale of labor-saving devices and the providing of welfare services to the poor through higher taxes on the rich); and (2) positions of power and wealth are open to all of ability to fill them. This DEMOCRATIC equality of opportunity mixed with CAPITALIST free enterprise (and differentiation of wealth) and with elaborate social welfare benefits to the poor, needy, and disabled.

Equality of individuals leads to equality of their opinions and ideas, so democratic equality tends to regard all views (religious, political, ethical) of equal value. This is opposed to moral HIERARCHY, which maintains that some beliefs, ideas, and values are superior to others. This inequality of values is preserved even in an egalitarian society by means of FREEDOM, whereby legally equal individuals are permitted freedom or LIBERTY of thought, belief, religion, speech, and so on, which may include believing that a certain system, faith, person, or action is better than others. This moderates the modern, scientific basis of equality (in biological species) and permits individual and group differences in democratic society.

This concept and issue of equality is in continual flux as public debates over discrimination, gifted-student programs, differential incomes, and alternative lifestyles continue. ARISTOTLE stated that justice is preserved when equals are treated the same and unequals are treated differently and that the challenge is to determine in which ways people are equal in certain ways and unequal in others.

Further Readings

Bedau, H. A., ed. *Justice and Equality.* Englewood Cliffs, N.J.: Prentice Hall, 1971.
Pennock, J. R., and Chapman, J. W., eds. *Nomos IX: Equality.* New York: Atherton Press, 1967.
Plato. *The Republic,* A. Bloom, transl. New York: Basic Books, 1968.
Rae, D. *Equalities.* Cambridge, Mass.: Harvard University Press, 1981.
Tawney, R. H. *Equality,* 4th ed. London: Allen & Unwin, 1952.

Erasmus, Desiderius (1466–1536)   *Dutch Christian humanist*

Erasmus is best known for his CLASSICAL scholarship, his integration of Greek and Roman philosophy and ethics into CATHOLIC European thought, and literary criticism of church decline (which contributed to the Protestant REFORMATION). Educated at a school of "The Brethren of the Common Life" at Deventer, in Paris at the College of Montaigu, and at the universities of Oxford and Cambridge in England, Erasmus became the most famous scholar of his lifetime and was revered throughout Europe by clerics and royalty (including Henry VIII, Charles V, Francis I, and Archduke Ferdinand of Austria).

Erasmus combined the best of classical "humanist" scholarship with biblical Christianity. He denounced the formalism, decadence, and superstition of the late MEDIEVAL church (for example, in his book, *In Praise of Folly*) and urged a return to a New Testament basis of the CHRISTIAN faith instead of the dry and sterile scholasticism of the Catholic academics. These ideas of a reformed, evangelical church contributed to those Protestant Reformation ideas of Martin LUTHER and John CALVIN, which finally broke from the Roman Catholic hierarchy. Erasmus never left the Catholic Church, however, and eagerly sought reconciliation between the warring camps of the Reformation. In the end, he was denounced by both sides, rejected by the Protestants for remaining with the Catholic Church, censured by Popes Paul IV and Sixtus V.

Erasmus edited classical Greek and Latin proverbs in his book *Adagia* (1500), writings of the early Christian fathers (St. Jerome, St. Irenaeus, St. Ambrose, St. AUGUSTINE), and did a new translation of the Bible (New Testament) from the original Greek into Latin. His political writings, *Manual of the Christian Knight* (1503) and *The Education of a Christian Prince* (1515), emphasize the need for religious faith and ethics in rulers. Ordained a Catholic priest, Erasmus was close friends with many secular and Christian scholars, including Thomas MORE (whose *Utopia* or ideal Christian commonwealth, Erasmus influenced).

Further Reading
Binns, L. E. *Erasmus the Reformer.* London: Methuen, 1928.

ethics/ethical

In political theory, *social ethics* refers to the standards for good or moral conduct in a political community. All major political thinkers have a social ethics or belief in what constitutes a good society, healthy social relations, and proper conduct of individuals. For example, the Greek philosopher SOCRATES (Plato's *Apology*) questions and criticizes his fellow Athenean citizens for their over-concern with money, pride, and prestige. He urges them to care about more important things: duty, patriotism, and love of God. A strong, healthy republic, for Socrates, requires citizens who practice high social ethics: self-sacrifice, humility, and honesty. PLATO's *Republic* speaks of ethics in terms of

the VIRTUE of different social classes: Rulers are wise and good, the military is courageous and honorable, and the workers are moderate and efficient.

Platonic social ethics are then being in one's "place" and doing a good job. ARISTOTLE's ethics include both functional excellence and moral excellence. The latter revolves around the ethics of a good character that habitually chooses the "Golden Mean"—the moderate good in human relationship (e.g., generosity rather than stinginess or extravagance). An ethical person has such a character, and a good society is full of such people (and prepares them through education, economics, and political participation). St. AUGUSTINE's ethics revolve around the CHRISTIAN virtues of humility, reverence for God, and love for others. A good society will have many such Christians, including in the government. St. Thomas AQUINAS views ethics through both the classics of Aristotle and Christian theology, through divine law, natural law, and human law. Ethical conduct is conforming to God, nature, and state. Modern political "realism," as in MACHIAVELLI, sees POWER (gaining and keeping) as the only worldly ethic; he advises in *The Prince* a ruler to break traditional morality to maintain order and personal power. Reformation political thinkers LUTHER and CALVIN emphasize the individual's direct guidance from God in ethics through reading the Bible and prayer. Modern liberals HOBBES and LOCKE place ethics in terms of individual rights and interests—pursuing private goals and respecting the individual natural rights of others. COMMUNISM (in Karl MARX) situates ethics in historical economic class interests, the only social good being working for the progressive revolutionary social class, helping it take over the government. FASCISM (in Giovanni GENTILE) holds obedience to the state as the highest ethical value.

Most political ethics, or view of the good person, good citizen, and good society, derive from some religious or philosophical source—a view of HUMAN NATURE and the just state. The United States, with a mix of traditions, draws its ethics from a variety of sources (primarily Judeo-Christian religion, British liberalism of John Locke, classical republicanism, and Enlightenment ideals). Ethics is studied in theology, philosophy, and political theory and is applied to law, business, economics, and psychology, as well as government.

In general, ethics can be divided into positive and negative. Negative ethics defines social and individual goodness in terms of what is "not" done (e.g., "Thou shalt not steal"). Positive ethics considers active benevolence and charity necessary to individual and social virtue (e.g., "Love thy neighbor as thyself"). These two (positive ethics in classical and religious ethics; negative ethics in Lockean liberalism) often conflict. An emphasis on respecting rights, leaving others alone, and diversity is most common in negative ethics; a concern with others' moral well-being is characteristic of positive ethics.

Further Reading
Sheldon, G. W. *The History of Political Theory.* New York: Peter Lang Publishing, 1988.

euthanasia

Euthanasia describes an act of causing a person's death painlessly to end his or her suffering. There are two categories of euthanasia to be considered—active euthanasia and passive euthanasia. Active euthanasia requires the deliberate killing of a person, using medical skills and knowledge as the instrument of death. Passive euthanasia refers to the practice of ceasing medical treatment so as to allow death. In addition to these categories, we distinguish between voluntary and nonvoluntary euthanasia. The former occurs when a patient chooses and so consents to die. The latter occurs when an act of euthanasia is carried out on a patient who is unable to decide, usually because the patient is incompetent and so cannot consent.

These categories and distinctions enable us to identify four types of euthanasia:

1. Passive voluntary euthanasia
2. Passive nonvoluntary euthanasia
3. Active voluntary euthanasia
4. Active nonvoluntary euthanasia

Acts of euthanasia raise moral and political issues: first, whether respect for individual autonomy should allow patients to decide life-and-death issues for themselves; second, whether medical practitioners should use their skills and available technology to end life rather than to preserve it; and third, whether others (and which others) should decide life-and-death issues for patients who are incompetent. The most prominent issue in recent times has been the controversy of cases of doctor-assisted suicide, where a physician provides medication and instruction to individuals so that they may take their own lives. In nearly all countries, active euthanasia, including doctor-assisted suicide, is out-

lawed. The most notable exception is Holland, where active voluntary euthanasia is, in some circumstances, permitted.

There are a number of common arguments against euthanasia. First, it is argued that there are moral and practical grounds for a general rule or practice that universally prohibits the killing of others and respecting the sanctity of life. To allow euthanasia is to challenge and thereby weaken an absolute prohibition on killing. This is the position held by the Catholic Church and others. The utility of maintaining this rule outweighs the benefit to those whose suffering is ended by acts of euthanasia. Second, it is argued that errors in diagnosis and in determining the prognosis for recovery of a patient are possible; thus, patients who would otherwise live are needlessly killed by euthanasia. Finally, a patient may be beyond current medical help now but within its scope in the future. A sanctioned practice of euthanasia, too, readily supposes that medicine can no longer help.

These arguments are opposed by those who claim that what should be preserved is not life but rather a minimum quality of life. Death then is sometimes a benefit rather than a harm to the person who dies. Also, voluntary euthanasia respects the autonomy and self-determination of patients: It allows individuals to make their own choice in the most crucial question instead of being subject to the decisions of third parties.

In cases of nonvoluntary euthanasia where a patient is unable to render a competent decision, the difficulty is in determining who makes the choice to end life-preserving treatment and on what grounds. In practice, passive nonvoluntary euthanasia is usually a joint decision between family and doctors. There are several grounds for ending life-preserving treatment: First, the existence of a "living will," or advance directive, that directs others to treat its author according to his or her wishes should the author become incompetent; second, by "substituted judgment," where others decide according to how they think he or she would have decided for herself; finally, by basing a decision on what others take to be in the patient's best interests.

There are a number of deep controversies on the topic of euthanasia other than whether its practice, in any form, is morally and politically acceptable. It is common in practice to draw a very sharp distinction between active and passive euthanasia. The former is most often legally forbidden; the latter is permitted. James Rachels has argued that the distinction fails to indicate a morally relevant difference; that acts of killing and letting die are both of equal moral weight, both bringing about a patient's death, with the same purposes and intention; and, moreover, that there are cases where active euthanasia is more humane because it would end suffering earlier. Given the purpose of euthanasia, which is to end suffering, and given the lack of a real moral difference between active and passive euthanasia, he propounds that active euthanasia ought to be allowed and practiced.

Another difficult issue concerns who should be allowed to die by an act of euthanasia. In Holland, there have been requests for euthanasia from people who are not in immediate danger of death and whose suffering is not immediate or not physical, for example, people who are HIV-positive but who wish to die before the onset of full-blown AIDS, and anorexic patients who do not respond to treatment. There have also been requests for euthanasia from people whose suffering is psychological rather than physical.

The moral and political issues surrounding euthanasia, like those of abortion, concern very deep questions about death and quality of life, as well as questions about the traditional aims and purposes of medical practice. Important values conflict in this debate, including the sanctity of life versus respect for the autonomy and agency of individuals. This lack of conceptual clarity is made more difficult by quick advances in medical technology.

Further Reading
Dworkin, G., Frey, R. G., and Bok, S. *Euthanasia and Physician-Assisted Suicide (For and Against).* New York: Cambridge University Press, 1998.

evangelical

A branch or movement in CHRISTIANITY, most often associated with REFORMATION Protestants, with distinct political consequences. EVANGELICAL Christians hold the Bible as the main source of God's truth, salvation through faith in Jesus Christ, the DEMOCRATIC "church of all believers" and the need to "evangelize," or spread the truths of Christianity around the world. Most Evangelicals also emphasize a personal or "born-again" religious experience to prove one's Christian faith. This INDIVIDUALISM, allowing the person to commune directly with God through the Bible and prayer, leads to a natural EQUALITY and democracy in the church and society. So, the PURITAN, early English evan-

gelicals, advocated independent congregational churches (freed from pope and bishops) along with REPUBLICAN secular government.

In contemporary U.S. politics, "Evangelicals" are often associated with the CONSERVATIVE RELIGIOUS or CHRISTIAN RIGHT, which advocates traditional Christian moral policies in government (religious education in schools; laws against ABORTION, divorce, pornography, and HOMOSEXUALITY) along with reductions in taxes, welfare programs, and increased military spending. Evangelical Christians often take a providential or COVENANT view of politics. Leaders include Billy Graham, Jerry Falwell, and Marion "Pat" Robertson. U.S. president Jimmy CARTER was an evangelical Christian.

Further Reading
Dayton, D. W. *Discovering an Evangelical Heritage.* New York: Harper & Row, 1976.

existentialism/existential

A philosophy developed in 20th-century Europe associated with thinkers Sören KIERKEGAARD, Friedrich NIETZSCHE, Edward Husserl, Martin HEIDEGGER, and Jean-Paul SARTRE, Politically, existentialism has been aligned with MARXIST COMMUNISM in France and NAZI FASCISM in Germany.

The main theme of existentialism is that the individual is alone, suffering from meaninglessness and ALIENATION. No rational order, NATURAL LAW, or divine providence exists, only self-made reality. The world and society are chaotic, unpredictable, and incomprehensible. This leaves the individual to "make" his or her own reality, to take personal responsibility for one's FREEDOM, never relying on any external objective religious or moral system or institution (such as CHRISTIANITY or the church). To live this independent way is "authentic" and "courageous" but is inevitably filled with dread, anxiety, and fear of death. Most existentialist thinkers are atheists, finding no meaning or comfort in God and seeing the faithful as weak and ignorant. People must make their own reality intentionally and responsibly. The emphasis on self and HUMANISM may explain the tendency of some existentialists to embrace Adolf HITLER and Nazism because it claimed to be bold and unsentimental. Others (like Frenchmen Sartre and Maurice Merleau-Ponty) embraced LEFT politics, seeing Marxist SOCIALISM as taking the world realistically.

The depressing, alienated thought of existentialism probably reflects the alienation in European society (especially among intellectuals) during the tumultuous 19th and 20th centuries when radical economic and political change and two world wars challenged everything stable and orderly in their culture. In many ways, it is the way a sensitive European mind tried to cope with modernity (industrialism, secularism, INDIVIDUALISM). Having abandoned any traditional religious faith or sense of social order, existentialists fell on themselves as the only reality; their subjective "feelings" were the only truth known to them.

By the late 21st century, existentialism was no longer a prominent philosophy, being replaced either by individualist hedonism or some return to belief in social order and religious truth.

Further Reading

Kotarba, Joseph A., and Fontana, Andrea, eds. *The Existential Self in Society.* Chicago: University of Chicago Press, 1984.

exploitation

To use or "exploit" someone or a group of people without fairly compensating them. Most prominent in the LEFT political theory of Karl MARX, exploitation is usually taking advantage of one economic class by another. So, for example, slave labor is said to be exploited by the masters because slaves work very hard for little pay or return. Marxism claims that all "oppressed" workers are exploited throughout history (e.g., peasants by landlords during the FEUDALISM of the MIDDLE AGES; industrial workers or the proletariat by CAPITALISTS; etc.). Marxist Sociology takes this concept of exploitation (or unfair use of others) and applies it to other social groups (men exploit women, whites exploit people of color, the advanced industrial nations exploit the poor Third World countries, etc.). This perspective sees most relationships as characterized by exploitation—someone is being used and treated unfairly. This leads to the LIBERAL DEMOCRATIC and SOCIALIST political movements to fight on behalf of the exploited and oppressed; to redistribute PROPERTY, power, and status to those who have been exploited; and to establish a society where exploitation will no longer occur (such as in COMMUNISM). In line with Marxism, the source of exploitation is identified with external social systems rather than internal (evil) HUMAN NATURE, so its solution is in social engineering rather than psychological or spiritual transformation.

This predominantly MODERN view of exploitation contrasts with much of ancient and medieval political thought, which sees such unfair use of others as emanating from cruel and selfish human nature or actually being a fair exchange between unequals in society. Who defines whether an act is exploitative (the "victim," the law, the perpetrator, or some dominant culture) affects the outcome of the definition. But the prevalence of this Leftist perspective on exploitation, especially in EGALITARIAN, democratic cultures, has tended to render any one or group with power suspected of exploiting others. Thus the rich, prominent, white, male, heterosexual, First World, and well-educated people are perceived in this view as inevitably privileged oppressors and exploiters.

A further application of this concept occurs in the ENVIRONMENTAL and ANIMAL RIGHTS movements, which present the Earth or "Mother Nature" as being exploited by humans. In this view, people unfairly use up and pollute the natural realm and resources by their superior power. Thus, environmentalists seek to defend Nature from exploitation by humanity.

Further Readings

Elster, J. *Making Sense of Marx,* chap. 4. Cambridge, Eng.: Cambridge University Press, 1985.

Lukes, S. *Marxism and Morality.* Oxford: Clarendon Press, 1985.

Steiner, H. "A liberal theory of exploitation," *Ethics* 94 (1984): 225–41.

F

Fabian/Fabianism

A SOCIALIST movement, prominent in late 19th- and early 20th-century Britain. Formally associated with the Fabian Society (1884–1939) in London, its ideas affected socialist and SOCIAL DEMOCRATIC thought in Europe and the United States. A diverse movement, it included such notable members as author and playwright George Bernard Shaw, author H. G. Wells, writer and social reformer Beatrice Potter Webb, Theosophist Annie Besant, and civil servant/social scientist Sidney Webb.

Named after the Roman general Fabian, who defeated the army of Hannibal by patient resistance, firm resolve, and sudden attack, Fabian socialism believed in the gradual transformation of society from CAPITALISM to socialism by means of talented socialists and technocrats working within the government. Well-educated, highly trained economists and administrators would gradually take over key areas of the government, media, and educational institutions, infuse socialist ideas and practices, and eventually take over the country. Many early LIBERAL Democrats in the United States (1930s–60s) saw themselves in this Fabian strategy, slowly infusing socialism into the United States through peaceful, gradual means. Regulation of business and national standards for education, media, and culture expressed the Fabian goal.

The Fabians saw themselves as enlightened, righteous reformers who brought civilization to the ignorant masses and achieved positions of leadership through their own merit and goodness. In general, they were liberal in extending SUFFRAGE and social benefits to women and the poor, though they eschewed MARXIST ideas of a workers' revolution or the "dictatorship of the proletariat" as vulgar and common. The union between LEFTIST politics and artistic refinement in liberalism found its early expression in Fabian socialism: Both socialist government by an enlightened elite and the sophistication of artistic elegance formed the ideal Fabian society. This image of the ARISTOCRACY of administration and art serving the common good of society was expanded to include civilized northern Europeans taking care of less-advantaged developing-world peoples under a benign paternalism. Most Fabian socialists and liberals rejected traditional religious categories and faith; confident in their own abilities and righteousness, they saw no need for reliance upon God or for doubts about the human ability to improve the world.

Fabianism was criticized by Marxist socialists as too middle class, gradual, and moderate. It was ridiculed by CONSERVATIVES as romantic and self-righteous. Despite these criticisms, Fabianism exercised an enormous influence in Britain, Europe, and the United States through social democratic, Labour Party, and liberal Democratic Party politics from 1900 to the present.

Further Readings

Crossman, R. H. S., ed., *New Fabian Essays*. New York: Praeger, 1952.

Durbin, E. *New Jerusalems*. London: Routledge, 1985.

MacKenzie, N., and MacKenzie, J. *The First Fabians*. Weidenfeld & Nicholson, 1977.

McBriar, A. M. *Fabian Socialism and English Politics 1884–1914*. Cambridge, Eng.: Cambridge University Press, 1966.

Pimlott, B., ed. *Fabian Essays in Socialist Thought*. London: Heineman, 1984.

Pugh, P. *Educate, Agitate, Organize: A Hundred Years of Fabian Socialism*. London: Methuen, 1984.

Shaw, G. B., ed. *Fabian Essays*. London: Allen & Unwin, 1889, 1962.

Webb, S., and Webb, B. *A Constitution for the Socialist Commonwealth of Great Britain*. London: Longmans, Green & Co., 1920.

———. *Industrial Democracy*, 2 vols. London: Longmans, Green & Co., 1897.

Wolfe, W. *From Radicalism to Socialism: Men and Ideas in the Formation of Fabian Socialist Doctrines 1881–1889*. New Haven, Conn.: Yale University Press, 1975.

fascism/fascist

A political theory that emphasizes a unified powerful state to which all individuals and groups submit. Fascist governments existed in NAZI Germany, Italy, and Spain in the 1920s–40s. World War II was largely a war between the fascist countries (with Japan) and the rest of the world. Fascist political parties existed in most other nations (including Britain Ireland, France, and the United States), but they did not take over the government. Fascist governments were led by Adolf HITLER (Germany), Benito MUSSOLINI (Italy), and Francisco Franco (Spain).

Derived from the philosophy of HEGEL, fascism conceives of the nation as an organic unity that subsumes all divisions (classes, individuals, groups) and conflict in society and produces social harmony and peace. The individual and private organizations are to find their fulfillment in this unity of the STATE. Fascism, often called NATIONAL SOCIALISM, rejected both the LIBERAL, CAPITALIST DEMOCRACIES of Britain and the United States and the MARXIST COMMUNISM of the SOVIET UNION. Both liberalism and communism are unjust in the fascist view because they do not represent the interest of the whole nation but rather are the rule of a particular group or class. Historically, fascism was very nationalistic, militaristic, and internationally aggressive; in Germany, it also was highly anti-Semitic and led to the murder of 6 million Jews and 9 million others.

Giovanni GENTILE, the leading Italian fascist philosopher, employed Hegel's DIALECTIC in justifying fascist policy. For him, the human individual is made up of two opposing identities: (1) the particular will (personal desires, interests, goals); and (2) the universal will (the nation's culture, heritage, race, and mission). To be fully "self-realized," the individual must "get in touch" with his universal will, which is the state. Subordination to the fascist state's laws and leader become the way that individuals fulfill their destiny. Fascism used a lot of quasi-religious imagery, while twisting it to cause citizens to worship the state as God. For example, instead of saying, in the Judeo-Christian sense, that the faithful should seek God's will in their lives and find their true God-given identities in serving him, fascism made the state a god that the citizens should serve and, through it, find fulfillment. Fascism, then, becomes a kind of idolatry or worship of false gods. The fascist governments, following NIETZSCHE's idea of a "superman," invariably had a strong, charismatic leader (or Führer in Germany) who supposedly embodied the universal will of the state and stood as a kind of national "messiah."

Fascist governments in Germany, Italy, and Spain claimed to be supportive of religion and the church but only if those religious institutions obeyed the state. Any criticism of the fascist state by Christians led to their prosecution (such as Dietrich BONHOEFFER and The Confessing Church in Nazi Germany) and execution. Fascism favored religions that were nationalistic and submissive and that encouraged citizens to obey the state (CIVIL RELIGION). Similarly, fascist theory supported the traditional family, not because it was divinely ordained, but because it taught loyalty, devotion, and sacrifice outside the self to an "other" (which trained young people to be patriotic and obedient to the state). Fascist societies were TOTALITARIAN in that all private associations became tied to the official government (so the Boy Scouts became the Hitler Youth).

In international relations, the fascist dialectic provided a basis for fascist states invading their neighboring countries and dominating them. Gentile claims that "opposition" and "conciliation" through military defeat is "the eternal rhythm of human social life." Foreign peoples "offend" the fascist nation by hindering the stronger nation's development or rights. So, the fascist nation "overcomes" this "opposition" by attacking

Three-headed monster in armor trampling on religion, literature, and culture amid death and devastation, 1947. Painting by Harry Sternberg. (LIBRARY OF CONGRESS)

them militarily and forcing them to submit to the fascist state's power. Then "unity" is achieved. This fascist reasoning rationalized Germany's invasion and conquest of Poland, France, Austria, and other countries. Such fascist logic justified the brutal murder and oppression of many innocent peoples. Its diabolical theories convinced many in those fascist counties that their aggressive war policies were just and that robbing people of their property was part of the "dialectic of nature." Such twisted logic was supposedly confirmed by the early military successes of the fascist countries and its "might makes right" philosophy.

The swift destruction of fascist states and philosophy after World War II ended this ideology, except in Spain, where it continued into the 1970s. Some Latin American countries (such as Argentina) with close ties to Germany and Spain had fascist military governments but lacked the influence of European fascist regimes.

Seeing fascism as a just alternative to decadent liberal capitalist democracies or to the "dictatorship of the proletariat" in communism, some Western intellectuals (such as T. S. Eliot) sympathized with fascism in the 1930s. Only minority, extremist RIGHT-wing groups (such as the KKK, certain "skinheads," and neo-Nazi groups) adhere to fascist ideals now, as their deceptive and destructive qualities are widely recognized.

Further Readings

Gregor, A. J. *Young Mussolini and the Intellectual Origins of Fascism.* Berkeley: University of California Press, 1979.

Hamilton, A. *The Appeal of Fascism: A Study of Intellectuals and Fascism 1919–1945.* New York: Macmillan, 1971.

Laqueur, W., ed. *Fascism: A Readers' Guide: Analyses, Interpretations, Bibliography.* Berkeley: University of California Press, 1979.

Lyttelton, A., ed. *Italian Fascism from Pareto to Gentile.* London: Cape, 1973.

Mosse, G. L. *Masses and Man.* Detroit: Wayne State University Press, 1980.

Mussolini, B. *Fascism: Doctrine and Institutions.* Rome: Ardita Publishers, 1968.

Nolte, E. *Three Faces of Fascism: Action Française, Italian Fascism, National Socialism.* New York: Mentor, 1969.

Payne, S. G. *Fascism: Comparison and Definition.* Madison: University of Wisconsin Press, 1980.

Primo de Rivera, J. A. *Selected Writings,* Intro. by H. Thomas, ed. London: Cape, 1972.

Rocco, A. *La dottrina politica del fascismo.* 1925.

Sternhell, Z. *Neither Right nor Left: Fascist Ideology in France.* Berkeley: University of California Press, 1986.

Turner, H. A., Jr., ed. *Reappraisals of Fascism.* New York: New Viewpoints, 1975.

Weber, E. *Varieties of Fascism.* Princeton, N.J.: Van Nostrand, 1966.

federalism/federalist/federal

A governmental structure in which two levels of government (central or national and decentralized or state/province) exist within the same country. This double-tiered government is set up by a CONSTITUTION that defines the authority and limits of each level of STATE. For example, in the United States of America, a federal REPUBLIC is established by the U.S. Constitution, which divides power between the national (or federal) government, located in Washington, D.C. (CONGRESS, the president, and the Supreme Court) and the 50 state governments (Virginia, New York, Texas, California, etc.). The decentralized state governments have their own constitutions, delineating the state government's structure (legislature, executive, judiciary). Thus, in federalism, the citizens are under two sets of government (regional and national). Several nations in the world have federal systems, including Canada, Germany, Australia, and India.

Federalism, with its dual government, can be contrasted with "unitary" government, in which all political authority is in the central government (as in parliament in Great Britain), and "confederate" government, in which political authority is entirely in decentralized regimes (such as the ancient Greek or MEDIEVAL German confederations). In each case, any alternative government (provincial in Britain or central in confederacies) is derived from the ultimate source of government. For example, prior to the U.S. Constitution that established American federalism, the country was governed by the Articles of Confederation that recognized sovereignty only in the states, leaving the central, national Congress only with power granted by those states. This lack of independent political authority rendered the conduct and financing of national policy (war, military, trade, commerce, treaties) extremely difficult, so the U.S. Constitution gave specific authority to the central government and left other (primarily domestic or internal) policies to the state governments. This division was partly designed by James MADISON from a Calvinist suspicion of governmental power and its corrupting influence on rulers and from an attempt to divide and distribute power to prevent TYRANNY (either local tyranny of the community or national tyranny of the president). Such CHECKS AND BALANCES are a main motive of federalism. Another reason for establishing federalist states is the attempts to maintain DEMOCRACY over a large territory. By breaking up the large country into regional jurisdictions, the citizens can be closer to government and more involved. Thus, Thomas JEFFERSON advocates a "pyramid of republics" in American federalism. In reality, power in federal systems tends to drift toward the national government, which assumes more and more of the duties and functions of the state governments. By conferring more authority to the national government over CIVIL RIGHTS, education, business regulation, and commerce, the U.S. Supreme Court has effectively created a unitary government in the United States. The tendency toward greater uniformity and efficiency has always caused power to drift toward the central governmental authority. CLASSICAL REPUBLICAN theory warns that this tendency threatens democracy and individual RIGHTS. Various STATES-RIGHTS movements in U.S. history (especially the secession of the Southern states during the American Civil War) resisted this tendency but have not prevented the increasing concentration of political power in the federal government.

Further Readings

Antieau, Chester James. *States' Rights under Federal Constitutions.* London: Oceana Publishers, 1984.

Livingston, W. S. *Federalism and Constitutional Change.* Oxford: Clarendon Press, 1956.

Sawer, K. *Modern Federalism.* London: Pitman Publishing, 1969.

Vile, M. J. C. "Federalism in the United States, Canada and Australia." In *Royal Commission on the Constitution,* I, Cmnd 5460, Research Paper 2. London: H. M. Stationery Off., 1973.

Wheare, K. *Federal Government,* 4th ed. London: Oxford University Press, 1963.

Wheare, K. C. (Kenneth Clinton). *Federal Government,* 3rd ed. London: Oxford University Press, 1953, repr. 1956.

Federalist Papers, The

A series of 85 essays written by Alexander HAMILTON, James MADISON, and John Jay in support of the ratification of the new United States CONSTITUTION. Originally published in various New York newspapers from 1787–88, *The Federalist Papers* were soon being reprinted in newspapers throughout the states and together in book form. They greatly influenced the proratification debate by arguing forcefully and persuasively for the wisdom and efficiency of the new constitutional government. They addressed the common ANTIFEDERALIST, STATES RIGHTS criticisms of the Constitution by showing that the Constitution established a FEDERAL REPUBLIC (not a unitary centralized TYRANNY), giving increased power to the national military and economy but leaving the states considerable control over domestic policy. They explained in detail the philosophy and rationale for the new American REPUBLIC as well as the specific provisions for the national government's structure and limits. *The Federalist Papers* reflected both a SOCIAL CONTRACT view of the state (from John LOCKE) and a Protestant CHRISTIAN perspective (from John CALVIN) on human nature, politics, and society. In the most famous philosophical Paper (#10), James MADISON shows how the Constitution's system of divided powers and CHECKS AND BALANCES comes from a Calvinist appreciation of human sin, envy, and greed, necessitating a limit on the terms and power of people in the government. Madison's famous argument for PLURALISM (that enlarging the social sphere and number of competing interest groups will prevent tyranny and ensure individual liberty) is found in this federalist paper. The ideals of religious LIBERTY, private PROPERTY, free enterprise, FEDERALISM, limited government, and public VIRTUE are expressed throughout *The Federalist Papers*. Consequently, they are considered the classic early commentary on U.S. constitutional government and are frequently consulted by scholars and U.S. Supreme Court justices for the original meaning and intent of the framers of the United States system.

Hamilton wrote the majority of the federalist papers (51), Madison wrote 24, and Jay wrote five. All were published under the pseudonym "Publius." They are credited for persuading a majority of the American colonies (nine of the 13 were required to ratify) to accept the new Constitution and abandon the old confederacy under the Articles of Confederation.

Further Reading

Main, J. T. *The Anti-Federalists*. Chapel Hill: University of North Carolina Press, 1961.

feminism/feminist

A social ideology associated with the women's movement in the Western world during the 19th and 20th centuries. Although a diverse movement, feminists generally agree on three propositions: (1) Men and women are fundamentally equal in rationality and ability; (2) society has historically denied women's EQUALITY with men and has prevented them from fulfilling their human capacities; and (3) women should engage in political ACTIVISM to secure legal, political, and economic equality with men. This feminist theory began during the MODERN, LIBERAL ENLIGHTENMENT, which attacked the traditional MEDIEVAL, patriarchal, and Judeo-CHRISTIAN view of woman as man's "helpmeet" and as primarily devoted to husband and children. An early literary expression of feminism occurred in Mary Wollstonecraft's *Vindication of the Rights of Woman* in 1792. This advocated equal educational, economic, and political RIGHTS and activities for women. During the 19th century in Europe and Britain, the feminist movement focused primarily on SUFFRAGE, or the right of women to vote. John Stuart MILL's *The Subjection of Women* (1869) argued that for purposes of political participation one's sex made no more difference than having red hair. During this period, feminism was largely a middle-class movement, but during the 20th century (as with Rosa LUXEMBURG) a MARXIST or SOCIALIST feminist movement emerged that identified the oppression of women with economic class oppression and EXPLOITATION. In this radical COMMUNIST feminism, the only solution to sex discrimination is the overcoming of CAPITALISM, private PROPERTY, the traditional family, and religion.

In the West, most feminism has involved achieving equal economic opportunity: education, employment, and professional advancement—equal pay for equal work, equal access to traditionally male professions (law, medicine, clergy, military), and executive and administrative positions. This concern for equal status for women has led to social policy concerning such issues as divorce laws, birth control, ABORTION rights, and lesbian rights. These liberal feminist positions are presented as giving females equality and LIBERTY similar to men. The Liberal wing of the American DEMOCRATIC PARTY has adopted most of this feminist agenda; the more conservative REPUBLICAN PARTY has not endorsed it fully.

Contemporary feminist (and postfeminist) theory varies widely from claiming total equality of the sexes to a unique distinctiveness (and superiority) of women, to rejection of all gender identifications (as in

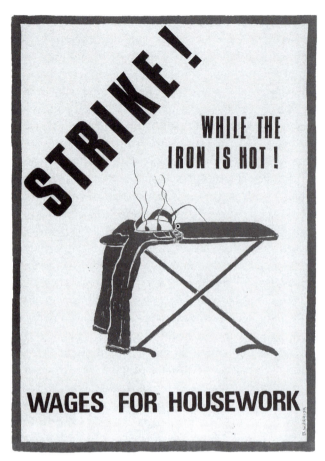

Poster from the Battered Women's Directory Project; Betsy Warrior, artist. (LIBRARY OF CONGRESS)

HOMOSEXUAL, bisexual, and transsexual movements). Other variants include developing-world feminism (which insists that neocolonial women are more oppressed than Northern Hemisphere, Eurocentric women) and ecofeminism (which combines women's rights with ENVIRONMENTALISM). All these forms of feminism are premised on giving women more power.

Further Readings

Beauvoir, S. de. *The Second Sex*, H. M. Parshley, transl. and ed. New York: Vintage Books, 1953, 1968.

Fuller, M. *The Writings of Margaret Fuller,* New York: Viking, 1941.

Leach, W. *True Love and Perfect Union: The Feminist Reform of Sex and Society.* New York: Basic Books, 1980.

Mill, J. S. "The Subjection of Women" (1869). In *The Collected Works of John Stuart Mill,* J. M. Robson, ed., vol. XXI. 1984.

Mitchell, J. *Woman's Estate.* New York: Pantheon Books, 1973.

Richards, J. R. *The Sceptical Feminist: A Philosophical Inquiry.* London: Routledge & Kegan Paul, 1980.

Taylor, B. *Eve and the New Jerusalem.* New York: Pantheon Books, 1983.

Wollstonecraft, M. *A Vindication of the Rights of Woman,* New York: Penguin, 1993.

feudalism/feudal

A political and economic system and culture in Europe during the MIDDLE AGES (roughly 800–1600).

Developed during CHARLEMAGNE's empire, feudalism was essentially a military system to protect Europeans from the invading Magyars and Vikings. This protection was provided by the king by dividing his territory among knights or nobility who usually resided in a walled castle. The nobleman (or prince) ruled the agricultural district around him and provided military protection to the agrarian peasants, who, in return, gave a portion of their agricultural produce and service to this landlord.

The social and political relations that developed in this feudal system, then, involved mutual OBLIGATIONS and honor. Over the years, they became traditions and customs, often accompanied by festivals and religious observances. Because Europe was CHRISTIAN by this time, this medieval social order was integrated into the CATHOLIC faith and even regarded as a holy Roman empire. Social conduct was highly personal (as opposed to formal or legal), and individual or family loyalty duties and TRADITIONS took precedence over purely legal codes. Separate regions were distinguished by often complex social practices and conventions. Society was HIERARCHICAL (by strict order and rank), with the higher ranks (aristocracy, clergy, patriarchs) showing paternalistic authority and care over their subjects and those of lower rank showing respect and deference to their superiors. Thus, feudal society was not marked by INDIVIDUALISM, EQUALITY, or DEMOCRACY. Subjects had no *natural rights* or mobility. This kind of society is often called organic and is compared to the human body (the king as head, the church as heart, peasants and guilds members as hands and feet). MODERN REPUBLICANISM, CAPITALISM, and Protestant Christianity radically altered this feudal system, and by the 19th century, it was supplanted by modernity. The rise of CORPORATISM and fascism in the 20th century was an attempt to restore some aspects of feudalism, but except for a period in Spain, it was unsuccessful. European feudalism is often romanticized (as in the English legends of King Arthur and the knights of the Round Table), but its social unity often masked severe injustices, cruelty, and economic stagnation. Its personal code of honor, the goodness and public service of "the Christian gentleman," and its peaceful agrarian lifestyle, however, seem attractive when compared with modern commercialism, individualism, and INDUSTRIALISM. This nostalgic quality of feudalism reappears in various CONSERVATIVE and Tory movements, including, to some extent, ROMANTICISM and the Green (ENVIRONMENTAL) movement.

Further Reading
Bloch, M. *Feudal Society,* 2 vols., L. A. Manyon, transl. Chicago: University of Chicago Press, 1962.

Fichte, Johann Gottlieb (1762–1814) *German philosopher*

Johann Gottlieb Fichte is best known for his development of transcendental IDEALISM. He was the most influential German philosopher in the period between KANT and HEGEL. Fichte was also a prominent German nationalist; especially in his later years, he abandoned his early emphasis on INDIVIDUALISM and became a proponent of STATE control of education and trade.

The son of a poor weaver, Fichte's education through the gymnasium was financed by a local wealthy farmer who was impressed by the boy's intellectual capabilities. Fichte studied philosophy, theology, and classical literature at Jena and Leipzig Universities, but his sponsor died, and the young philosopher was forced to tutor to support himself. During his studies and tutoring, Fichte became a disciple of Immanuel Kant. In 1791, Fichte met the prominent philosopher, and in an attempt to ingratiate himself, he wrote *Versuch einer Kritik aller Offenbarung (An Attempt of the Critique of All Revelations).* This work applied Kant's philosophy to religion. Kant was so impressed that he helped Fichte get the essay published. Fichte became renowned as a result of the essay.

Although a devotee of Kant, Fichte believed that Kant's philosophy was unfinished and that it was his duty to remove the dogmatism that contemporary thinkers ascribed to Kant's idealism. For Fichte, Kant had worked to prove the objective nature of knowledge but had not developed a philosophical foundation for his idealism. Fichte's theory asserted that only two branches of philosophy are possible: realism and idealism. Realism attempts to deduce knowledge from the material world; idealism develops knowledge

through the powers of REASON. Fichte's idealism was based on the premise that knowledge could only be produced through intuition (the ability of the self to recognize the self as being). Idealism could explain realism, but realism could not explain or measure idealism.

Fichte went on to write on the French Revolution and practical philosophy. From 1794–99, he taught at Jena University. Fichte asserted that the existent moral order in the world confirmed the existence of God and that there was no need to recognize a specific special or material being. By endeavoring to attribute a consciousness to God, Fichte contended that people limited the deity. In the transcendentalist tradition, he argued that people should look within themselves to find their true nature: Morality necessitated autonomy of thought. However, this viewpoint led to the philosopher to be accused of being an atheist, and he was fired from Jena University in 1799. He moved to Berlin, where he became more mystical in his writings, partially as a result of friendships with prominent Romantics of the day.

During the Napoleonic period, Fichte became a German nationalist and presented a series of lectures in support of patriotism. In 1810, he joined the new Prussian University in Berlin, where he taught until his death. In spite of his earlier emphasis on individual autonomy, in his later years, Fichte contended that individuals were actually "echoes" of the state and needed to be molded through education and state propaganda. Fichte also argued that the state should control commerce and trade.

Further Reading
Breazeale, D., and Rockmore, T., eds. *Fichte: Historical Contexts/Contemporary Controversies.* Amherst, Mass.: Humanity Books, 1994.

Filmer, Sir Robert (1588–1653) *English political theorist and royalist*

Filmer developed the theoretical defense of DIVINE RIGHT OF KINGS and royal ABSOLUTISM in England. Against the REPUBLICAN and SOCIAL-CONTRACT theories of John LOCKE, Filmer argued that all government is based in the authority of the father, and so the patriarchal (male MONARCHY) government is ordained by God. Like the French absolutist theorist BODIN, Filmer supported his arguments with the Bible, English constitutional history, and inferences from the nature of the human family. He claimed that God granted authority to Adam and his descendants, so patriarchal rule was evident throughout Hebrew, Greek, Roman, and European civilizations. DEMOCRATIC EQUALITY violated this natural and divine order and would lead to chaos and anarchy. Filmer attacked a wide rage of MODERN thinkers, including Locke, HOBBES, MILTON, and GROTIUS. Taking an extreme view of the ruler's absolute SOVEREIGNTY, Filmer claimed that absolute obedience to the state was just and that any resistance or even criticism of the king was contrary to God's will. This went far beyond the traditional CHRISTIAN view of civil obedience (as expressed by St. AUGUSTINE and St. Thomas AQUINAS). By using a family model of the polity, Filmer imposed patriarchal authority on all "subjects as children." The Calvinist system of CHECKS AND BALANCES, dividing power, was unworkable to Filmer. Even the church could not serve as a balance on secular political power.

Sir Robert Filmer lived as a typical MEDIEVAL English gentleman. He attended Trinity College, Cambridge, was knighted by King James I in 1618, married an heiress of the bishop of Ely, and spent his life on an estate in Kent. He associated with prominent clergy, antiquarians, and political and literary figures. His chief work was the book *Patriarcha* published posthumously in 1680.

Filmer expressed his royal absolutist ideas just as British monarchy and patriarchy were coming to an end. In 1688, the Glorious Revolution established parliamentary supremacy in Great Britain. Except for occasional nostalgic remembrances and a few limited revivals (as among such slave-owning U.S. southerners as George FITZHUGH), Filmer's ideals of patriarchal government went out of fashion by the late 17th century.

Further Readings

Daly, J. *Sir Robert Filmer and English Political Thought*. Toronto: University of Toronto Press, 1979.

Filmer, Robert, Sir. *Patriarcha and other writings*, Johann P. Sommerville, ed. Cambridge, Eng.: Cambridge University Press, 1991.

———. *Patriarcha and Other Political Works*, P. Laslett, ed. and intro. Oxford, Eng.: Basil Blackwell, 1949.

Laslett, P. *Sir Robert Filmer: The Man Versus the Whig Myth*. 1948.

Locke, J. *Two Treatises of Government (1689)*, P. Laslett, ed. and intro. Cambridge, Eng.: Cambridge University Press, 1965, 1970.

Schochet, G. J. *Patriarchalism in Political Thought*. New York: Basic Books, 1975.

———. "Sir Robert Filmer: some new bibliographic discoveries." In *The Library*, 5th ser., 26 (1971).

Sidney, A. *Discourses Concerning Government*, (1968; written ca. 1682), J. Robertson, ed. 1772.

First Amendment

In the U.S. CONSTITUTION, the first provision added to the founding political document guaranteed FREEDOM of religion, speech, press, and assembly. This amendment was added in 1789, almost immediately after the ratification of the original Constitution (and was a condition for several states ratifying the U.S. Constitution), to allay fears that the new national government might violate individual RIGHTS to LIBERTY of conscience, thought, expression, and popular assembly. The amendment reads: "Congress shall make no law respecting an establishment of religion, or prohibiting the free exercise thereof; or abridging the freedom of speech, or of the press; or the right of the people peaceably to assemble, and to petition the Government for a redness of grievances." These First Amendment rights (sometimes called CIVIL RIGHTS) became the basis for a whole body of constitutional law, in which, for more than 200 years, the U.S. Supreme Court applied these principles to practical matters of religious liberty, freedom of speech and press, and popular assembly. U.S. constitutional law interpretation is largely over this First Amendment.

Further Reading

Sheffer, Martin S. *God Versus Caesar: Belief, Worship and Proselytizing under the First Amendment*. Albany: State University of New York Press, 1999.

Fitzhugh, George (1806–1881)   *U.S. political theorist and proslavery advocate*

Born into a southern plantation family (in Virginia), George Fitzhugh became a leading proslavery writer before the American Civil War. Combining English Tory CONSERVATISM with an almost MARXIST critique of northern CAPITALIST society, Fitzhugh is unique in U.S. political thought. He attacked all MODERN political thought (including that of John LOCKE and Thomas JEFFERSON) for its INDIVIDUALISM, LIBERTY, and SOCIAL-CONTRACT perspectives. From a MEDIEVAL patriarchal view of society as made up of organic dependencies and HIERARCHICAL personal relationships, Fitzhugh defended black slavery as natural (and beneficial for African Americans) and feared that DEMO-

CRATIC LIBERALISM would lead to ANARCHY and chaos. If the slaves were freed, Fitzhugh argued, women would demand equality, and the traditional family and society would be destroyed. This reactionary attitude, like Sir Robert FILMER's, was premised on the patriarchs of the Hebrew Bible, CLASSICAL Greek and Roman civilization, and the CATHOLIC Middle Ages. Like the British conservatives and ROMANTICS from which Fitzhugh derived much of his philosophy, he identified the problems of Modern society not with insufficient FREEDOM, but with insufficient AUTHORITY.

From this hierarchical philosophy, Fitzhugh claimed that southern slavery was more humane than northern capitalism. The relationship of master to slave in the South was open, honest authority; the tyranny of capitalism over "wage slaves" was hidden and hypocritical. Institutionalized slavery was paternalistic and beneficent; free-market labor was cruel and EXPLOITATIVE. The southern slaveholders accepted their responsibility to take care of their workers; heartless capitalism used workers and cast them aside. The "freedom" of wage labor was an illusion, and democratic liberty a deception. "The Negro slaves of the South," Fitzhugh wrote in *Cannibals All!* (1854), "are the happiest, and in some sense, the freest people in the world." By contrast, the workers in northern industrial cities "must work or starve. He is more of a slave than the Negro because he works longer and harder for less allowance. . . ." Modern freedom then is "an empty and delusive mockery."

Fitzhugh was unique among proslavery southern writers in not only defending his institution but going on to attack northern society and hypocrisy. He saw the tendency of democratic liberalism to rebel against any authority, ending in equalitarian anarchy. "All modern philosophy converges to a single point—the overthrow of all government. . . .," stated Fitzhugh. If black slavery were abolished, feminism, socialism, and children's rights would follow.

Fitzhugh's traditional hierarchical organic philosophy was defeated with the Northern Union victory over the South in the American Civil War, but it continued to influence radical conservative thought in the United States.

Foucault, Michel (1926–1984) *French philosopher*

Born in Poitiers and educated at the École Normale Supérieure in Paris, Foucault became one of the leading French intellectuals of the 20th century. After serving in the philosophy departments at the University of Clermont-Ferrand and the University of Vincennes in the 1960s, Foucault was elected in 1970 to the highest academic post in France, the Collège de France, where he assumed the chair of professor of the history of systems of thought. During the 1970s and 1980s, his international reputation flourished as he taught and lectured all over the world. Foucault died from an AIDS-related illness in 1984.

Foucault's philosophy was greatly influenced by the German philosopher Friedrich NIETZSCHE. As a historian of knowledge, Foucault sought to show that there is no essential meaning to things. History does not possess an inherent order by which it unfolds; rather order is a product of the writing of history itself. To write a history of the past is to view it from a particular perspective in the present and to interpret past events in light of current concerns. Foucault referred to this understanding of the historically changing frameworks of knowledge as "genealogy." Through genealogical analyses, Foucault examined how "regimes of practices" come to define the rules by which certain ideas and beliefs are defined as true or false at different times in history. He was especially concerned with the ways in which POWER is employed within a society to structure relationships of domination or exclusion as well as to affect the formation of self-identities.

In his first major work, *Madness and Civilization* (1961), Foucault analyzed the distinction between reason and madness as defined during the early MODERN period. Prior to this period, madness was regarded as a form of experience with its own reason, often associated with genius, art, and religion. In the Modern era, however, madness came to be regarded as the complete opposite of reason and as the sign of antisocial tendencies that required medical treatment for their elimination. Concomitant with the rise of therapeutic practices in the 17th and 18th centuries was the development of punitive institutions and practices. In *Discipline and Punish* (1975), Foucault reviewed the "birth of the prison" in conjunction with other "disciplinary" practices that deploy power within assorted institutions—the army, the school, and the factory—to train the bodies of individuals. The modern prison (or school), for example, utilized the technology of constant surveillance (either real or perceived) to shape the embodied behavior of the prisoner (or student) toward the goal of self-discipline. For Foucault, such disciplinary techniques demonstrate the intimate linkage of knowledge to power. Foucault later referred to government techniques that seek to harness and control the bodies of citizens, even through health care and welfare systems, as forms of "bio-power."

Foucault also argued that the post-MODERN critique of political LEGITIMACY is not merely a simple skepticism about ENLIGHTENMENT ideals, but a recognition that reason and power are not inherently distinct. A significant facet of POST-MODERNISM is its criticism of the controversial assumption of modernity that legitimate AUTHORITY is necessarily opposed to domination and repression. Yet Foucault was careful to note that this does not mean that there is no distinction between authority and domination. Instead, what must be realized is that there are distinct and heterogeneous modalities of exercising power that are characteristic of authority as well as of freedom and domination. Consequently, authority cannot be regarded either as a form of action opposed to power or as an institution that merely wields power, but as a mechanism of political management that is composed by the fluid exercise of power throughout society. For Foucault, there is no justification for authority that completely transcends power and no guarantee that the exercise of authority will be constrained by the demands of a universal rationality.

The general thrust of Foucault's analysis of social and political institutions, then, was not the elimination of authority—that would presume the elimination of power—rather, it was the recognition that authority is constituted through the historically shifting and contextual uses of power, such that its legitimacy does not transparently derive from either NATURAL RIGHTS or rational consent.

Further Reading

Dreyfus, H., and Rabinow, P. *Michel Foucault: Beyond Structuralism and Hermeneutics.* Chicago: University of Chicago Press, 1983.

Fourier, Charles (1772–1837) *French social theorist*

Born and educated in Besançon, Fourier developed his social theory while working for much of his life as a minor business employee. His first major work, *Théorie des quatre mouvements et des destinées générales*
(*The Social Destiny of Man; or Theory of the Four Movements*), was published in 1808. Fourier argued that the social world and the physical universe were created by a benevolent deity and ordered according to a divine plan, although the plan had not been carried out practically in the social realm. According to Fourier, the social world and natural universe would evolve through eight ascending stages. Within the social evolutionary process, happiness, unity, and harmony would replace misery, division, and civilization. Social transformation must be driven by the complete release of the 13 passions implanted in human beings, yet repressed in civilization. These passions include the five senses; the "social" passions of friendship, love, ambition, and family feeling; the "distributive" passions for intrigue, diversification, and combination of pleasures; and the supreme passion of harmony, which synthesizes all of the lower passions.

Fourier advocated reconstruction of society based on the release of the passions and the attainment of harmony. Known as Fourierism, Fourier's doctrine of social change recommended the division of society into *phalanges,* or phalanxes. As conceived by Fourier, the *phalange* was to be a small cooperative community of fewer than 2,000 people. Each *phalange* was to be independent and self-subsistent and organized in such a way that the different interests, capabilities, and tastes of each member could be freely expressed and productively combined. Fourier was critical of the extreme inequality of wealth that resulted from the competitive nature of CAPITALISM and believed that small, cooperative communities would distribute wealth more equitably. Indeed, Fourier suggested that *phalanges* would be highly successful economic systems insofar as each member of the community would contribute his or her unique talent to the means of production and would receive compensation based on the productivity of the *phalange* as a whole. *Phalanges* would therefore be less wasteful than large capitalist economies and provide each member with incentive for contributing to the success of the entire community.

Fourier maintained that *phalanges* would both perfect humanity's social passion and provide for the pursuit and satisfaction of individual desires. The communal character of the *phalange* would inspire respect for the diversity of individual interests and passions and would also prevent social oppression and the "civilized" demand for bland conformity. Ultimately, Fourier believed, numerous *phalanges* would form loose associations around the world, and all people would live together harmoniously.

Attempts were made to put into practice Fourier's ideas of utopian SOCIALISM, most notably at Brook Farm in Massachusetts, between 1841 and 1847.

Further Reading
Beecher, J. *Charles Fourier: The Visionary and His World.* Berkeley: University of California Press, 1987.

Frankfurt School

The members of the "Frankfurt School" were inspired by the writings of Karl MARX. The school was formed in 1923 as part of the University of Frankfurt in Germany, taking the formal name of the *Institut für Sozialforschung* (Institute for Social Research). Established by Felix Weil, the first director of the institute was Carl Grünberg. The unique identity of the institute began to take shape after Max HORKHEIMER assumed the directorship in 1930. Horkheimer recruited a number of leading German intellectuals whose names are now permanently linked with the Frankfurt School, including Theodor W. Adorno, Erich Fromm, and Herbert MARCUSE. Jürgen HABERMAS is generally considered to represent the "second generation" of the Frankfurt School.

Although informed by a number of disciplines ranging from philosophy to psychology, sociology and political science, the work of the Frankfurt School has come to be referred to as CRITICAL THEORY. As developed by the members of the Frankfurt School, critical theory provides an analysis of existing conditions in society, a diagnosis of its faults, and recommendations for its radical transformation. The different approaches characteristic of critical theory were unified by the influence of Marxist philosophy, finding expression in strong critiques of CAPITALISM and the fetishism of technology in MODERN society.

Following the NAZI rise to power, the institute was forced to leave Germany. From 1933 to 1935, it was located in Geneva, Switzerland, after which it moved to New York City. In 1941 the institute was again relocated to California, eventually returning to the University of Frankfurt in 1953. The early work of the institute focused on the development of authoritarianism and FASCISM, and studies were conducted to examine the influence of AUTHORITY on the cultural and political attitudes of the German working class. These studies led to the later elaboration of the "authoritar-

ian personality" as a feature of individuals in modern society. The Frankfurt School theorists argued that individuals become indoctrinated through mechanisms of power to desire conformity and self-repression. The widespread existence of the authoritarian personality was then used to account for the popular support of contemporary TOTALITARIAN regimes.

The members of the Frankfurt School also extensively analyzed the "rationalization" of society. They maintained that, concomitant with the rise to dominance of the natural sciences, modern society has become obsessed with "instrumental" rationality, that is, the function of reason for the purpose of organizing efficient means for a given end. Within modern economic and political systems, efficiency is considered the only lens through which to view human activity. One result of the emphasis on instrumental rationality has been the gradual impoverishment of human existence. Creativity, imagination, pleasure, and individual autonomy are now regarded as obstacles to the efficient production of consumer goods and an increasingly inhuman technology. Another result described by the Frankfurt School was that a narrow focus on instrumental rationality undermines the role of moral reason in evaluating the goals of human activity, as well as the means used to achieve them. They pointed out that, in itself, efficiency cannot guarantee the morality of any desired goal or means used to achieve that goal. The Nazis, for example, developed and employed advanced science and technology for the purpose of exterminating millions of human beings in the most efficient way possible. Surely, the barbarity of the Nazis' actions demonstrates the irrationality of treating all things, including human beings, as mere objects.

The later work of the members of the Frankfurt School continued to explore the various ways that power and authority are utilized to control nearly all aspects of social life. The "culture industry," formed by the extension of technology into the mass media (radio, newspaper, television, and film), constitutes one especially effective system through which capitalism is able to maintain an all-pervasive influence on individuals' opinions, needs, and desires. According to the Frankfurt School, the culture industry has contributed to the entrenchment of the status quo and to the formation of a homogeneous, "one-dimensional" society. Given the conclusions reached in their works, it should come as no surprise that the members of the Frankfurt School became increasingly pessimistic about the prospects for revolutionary social change and human liberation.

Further Reading

Wiggershaus, R. *The Frankfurt School: Its Histories, Theories, and Political Significance.* Cambridge, Mass.: MIT Press, 1995.

Franklin, Benjamin (1706–1790) *American statesman, scientist, and writer*

Benjamin Franklin is best known for his active role in the American Revolution and the founding of the CONSTITUTION and as providing a classic American philosophy of DEMOCRACY, EQUALITY, hard work, and CHRISTIAN ETHICS. He was raised a Quaker in Philadelphia and served in both the Continental Congress during the American Revolution and the Constitutional Convention. In the latter, he is remembered, during a difficult conflict in the proceedings, for urging the delegates to prayer and the seeking of God's guidance in forming the new government. When a citizen asked Franklin what form of government the new Constitution created he said "A REPUBLIC, if you can keep it." Alternately advocating popular government; freedom of speech, press, economics, and religion; progress; and scientific knowledge, Franklin still remained skeptical of human motives and VIRTUE. He expressed the common American culture of realism, humor, the Protestant work ethic and faith in PROGRESS through his publications *The Pennsylvania Gazette* and *Poor Richard's Almanac*. Simple homespun wisdom, unpretentious manners, and common sense found expression in Franklin's thought. It affected generations of young Americans who read his *Autobiography* in which his life showed the success of following 13 virtues: temperance, silence, order, resolution, frugality, industry, sincerity, justice, moderation, cleanliness, tranquility, chastity, and humility. This distillation of CLASSICAL and CHRISTIAN virtues formed the American creed until the latter 20th century, when consumerism, moral decadence, and rebellion ridiculed these virtues as quaint and ridiculous. Still the American ethic of honesty, hard work, and piety draw from Franklin's legacy. The American culture that sees material success resulting from moral conduct is embodied in Franklin's life.

Politically, he favored universal SUFFRAGE, free public education, unicameral legislatures, and a government-stimulated economy. He opposed slavery,

Benjamin Franklin, portrait by Charles Willson Peale. (LIBRARY OF CONGRESS)

encouraged benevolent projects (libraries, hospitals), and rejected welfare programs that caused sloth and laziness. A self-made man, he became wealthy through hard work, invention, and political connections. As a colonial trade diplomat to England and ambassador to France, Franklin associated with the famous and prominent leaders in Europe and gained a cosmopolitan sophistication. His scientific discoveries in electricity made him world famous. A deist in religion, he nevertheless supported the Christian revivalist George WHITEFIELD and saw Christian morality as essential to American democracy and social harmony.

Further Readings

Becker, C. *Benjamin Franklin: A Biographical Sketch.* Ithaca, N.Y.: Cornell University Press, 1946.

Conner, P. *Poor Richard's Politics: Benjamin Franklin and the New American Order.* New York: Oxford University Press, 1965.

Franklin, B. *The Autobiography of Benjamin Franklin,* L. W. Labaree et al., eds. New Haven, Conn.: Yale University Press, 1964.

———. *The Complete Poor Richard's Amanacks published by Benjamin Franklin,* W. J. Bell, ed. Barre, Mass.: Imprint Society, 1970.

———. *The Papers of Benjamin Franklin,* L. W. Labaree et al., eds. 23 vols. New Haven, Conn.: Yale University Press, 1959– .

Stourzh, G. *Benjamin Franklin and American Foreign Policy.* Chicago: University of Chicago Press, 1954.

Van Doren, C. *Benjamin Franklin.* New York: Viking Press, 1938.

fraternity

Literally "brotherhood," or the political idea that all citizens or members of a group are close and related like brothers in a family. This has been applied in Western political thought in numerous ways. In the Bible, the supposedly warm ties between kin brothers is destroyed by envy and murder (when one of the first two brothers Cain murdered his brother Abel, another son of Adam and Eve, committing fratricide [Genesis 4:7; 33:1–11; 50:19–20]). Similarly, the intended love and mutual protection of brothers is violated when Joseph's brothers (again out of envious malice) sell him into slavery. In the CHRISTIAN Bible, the saints, who acknowledge Jesus as their lord and savior, become spiritual brothers, siblings in the faith (Galatians 3:38; Colossians 3:11; I Peter 2:17). Christ himself declares that his brothers are those who obey the will of God (Matthew 12:50). The church designation in Holy Orders of men (monks) as "friars" signifies this spiritual brotherhood. An imitation of this in pagan religious orders, like the Masons and other secret societies, often refer to themselves as a brotherhood: All imply a bond to each other and loyalty to a common group and purpose as strong as blood or family relations.

In ancient Greek political thought (as in ARISTOTLE), this is closely associated with "friendship" (or *philia*)—a particularly close intimate relationship that can occur between fellow citizens, family members, and even master and slave. Often, *adelphia* (brotherhood) is linked to the military, fellow-warriors or soldiers tied to each other by honor, patriotism, and common sacrifice (even to death). Roman thought emphasizes this military element.

Each of these conceptions of fraternity employs an exclusive view of the membership. Like modern collegiate fraternities, the brotherhood is distinctive by excluding others, forming a tight bond among those exclusively included. The bond of Israel (God's chosen people) is defined by the exclusion of outsiders (the gentile). The "saved" Christians become adopted brothers through the Son of God, Je-

sus Christ; the brotherhood of Greek citizens is contrasted with non-Greek barbarians; an ISLAMIC brotherhood is united against "the infidel" non-Muslims.

MODERN EGALITARIAN DEMOCRACY tends to diminish fraternity by attacking any exclusiveness, insisting that all humans are equal despite differences and that fraternities' separateness denies universal humanity. So, for example, the LIBERAL American trend toward prohibiting all discrimination against any individual by clubs, churches, civic organizations, or private groups on the basis that any exclusion is wrong prevents fraternal relationships from developing. The backlash against this legally imposed uniformity is sometimes expressed in radically racist or nationalist groups similar to FASCISM. Because the strong affectionate ties of fraternity are rejected by liberal egalitarian democracy, they sometimes come out in exaggerated group loyalties, such as CULTS.

The leading scholar of this concept, Wilson Carey MCWILLIAMS, traces its influence in the social, religious, cultural, and political history of the United States in his book *The Idea of Fraternity in America* (1973). Included in McWilliams's analysis are the themes of brotherhood in the CIVIL RIGHTS movement, various religious revivals, and several political philosophies in the United States.

Further Readings
Freud, S. "Totem and Taboo." In *The Complete Psychological Works of Sigmund Freud,* J. Srachey, ed., transl, vol. XIII. London: Hogarth Press, 1971.

Hutter, H. *Politics as Friendship.* Waterloo, Ont.: Wilfrid Laurier University Press, 1978.

Ignatieff, M. *The Needs of Strangers.* New York: Viking Press, 1985.

McWilliams, W. C. *The Idea of Fraternity in America.* Berkeley: University of California Press, 1973.

Nelson, B. *The Idea of Usury: From Tribal Brotherhood to Universal Otherhood.* Chicago: University of Chicago Press, 1949.

Simmel, G. *The Sociology of Georg Simmel,* K. Wolff, ed., transl. New York: Free Press, 1950.

Stephen, J. F. *Liberty, Equality, Fraternity.* London: Cambridge University Press, 1875.

freedom

One of the most important and complex ideas in political thought; in MODERN philosophy possibly the most central concept along with its corollaries, INDIVIDUALISM, EQUALITY, and DEMOCRACY. *Freedom* is also expressed as LIBERTY.

A helpful approach to defining freedom was offered by Sir Isaiah Berlin in his piece "Two Concepts of Liberty" (1957), which divides freedom into negative and positive freedom. Negative freedom is the individual's freedom *from* some obstacle (slavery, bondage, prison, legal, moral or cultural restraint) to free movement. Freedom, then, is the absence of external control. The liberty of movement, action, thought, impulse, passion, and so on, without someone, institution, culture, or law saying "you can't do that." Such unrestricted freedom characterizes Thomas HOBBES's vision of the STATE OF NATURE, which leads to competition, conflict, and self-destruction. Positive freedom is the individual's freedom *to* some accomplishment or substantive achievement. So, the freedom to be well educated or to have a job or wealth or medical care is positive freedom. An example of these contrasting views of liberty might be between the economic systems of CAPITALISM (or free enterprise) and SOCIALISM (or a planned economy). In the capitalist United States, anyone is free to start a business, but there is no guarantee he or she will succeed or become wealthy; no law prohibits you from trying, but society doesn't provide substantive support. In the socialist former SOVIET UNION, by contrast, individuals were forbidden from starting private businesses (that is, denied negative freedom) but were guaranteed employment, housing, health care, and retirement by the STATE (so they had positive freedom). The negative freedom system claims that economic freedom, intellectual and religious, actually leads to substantive abundance of PROPERTY, knowledge, or goodness. The positive freedom view claims that only results-oriented liberty is true freedom.

Various major political thinkers have approached the subject of political freedom in different ways. PLATO's *Republic* sees individual freedom best realized in the knowledge of and training of one's innate capacities and their use in the service of the whole society. Thus one's freedom must be strictly ordered and directed to the good of the just state. Purely individual freedom leads to frustration and delusion. Only the disciplined, well-educated person is truly free. An undisciplined individual freedom (as in DEMOCRACY) produces unhappy, foolish people and unjust government. Freedom, as a concept, is relatively unimportant for the CLASSICAL thinkers, who regard VIRTUE, JUSTICE, and harmony as more significant. ARISTOTLE discusses freedom in substantive terms of the Greek citizen being free by rising above "mere" economic (animal) existence to rational, ethical (human) activity. Real freedom is the realization of one's human telos, or potential, in fully developed reason, speech, and moral choice and action. This requires much education, modeling, and participation in the public realm. For the CHRISTIAN thinkers, St. Paul, St. AUGUSTINE and St. Thomas AQUINAS (as well as, later, John CALVIN, Martin LUTHER, and John WINTHROP), a person's natural liberty is prone to evil (murder, theft, adultery, etc.) because human nature is sinful. Obedience to God's will produces true freedom or "the liberty where with Christ hath made us free." So, Christian liberty involves escaping the bondage or slavery of sin through faith in Jesus Christ and the transformation of the individual through the Holy Spirit. This freedom is internal and can exist even in oppressive political social circumstances. The government should protect "moral liberty" (the right to do good) but not "natural liberty" (to individual sinful preferences).

John LOCKE, the archetypical modern British LIBERAL, declares that people are "free, equal, and independent." This human freedom to follow one's economic, religious, and social interest is not, for Locke, "license" to do whatever one wants but is constrained by the law of nature, which reason tells you is to never use your freedom to harm anyone else's rights to life, liberty, or property. For Locke, reasonable people restrain their freedom so as not to hurt others in their lives, health, liberty, or possessions; that is, individual freedom is not to kill, steal, or enslave. The state is established to punish those (criminals) who do not respect the RIGHTS of others and therefore abuse their freedom.

ROUSSEAU, the French liberal, sees freedom in the positive social sense: Freedom is "obeying laws one has had a part in making." This collectivist GENERAL WILL conception of freedom goes into MARXISM and FASCISM—freedom as obedience to the totality or state. BURKE criticizes this notion of liberty as alternately licentious and barbaric; his liberty is within historic British TRADITIONS.

John Stuart MILL applies British liberalism to the freedom of the mind. His arguments for intellectual liberty (in *On Liberty*) against custom and convention include these: (1) A new or controversial viewpoint may be true, and suppressing it will rob humanity of useful truth; (2) even if the obnoxious view is false, the defeating of it by truth will strengthen the correct view. The best society, for Mill, will be full of such critical thinkers and tolerant social liberty of conscience and intellect.

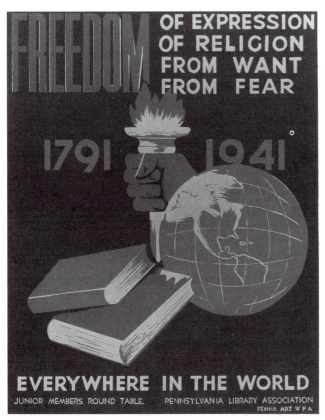

OF EXPRESSION
OF RELIGION
FROM WANT
FROM FEAR

1791 1941

EVERYWHERE IN THE WORLD
JUNIOR MEMBERS ROUND TABLE. PENNSYLVANIA LIBRARY ASSOCIATION
PENNA ART W P A

Poster promoting President Franklin Delano Roosevelt's "Four Freedoms." (LIBRARY OF CONGRESS)

Much of Western "freedom of the press" and academic freedom is premised in this Millian perspective.

For Marxist COMMUNIST thought, "bourgeois" CAPITALIST freedom is an illusion that enslaves the working class and trivializes true human liberty. Only in communism will the individual be truly free from ALIENATION, meaningless labor, and oppression. The temporary tyranny of the "dictatorship of the proletariat" is worth this ultimate heaven of communist society.

EXISTENTIALISM asserts the necessity of individual freedom in a meaningless universe and the personal responsibility to make meaning out of one's life.

In contemporary political thought, LIBERTARIAN theorists argue for absolute freedom of the individual from government taxation and laws to protect the citizen from himself (such as the "victimless crimes" of drug use, prostitution, and suicide). For Libertarians, such as Robert NOZICK, the state should not tax some (wealthy) people to aid other (poor) ones or protect individuals from themselves. Earlier, SOCIAL DARWINISM made a similar argument that the weak and foolish

should be free to destroy themselves, die out, and leave the strong and clever to survive and succeed.

Freedom will remain a prominent topic for political discussion and debate because it touches the very essence of human nature.

Further Readings

Berlin, I. "Two Concepts of Liberty." In *Four Essays on Liberty.* London: Oxford University Press, 1969.

Gray, J., and Pelczynski, Z., eds. *Conceptions of Liberty in Political Philosophy.* New York: St. Martin's Press, 1984.

Rawls, J. *A Theory of Justice.* Cambridge, Mass.: Belknap Press of Harvard University Press, 1972.

Ryan, A., ed. *The Idea of Freedom.* Oxford, Eng.: Oxford University Press, 1979.

French Enlightenment

An intellectual movement in France from roughly 1715 to 1789 that advocated REPUBLICANISM, human EQUALITY, reason as the true source of knowledge, social progress through science and education, and optimism over human improvement and perfection. Like the ENLIGHTENMENT generally, the French variant was critical of political ABSOLUTISM (MONARCHY), traditional religion (especially CATHOLIC CHRISTIANITY), social HIERARCHY (MEDIEVAL class system) and economic monopoly, luxury, and decadence. The leading thinkers of this French Enlightenment included VOLTAIRE, ROUSSEAU, MONTESQUIEU, DIDEROT, and CONDORCET (sometimes referred to as the *philosophes*). They produced an *Encyclopédia,* which embodied their enlightenment view of life and the world. It relied heavily on scientific materialism, empiricism, and radical social theories. Claiming to advance LIBERTY, it challenged all traditional family, social, governmental, and religious standards, elevating irreverence to a high status. It ridiculed the hypocrisy of the church, the foolishness of rulers, and the superstitions of common people. Its faith in humanistic PROGRESS drew from Sir Francis BACON and its REPUBLICANISM from John LOCKE. Most French Enlightenment thinkers were not Christians, but Unitarians, deists, or atheists. Their ideas culminated in the French Revolution of 1789 and were spread across Europe by the French invasions led by Napoleon. They believed their ideas would advance civilization, but more traditionally minded people saw their enlightenment as darkness.

Further Readings

Brumfitt, J. H. *The French Enlightenment.* London: Macmillan & Company, 1972.

Cassirer, E. *The Philosophy of the Enlightenment.* Princeton, N.J.: Princeton University Press, 1951.

Cranston, M. *Philosophers and Pamphleteers.* Oxford, Eng.: Oxford University Press, 1986.

Hampson, N. *The Enlightenment.* New York: Pelican, 1968.

Hazard, P. *European Thought in the Eighteenth Century.* Cleveland: World Publishing Co., 1954.

Wade, I. O. *The Intellectual Origins of the French Enlightenment.* Princeton, N.J.: Princeton University Press, 1971

Freud, Sigmund (1856–1939) *Austrian psychiatrist, founder of psychoanalysis, and social philosopher*

Freud is best known for developing the psychoanalytic method of psychological therapy, including examination of the subconscious mind, dream interpretation, and hypnosis. He divided the human psyche (or nature) into three parts: (1) the id, or the primitive animal impulses toward survival, sexual satisfaction, consumption, and violence; (2) the ego, or human reason and intelligence that orders and restrains the id to allow a person to function normally; and (3) the superego, or internalized authority from social morals (in family—especially father—government, church, and God). For Freudian psychoanalysis, an emotionally "healthy" person has a balanced psyche: The rational ego controls the worst animal instincts of the id but is not overly repressed by the superego. If the id is excessively active, an individual acts like a criminal, following animal passions to kill, steal, and rape. If the superego is overbearing, the individual is obsessed with order, rules, and guilt. Freud's theory that humans are driven primarily by libidinal (sexual) drives (egos) that lead to EXPLOITATION and destruction of others and that require social restraint leads to his social philosophy.

Sexual drives, or the "life impulse," can be channeled constructively into work and artistic creativity, but these are usually a competitive, destructive force. In *Civilization and Its Discontents* (1930), Freud portrays human history and society as violent, cruel, oppressive, and vicious because of humanity's evil nature. This pessimistic view of human nature caused him to ridicule political systems (like COMMUNISM) that presumed that people are naturally good and capable of creating a just, peaceful society. Freud rejected that ENLIGHTENMENT optimism (as in ROUSSEAU) that assumed that changing a human's social environment would improve one's character. Although raised Jew-

ish, Freud was a scientific atheist, calling religion an "illusion" used to dupe and control the masses (see *The Future of an Illusion*). His emphasis on human evil and sin compared with that of St. AUGUSTINE, but Freud's atheism offered no hope of redemption through Christ or a future heaven. Human life and society, for Freud, is a kind of hell, the individual torn between conflicting impulses; ". . . the bearer and . . . the victim of civilization;" loaded down with unsatisfied desires, frustrated impulses, and guilt feelings, unameliorated even by worldly accomplishments or getting drunk. When Freud was dying with mouth cancer, he willingly submitted to being killed by a drug overdose.

The modern world was for him a mixture of lazy, stupid masses and ruthless dictators. Only low expectations, the rule of rational men, and realistic economics (market CAPITALISM) could lead to a moderately healthy state. A "good" society, for Freud, would be one with sufficient order and authority to prevent the mass crime and ANARCHY of the unrestrained id, but not so controlling that it produced massive guilt and psychological neuroses.

Although not strictly a political thinker, Freud's psychological therapy methods (widely adopted in the West) and the sociological assumptions underlying them greatly affected 20th-century political culture in Europe and America.

Further Readings
Freud, S. *Civilization and Its Discontents,* J. Rivière, transl. London: Hogarth Press, 1930.

———. *The Future of an Illusion,* W. D. Robson-Scott, transl. London: Hogarth Press, 1962.

———. *Two Short Accounts of Psychoanalysis.* Harmondsworth, Eng.: Penguin, 1957.

Fromm, E. *The Crisis of Psychoanalysis.* London: Cape, New York: Holt, Rinehart, Winston, 1970, 1978.

Marcuse, H. *Eros and Civilization: A Philosophical Inquiry into Freud.* Boston: Beacon Press, 1955, 1966.

Roazen, P. *Freud: Political and Social Thought.* New York: Knopf, 1968.

fundamentalism/fundamentalist

A movement in the protestant CHRISTIAN church beginning early in the 20th century that sought to defend orthodox religious faith from theological LIBERALISM, theories of evolution, SOCIALISM, FEMINISM, and secular HUMANISM; one who believes in this movement. By adhering to certain "fundamentals" of the Christian religion (the virgin birth of Christ; the Atonement; the

Resurrection of Jesus; Christ's miracles; and the inspired Bible), these CONSERVATIVE believers rejected several tenets of MODERNISM. The movement caused splits in the American Protestant churches between conservative (mostly Baptist and evangelical) and liberal ("mainline," Episcopal, Presbyterian, Methodist) denominations. By the 1950s fundamentalism had become more narrow and contentious, viewed by many Christians as extremist.

Politically, fundamentalism has been associated with the CHRISTIAN RIGHT or Religious Right and its attacks on LIBERAL welfare policy, radical feminism, HOMOSEXUALITY, ABORTION, and humanist education. They have supported conservative political candidates (such as Ronald REAGAN) and conservative political parties (primarily the REPUBLICAN PARTY).

The future of fundamentalism as a political influence is uncertain. Often ridiculed by the media and liberal groups, its staying power has surprised many and its effect of moving certain churches and political policies to the RIGHT is widely acknowledged. Having lost power at the national level with the election of Bill Clinton as U.S. president, fundamentalists became increasingly active in state politics, where they affected changes in policies concerning education, crime, welfare, and family law.

Further Reading

Watson, Justin. *The Christian Coalition: Dreams of Restoration, Demands for Recognition.* New York: St. Martin's Press, 1997.

G

Gaius (A.D. 130–80) *Roman-law scholar and jurist*

The *Institutes* of Gaius divided the legal code into three areas: LAW concerning (1) persons (according to one's status in the state, society, and the family); (2) things or PROPERTY (such as title ownership, inheritance, contractual obligations, and reputation); and (3) actions (including legal procedures or court actions). An early work in ROMAN LAW, it influenced JUSTINIAN's great code of Roman law, which ruled the latter Roman Empire and continues in European law to this day. Appeal to a universal code of law in an entire nation (superseding local customary practice), reasoned arguments, case precedents, and procedural order affected Western notions of JUSTICE and government throughout the MEDIEVAL and MODERN periods.

Further Reading
Gaius. *The Institutes of Gaius,* transl. with an intro. by W. M. Gordon and O. F. Robinson, with the Latin text of Seckel and Kuebler. Ithaca: Cornell University Press, 1988.

Gandhi, Mohandas K. (Mahatma) (1869–1948) *Political philosopher and activist, founder of modern India*

Famous for his development of *satyagraha,* or nonviolent resistance, Gandhi used this method of social protest to lead the Indian independence movement and to secure nationhood for modern India from the British EMPIRE. This use of CIVIL DISOBEDIENCE proved that armed, violent revolution was not necessary to change society and has been a model for many other nonviolent reformers (notably U.S. CIVIL RIGHTS leader Martin Luther KING, Jr.).

Educated as a lawyer, Gandhi began his social activism in South Africa. From 1915, he led the nationalist movement in India, achieving independent nationhood in 1947. He was revered as the liberator of India from foreign imperial domination but was depressed to see the immediate outbreak of domestic warfare between the Hindu and Muslim populations in India. A radical Hindu assassinated him in 1948.

Gandhi's political thought grew out of a reformed Hindu worldview with elements of animism. The universe, in this view, is ruled by a supreme intelligence or truth, which as spirit inhabits all living things. The material world, including the human body, PROPERTY, and the STATE, are just the shell of this spiritual essence. So, goodness consists in renouncing the sensual, worldly sphere and getting in touch with the "oneness" of the spirit realm. Politics and government,

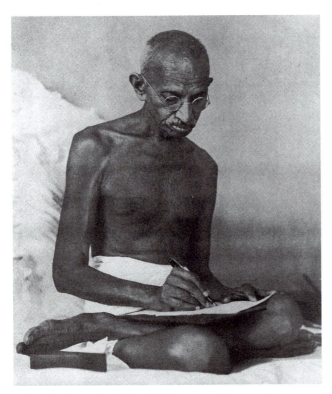

Mohandas Karamchand Gandhi. (LIBRARY OF CONGRESS)

for Gandhi, represented "violence in concentrated form"; it degrades the human spiritual essence and oppresses humanity. A very limited state (almost ANAR-CHY) is the best government because coercion should be left to a minimum and FREEDOM to a maximum.

Gandhi's ideal Indian state would be composed of small, self-governing, self-sufficient village communities, ruled by social custom and moral conformity and linked to regional and national assemblies through elected representatives (not unlike Thomas JEFFERSON's system of ward republics). Because he considered human (spirit) essentially good, Gandhi treated crime as simply a disease, requiring understanding and help rather than punishment. Without a Judeo-CHRISTIAN notion of sin, he could not conceive of a human evil unable to be cured by educative enlightenment. Although basically DEMOCRATIC, his political theory respected minority RIGHTS, religious FREEDOM, and individual LIBERTY of conscience. Embracing poverty and an ascetic lifestyle, Gandhi saw excessive wealth in the midst of starvation as a moral crime against humanity. At first, he encouraged the rich and prominent to hold their property in stewardship voluntarily, giving to the poor all beyond their basic needs. Later, he saw a more intrusive role for the state in redistributing wealth

through high taxation, restrictions on inheritance, state ownership of land, and large industries that led to SOCIALISM in India).

Gandhi was extremely critical of the West, especially the British for their worldly wealth, materialism, pomp, pride, and IMPERIALISM. When once asked what he thought of Western civilization, Gandhi quipped, "I think it would be a good idea." Although not a Christian, Gandhi admired Jesus Christ, especially his teachings in the Sermon on the Mount (Matthew 5–7).

Gandhi remains one of the greatest political figures of the 20th century, whose ideals of love and human dignity, spirituality and nonviolent social change have inspired many later political activists.

Further Readings

Bondurant, J. V. *Conquest of Violence: The Gandhian Philosophy of Conflict*. Princeton, N.J.: Princeton University Press, 1958.
Dhawan, G. *The Political Philosophy of Mahatma Gandhi*. Ahmedabad, India: Navajivan Publishing House, 1951.
Gandhi, M. K. *The Collected Works of Mahatma Gandhi*. New Delhi: Publications Division, Ministry of Information and Broadcasting, Govt. of India, 1958.
———. *Hind Swaraj or Home Rule*. Ahmedabad, India: Navajivan Publishing House, 1938.
———. *Non-violent Resistance*. New York: Schocken Books, 1951, 1961.
Iyer, R. N. *The Moral and Political Thought of Mahatma Gandhi*. New York: Oxford University Press, 1973.
Woodcock, George. *Mohandas Gandhi*. New York: Viking Press, 1971.

general will

A concept usually associated with the French ENLIGHT-ENMENT thinker Jean-Jacques ROUSSEAU, but of more ancient origin.

In Rousseau's political theory (in his book *The Social Contract*) the general will is the will of the whole society properly encoded in LAW. Similar to the CLASSICAL Greek and Roman (e.g., in ARISTOTLE and CIC-ERO) ideal of the common good, Rousseau contrasts this universal societal interest with both the particular will of the individual (private desires, goals, property, etc.) and the will of all (the mere collection of particular wills in pluralistic society). So, for example with respect to social health-care policy, an individual's particular will might be high-quality medical care for oneself at no cost; the will of all may be the majority getting good care at moderate cost, but the general will would be a system of health care which the entire society agreed by consensus is best for everyone. This involves a political process involving all citizens' participation. Through discussion, the particular interests of individuals are expressed and weighed with others, cancelled out, and the general will emerges. As Rousseau wrote ". . . take away from these same [particular] wills the pluses and minuses that cancel one another, and the general will remains as the sum of the differences." This presumes a social or community sense beyond private, individual interest, which British and American LIBERALISM denies. Western INDIVIDUALISM regards Rousseau's general will as a progenitor of TOTALITARIANISM, later emerging in the FASCIST "universal will." See Giovanni GENTILE.

An earlier theological meaning of *general will* (*volonté générale*) refers to the CHRISTIAN notion that God wills all people to be saved through Jesus Christ. St. AUGUSTINE holds that this original intent of God is frustrated by Adam's disobedience (Genesis) and replaced by the Lord's grace to the elect through Jesus Christ.

Further Readings

Riley, P. *The General Will before Rousseau: The Transformation of the Divine into the Civic.* Princeton, N.J.: Princeton University Press, 1986.

Shklar, J. N. "General will." In *Dictionary of the History of Ideas.* New York: Scribner, 1975.

———. *Men and Citizens.* Cambridge, Eng.: Cambridge University Press, 1969.

Wokler, R. *The Influence of Diderot on Rousseau,* 1975.

Gentile, Giovanni (1875–1944) *Italian fascist philosopher*

A professor of philosophy at the universities of Rome, Pisa, and Palermo, Gentile served as minister of public instruction in Mussolini's FASCIST government in the 1930s and edited the *Encyclopedia Italiana*. After Mussolini's fall in 1944, Gentile was assassinated by Italian COMMUNISTS.

Influenced by the DIALECTICAL philosophy of HEGEL, Gentile developed his fascist theory of politics in the book, *Genesis and Structure of Society*. In it, he divides human nature into a particular will (of private desires, INTERESTS, PROPERTY, etc.) and a universal will (of nation, heritage, race, community within the individual). The individual comes to know himself by getting in touch with the universal will within, which is expressed through the STATE and LAW. Therefore, obedi-

ence to the state is the fulfillment of the INDIVIDUAL. This explains how the state under fascism becomes so powerful but claims to not oppress the individual or his RIGHTS. In fact, personal rights, in Gentile's theory, are part of the particular will that must be subordinated to the universal will. The private will and personal interests must be transcended by the community will, which is expressed in state law, and the strong political leader. Using the dialectic, Gentile insists that AUTHORITY promotes FREEDOM, DICTATORSHIP is true DEMOCRACY, and international military aggression is peace.

Gentile argued that fascist unity serving the good of the total or whole nation is more just than liberal (CAPITALIST) democracy or MARXIST communism (because each of those serve a certain group or class in society). He justified military aggression by stating that the dialectic divided the world into dominant peoples and dominated peoples. If a weaker (nonfascist) country is hindering the development of stronger (fascist) country, it is natural, dialectically, for the more powerful nation to invade and conquer the less powerful nation. The fascist state is "overcoming" the opposition of a neighboring country that is "offending" it by not submitting to its will. The fascist state's military destruction of other nations is justified as securing its rights. Fascist Italy and NAZI Germany used this argument to justify their military conquest of Ethiopia, France, Poland, Russia, and other countries.

Gentile's fascism favored the traditional family and religion, but only as institutions that taught obedience and self-sacrifice aiding the state. Both family and faith are subordinated to the state, according to fascist theory. Any loyalty to family or God that opposed the government was to be suppressed. Consequently, the state becomes the highest authority in Gentile's fascist theory. In fascist society, the state becomes a kind of God, demanding absolute obedience and submission. Any questioning or criticizing of the government is considered treasonous and is punished by death. The brutal dictatorships in Nazi Germany and Fascist Italy followed from this fascist idea. The dialectical logic of fascism, which combined opposites and synthesized contradictions, made it difficult for Western democracies using CLASSICAL (Aristotelian) reason and logic to negotiate with fascist governments. Because standards of logic, truth, and the meaning of words were not shared by fascist and nonfascist countries, discussion was difficult, resulting ultimately in war. So, among other lessons, Gentile's ideas show how a philosophical outlook can greatly affect politics and international relations.

Further Reading
Gentile, Giovanni. *The Philosophy of Art,* transl. with an intro. by Giovanni Gullace. Ithaca, N.Y.: Cornell University Press, 1972.

Gibbon, Edward (1737–1794)   *English historian of the Roman Empire*

Gibbon's *The Decline and Fall of the Roman Empire* remains the classic study of the end of the Latin world and beginning of the European MIDDLE AGES. Besides the breadth of this seven-volume work (employing many original Roman documents and contemporary scholarship), Gibbon's analysis reflects CLASSICAL REPUBLICAN presuppositions of the moral decadence and political decay of the Roman Empire. He also explains the reasons for CHRISTIANITY's survival in the midst of the Empire's collapse. The early church, Gibbon insists, survived and expanded because of (1) the principled zeal of its faithful, (2) its doctrine of a future life in heaven won by Christ, (3) the impressive miracles and spiritual power of the early church, (4) the pure morals and lifestyle of its members, and (5) the discipline early Christians imposed on their community.

Gibbon's fame as a historian caused him to move in the high society and literary circles of 18th-century London. Although vain and pompous personally, his doctrines were inherently critical of British wealth, power, and prestige. Imperial luxury and lax morals could lead to the "decline and fall" of the British Empire as easily as they did the Roman Empire, so Gibbon's historiography began a tradition of treating past civilizations in such a way as to warn and reform current society. His exposure of the military and political disasters attending the decline of social morality and discipline in Rome served to warn MODERN culture about the dangers of moral decline, economic self-indulgence, political TYRANNY, and excessive luxury and pride. If the mighty 1,000-year Roman Empire could fall, any powerful, self-confident civilization could end.

Further Reading
Braudy, Leo. *Narrative Form in History and Fiction:* Hume, Fielding & Gibbon. Princeton, N.J.: Princeton University Press, 1970.

Gierke, Otto Friedrich von (1841–1921)
German legal philosopher

Otto Friedrich von Gierke was a prominent legal scholar and leader of the Germanist school of jurisprudence. He was one of the foremost opponents of the Romanist school of German law. A staunch German nationalist, von Gierke became an advocate for national unity in his later years.

Von Gierke has a long and distinguished academic career and taught at a variety of prestigious universities. He served as a professor at Breslau (1871–84), Heidelberg (1884–87), and, finally, Berlin (1887–1921). Early in his career, von Gierke earned a reputation as a legal historian.

Initially, von Gierke promoted a decentralized and pluralistic society. He asserted that the ideal state would be a combination of *Genossenschaften* (cooperative associations) and *Herrschaften* (groups that were subordinated to an individual imperious will). Hence, it would be a blend of autocracy and democracy and, on a theoretical level, a rejection of methodological individualism. Von Gierke believed that the formation of the German Empire in 1871 marked a close synthesis of this concept. He had a profound impact on his pupil, Hugo Preuss, who was instrumental in drafting the constitution of the Weimar Republic in 1919.

In 1888, when the first draft of Germany's civil law code was promulgated, von Gierke roundly criticized the effort. Following German unification in 1871, efforts to codify German law intensified. The legal system up to that time was based on both Roman law and customary German law, based primarily on tribal law. Although Roman law had been dramatically modified through the centuries, it was accepted that customary, or common, law still prevailed in areas of conflict. Individual states of Germany, including Bavaria and Prussia, already had codified their civil law, and some regions, such as Alsace and Westphalia, retained elements of the Napoleonic Code.

Von Gierke supported the effort for legal codification and would later cite the formation of the *Reich,* or empire, under Otto von Bismarck as the foundation for legal reform. He opposed the first civil code, however, on the basis that it relied too heavily on Roman law. Von Gierke emerged as one of the leaders of the historical jurisprudence school that opposed the so-called Romanist school; eventually, the code was revised and many of the Roman elements were removed. A new proposal was issued in 1896 and went into effect in 1900. Von

Gierke's efforts led him to write a massive three-volume opus, *Deutsches Privatrecht* (*German Private Law*) between 1895 and 1917. His concepts played a major part in the new code, which, with modifications, remains the foundation for the German legal system.

In 1900, the British jurist Frederic William Maitland wrote a partial translation of von Gierke's four-volume *Das deutsche Genossenschaftrecht* (*The German Law of Associations*) and published it as *Political Theories of the Middle Ages*. In the work, von Gierke contended that feudalism led to a synthesis of land ownership and rule. Nonetheless, during the same period, the role of the individual became strengthened through the recognition of natural law. Many pluralists used Maitland's translation to bolster their arguments for more decentralized political systems, although in doing so they disregarded von Gierke's emphasis on political authority.

Further Reading
Cameron, R. *Frederick William Maitland and the History of English Law.* Norman: University of Oklahoma Press, 1961.

Gladstone, William (1809–1898) *British statesman and Prime Minister*

William Gladstone was a British statesman and the dominant personality of the Liberal Party from 1868 to 1894. As chancellor of the exchequer, he actively pursued a free-trade agenda; he was prime minister four times and achieved notable reforms. Among his many achievements were the passage of the Irish land act, the establishment of competitive civil-service examinations, a closed voting system, parliamentary reform, and reform and expansion in education.

One of his earliest successes was the 1867 Reform Act. Specifically, the act accorded suffrage to every male adult householder living in a voting district. In addition, male renters in some cases were also granted the vote. The act also reapportioned members of Parliament based on population distribution. In sum, the 1867 Reform Act gave the vote to about 1,500,000 men. The following year in the general election 1868, the Conservatives were defeated and Gladstone, leader of the Liberal Party, became prime minister. In 1870, Gladstone and his education minister, William Forster, persuaded Parliament to pass the government's Education Act, which established school boards in Britain.

After the passage of the 1867 Reform Act, blue-collar men formed the majority in most political districts; however, employers were still able to influence voters because of the open system of voting. In parliamentary elections, people still had to mount a platform and announce their choice of candidate to the officer, who then recorded it in the poll book. Employers and local landlords therefore knew how people voted and could seek retribution for not supporting their preferred candidate. In 1872, Gladstone removed this level of intimidation when his government brought in the Ballot Act, which introduced a secret system of voting.

From 1874 to 1880, the Liberal Party lost POWER to Benjamin Disraeli and the Conservatives. Now in the role of opposition, Gladstone decided to bide his time and turn his attention to writing. During this time, he completed two books, titled *An Inquiry into the Time and Place of Homer in History* (1876) and *Bulgarian Horrors and the Question of the East* (1876). When Parliament was dissolved in 1880, the Liberal Party reclaimed the majority under Gladstone's direction.

During this term, Gladstone renewed his reform efforts in the form of three measures. First, the Corrupt Practices Act, in contemporary terms known as campaign finance reform, specified how much money candidates could spend during an election and banned such activities as the buying of food or drink for voters. Second, in 1884 Gladstone introduced proposals to extend voting RIGHTS further to additional male voters who resided outside of urban centers. The net effect was to add approximately six million to the total number who could vote in parliamentary elections.

Finally, Gladstone turned his attention to the issue of Irish home rule. The proposal was unpopular in the Liberal Party, dividing it nearly evenly. The measure was defeated in Parliament but did not serve to prevent Gladstone's reelection in 1892. The following year, the Irish Home Rule Bill was passed in the House of Commons but was defeated in the House of Lords. In his last reform effort, Gladstone had gained considerable enmity from Queen Victoria who criticized his position on home rule. William Gladstone resigned from office in March 1894 and died in 1898.

Further Reading
Stansky, Peter, and Gladstone, William Ewert. *Gladstone, A Progress in Politics.* New York: W. W. Norton, 1981.

Godwin, William (1756–1836)   *British political philosopher, novelist, and anarchist*

In his book *An Enquiry Concerning Political Justice,* Godwin puts forth his radical anarchist idea that all government AUTHORITY is corrupt and oppressive and that it should be eliminated. From his very positive view of human beings as naturally rational, peaceable, and virtuous, Godwin asserts that evil behavior is not from innate sin but from mistaken beliefs. All a society has to do to become perfectly just is provide LIBERTY and enlightened education to citizens. This will produce happy, moral individuals and social harmony. All social ills results from people in authority who coerce and frustrate others and incite passions and conflict in society. Then, to retain their power, governments keep their citizens ignorant, poor, and contentious. The sooner they are overthrown, the better for humanity.

In typical ENLIGHTENMENT fashion, Godwin has faith in the PROGRESS of reason and knowledge: People are rational, and the truth will ultimately prevail, producing FREEDOM and JUSTICE. History is progressively improving humanity's condition and ultimately will perfect human beings. He even believed that eventually humans' intelligence will allow them to control their natural lives completely—to avoid all sleep (which comes from inattention) and conquer death by medical means. Such scientific optimism and individual control of one's destiny (and rejection of tradition NATURAL LAW and religion) represents the radical modern materialism of Godwin's time. His arguments for redistribution of private PROPERTY foreshadow both UTILITARIANISM and SOCIALISM. Like his contemporary Thomas PAINE, Godwin's radical attack on TRADITION and authority lends itself to political DEMOCRACY, social EQUALITY, and FEMINISM.

Originally a Presbyterian minister, Godwin left the church and his Christian faith by 1783. He married Mary Wollstonecraft (an early advocate of feminism), who died in childbirth. Their child was Mary Shelley, who wrote the novel *Frankenstein.* Godwin's novel *Caleb Williams* influenced a generation of English writers, notably Robert Southey, Wordsworth, Coleridge, and Percy Shelley, but with the end of radical literature in the 1790s, Godwin declined into poverty and obscurity in his last 30 years.

Further Readings
Clark, J. P. *The Philosophical Anarchism of William Godwin.* Princeton, N.J.: Princeton University Press, 1977.

Godwin, W. *An Enquiry Concerning Political Justice,* I. Kramnick, ed. Harmondsworth, Eng.: Penguin, 1976.

———. *Caleb Williams,* D. McCracken, ed. New York: W. W. Norton, 1977.

Locke, D. *A Fantasy of Reason: The Life and Thought of William Godwin.* London: Routledge, 1980.

Goldman, Emma (1869–1940)   *Russian–American anarchist feminist socialist*

As a Russian Jewish immigrant to the United States of America, Goldman became a leading writer and activist for ANARCHISM, FEMINISM, and COMMUNISM. She held that all evil comes from AUTHORITY: in the government, the church, the family, and people. Freed from these oppressive authority structures, humans, for Goldman, will be happy, moral, cooperative, and loving. Government, she wrote, is "the dominion of human conduct"; religion is "the dominion of the human mind"; private PROPERTY is "the dominion of human needs"; and the traditional family is "slavery" for women. Through the revolutionary overthrow of the STATE, CAPITALISM, the church, and the family and establishment of anarchism, "the freest possible expression of all the latent powers of the individual will emerge," for Goldman. This emphasis on individual LIBERTY and the belief that only the destruction of authority is needed to accomplish social harmony, peace, and abundance reveals the Russian anarchist roots of Goldman's political thought. Anarchy will usher in a kind of "Heaven on Earth" for her: "It is the philosophy of the sovereignty of the individual. It is the theory of social harmony. It is the great, surging, living truth that is reconstructing the world, and that will usher in the Dawn." This passionate, quasi-Messianic message (anarchism or human salvation and heavenly peace) caused some to follow the movement, especially from among poor, European, immigrant industrial workers in New York early in the 20th century. However, with the increasingly violent tactics of some anarchists, the failure of anarchism in the Russian Revolution of 1917, and the increased prosperity in the U.S. economy, Goldman's philosophy went out of favor by the 1920s. Some of its themes (SOCIALIST redistribution of wealth, women's liberation, secular anti-Christianity) continued in the U.S. labor movement, the feminist movement, and the LIBERAL DEMOCRATIC PARTY throughout the 20th century.

Emma Goldman, 1934. (LIBRARY OF CONGRESS)

Further Readings

Goldman, Emma. *Living My Life*. New York: Dover Publications, 1970.
———. *My Further Disillusionment in Russia,* being a continuation of Goldman's experiences in Russia as given in *My disillusionment in Russia*. Garden City, N.Y.: Doubleday, 1924.
Drinnon, Richard. *Rebel in Paradise: A Biography of Emma Goldman*. Chicago: University of Chicago Press, 1961.

Gramsci, Antonio (1891–1937) *Italian communist*

Born in the province of Cagliari in Sardinia, Gramsci was educated at the University of Turin. While a student at the University, Gramsci became involved in the Socialist Youth Federation and, in 1914, joined the Italian Socialist Party (PSI). Gramsci also began to work as a journalist during World War I. He had started an intensive study of the work of Karl MARX, and he was a frequent speaker at workers' study circles on historical and political topics. Gramsci became convinced during the latter stages of the war, during which the Bolshevik revolution occurred in Russia in October 1917, that CAPITALISM must be assailed by the forces and strategies of revolutionary SOCIALISM. Gramsci utilized his journalistic skills to promote the cause of radical social

transformation. In 1919, he established with several colleagues a new periodical called *L'Ordine nuovo* (*The New Order*), which published critical reviews of cultural and political ideas and events throughout Europe, the Soviet Union, and the United States.

In 1921, while attending the Italian Socialist Party Congress at Livorno, Gramsci participated in a walkout by the communist minority within the PSI. He then played an instrumental role in helping to found the Italian Communist Party (PCI), becoming a member of its central committee. A strong supporter of Soviet communism at this time, Gramsci spent 1922 and 1923 living in Moscow as an Italian delegate to the Communist International. After his return to Italy, he was elected to the chamber of deputies and soon became the general secretary of the PCI. In the interim, Benito Mussolini, the leader of the Italian Fascist Party, had assumed control of the Italian government. In consolidating his DICTATORSHIP, Mussolini outlawed political opposition, including the Italian Communist Party. Because of his position and activities with the PCI, Gramsci was arrested and imprisoned by the fascists in 1926. He spent the next 11 years in various prisons, suffering from poor conditions and failing health. He died from a cerebral hemorrhage in Rome a week after being released from prison.

Gramsci made several important contributions to Marxist theory. Much of his significant writing is contained in the notebooks and letters he wrote while confined to prison. Probably the most notable of Gramsci's ideas is his concept of *hegemony*. According to Gramsci, *hegemony* refers to the process whereby a ruling class solidifies its political, intellectual, and moral authority or leadership over the rest of society. Hegemony can be established through consent or coercion. Under capitalism, the dominated masses come to adopt the ideology and values imposed on society by the dominant economic ruling CLASS. For Gramsci, the communist revolution requires that the proletariat achieve hegemony. Indeed, the success of hegemony consists of the dominated perceiving the instruments of domination as being in their best interests, thereby reinforcing the AUTHORITY and control of the dominating class. In essence, then, the concept of hegemony develops the Marxist insight that the ideas of a culture are the ideas of its ruling class. For this reason, Gramsci also advanced the notion that culture, in addition to politics and the economy, is a fundamental element of social change that deserves not only increased theoretical analysis, but also an enhanced role in political strategy. A successful revolutionary movement, argued Gramsci, must be able to replace the existing authoritarian capitalist culture with an EGALITARIAN proletarian culture, changing and shaping the way people live, think, and feel.

Further Reading
Martin, J. *Gramsci's Political Analysis: A Critical Introduction.* New York: St. Martin's Press, 1998.

Great Awakening, The

A series of CHRISTIAN religious revivals in North America from about 1740 to 1770. Key EVANGELICAL leaders of these spiritual revivals were English minister George WHITEFIELD and American minister Jonathan Edwards. Occurring primarily among PRESBYTERIAN, Methodist, and Congregational churches, the Great Awakening effectively Christianized the British North American colonies (later the United States of America).

Politically, this religious revival had several significant effects. The practice of itinerate and uneducated lay Christians preaching the Bible in nontradition settings (such as houses and outdoors rather than in church buildings) had a democratizing effect on American society. Through EGALITARIAN DEMOCRACY in religion and ETHICS, the American culture became more democratic generally, preparing the populace for the American Revolution (1776–84) and the establishment of the American Republic (1789). The HIERARCHY and monopoly of the established churches was changed by the Great Awakening into a lively, POPULIST Christianity ruled from bottom (congregational community) up (electing clergy) rather than the traditional from top (ordained clergy) down (to passive masses). With ordinary people leading the revivalist churches, the protestant doctrine of "priesthood of all believers" was realized, preparing citizens for economic and political democracy. Rather than a limiting, repressive force, the Christian church became a democratic liberating force in American life. The legal restraints on religious FREEDOM (and, consequently, on freedom of speech) were abolished in practice, and common citizens became confident of their ability to be self-governing.

The advocates of this religious/social revival saw it as a genuine outpouring of the Holy Spirit of Christ, as evidenced by massive conversions, increased religious sincerity, and morality and public responsibility. Rev. Edwards described it as "a divine and supernatural light," transforming many communities. Its emphasis on "the New Birth" or Christian transformation of the individual, conformed to past evangelical PURITAN theology. That emphasis upon a personal relationship to Christ and salvation emboldened Americans to break ties to traditional English society and class structures. More aristocratic clergy in Boston and at Harvard University rejected this populist Christianity and eventually retreated to Unitarian thought. But the effects of the Great Awakening were widespread throughout the American colonies advancing a more democratic religious, social, and political life.

Further Readings
Bushman, Richard L., ed. *The Great Awakening: Documents on the Revival of Religion, 1740–1745.* New York: Atheneum, 1970.
Gewehr, Wesley Marsh. *The Great Awakening in Virginia 1740–1790.* Gloucester, Mass.: P. Smith, ca. 1930, 1965.
Hall, Timothy D. *Contested Boundaries: Itinerancy and the Reshaping of the Colonial American Religious World.* Durham, N.C.: Duke University Press, 1994.
Miller, P., and Heimert, A., eds. *The Great Awakening: Documents.* Indianapolis: Bobbs-Merrill, 1967.
Wood, Gordon. *The Radicalism of the American Revolution.* New York: Knopf, 1991.

Greek political theory

The political ideas developed in ancient or "CLASSICAL" Greece (400–200 B.C.) especially around Athens. Leading Greek political thinkers are SOCRATES, PLATO, and ARISTOTLE, great classical Western philosophers who first developed written concepts of JUSTICE, DEMOCRACY, VIRTUE, RIGHTS, EQUALITY, LIBERTY, and ETHICS. Their brilliance in framing these fundamental political ideals and questions (as in Plato's *Republic* and *Laws;* Aristotle's *Politics* and *Nicomachean Ethics*) influence the rest of Western political thought to the present day. Later CHRISTIAN thinkers (St. AUGUSTINE, St. Thomas AQUINAS, John CALVIN), Roman philosophers (CICERO, JUSTINIAN) and MODERN REPUBLICANS (James HARRINGTON, ROUSSEAU, Thomas JEFFERSON, John MILTON) to contemporary American political theorists (John RAWLS, Benjamin BARBER, Leo STRAUSS, Wilson Carey MCWILLIAMS) have been influenced by these original Greek political philosophers. Our intellectual debt to Greek political thought in the West is immeasurable.

Although diverse in ideas and emphases, most Greek political theorists provide a NATURAL LAW view of humanity and society (that humans operate within natural abilities and limits) that commends an ideal of public virtue (individual self-sacrifice for the common good), justice (the harmonious ordering of parts within the whole society), HIERARCHY (distinct ranks in family, economy, and politics), and PARTICIPATION (active involvement in governing). A classic example of this is Aristotle's statement that "man is by nature a social and political animal" by virtue of his unique human faculties of "reasoned speech and moral choice" (which cannot be used or developed in isolation). Consequently, the citizen must be prepared (socially, economically, morally, and politically) to participate in the direct rule of the REPUBLIC (*polis*) and develop a noble character that knows and practices justice. This classical Greek emphasis on ethical character in service of the public good flows directly to the MEDIEVAL "English gentleman" who is bred to noblesse oblige and serving the common good.

This "public-spirited" quality of ancient Greek thought contrasts with the modern LIBERAL concentration of private interest, selfish PLURALISM, and WELFARE-STATE views of politics. Even in later Greek thought (Zeno the Stoic), the trend was toward "self" realization and private concerns, but the enduring nature of Greek theory is its social view of justice. For the ancients, politics was to bring out the best in human nature, not the most sordid, and political service was to be "the good life" of reason and ethics above the "mere life" of physical urges and economics. To be self-centered or obsessed with money was a kind of slavery to one's lowest nature, for Aristotle. Humans reside between the gods and the beasts; political life fulfills the human's proper place between contemplation (divine) and biological life (animal). Without proper training and cultivation of the higher faculties, humans become worse than beasts. So, it is society's responsibility to promote education and virtue in its citizens. Unlike later Christianity, with its emphasis on human weakness and sin, classical Greek thought was confident that people could become truly excellent (even perfect) through the best education and moral example. This ancient optimism over human nature is revived in MODERN ENLIGHTENMENT thought.

Further Readings

Aristotle. *The Nicomachean Ethics*, H. Rackham, transl. 1934.

Barker, E. *From Alexander to Constantine.* [An anthology, with massive commentary on passages and documents, 338 B.C. to A.D. 337.] Oxford: Clarendon Press, 1966.

Ehrenberg, V. *The Greek State*, 2nd ed. London: Methuen, 1969.

Euripides. *The Suppliant Women*, F. Jones, transl. 1958.

Finley, M. I. *Politics in the Ancient World.* Cambridge: Cambridge University Press, 1983.

———. *Democracy Ancient and Modern*, 2nd ed. New Brunswick, N.J.: Rutgers University Press, 1985.

Guthrie, W. K. C. "A History of Greek Philosophy," vol. III, pt. 1. In *The Fifth-Century Enlightenment.* Cambridge, Eng.: Cambridge University Press, 1981.

Kerferd, G. B. *The Sophistic Movement.* Cambridge, Eng.: Cambridge University Press, 1981.

Nippel, W. *Mischverfassungstheorie und Verfassungsrealität in Antike und früher Neuzeit,* pt. 1. Stuttgart: Klett-Cotta, 1980.

Ober, Josiah. *The Athenian Revolution: Essays on Ancient Greek Democracy and Political Theory.* Ithaca, N.Y.: Cornell University Press, ca. 1996.

Raaflaub, K. *Zum freiheitsbergriff der griechen.* In *Soziale Typenbegriffe im alten Griechenland,* vol. IV, E. Weskopg, ed. Berlin: Akademie-Verlag, 1981.

Vlastos, G. "Isonomia politike" (in English). In *Isonomia,* J. Mau and E. G. Schmidt, eds. Berlin: Akademie-Verlag, 1964.

Winton, R. I., and Garnsey, P. "Political theory." In *The Legacy of Greece,* M. I. Finley, ed. Oxford: Oxford University Press, 1981.

Green, Thomas Hill (1836–1882)   *Liberal reformist and philosophical idealist*

Thomas Hill Green was an important influence on late Victorian and early 20th century liberal political thought. His significance at that time is said to have superseded John Stuart Mill's importance. His work is seldom cited in contemporary debates, although Green provides an interesting counterpoint to current liberal orthodoxies.

Green's first publication was an introductory essay to an edited volume of Hume's philosophy, in which he sets out a lengthy argument against empiricism. The general framework of this argument is important because it is applied later to his critique of utilitarianism and the contract tradition of liberalism. First, Green argues that ideas do not originate in mere sensation. In this, he follows Kant in arguing that ideas presuppose conceptions such as of causality, time, space, and so on. Second, Green claimed that conceptions and ideas are always in relation to other ideas and conceptions. This antinominalism, or holism, allowed the mind to be active and creative in knowing, thus constituting reality. This is Green's idealism.

Green thought of utilitarianism as a moral analogue of empiricism. He argued that a feeling or sensation such as pleasure cannot be the source of moral goodness. A conception of goodness is required for pleasure *to be taken* as good. Furthermore, this conception of goodness arises only in our relations with others within a common society. Green's idea of the good was that of individual self-perfection toward a Christian end. The idea that individuals can only approach goodness through social relations naturally brings into question the role of the state, politics, and power. Here, Green distinguishes between negative and positive freedoms. The former he associated with the contract tradition of liberalism, in particular with Hobbes and Locke. Negative freedom diminishes, rather than increases, our capacity to seek self-perfection by isolating us instead of binding us within the social whole and casting individuals as mere competitors for material goods. Positive freedom, on the other hand, is a freedom exercised within society, with and through the support of the state and social and political institutions. The state thus has a duty to provide the bases of support that enable citizens to seek the moral good.

Although Green emphasized the role of government and the social character of moral and political ideals, he was not a communitarian, and neither was he a perfectionist. The foundation of moral and political values is the individual; there are no *sui generis* social values, and in spite of the role he assigns to the state, he did not think it was its task to instruct or foster particular moral values. He believed that citizens should find their own way toward self-perfection and that given the opportunity they would find their way to the Christian ideal to which Green himself subscribed.

Green's own life reflected his liberal philosophy. He was very active as a citizen in political life, serving in elected office, supporting progressive reforms in working conditions, and promoting education. He was born in Birkin, Yorkshire, England, the child of a minister. He spent his academic career at Oxford becoming the Whyte's professor of moral philosophy in 1878. He died very young at the age of 44. Nearly all his work was published posthumously, including his unfinished *Prologomena to Ethics*. His political and other writings are collected in three volumes, *The Works of Thomas Hill Green*, edited by R. L. Nettleship.

Further Reading

Richter, M. *The Politics of Conscience: T.H. Green and His Age.* Cambridge, Mass.: Harvard University Press, 1964.

Grotius, Hugo (1583–1645)   *Dutch jurist and political philosopher*

Famous for his early formulation of MODERN NATURAL-RIGHTS political philosophy that greatly influenced British REPUBLICANISM (John LOCKE) and American DEMOCRACY (Thomas JEFFERSON). He argued that two principles underlie all political morality: (1) self-preservation of human life is always legitimate, and (2) harm or injury of others (except in self-defense) is always illegitimate. This materialist view of human ethics contrasted with CLASSICAL (ARISTOTLE) and MEDIEVAL (St. Thomas AQUINAS) political theory, but it formed a basis for LIBERAL CIVIL-SOCIETY, SOCIAL-CONTRACT government and private PROPERTY rights. These "laws of nature" are fully developed in John Locke's *Second Treatise of Government* in the 1680s where they justified the parliamentary revolution of 1688. Thomas Jefferson's DECLARATION OF INDEPENDENCE similarly draws on these ideas.

In his own country of Holland, Grotius advanced an aristocratic IMPERIALIST republicanism, justifying both a limited MONARCHY in the Netherlands and foreign expansion of Dutch trade and colonialism. Much of his political writings dealt with INTERNATIONAL LAW (just-war doctrine, foreign relations, etc.). As a HUMANIST scholar, he edited classical Greek and Latin texts and wrote about ancient history. He served in the government of the United Provinces, culminating in chief executive of Rotterdam. His career came to an unhappy end when he was tried and convicted of treason and sentenced to life in prison. Escaping, he lived in Paris, served as Sweden's ambassador to France, and was finally killed in a shipwreck. A prolific author and political activist, Grotius became a hero of the ENLIGHTENMENT. His religious skepticism and advocacy of LIBERTY of conscience led to religious FREEDOM and TOLERATION.

Further Readings

Grotius, Hugo. *De iure praedae*, G. L. Williams, transl. 1950.
———. *De iure belli ac pacis*, F. W. Kelsey, transl. 1925.
Knight, W. S. M. *The Life and Works of Hugo Grotius.* London: Sweet and Maxwell, 1925.
Tuck, R. *Natural Rights Theories.* Cambridge, Eng.: Cambridge University Press, 1979.
———. *Grotius, Carneades and Hobbes*, Grotiana new ser. 4. 1983.

guild

An economic group of shared activity or trade with political influence, especially during the European MIDDLE AGES. Examples of guilds are merchant guilds, such as all the commercial stores in a given city (such as Florence, Italy) and craft guilds (such as all the cloth weavers in England). Most nonagricultural businesses were organized as guilds in MEDIEVAL Europe (e.g., shoemakers or cobblers, masons, printers, plumbers, tailors, jewelers, etc.). Guilds regulated the quality, sale, and personnel of certain specialized goods. They created an effective monopoly in these areas of the economy that they controlled. Training of skilled workers was accomplished through the guilds (through a system of apprentices, journeymen, and masters). Dominating industry in Europe from the 10th through the 17th centuries, guilds exercised considerable political influence in many cities and towns, providing a regional governance, checking the national power of the king and continental power of the church. Sometimes called colleges or corporations, medieval guilds also existed in educational and religious bodies (academic institutions were originally guilds of scholars). Guilds tended to be CONSERVATIVE organizations, valuing routine, TRADITION, and stability over economic development and technological change (which was seen as threatening their economic livelihood and political influence). With mechanized industrial CAPITALISM in the 17th and 18th centuries, the economic and political power of the European guilds was destroyed. Technology, free trade, and competition eroded their influence. Some MODERN labor and trade unions modeled their structures on medieval guilds, as did new trade professions (such as electrician). But only in FASCISM in Italy and Spain (through the ideas of CORPORATISM and SYNDICALISM) did guilds continue into the 20th century. A movement called guild SOCIALISM in Britain tried, in the early 1900s, to improve the conditions of industrial workers by reintroducing guild systems and monopolies (in cooperation with the state), but it tended to be supplanted by more nationalistic, MARXIST workers' socialism. Guilds came to be associated with the past and reactionary social movements. The term *guild* now signifies mostly an honorary or professional association.

Further Readings

Cole, M. "Guild socialism and the labour research department." In *Essays in Labour History 1886–1923*, A. Briggs and J. Saville, eds. Hamden, Conn.: Anchor Books, 1971.

Glass, S. T. *The Responsible Society: The Ideas of the English Guild Socialist.* Longmans, London: 1966.

Russell, Bertrand. *Proposed Roads to Freedom: Socialism, Anarchism and Syndicalism.* New York: Henry Holt and Co., 1919.

Wright, A. W. *G.D.H. Cole and Socialist Democracy.* Oxford, Eng.: Clarendon Press, 1979.

Gutiérrez, Gustavo (1928–)   *Latin American Catholic theologian and philosopher of liberation theology*

In his book, *A Theology of Liberation* (1973), Gutiérrez presents the classic theory of LIBERATION THEOLOGY that dominated the LEFT of the CATHOLIC Church in Latin America (and mainline LIBERAL protestant churches) in the 1970s and 1980s. It seeks to address the poverty and misery of the Third World by combining MARXIST-LENINIST social analysis with CHRISTIANITY. According to this view, contemporary politics is understood in terms of the wealthy CAPITALIST IMPERIALIST countries of the Northern Hemisphere (such as the United States, Britain, and Germany), exploiting and oppressing the poor "neo-colonies" of the Southern Hemisphere (South America, Africa, Asia, etc.). The only solution to this economic injustice is the revolutionary overthrow of the developing country governments, expulsion of imperialist corporations, and establishment of SOCIALISM. The church, in its Christian role to help the poor, should assist these socialist, anti-imperialist revolutions, thereby achieving "salvation in history." So, liberation theology sees fighting for radical revolution as serving God. Its goal, as Christ's, is the realization of "true human existence." Gutiérrez advocated a "broad and deep aspiration for liberation from all that limits or keeps man from self-fulfillment, liberation from all impediments to the exercise of his freedom."

This expression of worldly, economic, and political FREEDOM differed from traditional Catholic views of human nature and politics. Although liberation theology cared for the poor (and affected reforms benefiting them, especially in socialist Nicaragua under the Marxist Sandinista government), the Roman Catholic hierarchy criticized it for distorting traditional Christian theology. By drawing on ENLIGHTENMENT and COMMUNIST ideas of people and society, Gutiérrez saw sin in terms of social *systems* rather than the individual will, and salvation in material rather than spiritual terms. In turn, he criticized the Catholic Church in Latin America for being aligned with the economic and political establishment and sanctifying the oppression of the poor and helpless. He claimed the Catholic hierarchy was aiding the rich imperialists in preventing the masses from getting "dignity, liberty, and personal fulfillment." By remaining neutral in the world economic class struggle, the church, in effect, is siding with the wealthy and powerful. The church should take the side of the revolutionary masses and radical socialism.

Some radical priests and nuns followed this program and fought with Marxist guerrilla groups in Latin America. The papacy denounced this revolutionary, violent involvement, but under Pope John Paul II, it also called for political reform and concern for improving social justice for the poor in Latin America. The democratic component of liberation theology also called for a loosening of church HIERARCHY (priests from bishops) and allowing Catholic lay involvement in politics without the intermediary of the church.

By the late 20th century, liberation theology was less popular in South America, as democratic movements and economic development emerged there. But it affected the liberal, mainline Protestant churches in the United States and Europe (Episcopal, Presbyterian, United Church of Christ), which adopted much of the Marxist class-struggle rhetoric in their policies on CIVIL RIGHTS, women's rights, and "economic JUSTICE" (or "racism, sexism, and classism"). This caused the liberal North American churches to sympathize with socialist Cuba, Nicaragua, the Soviet Union, and China. Among CONSERVATIVE Catholics and EVANGELICAL Christians, liberation theology was rejected as heretical and socialistic. It did heighten the Vatican's sensitivity to poverty in the developing countries and the church's call to help the poor and oppressed of the world.

Gutiérrez studied at the National University of Peru and the Universities of Louvain and Lyon in France and was ordained a Catholic priest in 1959. He taught theology at the Catholic University in Lima, Peru.

H

Habermas, Jürgen (1929–) *German philosopher*

Named "the most powerful thinker" in Germany by *Der Spiegel* magazine in 1979, Habermas is the most distinguished scholar of the second generation of the FRANKFURT SCHOOL. Born in Düsseldorf, Habermas was raised in NAZI Germany, an experience that had a profound affect on his later work in moral and political theory. After studying at several universities in Germany, Habermas completed his Ph.D. in philosophy at the University of Bonn in 1954. Shortly thereafter, he became the assistant to Theodor Adorno at the Institute for Social Research in Frankfurt, serving in that capacity until 1959. Since that time, he has been a professor of philosophy at the universities of Heidelberg and Frankfurt, as well as the director of the Max Planck Institute in Starnberg. He is presently professor emeritus at the University of Frankfurt and permanent visiting professor at Northwestern University.

Following in the tradition established by the members of the Frankfurt school, Habermas's work embodies a form of CRITICAL THEORY that combines philosophy and social science. However, Habermas is less dependent upon the writings of Karl MARX than the early Frankfurt School, and he has been receptive to the contributions of contemporary analytic philosophers. In his early writings, Habermas criticized the instrumental-rationality characteristic of modern science and the way science enabled CAPITAL-ISM to dominate the everyday cultural environment, or "lifeworld," in which individuals interact. He also described the "legitimation crisis" that the modern state confronts when it is unable to protect citizens from the negative effects of economic collapse under capitalism. According to Habermas, critical theory should illuminate the emancipatory potential of labor and cultural activities that are able to carry out social and political reform.

In *The Theory of Communicative Action* (1981), Habermas developed an extensive account of social interaction based on theories of language and communication. Following a critique of the traditional conception of reason based on the paradigm of "isolated" self-consciousness, Habermas built an alternative paradigm based on the intersubjective relationships of individuals within communities. In the lifeworld of everyday experience, individual identity and consciousness are shaped by various structures of beliefs, values, and practices, generally mediated through the activity of communication. For Habermas, *communicative action* refers to the cooperative process whereby individuals represent states of affairs to one another through utterances, establish interpersonal relationships based on the mutual recognition of their utterances, and interpret and modify the social system in which they are immersed.

The theory of communicative action was then used by Habermas to formulate his theory of discourse ethics. Like many theories of JUSTICE, discourse ethics focuses on questions of the right and the good and on how ethical norms can be justified through a procedure of moral argumentation and reasoned agreement. The goal for Habermas is to allow for undistorted communication between all participants in a practical discourse so that understanding of, and agreement on, valid norms can occur. Social systems that do not provide public, participatory access to norm formation and the creation of consensus through communicative action thereby restrict the potential for individual and societal emancipation. In his most recent writings, Habermas extends his theory of discourse ethics into an account of what he calls deliberative politics. Habermas insists that genuine DEMOCRACY must consist of, and encourage, public processes of communicative action. In other words, democracy can only function within a constitutional framework that guarantees the equal RIGHTS of political participation throughout the public sphere. Democratic governments thus have an obligation to develop the social, legal, and political institutions necessary for individuals to interact freely in pluralistic societies.

Further Reading

Outhwaite, W. *Habermas: A Critical Introduction.* Stanford, Calif.: Stanford University Press, 1994.

Hamilton, Alexander (1755–1804)   *U.S. statesman and political philosopher*

A leading FEDERALIST in the early American REPUBLIC, Hamilton served as an officer in Gen. Washington's army during the Revolutionary War, as a delegate to the Constitutional Convention, and as the secretary of the treasury in President Washington's administration. He wrote a majority of *The* FEDERALIST PAPERS, arguing for ratification of the new U.S. CONSTITUTION and providing the authoritative exposition of the new federal system of U.S. government. As a proponent of a powerful central government (contrary to STATES

RIGHTS), a strong executive, and public support of industrial CAPITALISM, Hamilton and other "high federalists" became the political opponents of Thomas JEFFERSON and the agrarian democrats.

Hamilton expressed a pessimistic view of human beings as selfish and petty. Ambition and enlightened self-interest could lead people to care about greater things, so acquisition of wealth and fame are noble. A political system that encouraged and rewarded prosperity and notoriety was the best, in his view. Most common people are unable to strive for anything above their personal desires, so DEMOCRACY should be checked by aristocratic institutions that attract the better sorts of people into government. Consequently, Hamilton favored the U.S. constitutional provisions for a strong executive and SUPREME COURT, as well as a powerful Senate. A powerful national government would also aid in creating a wealthy country through commerce and a strong military to protect and expand the national interest. Hamilton admired the British IMPERIALISM, and he hoped to replicate those institutions in the United States. He believed in NATURAL RIGHTS, but after David HUME and William BLACKSTONE, Hamilton maintained that state power is necessary to secure individual RIGHTS. He often referred to this healthy, strong government as "energy in the executive." Those fearing TYRANNY from the federal government (see ANTIFEDERALISTS) resisted Hamilton's nationalism. Thomas Jefferson wished to keep most state power decentralized and limited, reserving the national regime for international affairs.

This led to a conflict over early interpretations of the U.S. Constitution. Hamilton and the federalists wanted "expansive implied powers" for the central government; Jefferson favored limited "strict construction" of specifically enumerated national powers. Through the Supreme Court's Hamiltonian interpretation of Constitutional FEDERALISM under John MARSHALL, the federal government has assumed more authority throughout U.S. history. So, although the United States is culturally a Jeffersonian democracy, both economically and politically it has taken the road of Hamilton. Hamilton was killed in a duel with Aaron Burr.

Further Readings

Kenyon, C. "Alexander Hamilton: Rousseau of the Right," *Political Science Quarterly* 73 (June 1958): 161–178.

Miller, J. C. *Alexander Hamilton: Portrait in Paradox.* New York: Harper, 1959.

Harrington, James (1611–1677)   *English political philosopher*

Representative of CLASSICAL REPUBLICANISM, Harrington adopts ARISTOTLE's view that citizens must be economically independent to be virtuous rulers. In his book, *The Commonwealth of Oceana,* Harrington argued that political AUTHORITY always follows from economic power through PROPERTY ownership. So, MONARCHY exists where the royal family monopolizes all property (as in feudal landed tenure); aristocracy is land ownership by a few wealth persons; and a commonwealth (or REPUBLIC) occurs when property is widely dispersed. That a republic cannot exist without a large middle class is a theme of Harringtonian political theory. He also links sovereignty with the right to bear arms (or own guns). A monarchy keeps weapons away from the general population and uses a standing paid army; a republic, or commonwealth, allows citizens to possess arms and relies on a citizen militia. So, for Harrington, as a state becomes corrupt, it takes property from the average citizens (through higher taxes), concentrates power in the central administration (through patronage), and disarms the citizenry (relying on mercenaries). All of these corruptions to republicanism make people dependent on the government and destroy public VIRTUE. These ideas influenced later British and American classical Republicans, notably Thomas JEFFERSON.

Further Readings

Russell-Smith, H. F. *Harrington and His Oceana.* Cambridge, Eng.: The University Press, 1914.
Tawney, R. H. *Harrington's Interpretation of His Age.* 1942.

Hayek, Friedrich August von (1899–1992)   *Economist and liberal political philosopher*

Hayek's economic theory, for which he was awarded the Nobel Prize in 1972, is concerned chiefly with arguing against various forms of state control and intervention. His early target was the TOTALITARIAN states of the 1930s and later SOCIALIST and WELFARE STATES. His criticisms rest on the following claims: First, economics is the science of coordinating ends rather than distributing resources; second, value is subjective, which is to say that value is a function of individual preferences; third, given the multiplicity of ends and the subjectivity of value, no individual or state can or should plan for an entire economy. In short, Hayek rejected economic models that were based on the ideas of perfect competition between perfectly rational economic agents who are in possession of a complete knowledge of their own and others' ends. It followed from this that any attempt by a state to organize an economy rested on a profound error about the nature of value and its own ignorance of the actual economic ends and purposes of its citizens. According to Hayek, this ignorance extended to the agents themselves, who are incapable of any exact expression of their own ends, and so these ends are not, even in principle, capable of being known and thus used and organized by a centralized BUREAUCRACY.

Hayek's arguments were important at a time when theories of central planning in socialist, communist, and welfare states were generally accepted as both economically feasible and politically desirable. In place of an economics of planning, Hayek constructed an economics founded on the idea of a spontaneous order. Such an order emerges in an economy through the activities and choices of discrete individuals, not as a consequence of intention and control. Hayek's LIBERALISM comes through at this point. He argues that centralized economic planning threatened both the material welfare of citizens and their liberties and FREEDOMS. What is crucial, according to Hayek, in protecting the welfare of citizens and their freedoms is EQUALITY before the LAW. The chief role of the government is to ensure equality before the law and not attempt to impose other economic measures to achieve political ends such as a particular favored economic distribution. Hayek stops short of a LIBERTARIAN position assigning functions to government beyond the minimalist conceptions advanced by theorists such as Robert Nozick. He argued for example that the state has a role in providing support to those on the margins of the market economy. It is not always clear, however, by what principle Hayek determines when the state has a legitimate role in adjusting the spontaneous order of the market economy.

Hayek was born in Vienna, Austria, to a family of academics. He studied at the University of Vienna, graduating in law and political science. After teaching in Austria, Hayek took up a position at the London School of Economics in 1931, entering into debate with Keynes and other welfarist economists. In 1950, he moved to the University of Chicago and, in 1967, to the University of Salzburg.

Hegel, Georg Wilhelm Friedrich (1770–1831)
German philosopher

Most famous for his development of the idea of the DIALECTIC, which he learned from Eastern mysticism and religion, that posits that all reality is made up of opposites (day/night; light/dark; freedom/authority; etc.). Hegel's dialectical view of society leads to both MARXIST COMMUNISM and state FASCISM. In Hegel's main political book *The Philosophy of Right* (1821), the dialectic occurs in three social "moments" or institutions: the family, CIVIL SOCIETY, and the STATE. The family is a unit of primitive or natural unselfish altruism as the individual identifies with its interests and sacrifices for it. Civil society is the competitive economic realm where individuals have to look after themselves, are self-interested, and are antagonistic to others. The state is to be a unity that subsumes differing interests into one totality, serving the universal national good and producing real FREEDOM. This organic state "synthesizes" other family, business, and class antagonism, producing the CITIZENSHIP that transcends religion, class, and region. The ideal government, for Hegel, would be an assembly of estates (classes, groups, corporations), a professional civil service, and a limited MONARCHY. For him, history moves dialectically toward this ideal state and the consciousness of freedom. Examples of this historical development include: (1) the Oriental world, in which one (ruler) was free but all others were unfree; (2) the CLASSICAL world, in which a few were free, but most were unfree; and (3) the Germanic world in which through universal citizenship all are free. This universal freedom was advancing through democratic movements and PROTESTANT CHRISTIANITY. Hegel extolled the French Revolution, Napoleon, the English PARLIAMENT, and German nationalism as signs of this social progress.

Hegel, whose writings are extremely obscure and difficult to comprehend, taught philosophy at the universities of Heidelberg and Berlin.

Further Readings

Avineri, S. *Hegel's Theory of the Modern State.* New York: Cambridge University Press, 1972.

Harris, H. S. *Hegel's Development.* Oxford, Eng.: Clarendon Press, 1972.

Shklar, J. N. *Freedom and Independence: A Study of the Political Ideas of Hegels' Phenomenology of Mind.* Cambridge, Eng.: Cambridge University Press, 1976.

Taylor, C. *Hegel.* Cambridge, Eng.: Cambridge University Press, 1975.

Heidegger, Martin (1889–1976)   *German philosopher*

Heidegger was born and died in the town of Messkirch, in the Black Forest region of Germany. Raised as a CATHOLIC, he attended a Jesuit seminary and spent a brief period as a Jesuit novice. He later studied philosophy at the University of Freiburg and received his doctorate for a thesis on the medieval philosopher Johannes DUNS SCOTUS. Heidegger taught at Freiburg from 1916 to 1923 and then spent the next four years at the University of Marburg before returning to Freiburg to assume the chair of philosophy on the retirement of Edmund Husserl. Hannah ARENDT and Herbert MARCUSE were students of Heidegger.

While at Marburg, Heidegger published his most famous work, *Being and Time* (1927) in which he offered a phenomenological analysis of human existence, which for Heidegger was the means for addressing the metaphysical question of "the meaning of Being." According to Heidegger, the world is not simply an array of objects against which we are set as individual thinking subjects; rather, we are "beings-in-the-world" insofar as we inhabit and engage with a worldly environment that provides the conditions for a meaningful existence. Heidegger argued that we find ourselves "thrown" into the world and that our human reality is shaped by the various ways that we encounter and question our mode of Being. We can live "inauthentically" by ignoring our individuality and becoming part of the "they," or crowd, and its conformist conventions, or we can live "authentically" by assuming responsibility for our individual choices and actions, thereby understanding that we give meaning and value to our lives. Because of Heidegger's philosophy of being, he is often, though controversially, regarded as a proponent of EXISTENTIALISM.

Still more controversial is Heidegger's relationship to politics. In 1933 he was appointed rector of the University of Freiburg by the NAZI government. In his inaugural address as rector, Heidegger stated that "'Academic Freedom' . . . is banished from the German university," and in an article in the student newspaper later that year he wrote "The Führer himself, and only he, is the current and future reality of Germany, and his word is your law." Heidegger's early enthusiasm for national socialism apparently abated, however, and he resigned the rectorship in 1934. Nevertheless, Heidegger was not permitted to teach in

Germany by the allied occupation forces between 1945 and 1951. Heidegger never issued a clear apology for his support of the Nazis, although in a 1966 interview with *Der Speigel* magazine, he claimed "I would today no longer write the sentences which you cite [quoted above]. Even by 1934 I no longer said such things." There is today an extensive and lively debate among scholars about both the extent of Heidegger's sympathy for the Nazi movement and the relevance of his political actions with respect to the integrity of his body of thought. Although it may be possible to overstate Heidegger's support of the Nazis, it surely is too simple to dismiss his activities, especially given his philosophy of existential authenticity and moral responsibility.

Heidegger's later writings contain a critique of HUMANISM. In the "Letter on Humanism" (1947), Heidegger responded to the claim by Jean-Paul SARTRE that existentialism was a humanism in that it sought to place human beings at the center of history. Heidegger rejected Sartre's position of starting from the subjectivity of individual consciousness, a move that also constituted the famous "turn" in Heidegger's own thought away from his earlier individualistic existentialism. Heidegger argued instead that we must allow our thinking to transcend the individual toward a greater attentiveness to Being and the way that language, which itself transcends individual consciousness, reveals or discloses Being. Heidegger thus warns against the claims of humanism, particularly those of political action based on the idea of rational, freely choosing, and authentic human subjects.

Further Reading
Young, J. *Heidegger, Philosophy, and Nazism.* Cambridge, Eng.: Cambridge University Press, 1997.

Helvétius, Claude-Adrien (1715–1771) *French philosopher and encyclopedist*

Claude-Adrien Helvétius was a French philosopher whose work influenced later thinkers such as Jeremy BENTHAM and James Mill. He was one of the French encyclopedists and believed in the materialism common to that group. His most significant work was *De l'espirit* (*Essays on the Mind*), which was condemned by both the French government and the pope, but, along with many of his other essays, was translated after his death and widely read throughout Europe.

Helvétius was born in Paris and studied at the Collége Louis-le Grand. In 1738, he became the farmer-general, a prominent and lucrative tax-collecting position. He later was appointed chamberlain to the queen. Helvétius served in this post until 1751, at which point he retired to the country. Frustrated with the intrigue and trivialities of court life, Helvétius moved to a small estate at Vore and married. He devoted the rest of his life to philanthropy and philosophical discourse. The philosopher traveled to England in 1764 and Germany the following year. He was well received at the court of Frederick II as one of the leading voices of French intellectualism.

Like other encyclopedists, he was a staunch believer in materialism and contended that all human reasoning and emotions, including memory and judgment, were qualities derived from physical sensations. Like Locke, Helvétius believed that all humanity was born with their minds as essentially blank tablets (*tabula rasa*) and with equal intellectual capabilities. As such, all differences in later abilities were the direct result of variances in education, experience, and environment. This belief ran counter to the accepted class structure of monarchist France.

In *Essays on the Mind* (1758), Helvétius asserted that there was no real distinction between right and wrong, and moral choices were actually decided on the basis of self-INTEREST. Helvétius was an egoist who believed that self-interest took precedence over all other matters. He contended that humans never acted for the sake of others or in an altruist manner, unless such actions benefited their self-interest. This strong belief in hedonism led the encyclopedist to claim that all human actions are designed to maximize individual pleasure. However, ethical egoism is possible because self-sacrifice can result in great personal or societal rewards. Therefore, society enacts customs, laws, and traditions that reward actions that benefit the greater good.

This view of ETHICS, which placed self-satisfaction above all else, provoked a backlash by the government and the church. Helvétius's brand of utilitarianism led the Sorbonne to denounce *Essays on the Mind*, which was publicly burned in Paris. As with the *Encyclopédie*, there were efforts to suppress publication. However, overseas editions were broadly acclaimed, and the work became one of the most widely translated and read texts of the period.

Another major work, *De l'homme, de ses facultés intellectuelles et de son education* (*A Treatise on Man: His*

Intellectual Faculties and his Education) was posthumously published in two volumes in 1772. Interest in his writings remained acute even after his death, and a complete collection of his works was published in 1796.

Further Reading

Morley, J. *Diderot and the Encyclopaedists.* London: Macmillan, 1971.

Henry, Patrick (1736–1799)   *American revolutionary leader, lawyer, and politician*

Known for his stirring oratory, Patrick Henry uttered some of the most famous phrases of the American Revolution (such as "give me liberty, or give me death!"). Early in the colonial struggle against the British EMPIRE (the Stamp Act controversy), Henry advocated American independence. He was active in Virginia government (House of Burgesses, 1765–74; Continental Congress, 1774–76; governor, 1776–79; and Constitutional Convention, 1788).

He was a leading ANTIFEDERALIST, arguing against the new U.S. CONSTITUTION, especially with its leading proponent, James MADISON. Henry feared that the new national government would violate individual and STATES RIGHTS, and he was instrumental in the addition of the first ten amendments (The Bill of Rights) to the Constitution, protecting FREEDOM of speech, press, religion, and criminal rights. An EVANGELICAL CHRISTIAN, he supported the passage of the Virginia statute for religious freedom (1785). After the ratification of the federal Constitution, Henry was reconciled to the new government and became a FEDERALIST.

Largely self-educated, Henry had a gift of dramatic speech and became rich as a trial lawyer. He retired to a plantation farm in central Virginia but remained active in advising POPULIST politicians and church leaders. He represented the rising common people in the U.S. DEMOCRACY, especially the BAPTISTS, and encouraged ordinary people to become involved in politics. Remembered as a great Revolutionary patriot, his fervent speeches and ringing phrases are still taught to U.S. school children.

Further Reading

Mayer, Henry. *A Son of Thunder: Patrick Henry and the American Republic.* New York: Franklin Watts, 1986.

Henry VIII (1491–1547)   *English king, political and religious reformer*

Although a brutal dictator, King Henry VIII's reign as English monarch (1509–47) is considered significant for its moves toward MODERNITY in the increased power of PARLIAMENT and shift towards Protestant CHRISTIANITY. Fearful of not producing a male heir to continue the Stuart MONARCHY, Henry sought a divorce from his barren wife Catherine of Aragon. When the pope refused to grant an annulment, Henry led Parliament to pass legislation making the king of England head of the church. This followed the REFORMATION political theory of Martin LUTHER on the secular control of clergy. Henry remained doctrinally CATHOLIC (except for recognition of the papal supremacy) but opened the door for Protestantism in the English or Anglican Church polity. The pope excommunicated Henry with the support of Thomas MORE. The king proceeded to dissolve the Catholic monasteries in England, granting their PROPERTY to various nobles (and thereby gaining their political support). In 1536, he decreed the use of the English Bible (over the Latin) in churches, effecting a major Protestant principle of teaching religion in the vernacular.

Henry VIII's reign is chiefly remembered for causing England to separate from the jurisdiction of the Roman church ("The Bishop of Rome hath no authority in this realm of England" in the English Articles of Faith); the setting of the royal AUTHORITY over church affairs; the increased use and power of the REPUBLICAN Parliament; and the expansion of English influence in Ireland and the world. Henry was educated in Renaissance HUMANISM and took a keen interest in ecclesiastical matters as a youth. Engaging and bright during his early years, his adulthood is remembered as brutal, dictatorial, and cruel.

Further Reading

Ridley, Jasper Godwin. *Statesman and Saint: Cardinal Wolsey, Sir Thomas More, and the Politics of Henry VIII.* New York: Viking Press, 1961.

Herder, Johann Gottfried von (1744–1803)   *Philosopher and cultural historian*

Herder was one of KANT's students in the Prussian town of Köningsberg in the 1760s, and it was against the spirit of Kant's ENLIGHTENMENT ideas that Herder devoted his writings. In particular, Herder challenged the prevailing rationalist, universalist, and scientistic views of language, psychology, history, and culture.

Herder's most influential contribution to political thought is his philosophy of history and culture. His arguments are most fully set out in *Another Philosophy of History and Humanity*, 1774, and in *Ideas for a Philosophy of History and Humanity*, 1784–91. As with many of Herder's central themes, Herder's first interest in the opposition between history and REASON began with his study of language and literature. The latter, he argued, cannot be properly understood outside of the historical context of their development. To understand language and literature is to comprehend the particularities of the circumstances of their creation; it is this idea that Herder applies to understanding history. The enlightenment model of historical knowledge was the application of universal values and measures to all cultures. Cultures could be understood by standing outside and beyond them, using reason and objectivity as the tools of knowledge. Herder argued that cultures could only be understood by taking up a position inside the culture in question, abandoning one's own cultural prejudices, and seeing the world within the circumstances of that culture.

The political realization of the enlightenment ideal was, in Herder's view, the centralized, BUREAUCRATIC STATE, exemplified in his own time by the sprawling states of Austria and Russia. He objected to what he took to be the coercive character of these cosmopolitan states that incorporated diverse cultures and nations within their borders. He argued that political freedom required nations of people who shared a common culture, history, and most particularly language. Herder thus advocated NATIONALISM. He was, however, careful to argue that there was no hierarchy of cultures and that cultures were therefore of an equal value. It was a nationalism intended to promote freedom and agency within nations and between nations equal in worth.

Herder's philosophy avoided strict analytic divisions and reductive solutions. He thus argued against what he called faculty psychology, where the mind was neatly divided into parts, some concerned with reason, some with desire, and so on. He also resisted the idea that science was universal in its scope and methods. He was one of the first to argue that knowledge of human behavior and society required different scientific methods than those used for the natural world.

Herder's influence on political thought is inestimable. His historicist approaches to philosophical and political concerns continue to shape debates and mark the divisions between those who advocate a universalist agenda and those who oppose the paradigm handed down from the Enlightenment thinkers. His influence was most clear in the 19th century when his ideas found their way into the writings of FICHTE and HEGEL and through these to MARX and NIETZCHE.

Herder was the son of a schoolmaster. He studied at the University of Köningsberg under KANT, attending his lectures. His views on language and history were influenced by the anti-Enlightenment thinker J. G. Hamann. He in turn was an important influence on Goethe.

Further Reading
Berlin, I. *Vico and Herder.* New York: Viking Press, 1976.

hierarchy/hierarchical

A social organization based on higher and lower ranks, AUTHORITY, and power. Perhaps the easiest MODERN example of hierarchy is the military, with its strict order of rank and authority. In a hierarchical system, power is formal, official, and clearly obvious. The people higher on the hierarchical scale, or "superiors," have control and power over those lower on the hierarchy, or "inferiors." Another example is the CATHOLIC Church with its hierarchy of priests, bishops, cardinals, and the pope. In traditional hierarchical political theory (such as ARISTOTLE, St. Thomas AQUINAS), hierarchical authority is good because it represents superior VIRTUE, intelligence, goodness, skill, or honor having power over the less accomplished or less moral. Hierarchical theory also applies to ideas or values in which some philosophies or religions are better than others. In CLASSICAL thought (PLATO) the PHILOSOPHER-KING rules because of his superior virtue in wisdom and goodness, and this benefits everyone in society, including the lesser people. In Aristotelian philosophy, superior people, ideas, or values are characterized by being more complete or comprehensive (so politics is superior to economics because it encompasses it). CHRISTIAN theology holds that its religion is best because it includes the finest elements of all other faiths but goes beyond them ("I am the way, the truth and the life," in Jesus' words). This hierarchical approach to society and ideas is contrasted with EGALITARIAN views, which present all people and values as equally important and valid. This EQUALITY view, characteristic of most MODERN, ENLIGHTENMENT thought, naturally led to DEMOCRACY, in which, in JEFFERSON's phrase, "all men are created equal." Thus, although hierarchies exist in the modern world, the egalitarian culture of most REPUBLICS makes them difficult to justify. An authority separate from the egalitarian one of personal preference is required to justify hierarchy. This can come in TRADITION (as in hereditary monarchy or aristocracy), God (or the Bible), race, knowledge, or efficiency. In the democratic culture of most Modern, secular states, only functional (work) superiority is considered a valid reason for hierarchy, so a successful executive earns higher position and wealth as a consequence of greater productivity.

Only very CONSERVATIVE ideology embraces hierarchy in the contemporary world. Like the ancient and MEDIEVAL, they base superior rank on the basis of culture (Western civilization), gender (men over women), education (classical), and religion (Judeo-Christian). Such hierarchy is not widespread or POLITICALLY CORRECT. In egalitarian, democratic society, every person and every opinion is considered equal to every other. This view lends itself to a kind of ethical relativism in which no standard exists for judging competing ideas or values. One effect of this is to attempt a separation of fact (science) and values (morality), but the political consequences of this, as in NAZI Germany, have been troubling. U.S. PLURALISM solves this dilemma by allowing formal legal equality for all citizens (in the public sphere) but allowing considerable hierarchy in the private sphere (family, business, clubs, religious organizations, etc.). The political battle between egalitarian and hierarchy then takes the form of defining *public* and *private,* with LIBERAL egalitarians trying to expand the public to every aspect of life (e.g., family, private associations) and conservatives trying to expand the private sphere (free from government regulation).

For hierarchical thinkers, the debate will continue because hierarchy exists in the universe and nature and cannot be eliminated from society and politics. The most radical attempt to abolish hierarchy, MARXIST COMMUNISM (by seeing all people as common workers and "comrades"), ended in a most AUTHORITARIAN system.

Hindu political thought

The political viewpoint of regions (especially India) where the Hindu religion predominates. The Hindu religious tradition, with its multiple gods and goddesses (polytheism) and belief in many spirits that affect human life, has influenced the basic political worldview of Hindu cultures. But certain aspects of Hindu political thought (such as the class and caste system) suggest that some Western ideals (such as PLATO's *Republic*) may have influenced Eastern thought.

Most of Hindu political thought views the universe in animist terms as a cosmic whole that is animated by divine Truth or intelligence. So unlike Western Judeo-CHRISTIAN theology in which God is the creator of the universe and outside it, Hindus see the natural order itself as a deity and worship it. The individual has a God-given (and hereditary) "place" in this divine universe, so staying in one's place and performing the duties of that place is JUSTICE. This explains the rather static, fatalistic attitude of society and also explains the poor as just part of the divine natural order, to be accepting of their unchanging position in society and oblivious to improving their conditions. If people wish to improve their social and political situation, punishment and repression may be properly imposed; Hindus call this the path of rectitude—remaining in one's given place, performing one's function diligently, and not questioning this "divinely ordained" system.

The society is conceived as a collection of communities or classes, reflecting specific economic functions or occupations, into which one is born. A HIERARCHY controls and manages this society, so Brahmans or rulers, soldiers, workers and those performing the meanest, dirtiest tasks ("untouchables") are supposedly determined by a universal divine order. Any attempt to change or get out of this system is seen as sinful, self-love, pride, and corrupt INDIVIDUALISM; such self-assertion is creating a "bad karma" that will be punished later by being reincarnated as a lower being (or in a lower caste). In short, the poor wretched people can be shown contempt or cruelty because they are getting their just punishment.

This does not lend itself to sympathy for the poor and oppressed, but rather further abuse and EXPLOITATION of them. The CHRISTIAN view that this is oppressive and uncharitable is dismissed by Hindu thought as unenlightened. So, Hindu views of inevitable, static, caste order regards Western FREEDOM as confusion, chaos, and lawlessness. Government should suppress such dangerous freedom. The leader of the state, or ideal king, serves this stabilizing function: He should promote commerce, prosperity, and the "righteousness" of this Hindu order. He may properly use violence, intrigue, bribery, deception, and cruelty to accomplish this task. He rules with the "seven organs" of government: his MONARCHY; ministers; the territorial COMMUNITY; military fortifications; the treasury; the army; and allies. Punishing dissenters and traitors is an important function of the Hindu prince. Strict punishment of breakers of the universal order serves to deter other offenders and preserve the society against the "evils" of individual freedom and PROGRESS.

This central theme of Hindu political thought exists within a diversity of deities and cults that encourages relativism that preserves its central teachings while offering a surface image of TOLERATION. Both the rigidness and the polytheistic confusion explain recurrent conflicts in India between Hindus and monotheistic Muslims, as well as between India and the Western CAPITALIST democracies.

Further Readings

Ghoshal, U. N. *A History of Hindu Political Theories*. Bombay; New York, Indian Branch: Oxford University Press, 1959.
Jayaswal, K. P. *Hindu Polity*. Eastern Book House, 1924.

historical materialism

A theory of history developed by Karl MARX and Friedrich ENGELS (and carried on by later COMMUNISTS) that conceives of historical social change and progress as motivated by technological advances in economic production. Accordingly, all ideas, LAW, politics, art, education, religion, and philosophy as the "superstructure" reflect the fundamental, materialist "structure" of the economy. So, for example, Marxism sees the organic, hierarchical theology of MEDIEVAL CHRISTIANITY (St. Thomas AQUINAS) as simply reflecting the social class structure of the European Middle Ages and economic FEUDALISM. Thus, ideas are not autonomous or important by themselves but are determined by economic technology and "relations of production."

This theory further claims to be "scientific SOCIALISM" in discovering universal laws of history that prove that capitalism will inevitably lead to socialism and then to communism. Much like Darwin's theory of biological evolution, of which Marx approved, historical materialism sees human social progress as following natural laws. It rejects any supernatural, spiritual dimension to human history or any possibility of alternative developments in economic progress.

With the fall of communism as a world system (the end of the SOVIET UNION) in the 1980s, this philosophy is no longer widely subscribed to, except by certain Western academic philosophers and sociologists.

Further Reading

Lichtheim, G. *Marxism*. New York: Praeger Publishers, 1961.

historicism/historicist

A philosophy originally developed in Germany in the mid-1800s (see George HEGEL and Karl MARX) that views socials truth as historically relative. For historicism, then, there is no constant, universal human nature that exists in all times. Rather, HUMAN NATURE and social concepts (JUSTICE, FREEDOM, DEMOCRACY, etc.) are conditioned by people's historical and social context. So, the social environment really makes human beings what they are, and because social, economic, and political concepts change throughout history, humans are different at different times and places in the world. So, MODERN, 20th-century people in technologically advanced, CAPITALIST democracies cannot relate to people from ancient Israel, CLASSICAL Greece, MEDIEVAL CHRISTIAN Europe, and so on. This leads to a depreciation of the value of past literature on current intellectual life (e.g., the Bible, ancient philosophy such as that of PLATO and ARISTOTLE, the CATHOLIC Middle Ages). Historicism tends to view knowledge as progressing, so old books are inferior to newer writings; the knowledge of Solomon or Jesus has been superseded by superior recent studies. There is, therefore, a certain contempt for the past and arrogance of newness in historicism. It presumes that Modern people are unable to know ancient thinkers (because of their differing social contexts) and that civilization has advanced and progressed over time, so Modern ideas are necessarily better than older principles. It portrays old systems of thought as at best incomplete and naïve and at worst pathetic and dangerous. So, for example, historicist economics dismisses ancient warnings against usury as quaint and primitive; historicist, LIBERAL theology diminishes the value of the Bible and other sacred texts as archaic and outmoded. Simply by being "old," an idea (such as patriarchy or faithfulness) is considered wrong by historicism. The alternative to historicism is traditional, CONSERVATIVE religion, philosophy, and psychology that see humanity as constant, uniform, unchanged by historical and social circumstances and, therefore, benefiting from the wisdom of the past. This conservative view that "nothing is new under the sun" sees the same human capacities, emotions, reason, and dilemmas throughout history. So, the stories of human life in the Bible, Aristotle's ethics,

Shakespeare's plays, or John LOCKE's STATE OF NATURE all have something to teach contemporary people.

These differing perspectives (historicist versus conservative) show up in differing educational perspectives (for example, multiculturalism versus classical). For one, the past has nothing to teach us; for the other, it is the most reliable guide to the present.

MARXISM or COMMUNISM is the typical historicist approach. Because it sees people as determined by the way they produce or work, and because economic production techniques change in history (agricultural, industrial, etc.), then all past knowledge is premised in antiquated social systems. Only the most Modern philosophy, like the latest computer, is the best. Even better is what is becoming or is the revolutionary prophesy of radical communism: Real knowledge is based on prediction of what the future will become. So, SOCIALIST economic planning looked at future trends; the old was useless. CRITICAL THEORY and critical thinking are based in a historicist worldview. Conservative approaches (such as those of Edmund BURKE) are characterized by "reverent thinking," valuing past knowledge that has stood the test of time, perennial truths that always give wisdom (as in *Proverbs*), regardless of historical or political setting.

In Western thought, both historicism and conservative ideologies exist and are in tension. Contemporary democratic politics tends emphasize the new and innovative (historicism), but a nostalgic return to "basics" or "fundamental truths" also appears in Modern politics and political philosophy. See CULTURE WARS.

Further Reading

Ryan, Kiernan, ed. *New Historicism and Cultural Materialism: A Reader.* New York: St. Martin's Press, 1996.

Hitler, Adolf (1889–1945)   *German Nazi dictator*

As the leader of NATIONAL SOCIALISM, or the NAZI Party, Hitler's political thought represents German FASCISM, which subordinates the individual to the national (and the leader's) will. Influenced by the philosophy of Friedrich NIETZSCHE, the anti-Semitic (anti-Jewish) ideas of Karl Lueger, theosophy spiritism, and the occult, Hitler's ideas revolved around the supremacy of the German nation and the Aryan Master Race. In this nationalist fascism, CHRISTIANITY is seen as weak and passive, a "slave" religion to be rejected in favor of a neopagan state religion. The Nazi German Third Reich

Benito Mussolini and Adolf Hitler in Munich, Germany, ca. June 1940. (NATIONAL ARCHIVES)

claimed to be the "third Rome" of Holy Roman Empire controlling the world.

Hitler's ideology was based on hatred of many groups that he claimed had deceived and destroyed Germany: COMMUNISTS, Jews, the pope, Christian SOCIALISTS, and the Slavic races. Ruthless destruction of these groups was justified by his conspiratorial view of anti-German forces. Hitler's mad rhetoric, masterful psychological manipulation, and deceitful use of power gave him absolute authority in the German government by 1933. Like the classic dictator described by ARISTOTLE, Hitler quickly used his power to kill his political opponents, replace professional diplomats, put his party rivals in jail, enforce censorship, and spy on and terrorize the population. As a TOTALITARIAN regime, Nazi Germany controlled every aspect of life under politics: economics, the family, sports, education, and private groups or associations of CIVIL SOCIETY (e.g., the Boy Scouts became the Hitler Youth).

Like Italian fascist theory (Giovanni GENTILE), Hitler's national socialism justified military aggression against neighboring countries (Austria, Czechoslovakia, France, Poland) through pretenses of racial and national superiority and a historical mission to rule and dominate the world. Nazi foreign policy claimed to be invading and robbing other countries to liberate oppressed German populations in those countries. Still, Hitler's military strategy often failed; the voices or spirits that spoke to his "intuition" halted the German capture of Moscow and the defeat of Great Britain at crucial periods in the war. The destruction of World

War II that Hitler's Nazi regime unleashed caused the deaths of 50 million people, unprecedented human suffering, and material destruction. Its attempt to exterminate the Jewish people resulted in the death of 6 million Jews (the Holocaust). Together, the domestic tyranny, cruel atrocities, and international terror make Hitler the most horrifying name in Modern history, a monster of satanic proportions. This episode in a civilized European country in the 20th century challenged the MODERN ENLIGHTENMENT optimism over HUMAN NATURE and social PROGRESS. Philosophically, then, Nazi fascism led to a POST-MODERNIST rejection of Modernist reason and order, as well as a revival of traditional Judeo-CHRISTIAN appreciations of human sin and political evil.

The ultimate irony of Hitler's legacy was its short duration (12 years rather than the supposed thousand years) and its destruction of the nation that claimed to be the world's "master race." Hitler himself committed suicide in his underground Berlin bunker as the Russian and Allied armies conquered the city.

Further Reading
Bullock, A. *Hitler.* Harmondsworth, Eng.: Penguin Books, 1962.

Hobbes, Thomas (1588–1679)   *English philosopher and founder of British liberalism*

The MODERN LIBERAL concepts of RIGHTS, INDIVIDUALISM, LIBERTY, government by CONSENT, and SOCIAL CONTRACT begin with Hobbes's philosophy. A materialist, he looked at HUMAN NATURE and society from a scientific, biological perspective. For Hobbes, people are just like everything else in the universe: matter in motion. He applies this scientific method to humans through their physical senses (sight, smell, hearing, taste, touch), being their only source of knowledge. Thus, human action or behavior can be explained by either pain or pleasure: People have "appetite" to more *toward* something that pleases their senses (beauty, food, warmth, etc.) and "aversion" to move *away* from things that hurt their senses (excessive heat or cold, poverty, or boring lecturers). All human thoughts, therefore, are derived from sensory data. This empiricism forms the philosophical basis of BEHAVIORISM in social science. It contrasts with earlier Western social thought that explains human conduct in terms of VIRTUE or ETHICS (PLATO and ARISTOTLE) or moral reason. It reduces the human being to the status of any other animal except

for one thing: rationality. Rationality for Hobbes is a calculating faculty that humans use to add and subtract pleasures and pain. So, unlike other creatures who are wholly governed by their sensory feelings, human reason allows us to calculate the total pleasure or pain of an experience and sometimes endure some pain for a greater pleasure (like sacrificial saving, investing) or forgo a pleasure that causes greater pain later (such as drunkenness, illicit sex, "flying" off a rooftop).

This materialistic view of Hobbes leads him to define human relationships in terms of POWER. He divides power into natural (one's physical strength, intelligence, eloquence, beauty) and instrumental (money, fame, prestige, honor), but more power allows an individual to acquire more pleasure and avoid more pain. All humans, then, want more power. This is because the worth of a person in Hobbes's view is the amount of power the person has (or what another would pay to use it—leading to the labor market). So, the worth of a person in this materialistic philosophy is the person's price. This reduces people to being products to be bought or sold. It violates the CLASSICAL and CHRISTIAN view of human dignity as a moral being created in God's image, capable of noble deeds. Hobbes reduces human dignity to social prestige, especially honors (such as titles) conferred by the state (awards, knighthood, earldoms, etc.).

Such a view of humanity logically leads to an original society (or "state of nature") that is highly competitive and combative. All individuals seek their own pleasure, power, and prestige, and soon they are in conflict with each other. In this "natural" state, Hobbes says, everyone has a right to anything he or she can get, steal, or kill. Thus, our EQUALITY comes from each being able to murder another. Original human society is a jungle existence—full of violence and insecurity. This prevents higher development of economics, culture, art, luxury, or learning. So, in this dangerous setting, human reason comes to the rescue: it tells the person that it is better to give up some liberty in exchange for security.

The government is formed by a social contract of all those individuals (by consent) surrendering their rights to the sovereign state (preferably a monarch) who, in exchange, promises to protect them from theft, murder, kidnapping, and so on. The STATE, for Hobbes, must have ABSOLUTIST power to accomplish this because people are prone to break their promises. He advocates a strong, terrifying state to keep people in line. Rational citizens will recognize the advantage of social peace and give obedience to the government. Hobbes allows the state to regulate PROPERTY, censor speech and press, dictate jobs and residence—every aspect of society but killing the subjects, whom it was created to protect. So, this early philosophical liberalism does not allow individuals to retain many natural rights (as later, John LOCKE, John Stuart MILL, or Thomas JEFFERSON do), but Hobbes insists that this absolute authority is necessary to preserve social order. He ridicules "those democratical writers" who want to limit the power of the state, comparing their minds to the diseased madness of rabies. Any brutal authority is preferable to the "war of all against all" in the state of nature, where life is "solitary, poor, nasty, brutish and short." It is thought that Hobbes's experience of the disorder of the English civil wars led to a paranoid fear of freedom and ANARCHY.

Because of its authoritarian conclusions, Hobbes's political theory was soon out of favor, but his materialist premises continued to inform democratic liberalism and behaviorist social science. Most significant was Hobbes's materialistic influence on Modern ethical relativism. If all ethical value judgments are derived from knowledge, and all knowledge is from private sensory experience, definitions of *good* and *evil* are all personal and vary by individual. If one person takes pleasure in eating dirt, no universal moral standard can obviate that preference. Hobbes's scientific morality bases all ethical decisions in individual senses and choice, without any overriding definition of *right* and *wrong* (from the community in ARISTOTLE, the church in St. Thomas AQUINAS, God in John CALVIN, the Bible in Martin LUTHER). This leads in Modern EGALITARIAN democratic society to ethical relativism, where no shared common moral vision exists over the whole society. It develops into what James HUNTER calls the PROGRESSIVE mindset in contemporary United States.

Thomas Hobbes was born into a lower-middle-class family in England; his father abandoned the family when Thomas was young. He attended Oxford and served as tutor to the noble Devonshire family, which allowed him to travel to the intellectual centers of Europe (Paris, Venice). His main book in political philosophy is *The Leviathan* (1651). For its atheistic ideas, it was banned by the British Parliament and blamed, with other sacrilegious books, for God's wrath in the Great Fire of London in 1666. Hobbes's ideas offended both REPUBLICAN Parliamentarians (who wanted the state to be less absolutist) and royalist monarchists (who wanted to base their legitimacy in DIVINE RIGHT OF KINGS). Despite his unpopularity, Hobbes enjoyed a long life and had a worldwide reputation for his intellectual activities.

Further Readings

Brown, K. C., ed. *Hobbes Studies.* Cambridge, Mass.: Harvard University Press, 1965.

Goldsmith, M. M. *Hobbes's Science of Politics.* New York: Columbia University Press, 1966.

Warrender, H. *The Political Philosophy of Hobbes.* Oxford, Eng.: Oxford University Press, 1957.

Watkins, J. W. N. *Hobbes's System of Ideas.* London: Hutchinson, 1973.

Hobhouse, Leonard Trelawney (1864–1929)
English writer and sociologist

During his distinguished career, Leonard Trelawney Hobhouse produced a number of works that detailed the basis for the MODERN LIBERAL movement. Hobhouse became a sociologist after initially teaching philosophy and writing for the *Manchester Guardian.* In addition to his political works, Hobhouse also wrote extensively on the development of scientific thought and human REASONING.

Hobhouse was born in St. Ives, Cornwall, in 1864. He was educated at Marlborough and studied classics at Corpus Christi College at Oxford. In 1890, Hobhouse became an assistant tutor at Oxford, where he taught philosophy; he was eventually elected a fellow of Corpus Christi College. At Oxford, Hobhouse began to study the trade union movement. This sparked an interest in sociology, which led the young scholar to abandon philosophy for the social sciences. Hobhouse's first scholarly monograph, *The Labour Movement* (1893), reflected his newfound interest. This work was followed by another sociological piece, *The Theory of Knowledge* (1896).

In 1897, Hobhouse began to write for the *Manchester Guardian.* He ultimately became responsible for writing the newspaper's lead articles. While at this post, he also produced two important books, *Mind in Evolution* (1901) and *Democracy and Reaction* (1904). *Mind in Evolution* demonstrated Hobhouse's keen intellectual abilities. He studied the major stages of human mental development and concluded that evolution did not automatically imply PROGRESS toward greater mental performance. Instead, evolution marked a diffusion of knowledge and widening of scope, including the emergence of self-consciousness.

Hobhouse's success with these works led him to leave the *Manchester Guardian* to help cofound a new liberal newspaper, *The Tribune*. That same year, he also became the editor of the *Sociological Review*. In 1907, he was appointed a professor of sociology at London University. Although he was not a formal member of the staff, Hobhouse did continue to publish articles in the *Guardian,* and in 1911, he was made a director of the paper.

Also in 1911, Hobhouse published one of his seminal political works, *Liberalism,* in which he presented an overview of what has come to be known as welfare liberalism. Hobhouse echoed John Mill's warnings about the tyranny of the majority in DEMOCRATIC societies and of customs and traditions. He further argued that FREEDOM was only one component of a modern democratic society and that there needed to be social protections built into a nation's infrastructure and government to ensure EQUALITY. Hobhouse contended that government had a role to play in regulating industry to prevent corporations from gaining unfair competitive advantages over other companies that voluntarily adopted policies that were advantageous for workers, including higher wages, pension benefits, and fewer working hours.

Hobhouse was initially opposed to British participation in World War I but came to support the government after the outbreak of the war. He again switched positions as a result of the mounting casualties, and by 1917, he advocated a negotiated peace. He also was a staunch supporter of women's SUFFRAGE. Following the war, he wrote a number of other influential works, including *The Rational Good* (1921), *The Elements of Social Justice* (1922), and *Social Development* (1924).

Further Reading

Collini, S. *Liberalism and Sociology: L. T. Hobhouse and Political Argument in England, 1880–1914.* Cambridge, Eng.: Cambridge University Press, 1979.

Holbach, Paul-Henri-Dietrich, baron d'
(1723–1789)   *French philosopher*

Holbach was born Paul Heinrich Dietrich in Edesheim, Germany, but was raised and educated in Paris by his wealthy uncle, Franciscus Adam d'Holbach. He became a French national in 1749 and inherited the estate and title of baron d'Holbach after the death of his uncle in 1753. Holbach studied at the University of Leiden, but it was only after he settled into his Paris estate that he began to establish his reputation. It was at this time that Holbach began to associate with many of the most famous radical thinkers or *philosophes* of the period, including Marie-Jean CONDORCET, Denis DIDEROT, Claude-Adrien HELVÉTIUS, and Jean-Jacques ROUSSEAU. Holbach's *salon* became the center for intense intellectual debate, particularly the exchange of radical moral and political ideas and the critique of existing institutions.

Holbach contributed several hundred articles, mostly on science, to the massive *Encyclopédie* that was organized and published by the *philosophes*. He also wrote a number of treatises, the earliest of which included *Christianity Unveiled* (1761) and *The Sacred Contagion; or Natural History of Superstition* (1768). Holbach became notorious as the most vocal atheist among the Parisian intellectuals. He condemned organized religion as harmful nonsense and insisted that there is no such thing as the soul or spiritual substance. Instead, as Holbach argued in *The System of Nature* (1770), human beings are nothing more than the causally determined products of a mechanistic physical universe. All of reality consists of matter and motion, which assumes different forms according to natural laws of cause and effect.

Holbach's atheistic materialism served as the basis for his moral and political theories. According to Holbach, human beings are naturally driven to secure their self-preservation and happiness. However, because humans are imperfect and unequal in their capabilities, the only way to attain happiness for all is through social exchange and cooperation. Consequently, Holbach defined *ethics* as the human science of determining the needs of humans and of devising the most effective means for satisfying these needs. For Holbach, ethics was considered a form of practical knowledge in contrast to the illusory superstition of religion. The former, when taken as a type of UTILITARIANISM, was capable of securing human happiness, whereas the latter, when understood as supernatural dogmatism, can breed only unhappiness and conflict.

Holbach's political theory is an extension of his ethics. In Holbach's view, the proper role of politics is to insure the well-being of society. The state is to be established through a "social pact" that grounds political power on the will and consent of the public. The goal of the pact is to develop the cooperative interactions of citizens so that they may provide useful services necessary for the satisfaction of their individual and collective needs. The LEGITIMACY of a government, therefore, depends on its ability to organize social exchange and secure the happiness of the people. Consistent with the ideals of the ENLIGHTENMENT, Holbach believed that individual RIGHTS to LIBERTY, security, and PROPERTY must also be guaranteed and that church and state must be separated to avoid the dangers of TYRANNY and intolerance.

Further Reading

Topazio, Virgil W. *d'Holbach's Moral Philosophy: Its Background and Development*. Geneva: Institut et Musée Voltaire, Les Delices, 1956.

holistic/holism

A view of society as organic and interconnected. Applied to philosophy and politics in the ENVIRONMENTAL movement and certain social theories (see FASCISM, COMMUNISM), holistic thought derives from Eastern cosmology, which focuses on the "whole" or totality of reality. An image commonly employed by the holistic perspective is of the single drop of water becoming part of the whole ocean, or "one," as it drops into the sea. So, through meditation, getting in touch with nature, gaining consciousness of the community or the nation within the self, an individual can relate to the "other." Holistic approaches to the earth, society, and politics, and are critical of INDIVIDUALISM, CAPITALISM, private PROPERTY, and monotheism.

The Western intellectual tradition of the Ancients (ARISTOTLE) and British LIBERALISM (John LOCKE) reject COMMUNITARIAN holism by asserting the importance of the individual and reason that differentiates among separate things. The drop of water may become "one" with the ocean when it falls into the sea, but is ceases to be a single drop. Fear of the particular being subsumed within and oppressed by the universal state or community prevents the West from embracing holistic philosophy for sustained periods. G.W.F. HEGEL's DIALECTIC probably brought this Eastern religious slant to Western politics more than any other Modern thinker.

Holocaust, The

The Holocaust names the systematic destruction of European Jewry beginning in the early 1930s with the German NAZI Party's identification of and legalized discrimination against Jews and culminating in the Nazi genocide of Europe's Jews in the death camps.

The scale of the genocide and its presence in the heart of European civilization signaled an abrupt set of questions that postwar thinkers are forced to confront: How was evil on this scale possible? Where was God? Where was man? But at the same time as the Holocaust demands intellectual attention and thought, in the words of theologian and Holocaust writer, Arthur Cohen, "There is something in the nature of thought—its patient deliberateness and care for logical order—that is alien to the death camps." The first question therefore confronting writers on the Holocaust is whether their words, thought, and reflection can do justice to the irretrievable experience of those who suffered the events of the Holocaust. Although the answer to this question is, of course, "no," some philosophical, theological and political issues must be faced nonetheless.

One set of arguments concerns the place of the Holocaust in history, whether it was a unique event or another example, albeit on a very large scale, of the inhumanity of which we are capable. Richard Rubenstein, with others, has argued that what makes the Holocaust unique is its place in modernity. Rather than being an act of anger, the Holocaust was an industrial and bureaucratic event that required calculation and careful planning. It is this connection of the Holocaust with rationality—that most European of achievements—that makes it defining of the age of modernity and signifies, in the words of Hannah ARENDT, the "banality of evil."

From a political perspective, the Holocaust changes our perception of state power and, with it, the limits and legitimacy of the state's exercise of coercive force. The Holocaust brings into possibility an act of genocide as a government policy. In important ways, this internationalizes the question of government power and calls into ethical doubt absolute state SOVEREIGNTY.

From a theological perspective, the idea of God as omnipotent and as benevolent is placed in doubt by the fact of the Holocaust. Some Jewish theologians such as Richard Rubenstein have argued that the Holocaust is an empirical refutation of the existence of God. Emil Fackenheim argues that the Holocaust is compatible with God's existence and what is required is an articulation of a proper response to the Holocaust. Part of this response is not to be cynical and despairing, which would, he claims, be a way of completing Hitler's work for him. Arthur Cohen has argued that the idea of God must be reconceived in the aftermath of the Holocaust; more specifically, Cohen urges the idea that God should be understood as standing outside human history. More recently, Zachary Braiterman has employed a post-Modern perspective on these theological difficulties.

Further Readings

Braiterman, Z. *(God) After Auschwitz*. Princeton, N.J.: Princeton University Press, 1998.

Cohen, A. *The Tremendum*. New York: Crossroad, 1988.

Rubenstein, R. *The Cunning of History*. New York: Harper & Row, 1975.

Holy Roman Empire

The political empire of Western Europe from the coronation of CHARLEMAGNE in A.D. 800 to the conquest of Napoleon I in 1806. The "second thousand-year" empire saw itself as a successor to the first Roman Empire (500 B.C.–A.D. 500). As a political concept and image, the Holy Roman Empire represented Europe's nostalgic yearning for a universal, peaceful order, controlling strife within and defending from foreign invaders (especially Muslims of the Ottoman Empire). The image of a thousand-year empire was invoked by the NAZI German Third Reich (1933–45) under Adolf HITLER.

The Holy Roman Empire was distinguished from its pagan predecessor by the rise of the Roman CATHOLIC Church and papacy, which preserved CLASSICAL civilization and learning after the fall of the first Roman empire under Emperor Romulus Augustulus in A.D. 476. Just as the pope was seen as the vicar of Christ in spiritual matters, the emperor was seen as the vicar of Christ in temporal or worldly matters. But both had limits on their authority by the practical difficulties of managing a vast territorial empire made up of diverse nationalities, languages, and customs. Latin remained the language of the church and the court, partly to preserve this universal empire among Italians, Germans, Franks, and so on. The Eastern (BYZANTINE) empire, centered in Constantinople, also challenged the Holy Roman Empire's claim to succession of the earlier Roman empire.

Emperors were supposed to be elected under a procedure developed by the pope (with national "electors"), but the office tended to become hereditary from the kings of Germany, beginning with Otto I (the Hapsburg dynasty) in A.D. 936. A balance of power existed between the church, the emperor, various regional princes and independent towns, cities, and GUILDS. By 1648, there were more than 300 sovereign principalities or free imperial cities, so an informal system of CHECKS AND BALANCES existed in the Holy Roman Empire. The Protestant REFORMATION increased this division of power by breaking the Catholic monopoly over the church and aligned Lutheran princes against the emperor. By the 1700s, the imperial title had become largely honorific, but it contained considerable symbolic power. The current European Union is an economic and political form of the empire, devoid of a spiritual CHRISTIAN dimension.

Further Reading

Bryce, James Bryce, Viscount. *The Holy Roman Empire*. New York: St. Martin's Press, 1904.

homosexuality/homosexual

As a political issue, the debates over homosexual RIGHTS represent a serious conceptual and moral issue. By making sexual identity a public matter, the gay/lesbian/bisexual/transgender movement fulfills Hannah ARENDT's prophesy (in her book, *The Human Condition*) that traditionally private matters will become socialized in modernity. On a deeper level, the prohomosexual lobby, which seeks equal legal rights to nonheterosexual marriages and an end to all DISCRIMINATION on sexual orientation and activities grounds, reflects James Davison HUNTER's "PROGRESSIVE" mindset (in his book *Culture Wars*), which places personal individual preference above all objective and traditional moral standards and sees ethics as historically and personally relative. This is contrasted, by Hunter, with the more CONSERVATIVE "orthodox" perspective that rejects homosexuality on traditional moral, religious, and NATURAL-LAW grounds.

In contemporary U.S. politics, this takes the form of prohomosexuality in the LIBERAL DEMOCRAT PARTY, the liberal mainline Protestant churches (and Reformed Judaism), and the liberal media and educational institutions. The antihomosexual agenda groups include the CATHOLIC and EVANGELICAL Churches, the REPUBLICAN PARTY, and the conservative media and schools. Much of this public debate now coalesces on the issue of AIDS, a disease that affects male homosexuals disproportionately. Prohomosexual IDEOLOGY argues that laws forbidding homosexuals to have legal marriages (and therefore shared health-care insurance), military privileges, and social acceptance are discriminatory and unjust. Opponents of legal recognition of homosexuality argue the biblical denouncement of it as "an abomination to God" (Leviticus 18:22–30), the natural-law violation of its practice, the health consequences of its acceptance, and a fear of the decline of the traditional family and social fabric (not to mention for the CHRISTIAN RIGHT, COVENANT view of the wrath of God on a civilization that affirms immoral conduct).

Like the ABORTION issue, the political furor over legalized homosexuality is extremely volatile, often compared to the slavery controversy preceding the American Civil War. Proponents of homosexual rights view their cause as the logical conclusion of EGALITARIAN DEMOCRACY. Opponents see it as the moral decline of Western civilization, much like that which preceded the collapse of the Roman Empire. A complex social and psychological issue, it promises to continue as a prominent policy debate in the U.S. CULTURE WARS.

Hooker, Richard (1554–1600)   *English theologian and political philosopher*

In his classic book, *Of the Laws of Ecclesiastical Polity* (eight volumes), Hooker presented the Anglican royalist/Parliament theory of government. In it, he saw the English Church as a *via media,* or "middle way," between CATHOLIC and Protestant and the English state as a combination of the best of MONARCHY and REPUBLICAN government. Drawn from the MEDIEVAL, NATURAL-LAW perspective of St. Thomas AQUINAS, Hooker's political theory saw CHURCH AND STATE as both separate and related. He shared the Thomists' Aristotelian faith in reason and rejected the PURITAN belief that human intellect was hopelessly corrupted by sin. Still, he adopted the MODERN, LIBERAL belief in government by the CONSENT of the governed and the state as a SOCIAL CONTRACT (á la John LOCKE), which offended his monarchist colleagues who wanted to base the king's AUTHORITY in DIVINE RIGHT (see Robert FILMER). Hooker liked the British compromise of the king in Parliament, CHECKS AND BALANCES in a mixed CONSTITUTION, and the Established Church of England. The unique blending of religion and politics in England created the best society and government, for Hooker. Like Edmund BURKE later, he was a traditional CONSERVATIVE, seeing the accumulated wisdom of English culture and common law as forming the most just, stable regime. The church, as a political as well as a spiritual body,

conveyed an ethical tone to society and moderated the individual impulses of radical Protestantism. He feared the EVANGELICAL belief that every Christian can interpret scripture, seeing it as leading to ANARCHY and immorality. The church hierarchy must determine religious doctrine and practice, drawing on the wisdom of the past. A limited monarchy, a representative Parliament, and a state church created the wisest, fairest polity and culture.

Richard Hooker presents the classic British ethics of dignity, civility, and moderation; slow, balanced, compromising, he embodies high, aristocratic British taste and temperament. An archetypical "English gentleman," educated in Latin School at Exeter, he attended Corpus Christi College at Oxford. A teaching Fellow at Oxford, he also served as master of the temple church in London. As a scholar, churchman, and political writer, Richard Hooker displayed the attitudes and traits of a civilized, learned English Anglican clergyman. His idealization of the Late Middle Ages in England would not have predicted the social, religious, and political upheavals of the 1600s.

Further Reading
Faulkner, R. K. *Richard Hooker and the Politics of Christian England.* Berkeley: University of California Press, 1981.

Horkheimer, Max (1895–1973)   *German philosopher*

Horkheimer was the primary director of the Institute for Social Research, otherwise known as the FRANKFURT SCHOOL. Established in 1923, the Frankfurt School was a group of social theorists that developed a Marxist-inspired CRITICAL THEORY of modern CAPITALISM and culture.

Horkheimer assumed the position of the institute's director in 1930. He immediately began to recruit a number of important scholars to the institute, such as Theodor Adorno, Erich Fromm, and Herbert MARCUSE, and to formalize the Institute's research orientation. The Institute's theoretical approach was already dominated by Marxism, but Horkheimer was critical of the economic determinism exhibited by many orthodox Marxists who attempted to reduce all social phenomena to questions of the economic life of society. He insisted that science, art, religion, ethics, and the psychic structure of individual consciousness required analyses in their own right, although he also stressed that their interconnections with the economic system must be examined. Consequently, Horkheimer emphasized the necessity of both quantitative and qualitative social research of an interdisciplinary nature, with the goal of producing knowledge that was able to contribute to the struggle against all forms of political domination. Following the NAZI rise to power in 1933, Horkheimer facilitated the transfer of the institute from Frankfurt to Geneva and then to New York City and California. In 1953, the institute returned to Germany, and Horkheimer was appointed rector of the University of Frankfurt.

Horkheimer's own work in critical theory is generally divided into two stages. In the first stage, Horkheimer was careful to elaborate his notion of critical theory and to expound on its revolutionary potential. For example, in his essay "Traditional and Critical Theory" (1937), Horkheimer argued for a HISTORICAL MATERIALISM that viewed human activities within the changing contexts of concrete social situations. Out of material social life, particular human thoughts and practices emerge, and it is only by examining specific historical conditions that ideas and practices can be understood. From this perspective, Horkheimer claimed that the validity of ideas was to be assessed and confirmed through their application in practical human activities and historical struggle. Critical theory can then diagnose ideological discrepancies between theory and practice, such as the contradiction between LIBERALISM's support for the concept of EQUALITY and capitalism's creation of real conditions of inequality. Critical theory would also contribute to a revolutionary politics capable of transcending such contradictions by securing a genuine material equality and thereby "building a new world."

In the second stage, Horkheimer grew more pessimistic toward the possibility of revolutionary social progress and eventually focused his attention on theological experiences of the transcendent. In books such as *Dialectic of Enlightenment* (1947), co-authored with Adorno, and *Eclipse of Reason* (1947), Horkheimer analyzed the ways that modern culture is conditioned by a capitalist mode of production. Capitalism not only dominates working conditions, but also the personal lives of individuals by selling entertainment as a form of escapism from the stress of having to earn a living in a competitive marketplace. Mass culture is essentially meaningless, but it offers an illusory release from the drudgery of work. However, free time thus serves to sustain the capitalist wage-labor system by making individuals dependent upon the commodities produced and marketed by that system. The circular nature of capitalism helps maintain the status quo. In the end, Horkheimer regarded contemporary society as a "totally administered world" that had eroded the autonomy of the individual.

Further Reading
Stirk, P. M. R. *Max Horkheimer: A New Interpretation.* Lanham, Md.: Barnes & Noble, 1992.

Huguenots

French Protestant Christians, following the theology and political theory of John CALVIN and emerging in France during the mid-1500s. As critics of the Roman CATHOLIC (established) Church in France and being REPUBLICAN in IDEOLOGY, they caused a civil war that lasted for more than 30 years (1562–94). The most notorious persecution of the Huguenots occurred in 1572 on St. Bartholomew's Day (August 24) when 10,000 were massacred in Paris and other French cities. The Edict of Nantes (1598) led to FREEDOM of religion in France and an end to official persecution of the Huguenots. This, however, was revoked by King Louis XIV in 1685, forcing many French Protestants to flee to Holland, England, Switzerland, Prussia, and America. Only in 1802 was the Huguenot Church legally permitted, though it was again repressed by the Bourbon Restoration in 1815. Since 1819, it has enjoyed freedom and eventually formed the Protestant Federation of France.

The Huguenots represent a classic case of CHURCH-AND-STATE conflict, the disastrous effects of oppression of religious LIBERTY. The CHRISTIAN church (Catholic and Protestant) in France has never recovered from this religious/political strife, and the diminishing influence of faith and morals on French politics led to the turbulence of the revolution of 1789, the Napoleonic Wars, and governmental instability and betrayal well into the 20th century.

Further Reading
Konnert, Mark. *Civic Agendas and Religious Passion.* Kirksville, Mo.: Truman State University Press, 1997.

human nature

The definition of what human beings' nature is, or what makes humanity different from other animal species. Every political thinker and society has assumptions about the distinctive nature of people and builds society, economics, politics, and international relations on that vision of human essence.

For example, CLASSICAL Greek political thought generally sees humans as by nature social, always living in communities and requiring others to fulfill one's individuality. So, ARISTOTLE defines humans as distinct by two faculties: (1) reasoned speech and (2) moral choice. Both of these human qualities (rational conversation and ethical action) require other people to be developed and exercised. So, for Aristotle, to live alone is to be not fully human. One must be intellectually and morally engaged with others to develop one's uniquely human *telos,* or purpose in life. Political participation in the small democratic polis is necessary to completion of people's social nature, for Aristotle's *Politics.* PLATO's *Republic* goes even further in defining distinctive social functions (or VIRTUES) for each individual. Some are born to rule (the philosophic); some have a "spirited" military capacity by nature; and many people are by heredity economic (meant to work and produce in society). The just government, for Plato, must recognize and train these "natures" and harmonize them within a just society. The fulfillment of human nature forms the basis of JUSTICE in Plato's theory. Ancient Roman thought (CICERO) views human nature more in terms of patriotism and LAW, the social virtues appropriate to the Roman Empire. CHRISTIAN thinkers (St. AUGUSTINE, St. Thomas AQUINAS, LUTHER, CALVIN) present a biblical view of human nature: people created by God in his image (rational, creative, loving), but corrupted by willfulness and sin (selfishness, pride) and redeemed or forgiven by God by Jesus Christ. This Christian view of human nature as fallen and rebellious, yet potentially repentant, humble, and saved by God, leads to a complex vision of society and politics. The real end of human life is knowing and glorifying God (for which we were created), and no social or political activity can replace that, but humans now live in an imperfect world and are called to be like Christ, loving others, seeking peace. So most Christian views of human nature commend political participation and obedience but see the kingdom of heaven as humans' true community. People are to accept the world (and themselves) as imperfect things, yet strive for goodness (social justice and individual holiness). Unlike the Greek pagan philosophers, or MODERN COMMUNIST thinkers, however, St. Augustine believes that humans can never reach their completion in this world.

RENAISSANCE political thought (MACHIAVELLI) sees humans as mean, selfish, petty, and violent, but its HUMANISM allows for no hope of redemption. Instead, *The Prince* must be "realistic" and use deceit and force to rule these small minded, foolish creatures. Politics is POWER. Thomas HOBBES continues this materialistic realism by viewing human nature purely in biological terms, a human as "matter in motion" governed by sensory impulses, pleasure and pain. Only a calculating rationality saves one from destruction. John LOCKE develops this by defining the human being as "free, equal, and independent" but having a moral reason, self-restraining ethics, which allows for social harmony. CONSERVATIVE Edmund BURKE allows for a human nature shaped by the civilizing influence of tradition and aesthetics (beauty); radical romantic J. J. ROUSSEAU emphasizes human feelings, emotions, and sympathy for others.

COMMUNISM (Karl MARX) denies a permanent "human nature," seeing it fluid and changing with history. The one constant feature of humanity, for Marxism, is its productive capacity, but economic relations and technology advance and change people with it. Soviet thinkers believed that socialist Russia would create a "New Man" (intelligent, kind, peaceful, creative, loving) and end the old human nature of acquisitiveness, individualism, conflict, and greed. This was not actually realized in communism.

The great political thinkers have an explicit idea of human nature that explains, at least in part, human capacities and behavior. All political thought is premised in ideals of human nature.

Further Reading
Wilson, E. D. *Sociobiology: The New Synthesis.* Cambridge, Mass.: Belknap Press of Harvard University Press, 1975.

human rights

Rights attending the condition of being human. These usually include the right to life, or to not having a person's life terminated before its natural death. The defining of when human life begins and what *natural death* is immediately arises, as evidenced in the political debates over ABORTION and euthanasia. The human right to FREEDOM, or LIBERTY, is usually included in discussions of human rights. These relate to freedom of thought (intellectual freedom), belief (religious freedom), conscience, expression (speech and press), and movement. PROPERTY, or private ownership of land and possessions (which also is related to economic freedom, or CAPITALISM), is often included in human rights. These NATURAL RIGHTS of "Life, Liberty and Property" in John LOCKE's phrase, are the human rights supposedly attending human existence, or God-given rights that preexist society and cannot be taken by the state without violating divine law and NATURAL LAW. Government for British LIBERAL, SOCIAL-CONTRACT theory is formed to *protect* these rights, and any state that violates them is illegitimate (see LEGITIMACY).

Once government is formed, other human social rights emerge: the right to legal due process (or a fair trial); political participation (or having a say in the laws that govern you, such as voting); the right to education, employment, security, and protection from crime or foreign invasion. Such human rights are expressed in various political documents such as the U.S. CONSTITUTION's Bill of Rights, The UN Declaration of Human Rights of 1948, and the French Republic's Declaration of the Rights of Man (1789). President Jimmy CARTER made human rights a prominent goal during his administration.

Problems occur in human rights issues in two ways: (1) the achievement of some rights (e.g., freedom) may violate other rights (e.g., property), as when unregulated industrial development can impoverish certain populations or pollute the ENVIRONMENT; and (2) Western concepts of individual rights may not fit other cultures or communities (such as Chinese or Muslim nations). So, liberal democracies trying to force other countries (the former SOVIET UNION, Iran, India, Africa) to adopt rights to religious and economic freedom may violate their most firmly held values (community conformity, a single religious faith, etc.).

The presumption of human-rights philosophy is that substantive social good will follow the acceptance of abstract individual rights. So, for example, protection of human life will make a society healthier and just; allowance of freedom of religion will please God and render a society more moral; economic freedom and private ownership of property will enhance material prosperity; and democratic participation will make for a more peaceful, happy society and responsive government.

Further Readings
Brownlie, I., ed. *Basic Documents on Human Rights,* 2nd ed. Oxford, Eng.: Clarendon Press, 1981.

Cranston, M. *What are Human Rights?* New York: Taplinger, 1973.

humanism/humanist

A philosophy that places human beings, rather than God or other aspects of nature, at the center of the universe. For humanists, the human species is the most important reference point in ETHICS, politics, science, art, and economics. Rather than asking "What is God's will in this matter?" or "How will this affect the environment?" humanism asks "How will this benefit humanity?" It takes human beings as the measure of all things, partly because most humanism (such as secular humanism) is atheistic and, therefore, believes that humans are the best, most highly developed creatures in the universe. Both CLASSICAL political thought and ENLIGHTENMENT philosophy take this positive humanist view of humanity, contrary to the more negative Judeo-CHRISTIAN or Machiavellian REALISM view of humans as sinful and destructive. ARISTOTLE's humanism conceives of a human being as excellent and, even "perfect," when he or she fully develops his or her human *telos* (capacities) of reasoned speech and moral choice: The educated, prosperous, cultured, ethical, politically active Greek gentleman becomes the ideal of human goodness, the standard for VIRTUE and practical excellence. For Roman philosopher CICERO, the soldier–hero–statesman of the empire, with his valor, courage, strength, and patriotism, is the measure of human goodness. Enlightenment thinkers Jean-Jacques ROUSSEAU and Thomas JEFFERSON saw human reason and science civilizing the world and education ennobling humanity. With the right social order (democratic, EGALITARIAN, scientific, technological, middle-class, prosperous) humans would cease being brutal and ignorant, and history would usher in a new dawn of freedom and happiness. MARXIST COMMUNISM continued this humanist view by seeing human material production and economic advancement as creating a nonalienated individual who would soar to the level of gods: creative, benevolent, aesthetic, free, peace loving, and cooperative. SOCIALISM would bring the best out in humans; true human excellence in communism is the highest achievement of Nature.

Contrary to these optimistic humanist theories are not just traditional CHRISTIAN thinkers (St. AUGUSTINE, John CALVIN) who see human sin as predominant and

Jesus Christ as the only ideal person but also CONSERVATIVES (Edmund BURKE) who criticize humanist pretensions and utopian speculations as inaccurate in history and disastrous in the future.

Twentieth-century humanist thought is revealed in *The Humanist Manifesto* (1933 and 1973) and widespread premises of MODERN, LIBERAL society. The humanist assumptions about the goodness and value of people, the rejection of God, the glorification of humanity, hope in progress and humanmade technology undergird much of Modern Western society (education politics, media, business, science).

In the United States, the CHRISTIAN RIGHT began to challenge secular humanism in the culture, offering a religious alternative in education, politics, and media. CATHOLIC pope John Paul II criticized Modern humanism with actually degrading human life with a "Culture of Death" (ABORTION, HOMOSEXUALITY, EUTHANASIA). In 1961, the U.S. Supreme Court ruled that secular humanism had become a nontheistic "religion," taught in the public schools as a distinct worldview. This challenged the view that humanism was ethically neutral or objective and opened the door for alternative (Jewish, Christian, Muslim) religious worldviews in the public school curriculum. Conservatives welcomed this development as an honest recognition that humanism had replaced Christianity as the dominant religion in the contemporary United States. For a good discussion of these conflicting philosophies, see James Davison HUNTER's *CULTURE WARS*.

If traditional religions challenged humanism from "above," spiritually, ENVIRONMENTALISM criticizes it from "below": other animal species' rights, and the natural order. For environmentalists, humanism arrogantly places humans in a superior position to other animals and nature.

Further Reading

Flew, Anthony. *Atheistic Humanism.* New York: Prometheus Books, 1993.

Humboldt, Wilhelm von (1767–1835) *German philosopher, linguist, and educational reformer*

Humboldt was born in Potsdam, then part of the former kingdom of Prussia. He studied at the universities of Frankfurt an Oder, Göttingen, Weimer, and then the University of Jena, where he developed a close friendship with Friedrich von Schiller. From 1802 to 1808,

Humboldt served as the Prussian ambassador to the Vatican and in 1809 was appointed the Prussian minister of education, a position Humboldt used to make progressive reforms in the school and university system and to establish the University of Berlin (now Humboldt University).

Humboldt's educational reforms were grounded in the ideas of HUMANISM, especially those of the value and dignity of human beings. The German humanists of the period were advocates of the need to incorporate training in classical arts, literature, languages, and philosophy with new developments in the advancing social and natural sciences. Humboldt believed that the state has a responsibility to educate its citizens and to cultivate civic virtues while allowing for the diversity of individual tastes and interests. Humboldt's humanism, therefore, contained a form of perfectionism, that is, a morality that characterizes some states of human beings as intrinsically good and holds that right actions are those that most fully develop such states. In *The Sphere and Duties of Government* (1854), Humboldt wrote "The grand, leading principle, towards which every argument unfolded in these pages directly converges, is the absolute and essential importance of human development in its richest diversity." For Humboldt, the ideal of development that humans ought to pursue is based in the good of AUTONOMY, or the freedom of choice associated with LIBERTY. Politically, then, Humboldt argued that individual self-development can flourish to the maximum extent only when governmental activity is limited to providing security, that is, preventing harm to others. This view was to have a strong influence on the work of the British philosopher John Stuart MILL.

From his enthusiasm for classical studies, Humboldt argued for the importance of historical experience. In particular, Humboldt emphasized the role of ideas in shaping human history, and in a number of essays, he explored how ideas have informed great social and political developments in Western civilization. "Everything that is active in world history," Humboldt wrote, "is also stirring in the inner being of man." Humboldt's influential works on language sought to demonstrate how nature and history are connected through the ideas expressed in human language. According to Humboldt, language reflects the culture and character of its speakers and reveals the unifying worldview unique to each nation. Because humans perceive the world largely through the medium of language, the study of language must also incorporate the study of history and anthropology if an individual's and a nation's worldview is to be fully understood.

Further Reading

Sweet, P. R. *Wilhelm von Humboldt: A Biography.* Columbus: Ohio State University Press, 1978.

Hume, David (1711–1776) *Scottish philosopher and political historian*

This MODERN thinker developed important theories of skepticism, relativism, and UTILITARIANISM that affected later ethical, religious, and political ideas in the West. In his famous *Treatise of Human Nature* (1739), Hume challenges the rationalism of LIBERAL SOCIAL-CONTRACT views (such as John LOCKE's, that there are constant, reasonable, universal standards of RIGHT and JUSTICE). Although relying on sensory EMPIRICISM, Hume sees the knowledge derived from experience as historically variable and culturally relative, so, for example, he does not judge one form of government as better or more rational or just than any other; his standard of good politics is efficiency and custom. Convention rather than abstract principles establish "justice." Like CONSERVATIVE Edmund BURKE, Hume regards the workable, practical past as valuable. MONARCHY may be best in France, parliamentary DEMOCRACY in Britain; no facts can determine which is "morally" superior. Such utilitarian ideas made Hume appealing to Jeremy BENTHAM.

Prudence, pragmatism, and practicality were Hume's values. He saw advantages and disadvantages to all systems: free, democratic governments encouraged commerce but were in danger of contracting high public debts; monarchy is more dignified and orderly but threatens individual LIBERTY and PROGRESS. In general, as long as the regime was functioning fairly well, Hume supported it. He avoided party identification and conflict, preferring to remain above policy debates. He was basically CONSERVATIVE, not from philosophical principle but from skeptical relativism. He rejected both Whig reason and DIVINE RIGHT OF KINGS. His skepticism spread to religion, preventing Hume from being an orthodox CHRISTIAN. He found the ethical values of HUMANISM (dignity, intelligence, wit, eloquence, sophistication) preferable to his native Scots Protestant values of piety, hard work, abstinence,

self-discipline, and reverence for Christ. This Humean liberal skepticism and attraction to worldly culture and aesthetics made him appealing to the French philosophers, such as Jean-Jacques ROUSSEAU.

Educated at the University of Edinburgh, Hume failed as a lawyer and was prevented by the church from becoming an academic in Scotland. He worked as a law librarian and wrote an extensive *History of England* (eight volumes, 1754–61).

Further Readings

Forbes, D. *Hume's Philosophical Politics.* Cambridge, Eng.: Cambridge University Press, 1975.

Mackie, J. L. *Hume's Moral Theory.* London: Routledge & K. Paul, 1980.

Miller, D. *Philosophy and Ideology in Hume's Political Thought.* Oxford, Eng.: Clarendon Press, 1981.

Hunter, James Davison (1955–) *U.S. sociologist, political and religious theorist*

Best known for his analysis of U.S. society in terms of CULTURE WARS (in the book *Culture Wars: The Struggle to Define America* [1991]), Hunter has written extensively on religion and politics in the United States. An expert on Protestant EVANGELICALS, he has advised numerous foundations, churches, political parties, and organizations (including the White House). Author and editor of numerous scholarly books and articles, Hunter currently chairs the Department of Sociology at the University of Virginia and serves as executive director of the Institute for Advanced Studies in Culture.

Hunter's analysis of U.S. culture in his book *Culture Wars* is possibly the most brilliant description of society in the United States since Alexis de TOCQUEVILLE's *Democracy in America.* Rather than relying on dated MARXian notions of class, race, and gender, Hunter develops categories of attitudes (progressive and orthodox) that inform U.S. people's political stances on numerous fronts. Based in philosophical and moral worldviews, these attitudes transcend race, sex, class, and political party. The orthodox (CONSERVATIVE CATHOLICS, Jews, and Muslims, and Evangelical Protestants) hold some transcendent authority as a guide to positions on social issues (welfare, education, ABORTION, etc.), while progressives (LIBERAL Protestants, Reformed Jews, secularists) base their social attitudes on personal preference. Hunter shows how these alternative perspectives affect the U.S. media, education, art, medicine, and politics. An insightful and influential theory, Hunter's concept of culture wars has redefined U.S. society and history.

He was educated at Rutgers University and has lectured around the world (including at Notre Dame University Law School; Queen's College, Cambridge University; Harvard; the University of Chicago; and Columbia University). Active in both religious and political affairs in the United States, Hunter has been an exceptionally active and influential scholar in the world.

Further Readings

Hunter, James Davison. *Culture Wars: The Struggle to Define America.* New York: Basic Books, 1991.

———. *Evangelicalism: The Coming Generation.* Chicago: University of Chicago Press, 1987.

Hunter, James Davison, and Guinness, Os, eds. *Articles of Faith, Articles of Peace: The Religious Liberty Clauses and the American Public Philosophy.* Washington, D.C.: Brookings Institution, 1990.

I

idealism/idealist

In political thought, idealism is understood in two ways: (1) the common or colloquial meaning in which someone is idealistic, and (2) the ideas of 19- and 20th-century idealist philosophers KANT, HEGEL, FICHTE, and T. H. GREEN.

The common political meaning of *idealism* involves a person or a movement that has ideals or goals that are supposedly attainable through positive social reform. In this sense, Thomas JEFFERSON is often called an idealist because he believed in the ideals of EQUALITY, human dignity, PROGRESS, DEMOCRACY, FREEDOM, and so on and he believed that those positive ideals were attainable in the MODERN U.S. REPUBLIC. So, an idealistic person believes that people and societies are capable of improving and achieving noble ends; opposed is the pessimist or realist who doubts that humankind can ever improve or become more humane, generous, just, and so on. Among idealistic movements, we might include SOCIALISM (which believes greed and poverty can be eliminated through state economic planning and redistribution of wealth); ENVIRONMENTALISM (which focuses on the care and nonexploitation of nature); and ANIMAL RIGHTS (where people will stop eating and using other creatures). Most of these social movements are LIBERAL, so liberal idealism is a logical combination of terms. CONSERVATIVE thinkers (such as Edmund BURKE, St. AUGUSTINE, Ronald REAGAN) challenge idealism on two levels: (1) they see inherent limits to human capacities for goodness (through sin, historical culture, ignorance) that makes idealism an inaccurate, naïve view of humanity; and (2) those human limitations show themselves in idealists through their pride, self-righteousness, and intolerance. Thus, idealists are often frustrated by the world and their pessimistic critics. They see the nonachievement of their ideas as caused by pessimism and conservatism rather than their own unrealistic worldview.

Idealism is strong in the ENLIGHTENMENT, Jean-Jacques ROUSSEAU, Karl MARX, and FEMINISM. The United States is famous for its optimistic idealism, especially regarding patriotism, DEMOCRACY, and equality, as Alexis de TOCQUEVILLE noted in *Democracy in America.*

The second meaning of idealism is a formal philosophical school that locates reality in ideas, or the perceptions and conceptions of the human mind. For Kant, the external empirical world is ordered and systematized by the human brain, through categories of time and space, causality, substance, and so on, which do not occur in the natural objective universe. This HUMANIST view rejects a divinely ordered NATURAL LAW and so constructs order out of the human mind. So, ideas and the way people construct their reality (including social and governmental institutions) become the truth. Kant acknowledged an objective world outside the autonomous person; Fichte sees the whole of reality in the subjective perception of human beings. Hegel tries to reconcile these in his DIALECTIC which sees subject and object as interrelated realities, each affecting the other in a totality. History becomes the growing self-consciousness of this dialectical reality, which institutes political, economic, and social organisms. Green inserts a theological element in his philosophical idealism in which the mind of God (or "eternal intelligence") contains both subject and object in total reality.

The political consequences of these philosophical idealisms is to take seriously historical conceptions of democracy, JUSTICE, and so on and to understand how powerful ideas are in shaping political reality. Thus, political theory as a field of study is a form of idealism. IDEOLOGY and the study of historical ideologies is a form of intellectual idealism.

Further Readings

Milne, A. J. M. *The Social Philosophy of English Idealism.* London: Allen & Unwin, 1962.

Plant, R. *Hegel,* 2nd ed. Oxford, Eng.: B. Blackwell, 1983.

Richter, M. *The Politics of Conscience: T. H. Green and His Age.* Cambridge, Mass.: Harvard University Press, 1964.

ideology/ideological

A theory or a set of beliefs about the political world that order our perception of events and explain how society operates. For example, CONSERVATIVE ideology brings certain assumptions about HUMAN NATURE, history, politics, economics, and society that cause it to identify problems in a certain way, prescribe solutions, and explain occurrences in the world. LIBERAL ideology views the same environment by different categories. So where conservatives (BURKE) like tradition, the classics, AUTHORITY, and moderate change, they see the crises in the world as signs of RADICAL new ideas, rebellion against morality, and perversion. Liberal ENLIGHTENMENT ideology expresses an optimistic view of human nature and social PROGRESS, while seeing TRADITION and conservatives as causing the problems.

So, an ideology is simply a coherent worldview involving a pattern of symbols and beliefs that explain and evaluate society. Among the dominant ideologies in the West are (1) CHRISTIAN, (2) CLASSICAL REPUBLICAN,

(3) Enlightenment liberal, (4) MARXIST COMMUNISM, and (5) POST-MODERNISM. The study of these ideologies (by MANNHEIM, MARX, CRITICAL THEORY, GRAMSCI, Lukacs), or paradigms, tend to see them as attached to and justifying some individual or social interest. So Marxism, for example, sees all political theories as ideologies that support an economic ruling class. Karl Marx would judge the philosophy of John LOCKE (or British liberalism) as "bourgeois ideology" because it justifies private PROPERTY ownership, wage labor, and market economics, which support CAPITALISM. But the economic class theory of Marx with its emphasis on POWER, class conflict, and exploitation, itself becomes an ideology that underlies much of sociology and POLITICALLY CORRECT attitudes in academia (Michael FOUCAULT). James D. HUNTER's conception of ideologies in the book *Culture Wars* integrates them into moral attitudes and political activism.

Most often, ideology simply refers to a political slant or opinion (such as REPUBLICAN [PARTY] ideology as the ideology of conservative president Ronald REAGAN—free markets, reduced taxes, increased military spending, and so on; or DEMOCRATIC [PARTY] ideology of social-welfare programs, CIVIL RIGHTS activism, etc.). Ideology then is just a set of coordinated ideas or positions on correct policy matters (e.g., LEFTIST ideology; CHRISTIAN RIGHT ideology). In PLURALISM, it is considered normal that any interest group would have an ideological agenda, but in James MADISON's constitutional scheme, those competing ideologies will balance and cancel each other out.

Further Readings

Cox, R. H. *Ideology, Politics and Political Theory.* Stamford, Conn. Wadsworth, 1969.

Lichtheim, G. *The Concept of Ideology, and Other Essays.* New York: Vintage Books, 1967.

Mannheim, K. *Ideology and Utopia.* New York: Harcourt, Brace & World, 1936.

Ignatius Loyola, St. (1401–1556) *Religious and political leader, founder of the Jesuit Order in the Roman Catholic Church*

The Society of Jesus or Jesuits was founded in 1540 and spread Catholic doctrine through extensive educational and missionary activity. By the 20th century, Jesuits had infiltrated most countries or continents in the world, including India, China, Africa, Japan, Russia, South America, and Europe. Its principal aims were to support the pope's authority, to reform the Catholic Church through education, and to spread the gospel around the world. Organized along military lines, the head of the order is called the general, and strict discipline is enforced.

In Protestant countries, the Jesuits were often viewed with suspicion as deceitful, clever, and powerful instruments of the papacy to restore Catholicism as the official state religion. Their effectiveness and political involvement caused the Jesuits to be expelled from various regions, including France, Germany, Latin America, Portugal, and England. In every case, they were eventually able to reestablish themselves. In America, they are noted for founding schools and universities, providing rigorous CLASSICAL and religious education, and providing prominent scholars for the church.

Ignatius set an example of a disciplined, devout life to the Jesuit order. He left a military career and committed himself to be "a soldier for Christ." He studied in Spain and Paris and took pilgrimages to Rome and Jerusalem. His rigorous life of prayer, poverty, and mystical spirituality (expressed in his book, *Spiritual Exercises*) impressed others in the church and drew many men into the Jesuit order. He wrote the constitutions for the Society of Jesus between 1547 and 1550. In 1622, he was canonized or declared an official saint of the Catholic Church.

Further Reading
Ignatius Loyola, St. *The Autobiography of St. Ignatius Loyola* with *related documents,* introd. and notes by John C. Olin, ed., Joseph F. O'Callaghan, transl. New York: Harper Torchbooks, 1974.

imperial church

The official state church of an empire, whether the MEDIEVAL Western CATHOLIC Church of the HOLY ROMAN EMPIRE, the British imperial church of England, the BYZANTINE Eastern Orthodox Church, or the Russian ORTHODOX Church. Each of these imperial CHRISTIAN churches share the distinctions of being legally established by the government (persecuting other church denominations), acting directly on politics (often bishops serving as secular officials), and adopting the titles, pomp, dignity, and authority of the state. Critics of these imperial churches (both within and outside the official church institution) attack them as worldly and proud, a violation of Christ's humility

and the dictum that "my kingdom is not of this world" (John 18:36). REFORMATION Protestants Martin LUTHER and John CALVIN sought to reform the imperial church structures by simplifying the governance, architecture, titles, and dress of church leaders. Consequently, they had the political effect of advancing EQUALITY (the "priesthood of all believers") and DEMOCRACY (elected clergy, congregationalism) against the HIERARCHY of the imperial church. This influenced the development of MODERN REPUBLICANISM and LIBERALISM (as in the political theory of the PURITAN John LOCKE). Movements within the imperial church (such as the work of St. Frances of Assisi) attempted to reform its officious character and prevent a schism in the church.

Further Reading
Donfried, Karl P., and Richardson, Peter, ed. *Judaism and Christianity in First-Century Rome.* Grand Rapids, Mich.: William B. Eerdmans, ca. 1998.

imperialism/imperialist

A system of political domination and economic EXPLOITATION by an "imperial" nation (e.g., Rome, Britain) of a "colonial" area (India, Africa, North and South America). Before MARX's and LENIN's theories of the 19th and 20th centuries, imperialism was generally seen in positive, favorable ways. CICERO justifies the Roman Empire as bringing LAW, order, civilization, and advanced economics and culture to the savage areas of Germany and Britain. The CATHOLIC HOLY ROMAN EMPIRE of the MIDDLE AGES is seen as a noble, CHRISTIAN region protecting the faithful against barbarian invaders and Muslims. The early British Empire is presented (even by Karl Marx) as spreading DEMOCRACY, CAPITALISM, and economic development to a dark, AUTHORITARIAN, brutal, and impoverished Third World.

By the early 20th century, however, Marxism (especially the theories of V. I. Lenin) treated imperialism in less and less sympathetic terms. This Marxist-Leninist indictment of Western imperialism continues to the present in LEFTIST political IDEOLOGY, which sees all imperialism as evil domination. MULTICULTURALISM claims that all peoples and cultures are equally just and valid, so the idea that Western DEMOCRACY can give anything to Africa or Asia is seen as arrogant "cultural imperialism." This Marxist COMMUNIST view of Western imperialism extends to the spread of Christian missionaries, which it uses to justify persecuting and murdering those in religious missionary service.

Lenin and other 20th-century communists developed an elaborate theory of capitalist-imperialism. This was partly to explain why the SOCIALIST revolution predicted by Marx had not occurred in the advanced capitalist countries (Britain, Germany, the United States). According to Lenin, capitalism survives by "exporting" its contradictions to colonies. Colonies serve several purposes: (1) as markets for the sale of excess goods and production; (2) as a source of cheap natural resources and labor; (3) as a testing or dumping ground for new techniques or pollution. This economic imperialism further corrupts the colonial political leaders (who become the native arm of imperial domination) and the domestic (imperial nation) working class (preventing socialist revolution in the advanced countries). So, in capitalist imperialism, the neocolonies are so exploited that the businesses in the advanced countries can "bribe" their indigenous workers with higher wages, education, career advancement, and unions. So, workers in Europe or the United States live at a middle-class level, sharing the benefits of the exploitation of Third World labor and resources. This explains why workers in advanced countries are often CONSERVATIVE and patriotic, leaving the radical LEFT to exist among LIBERAL middle-class professionals. It also, for Marxism-Leninism, explains why the socialist revolutions occurred first in the colonial nations (Russia, China, Vietnam, Cuba) rather than the advanced capitalist countries. But, Lenin asserted, as more Third World countries became socialist, expelling the imperialists, the problems of capitalism would return to the host countries, eventually leading to socialist revolutions there. That this had not occurred by the end of the 20th century contributed to the decline of communism in the SOVIET UNION, China, and the Third World. Still, many poor African and Asian countries (for example, in the United Nations) employ the rhetoric of Marxism-Leninism to complain about the poverty of their own nations and wealth of the United States and Europe. Many Western liberals share in this perspective, blaming the prosperity of the advanced nations on the exploitation of poorer nations.

An important component of MODERN imperialist theory is the distinction between a colony (where the imperial country rules politically) and a neocolony (where imperial control, or hegemony, is informal and economic). Much of the resentment in Southern Hemisphere countries toward Northern Hemisphere (imperial) nations is the suspicion that control is subtle, commercial, and deceptive. This accounts for the widespread hostility toward the United States (and the CIA) around the world. Whether political or economic, modern theories of imperialism always charge that militarism accompanies foreign domination. The two world wars are seen as conflicts between rival imperial countries (Britain, France, Germany, Japan, the United States), and recent military actions by NATO (in Serbia or Iraq) are seen as evidence of Western imperialism.

Historically, the colonial regions often benefit from the legal, cultural, religious, and technological influences of advanced imperialism and eventually secure greater independence and prosperity from the relationship (as in India, the Arab Middle Eastern countries, and the Peoples Republic of China). They then often exercise imperial domination over their weaker neighboring countries, proving that imperialism is not a habit of only certain cultures but appears to be a feature of collective human nature.

Further Readings

Brewer, A. *Marxist Theories of Imperialism: a Critical Survey.* New York: Routledge, 1980.

Lenin, V. I. "Imperialism: the highest stage of capitalism" (1916). In *Selected Works*, vol. I. London: Institute of International Affairs, 1950.

Marx, K. *On Colonialism and Modernization*, S. Avineri, ed. Garden City, N.Y.: Doubleday Anchor, 1969.

individualism/individualistic

The political idea that the human individual is the most important entity in society. The source of this individualistic philosophy can be biological, religious, or economic. In MODERN philosophical materialism (the British LIBERALISM of Thomas HOBBES and John LOCKE), the human individual is central because, biologically, people are separate and autonomous and our private, physiological senses (from which we gain all knowledge) cannot be shared collectively. So, by nature we are individuals, and from that condition each possesses NATURAL RIGHTS (to life, LIBERTY, and PROPERTY). In the religious or spiritual source of individualism, the CHRISTIANS St. AUGUSTINE, Martin LUTHER, and John BUNYAN emphasize that God created each individual person as unique to relate to him personally and that salvation is individually chosen through Christ. An economic basis of individualism (as in the thought of Adam SMITH) says that individual invention, work, and trade make the most natural and productive economy. It is no coincidence, as Max WEBER showed, that individualism tends to converge in Modern, CAPITALIST, DEMOCRATIC, Protestant culture (Switzerland, Holland, Britain, the United States).

Individualism is contrasted with CLASSICAL "social" views of humanity (PLATO, ARISTOTLE); MEDIEVAL CORPORATISM (St. Thomas AQUINAS); and later SOCIALIST, FASCIST, and COMMUNIST thought in the West (Karl MARX Friedrich ENGELS); as well as more collectivist cultures and religions in the East (CHINESE, Japanese, ISLAM, HINDU culture). In these, group, family, race, nation, or community is the most important unit in society, to which the individual should be subordinated. Even contemporary U.S. COMMUNITARIAN theory (Benjamin BARBER) rejects the private individualism or "atomism" of the Modern United States.

So, individualism can be presented favorably (as in "rugged American individualism"): symbolizing independence, initiative, self-reliance, creativity, and personal piety and responsibility; or unfavorably (as in "selfish individualism"): representing greed, avarice, pride, selfishness, and arrogance. Most recent expressions of individualism in political thought occur in John Stuart MILL's idea of intellectual liberty within a "free market place of ideas"; Alexis de TOCQUEVILLE's analysis of American society in his book *Democracy in America;* Robert NOZICK's LIBERTARIAN ANARCHISM; Ronald REAGAN's CONSERVATIVE REPUBLICAN PARTY IDEOLOGY; and Jimmy CARTER's emphasis on HUMAN RIGHTS.

Because individualistic political ideals tend to emphasize FREEDOM of individual conscience, religious belief, action and movement, economic enterprise, and private PROPERTY, they are often associated with LIBERALISM, EQUALITY, CAPITALISM, and democracy.

Further Readings

Arieli, Y. *Individualism and Nationalism in American Ideology.* Cambridge, Mass.: Harvard University Press, 1964.

O'Neill, J., ed. *Modes of Individualism and Collectivism.* London: Heinemann, 1973.

industrial/industrialism

A MODERN economic system characterized by the use of industrial machinery, capital, advancing technology, a division of labor, wage labor, rational production, and market exchange. Since the emergence of industrial CAPITALISM in Europe in the 18th century (beginning with steam power and metallurgy in Britain), replacing the predominantly agricultural economy of the MIDDLE AGES, industrialism has featured prominently in Western political thought. The social and political effects of mass production, the rise of cities, increases in population, and increased exchange economics changed political thought to accommodate the new historical order. Industrial society becomes a major political concept in the writings of SAINT-SIMON, Herbert SPENCER, Adam SMITH, and Karl MARX.

The idea that societies were distinguished by their manner of economic production (as opposed to their political, military, or religious characteristics) began in the political theories of England and Scotland, where industrial capitalism first emerged. To describe a society in terms of its commerce, transportation, communication systems, average income, and so on began with the economic social analysis of Adam Smith's categorization of whole countries in terms of the goods produced there, the modes of trade, and the growth of wealth (as exemplified in the title of his famous book *The Wealth of Nations*). This was radically different from the religious worldview of the Middle Ages or the ethical approach of the ancient world (St. Thomas AQUINAS, ARISTOTLE). But that perspective has spread around the world.

Industrial society is marked by increasingly complex economic specialization. Where the traditional farmer performs many work tasks, requiring a multiplicity of skills, the modern worker assumes more and more minute and limited labor processes. This division of labor is seen as more productive and efficient but for Marx dehumanizes the worker with boring, routine, monotonous work. This causes ALIENATION and misery in the midst of material plenty. Such unhappiness in the midst of prosperity became both the CONSERVATIVE and the radical COMMUNIST criticism of industrial society. For Tory Conservatives (like Edmund BURKE), the solution is to preserve the past agrarian traditions and lifestyle as much as possible, a solution expressed in Thomas JEFFERSON and seen in Modern U.S. suburbs, where a preindustrial rural environment is encouraged. MARXISM sees the main problem of industrialism not with mass production or urbanization, but with private ownership of PROPERTY, which leads to EXPLOITATION and privation. The correspondence of social ownership (SOCIALISM) with socialized production humanizes industrialism, for Marxists. This may explain the unaesthetic development of industrialism in the SOVIET UNION, China, and Eastern

Europe as contrasted with the greater ENVIRONMENTAL concern in the LIBERAL democracies.

Both capitalist and socialist commentators on industrialism praise the way in which this Modern economic system encourages social (and international) interdependence, bringing people, classes, cultures, and different nations closer together. This elimination of national and cultural isolation makes the world seem more interconnected, as it certainly is under industrialism, international trade, the Internet, and so on. Other advantages of industrialism include its values of hard work, honesty, nonviolent competition, and productivity. Early advocates of industrialism noted its compatibility with EGALITARIAN democracy and social PROGRESS. They contrasted its commercial values with earlier (Medieval) military societies with their emphasis on honor, warfare, and patriotism. Critics in the 20th century bemoaned industrialism's tendency to subsume distinctive traditional cultures into a homogeneous "McDonald's" U.S. culture, cheapening human distinctiveness and reducing all human relationships to commodity exchange.

Further Readings

Aron, R. *Eighteen Lectures on Industrial Society.* London: Weidenfeld & Nicolson, 1967.

interest/interests

Things or activities that people have or want, such as PROPERTY, RIGHTS, positions, POWER, political participation, prestige, honor, fame, and so on. In Western political theory, the language of interests does not appear until the MODERN period, especially in the British LIBERALISM of Thomas HOBBES and John LOCKE. Prior to this, *VIRTUE* and *JUSTICE* are the dominant categories (see ARISTOTLE, PLATO, St. Thomas AQUINAS). There, in Modern philosophy, human interests attend the physiological condition of people (self-preservation) and concern "life, LIBERTY, and PROPERTY," in Locke's famous phrase. Then, human interests develop into rights to certain economic, social, intellectual, and political prerogatives and activities. Mostly individual, the concept of interests then extends to community interests (in ROUSSEAU, FASCISM, BARBER) and national interests (in GROTIUS). MARXISM, of course, speaks of class interests, where groups (owners versus workers, rural farmers versus industrial proletarians) have conflicting economic interests. James MADISON's PLURALISM in the United States assumes a multiplicity of social,

economic, and religious interests. The U.S. CONSTITUTION, with its system of CHECKS AND BALANCES, is constructed specifically to manage and balance such conflicting interests. Contemporary thinkers on interests include Ronald Dworkin, John RAWLS, and Robert NOZICK, who express philosophically the current LIBERAL, CONSERVATIVE, and LIBERTARIAN notions, respectively, of individual and social (or common) interests. The POST-MODERNISM of FOUCAULT, much like ancient and Medieval thought, challenges the Modern preoccupation of human interests as a historical customary formulation distorting the full human potential. Many other critics regard the contemporary overemphasis on interests as reducing people to selfish economic beings, thus trivializing their higher human essence, worth, or spirituality.

Further Readings

Barry, B. "The public interest," *Proceedings of the Aristotelian Society* supp., vol. 38, London: The Aristotelian Society, (1964): 1–18.

Benn, S. I. "Interests in politics," *Proceedings of the Aristotelian Society 60,* London: The Aristotelian Society, (1959–60): 123–40.

Connolly, W. E. "The public interest and the common good." In *Appearance and Reality in Politics.* Cambridge, Eng.: Cambridge University Press, 1981.

international law

The body of LAW that attempts to regulate relations between nations to prevent conflicts from becoming violent warfare. This includes (1) theoretical international law, or the study of philosophies of just relations among states, or international jurisprudence (which defines such general principles as nonaggression, respect for boundaries, and rules against murder, theft, and piracy, etc.); (2) customary international law, or the unwritten but commonly understood practices between nations (such as respect for diplomatic immunity, professional courtesy, etc.); and positive international law, or the formal agreements (treaties, conventions, organizations) that regulate contemporary international relations (such as the United Nations, the International Court of Justice, the General Agreement on Tariffs and Trade, the Geneva Convention on Treatment of Prisoners of War, etc.).

Historically, international law begins with the law of the Roman Empire and continues through the CANON LAW of the MEDIEVAL CATHOLIC Church. Modern thinker Hugo GROTIUS applies LIBERAL SOCIAL-CONTRACT theory to international relations. Jeremy BENTHAM first coined the phrase *international law* and applied his UTILITARIAN ethic to it. HUMAN RIGHTS has become a prominent theme in late 20th-century international law. Largely a construct of Western liberal CAPITALIST DEMOCRACIES, current international law seldom enjoins uniform compliance. Independent nations value their sovereign interests and tend to conform to international regulations selectively. Still, the ideal of a rational, peaceful resolution of international disputes has a civilizing and educational effect on the most barbaric past practices, and fears of a "New World Order" are allayed somewhat by the inefficiency and unenforceability of universal international law.

Further Readings

De Visscher, C. *Theory and Reality in Public International Law.* Princeton, N.J.: Princeton University Press, 1967.

Falk, R. A. *The Status of Law in International Society.* Princeton, N.J.: Princeton University Press, 1970.

Hyde, C. D. *International Law,* 2nd ed. Fred B. Rothman & Co., 1983.

Kelsen, H. *Principles of International Law,* 2nd ed. New York: Holt, Rinehart and Winston, 1966.

Lauterpacht, H. *The Function of Law in the International Community.* Oxford, Eng.: Clarendon Press, 1933.

Muslims worshiping the shrines sacred to Islam, in Mecca, Arabia. (LIBRARY OF CONGRESS)

Islam/Islamic/Islamic political thought

The political ideas emanating from the holy books of the Islamic religion (especially the Koran), the scholarly interpretation of those religious texts by Muslim writers, and the historical practices of government in Muslim countries. Islam is the third great monotheistic faith (along with Judaism and CHRISTIANITY), and its religion and politics resemble them in many ways, including confronting issues of CHURCH AND STATE (or how to relate the spiritual and the worldly realms). As in the other dominant theological systems in the world, Islamic political thought has a rich and diverse tradition, but generally it ties religious and governmental AUTHORITY more closely together than Christian political ideology. Originally, after the Muslim prophet MOHAMMED, who united both sacred and secular authority in himself, the "imam-caliph" combined worldly and godly power in one ABSOLUTIST ruler. Later, a division occurs in Islamic political thought (and practice) between the worldly, secular ruler (the sultan) and the religious leader (the caliph). Still, temporal and spiritual realms are closely linked, as Muslims see (much like CATHOLIC Christians) that

government cannot rule well without morals (which it gets from religious institutions) and spiritual entities cannot exist without the support, encouragement, and protection of the state. So, most of Muslim political history (as in the vast Ottoman Empire) is of close cooperation and interconnection between the political and religious establishments. This contributes to the strong emphasis on absolute obedience and submission to authority, divine and worldly (God–Allah, ruler–sultan, governor; religious leaders–caliph, imams; family–father, parents). Questioning of authority, much less than rebellion, is seen as unacceptable in traditional Islamic political culture. Obedience, respect for authority, submission, order, and staying in one's place reflect the values of the Muslim religious and political mentality. Much like PLATO's *Republic,* staying obediently in one's place or function is seen as the fulfillment of VIRTUE, JUSTICE, and the divine will. Resignation to the existing power structure, acceptance of whatever happens in the world, fatalism, patient suffering, and passivity represent the Islamic worldview. Western, ENLIGHTENMENT notions of questioning, ACTIVISM, PROGRESS, change, independence, and REVOLUTION are seen as morally decadent and socially disruptive. This produces a basic CONSERVATIVE outlook that permeates the Muslim world and explains the rise of Islamic fundamentalism in the late 20th century as a reaction to radical economic, technological, and social changes in the world. Until the whole world is Islamic, Muslim political thought holds, Earth will be disordered and chaotic. This leads to a tendency toward Islamic evangelism that seeks to spread Islam to the world, especially Europe and the United States.

Another strain of Islam (MODERNISM) sees a more flexible religion which can accommodate DEMOCRACY, CAPITALISM, religious FREEDOM, individual LIBERTY, and EQUALITY. First expressed by Turkish leader Kemal ATATÜRK with the founding of the Republic of Turkey, Kemalism, like Jeffersonian American democracy, sees religion separate from the state and the human individual pleasing God by freely investigating all religious faiths and, guided by liberty of conscience, choosing the belief that he or she is led by God to accept. This has allowed religious and political PLURAL-ISM, democracy, economic development, and modern scientific education to flourish in Turkey. On the other end of the political spectrum, Iran under the Ayatollah Khomeini restored a conservative Islamic state ruled directly by Muslim religious leaders, suppressing all political and religious DISSENT.

Like other theological cultural traditions, Islamic political thought is evolving and diverse, both influencing and being influenced by non-Islamic traditions.

Further Readings

Hafeez Malik, ed. *Central Asia: Its Strategic Importance and Future Prospects*, 1st pbk. ed. New York: St. Martin's Press, 1996.

Enayat, H. *Modern Islamic Political Thought.* Austin: University of Texas Press, 1982.

Lambton, Ann Katharine Swynford. *State and Government in Medieval Islam: An Introduction to the Study of Islamic Political Theory: The Jurists.* Oxford, Eng.: Oxford University Press, 1981.

Rosenthal, E. *Political Thought in Medieval Islam.* Cambridge, Eng.: Cambridge University Press, 1958.

J

Jackson, Andrew (1767–1845) *American politician, president, and soldier*

"Andy" Jackson's political legacy is the POPULIST American DEMOCRATIC PARTY or Jacksonian Democracy. This involved the expanding of SUFFRAGE (voting) rights to poor or common people (mostly farmers) and the extensive use of federal PATRONAGE employment (giving government jobs to political party supporters). Such radical EGALITARIAN democracy made the Jacksonian Democratic Party the party of the people as opposed to the more elitist or ARISTOCRATIC FEDERALIST and Whig (later REPUBLICAN) parties. Jackson as U.S. president further advanced the cause of common folk by ending the official national bank and putting government funds into various private state banks. He furthered population expansion into the Western frontier, benefiting average U.S. farmers but displacing Native American Indian tribes. He advocated more power in the federal government and offended the nullification Southern Democrats who wanted STATES RIGHTS over national legislation (causing the resignation of John C. CALHOUN as vice president).

A colorful, rustic figure from Tennessee, Andrew Jackson, nicknamed Old Hickory, was revered as a military hero (winning a decisive battle against the British in the War of 1812), an effective spokesman for the common people, and a shrewd national politician and party leader. He descended from Irish immigrants; his informal style and democratic principles made him popular among U.S. farmers, workers, BAPTISTS, and southerners. He retired to his plantation in Tennessee, The Hermitage.

Further Readings

Remini, Robert Vincent. *Andrew Jackson and the Course of American Democracy, 1833–1845.* New York: Harper & Row, 1998.
———. *Andrew Jackson and the Course of American Empire, 1767–1812.* New York: Harper & Row, 1998.

Jackson, Jesse, Rev. (1941–) *African-American political activist, minister*

Most noted for his Operation PUSH (People United to Save Humanity), Jesse Jackson is a prominent LIBERAL DEMOCRATIC civil rights leader and LEFTIST political ACTIVIST. Combining traditional black CHRISTIAN church oratory with radical political theory, Jackson attacks the American corporate establishment and advocates major restructuring of the United States's economic, military, and political system. His liberal policy statements drew a coalition of disenfranchised, poor, minority, HOMOSEX-UAL, and FEMINIST women voters in the Rainbow Coalition, supporting his U.S. presidential candidacy in 1984 (the first African-American candidacy as part of a mainstream party in U.S. history). Jackson's "anti-American corporate–militarism–imperialism" theme made him a favorite among developing countries, especially among Africans and Arabs. But this radical appeal diminished his influence with other contingents in the Democratic Party (notably Jewish Americans and CATHOLICS). His association with the radical leader of the black Nation of Islam, Louis Farrakhan, further eroded Jackson's appeal to mainstream U.S. voters.

However, Jackson is held in tremendously high esteem among African Americans, partly due to his close association with civil rights leader Dr. Martin Luther KING, Jr. Accused of personal vanity and political opportunism, Jackson nevertheless articulates the politics of inclusion.

Further Readings

Frady, Marshall. *Jesse: The Life and Pilgrimage of Jesse Jackson*, 1st ed. New York: Random House, 1996.

Hertzke, Allen D. *Echoes of Discontent: Jesse Jackson, Pat Robertson, and the Resurgence of Populism*. Washington, D.C.: Congressional Quarterly, 1993.

Jacobin

A member of the French Revolution Jacobins political party, led by Maximilien Robespierre, which constituted the most RADICAL and extremist group during that revolution. The Jacobin period was known as the Reign of Terror because of the mass executions carried on during its rule (1793–94). The term *Jacobin* then became generally applied to any ruthless, radical revolutionary who used violence and dictatorship to accomplish ends. So, for example, the Russian COMMUNIST revolutionary, V. I. LENIN was often called a Jacobin by his critics. MAO TSE-TUNG's CHINESE Cultural Revolution, which used radical threats, humiliation, torture and execution of "enemies of the People," was often accused of Jacobinism. So, any extremely brutal revolutionary change may be termed *Jacobin*, even though it was not a formal part of the French revolutionary group that gave rise to the title.

Further Reading

Cole, C. Robert, and Moody, Michael E., eds. *The Dissenting Tradition: Essays for Leland H. Carlson*. Athens: Ohio University Press, 1975.

Jefferson, Thomas (1743–1826) *American statesman, revolutionary, and political philosopher*

Possibly the most famous thinker of the American Revolution and early American Republic, this author of the DECLARATION OF INDEPENDENCE and founder of Jeffersonian Democracy is the quintessential American political philosopher. His ideals of individual LIBERTY and RIGHTS, popular DEMOCRACY, economic EQUALITY, public education, and religious freedom underlie U.S. political culture. Americans revere Jefferson so much that one scholar said that their image of him is a reflection of their own identity. A Renaissance man and ENLIGHTENMENT LIBERAL, Thomas Jefferson's brilliance covered politics, economics, religion, LAW, science, education, art, music, and literature. His genius and wide range of interests and accomplishments make him a fascinating figure to study. Numerous books have examined every aspect of his life. A wealthy plantation owner in Virginia, Jefferson served as governor of that state, as a delegate to the Continental Congress, ambassador to France, secretary of state under President Washington, vice president in John Adams's presidency, and third president of the United States (1801–09). He authored the Virginia statute for religious freedom and *Notes on the State of Virginia* and founded the University of Virginia in Charlottesville.

Jefferson received a CLASSICAL education from clergy of the Church of England and at William and Mary College, before reading the law under George Wythe. His political thought drew upon an exceedingly broad range of thinkers, including John LOCKE, ARISTOTLE, James HARRINGTON, MONTESQUIEU, BOLINGBROKE, and Jesus Christ.

Early in his career he wrote from the SOCIAL-CONTRACT, NATURAL-RIGHTS philosophy of John Locke and the ANCIENT CONSTITUTION. He used these ideas of individual LIBERTY, private RIGHTS, limited government, and "the Right of Revolution" to justify the American Revolution in his Declaration of Independence. Jefferson adapted Locke's conception of a STATE OF NATURE made up of "free, equal, and independent" individuals to the British Empire made up of free, equal, and independent political communities (including the North American colonies). This theory rationalized the United States separating from Britain and becoming an independent nation. Such reasoning inspired many imperial dominated nations (including India, Mexico, Vietnam, China, and many African and South American countries).

In founding the new American republic, Jefferson drew upon Aristotle's theories of an independent, educated, economically self-sufficient citizenry. He tried to replicate the ancient Greek polis in the small participatory democracies, or wards, in Virginia, where every citizen would engage in some form of rule or self-governance. This small scale, direct democracy would be linked to the state and national levels of state by an elected "Natural Aristocracy" of "wisdom and VIRTUE." Much like PLATO's *Republic*, Jefferson conceived of American public education as elevating all citizens into their natural "places" in society, to the benefit of all humanity. He saw CHRISTIAN ethics as essential to the harmonious social relations in the U.S. democracy and believed that freedom of religion would promote tolerance, morality, PROGRESS, and "the ethics of Jesus." His conception of the separation of CHURCH AND STATE made America both the most diverse, religious society and the most EVANGELICAL Christian nation in the world. His ambiguity on the SLAVERY issue (denouncing it as an institution but owning African-American slaves himself) and alternating views on nationalism versus STATES RIGHTS caused Jefferson's critics to accuse him of hypocrisy. But he remained consistent in regarding human slavery as immoral and seeing the state governments as controlling domestic policy (relegating the federal government to foreign relations). With ample aid from his secretary of state, James MADISON, he accomplished the Louisiana Purchase, thereby doubling the size of the United States. His use of the national government during the embargo led to fierce opposition in New England.

Jefferson subscribed to classical REPUBLICAN ideals of an agrarian economy; local governance of virtuous yeoman farmer–citizens; and suspicion of centralized government, standing armies, capitalist finance, public debt, and political patronage. He compromised his ideals, however, to build a strong military to protect U.S. trade interests and nascent industrialism.

Jefferson's influence has been worldwide, from developing-world national liberation movements to democracy movements in the former Soviet bloc countries. Because of his wide-ranging writings, he is cited as an authority by widely divergent groups and ideologies: from CONSERVATIVE LIBERTARIANS to RADICAL SOCIALISTS. He himself was a complex thinker and personality: aristocratic yet progressive; dignified but EGALITARIAN; democratic yet elevated; morally conservative, but politically radical. In the end, Jefferson and

Thomas Jefferson. Painting by Thomas Sully. (NATIONAL ARCHIVES)

his political thought defy simple explanation, and they remain a fascinating enigma.

Further Readings
Koch, A. *The Philosophy of Thomas Jefferson.* Gloucester, Mass.: Peter Smith, 1957.
Sheldon, G. W. *The Political Philosophy of Thomas Jefferson.* Baltimore: Johns Hopkins University Press, 1991.

Jehovah's Witnesses

A religious group known for its political involvement, especially in U.S. CONSTITUTIONAL LAW. Originally founded from a CHRISTIAN group led by Charles Raze Russell, the sect deviated from traditional Christianity by denying the divinity of Jesus. Rather like Jewish and Muslim believers, Jehovah's Witnesses worship one God (Jehovah) and spread their doctrines through aggressive evangelism.

Politically, this group became active in the 1930s in challenging state authority (as idolatrous) through numerous SUPREME COURT cases, most notably cases concerning religious freedom (the right to evangelize door-to-door) and separation of CHURCH AND STATE (exempting public school students from saluting the flag and reciting the Pledge of Allegiance).

Further Reading
Watchtower Bible and Tract Society. *The New World*. . . . New York: Watchtower, ca. 1942.

John Birch Society

An ultra-CONSERVATIVE, far RIGHT-wing, American political group noted for its fervent anti-COMMUNISM. Founded in 1959 by Robert Welch, a Massachusetts businessman, the society is named after a BAPTIST missionary who was killed by the Communist Chinese in 1945. The John Birch Society advanced strongly anti-LIBERAL policies through its publications *The New American* magazine and *The Blue Book,* as well as members who served in the U.S. government. It expressed an extremely antistatist and conspiratorial view of politics, accusing presidents Franklin ROOSEVELT, Harry Truman, and Dwight Eisenhower of being sympathetic to communism, identifying the United Nations as a tool of the Soviet and Chinese Communist governments. Committed to "God, family, country, and strong moral principles," the John Birch Society, like some of the CHRISTIAN RIGHT, advocated restoration of prayer in public schools, U.S. boycotting of UNICEF, opposition to civil rights legislation and liberal Supreme Court rulings, and cutting the U.S. welfare system. Taking an apocalyptic view of history, Welch saw the imminent takeover of the United States and the world by communists through liberal educators and "communist sympathizers" in the national government. Although a small fringe group (100,000 members), it exerted influence on conservative parties, organizations, and politicians.

Further Readings
Epstein, Benjamin R., and Foster, Arnold. *Report on the John Birch Society.* New York: Random House, 1966.
Grove, Gene. *Inside the John Birch Society.* New York: Gold Medal Books, 1961.

John of Paris (1250–1304)   *French political and ecclesiastical philosopher*

Of great influence on MODERN LIBERAL, SOCIAL-CONTRACT political theory (especially that of John LOCKE) and separation of CHURCH AND STATE ideas, John's philosophy grew out of a unique conception of PROPERTY. Contrary to much MEDIEVAL European thought, he viewed private material possessions as existing in nature prior to temporal (state) and ecclesiastical (church) institutions. This NATURAL RIGHT to property derived from God's granting people physical power (labor) and needs, as well as the common store of nature. Mixing one's work with divine creation produces individually held property. This LABOR THEORY OF VALUE, later adapted by Locke, RICARDO, and Karl MARX, makes economic activity rather than secular or religious AUTHORITY the basis of privately held wealth. Governments and churches should respect and protect such industry and material prosperity. The corporate structure of the (CATHOLIC) church may hold land and property with papal control over its dispensation and stewardship. The just ruler serves the common good of his or her subjects, and states can be overthrown if that trust is violated (compare to Locke's "right to revolution"). Even a pope can be displaced, in John's view, by a sovereign council of the whole church. These Modern REPUBLICAN ideas are later developed by the Protestant REFORMATION.

Much like Martin LUTHER 200 years later, John of Paris conceives of the separation of the spiritual and temporal powers, church and state, with the secular government enjoying autonomous SOVEREIGNTY over the realm's material concerns (economics, education, military, etc.). The church occupies a separate but related sphere of religion and morals but without coercive authority over politics.

John of Paris was a member of the Dominican religious order and contributed (in his book, *De Potestate regia et papali*) to the discussion between King Philippe of France and Pope Boniface VIII over their respective rights and powers.

Further Reading
John of Paris. *On Royal and Papal Power,* J. A. Watt, transl. Toronto: Pontifical Institute of Medieval Studies, 1971.

John of Salisbury (1115–1180)   *Medieval English political philosopher and cleric*

A classic representative of CHRISTIAN political thought of the MIDDLE AGES, John of Salisbury provided the famous analogy of the state to a body (the king as head, church as heart and soul, peasants as hands and feet, etc.). He related CHURCH AND STATE in a typical Augustinian way: Society is both a natural entity and a spiritual realm (a mixture of the City of Man and the City of God), and Christians are both animals and saints. Human and divine must work together for JUSTICE to survive; the ruler must conform to godly principles and CANON LAW. Government (as John CALVIN later described it) is a combination of worldly and spiritual concerns, and rulership is a kind of divine ministry, accountable to God. Evil tyrants will be dealt with most severely by the Lord. In his book, *Policraticus* (1156–59), John of Salisbury describes many historical examples of bad rulers being punished by God and destroyed for their iniquity and unfaithfulness. These examples include many instances of unjust rulers being murdered, but John does not advocate violent revolution or tyrannicide; rather, the godly citizenry "resists" an evil prince through suffering, prayer, and patience. John's advice is a warning to weak or wicked princes, that they cannot enjoy God's peace, safety, and blessings unless they repent and return to just, godly governance.

John of Salisbury drew upon the Christian classics and ancient Greek and Roman philosophy and law (especially CICERO). His emphasis on human reason as a source of moral knowledge reflects this CLASSICAL education. Trained in France, he returned to serve Archbishop Thomas BECKET in England, ending his career as bishop of Chartres. Traveling extensively in France and Italy, John of Salisbury was acquainted with the great scholars of his time and observed personally the drift of power to the papacy through increased appeals to the Roman curia.

The ideal polity provides a balance between material and spiritual, worldly, and Christian, and a ruler has the responsibility (as a blending of natural and divine) to maintain that balance. Church and state should respect each other, neither invading the purview of the other, for achievement of a healthy, balanced state.

Further Readings

Chibnall, Margorie, trans. *The Historia Pontificalis of John of Salisbury*. Edinburgh: Thomas Welson and Sons,1956.

Wilks, M., ed. "The World of John of Salisbury." *Studies in Church History*, subsidia 3. Oxford, Eng.: Blackwell Publishers, 1984.

just-war doctrine

In Western political thought, the ideals and values surrounding the definition of when warfare is justified and how it should be conducted in a just manner. This includes what the just causes of war are, who has AUTHORITY to determine appropriate responses to war, and how warfare should be conducted to respect morals and JUSTICE.

For example, in the MIDDLE AGES, the CATHOLIC Church defined justified war as that in defense of one's nation or property when invaded; when it is initiated by a valid political authority; when it is taken as a last resort (after attempted peace negotiations, compromise, etc.); when it is carried on in a proportional manner (using only enough force to repel the invader and restore justice, but not to exercise vengeance or retribution); when its end or purpose is the restoration of peace; and when it has a reasonable hope of success. Other components of just-war doctrine include the treatment of noncombatants or civilian populations. In general, Medieval doctrine exempted women, children, the aged and infirm, priests, peasants, pilgrims, townspeople, and all who did not bear weapons from the attack of military force. This confined warfare to military personnel and limited the ravages of war to those directly engaged in combat. St. AUGUSTINE, St. Ambrose, and Gratian developed these CHRISTIAN doctrines of limited war, drawing from earlier ROMAN LAW and Catholic conceptions of godly love (*caritas*). St. Thomas AQUINAS further developed this church doctrine, which influenced Medieval knights' notions of honor and chivalry.

Prior to the Christian Middle Ages, warfare was much more brutal and extensive. The Hebraic tradition of genocide of opponents of ancient Israel as detailed in the Jewish Bible, and early Greek and Roman imperial slaughter of innocents illustrates the restraining influence of Christianity on human warfare. The MODERN secular theorists SUAREZ and GROTIUS built on the Catholic just-war doctrine, without its religious foundations. Twentieth-century war returned to the barbaric practices of pagan warfare with mass genocide by NAZI Germany and civilian destruction by U.S. nuclear attacks on Japan. Despite numerous treaties and institutions of international law, warfare in the 19th and 20th centuries reached new levels of cruelty and mass destruction.

Further Readings

Johnson, James Turner. *Just War Tradition and the Restraint of War: A Moral and Historical Inquiry*. Princeton, N.J.: Princeton University Press, 1981.

Ramsey, Paul. *The Just War: Force and Political Responsibility*. New York: Scribners, 1968.

Russell, Frederick H. *The Just War in the Middle Ages.* Cambridge, Eng.: Cambridge University Press, 1975.

justice

A central concept in Western political theory, but one that has been defined in various ways. Two main ways of defining *justice* are: (1) the harmonious and healthy ordering of persons within the whole society; and (2) the individual RIGHTS and benefits of each citizen in a community. The first orientation of *justice,* exemplified in CLASSICAL (especially PLATO) and MEDIEVAL (St. Thomas AQUINAS) political thought, focuses on the justice of the entire nation or whole community and subordinates the individual's interests to the common good. The second, MODERN conception of *justice* (as in John LOCKE, Karl MARX) emphasizes the individual's economic interests and benefits against the larger society. Plato's *Republic* gives the classic definition of *justice* as "giving each person his due" or every individual receiving what he or she "deserves." For Plato, this means having one's innate abilities (to be a ruler or soldier or worker) recognized, properly trained, and used by society. From this "justice as deserts," every individual is fulfilled, everyone is in one's proper place, and the whole society is a harmonious, cooperative unity. Thus, the emphasis in this Platonic definition of *justice* is on a certain *ordering* of parts within the whole, the individuals within a certain *place* where each is needed, useful, and fulfilled (which is determined by others—parents, elders, rulers). This system of justice subordinates individual preference to the common good and requires wise rulers (PHILOSOPHER-KINGS) to structure it. Such a holistic view of justice continues in the Roman Empire (CICERO) in which service to Rome (as senator, soldier, citizen) is considered noble and just. The CATHOLIC Middle Ages employs this organic notion of justice in St. Thomas Aquinas's *Summa Theologica,* which combines CHRISTIAN and Aristotelian concepts of order and virtue. The just realm is one ultimately ruled by God with each social component (church, king, nobility, GUILDS, peasants) in its "place," working harmoniously together—"God's in his heaven, all's right with the world." This medieval HIERARCHY is presented as natural and divine (NATURAL LAW) and finds literary expression in Shakespeare's plays. *Injustice,* from this classical view, is a society where individuals are *not* in their places, are out of order, and everyone is considered equal and

capable of determining his or her individual destiny. Plato depicts such injustice as a lower person (soldier, child, woman) ruling over his or her "betters" or superiors; it is "unjust" to treat a soldier like a businessman or a ruler like a soldier. Shakespeare depicts this as a peasant or rebellious-prince position in which the person does not belong. Disaster results in such "unjust" assertive individualistic behavior.

Modern, LIBERAL, and SOCIALIST definitions of *justice* take the individual and her or his economic desires as the basis for justice. In this perspective, all individuals are equal, self-determining, and deserving of the same social benefits and conditions in society. This makes DEMOCRACY the most just regime and competition for social benefits the norm. CAPITALISM promises the just reward of productive merit, and COMMUNISM promises the social justice of equal economic benefits to all. Injustice, in this view, is any inequality, discrimination, or unfair treatment of anyone.

Most contemporary countries blend these Ancient HIERARCHICAL and Modern EGALITARIAN notions of the ideal state. John RAWLS's *Theory of Justice* combines these standards of justice by employing a Modern Lockean ideal of individual EQUALITY within a society; equal opportunity with social differences and responsibility provide a theory reflecting the U.S.'s mixed regime of capitalist individualism and Judeo-CHRISTIAN morality. Private business and religious organizations allow considerable organic justice, while LIBERAL social programs give equality to all. Thus, traditional and Modern ideals of justice reside within the same civilization in an uneasy balance but with each tempering the excesses of the other. Such a PLURALISM of values and systems of justice produce confusion and controversy but, in MADISON's ideal constitutional REPUBLIC, prevent the worst form of tyranny. Individuals, as in Robert NOZICK's *Anarchy, State and Utopia,* are free to choose a system of justice, but a common standard eludes the entire society.

Justice, then, is an evolving and complex concept in political thought, but one which benefits from knowledge of the past.

Further Readings

Miller, D. *Social Justice.* Oxford, Eng.: Clarendon Press, 1976.
Pettit, P. *Judging Justice.* London: Routledge, 1980.
Rawls, J. *A Theory of Justice.* Cambridge, Mass.: Belknap Press of Harvard University Press, 1971, 1972.

Justinian I (A.D. 482–565) *Byzantine emperor and law-code founder*

Famous for the Justinian code of ROMAN LAW, which he developed in the Eastern Empire in Constantinople, Justinian influenced much of later European law. His *Institutes* compiled much of ancient Roman law and integrated it into orthodox CHRISTIAN culture. For example, as emperor, Justinian I saw himself as supreme ruler over CHURCH AND STATE, uniting the spiritual and worldly orders that were separated by the Western CATHOLIC European order. This pattern of combining political and religious authority in one person (sometimes called Caesaro-Papism) led the Eastern Orthodox Church (in Greece, Armenia, Russia) to declare the secular ruler (e.g., Russian czar) as "Christ on earth." As such, Justinian I dictated church doctrine as well as secular law. The idea of separation of church and state or religious FREEDOM as understood by Protestant Christianity (especially PURITAN) is lost. A formal, official Christian religion emerged, and worldly corruption of the church followed. The state and the church became indistinguishable. For the Western church, this blending of earthly and divine corrupted the Christian faith more than outright persecution, as the pride, emoluments, and formality of the official religion deformed the simple teachings of Jesus. (See IMPERIAL CHURCH.)

Justinian I also expanded the Eastern Roman Empire into Northern Africa and the Middle East, areas later conquered by ISLAM.

Further Reading

Jones, A. H. M. *The Later Roman Empire, 284–602: A Social, Economic and Administrative Survey,* 3 vols. Baltimore: Johns Hopkins University Press, 1964.

K

Kant, Immanuel (1724–1804) *German philosopher*

Immanuel Kant was born, lived, and died in Königsberg, eastern Prussia. He studied science, history, and philosophy at the University of Königsberg from 1740 to 1747 and, after working as a private tutor for several years, served as a *Privatdozent* (a lecturer paid by the students who attended his lectures) at the university until 1770. That same year, Kant was appointed professor of logic and metaphysics by the university, where he taught until 1796. Although Kant published several works as a young scholar, his most important writings appeared in his middle and later years. In 1781, he published the *Critique of Pure Reason,* which had a major impact on epistemology and metaphysics during his lifetime as well as throughout the MODERN period. Kant's subsequent publications attempt to work out the implications of his critical analysis of human reason for the areas of aesthetics, morality, and politics.

In the *Groundwork for the Metaphysics of Morals* (1785), Kant presented his basic moral theory, arguing that the only thing that is unconditionally good is a good will. According to Kant, a person who acts with a good will acts on the basis of neither the desires that influence the action nor the consequences that result from it, but instead on the recognition that the action is obligatory or necessary. This means that the person acts in accord with what Kant calls the categorical imperative, which can be formulated as "Act only on that maxim that you can, at the same time, will that it should be a universal law," that is, a law that everyone should obey. Kant's categorical imperative represents a form of deontological ethical theory (from the Greek *deon,* meaning "duty"), which is the view that defines *right action* in terms of obligations and duties rather than the consequences or results of an action. This is in contrast to teleological ethical theories (from the Greek *telos,* meaning "end" or "goal"), which hold that the best consequences or results determine the rightness of an action. Kant believed that an action willed from the categorical imperative is done with a necessary view to treating all persons, including ourselves, as ends in themselves and not merely as means to other ends. Only in this way is it possible to respect the intrinsic freedom, equality, autonomy, and dignity of human beings.

In several later essays, Kant sought to clarify the relationship of his moral theory to political practice. In the famous essay "On the Common Saying: This May be True in Theory, But It Does Not Apply in Practice," published in 1793, Kant discussed how a civil state is justified on the basis of a SOCIAL CONTRACT that expresses the moral conception of humanity as an end in itself. In a just civil government, the rights of humanity are secured, establishing a reciprocal obligation on the part of each citizen to respect the RIGHTS of all others. Thus, some limitations on FREEDOM do exist through the RULE OF LAW and the state's right to punish, but these limitations are legitimate because they actually increase freedom by prohibiting (and redressing) the types of wrongs characteristic of the lawless STATE OF NATURE. For Kant, then, the value of legitimate government is that it guarantees our NATURAL RIGHTS to freedom and equality and provides us a foundation from which to acquire other rights. Kant referred to his ideal of the perfect moral community, in which autonomous persons legislate together according to the categorical imperative, as the "Kingdom of Ends." In *The Metaphysics of Morals* (1797), Kant argued that the Kingdom of Ends establishes a sphere of public JUSTICE within which all persons are obligated to respect everyone else's rights.

Kant also argued that, in matters of international justice, the real relations between nations is analogous to the hypothetical relations between individuals in the state of nature. Just as public justice must be established in the single, domestic state to secure each individual's right to freedom within that state, so too public justice must be established on a global scale to secure the rights of all humanity. Although he expressed concerns regarding the formation of a world government, Kant proposed a voluntary federation of states, or a "league of nations," whose common law would preserve equality and mutual respect among nations. Ultimately, Kant suggested in *Perpetual Peace* (1795) that only such a world federation would bring an end to war and lead to the realization of justice and the guarantee of CIVIL LIBERTY.

Further Reading
Shell, S. M. *The Rights of Reason: A Study of Kant's Philosophy and Politics.* Toronto: University of Toronto Press, 1980.

Kautsky, Karl (1854–1938) *German Marxist theorist and social democrat*

Kautsky's SOCIALIST theory represented the gradual (rather than sudden) and peaceful (rather than violent revolution) wing of the LEFTIST political thought in the 20th century. This moderate MARXISM saw socialism evolving out of CAPITALISM through DEMOCRATIC processes, as opposed to working class revolution led by a radical militant COMMUNIST Party (contrast V. I. LENIN). Such gradual socialism through parliamentary means came to be associated with the social democratic political parties in Europe (especially Germany, France, Italy, and the Labour Party in Britain). This caused the more militant communist revolutionaries to accuse "Kautskyites" of compromise and betrayal of the proletarian cause. To radicals like Lenin, such legal socialism was middle-class, intellectual, bourgeois compromise and would never lead to true communism. At worst, other Marxists accused Kautsky's social democrats of being allied with the capitalist oppressors, weakening the working class cause, and being tools of the IMPERIALISTS. Similarly, Kautsky's belief that socialism would lead to a more democratic government (rather than the DICTATORSHIP of the proletariat) was ridiculed by more radical communists as a weak compromise with the system.

In a more-orthodox Marxist manner, Kautsky saw the economic CLASS of German peasants as having social INTERESTS (in landed property, agriculture, small-scale production) contrary to the industrial working class (compare MAO TSE-TUNG, CHINESE POLITICAL THOUGHT). He also developed a theory of ultraimperialism (stabilizing capitalist economics and preventing war through monopolies and cartels) that conflicted with Lenin's theory of imperialism.

Kautsky's emphasis on socialist consciousness developed by communist intellectuals (like himself) diminished the role of the working class in revolutionary politics and furthered a certain passivity that Lenin also denounced. Kautsky, then, represents a kind of tame, domesticated Marxism, seen as ineffective by his more radical colleagues, but realistic by his fellow social democrats.

Further Reading
Salvadori, M. *Kautsky and the Socialist Revolution.* London: NLB, 1979.

Kennedy, John F. (1917–1963) *President of the United States*

John Fitzgerald Kennedy, the 35th president of the United States, was the youngest ever elected to the presidency and the first of the Roman CATHOLIC faith.

Elected in 1960 by a narrow margin, Kennedy's popularity grew quickly among most Americans. During his relatively brief term of office, President Kennedy dealt with a range of both domestic and international critical issues, including the Berlin airlift, the Cuban missile crisis, and the growing CIVIL RIGHTS movement. The U.S. space program, however, surged ahead during the Kennedy administration, scoring dramatic gains that benefited U.S. prestige worldwide.

Kennedy's political career began as a representative from Massachusetts's 11th Congressional District. As a representative, Kennedy had a mixed voting record. On domestic affairs, he followed the administration's Fair Deal policies in most matters, fighting for slum clearance and low-cost public housing. As a member of the Education and Labor Committee, he wrote his own temperate report concurring with the minority that opposed the Taft-Hartley bill. On foreign affairs he backed the Truman Doctrine, a policy of the containment of COMMUNISM, but was critical of the president for not stemming the advance of communism in China.

In November 1952, while the Republican Dwight D. Eisenhower carried Massachusetts, Kennedy defeated Henry Cabot Lodge by more than 70,000 votes for U.S. Senate. As senator, Kennedy was an active legislator uniting New England senators into an effective voting bloc. By 1957, he was taking mildly liberal positions on the difficult question of CIVIL LIBERTIES. He helped arrange a compromise between northern and southern positions on the civil rights bill passed in 1957. Also in 1957, Kennedy was appointed to the Senate Foreign Relations Committee. His emphasis on domestic issues shifted to military programs, foreign aid, and underdeveloped areas.

Kennedy was inaugurated as president on January 20, 1961. Kennedy chose his cabinet to represent the country's main sections and INTERESTS. To reassure business, a Republican, C. Douglas Dillon, was appointed secretary of the treasury, and another Republican, Robert S. McNamara, who had been president of the Ford Motor Company, was named secretary of defense. Dean Rusk, who had headed the Rockefeller Foundation, became the new secretary of STATE, and Adlai Stevenson was appointed ambassador to the United Nations. Robert Kennedy, the president's brother, became attorney general.

Although interested in domestic affairs, Kennedy's brief tenure as president was dominated by international crises. Arguably, most serious among these was the Cuban missile crisis. On October 6, 1962, the United States took aerial reconnaissance photographs of Soviet missile bases under construction in Cuba. Just 90 miles from the U.S. coast, it was conceivable that from these bases a nuclear attack could be launched on much of the United States and the Western Hemisphere. Addressing the nation on October 22, President Kennedy announced an embargo on all offensive weapons bound for Cuba. This meant that U.S. warships would halt and search Soviet ships. The crisis was averted when Cuba-bound Soviet vessels returned to Russian ports.

In November 1963, President Kennedy and his wife, Jacqueline Kennedy, traveled to Texas. In Dallas on November 22, while touring Dallas, an assassin fired several shots, striking the president twice, in the base of the neck and the head, and seriously wounding Texas governor John Connolly, who was riding with the Kennedys. On November 24, amid national and worldwide mourning, the president's body lay in state in the rotunda of the U.S. Capitol. The next day, leaders of 92 nations attended the state funeral, joining millions of Americans in mourning. The president was buried in Arlington National Cemetery, where an eternal flame marks his grave.

Further Reading
Reeves, Thomas C., ed. *John F. Kennedy: The Man, the Politician, the President.* Melbourne, Fla.: Krieger Publishing Company, 1990.

Keynes, John Maynard (1883–1946)   *British economist and social thinker*

Keynesian economics became the foundation of LIBERAL DEMOCRATIC Party social policy in the United States from the 1930s (President Franklin D. ROOSEVELT'S NEW DEAL) until the present. To solve the Great Depression of the 1930s, Keynes recommended increased government spending, public debt, and social employment. By borrowing and spending money on public-works projects, Keynes argued, the depressed economy would be restimulated ("priming the pump"), and CAPITALISM would be saved. Social programs by the federal government would provide public employment and social services to get business going again. This would be an alternative to pure SOCIALISM (state-owned and -planned economy) or FASCISM (total state control of the private economy).

Keynes saw the favorable side of capitalism (innovation, reward for invention and hard work, market efficiency, and personal liberty) and sought to correct its deficiencies (the extreme business cycle of "boom and bust," high unemployment, poverty in certain sectors of the economy) with government monetary control and regulation. Britain and the United States employed Keynesian economics more than other nations, and some attribute this to their preserving their democracies and free-market economics. But critics of Keynesian views (CONSERVATIVE economists such as Milton Friedman) claim that these policies led to monetary inflation, high taxes, and excessive federal government regulation of business. Still, the Liberal Democratic policy premised in Keynesian economics ("mixed economy" of public/private) dominated U.S. national politics for 50 years (1930–80) until the presidency of Ronald REAGAN shifted policy back to more laissez-faire capitalism, and returning greater policy control to the states. But the principal policies of Keynes (Social Security, central-government monetary control, public debt, and regulatory agencies) continue to dominate the U.S. political system.

Further Reading

Harrod, R. F. *The Life of John Maynard Keynes.* New York: Harcourt, Brace and Co., 1951.

Kierkegaard, Sören (1813–1855) *Danish philosopher and existentialist*

As a progenitor of EXISTENTIALISM, Kierkegaard criticized the DIALECTICAL philosophy of HEGEL by asserting that "Truth is subjectivity," by which he meant that until a philosophic, political, ethical, or religious principle was known personally, it did not exist for the individual. This reflects his EVANGELICAL Protestant CHRISTIANITY, emphasizing personal commitment to living a Christlike life rather than the formal institutional church and cold religion he witnessed in Denmark. His emphasis on individual responsibility in morals led to secular philosophical Existentialism (*see* SARTRE). But Kierkegaard approached truth from various perspectives: (1) aesthetic (sensory stimulation and beauty); (2) ETHICAL (moral views and conduct); and (3) religious (the individual's relationship to God). His approach ended with a profoundly personal Christian sense of humility and faith in *Christian Discourses*

and *Training in Christianity* (1850). This INDIVIDUALIST, CONSERVATIVE, and mystical dimension of Kierkegaardian thought made him a target for more "ACTIVIST" philosophers, especially LIBERALS and MARXISTS. His introspective psychology in *The Concept of Dread* (1844) and *Sickness Unto Death* (1849) made him appealing to political writers with a religious bent, such as Karl Barth and Martin HEIDEGGER.

Further Reading

Polk, Timothy. *The Biblical Kierkegaard.* Macon, Ga.: Mercer University Press, 1997.

King, Martin Luther, Jr. (1929–1968) *African-American minister and social activist*

The Reverend Martin Luther King, Jr., was the foremost leader of the civil rights movement in the United States, which fought against legalized segregation and racial injustice. King was born in Atlanta, Georgia, the son and grandson of Baptist ministers. At the age of 15, he entered Morehouse College and received his B.A. in 1948. That same year, King was ordained a Baptist minister. He spent the next three years at the Crozer Theological Seminary, where he was elected student body president and graduated with the highest grade average in his class. King then attended Boston University and continued his study of theology, philosophy, and ethics. He received a Ph.D. in 1955 in philosophical theology for a dissertation titled "A Comparison of the Conceptions of God in the Thinking of Paul Tillich and Henry Nelson Wieman." During this period King was greatly influenced by the works of a number of major thinkers, including SOCRATES, St. AUGUSTINE, St. Thomas AQUINAS, Sören KIERKEGAARD, Frederick DOUGLASS, and Mohandas GANDHI.

Following his marriage to Coretta Scott, King became pastor of the Dexter Avenue Baptist Church in Montgomery, Alabama. In December 1955, Rosa Parks was arrested for refusing to surrender her bus seat to a white passenger. Black activists in Montgomery then formed a boycott of the city's public bus system and selected King to lead the boycott. The boycott brought the first public attention to King as a leading social activist. His speeches were passionate and uncompromising in their demand for FREEDOM and justice for blacks and foreshadowed the great rhetorical skill that made King famous both nationally and internationally in the years to come. By early 1957, the boycott had succeeded in forcing the desegregation of the Montgomery bus system.

To build on the success of the Montgomery boycott, King organized the Southern Christian Leadership Conference (SCLC). The SCLC enabled civil rights activists and religious leaders to coordinate their efforts and provided King with greater visibility and support. In 1959, King met with Indian Prime Minister Jawaharlal Nehru and other followers of Gandhi's philosophy of *satyagraha,* or the power of truth to liberate the oppressed through active nonviolence. These meetings reinforced King's conviction that freedom from racial oppression must be achieved through nonviolent resistance. The essence of King's thought was that all individuals have a moral obligation to refuse to cooperate with evil. King argued that because evil laws, such as those enforcing racial segregation and inequality, are neither morally nor politically legitimate, resisters are justified in disobeying those laws. To retain their moral authority, however, resisters must always pursue nonviolent forms of noncooperation because violence destroys the value and dignity of human life. Consequently, King advocated nonviolent CIVIL DISOBEDIENCE as the only morally and practically acceptable path to freedom from oppression.

King moved to Atlanta in 1960 and continued his intense activism for civil rights, despite the threats continually directed at himself and his family. Organizing and participating in numerous marches and sit-in demonstrations, King was often arrested and jailed. While in jail following his arrest for protesting segregation policies in Birmingham, Alabama, in early 1963, King wrote his famous essay, "Letter from a Birmingham Jail." In this letter, King defended the philosophy and tactics of nonviolent civil disobedience against numerous critics: "Nonviolent direct action seeks to create such a crisis and foster such a tension that a community which has constantly refused to negotiate is forced to confront the issue. It seeks so to dramatize the issue that it can no longer be ignored . . . We know through painful experience that freedom is never voluntarily given by the oppressor; it must be demanded by the oppressed."

In August 1963, King helped organize the historic March on Washington, where several hundred thousand people gathered to demand equal justice for all citizens under the law. Here, King delivered his stirring "I Have a Dream" speech, in which he described his

Dr. Martin Luther King, Jr., at the civil rights March on Washington, 1963. (NATIONAL ARCHIVES)

faith in the vision of all people united together in love and brotherhood. Shortly thereafter, the federal government passed the Civil Rights Act of 1964, which outlawed racial discrimination in publicly owned facilities and employment practices. In December 1964, King was awarded the Nobel Peace Prize in recognition of his contributions to peaceful social change.

During the next several years, King sought to broaden his activism by opposing the Vietnam War and by building coalitions among poor communities of all colors in the United States. These activities reflected King's growing awareness of the international dimensions of racism and of how CAPITALISM contributed to racial violence and social injustice. King was concerned that the focus on civil and political freedom too often overlooked the importance of social and economic equality. The great economic divisions found in the United States and elsewhere undermined the conditions needed to make equality and freedom real for the poor. King argued that economic inequality was a problem for both whites and blacks who were exploited by an economic system that was determined to limit the power of working people. Therefore, he sought to expand the struggle for freedom to include both racial and economic justice, based on a theory of economic reconstruction inspired by democratic SOCIALISM.

While in Memphis, Tennessee, to support a strike by the city's sanitation workers, King was killed by a sniper's bullet on April 4, 1968, as he stood on the balcony of the motel where he was staying.

Further Reading
Oates, S. B. *Let the Trumpets Sound: A Life of Martin Luther King, Jr.* New York: HarperPerennial, 1994.

Knights of Labor

A CATHOLIC labor union in the United States, first condemned and later endorsed by the church. The central controversy, like that of LIBERATION THEOLOGY a century later, was the degree of anti-CHRISTIAN, COMMUNIST IDEOLOGY in this labor organization.

Founded in 1869, the Knights of Labor was the first national workers' union in America. Led by Uriah Stevens, it contained primarily immigrant (Irish) Catholic INDUSTRIAL laborers. Like other early unions, it employed secret rites, customs, and practices (similar to the Masonic Order). Such secrecy and potentially pagan rites were condemned by Pope Leo XIII (1884), prompting several U.S. Catholic bishops to condemn the Knights of Labor. However, in 1887, a majority of the archbishops in the United States criticized this blanket rejection of the Knights of Labor, warning the Vatican that it could result in a tragic loss of Catholic influence in the U.S. labor movement and among ordinary Catholics. The Rome hierarchy examined this economic/religious controversy and ruled that the union could continue if it removed any references to SOCIALISM or communism in the Knights' CONSTITUTION. This was seen as a victory among socially LIBERAL U.S. Catholics as a church accommodating MODERN industrial economic realities and conditions in the United States. The same compromise occurred in the latter 20th century in response to the Latin American liberation theology of Gustavo GUTIÉRREZ, when Pope John Paul II condemned the MARXIST-LENINIST components of that move-

ment but furthered the church's commitment to social JUSTICE and the poor in the developing world. An interesting episode in CHURCH AND STATE relations, the Knights of Labor controversy shows the evolving nature of religion and politics in America.

Further Reading
Fink, Leon. *Workingmen's Democracy: The Knights of Labor and American Politics.* Urbana: University of Illinois Press, 1985.

Knox, John (1513–1572)   *Scottish religious and political activist*

A leader of the Protestant REFORMATION in Scotland, Knox was alternately in and out of favor in the British government. Converted as a CATHOLIC priest to Calvinist theology, he led the Protestant movement in Scotland and England. This included the abolition of the pope's authority in Great Britain, idolatry of the Virgin Mary, and celebration of the mass. His virulent opposition to women in positions of authority in both church and state did not earn Knox favor with the new monarch, Queen Elizabeth I. He preached fervent sermons against Mary, Queen of Scots, for her "popery" and worldliness, which lost him favor during her reign. With the ascension to the throne of King James I, Knox enjoyed favor in court but soon lost it with the demise of the regent, Lord Murray.

A prolific writer, John Knox influenced Scottish reformed theology in Britain and America. Its EVANGELICAL and DEMOCRATIC themes appear in his works *The Scottish Confession; The First Book of Discipline; Treatise on Predestination; The Book of Common Order;* and *History of the Reformation of Religion within the Realm of Scotland* (1587). By influencing the Scots and Scots-Irish PRESBYTERIANS, many of whom settled in the American colonies, Knox's ideas on religion and politics greatly affected CHURCH-AND-STATE ideas in the later United States of America, including Founders such as John WITHERSPOON, James Wilson, and James MADISON.

Further Reading
MacGregor, Geddes. *The Thundering Scot: a Portrait of John Knox.* Philadelphia: Westminster Press, 1986.

Koran (Qur'an), The

The sacred book of the religion of ISLAM, which provides for its views of God (Allah), faith, morals, LAW, society, economics, and politics. This forms the spiritual and temporal basis of Muslim countries (predominantly in the Arab Middle East, Africa, Central Asia, and Indonesia). Islam holds that the Koran was dictated to the Muslim Prophet MOHAMMED (570–629) by an angel. It teaches monotheism (the doctrine of one God) and his goodness, awesomeness, omnipotence, and determination of all things. Other doctrines of Islam are held in varying interpretations by Muslims, but generally the Koran presents Jesus Christ as a prophet (along with Abraham and Moses) but not as the Son of God as understood by Christians, and it denies the Resurrection and the Holy Trinity.

The Koran presents a unity of religious and governmental authority as exemplified by Mohammad who, like the Hebrew king David, was a military, spiritual, and political leader. This continues in ISLAMIC POLITICAL THOUGHT, which denies the Western CHRISTIAN separation of religion and politics but sees faith and law united in the state. This is realized in varying degrees in contemporary Muslim countries from Iran—which claims to be an "Islamic Republic," deriving all its laws and social customs from the Koran—to Turkey—which is a MODERN secular REPUBLIC, formally separating religion from politics, incorporating Western European legal codes, education, science, and economics (including religious freedom) into a predominantly Muslim culture.

A contemporary political manifestation of the Koran is the idea of jihad, or "holy war," which can mean the individual's spiritual war against his own sin or an organized terrorist war against the non-Muslim "infidels" (Jews and Christians). Much of the current conflict in the Middle East (Arab-Israeli) centers around this concept. Many of Mohammad's recitations were probably written down during his lifetime, but the present text of the Koran was certainly in existence from the period of the Muslim caliph Uthman (643–656).

Further Reading
Sells, Michael. *Approaching the Quran*. Ashland, Oreg.: White Cloud Press, 2000.

Kropotkin, Peter (1842–1921)   *Russian anarchist*

Kropotkin was born in Moscow, the son of an army general and a descendent of a line of Russian princes dating back to the founding of the Russian empire. He was educated in the Corps of Pages in St. Petersburg and served as an aide to Czar Alexander II. Kropotkin then became an officer in the Mounted Cossacks. He was stationed in Siberia, where he conducted geographical surveys and developed important analyses of glaciation in east Asia during the Iron Age. Kropotkin also was exposed to the terrible conditions of the penal system in Siberia and to the writings of many radical political theorists, including the French anarchist Pierre-Joseph PROUDHON. In 1866, Kropotkin resigned his army commission and spent the next several years in scientific study of the glaciers of Finland and Sweden. In 1871 he was offered the secretaryship of the Russian Geographical Society, but Kropotkin refused, deciding to leave science and work instead for social justice and political change.

After visiting exiled Russian revolutionaries in Switzerland, Kropotkin returned to Russia an avowed adherent to ANARCHISM, the theory that coercive government, or the STATE, should be abolished. He became a member of an underground revolutionary group and was arrested in 1874 for distributing anarchist propaganda. Kropotkin escaped from prison two years later. He fled to France where he became an active member of the international anarchist movement, founding the anarchist paper *Le Révolté* in 1879. After serving nearly four years in prison following his arrest by French authorities in 1882, Kropotkin settled in England, where he spent the next 30 years developing his theory of anarchism in a number of influential writings. Kropotkin returned to Russia after the Bolshevik revolution of 1917 and remained there as a critic of the Bolsheviks' authoritarian tendencies until his death in 1921.

Kropotkin advanced a version of anarchism called anarchist communism. Several features of anarchist communism are shared with other forms of anarchism, such as its denunciation of state power and centralized government and its endorsement of self-managed communes. Kropotkin supported the practice of direct political action rather than parliamentary representation because the latter was believed to deprive the people of their ability to decide political matters for themselves. For Kropotkin, it was vitally important to protect the individual and his or her capacity to make decisions about his or her life from the "mutilating" power of the state. Recognizing the need, however, for some sort of administrative arrangement, even for small associations such as communes, Kropotkin advocated a type of FEDERALISM. In this arrangement, political decisions were to be made democratically through discussion and decision directly by the people, while the administration of these decisions were to be implemented by various boards and commissions.

Kropotkin's adherence to federalism is supported by his theory of mutual aid. In his book *Mutual Aid* (1902), Kropotkin utilized his scientific training to present an evolutionary theory that holds that human beings are naturally social animals whose sociability has been corrupted by authoritarian social institutions. In contrast to neo-Darwinian evolutionists, Kropotkin argued that cooperation rather than competition or conflict is the primary characteristic of both animal and human nature. Moreover, he suggested that social revolutions are a part of the evolutionary process and that anarchism seeks to bring humans back into a more natural form of social organization. This theme is presented also in his earlier *The Conquest of Bread* (1892), where Kropotkin described how an anarchist form of federalism grounded on mutual cooperation would be preferable to a form of centralized, state SOCIALISM. In a variety of areas, such as and agriculture the production of food and clothing, he then detailed how it was possible to avoid oppressive social arrangements by following the alternative of anarchism. In Kropotkin's view, an anarchist society would promote "a new harmony, the initiative of each and all, the daring which springs from the awakening of a people's genius."

Further Reading

Woodcock, G., and Avakumovic, I. *Peter Kropotkin: From Prince to Rebel*. Montreal: Black Rose Books, 1990.

Kulturkampf

An incident in 19th-century German CHURCH-AND-STATE relations in which the Prussian ruler (Bismarck) forced anti-CATHOLIC practices and legislation on the German confederacy. Fearing that the Roman Catholic HIERARCHY would weaken the German empire, Bismarck suppressed the Catholic department of the Ministry of Public Worship, expelled the Jesuits from the country, imposed state control over education, abolished monasteries, and imprisoned several Catholic bishops. Unlike similar actions in England under King HENRY VIII, this Kulturkampf met enormous resistance by the German Catholic population and was suspended. A concordat was made between Prussia and the Vatican, the expulsion of Jesuits was reversed, and by 1887 most anti-Catholic legislation was nullified. The CONSERVATIVE political elements in Germany saw the Roman Catholic Church as an ally against rising SOCIALIST, COMMUNIST, and SOCIAL DEMOCRATIC movements. This episode stabilized the traditional church and state relations in that part of Europe into the 20th century.

L

labor theory of value

The economic theory that value in things is produced or is a result of the amount of human work, effort, or labor in them. In other words, the worth of a piece of property (land, house, car, shoes, etc.) is determined by how much labor went into creating it. This labor includes both physical, mental, and mechanical work, so the labor in a car includes not just the auto workers on the assembly line, but also the miners who extracted the iron for the steel, the chemists, manufacture of the engine, the artists who drew the design of the car, and the advertisers who marketed the built automobiles. Thus, in this labor theory of value, almost everyone is a worker, except the CAPITALIST owners who do no work but collect dividends or profits—an idle, landed ARISTOCRACY.

The labor theory of value appears in several thinkers, including JOHN OF PARIS, John LOCKE, David RICARDO, and Karl MARX. Each used it to justify a certain kind of political/economic system (capitalism or SOCIALISM) and to attack certain economic classes. Locke emphasized title ownership to private property as coming from the labor mixed with common nature, giving the example of a field that earns value and owner entitlement through its human cultivation. He then admitted wage labor, or someone selling their labor to another for payment in a free contract; then the product of the labor becomes the property not of the worker, but of his employer. Karl Marx's COMMUNIST theory used this idea to claim that wage labor robbed the working class through economic EXPLOITATION. In MARXISM, the cost or price of labor itself becomes a commodity (as in the labor market) and is reduced to the subsistence level of producing workers: their food, clothing, housing, education, and so on. Because those worker's wages are less than the value of product they produce with their labor, the employer or capitalist steals value from the laborers in the form of profit. This is not simply unjust, in Marx's view; it causes the crises of economic overproduction and the economic collapse of capitalism, ushering in socialism. This radical conclusion of the labor theory of value prompted worker's revolutions in Russia, China, and other communist countries.

Contrasting theories of value include the utility theory that says that the value of a thing is its perceived usefulness by the consumer. Other challenges to the labor theory of value include its ignoring the value of capital (from deferred consumption); its overemphasis on physical, manual labor (as opposed to intellectual or managerial); its determinism; and its HISTORICISM. Because the capitalist economy continued

177

to grow and the socialist and communist economies stagnated, the labor theory of value declined in popularity. It remains in the basic Protestant work ethic and various equal-pay-for-equal-work movements, but with the increasing complexity of the world economy, it becomes harder to identify the sources of labor in any product, and therefore the labor theory of value loses much of its explanatory power.

Further Reading

Meek, R. L. *Studies in the Labour Theory of Value,* 2nd ed. New York: Monthly Review Press, 1973.

laissez-faire

The economic and political doctrine that government should "leave alone" business activity as much as possible. Accompanying MODERN CAPITALISM and free-market economics, laissez-faire policies allow businesses and individuals to produce, exchange, and consume economic products with a minimum of government regulation or interference. The STATE in this view performs the minimum duties outlined by John LOCKE of protecting individual NATURAL RIGHTS to "life, LIBERTY, and PROPERTY," otherwise leaving people alone. Government thus provides basically a judicial function: police catching thieves, killers, kidnappers, and so on and punishing them. The underlying assumption of laissez-faire policy is that the society and economy will work best (most harmonious, happy, prosperous) if left free. The state may provide for a few large, common enterprises or public utilities (roads, electricity, military defense, prisons) but leaves most economic activities in the private sector. This IDEOLOGY is often associated with the CONSERVATIVE Party in Britain and the REPUBLICAN PARTY in the United States (for example, President Ronald REAGAN), with their programs of reduced taxes, reduced government services and regulations, and probusiness policies. A logical philosophical expression of laissez-faire ideas occurs in LIBERTARIAN (Robert NOZICK) and ANARCHIST theories.

Critics of laissez-faire economics argue that complex modern society requires greater government regulation and help for the poor. U.S. LIBERAL Democrats and European SOCIALISTS often attack laissez-faire attitudes and programs as unrealistic, hypocritical, and unfair.

Most Western INDUSTRIAL democracies do not practice laissez-faire capitalism or total state socialism but a mixture of the two: a "mixed economy" of private business enterprise and government regulation and social programs in education, housing, banking, health care, and so on. Purely laissez-faire market economics probably never existed in any country, but they were more prevalent in early capitalism (18th-century Britain, 19th-century United States) than in recent years. The Modern labor movement was a principle influence on ending extensive laissez-faire economics. Only a few contemporary economists (such as Milton Friedman) advocate laissez-faire.

Further Reading

Emmett, R. B. *Selected Essays: Laissez Faire.* Chicago: University of Chicago Press, 2000.

Lassalle, Ferdinand (1825–1864)   *Political theorist and activist*

Lassalle was deeply involved in socialist politics and organization in Germany, participating in the revolution of 1848 and founding the first German socialist party, the General German Workingmen's Association, in 1863. He was a sometime friend and correspondent of Karl Marx, led a flamboyant life, and died at age 39 in a duel.

Lassalle contributed to socialist political thought in two areas: In economic theory Lassalle developed what he called the iron law of wages; in the theory of socialist revolution, he advanced the idea that the state could be transformed into an ally of the working classes. The iron law of wages determined that the capitalist market would depress workers' wages until they reached the minimum level required to keep the worker and his family alive. The only remedy to this was for workers to exit the wage-labor system and to work in producer cooperatives that the workers owned and that would return the full value of their labor.

Lassalle's understanding of the state and the role it played differed radically from Marx's own understanding and was the chief source of Marx's increasing antagonism toward Lassalle and his followers. Lassalle denied that the state was necessarily against the interests of the working classes. He argued that the state could and should reflect the interests of workers and that this could be achieved through universal and direct suffrage.

Marx's *Critique of the Gotha Program,* where he sets out his only systematic account of a future communist society, is Marx's response to Lassalle's ideas, particularly those concerning the role of the state and the idea that workers should receive the full value of their labor.

Lassalle's economic and political views were influenced by Hegel and the economist Ricardo. He published a study of the ancient Greek philosopher Heraclitus in 1858. His other writings cover the question of rights, economic theory, and political activism.

Further Reading
Bernstein, E. *Ferdinand Lassalle as a Social Reformer.* St. Clair Shores, Mich.: Scholarly Press, 1970.

law

An official rule or ordinance of the STATE or government, binding CITIZENS through threat of punishment. Common laws punish crime (originating in COMMANDMENTS against murder, theft, kidnapping, assault, etc.) and regulate society (laws on marriage, family, property, education, etc.). Most state laws originate in moral and religious precepts (the Bible, the Torah, the KORAN, the church, etc.).

Government by laws (or the "RULE OF LAW") has been an ideal since the earliest political theories. CLASSICAL Greek and Roman thinkers (PLATO, ARISTOTLE, CICERO) held that laws were made when people were most reasonable, thoughtful, and deliberate, so they were more wise and just than the "rule of men" who could at times be moved by passion, interests, or other destructive forces. So the rule of law was preferred over the rule of men. A ruler's personal power should be limited by rules and laws so that he or she will not become a DICTATOR or TYRANT. This contrasts with another school of Western political thought (also in Plato and Aristotle) that holds that the rule of the best persons (the ideal citizen or PHILOSOPHER-KING) is preferable to legalistic government. To some extent, the classical REPUBLICAN tradition relies more on the quality of the citizenry than on formal rules and laws. The Lockean LIBERAL school (as in James MADISON) favors formal legislation over the character of citizens.

For Cicero and the Roman Empire, "every wise thought of the philosophers is encoded in law," so ROMAN LAW can create justice across a diverse EMPIRE (*Lex romana*). The British Empire assumes this lofty view of the British law (*Lex Britannia*), civilizing the world; the CATHOLIC Church of the Middle Ages adopts this view in CANON LAW, as do MODERN Americans in CONSTITUTIONAL law. St. Thomas AQUINAS discusses politics in terms of a series of ever-encompassing laws (divine law, NATURAL LAW, human or positive law). In this Thomist perspective, God's eternal law is revealed in scripture (the Bible) and the natural world (natural law), and public or state laws must conform to these "higher laws" to achieve justice.

Modern LIBERALISM similarly posits NATURAL RIGHTS as derived from God and nature; governments are created to preserve and protect them (see HOBBES, LOCKE, and JEFFERSON).

Given the prominence and prestige of law in political thought, much study has occurred on how laws are made, who is involved in forming them, and how they are enforced. Generally, laws are respected when people feel they have had a part in making them (as in a DEMOCRACY or a REPUBLIC), the rulers carrying them out are honest and just, and the laws are applied equally to all. Corruption becomes laws being forced through without popular CONSENT, or enforced by immoral leaders, or applied indiscriminately. One solution for keeping laws effective is the CHECKS-AND-BALANCES system of MONTESQUIEU and James Madison, which divides and distributes legal power and institutions, preventing their manipulation or misuse. In the United States, this takes the form of constitutional law (or fundamental law, which constricts ordinary statutory law), FEDERALISM (which divides levels of government), and branches of government (legislative, judicial, executive).

A further division of law develops in CHURCH-AND-STATE theories, in which CIVIL DISOBEDIENCE to a public law can be justified on religious and moral grounds. Modern legal systems now proliferate law into civil law, criminal law, military law, commercial law, maritime law, administrative law, tax law, and constitutional law. This may explain the emergence of the philosophy of law and the proliferation of lawyers.

Further Readings
Cotterell, R. *The Sociology of Law: An Introduction.* London: Butterworths, 1984.
Dworkin, R. *Taking Rights Seriously.* Cambridge, Mass.: Harvard University Press, 1977.
Finnis, J. M. *Natural Law and Natural Rights.* Oxford, Eng.: Clarendon Press, 1980.
Fuller, L. L. *The Morality of Law,* rev. ed. New Haven, Conn.: Yale University Press, 1969.

Left/Leftist/Left-wing

A designation of a political or IDEOLOGICAL stance or position associated with LIBERAL, SOCIALIST, and COMMU-

NIST ideals. So, MARXISM, SOCIAL DEMOCRACY, and American liberal Democrats are Left to varying degrees. The Left politically tends to be PROGRESSIVE (for social change), in favor of central government control or regulation of the economy (especially to benefit the poor and working class), and sometimes to champion the cause of the downtrodden or "oppressed" people and minorities (blacks, women, Native Americans, homosexuals, gays, lesbians, transsexuals, the disabled, the poor of the developing world). Left-wing politics began in the United States with the Progressive era in the early 1900s, deepened with the NEW DEAL Democratic Party under President Franklin ROOSEVELT in the 1930s, and continued under the liberal Democratic governments of John KENNEDY, Lyndon Johnson, and Bill Clinton. Often, Leftist policies embrace loosening TRADITIONAL moral social practices (on ABORTION, divorce law, sexual roles, etc.). Strongly favoring civil rights, Left politics usually also oppose military spending and warfare. The A.C.L.U. (American Civil Liberties Union) is a premier Leftist political organization. Left theory is often antibusiness and pro-ENVIRONMENTALISM and pro-FEMINIST, so Left is a broad ideological category that includes a variety of movements and stances. Generally, however, a Leftist is in favor of using the state to regulate the economy and to provide extensive social programs (in education, medicine, housing, mass transportation, etc.). It is contrasted with the RIGHT, or CONSERVATIVE MODERN ideology, which advocates less central state regulation over the economy, more private individual FREEDOM, and more traditional moral values. James Davison HUNTER's book *Culture Wars* describes the Left and Right positions in terms of cultural progressives and orthodox. His analysis illuminates the ethical bases of these political stances and shows why the Left tends to be more secular and hostile to religion while the Right is more favorably inclined to traditional religious standards. A contemporary critical term for the Left is *p.c.* (POLITICALLY CORRECT).

Although Leftist ideology enjoyed widespread popular acceptance and political dominance in the West during most of the 20th century, it began to be identified with high government spending, public debt, economic inflation, and social breakdown by the 1970s and has been largely superseded by MODERATE policies and leaders since the 1980s. With the collapse of Soviet COMMUNISM, extreme Leftist politics and economics have been largely discredited as social solutions. For the socioreligious expression of the left, see LIBERATION THEOLOGY.

Further Reading
Long, P. *The New Left*. Boston: P. Sargent, 1969.

legitimacy/legitimate

The concept of whether a STATE, ruler, system, or movement is valid, right, just—legitimate (as opposed to illegitimate—improper, unjust, arbitrary, or invalid). Political legitimacy is a concern throughout the history of political theory, but it receives special importance in the MODERN, LIBERAL SOCIAL-CONTRACT theories of Thomas HOBBES, John LOCKE, and Jean-Jacques ROUSSEAU. The central questions of political legitimacy are: What characteristics make an institution or government justly exercise POWER and AUTHORITY over others? Who determines if a state is legitimate or illegitimate? What are the remedies if a person or government ceases to be legitimate?

CLASSICAL political philosophy places political legitimacy in the character of those who rule and in the purpose of the state. ARISTOTLE considers the purpose of the state to be to serve the common good, so several regimes can be legitimate (MONARCHY—the ruler of one for the common good; ARISTOCRACY—the rule of a few for the common good; polity—the rule of the many for the common good). An illegitimate state is one where those in power govern for their own selfish INTERESTS. So, Aristotelian legitimacy resides in the character of the rulers and in the nature of their governance; it is determined by the excellent moral person, not the subjects who are ruled over. Similarly, PLATO's *Republic* details an ideal polis ruled by the wise and good PHILOSOPHER-KING, whose knowledge and VIRTUE establish a harmonious society of JUSTICE. All other regimes (military rule; government by the wealthy; democracy; tyranny) are increasingly illegitimate and unjust. In CHRISTIAN political thought (St. AUGUSTINE, St. Thomas AQUINAS), the only perfect and fully legitimate regime is the City of God, or kingdom of heaven, ruled by Christ; all earthly governments are characterized by worldly power and sin, greed, dominance, and violence. But some states are more just than others and therefore are more legitimate. A regime led by virtuous, godly men, advised by the church, and viewing their authority in stewardship as a gift from the Lord will tend to be more just and deserving of the peoples' allegiance and respect. DIVINE RIGHT OF KINGS comes from this MEDIEVAL Christian perspective.

With the breakdown of monarchies in Europe and the rise of popular REPUBLICAN governments, the social-contract school of thought based political legitimacy in the consent of the people. Legitimate government in Hobbes and Locke are those formed by an agreement among the people (or social contract) to set up a state or ruler to serve certain ends (military defense, protection of NATURAL RIGHTS, social peace, promotion of INDUSTRY, etc.). America adopts this British liberal view of political legitimacy through Thomas JEFFERSON's Declaration of Independence (declaring the British parliamentary rule in America illegitimate) and James MADISON's United States CONSTITUTION, a legitimate social contract of limited powers, republican principles, and democratic SOVEREIGNTY. Most Modern industrial democracies premise state legitimacy in such popular election of leaders, constitutional guarantees of individual freedom, natural rights, and liberty. Rousseau extends this to the radically democratic GENERAL WILL, or legitimacy only through social consensus or COMMUNITARIAN democracy.

MARXIST COMMUNIST theory rejected this liberal view of legitimate government, calling it the DICTATORSHIP of the capitalist economic class. For SOCIALISTS, legitimacy in the Modern industrial period of history requires rule by the working class or the "dictatorship of the proletariat." Political legitimacy is determined by the most progressive and oppressed economic social class. This DIALECTICAL philosophy in Marxism (or CRITICAL THEORY) challenges all traditional authority as illegitimate unless it embraces radical EGALITARIAN democracy and communist economics. As V. I. LENIN shows in the Soviet Union, a minority political party can rule as a "legitimate" TOTALITARIAN DESPOT if it embodies these Marxist principles.

Twentieth-century ANARCHISM denies any legitimate state authority, seeing all governmental authority as corrupt and oppressive. Communitarian democrats such as Benjamin BARBER view participatory classical democracy only as fully legitimate, given human social nature. John RAWLS *Theory of Justice* provides a philosophy of liberal American legitimacy that is based in a Lockean constitutional republic and a social welfare state. In Rawls, inequalities of wealth, authority, and position are legitimate if they are open to all and serve the common good. POST-MODERNIST thinking, like

anarchism, questions any legitimacy outside individual perception and preference.

As long as order and government are necessary, some basis for legitimacy will be required. People need a sense that rule is fair and just, so theories of legitimacy provide that assurance.

Further Readings

Connolly, W. E., ed. *Legitimacy and the State.* New York: New York University Press, 1984.
Habermas, J. *Legitimation Crisis,* T. McCarthy, transl. Boston: Beacon Press, 1973.
Hirschman, A. O. *The Passions and the Interests.* Princeton, N.J.: Princeton University Press, 1977.

Leland, John (1754–1841)   *American activist for religious freedom*

Rev. John Leland was active in the early Virginia and United States CHURCH-AND-STATE controversies with Thomas JEFFERSON and James MADISON. A BAPTIST minister, Leland worked in Virginia (1777–92) when the Anglican Church was the legally established official church in that British colony. As such, DISSENTER Christians like Leland were persecuted by the STATE, fined, imprisoned and humiliated. Leland led the Baptists, PRESBYTERIANS, and Mennonites in their political effort to achieve religious FREEDOM in the commonwealth. He petitioned the Virginia legislature for laws disestablishing the Episcopal Church, supported Jefferson's proposed statute for religious liberty, and urged James Madison to ensure a Bill of Rights in the new U.S. CONSTITUTION (especially the FIRST AMENDMENT, providing for freedom of religious belief). As such, Leland tied the rising EVANGELICAL CHRISTIAN population in the United States with the emerging Jeffersonian DEMOCRACY and Democratic-Republican Party. The shared views of EQUALITY, INDIVIDUALISM, and democratic government forged a coalition of farmers, workers, Protestants, and southerners that dominated U.S. politics from 1800 to 1840.

Leland's political theory held that democracy was the best system for both church and government. Influenced by the English PURITAN John BUNYAN, Leland saw the individual's personal relationship to God and spiritual development best accomplished in a free environment. A government dominated by ARISTOCRACY would inevitably become corrupt, and a church aligned with the government would be compromised. As a radical Protestant, Leland believed in "the priesthood of all believers" and in a church congregation's right to elect their own minister. As a Jeffersonian democrat, he believed the common people should run the government. This ecclesiastical and political EGALITARIANISM has permeated U.S. popular culture from 1800 to the present.

Further Reading
Butterfield, L. H. *Elder John Leland, Jeffersonian Itinerant.* 1953. Reprint, New York: Arno Press, 1980.

Lenin, Vladimir Ilyich (V. I.) (1870–1924)
Russian Marxist thinker, leader of the Bolshevik Communist Party and the Soviet Union

V. I. Lenin brought the COMMUNISM of Karl MARX into the 20th century with his theories of CAPITALIST IMPERIALISM, "the role of a vanguard revolutionary Communist Party," and SOCIALIST governance through "DEMOCRATIC centralism." Thereafter, communist thought becomes MARXISM-LENINISM.

By the turn of the century (1900), Marxism's prediction of working class revolution in the advanced capitalist countries (Germany, Britain, United States) had not occurred. Lenin explained this by pointing to the development of economic imperialism, growing out of monopoly capitalism, especially finance capital or banking. In his book, *Imperialism, the Highest Stage of Capitalism* (1916), Lenin explained that the industrial capitalist nations had "exported" their problems (over production, CLASS conflict, poverty) to the Third World colonies. These "neocolonies" in Africa, South America, China, and the Middle East provided cheap labor and raw materials, markets for manufactured goods, and places for economic experimentation. Thus, the owner-worker class struggle, he continued, becomes global. Competing capitalist-imperialist nations fight wars (such as World War I) for control of these colonies. The great profits accrued from this arrangement allows capitalist corporations to "bribe" their domestic (British, French, American) workers with high wages and benefits and to keep them passive and CONSERVATIVE. But as the neocolonies (China, Asia, Latin America) have socialist wars of liberation, he concluded, the crises of capitalism return to haunt the imperialist host nations, causing lower wages in those countries, leading to socialist revolution at home.

This Marxist-Leninist theory affected much of 20th-century international politics. African, South American, and Asia countries fought wars of socialist national liberation (e.g., Vietnam) and explained their poverty (in the UN and elsewhere) by blaming the "imperialist" Northern Hemisphere nations. Employing a "labor theory of value," such Leninist rhetoric continues in attacks on the United States, multinational corporations, the World Bank, militarism, racism, and so on. The American LEFT still embraces much of this perspective. By the turn of the 21st century, however, with the fall of the SOVIET UNION's communist system, the failure of socialism in Cuba, Africa and China, and the move toward democracy and market capitalism in Latin America, the Marxist-Leninist thesis had lost influence.

Internally, Lenin developed Marxist theory in the Russian Revolution of 1917. His book *The Development of Capitalism in Russia* (1899) analyzed economics in his homeland. Although Russia was less developed in capitalism than Western Europe, Lenin said it had enough of a revolutionary proletariat (factory workers) to lead a socialist revolution. They could inspire other disaffected, impoverished classes (peasants, lower middle class) to overthrow the czarist system. What was needed was a professional revolutionary party (or cadre) to motivate this vanguard, revolutionary working class. Thus was born the highly disciplined, conspirational, and terrorist Leninist Communist Party. In his book *What Is To Be Done?* (1902), Lenin formulated the theoretical basis of this revolutionary organization, its strategy and tactics for taking power, and a blueprint of the new socialist order. This work became a handbook for communist revolutionaries around the world. It covers how the "Reds" (Marxists) can infiltrate the government and other established social groups (the media, education, the military, even the church) and gradually move them toward communist ways of thinking. Such tactics (including violent terrorism, assassination, and blackmail) were justified by Lenin and other communists on the grounds that their goal (socialism) was worth any means employed, even murder, lying, and theft. Adherence to common moral standards, for communist revolutionaries, would maintain the oppressive, exploitative system of capitalist-imperialism. However, these methods aroused the suspicion of CONSERVATIVES in Europe and America (such as the JOHN BIRCH SOCIETY and the McCarthy hearings) to any Leftist or LIBERAL organizations, causing persecution of many people whom were not actually communist.

Lenin's BOLSHEVIK Communist Party took over the Russian government in October 1917. It quickly aban-

Vladimir Ilyich Lenin, ca. 1920. (LIBRARY OF CONGRESS)

most ruthless follower, Joseph Stalin, took over the Soviet leadership and instituted a terrible TOTALITARIAN state that terrorized its own people and dominated its (East European) neighbors. The dreams of liberation and prosperity in Marxism-Leninism turned into the nightmare of the USSR. Officially atheistic, the Soviet Union persecuted the CHRISTIANS, Jews, and Muslims within its borders. The deceit, foreign subversion, and imperialism of the USSR state made it difficult for other countries to deal or negotiate with it. The cold war of 1950–87 between the Western powers and the Soviet empire reflected this tension. After 70 years of DESPOTISM, poverty, and mistrust, the Russian people, led by Premier Gorbachev, abandoned the Soviet system for a MODERN REPUBLIC and a mixed economy. However, the legacy of Leninist violence and concentrated, arbitrary state power unfortunately persists in contemporary Russia.

Further Readings

Carr, E. H. *The Bolshevik Revolution,* 3 vols. New York: W. W. Norton, 1978.
Harding, N. *Lenin's Political Thought,* 2 vols. New York: St. Martin's Press, 1977, 1981.

Levellers

A political group in 17th-century England that advocated social "levelling" or EQUALITY. The most radical EGALITARIAN of these Levellers were the so-called Diggers, or agrarian COMMUNISTS, who sought to equalize all property and land. Gerrard Winstanley was a leading theorist of this agricultural commune-style of economy. He took his inspiration from a radical PURITAN reading of the Bible, holding that the early CHRISTIANS had "all things in common." For him, private ownership of property, especially excessive wealth, was a sign of original sin, greed, and injustice. These religious Levellers also saw the emergence of agrarian communism as ushering in a new millennium and the return of Christ.

Politically, these English radicals advocated popular rule, the abolishing of MONARCHY, the nobility, and the state church. Each community should be governed democratically, distinctions of rank and aristocracy eliminated, and the voting (SUFFRAGE) right extended. Political, economic, social, and religious independence was their ideal. Some of their notions of popular SOVEREIGNTY and government LEGITIMACY found their way into John LOCKE'S SOCIAL-CONTRACT ideas year later,

doned any practice of workers' democracy ("soviets") and instituted an autocratic DICTATORSHIP. Military, economic, and even family life was strictly controlled by the central STATE. The socialist government in Russia soon became more BUREAUCRATIC, cruel, and oppressive than the czarist regime. Poverty, a state secret police, massive executions, and imprisonments showed the vicious side of communism. Rivalries among Bolshevik Party leaders (especially STALIN, TROTSKY, and BUKHARIN) led to political purges, show trials, and brutality. Fear and misery spread in the country. Many upper- and middle-class Russians left the country, moving primarily to France. Leftists in Western Europe and America supported this new Soviet socialist system and advocated its establishment in other countries. Lenin recognized the destructive demise of his socialist ideal and attempted to reform it with more decentralized, free-market reforms, but he died soon after the revolution, and his plans were never implemented. Instead, his where they influenced the parliamentary revolution of 1688. Most of the English Levellers flourished in the 1640s–50s during the commonwealth period of English civil wars and Oliver CROMWELL. In fact, many of the Levellers came out of Cromwell's parliamentary "New Model Army" of small farmers, traders, artisans, and GUILD apprentices. John Lilburne, William Walwyn, John Wildman, and Richard Overton were their chief spokesmen; a prominent political pamphlet of Leveller literature was *Man's Moralitie* (1643).

Besides LIBERAL social-contract themes, much Leveller thought rested on the ideal of the ANCIENT CONSTITUTION, a REPUBLICAN society that supposedly existed in England before the Norman Conquest (1066) and that the Levellers sought to restore. Later, Algernon Sydney, Henry St. John BOLINGBROKE, and William BLACKSTONE (as well as Thomas JEFFERSON in America) developed these antimonarchy ideas. Opposition to royal charters, trading companies, the state bank, and IMPERIALISM became associated with the CLASSICAL republicanism paradigm developed by J. G. A. POCOCK.

Besides this particular group of political thinkers and activists, *leveller* is a term used to describe anyone who believes in evening out social, political, or economic inequalities. So, radical LEFTISTS, populists, liberals, socialists, and communists are often described as levelers—wanting to ban all distinctions and differences in society. CONSERVATIVES attack this philosophy of levelling all social distinctions as destructive of excellence, TRADITION, and well-earned merit and wealth. Edmund BURKE responds this way toward the radical democrats of the French Revolution of 1789 (as punishing the prominent, accomplished people), and James MADISON regards this COMMUNITARIAN egalitarianism as reflective of sinful pride and social envy (and designs the U.S. CONSTITUTION to avoid such "tyranny of the majority"). Jefferson accepts the Leveller critique of hereditary aristocracy but believes that a "Natural Aristocracy" of merit and VIRTUE exists in society and should be elevated to higher positions in government. Joseph STALIN and MAO TSE-TUNG's communist attacks on all social HIERARCHY and distinction can be seen as 20th-century expressions of Leveller philosophy.

Further Readings
Bernstein, Eduard. *Cromwell & Communism.* New York: Schocken Books, 1963.
Haller, William. *The Leveller Tracts, 1647–1653,* William Haller and Godfrey Davies, eds. Gloucester, Mass.: Peter Smith, 1964.

Lewis, Clive Staples (C.S.) (1898–1963)   *British classicist and Christian apologist*

A teacher at Oxford (and later Cambridge) University, C. S. Lewis is regarded as one of the greatest MODERN CHRISTIAN philosophers, who especially appealed to intellectuals. Author of numerous theological treatises and books, (*Mere Christianity, Screwtape Letters*), children's fantasy stories (*Chronicles of Narnia*), and works of scholarship (*Oxford History of English Literature, The Allegory of Love: a Study in Medieval Tradition*) Lewis's writings have sold in the millions. His contribution to political thought was to apply EVANGELICAL Christianity to 20th century politics. Like Reinhold NIEBUHR, he rejected the subordination of religion to political ideology (of the LEFT or RIGHT) and insisted that the politics of the Gospels of Jesus would be very radical in some ways (economic EQUALITY, charity, SOCIALISM), but very conservative in other ways (respect for AUTHORITY, reverence, moral purity), what today would be called a "fiscal LIBERAL" but "moral CONSERVATIVE." This political orientation most resembles that of contemporary CATHOLIC social thought. Though Lewis was an Anglican PROTESTANT Christian, his basic writings on theology, psychology, and social problems are read by a wide range of religious denominations.

Further Readings
Hart, Dabney Adams. *Through the Open Door: A New Look at C. S. Lewis.* Tuscaloosa: University of Alabama Press, 1984.
———. *The Great Divorce.* New York: Macmillan, 1963.
Lewis, C. S. *Mere Christianity.* New York: Macmillan, 1960.
———. *The Screwtape Letters.* New York: HarperCollins, 1962.
Mills, David, ed. *The Pilgrim's Guide: C. S. Lewis and the Art of Witness.* Grand Rapids: Eerdmans, 1998.
Schakel, Peter J., and Hutar, Charles A., eds. *Word and Story in C. S. Lewis.* Columbia: University of Missouri Press, 1991.
Sims, John (John A.). *Missionaries to the Skeptics: Christian Apologists for the Twentieth Century: C. S. Lewis, Edward John Carnell, and Reinhold Niebuhr.* Macon, Ga.: Mercer University Press, 1995.
Walsh, Chad. *C. S. Lewis: Apostle to the Skeptics.* New York: Macmillan, 1949.

liberalism/liberal

A major school of political thought dating from the 1600s, often referred to as British liberalism or philosophical liberalism. Its main thinkers are John LOCKE, Thomas HOBBES, John Stuart MILL, Robert NOZICK, and John RAWLS ("liberals"). This strain of political thought is not to be confused with "American LIBERALISM" that arose in the 20th century and is very different in its view of humanity and government. A 20th-century equivalent of this philosophical, Lockean liberalism, would be a CONSERVATIVE, LAISSEZ-FAIRE, REPUBLICAN PARTY IDEOLOGY (as in the administration of Ronald REAGAN).

The distinctive features of MODERN liberalism include INDIVIDUALISM, materialism, an emphasis on NATURAL RIGHTS, LIBERTY and FREEDOM, EQUALITY limited for some by SOCIAL CONTRACT, private PROPERTY, separation of religion and politics (or CHURCH AND STATE), and REPUBLICAN DEMOCRACY. Prominent liberals in this sense include Thomas JEFFERSON, James MADISON, and Alexander HAMILTON. This liberalism tends to accompany economic CAPITALISM (free market, free enterprise), as in Adam SMITH, and protestant CHRISTIANITY (as in John CALVIN). So, liberalism is most manifest in the society and politics of the United States of America. Its prominent critics on the RIGHT include traditional CATHOLIC philosophy (John Henry Newman), FASCISM, and CLASSICAL republicanism; and on the LEFT, MARXISM, COMMUNISM, SOCIALISM, SOCIAL DEMOCRACY, COMMUNITARIANISM, and American liberalism. Both Left and Right critics of philosophical liberalism attack its emphasis on private individualism, private rights and property, a lack of morality and social VIRTUE, and its competition. The most extreme ideological expression of British, Lockean liberalism is LIBERTARIAN thought or ANARCHISM.

Hobbes and Locke are typical liberal thinkers. They conceive of human beings in Modern scientific, materialistic terms, as biological "matter in motion," led by physical "pleasure-and-pain" impulses, guided by sensory stimulation. This natural condition gives rise to the natural rights of "Life, Liberty, and property," to continue that existence. Human reason leads people to institute government through a social contract of free individuals to protect their rights from murder, theft, slavery, and so on. Government is limited to this criminal-justice role and an any more intrusive state is not LEGITIMATE. Most human business is to be conducted privately (though business and contracts), not publicly (through the government). People are best left free to pursue their own INTERESTS. Only the individual knows what is best for him- or herself. Consequently, moral judgment is individual and relative. No one can dictate ideals to another person. Personal autonomy and freedom are of the highest value.

The benefits of this liberal ideology are great individual liberty (freedom of thought, conscience, speech, press, movement, religious belief, economic activity), prosperity, and democracy. The disadvantages of liberalism include privatism, selfishness, loneliness, and a lack of community identity, AUTHORITY, and moral certainty. Because of its economic and technological development and political freedom, liberalism has advanced around the world since its inception in 17th-century Europe. However, cultural, regional, and religious reactions to liberalism have resisted its expansion (as in fundamentalist ISLAM in Iran, Confucian and communist ideology in China, reactionary czarist nationalist movements in Russia, neofascism in Germany, and conservative Catholic and EVANGELICAL Christian thought). All of the opponents of philosophical liberalism blame modern ALIENATION, social dysfunction, and the breakdown of the family and declining moral values on liberal society. Benjamin BARBER's book Strong Democracy critiques U.S. liberal individualism from a classical and communitarian perspective.

Contemporary defenders of liberalism (like Robert Nozick) claim that more benefits than costs result from liberal society, that humans value freedom more than order or security, and that the greatest cultural and religious achievements have historically occurred in an atmosphere of individual LIBERTY. The controversy over liberalism and its effects promises to continue into the next millennium.

Further Readings
Arblaster, A. The Rise and Decline of Western Liberalism. Oxford, Eng.: Blackwell, 1984.
Bramsted, E. K., and Melhuish, K. J., eds. Western Liberalism: A History in Documents from Locke to Croce. London: Longman, 1978.
Dworkin, R. Taking Rights Seriously. Cambridge, Mass.: Harvard University Press, 1977.
Gray, John. Enlightenment's Wake: Politics and Culture at the Close of the Modern Age. New York: Routledge, 1995.
MacLean, D., and Mills, C., eds. Liberalism Reconsidered. Totowa, N.J.: Rowman & Allanheld, 1983.
Manning, D. J. Liberalism. New York: St. Martin's Press, 1976.
Mansfield, H. C., Jr. The Spirit of Liberalism. Cambridge, Mass.: Harvard University Press, 1978.
Ruggiero, G. de. The History of European Liberalism. Boston: Beacon Press, (1925) 1959.
Walsh, David. The Growth of the Liberal Soul. Columbia: University of Missouri Press, ca. 1997.

liberalism, American

A 20th-century U.S. political IDEOLOGY associated with the LEFT WING of the DEMOCRATIC PARTY, emphasizing central or federal government regulation of the economy, extensive social-welfare programs (for the poor, elderly, minorities, women, etc.) in education, housing, health care, and job training. Liberalism is the

United States version of European SOCIAL DEMOCRACY, often associated with the economic theories of John Maynard KEYNES. It began during the Progressive Era around 1900 with federal laws regulating business health and safety regulations, labor laws, and programs for the poor. This was largely motivated by the Calvinist or PURITAN social conscience of leaders like Woodrow WILSON. During the Great Depression of the 1930s, Liberalism greatly expanded under President Franklin D. ROOSEVELT'S NEW DEAL, which gave the national government tremendous powers to regulate business and citizens' everyday lives. Massive federal programs in welfare, education, public housing, defense, highway construction, agriculture, banking, and health care transformed the United States from a CAPITALIST economy to a mixed public/private economy. The New Deal Democratic Party coalition included labor unions, blacks, Jewish Americans, CATHOLICS, FEMINIST women, SOCIALISTS, and COMMUNISTS. This coalition continued liberal policies in the presidential administrations of John F. KENNEDY, Lyndon Johnson, Jimmy CARTER, and William Clinton. A corollary liberal movement in the U.S. Supreme Court, beginning under Chief Justice Earl Warren in the 1950s, affected much of U.S. CONSTITUTIONAL law (toward liberal decisions on ABORTION, FEDERALISM, criminal due process, religious PLURALISM, and women's, minority, and HOMOSEXUAL rights). Corollary liberal movements in religion, education, art, and entertainment are described by James D. HUNTER'S book *Culture Wars* as "progressive" thought.

Liberalism dominated U.S. politics for about 50 years (1930–80). When the fiscal policies of high federal taxes and government deficits caused economic recessions in the 1970s and liberal social policy favoring minorities, and women (affirmative action) prompted resentment, a CONSERVATIVE trend entered the United States with the presidency of Republican Ronald REAGAN. Later, the Republican-dominated Congress led by Newt Gingrich modified many liberal programs (welfare, health care, Social Security). Even ideologically Liberal Democrat president Bill Clinton compromised on many traditional liberal positions, moderating the national party's platform.

Further Readings

Burner, David, and West, Thomas R. *The Torch Is Passed: The Kennedy Brothers & American Liberalism,* 1st ed. New York: Atheneum, 1984.

Filler, Louis. *Crusaders for American Liberalism.* Yellow Springs, Ohio: Antioch Press, 1950.

Gettleman, Marvin E. *The Great Society Reader: The Failure of American Liberalism,* Marvin E. Gettleman and David Mermelstein, eds. New York: Random House, 1967.

Hamby, Alonzo L. *Beyond the New Deal: Harry S. Truman and American Liberalism.* New York: Columbia University Press, 1973.

liberation theology

An approach to politics and religion (or CHURCH AND STATE), first developed in Latin America by Gustavo GUTIÉRREZ, which combines MARXISM-Leninism with CHRISTIANITY. Adopting the imperialist theory of V. I. LENIN, liberation theology asserted that the cause of Third World poverty and oppression was CAPITALISM in the advanced Northern Hemisphere nations (Europe, the United States, Canada, etc.). Because Christ identified with the poor, liberation theology advocated that the church lead radical SOCIALIST revolutions in poor countries, establishing COMMUNIST systems (like Cuba, China) that would redistribute wealth, expel imperialist powers, and achieve workers' DEMOCRACY.

A movement beginning in the Roman CATHOLIC Church of South America, liberation theology spread through that continent in the late 1960s and 1970s. It contributed to the communist takeover by the Sandinista government in Nicaragua. By 1980, more than 100,000 "base communities" of small revolutionary groups that applied liberation theology principles to their areas had emerged in South America. Radical priests and nuns accepted Gutiérrez's thesis, in his book *A Theology of Liberation,* that the church could not remain neutral in the social CLASS struggle or leave politics to the Catholic Church HIERARCHY. Even violent revolution was seen as a part of this radical religious "salvation in history." The Bible was read through Marxist-Leninist categories and revolutionary "praxis" was seen as the only valid form of Christianity. The official Catholic Church under Pope John Paul II rejected this liberation theology, especially its portrayal of human sin in economic systems and classes rather than individuals; though it also called for greater social justice in the Third World.

Liberation theology entered the North American churches through FEMINIST, black, and social-justice movements, especially in the older Protestant denominations (Episcopal, Presbyterian, Methodist, U.C.C.). It cast Christian politics in terms of the social oppression of women and other minorities. Worldly power controlled by white male citizens was to be attacked, defeated, and transferred to oppressed peoples. Power structures in government, business, education, the military, and the church were to be abolished or restructured (with affirmative action, etc.) to transfer authority to the dispossessed "peoples of color." This caused a reaction from the more CONSERVATIVE politicos (e.g., the REPUBLICAN PARTY under President Ronald REAGAN) and EVANGELICAL Christian churches (e.g., BAPTIST), which reaffirmed the preeminence of values such as FREEDOM, PROPERTY, and the TRADITIONAL role of men in society. By the turn of the 21st century, liberation theology had lost much of its influence in the world as conventional democratic movements spread in Latin America, but its values continue in many Liberal circles.

libertarian

A 20th-century (primarily U.S. and British), RIGHT-WING, political IDEOLOGY and movement, akin to ANARCHISM and LIBERALISM, that advocates little or no government and absolute INDIVIDUAL social, economic, and moral FREEDOM. Libertarians such as Robert NOZICK assert that it is not legitimate for the state (1) to tax some people (the wealthy) to help other people (the poor) or (2) to declare illegal activities (such as drug use and prostitution) that have no victim (except the individual participating in those activities). In other words, libertarians would end all taxes except those needed to fund the minimal legitimate state functions (police and defense) and eliminate all laws against victimless crimes. This radical individual, personal freedom and antistatism emerges from a Lockean view of human nature as materialist, independent, free, and possessing NATURAL RIGHTS to life, liberty, and property that no government can take away. The ideal society for libertarians, as outlined in Nozick's book *Anarchy, State and Utopia,* is of free, autonomous individuals relating to each other on a voluntary, consensual basis with minimal interference from the state. Allied with LAISSEZ-FAIRE CAPITALISM, libertarian views gained popularity with some CONSERVATIVE business people and REPUBLICAN PARTY members (such as President Ronald REAGAN). In Britain, Conservative Prime Minister Margaret Thatcher espoused some libertarian sentiments. Besides Nozick, leading libertarian writers include economists Milton Friedman, Ludwig von Mises, Frederick von HAYEK and

Murray Rothbard, and novelist Ayn Rand. An earlier U.S. SOCIAL-DARWINIST philosopher, William Graham SUMNER, expressed quasi-Libertarian ideals in the 19th century. Much like EXISTENTIALISM, libertarianism sees humans as essentially alone, enjoying both the freedom and responsibility that nature gave them. State or social coercion violates that individuality and should be eliminated.

Critics of libertarian thought assert that it is an inaccurate representative of human nature (which is social and collective) and of contemporary society (which is corporate and interdependent). At worst, critics of libertarian views assert it is selfish and hedonistic, an ideological justification of greed and license for the rich and powerful to exploit the weak and poor and to avoid their social responsibilities.

As an actual social movement, libertarianism is a small group; a Libertarian Party in the United States routinely runs presidential and other official candidates for election, but they never win. More significant is the ideology's influence on the conservative probusiness wing of the U.S. Republican Party. There, it has managed to reduce taxes on the rich and regulations on corporations. The morally conservative CHRISTIAN RIGHT of the Republican Party has counteracted its effects on lifting laws against victimless crimes, however.

Libertarian ideology is largely an extreme version of traditional liberalism, which conditions but does not control modern democratic thought.

Further Readings

Machan, Tibor R., ed. *The Libertarian Alternative: Essays in Social and Political Philosophy.* Chicago: Nelson-Hall Co., 1974.

Narveson, Jan. *The Libertarian Idea.* Philadelphia: Temple University Press, 1988.

Newman, Stephen L. *Liberalism at Wits' End: The Libertarian Revolt Against the Modern State.* Ithaca, N.Y.: Cornell University Press, 1984.

Rothbard, Murray N. *The Essential Von Mises,* 4th ed. South Holland, Ill.: Libertarian Press, 1980.

Von Mises, Ludwig. *Planning for Freedom and Sixteen Other Essays and Addresses.* Libertarian Press, 1974.

liberty

Like FREEDOM, *political liberty* means unrestrained, uncontrolled individual thought, action, and choice. Emerging in the Western world with the philosophical LIBERALISM of Thomas HOBBES, John LOCKE, and John Stuart MILL, liberty becomes a premier social value in

MODERN DEMOCRACY. The United States of America was born with a number of conceptions of liberty: political, economic, social, and religious. Thus, liberty became the rallying cry of a diverse number of groups, classes, and regions in the American Revolution and in formulation of the U.S. constitutional republic. For example, the North American colonists' political liberty meant local community self-governance against the distant British Parliament and MONARCHY. Social liberty meant freedom from the bonds of traditional British HIERARCHICAL class social structures. Economic liberty of free-market CAPITALISM meant individual property ownership and free-enterprise commerce instead of the controlled trade and monopolies of the British Empire. Religious liberty meant the freedom to believe, worship, and evangelize as different churches and individuals chose, rather than the legal conformity of the established, official, state church of England. So, despite differences of region, faith, class, and nationality, the American colonists could agree on their desire for liberty. Since then, the term has signified claims of individual RIGHTS (CIVIL LIBERTY) and individual preferences. Primarily CONSERVATIVE groups (businesses, Republicans, EVANGELICAL CHRISTIANS) employ the language of liberty, but LIBERAL groups also use it at times (the American Civil Liberties Union, abortion rights supporters, HOMOSEXUAL rights lobby, etc.).

The ideal of liberty has always been ambiguous. Taken to an extreme, individual liberty leads to ANARCHISM or LIBERTARIAN thought. Others value order, EQUALITY, JUSTICE, and morality. So, the early American PURITAN political thought of John WINTHROP defined two kinds of liberty: moral liberty and natural liberty. In his Calvinist theology, *natural liberty* was the human sinful, selfish desire to do whatever one wanted, even to kill, steal, and lie. This liberty should be restrained by LAW. The moral liberty is "freedom where with Christ hast made us free"—the liberty God has given us to choose the good and to do it by the power of the Holy Spirit.

John LOCKE argued that human reason taught humans a law of nature to never use their liberty to harm others. This made widespread social freedom possible because individuals were self-governing. Republics rely on such personal self-restraint; TOTALITARIAN regimes require more external pressure on individuals. Thus, liberty is not a value in FASCIST, COMMUNIST, and aristocratic states, but is a value primarily in DEMOCRATIC governments.

Formal, CONSTITUTIONAL liberties are often declared and protected in a Bill of Rights.

Further Readings

Garvey, John H. *What Are Freedoms For?* Cambridge, Mass.: Harvard University Press, 1996.

Hayek, F. von. *The Constitution of Liberty.* Chicago: University of Chicago Press, 1960.

Machan, T. *Human Rights and Human Liberties.* Chicago: Nelson Hall, 1975.

Skinner, Quentin. *Liberty before Liberalism.* Cambridge: Cambridge University Press, 1998.

Lincoln, Abraham (1809–1865)   *U.S. political philosopher, lawyer, statesman, and president of the United States (1861–1865)*

Known chiefly for freeing the African-American slaves during the American Civil War, Lincoln's emancipation of enslaved Southern blacks grew out of deeply held religious, philosophical, and political ideals.

Abraham Lincoln saw the enslavement of human beings in the United States as undermining the foundations of the U.S. REPUBLIC: respect for basic HUMAN RIGHTS to life, LIBERTY, and PROPERTY. If a social practice violates the fundamental NATURAL RIGHTS that John LOCKE said formed CIVIL SOCIETY, the whole system of DEMOCRATIC self-government is endangered. Just as contemporary opponents to ABORTION argue that disregard for preborn life threatens regard for all human life, Lincoln argued that violation of African-Americans' liberty threatens every citizen's liberty.

Lincoln specifically attacked the non-natural-rights philosophies of his day: John C. CALHOUN's concurrent-majority theory that placed a regional majority's desire over individual human rights, and Stephen Douglas's theory of popular sovereignty, allowing expansion of slavery into the Western territories. In terms of philosophical ETHICS, Lincoln held that right and wrong are moral absolutes even if a sizeable majority reject or are apathetic about them. If an indifferent or apathetic (or evil) majority can deny the traditional Judeo-CHRISTIAN moral standards underlying the United States, God's wrath could destroy the country. Sounding like the Old Testament prophets Jeremiah or Isaiah, Lincoln described the terror and bloodshed of the American Civil War as God's terrible punishment for the sin of slavery. "The Almighty, has his own purposes. 'Woe unto the world because of offenses! . . . woe to that man by whom the offense

President Abraham Lincoln. (NATIONAL ARCHIVES)

Further Readings

Jaffa, H. V. "Abraham Lincoln." In *American Political Thought: The Philosophical Dimension of American Statesmanship,* M. J. Frisch and R. G. Stevens, eds. New York: Scribner, 1983.

———. *Crisis of the House Divided: An Interpretation of the Issues in the Lincoln-Douglas Debates.* New York: Doubleday, 1959.

Lincoln, A. *The Collected Works of Abraham Lincoln,* R. P. Basler, ed., 9 vols. New Brunswick, N.J.: Rutgers University Press, 1953.

Neely, Mark E. *The Fate of Liberty: Abraham Lincoln and Civil Liberties.* New York: Oxford University Press, 1991.

———. *The Last Best Hope of Earth: Abraham Lincoln and the Promise of America.* Cambridge, Mass.: Harvard University Press, 1993.

Tap, Bruce. *Over Lincoln's Shoulder: The Committee on the Conduct of the War.* Lawrence: University Press of Kansas, 1998.

Thurow, G. E. *Abraham Lincoln and American Political Religion.* Albany: State University of New York Press, 1976.

cometh!" He prayed for a speedy conclusion of the War Between the States, but he said, "if God wills that it continue until all the wealth piled up by the bondman's two hundred and fifty years of unrequited toil shall be sunk, and until every drop of blood drawn by the lash shall be paid by another drawn with the sword, . . . 'The judgments of the Lord are true and righteous all together.'" This relating of the Bible to U.S. political history places him within the COVENANT religious tradition of the PURITANS: that no social evil will go unpunished by God; so Americans must live moral lives to avoid destruction.

Besides his blending of CHURCH AND STATE, Abraham Lincoln revived the earlier American ideal of equality in JEFFERSON'S DECLARATION OF INDEPENDENCE. As U.S. INDUSTRIALISM created greater economic inequalities and threatened to turn the government over to a CAPITALIST ARISTOCRACY, Lincoln's revival of Jeffersonian EQUALITY and rights foreshadowed the LIBERAL Progressive Era.

Although not immune to the racial prejudices of his times, Lincoln, for his emancipation of black slaves, remains a hero to African Americans. Tragically, he was assassinated shortly after the successful restoration of the American Union.

Locke, John (1632–1704)   *British political philosopher and activist*

The most prominent theorist of British LIBERALISM, John Locke's ideas of NATURAL RIGHTS, government by the CONSENT of the governed, SOCIAL CONTRACT, the limited state, private PROPERTY, and revolution greatly influenced all MODERN DEMOCRATIC thought, especially in the United States of America. Thomas JEFFERSON cites Locke's ideas in the DECLARATION OF INDEPENDENCE, and the U.S. CONSTITUTION contains many Lockean principles.

Like Thomas HOBBES, Locke's political theory is based on materialist, scientific premises (he was a medical student at Oxford). Humans in their original condition, or STATE OF NATURE, are "free, equal and independent." From this state of physical FREEDOM, equality, and autonomy, Locke asserts that humans possess the natural rights to "Life, LIBERTY and Estate (property)," or continued existence (self-preservation). This means that murder, theft, slavery, and kidnapping violate a person's rights, but by human reason, Locke believes, each INDIVIDUAL knows the law of nature that, like the Golden Rule, tells people that they cannot exercise their freedom to harm anyone else's rights to life, liberty, or property. Most people are reasonable, respecting others natural rights, but some violate others' person or property in criminal ways. Such criminals can be killed by their victims as "beasts of prey" in the state of nature. However, Locke, the Calvinist PURITAN, perceives a problem with individuals enforcing the law of nature themselves: human sin.

This selfish sin will tend to punish transgressors of rights too harshly, unleashing retaliation and escalating violence. Our "self love" makes us incapable of being judges in our own cases. This dilemma gives rise to government, in Locke's theory.

Government is created by the consent of the governed when they realize the "inconveniences" of keeping private justice in the natural state. A social contract is formed whereby the citizens delegate to the STATE the judicial function, protecting their natural rights by establishing police, courts, prisons, and so on. This Lockean liberal government is "limited" to protecting an individual's natural rights to life, liberty, and property by adjudicating disputes over rights, punishing criminal violators of others' rights, and maintaining social peace.

If the state itself invades the rights of citizens by killing them, taking their property, or imprisoning them unjustly, it is the right of the people to abolish it and establish a new government that will perform its duties properly. This is Locke's famous "right of revolution," which British Parliamentarians used in the revolution of 1688, and Jefferson used to justify American colonial independence from Great Britain. The idea of a peoples' right to overthrow an oppressive, TYRANNICAL government has justified numerous revolutions since Locke's time.

One of the main purposes of the state for Locke is the preservation of private property, which has caused critics to accuse him of being an apologist for early CAPITALISM. Locke's LABOR THEORY OF VALUE maintains that a person's mixing labor or work with nature gives the person legitimate title to its produce. This is bound by the MEDIEVAL "spoilage limitation"—that no one can possess more property than he or she can use before it spoils, but the invention of money in imperishable metals (gold and silver) allows unlimited accumulation of wealth. Hiring the labor of another allows wage-capital relations indicative of MODERN market, INDUSTRIAL economics. Because the state is supposed to protect property, and because the employer-employee contract is a kind of property, this obliges all with work (or any use of the country's facilities) to obey the LAW. Hence, all people living in a nation give tacit consent to the laws. Critics of Lockean liberalism claim that most workers have little choice in the matter, and therefore the capitalist state is not LEGITIMATE (see Karl MARX). But this view of free humans, rights, EQUALITY, and private property protected by a limited state continue to have appeal with CONSERVATIVE, LAISSEZ-FAIRE REPUBLICANS (like Ronald REAGAN), LIBERTARIANS (Robert NOZICK), and liberal individualists generally.

John Locke also advocated religious freedom and separation of CHURCH AND STATE. For him, in *A Letter Concerning Toleration* (1689), a government compelling religious faith and persecuting unbelievers is a violation of the spirit of Christ and infringes on personal liberty of conscience. The proper CHRISTIAN means of salvation are persuasion and prayer, not legal requirements and punishments.

The son of an English Puritan soldier in Oliver CROMWELL's parliamentary army, John Locke attended Christ Church (College), Oxford University. His primary work on political philosophy is the book, *The Second Treatise of Government* (1689).

Further Readings

Coleman, J. *John Locke's Moral Philosophy.* Edinburgh: Edinburgh University Press, 1983.

Cox, R. H. *Locke on War and Peace.* Oxford, Eng.: Clarendon Press, 1960.

Gough, J. W. *John Locke's Political Philosophy.* Oxford, Eng.: Clarendon Press, 1973.

Grant, Ruth Weissbourd. *John Locke's Liberalism.* Chicago: University of Chicago Press, ca. 1987.

Harris, Ian. *The Mind of John Locke: A Study of Political Theory in Its Intellectual Settings.* Cambridge, Eng.: Cambridge University Press, 1994.

Martin, C. B. (Charles Burton). *Locke and Berkeley: A Collection of Critical Essays.* C. B. Martin and D. M. Armstrong, eds. Notre Dame, Ind.: University of Notre Dame Press, 1968.

Pangle, Thomas L. *The Spirit of Modern Republicanism: The Moral Vision of the American Founders and the Philosophy of Locke.* Chicago: Chicago University Press, 1988.

Yolton, John W. *John Locke & Education,* 1st ed. New York: Random House, 1971.

Lollards

An early Protestant group in England that led into the PURITAN movement of Oliver CROMWELL and REPUBLICAN IDEOLOGY. Originally followers of religious reformer John WYCLIFFE in the 14th century. The Lollards took an INDIVIDUALISTIC and DEMOCRATIC view of CHRISTIAN politics (in CHURCH AND STATE) including an emphasis on a personal faith (relationship to God through Jesus Christ without intermediate priestly function); private revelation from the Bible (without interpretation from the official church); divine election (the predestination view of St. AUGUSTINE and John CALVIN); and the EQUALITY of believers. Like later

Reformation thinker Martin LUTHER, the Lollards rejected CATHOLIC doctrines of celibate clergy, papal indulgences, pilgrimages, and HIERARCHY. Persecuted by the church and the royal state, the Lollards dwindled by the end of the 15th century, but their ideas reemerged in the MODERN Protestant churches.

Further Reading
Trevelyan, George. *England in the Age of Wycliffe*, new ed. London: Longmans Green, 1904.

Luther, Martin (1483–1546) *German Protestant reformer and writer on religion and politics*

The first widely influential CHRISTIAN Protestant thinker, Luther (along with John CALVIN) radically altered the Western view of CHURCH AND STATE.

Drawing on the theology of St. Paul (in *Romans*) and St. AUGUSTINE, Luther emphasized Christianity based on personal faith and God's grace, rather than the CATHOLIC emphasis on religious rituals and works. He attacked the church official HIERARCHY through a DEMOCRATIC doctrine of "the priesthood of all believers," the EQUALITY of all Christians. Although this was a spiritual equality, it obviously affected worldly conceptions of politics, away from MEDIEVAL MONARCHY of the HOLY ROMAN EMPIRE and toward REPUBLICAN government in MODERNITY. Luther's emphasis on INDIVIDUAL relations with God through the Bible and Christ becomes the dominant evangelical worldview.

Luther then reverses the order of church and state (from that given by St. Thomas AQUINAS) by placing the government above the church in worldly authority. This later is adopted in England by King HENRY VIII, who assumes the role of appointing bishops in the Church of England. Strict separation of religion and politics follows, with the church primarily concerned with spiritual matters (worship, prayer, religious education, etc.) and the state with secular matters (economics, law, punishment of criminals—the "Sword" or "hangman"). Such separation of church and state leads to Modern religious FREEDOM, LIBERTY of conscience, and religious diversity as developed in John LOCKE, Thomas JEFFERSON, and others. The noninvolvement of the Lutheran Church is often blamed for the passive acceptance of the NAZI government in Germany of the 1930s. But for Luther, the church deals primarily with the soul, the "inner man," and the state with the body or "outer man." Chris-

tians are best made by a free, evangelical church, and then they will, informally, affect the secular society and politics, in Luther's view. This is contrasted with the traditional imperial Catholic Church where ecclesiastical and governmental officials engage each other directly.

Luther's reformed emphasis on human sin and an active Satan suspects any goodness from reason or high human motives and doubts worldly leaders' ability to affect good, except through the spirit of Christ working through them. Christians should serve in government if called to by God but not expect much from earthly regimes, which are invariably evil and corrupt. This leads to the predominant evangelical (and especially BAPTIST) "removal" from the world and its supposed vanity, pomp, and wicked corruption. If all politics is more or less corrupt, there is little difference between forms of government or political leaders, in this Lutheran perspective.

If the STATE forces citizens to perform actions that are clearly contrary to Christian teaching (worshiping idols, killing innocents, lying, and stealing), unless supported by a JUST-WAR doctrine, the individual Christian can disobey the state, but this is a matter of individual conscience, not official church direction (which remains neutral). In this sense, Dietrich BONHOEFFER, Lutheran minister, contradicted this traditional Lutheran doctrine by organizing the church to resist the Nazi German government openly.

Luther's Protestant political theory led to long religious wars in Europe and transformed Western Christianity. American conceptions of religious freedom and the separation of church and state are largely derived from Luther's thought. His main political writings include *On Secular Authority* (1523), *On Christian Liberty* (1520), and *To the Christian Nobility of the German Nation* (1520).

Further Readings
Atkinson, J. *Martin Luther and the Birth of Protestantism*, rev. ed. Atlanta: Knox Press, 1982.
———. *Martin Luther and the Birth of Protestantism*. Harmondsworth, Eng.: Penguin, 1968, 1981.
Cargill Thompson, W. D. J. *The Political Thought of Martin Luther.* New York: Barnes & Noble, 1984.
Thompson, W. D. J. Cargill (William David James). *The Political Thought of Martin Luther,* Philip Broadhead, ed., preface by A. G. Dickens. New York: Barnes & Noble, 1984.
Zachman, Randall C. *The Assurance of Faith: Conscience in the Theology of Martin Luther and John Calvin*. Minneapolis: Fortress Press, 1993.

Luxemburg, Rosa (1871–1919)   *Polish and German communist thinker and activist*

Active in the early European MARXIST SOCIALIST revolutionary movements, Luxemburg's ideas reflected the radical but DEMOCRATIC socialism of her time. Like V. I. LENIN, she insisted that a violent workers' revolution would be necessary to overthrow CAPITALISM and the "bourgeois" government (rather than the gradual, peaceful, parliamentary methods of SOCIAL DEMOCRAT Karl KAUTSKY), but she envisioned considerable debate, democracy, and flexibility with that "DICTATORSHIP of the proletariat," or COMMUNIST state. In this way, she was critical of the DESPOTIC and TOTALITARIAN qualities of the Russian (Soviet) communist revolution and BOL-SHEVIK state. She wanted the working class itself to accomplish the revolution and socialist regime, rather than a "vanguard" Communist Party of the Leninist (democratic-centralism) type. Revolutionary politics was to be the "school" of workers' democracy, with much learning through experiments, mistakes, and change. "Revolution," she wrote, "is the sole form of 'war' . . . in which the final victory can be prepared only by a series of 'defeats'."

Born into a middle-class Polish Jewish family, Luxemburg spent most of her adulthood in Germany and LEFTIST politics. She was assassinated during the 1918 German revolution.

Further Readings

Dunayevskaya, Raya. *Rosa Luxemburg, Women's Liberation, and Marx's Philosophy of Revolution,* foreword by Adrienne Rich, 2nd ed. Urbana: University of Illinois Press, 1991.

Rosa Luxemburg, ca. 1900. (LIBRARY OF CONGRESS)

Luxemburg, Rosa. *The Crisis in the German Social-Democracy.* New York: H. Fertig, 1969.

Nettl, J. P. *Rosa Luxemburg,* abridged ed. New York: Schocken Books, 1969.

Tyrmand, Leopold. *The Rosa Luxemburg Contraceptives Cooperative; A Primer on Communist Civilization.* New York: Macmillan, 1971.

M

Macaulay, Thomas Babington (1800–1859)
Historian and politician

Macaulay is most widely known as a historian, in particular for his *History of England*. He was, however, an important political essayist and politician who vigorously defended Whig and LIBERAL views in his writings and speeches.

Macaulay's approach was one of moderation between the extremes of RADICALism and despotism. In his historical writings, he admired those figures who exemplified the "middle ground," in particular the English king William III. This pursuit of moderation was known as trimming, and is most clearly articulated by George Saville. He opposed the elaborate doctrines of the Roman CATHOLIC Church and the policies of the RIGHTIST Tory party, as well as the LEFT-WING radicals. He opposed the practice of slavery, spoke in favor of the reform bill in the English parliament in 1832, and wrote the first criminal code for the colony of India.

In numerous essays, many of which were published in the *Edinburgh Review*, Macaulay argues for religious TOLERATION, FREEDOM of expression, and a commonsense understanding of the politics and government. In an essay on MACHIAVELLI, for example, he attempts to restore the reputation of Machiavelli, and at the same time, he offers remarks and arguments on the topic of morality, politics, and history. He wrote a number of essays critical of UTILITARIANISM and its account of the ends of government, and in an essay on the poet MILTON, Macauley defends the idea of public LIBERTY as basic to a system of JUSTICE.

One of the central features of Macaulay's discussion of issues in political theory is his insistence on the perspective of history as a way of correcting the prejudices of the present. One of his main criticisms of the utilitarian James MILL, for instance, is the latter's attempt to theorize politics a priori. Macaulay's political views and philosophy are very evident in his historical writings, where his dramatic and rhetorical style of writing clearly distinguishes political and historical villains and heroes.

Macaulay was born in Leicestershire, England. His father was a leading antislavery spokesman. A precocious child who read from the age of three and "spoke in printed words," he studied at Cambridge, was elected to the House of Commons on several occasions, where he had a reputation as an orator, and spent three and a half years in India as a representative of the colonial government. He was devoted to his family, especially his sisters and their children, although he himself never married.

Further Readings

Hamburger, J. *Macaulay and the Whig Tradition*. Chicago: University of Chicago Press, 1976.

Trevelyan, George. *The Life and Letters of Lord Macaulay*. London: Oxford University Press, 1876.

Machiavelli,   Niccolò (1469–1527)   *Italian Renaissance political philosopher and official in Florence*

Known as the father of political realism and secular power politics, Machiavelli earned the nickname "Old Nick" (or Satan). His book *The Prince* is a handbook of ruthless DICTATORSHIP and political cunning. It is believed that Machiavelli's experience as a diplomat for the Florentine republic (with other Italian states and the French and German monarchies) and his witnessing of international intrigue contributed to his negative view of humanity and politics. Unlike the CLASSICAL emphasis on VIRTUE and JUSTICE (PLATO, ARISTOTLE) or the MEDIEVAL CHRISTIAN emphasis on faith and morals (St. AUGUSTINE, St. Thomas AQUINAS), Machiavelli emphasized the necessity of brute power, deceit, and violence in governing. A Machiavellian leader becomes identified with one who uses political power deceitfully, ruthlessly, and manipulatively. Adolf HITLER and Joseph STALIN were admirers of Machiavelli.

Machiavelli's pessimistic view of human nature comes from his opinion that people are greedy, selfish, petty, dissatisfied, and disloyal and have no hope of redemption. They have infinite wants and no means to satisfy them, so they are continually frustrated and resentful. Their resentment is always directed at the ruler, whom they expect to make them happy, and they blame the government (or prominent people) when they don't get what they want. People are vain, jealous, proud, and stupid in Machiavelli's view. How does a ruler deal with such people? *The Prince* gives step-by-step guidelines for governing such foolish, fickle human beings. He claims to have discovered a scientific principle of politics that fits all times and every society. The key to this "science of politics" (later developed by Thomas HOBBES's LIBERALISM) is to focus on POWER: getting and keeping it. Every other value or virtue must be subordinated to the acquiring and maintaining of state power. After all, Machiavelli reasons, without power you can't do much else. This subordination of all morals to worldly power earns him the nickname of the devil.

A Machiavellian politician, then, must learn to *appear* to be good when he isn't, *appear* to be virtuous, generous, kind, trustworthy, honest, and religious when in fact (when necessary for keeping his power and position) he is vicious, stingy, mean, duplicitous, and cynical. Being truly good, Machiavelli insists, can "lead to one's ruin," so it is better to survive by any means; for example, it would be nice to govern gently from the love of one's subjects, but because people are easily offended and unreliable, the successful Prince must instill a degree of fear in the people to gain respect and obedience. Other practical advice from Machiavelli includes: (1) rigging elections or candidates; (2) appealing to a country's origins and past traditions (e.g., celebrating holidays); (3) employing religion to gain reverence for the state; and (4) using other officials to carry out unpopular policies (and then destroying them). Such tactics make it dangerous to work for the Machiavellian Prince, but there are always enough people who want to be close to power to supply needed helpers and pawns. In a famous phrase, Machiavelli advises the ruler to be "a beast," or rather two animals: a lion and a fox (the first to strike terror into opponents, the second to wisely recognize traps and tricks). Finally, Machiavelli justifies this political realism with the statement that other peoples' evil requires us to treat them badly. This ethical reversal of ancient and Christian morality rendered Machiavelli a villain in most political literature (including Shakespeare) afterwards.

Some scholars (such as J. G. A. POCOCK) have tried to redeem Machiavelli by pointing to his classical REPUBLICANISM, but even in *The Discourses on the First Ten Books of Titus Livy* (1513), Machiavelli examines the Roman Empire to learn "Modernman's" rules for power politics. He may also have wished Lorenzo de' Médici of Florence to use his precepts to reunite Italy and save it from humiliating civil war and foreign domination, but his principles seemed, to most, despicable.

Further Readings

De Grazia, Sebastian. *Machiavelli in Hell*. Princeton, N.J.: Princeton University Press, 1989.

Hulliung, M. *Citizen Machiavelli*. Princeton, N.J.: Princeton University Press, 1983.

Jensen, De Lamar. *Machiavelli: Cynic, Patriot, or Political Scientist?* Boston: D.C. Heath, 1960.

Meinecke, F. *Machiavellianism: The Doctrine of Raison d'Etat and its Place in History*, D. Scott, transl. New York: Praeger, 1957.

Skinner, Q. *The Foundations of Modern Political Thought,* vol. I: *The Renaissance.* Cambridge, Eng.: Cambridge University Press, 1978.

Madison, James (1751–1836) *American statesman, political philosopher, U.S. president, and "Father of the Constitution"*

Madison's political thought was representative of Calvinist or PROTESTANT CHRISTIANITY, Lockean LIBERALISM and CLASSICAL REPUBLICANISM. Raised on a typical Virginia plantation, his education (by PRESBYTERIAN ministers and at Princeton under John WITHERSPOON) was heavily classical and Calvinist; that taught him that humans are basically sinful (even the "elect" of God) and prone to display their envy, greed, jealously, and oppression in politics. Therefore, a just society must divide power, encourage PLURALISM, and have CHECKS AND BALANCES in government. In his famous *Federalist Paper #10,* Madison describes this basic theory of a large REPUBLIC with diverse groups competing for POWER, none large or powerful enough to dominate the other. The U.S. CONSTITUTION with its FEDERALISM (dividing power between central national and decentralized state governments, and breaking the state into three branches: executive, legislative, and judicial) accomplishes the distribution of power that for Madison will prevent TYRANNY. Unjust, DESPOTIC government can come from local DEMOCRATS' communities (which oppress minorities) or concentrated national ELITES (which rob the people with high taxes and rule with autocratic patronage). The Madisonian system strives to balance these potential tyrannies, "pitting ambition against ambition" to protect INDIVIDUAL RIGHTS (to life, LIBERTY, and private PROPERTY). Depending on the time in U.S. history, Madison saw the threat to liberty from a different quarter: During the American Revolution, when he served in the Continental Congress (or national government), he perceived the petty, jealous, and stingy decentralized state governments as the worst expression of human sin, so he advocated a stronger central government (the U.S. Constitution rather than the Articles of Confederation), but when the national government became too powerful during the FEDERALIST administration of John ADAMS, Madison argued for greater STATES RIGHTS. As secretary of state under President Thomas JEFFERSON, Madison reasserted a strong nationalism with the Louisiana Purchase and Embargo Act. As fourth president of the United States, he balanced nationalism and a liberal interpretation of the Constitution with an ANTI-FEDERALIST CONSERVATIVE, or "strict," interpretation of federal power. When arguing for national protection of individual rights, Madison often employed the philosophical liberalism of John LOCKE; when he advocated localized democratic communities, he used the classical Republican language of ARISTOTLE, CICERO, and HARRINGTON.

Madison is also notable for his advocacy of religious FREEDOM in Virginia. His "Memorial and Remonstrance" provides a classic separation of CHURCH-AND-STATE IDEOLOGY. An EVANGELICAL CHRISTIAN, Madison saw the official state religion of the Anglican (English) Church as stifling and persecuting faithful Christians (especially BAPTISTS). Religious liberty, he thought, would allow simple Christianity to grow and flourish, making the U.S. republic more moral and productive. Religious diversity, like economic free-market capitalism and political pluralism, would prevent the oppression of one established church or monopoly industry or MONARCHY. This becomes the American creed.

James Madison is considered the "Father of the United States Constitution" for his pivotal role in the Constitutional Convention and his persuasive arguments for ratifying the Constitution in his FEDERALIST PAPERS. His intellect was extremely keen, earning him the respect and confidence of his fellow delegates. A vast knowledge of historical politics, confederacies, and political philosophy and theology made him an extremely valuable member of the group that created the U.S. government. Beginning as an ally of Alexander HAMILTON, Madison became the fiercest opponent of Hamiltonian Federalism in the 1790s. A lifelong friend and political ally of Thomas Jefferson, Madison displayed a cooler, more disciplined mind than the third president.

Critics of Madisonian, pluralistic democracy disparage its slow, deliberate checks and balances, but 200 years of successful constitutional history in the United States seems to confirm the wisdom and practicality of Madison's Calvinist skepticism over human nature, human motives, and the reality of potential misuse of political power by sinful human beings. Madison's legacy is of the oldest, most stable written constitutional government in history.

Further Readings

Alley, Robert S. *James Madison on Religious Liberty,* intro. and interpretations by the author. Buffalo, N.Y.: Prometheus Books, 1985.

Ketcham, Ralph Louis. *James Madison: A Biography,* 1st pbk. ed. New York: Macmillan, 1990.

Madison, J. *The Mind of the Founder,* M. Meyers, ed. and intro. Indianapolis: Bobbs-Merrill, 1981.

Miller, William Lee. *The Business of May Next: James Madison and the Founding.* Charlottesville: University Press of Virginia, 1992.

Morris, Richard Brandon. *Witnesses at the Creation: Hamilton, Madison, Jay, and the Constitution,* 1st ed. New York: Holt, Rinehart, and Winston, 1985.

Sheldon, Garrett Ward. *The Political Philosophy of James Madison.* Baltimore: Johns Hopkins University Press, 2001.

Magna Carta

A major document in British CONSTITUTIONAL history, limiting the absolute power of the king and guaranteeing certain basic RIGHTS. Written by English nobility (barons) in 1215 and signed by King John at Runnymede, the Magna Carta came in response to royal oppression and excessive taxation. It asserted the authority of the English aristocracy, feudal common-law custom, the independence of the church, and the privileges of free towns (such as London). It implied rights of subjects, such as trial by jury and habeas corpus (not being jailed without charges). Many later-citizens' rights and liberties were later attributed to the Magna Carta, especially by PURITANS and parliamentarians in the 1600s. This famous legal document primarily checked the authority of the MONARCHY and distributed power to the nobility and clergy, but it set a precedent for later expansions of INDIVIDUAL rights, as in the British and U.S. Bill of Rights.

The Magna Carta becomes a symbol of English LIBERTY from excessive government taxation, regulation, and arbitrary POWER. It provides the first Western legal document limiting the absolute AUTHORITY of the STATE. The MODERN LIBERALISM of John LOCKE, Thomas JEFFERSON, and John RAWLS grows out of this historic document.

Further Readings

Adams, G. B. *Constitutional History of England.* New York: H. Holt, 1936.

Holt, James Clarke, ed. *Magna Carta and the Idea of Liberty.* Wiley, 1972.

Jones, J.A.P. *King John and Magna Carta.* London: Longman, 1971.

Stenton, Doris Mary Parsons, Lady. *After Runnymede; Magna Carta in the Middle Ages.* Charlottesville: University Press of Virginia, 1965.

Thompson, Faith. *Magna Carta: Its Role in the Making of the English Constitution.* Minneapolis: University of Minnesota Press, 1972.

Maistre, Joseph Marie de (1753–1821)
French conservative philosopher

Joseph de Maistre was a philosopher and writer who was appalled at the VIOLENCE of the French Revolution. He defended the traditional order and the role of the CATHOLIC Church in society. Exiled in 1792, Maistre spent most of his life as a diplomat and official for the Kingdom of Sardinia. His most influential work was the momentous two-volume *Du Pape* (Of the pope) in which he asserted the power of the papacy and endeavored to justify the doctrine of papal infallibility.

Joseph de Maistre was born into a noble French family in Savoy. He studied under Jesuits in a convent and developed an intense religiosity and dislike of the RATIONALISM of the 18th-century ENLIGHTENMENT. He served in a variety of local posts, including service as a magistrate and assistant advocate general. In 1787, de Maistre became a member of the provincial senate of Savoy. After Napoleon invaded Savoy at the head of a revolutionary army in 1792, de Maistre went into exile for the remainder of his life. He fled to Switzerland and then entered the service of the king of Sardinia where he served in a variety of posts. After four years representing Sardinia at Lausanne, in 1799, de Maistre became keeper of the great seal of the kingdom. He was subsequently appointed plenipotentiary to the czar at St. Petersburg, a post he held for 14 years. He then returned to Sardinia and served as minister of state and keeper of the seal until his death in 1821.

All of de Maistre's works were in French. Although he wrote some minor essays and speeches, his first major piece was written during his time in Switzerland. De Maistre wrote in support of the American war of independence, but he fervently opposed the French Revolution. His writings reflected the contention that France had a unique mission in the world as a civilizing force and instrument of God. He asserted that the revolution was foreordained because the ARISTOCRACY had supported the rationalism of the Enlightenment and had turned its back on religion. Therefore, the bloodbath of the Reign of Terror was justified as punishment for their lack of religiosity.

In 1819, de Maistre published his most substantial work *Du Pape* in two volumes but four parts. In the first section, the author argues that within the church, the pope is sovereign and that papal SOVEREIGNTY is infallible. De Maistre devotes the remainder of his opus to the relationship between the pope and the world's nations. He believed that the papacy provided the only supranational force that could protect individual nations and states from outside powers. De Maistre also asserted that the various forms of PROTESTANTISM were doomed to fall into "indifference" because they could not resist science and rationalism. His other writings continued his defense of MONARCHY and the church. Many consider him one of the best stylists of his time, and his works are marked by precise reasoning and dialectical insight. De Maistre died while writing *Les Soirées de Saint-Petersbourg* (Evening parties of Saint Petersburg).

Further Reading
Lebrun R., *Throne and Altar: The Political and Religious Thought of Joseph de Maistre.* Ottawa: University of Ottawa Press, 1965.

Malthus, Thomas Robert (1776–1834) *Political economist and moral philosopher*

Malthus argued that human populations outstrip their food supplies if reproduction is left unchecked. This antiutopian, politically CONSERVATIVE view encouraged fierce argument that continues to the present.

The argument was first presented by Malthus in a pamphlet published anonymously in 1798, titled *An Essay on the Principle of Population as It Affects the Future Improvement of Society, With Remarks on the Speculations of Mr. Godwin, M. Condorcet, and Other Writers.* In it, Malthus claimed that human populations increase at a geometrical rate (1, 2, 4, 8, 16, 32, 64, 128, 256, etc.) while agricultural output increases at an arithmetical rate (1, 2, 3, 4, 5, 6, 7, 8, 9, etc.). It follows from this that without some check on population growth, the number people to be fed will be greater than the food supply available to feed to them. Malthus proposed two kinds of checks on birthrates—misery and vice. The motivation for Malthus's stark "scientific" presentation of this idea can be seen in the title of the pamphlet: He wanted to counter what he saw as the unwarranted optimism of his intellectual contemporaries, most particularly William GODWIN's as expressed in his *Enquirer.*

In 1803, Malthus published a very much expanded second edition titled *An Essay on the Principle of Population, or a View of Its Past and Present Effects on Human Happiness with an Inquiry Into Our Prospects Respecting the Future Removal or Mitigation of the Evils Which It Occasions.* The second edition is usually described as the "Second Essay," and the first edition as the "First Essay." Although the Second Essay is much longer, the most significant theoretical addition is the claim that in addition to vice and misery as checks on population growth should be added "moral restraint." This third check Malthus understood as delayed marriage—couples would not marry and therefore not reproduce until a later age. What is important here is the idea that what appears in the First Essay as an inevitable, scientifically determined human tragedy can now, in the Second Essay, be controlled in some measure by human intervention. Malthus translated his ideas into particular policy proposals, including the suggestion that poor children should not receive assistance. Of course, these proposals looked to the long-term benefit of societies, but they appeared harsh and, as things turned out, unnecessary.

The reception of Malthus's argument was overwhelmingly hostile. Many, including Godwin and later MARX, were committed to the idea that political and social PROGRESS would overcome nature and were unwilling to contemplate the thought of naturally imposed limits on their optimism. In literature, Malthus is mocked and portrayed as cruel and heartless. Others though recognized the importance of his thought, including Ricardo, John Stuart MILL, and KEYNES. Darwin acknowledges the importance of Malthus's work in the development of his ideas.

One objection to Malthus's argument has been to the claim that food production can grow only arithmetically. He was unable to foresee the role of technology in increasing agricultural output, and so his argument seemed to rest on an untrue premise. However, whether or not the technology of food production can continue to keep us free of Malthus's conclusions remains unclear. A second objection concerns Malthus's moral refusal to consider the role of contraception as way of controlling population growth.

Malthus was born in Surrey, England, and studied at Jesus College, Cambridge. He married in 1804 and took up a position as professor of history at Haileybury College in 1805.

Further Reading
Keynes, J.M. *Essays and Sketches in Biography.* New York: Meridian Books, 1956.

Mandeville, Bernard (1670–1733) *Moral and economic theorist*

Mandeville argued that nations prospered and became great through the vices of their individual members.

This view brought notoriety to Mandeville and frequent condemnation of his arguments and opinions by leading philosophers and theorists of his time.

Mandeville's most famous work is *The Fable of the Bees: or, Private Vices, Publick Benefits*. This combined the poem "The Grumbling Hive: Or, Knaves Turned Honest," originally composed 24 years earlier, and a number of essays defending and expanding on his opinions. The topics covered in the work include the origin of moral virtue, economics, and education. The central idea is that for a nation to attain greatness, it must first promote and encourage a particular form of economic activity. In particular, it must encourage the vices of greed, desire, and deceit. Greed and desire are required because the consumption of luxuries created employment and trade, and this in turn created a wealthy nation. Deceit is required because the nature of a successful economic transaction in an unregulated market required buyers and sellers to withhold information from each other. Mandeville backed up his claims by showing how frivolous fashions created employment, more economic activity, and ultimately wealth. He joined this analysis to a deflationary account of the moral virtues. He pointed out the contradiction in the views of those moralists who wanted both national greatness and a citizenship of morally exemplary people. In *The Fable of the Bees* he has the bees, which had previously enjoyed prosperity and greatness, turned into virtuous bees, and consequently their society declines into poverty. Prosperity and moral virtue are therefore incompatible. It was this paradox that most scandalized his interlocutors. The function of morality, for Mandeville, is to encourage and reward people's sacrifices by flattering them and provoking feelings of admiration and satisfaction.

Mandeville also held progressive views on the status of women that were published, for example, in *The Virgin Unmask'd*. He argued for the equality of women with men and against marriage.

Mandeville's arguments and opinions were influential and widely known among the intellectuals of his time. His work received comment from the leading minds of the 18th century including Jean-Jacques Rousseau, David Hume, and the economist Adam Smith.

Mandeville was born in Holland, where he studied medicine. He moved to England as a young man and practiced medicine while writing both on medical and political issues.

Further Reading
Goldsmith, M. *Private Vices, Public Benefits: Bernard Mandeville's Social and Political Thought*. Cambridge, Eng.: Cambridge University Press, 1985.

Manifest Destiny

An idea developed in 19th-century America that the United States had a God-given, providential destiny to occupy the entire North American continent. This CHRISTIAN destiny was "manifest," or realized, by the Westward migration of Americans, the annexation of Texas from Mexico, the successful military campaigns against the Indians (Native Americans), the missionary activity of Christian ministers, and eventually the control of the Philippine Islands during the Spanish-American War. First cited in 1845 in *The United States Magazine*, the idea of Manifest Destiny justified U.S. territorial expansion. Though later criticized as IMPERIALISM, the principle held that the FREEDOM, DEMOCRACY, and religion of the United States was ordained of God to spread to and liberate other peoples. The acceptance of U.S. "aggression" by many inhabitants of other dominions (as in the Louisiana Territory and California) seemed to confirm the accuracy of the doctrine. Although used at times to rationalize military conquest of areas and peoples, Manifest Destiny reflects the moral and political culture of the United States, its civil religion of bringing U.S. values of freedom and RIGHTS to oppressed peoples and the righteousness of that cause. Its continuing relevance was revealed in the presidencies of Jimmy CARTER and Ronald REAGAN, which strove to extend U.S. notions of economic development, religious freedom, representative democracy, and individual rights to all countries in the world. The LEFTIST, MARXIST-LENINIST, MULTICULTURAL, and POLITICALLY CORRECT rejection of this idea of a providential view of the United States claims it is naked, hypocritical imperialism and domination.

The term *Manifest Destiny* is not now used often because of these negative (imperialist) connotations, but its theme of a unique U.S. destiny or divine "calling" continues in other ways in U.S. political culture.

Further Readings
Horsman, Reginald. *Race and Manifest Destiny: The Origins of American Racial Anglo-Saxonism*. Cambridge, Mass.: Harvard University Press, 1981.
Manifest Destiny and the Coming of the Civil War, 1840–1861, compiled by Don E. Fehrenbacher. New York: Meredith Corporation, 1970.

Merk, Frederick. *Manifest Destiny and Mission in American History: A Reinterpretation,* with the collaboration of Lois Bannister Merk, 1st ed. New York: Knopf, 1963.

Mannheim, Karl (1893–1947) *Hungarian social theorist and sociologist*

Mannheim related political thinking and social context with more subtlety than Karl MARX, but he agreed with HISTORICISM that attitudes and IDEOLOGY are conditioned by the group membership of the philosophers. One's social class, education, and institutional framework affect the way one perceives politics. However, with that recognition, Mannheim hoped to establish a politically neutral "scientific" sociology of knowledge. Social groups might be able to recognize the biases of their perspectives and the validity of their opponents' views and together develop a shared program for social improvement (like John Stuart MILL's ideal "free marketplace of ideas"). He implemented these ideas during his period in England (1933–47) when he advocated social and economic planning as well as comprehensive public education.

Mannheim taught at universities in his native Hungary (Budapest), in Germany (Heidelberg and Frankfurt), and in Great Britain (the London School of Economics and the Institute of Education at the University of London). He wrote on CONSERVATIVE thought, on economic ambition, and on UTOPIAS. The complex and many-sided perspectives in Mannheim's thought show a subtle, objective intellect, but his ability to see issues from all philosophical perspectives has made it difficult to categorize him. This has caused some critics to accuse him of relativism and paradoxical attitudes (that is, inconsistency).

Further Readings

Mannheim, Karl. *Ideology and Utopia: An Introduction to the Sociology of Knowledge,* preface by Louis Wirth. London: K. Paul, Trench, Trubner & Co., Ltd., 1936.

Simonds, A. P. *Karl Mannheim's Sociology of Knowledge.* Oxford, Eng.: Clarendon Press, 1978.

Mao Tse-Tung (1893–1976) *Chinese Communist thinker and political leader*

Mao was the theoretical and practical leader of the COMMUNIST Chinese Revolution (1949) and People's Republic of China. His ideas blend MARXIST-LENINIST IDEOLOGY with classical Chinese philosophy (Confucianism and legalism). One modification of Marxism in "Mao Tse-tung Thought" was his emphasis on the revolutionary potential of the rural peasantry (as opposed to the industrial proletariat) and guerilla warfare in the countryside. His agricultural reforms toward communal production reflect this emphasis. Mao's cultural insularity (he never traveled abroad or became widely acquainted with foreign ideas) also contributed to his strong anti-Western bias, a tendency toward isolationism, and brutal persecution of Western intellectuals and Christian missionaries.

He broke from Soviet communist orthodoxy over the DICTATORIAL and BUREAUCRATIC quality of the new SOCIALIST state. Seeing a new ruling class emerging from the Communist Party leaders in government, Mao attempted (in the Cultural Revolution of the late 1950s) to decentralize power, break down newly emerging social HIERARCHY, and democratize socialism. This led to widespread disorder and violence, causing Mao's communist successors to denounce it. The move of contemporary China to a combination of DESPOTIC centralized government and greater free-market economics represents a rejection of Maoism. He is revered as a great nationalist revolutionary leader, but his social theories did not achieve wide success.

Marcus Aurelius (121–180) *Roman emperor and Stoic philosopher*

In his book, *Meditations,* the emperor Marcus Aurelius elaborated his stoical philosophy of patient suffering, human dignity, dedication to duty, wisdom, and respect for reason and the LAW of the universe. This meshed well with a Roman Empire already going into decline and became almost the official philosophy of the Western empire. Aurelius also dedicated his life to the economic prosperity, military expansion, and public VIRTUE of Roman culture. Stoicism tends to be inward-looking and private, but Marcus Aurelius believed that it would also strengthen the morality and power of Rome. His elevation of Roman religion and superiority put him at odds with the early CHRISTIAN church, which regarded the pagan STATE religions as idolatry and believed in the EQUALITY of Roman and barbarian peoples. Despite his brutal persecutions of Christians and campaigns against Britain, Germany, and the Parthians, Marcus was a humane emperor toward the poor (lowering their taxes), lenient to political criminals, and decreased the brutality of gladiator matches. He is remembered as a rarely philosophical, civilized Roman emperor, interested in wisdom and justice as ideals. He spent much of his reign suppressing rebellions in Germany but brought a plague back to Rome.

Further Reading

Birley, Anthony Richard. *Marcus Aurelius, A Biography,* rev. ed. New Haven, Conn.: Yale University Press, 1987.

Marcuse, Herbert (1898–1979) *German Marxist thinker and Critical Theory founder*

As part of the FRANKFURT SCHOOL of MARXISTS, Marcuse rejected the strict Soviet orthodoxy that focused on economic class analysis to explain all social problems. Drawing on Karl Marx's early *Economic and Philosophic Manuscripts,* Marcuse emphasized other aspects of society (notably abstract art and sex) for liberation from the dominant oppression of CAPITALIST technological RATIONALISM. Marcuse became the guru of the U.S. 1960s New LEFT, which challenged all conventional morality and protested the Vietnam War.

A consequence of Marcuse's modification of Marxism's historical materialism was to allow nonworkers (middle-class intellectuals) to gain socialist praxis through correct consciousness. This meant that university professors could be the vanguard of the communist revolution.

A German Jewish intellectual, Marcuse studied with Martin HEIDEGGER at the University of Freiburg. There, Marcuse wrote extensively on the DIALECTIC of HEGEL but was forced to leave Germany with the rise of the NAZI FASCIST state led by HITLER. He immigrated to the United States, where he taught at Brandeis University and the University of California.

Further Readings

MacIntyre, Alasdair C. *Herbert Marcuse: An Exposition and a Polemic.* Frank Kermode, ed. New York: Viking Press, 1970.

Schoolman, M. *The Imaginary Witness: The Critical Theory of Herbert Marcuse.* New York: Free Press, 1980.

Marshall, John (1755–1835) *American jurist, statesman, and Federalist*

Most famous as chief justice of the U.S. Supreme Court, Marshall developed the U.S. federal judiciary (courts) into a powerful branch of national government through his doctrine of judicial review. Under Chief Justice Marshall's leadership, the U.S. Supreme Court assumed the POWER to review federal congressional statutes and executive (presidential) actions. By giving itself the power to interpret the founding document of the government (the U.S. CONSTITUTION), Marshall made the Supreme Court a premier institution in the United States. This had the effect of making the American national state more aristocratic because the judges (justices) of the Supreme Court (usually only nine) are not elected by the people but are appointed by the president for life tenure (permanently).

A staunch FEDERALIST, Marshall used this expansion of Supreme Court power explained in the case ruling of *Marbury v. Madison* (1803) to increase the power of the national government over the states. In the Supreme Court cases of *Gibbon's v. Ogden* (1824) and *McCulloch v. Maryland* (1819), Marshall used the U.S. constitutional "commerce clause" to expand federal jurisdiction over state economic regulation. This brought him into IDEOLOGICAL conflict with Thomas JEFFERSON, who feared excessive concentration of political power in the central regime and in the Supreme Court. Jeffersonian DEMOCRACY preferred the more democratic levels of government (the states) and branches of government (legislature). Marshall also was associated with the wealthier classes of U.S. society and interpreted the Constitution to protect private property through the "contract clause" (Dartmouth College Case, 1819) against state regulation.

John Marshall was born into humble circumstances and received little formal education, but through hard work and a keen intellect, he rose in U.S. government and national prestige. He is still considered to be the greatest Supreme Court justice in history. He read the law and was admitted to the Virginia bar in 1780, served in the Virginia assembly, was commissioner to France, congressman, secretary of state, and finally chief justice of the Supreme Court. A long and distinguished career included his literary production of a biography of George Washington and an autobiography.

Further Readings

Beveridge, Albert Jeremiah. *The Life of John Marshall.* Boston: Houghton Mifflin, 1944.

Konefsky, Samuel Joseph. *John Marshall and Alexander Hamilton, Architects of the American Constitution.* New York: Macmillan, 1964.

Newmyer, R. Kent. *The Supreme Court under Marshall and Taney.* Wheeling, Illinois: Harlan Davidson, 1968.

Stites, Francis N. *John Marshall, Defender of the Constitution,* Oscar Handlin, ed. Boston: Little, Brown, 1981.

Marsilius of Padua (1275–1342)   *Italian political philosopher*

As part of the CONCILIARISM movement in the MIDDLE AGES, Marsilius argued against papal supremacy in the CATHOLIC Church and developed an early secular conception of politics. In his *Defensor pacis* (*Defender of the Peace*), Marsilius asserted a view of CHURCH AND STATE relations later associated with the Protestant reformer Martin LUTHER. He stated that churchmen (priests, bishops) should be subject to the temporal rulers in both worldly and spiritual matters. Clergy activity should be confined to church services and teaching Christianity. The state should be controlled by the people; hence, the popular will should regulate the church. This contradicted traditional Catholic teaching on religion and politics (St. AUGUSTINE, St. Thomas AQUINAS), which made the church superior to the state in all matters and the pope supreme. Pope John XXII denounced him as a heretic.

Marsilius derived his political and ecclesiastic theory from ARISTOTLE'S TELEOLOGY, UTILITARIAN philosophy, and REPUBLICANISM. As such, his secular DEMOCRATIC principles foreshadow MODERN, LIBERAL political thought, such as the SOCIAL-CONTRACT ideas of John LOCKE.

Educated in medicine at the University of Padua, Marsilius became the rector of the University of Paris in 1313.

Further Reading
Gewirth, A. *Marsilius of Padua and Medieval Political Philosophy.* New York: Columbia University Press, 1951.

Marx, Karl (1818–1883)   *German political and economic philosopher, the father of Modern communism*

The COMMUNIST systems of the 20th century owe their origins to the ideas of Karl Marx. Millions of people in the former SOVIET UNION, the People's Republic of China, Vietnam, Cuba, and Western Europe have lived with the consequences of Marx's theories. The combination of fatal attraction and disastrous results make MARXISM one of the most interesting but tragic of political philosophies, and Marx's influence extends beyond the formal communist and SOCIALIST nations.

His concepts of CLASS conflict, HISTORICISM, materialism, and ethical relativism have had enormous influence. No other ideology, except LIBERALISM and CHRISTIANITY, has exercised such a history-changing effect as Marxism.

Karl Marx grew up in a traditional Jewish family (from a long ancestry of teachers or rabbis), though his German father converted to Protestant Christianity to be able to enter the legal profession. Marx studied philosophy (especially HEGEL) at the University of Berlin, eventually receiving a Ph.D. degree. Refused academic employment in CONSERVATIVE Germany, he became involved in radical politics, finally emigrating to France and then Great Britain. Much of his adult life was spent in London, unemployed and supported financially by his fellow communist thinker, Friedrich ENGELS. In his notable writings (*The Communist Manifesto, Capital, The German Ideology,* etc.), Marx developed an original and highly coherent theory of history, politics, economics, and revolution. His antireligious, antitradition perspective kept him a social outcast in conventional European society all his life, but he was the hero of radicals everywhere.

Marx begins his political thought with a view of HUMAN NATURE that conceives of human beings (or "species-being") as production. Humans differ from other creatures in producing their material subsistence and, in the economic process, their own identity. Historical technology becomes the key to understanding humanity, in Marx's mind. People may think that their social, psychological, artistic, or spiritual lives define humanity, but Marx reduces all life to work. The way people work determines their nature. Like the Old Testament God, people create.

But throughout history, this human creativity has been stifled, frustrated, and alienated. Humanity is meant to produce freely, happily but is bound to social institutions and activities that oppress people. Humans are supposed to be in control of their destiny, like gods, but they are controlled, like slaves. In capitalist society, they experience ALIENATION: fearful separation from the object of their production (which they do not know), from their subjective nature (as producer), from nature and society (which they should dominate, but dominates them), and from other humans (with whom they should cooperate, but who compete and conflict with them). Communism will overcome all these agonies and make a free, productive, just, and happy society. All problems will fade with communist society. The state ownership of

PROPERTY and economic planning will liberate people to enjoy their true creative natures and social harmony. Furthermore, for Marx, this progress to communism is inevitable: Human history and technology is moving inexorably, by scientific laws, to communism.

This view of historical inevitability of communism comes from Marx's materialism, which sees reality as the tangible, economic activity of life (production and consumption). Applying Hegel's DIALECTIC, Marx sees history as the clashing of opposites: modes of production, social classes, and ideas. All thought (philosophy, law, art, religion) come from certain ways of working and economic structures. So when agriculture is the main way of working in the European MIDDLE AGES, and that economy is made up of working peasants and land-owning nobility, all politics, theology, art, and science evolve from that system of social production. Marx says that CATHOLIC Christianity (St. Thomas AQUINAS) of the medieval period simply reflects the HIERARCHY, chivalry, and MONARCHY of European economics of the Middle Ages (FEUDALISM). Protestant Christianity, with its individualistic views of Christ and salvation, its work ethic and piety, reflect emerging CAPITALISM.

History flows through economic systems with corresponding social classes, for Marx: (1) primitive (tribal) communism where all are "hunters and gatherers"; (2) antiquity (Greek and Roman) where owners are slave owners and workers are slaves: (3) medieval feudalism with peasants and landlords: (4) capitalism with INDUSTRIAL working proletarians and industrial-owning capitalists or "bourgeoisie"; (5) socialism when the working-class revolution sets up the "DICTATORSHIP of the proletariat" and (6) communism, in which technology produces such abundance that no work is necessary and all economic classes disappear. Marx's vision of future communist society is so heavenly (prosperity, leisure, freedom, happiness, harmony) that it is no wonder that many people followed it. The realities of poverty, disease, war, and work paled next to Marx's vision of a bright future in communism.

Of course, to get to this perfect society, one had to overthrow capitalist DEMOCRACY first. This would require the unutopian practices of conspiracy, sabotage, violent revolution, and brutal suppression of resistance and dissent; but for Marx, this was necessary to reach the heaven of the communist STATE. People were not sinful or imperfect, and once the ideal society was achieved, they would become unselfish, kind, loving, and cooperative.

Most of Marx's historical analysis has to do with the next great social transition—from capitalism to socialism. This results from the "forces of production" (socialized technology) outstripping the "relations of production" (private property and wealth, wage labor, and social classes). Specifically, utilizing the LABOR THEORY OF VALUE, Marx sees the workers not getting the full payment for their work, causing a "crisis of overproduction" (or recession/depression) that shuts down the economy, causing a workers' revolution, establishing socialism. The government of dictatorship of the proletariat leads society from socialism to communism, following an outburst of productivity by "liberated" workers. Because all economic periods have states that are dictatorships of the ruling (owning) class, this socialist dictatorship is really more democratic than LIBERAL democracy. Unemployment is eliminated; universal education, medical care, housing, and old age pensions are instituted; and the prosperity of socialism leads other capitalist societies to collapse.

The historical relativism of morals and ethics makes adhering to bourgeois values (honesty, respect for RIGHTS, nonviolence) unnecessary for socialist revolutionaries: Stealing, killing, kidnapping, lying, terrorism are all justified if they advance the revolution. A new socialist ethics (and New Socialist Man) will emerge in this new historic epoch. The old capitalist, acquisitive, greedy, selfish, individualistic human will become the socialist, sharing, caring, collectivist, generous, peaceful, humane person. War will end.

The experience in the socialist countries did not confirm Marx's positive vision. Instead, they displayed economic stagnation, oppressive governments, and social alienation far worse than that experienced in liberal capitalist countries. Marxism—the ideological development of Marx's theories and their practice in different nations—attempts to explain this disparity between Marx's ideal and communism's reality. Some blame the surrounding capitalist-imperialist countries; others blame poor leadership (Stalin) or bureaucracy. But after 70 years of disaster, communist regimes abandoned the Marxist system. The Soviet Union returned to a quasi-capitalist, REPUBLICAN system; China instituted free-market reforms; and Cuba declined into poverty and despair.

The theories of Karl Marx seduced and deceived millions of people and caused enormous human suffering. Questions remain as to why the promise of

Marxist communism failed so miserably. Traditional CHRISTIAN political thought (St. AUGUSTINE) would say it ignored the reality of human sin; British liberalism (John LOCKE) would say it denied NATURAL RIGHTS; Freudian psychoanalysis would say it did not understand human nature. Whatever the answer, the political thought of Karl Marx is one of the great episodes in Western political theory.

Further Readings

Avineri, S. *The Social and Political Thought of Karl Marx.* London: Cambridge University Press, 1968.

Balibar, Etienne. *The Philosophy of Marx.* 1995.

Cohen, G. *Karl Marx's Theory of History: A Defense.* Princeton, N.J.: Princeton University Press, 1978.

Derrida, Jacques. *Specters of Marx: The State of the Debt, the Work of Mourning, and the New International,* Peggy Kamuf, transl., intro. by Bernd Magnus and Stephen Cullenberg, 1994.

Elster, J. *An Introduction to Karl Marx.* Cambridge, Eng.: Cambridge University Press, 1986.

———. *Making Sense of Marx.* Cambridge: Cambridge University Press, 1985.

Hunt, R. *Marxism and Totalitarian Democracy,* 2 vols. Pittsburgh: University of Pittsburgh Press, 1974, 1985.

Isaac, Jeffrey C. *Power and Marxist Theory: A Realist View.* Ithaca, N.Y.: Cornell University Press, 1987.

Manuel, Frank Edward. *A Requiem for Karl Marx.* Cambridge, Mass.: Harvard University Press, 1995.

McLellan, D. *The Thought of Karl Marx,* 2nd ed. New York: Harper & Row, 1981.

Lovell, David W. *Marx's Proletariat: The Making of a Myth.* London: Routledge, 1988.

Marxism/Marxist

The historical development of the social theories of Karl MARX by other thinkers, and the application of those ideas in the practices of SOCIALIST and COMMUNIST parties and countries. The political thought of Marx was so complex and its impact on the 20th century was so enormous that it is natural that it would develop in several different themes and directions.

The prevalent form of Marxism is Soviet Russian or "orthodox" MARXISM-LENINISM. Sometimes called Stalinist or state capitalism, this historical strand of Marxism emphasizes the dominant Communist Party, the TOTALITARIAN control of a planned economy, education, culture, science, and art by the state, and the world class struggle and revolution. The restrictions on personal LIBERTY (of thought, action, belief, religion) and harsh secret police of this Soviet-style Marxism soon alienated Western LEFTISTS. An alternative "Humanist" Marxism emerged in the CRITICAL THEORY of the Frankfurt School, which allowed greater DEMOCRACY and individual FREEDOM in socialism. This continued the views of earlier thinkers who criticized Soviet communism (such as Rosa LUXEMBURG, Leon TROTSKY, Nikolay BUKHARIN, and others), other SOCIAL DEMOCRATIC parties of European nations (Germany, Italy, France), and the Labour Party in Great Britain. These political thinkers (such as Karl KAUTSKY) and movements (such as British Socialism) worked within the parliamentary electoral system and, when gaining political power, used it to nationalize industry, raise taxes on the wealthy, aid labor unions, and so on. Another development in Marxism is its application to economically underdeveloped (Third World) countries through LENIN's theory of capitalist IMPERIALISM. This led poor neocolonial nations in Africa, Asia, and Latin America to have Marxist-Leninist socialist revolutions (as in China, India, Vietnam, Iraq, Cuba, Mozambique), expelling the exploiting imperialists and attempting socialized economics. Finally, Marxist ideas filtered down into liberal academic fields, such as sociology, philosophy, and English, looking at society in terms of the dominance of powerful elites, EXPLOITATION, class conflict (racism, sexism, classism), and ENVIRONMENTAL degradation.

The decline of world communism has diminished the influence of Marxism as a system and an ideology. Its materialist emphasis on economics and fascination with social group conflict persists in modified form in other political thought (radical environmentalism, FEMINISM, liberalism).

Further Readings

Aronson, Ronald. *After Marxism.* New York: Guilford Press, 1995.

Guarasci, Richard. *The Theory and Practice of American Marxism, 1957–1970.* Lanham, Md.: University Press of America, 1980.

Meisner, Maurice J. *Marxism, Maoism and Utopianism: Eight Essays.* Madison: University of Wisconsin Press, 1982.

Bernd Magnus and Stephen Cullenberg, eds. *Whither Marxism? Global Crises in International Perspective.* Introduction. New York: Routledge, 1995.

Wright, Anthony. *Socialisms: Theories and Practices.* Oxford, Eng.: Oxford University Press, 1986.

Marxism-Leninism

The 20th-century development of Karl MARX's COMMUNIST theory by V. I. LENIN emphasizing worldwide CAPITALIST IMPERIALISM, SOCIALIST revolution in economically underdeveloped countries (neocolonies), and the decline of the advanced industrial nations. Also the official ideology of the SOVIET UNION, or Russian Stalinist Orthodoxy.

Mass Society

The emergence of mass society is mainly a late 19th- and 20th-century phenomenon. The term refers to a society or nation where linguistic, regional, economic, religious, and other differences have been blurred and a majority class that embraces similar values and norms has emerged. There is also a strong economic component in that the populations in mass societies use the same or similar products and respond to mass marketing. Politically, leaders and political ELITES in the 20th century have taken advantage of new media such as radio and television to control ideas and news and to distribute propaganda in highly effective means.

Concurrent with the increase in wages and decrease in working hours (all the result of the industrial revolution in Western Europe and the United States), there began to emerge a leisure class that had both disposable income and a significant amount of time to devote to activities other than work. In many ways, the evolution of the MODERN mass society would be spearheaded by the United States and its growing middle class. Spurred by the economic boom of the 1920s, new technologies, such as the radio and the Hollywood movie, and new forms of advertising created a consumer culture that promoted specific products and lifestyles. The impact of advertising on society did not go unnoticed by political leaders who began to use propaganda to great affect, especially as society became more uniform in its expectations and goals. In Germany and Italy, the FASCIST regimes' use of propaganda, and even Franklin D. ROOSEVELT's use of techniques such as the press conference and the "fireside chat," were demonstrative of the effectiveness of reaching mass societies through emerging media.

The cold war can be viewed as a contest between two competing visions of mass society. The SOVIET UNION endeavored to create a state, based on Marxism, that would eliminate economic classes and instead form one mass class. Concurrently, the progressive tax system of the United States and growing antipoverty programs contributed to an enormous middle class that has dominated American politics since the 1950s.

The continuing trend toward mass society and mass culture is not without its critics. For instance, writing in the 1940s, Theodor W. ADORNO correctly forecast the eventual emergence of a giant "culture industry" in which advertising, politics, and the various forms of entertainment would be merged together. Other critiques of mass society have centered on the philosophical merits of the movement. For instance, one of the main themes of U.S. culture has traditionally been INDIVIDUALISM. By its very nature, however, mass society tends to lessen the value of individual choice and distinctiveness by promoting uniformity in appearance and habit. Concurrently, mass society also reinforces the tyranny of the majority through various mechanisms. Hence, the counterculture of the 1960s United States, which was initiated as a protest against the mainstream, eventually became coopted by the mass society so that its music, dress, language, and so forth were absorbed into the mainstream.

The increasing globalization of the world's economy also reflects such trends as the exchange of music, ideas, and other aspects of culture through new media such as the internet and, as increasingly large multinational corporations come to dominate markets, may mark the emergence of a global mass society. The demise of MARXISM as a viable political entity has meant that the main values of the United States—democracy and free-market capitalism—have been broadly accepted by the world community. Francis Fukuyama writes that this new era marks the "end of history" as we know it (and in the Hegelian sense), in that history thus far has been centered around the struggle for equality and full participation in government. With these ideals now generally accepted, the mass societies of the world have formed a political consensus on government.

Further Reading
Fukuyama, F. *The End of History and the Last Man.* New York: Free Press, 1992.

Mayflower Compact

The political document written by the PURITAN American settlers in New England in 1620 and considered the first SOCIAL CONTRACT in the United States. Reflecting the Calvinist CHRISTIAN outlook of these English immigrants to America, the compact declares the settlement to be "For the glory of God, and advancement of the Christian faith." Adhering to a COVENANT view of religion and politics, these Puritans agreed to "covenant and combine ourselves together into a body politic . . . for the general good of the colony." Forty-one members of the ship *Mayflower* signed the compact. It formed the basis of the Plymouth (Massachusetts) government for 10 years and the foundation of later government covenants in New England.

Further Reading

Heath, D. *Mourt's Relation.* Cambridge, Mass.: Applewood Books, 1963.

McCarthyism

A term named after U.S. Senator Joseph McCarthy, signifying any persistent and unfair persecution of political opponents, especially COMMUNISTS or LEFTISTS. In the 1950s, Senator McCarthy, a REPUBLICAN from Wisconsin, accused the U.S. State Department of harboring communists and SOCIALISTS who were undermining U.S. foreign policy during the cold war. As chairman of the Senate permanent investigations subcommittee, McCarthy conducted hearings that accused a wide range of U.S. civil servants, academics, and media Hollywood figures of pro-Communist, anti-American subversive activity. This caused widespread panic in the United States and enormous suspicion of anyone on the LIBERAL LEFT.

McCarthyism has come to mean any hysterical, unprofessional, unfair accusation and persecution of others for political reasons. McCarthyism can be practiced by the whole range of IDEOLOGIES, from CONSERVATIVE RIGHT to Liberal Left. The U.S. Supreme Court has upheld the FIRST AMENDMENT right to free speech against McCarthyite extremist persecution.

McWilliams, Wilson Carey (1933–) *American political philosopher, academic, and scholar on religion and politics*

Most famous for his writings on FRATERNITY, especially his book *The Idea of Fraternity in America*, McWilliams is an internationally renowned scholar on AMERICAN POLITICAL THEORY, CLASSICAL political philosophy, and religion and politics. His approach is almost equally beholden to PLATO, ARISTOTLE, St. AUGUSTINE, and John CALVIN. He illuminates U.S. political culture in terms of the competing theoretical strains in the United States, especially MODERN LIBERALISM versus Protestant CHRISTIANITY. Of a caliber of Alexis de TOCQUEVILLE's *Democracy in America*, with the humor of Mark Twain, and the sensitivity of DANTE, McWilliams's insights into the

profound questions of political life have made him a modern-day prophet.

McWilliams has taught at Rutgers University, Yale, and Harvard. His many graduate students in political theory occupy academic positions around America and the world. Known as a deeply committed teacher and mentor, McWilliams effectively founded a school of U.S. political thought without intending to do so.

An active member of the DEMOCRATIC PARTY and a prominent PRESBYTERIAN churchman, McWilliams is highly regarded in academic, political, and ecclesiastical circles. In 1989, he received The John WITHERSPOON Award from the New Jersey Committee for The Humanities.

Further Readings

McWilliams, Wilson Carey, and Gibbons, Michael T. eds.*The Federalists, the Antifederalists, and the American Political Tradition.* Westport, Conn.: Greenwood Publishing Group, 1992.

McWilliams, Wilson Carey. *The Idea of Fraternity in America.* Berkeley: University of California Press, 1975.

———. *The Politics of Disappointment: American Elections 1976–94.* Chatham, N.J.: Chatham House, 1995.

———. "The Wearing of Orange." *Worldview* 26 (March 1983).

Medieval political theory

The political ideas in Western Europe from approximately the fall of the Roman Empire (A.D. 500) to the Protestant REFORMATION and MODERNITY (A.D. 1500). Much of the political thought of the Middle Ages concerns competing images of JUSTICE and claims to STATE power of the CATHOLIC Church, the HOLY ROMAN EMPIRE, feudal kings and princes, CORPORATISM, and popular SOVEREIGNTY.

The Early Middle Ages (A.D. 500–1000) saw the destruction of Roman LAW and EMPIRE with its universal worldly AUTHORITY and the rise of an alternative CHRISTIAN political philosophy (St. AUGUSTINE) of the Two Cities (City of God and City of Man). The Roman Catholic Church provided some semblance of unity and order in Europe and preserved remnants of civil justice and moral codes. The centralization of power in the bishop of Rome (pope) replicated the Roman CAESAR but with transcendent religious authority. An early political conflict at this time was between this centralized church and the decentralized barbarian kingdoms. The Catholic Church attempted to extend a uniform

Christian polity based on universal truth, while the separate kingdoms (e.g., in Germany) based law and principles on kinship, regional loyalty, and custom. By the ninth century, the church had developed the "Two Swords" doctrine, with the spiritual realm (superior) ruling the temporal (inferior) through the papacy and emperor (as in CHARLEMAGNE). The cooperation between these two realms helped to spread a uniform Christian civilization through education, a shared church liturgy, and recognized administration of ecclesiastical and governmental systems.

With the death of Charlemagne, Europe again was torn by localized strife (and Viking invasions) that diminished the power of the central church and the empire. Local princes resumed autonomous power, and local religious corporations (monasteries) elected their own leaders.

By the 12th century, Rome reasserted authority through universal CANON LAW in Europe. Revived CLASSICAL (ARISTOTLE) studies affected the Catholic Church in the theories of St. Thomas AQUINAS. Basing authority on a series of laws (divine, natural, and human) Thomist political philosophy became more RATIONAListic and HIERARCHICAL. Still, GUILDS and town emerged with independent structures and CONCILIARISM advocated a more DEMOCRATIC structure for church governance. JOHN OF SALISBURY and MARSILIUS OF PADUA formulated early Modern notions of popular sovereignty and representative government.

The 13th-century popes Innocent III and Gregory IX claimed power to resolve disputes between European monarchies, and by the 14th century, the papacy was explicitly identifying itself as the vicar of Christ on earth. JOHN OF PARIS challenged this papal supremacy, and other REPUBLICAN movements predated the final break with the Catholic Church in the Protestant reformations of John CALVIN and Martin LUTHER.

It is easy to see the conflicts and assertions of power in Medieval politics and political thought as self-interested claims. Although ambition and pride often motivated these combatants, most deputes were genuine concerns over justice, right, and responsibility to God and people. The Medieval church genuinely believed that it was best for Europe to have a uniform creed and governance.

Further Readings

Lambton, Ann Katharine Swynford. *State and Government in Medieval Islam: An Introduction to the Study of Islamic Political Theory: The Jurists.* Oxford, Eng.: Oxford University Press, 1981.
Milson, S.F.C. *The Legal Framework of English Feudalism* (the Maitland lectures, 1972). Cambridge, Eng.: Cambridge University Press, 1976.
Nederman, Cary J., and Forhan, Kate Langdon, eds. *Medieval Political Theory: A Reader: The Quest for the Body Politic, 1100–1400.* London: Routledge, 1993.

Menshevick

The majority political party of the Russian COMMUNISTS that broke with LENIN and the BOLSHEVIKS. Menshevicks advocated a more open DEMOCRATIC party against the more exclusive, militant democratic-centralism of the Bolsheviks.

Mercantilism

An economic system in Europe in the 1600–1700s that relied on foreign trade, protection of domestic INDUSTRY (protectionism), government monopolies, and banking. The main mercantilist principle was that a nation's wealth will increase by a favorable balance of trade (importing fewer goods than exporting). The British EMPIRE of the 18th century did this by importing cheap raw materials (like cotton) from the colonies (North America, India, Egypt) and exporting expensive manufactured goods (cloth, pottery, etc.). The government supported this policy with restrictive trade laws (e.g., British Navigation Acts) that punished unregulated or free trade. The Dutch, French, and German governments also adopted this policy at times (leading to European trade wars). Adam SMITH criticized mercantilism and advanced the thesis that free trade would actually be more productive and create more prosperity.

Further Readings

Gomes, Leonard. *Foreign Trade and the National Economy: Mercantilist and Classical Perspectives.* New York: St. Martin's Press, 1987.
Heckscher, E. *Mercantilism.* London: Allen & Unwin, 1935.

Michels, Robert (1876–1936)   *Italian political sociologist*

Robert Michels was a noted Italian political economist and sociologist whose development of the "iron law of oligarchy" reflected the trend by other academics in the early 1900s to support the trend toward AUTHORI-

TARIANISM. Their work would be used to provide the intellectual basis for fascism.

Michels was born into a wealthy German family. During his youth, he became a SOCIALIST and moved to Italy, where he spent his life as an academic. His training was in sociology and economics, and he became noted as a political sociologist. Michels held posts at a variety of prominent Italian universities, including Turin, Basel, and Perugia. He wrote a number of works, the most celebrated being *Zur Soziologie des Parteiwesens in der modernen Demokratie* (*Political Parties: A Sociological Study of the Oligarchical Tendencies of Modern Democracy*) published in 1911. Ultimately, his major essays were translated into English as *First Lectures in Political Sociology* (1949).

One of the main themes of Michels's work was the inevitable rise and dominance of oligarchies in political systems. Michels asserted that, even in DEMOCRATIC systems, the need for rapid decision making and the large-scale BUREAUCRACIES necessary to implement policy in the modern nation-state would give rise to political oligarchies that he defined as government by the most capable few: Within the organization of government, the most talented and capable would rise through the ranks and dominate agencies and policy development. Their rule would be accepted by people because they were the best suited for the posts. Michels termed his system the *iron law of oligarchy* and held that it applied to all types of political organizations, including political parties and governmental bureaucracies.

Just as DEMOCRATIC organizations were bound to become oligarchic, LIBERAL or RADICAL organizations were destined to become CONSERVATIVE. As trade unions or even MARXIST political parties developed large bureaucracies to carry out their functions, oligarchies came to dominate the organizations. Inevitably, the oligarchies enacted policies and governed in such a way as to maximize their power and further the interests of the elite group, became highly centralized and autocratic in nature, and also became more entrenched and resistant to change, reform, or alternative viewpoints.

Michels's work was similar to theories developed by other Italian academics and social philosophers, such as Gaetano Mosca and Vilfredo Pareto, who developed elite theory. These intellectuals maintained that all societies and governments were hierarchical in nature and that a small ruling elite held political power over the majority. Changes in the nature of government were simply changes in the ruling elite, and the new oligarchies reflected the values of the new powers. Other writers expanded on Michels's concept and endeavored to apply it to diverse groups such as governmental cabinets, religious denominations, and community groups.

Several of his contemporaries rejected the overt racism and TOTALITARIANISM of the FASCIST movement, but Michels supported the rise of Mussolini in Italy and believed that his regime was a welcome change from the weak governments that preceded it. It was thus with Michels's consent that his writings were to provide justification for the fascist government.

Further Reading
Mitzman, A. *Sociology and Estrangement: Three Sociologists of Imperial Germany.* New York: Knopf, 1973.

Middle Ages

The historical period in Western Europe between the fall of the ancient Roman Empire and the rise of the Protestant Reformation and MODERNITY; roughly, the thousand years between A.D. 500 and 1500. Dominated by MONARCHY, the CATHOLIC Church, and FEUDALISM, the political thought of the European Middle Ages is characterized by order, HIERARCHY, and religion (see St. Thomas AQUINAS). Also known as the Medieval period. See MEDIEVAL POLITICAL THEORY.

Mill, James (1773–1836) *British political philosopher, economist, and utilitarian*

As a philosopher of UTILITARIAN ETHICS and politics, Mill, like Jeremy BENTHAM, claimed to advance the "greatest happiness for the greatest number." By this, he meant widespread material, economic prosperity and DEMOCRATIC, EGALITARIAN government. Mill used this measure to attack the aristocratic British establishment and was therefore considered a RADICAL. Relying on the political and psychological INDIVIDUALISM of Thomas HOBBES, the free-market CAPITALISM of Adam SMITH, and the religious skepticism of the ENLIGHTENMENT, James Mill challenged the traditional organic realm of William BLACKSTONE and Edmund BURKE. His book *Essay on Government* asserted that the hierarchies in British life (MERCANTILISM, the English church, private schools, Parliament) obstructed the happiness of the majority of people. He advocated sweeping democratic reforms, extending voting rights to common people, frequent elections, and secret ballots. Mill's utilitarianism, then, was the early form of democratic LIBERALISM and WELFARE-STATE Liberalism (public education, social services to the needy, etc.). He tended to favor the educated middle class as the best leader of society; professional, scientific Britons would make the best rulers, in his view.

Educated at the University of Edinburgh, Scotland, James Mill trained to become a PRESBYTERIAN clergyman, but his unbelief in CHRISTIANITY ended that career. He worked for the British East India Company, afterward writing a *History of British India* (1817). Much of Mill's political writings were in the form of popular pamphlets.

Further Reading
Bain, A. *James Mill: A Biography.* London: Longmans, 1882.

Mill, John Stuart (1806–1873)   *British political philosopher, utilitarian, and advocate of liberty*

As the oldest son of James MILL, John Stuart Mill was educated in the RADICAL analytical school of his father. He was taught Greek at the age of three, Latin by eight, and a full Liberal Arts education by age 14. After this, he had a nervous breakdown.

John Stuart Mill applied the British LIBERALISM of Thomas HOBBES and John LOCKE to 19th-century society, especially intellectual LIBERTY. His belief in materialism, PROGRESS, women's rights (FEMINISM), DEMOCRACY, and SOCIALISM paved the way for 20th-century WELFARE-STATE liberalism. His inductive logic formed the basis of much modern social science and BEHAVIORISM.

Mill conceived of HUMAN NATURE as both rationally independent and individual and emotionally social. Like Jean-Jacques ROUSSEAU, Mill resented the cold, calculating reason of Hobbes and Locke, concerned only with personal, selfish INTERESTS. He perceived a human capacity for sympathetic feelings for others' suffering. ". . . [T]he good of others becomes . . . a thing naturally and necessarily attended to, like any of the physical conditions of our existences," he said. This human altruism should be developed by society and institutionalized in benevolent government (welfare state). Social PROGRESS requires civilized, sensitive human beings, and this depends on "liberty." By *liberty,* Mill means more than FREEDOM from arbitrary authority or formal restrictions. Even with political and legal lib-

erty, one's freedom can be inhibited by social prejudices and conventions. The majority's attitudes can become a TYRANNY against the individual's free thought. In his famous essay *On Liberty,* Mill argues for complete freedom of opinion, conscience, and expression, even of socially obnoxious ideas. The most radical or crazy ideas should be allowed to be expressed because (1) they may turn out to be correct and may lead to great progress and social benefits, and (2) even if they are wrong, the correct opinion will be strengthened by meeting and defeating the erroneous opinion. This Socratic view of the benefits of absolute liberty of thought and speech underlies Mill's idea of the civilized, progressive society and individual. Sometimes called "the free marketplace of ideas," it assumes that the competition of different perspectives will lead to the victory of the truth. The adversarial trial system of Anglo-American law (with competing prosecution and defense lawyers), the principle of a "free press" (with competing political publications and media), and "academic freedom" (where universities teach all sides of an issue) reflect J. S. Mill's advocacy of pure liberty. For him, a person is not truly educated unless he or she can present *all* angles of an issue, even those with which they disagree. To be able to serve as a devil's advocate—presenting persuasively one's opponent's argument—is the ideal intellectual for Mill. A DEMOCRACY full of such detached, objective intellectuals will be the most free, happy, prosperous, and progressive society.

A step towards this, for Mill, is the objective, value-free social science described in his book *A System of Logic,* in which he asserts that economics, politics, and sociology can be studied scientifically and that "intuition" or "given" truths are simply prejudices to be dismissed. Only factually proven assumptions are valid. This rejects the CONSERVATIVE, religious, cultural, and racial basis of much of traditional British knowledge.

Politically, this led Mill to advocate extending the SUFFRAGE (voting rights) to the middle classes, the poor, the working class, and women. An early FEMINIST, he said that discriminating between men and women made no more sense than judging people by their hair color. Still, he proposed a "proportional representation," where the better-educated citizens would have more than one vote. A simple majority rule would not lead to better, wiser government or public policy; the mass of people remains ignorant and self-seeking, selfish, and foolish.

A moderate critic of CAPITALISM, Mill nevertheless rejected centralized state SOCIALISM or COMMUNISM (MARXISM) but hoped for an economy of worker-owned enterprises, run democratically and operating in a free market. He favored gradual socialism through increased taxes on the wealthy, inheritances, and land.

J. S. Mill moderated the utilitarian philosophy of Jeremy BENTHAM by adding a qualitative dimension to human happiness. As social, moral, and intellectual beings, humans cannot be made happy with simply more and more quantities of goods; they must advance in quality. From this came his famous phrase: "It is better to be a human being dissatisfied than a pig satisfied; better to be Socrates dissatisfied than a fool satisfied."

John Stuart Mill brings liberalism up to the 19th and 20th centuries and greatly influences British and American notions of freedom of speech, press, and conscience; academic freedom; social welfare and progress; feminism; social science; and religious skepticism.

Further Reading
Mill, J. S. "Autobiography." In *The Collected Works of John Stuart Mill,* vol. I, J. Robson, ed. 1873.
Packe, M. St. J. *The Life of John Stuart Mill.* New York: Macmillan, 1954.
Ryan, A. *J. S. Mill.* London: Routledge, 1974.

Milton, John (1608–1674) *English political writer, Puritan, and religious poet*

Most famous for his classic Christian epic poetry (*Paradise Lost; Paradise Regained; Samson Agonistes*), Milton is significant as a PURITAN REPUBLICAN thinker during the period of the English Civil Wars (1640–60), CROMWELL'S commonwealth, and the CHURCH-AND-STATE controversies of that time. His political pamphlet *Areopagitica* is considered the classic MODERN defense of FREEDOM of the press. This greatly influenced later English and American conceptions of political and religious liberty.

Most of Milton's political writing concerned the legitimacy of the anti-MONARCHY, parliamentary system of England under Oliver Cromwell. As secretary of foreign tongues to the council of state, he wrote several treatises justifying the Puritan republic to other European states. His *Tenure of Kings and Magistrates* defended the trial and execution of King Charles I. This RADICAL thesis that monarchs are accountable to

the people and can be removed for treason, influenced later SOCIAL-CONTRACT thinkers such as John LOCKE and Thomas JEFFERSON. In religion, Milton was a firm Protestant, opposing a church institution (CATHOLIC, Episcopal, or PRESBYTERIAN) that interfered with the individual believer's right to LIBERTY of conscience. His belief that a true CHRISTIAN commonwealth would protect individual freedom to religious belief put him in the English Independent, Congregational or BAPTIST camp. A virtuous republic is ruled by people who are free to investigate and interpret the Bible for themselves and to live pious, peaceable Christian lives. The ideal form of this republican government varied, for Milton, from rule by the common "saints" to a benevolent oligarchy. His hopes for this Christian commonwealth were lost with the Restoration of the English monarchy in 1660. He thereupon retired to private life in the country, where he wrote his most famous religious poems. His final political treatise was *The Readie and Easie Way to Establish a Free Commonwealth* (1660).

Among Milton's most controversial writings were his essays favoring divorce on the grounds of incompatibility of mind and temperament. This un-Biblical argument for divorce may have grown from Milton's own very unhappy first marriage. This contributed to the Catholic European denunciation of Milton, Cromwell, and their republican ideas.

Further Readings
Davies, S. *Images of Kingship in 'Paradise Lost': Milton's Politics and Christian Liberty.* Columbia: University of Missouri Press, 1983.
Hill, C. *Milton and the English Revolution.* New York: Viking Press, 1977.

mixed constitution

Originally, in ARISTOTLE, a government that combines the three main forms of state: MONARCHY or kingship (the rule of one); ARISTOCRACY (the rule of a few); and polity (the rule of the many). Aristotle and later thinkers (CICERO, James HARRINGTON, John LOCKE, James MADISON, Baron MONTESQUIEU) viewed this "mixed" constitution as the most stable (if not most excellent, wise, or efficient) of governments. The assumption is that it will represent all sectors of a society (the few rich and noble with the majority poor and ignorant), preventing social unrest and REVOLUTION. The British CONSTITUTION of king, House of Lords, and

House of Commons embodies this mixed ideal, as does the U.S. Constitution (president, Senate, House of Representatives). The CHECKS AND BALANCES of this system are widely accepted in the MODERN period.

moderate

A political or IDEOLOGICAL position between LIBERAL and CONSERVATIVE, LEFT and RIGHT, which draws upon policy stances of both. For example, President Jimmy CARTER was considered a "moderate Democrat"; President George Bush was a "moderate REPUBLICAN." Both subscribed to some Conservative positions (on welfare, defense, ABORTION, etc.) and some Liberal positions (CIVIL RIGHTS, taxes). As extreme ideological positions (of Left or Right) make it difficult to win a majority vote in democratic elections, most U.S. politicians become moderate.

Modern/modernity

The historical period in the Western world from the end of the MIDDLE AGES to the 20th century (roughly 1500–1900). Characterized by the rise of Protestant CHRISTIANITY, political REPUBLICANISM, and INDUSTRIAL CAPITALISM, the Modern period differs substantially from previous ancient or CLASSICAL civilization, Medieval society, and "POSTMODERN" contemporary life. In political thought, Modern ideas are associated with LIBERALISM, SOCIAL-CONTRACT theory, INDIVIDUALISM, EQUALITY, and DEMOCRACY. The ENLIGHTENMENT in France is considered representative of modernity. Critics of Modern views include traditional CATHOLIC philosophy, classical Greek thought, FASCISM, Communitarianism, and some of COMMUNISM (though MARXISM is in some ways the logical conclusion of Modern thought). Prominent thinkers of modernity include Thomas HOBBES, John LOCKE and Jean-Jacques ROUSSEAU. Underlying much of the Modern perspective is a materialistic, scientific view of life, eschewing abstract ethical, religious, and spiritual perspectives.

Mohammed/Mahomet (570–632) *Founder of Islam; political, military, and religious leader*

Considered the last prophet of God (Allah) by Muslims, Mohammed grew up in Mecca, Arabia (now Saudi Arabia). At the age of 40, he began to have visions and revelations from an angel, which he preached (and which were later recorded in the *Koran*). These became the doctrines of Islam, including: There is only one God (monotheism); humans must submit to him (*Islam* means "submission"); heaven and hell await everyone on God's coming judgment. Mohammed prescribed many religious duties: frequent prayer and almsgiving, a pilgrimage to Mecca, and forbidding of usury. Developed Islam contains detailed prescriptions for almost every aspect of social, family, economic, and political life.

Mohammed at first was rejected by the pagan Arabs, but he defeated them militarily in 630. Islam spread rapidly, and Mohammed ruled a theocracy, which eventually spread from the Middle East to Africa and Western Europe (the Ottoman Empire). ISLAMIC POLITICAL THOUGHT still governs these regions in various ways. Early in his career, Mohammed reached out to the surrounding Jewish and CHRISTIAN populations, but when they rejected his teachings, Islam became increasingly hostile to these religions and their states. Much of contemporary political conflict in the Middle East is derived from these religious/political differences. Mohammed is revered by Muslims as the last and greatest prophet of God.

monarchy

Literally, the "rule of one" person (king, queen, etc.). ARISTOTLE discusses this form of government as potentially the best if the one ruler is wise and good, serves the common interest of society, and is efficient. Because the monarch is a single governor, he or she can make and implement decisions quickly, not having to take time to consult others (as in an ARISTOCRACY or DEMOCRACY). This absolute power of the monarch is also his or her weakness; if evil (TYRANT), the king or queen can do much more harm more quickly than a bad ruler in a mixed government.

Monarchy is a frequent government system in the world (kings David and Solomon in Israel; emperors in China; sultans in Arabia; European monarchs in France, England, etc.). Kingship dominated Europe during the CATHOLIC Middle Ages; St. Thomas AQUINAS wrote on CHRISTIAN monarchy and justified it on the logic "One God; one common interest; one ruler." With the rise of MODERN REPUBLICAN government, monarchy declined in Europe. Contemporary world politics diminished monarchical AUTHORITY leaving only symbolic or figurehead monarchies in Britain, Spain, Sweden, and a few other countries.

Montaigne, Michel de (1533–1592) *French essayist*

Born in a family mansion near Bordeaux, the young Montaigne received a classical education at home, made possible by his father's wealth and minor nobility. At the age of six, Montaigne was sent to the College of Guyenne at Bordeaux, and later he studied law at the University of Toulouse. In 1557, he became a member of the parliament of Bordeaux, where he served for 13 years. After retiring from public life, Montaigne devoted himself to writing, completing the first edition of his most famous and important work, the *Essais (Essays)*, in 1580. Following his travels throughout Europe, Montaigne became the mayor of Bordeaux in 1581, a position he held for four years. He spent the last years of his life attempting to mediate between CATHOLIC and PROTESTANT leaders and revising his *Essais (Essays)*, the final version of which was published posthumously in 1595.

Montaigne's mature thinking was informed by the works of the Greek skeptics, especially of Sextus Empiricus, and he adopted as his motto the phrase "What do I know?" The *Essays* reflect this influence in a series of learned and witty discussions of various topics, such as death, liars, the education of children, diet, sex, and friendship. As a whole, the *Essays* present Montaigne's attempts to think through his experience of life and his own self-understanding, including his skeptical doubt about the possibility of gaining secure knowledge. According to Montaigne, the intellect and the senses were fallible human faculties. All claims about the discovery of absolute truths and all judgments about the real nature of things were mere deceptions that inevitably resulted in contradictions and absurdities. We can apprehend the world only in terms of appearances, which are changing and uncertain; thus we can only try to live as best we can with life's contradictions while keeping faith in the possibilities of human achievement.

Montaigne's skepticism also led him to oppose religious, moral, and political dogmatism. Critical of accepted customs and values, which he often scorned as mere superstition, Montaigne displayed an admi-

rable ability to discuss and question openly nearly any subject related to how we live and what to live for. In several of the *Essays*, for instance, Montaigne condemned a number of legal practices common during the period, including torture, corporal punishment, and the persecution of witches. Montaigne's HUMANISM led him to speak against the cruelty found in human relationships, and he consistently argued for including more compassion in our treatment of one another. Montaigne was not an idealist, however, and he recognized the difficulty of achieving social and political TOLERATION due to the diversity of conflicting individual beliefs. In response, Montaigne suggested that toleration and the compassionate treatment of others required a stable system of laws in each country. Although complete JUSTICE was likely impossible even with the existence of good laws, Montaigne believed in the necessity of resisting dogmatic AUTHORITY for the sake of human LIBERTY.

Further Reading
Quint, D. *Montaigne and the Quality of Mercy: Ethical and Political Themes in the Essais.* Princeton, N.J.: Princeton University Press, 1998.

Montesquieu, Charles-Louis de Secondat, baron de (1689–1755) *French political philosopher and economist*

Most famous for his book, *The Spirit of the Laws* (1748), Montesquieu's ideas of a MODERN REPUBLIC, CHECKS AND BALANCES, and commercial VIRTUES made him celebrated in Europe and Early America. His principles of separation of powers in a CONSTITUTION greatly influence the Founders of the United States (especially James MADISON and Alexander HAMILTON in *The Federalist Papers*).

Montesquieu extolled the British constitution of a limited (figurehead) MONARCHY, representative parliamentary republic, and commercial EMPIRE. He felt that dividing and separating governmental powers (checks and balances) would form the most stable, just, and prosperous country. CAPITALIST ETHICS would promote the commercial virtues of "frugality, economy, moderation, work, prudence, tranquility, order, and rule." The British governments' promotion of commerce was a good thing, therefore. Modern republics, after ARISTOTLE's polis, encourage the virtues of EQUALITY, DEMOCRACY, and PATRIOTISM, as opposed to the predominant virtue of military honor in FEUDAL monarchies. But republics also enforce a dangerous kind of conformity and can stifle individual creativity and excellence. Also, Montesquieu asserted that a republic could not exist in a large country (which the U.S. FEDERALISM of Madison and Jefferson directly disputed) and so was confined to small states.

Montesquieu's emphasis on the "spirit" or culture of a nation's laws make him an early example of the sociological or anthropological approach to politics. Rather than the abstract principles of Lockean liberalism or MARXISM, his theory holds that a country's customs, religion, traditions, climate, size, and economy greatly affect its politics. ROUSSEAU later employed the view to explain why authoritarian Russia could not become democratic under Peter the Great. Britain's "spirit of commerce" (a peaceful, disciplined acquisition of PROPERTY and respect for LIBERTY) makes it an ideal prosperous republic.

This Modern, liberal, capitalist, republican ideal contrasted with Montesquieu's own France of monarchy and feudalism and caused him to lose favor in his own country. But he was celebrated as a noble and great political thinker throughout Europe and America in the 18th century.

His minor works include *The Persian Letters,* a satire of medieval Western values of CATHOLICISM and Aristotelian NATURAL LAW and informed by John LOCKE, SPINOZA, and Bayle. His *Consideration on the Causes of the Greatness of the Romans and Their Decline* (1734) addresses MACHIAVELLI'S REALISM and concludes that ancient pagan Rome was not representative of human evil, but rather was a perversion of humanity characteristic of degenerate republics. He does not embrace a CHRISTIAN or CLASSICAL Greek view of human moral and ethical capacities, but sees humans as animals with very limited intelligence, filled with desires and anxieties, longing for satisfaction, peace, and security. Unless this rather pathetic creature is directed to constructive activity of an economic sort (commercialism), he or she will become violent and destructive. Hence, Montesquieu's appreciation for the English—a peaceable, sturdy, republican people with limited, MODERATE, commercial and political aims. This British (and soon U.S.) MODERNITY is a standard for forward-looking diplomats and founders of governments. As Montesquieu proclaims in a famous quote: "The Greek political thinkers knew of no other power that could sustain popular government except that of VIRTUE; today we hear only of manufactures, commerce, finance, riches, and even luxury."

Consequently, he greatly influenced the ENLIGHTENMENT and Modern republics.

Further Readings
Pangle, T. L. *Montesquieu's Philosophy of Liberalism: A Commentary on "The Spirit of the Laws."* Chicago: University of Chicago Press, 1973.
Shackleton, R. *Montesquieu: A Critical Biography.* London: Oxford University Press, 1961.

Moral Majority

A CONSERVATIVE political group of the CHRISTIAN RIGHT in the United States. Founded in 1979 by BAPTIST leader Jerry Falwell, the Moral Majority championed RIGHT-wing causes (anticommunism and secular HUMANISM; profamily; prodefense; antipornography, antiabortion, pro-PRAYER IN SCHOOL, etc.). Representing about four million members (primarily white, fundamentalist Protestant Christians) the Moral Majority attacked LIBERAL, FEMINIST, HOMOSEXUAL, and social welfare policies in the U.S. government, media, schools, and business. Strong defenders of CAPITALISM, strict laws against crime (including capital punishment), and support for Israel, the Major Majority was largely ridiculed by the media, higher education, and the DEMOCRATIC PARTY. It was more accepted by the U.S. REPUBLICAN PARTY (especially under President Ronald REAGAN) and grass-roots conservatives. It registered an estimated three million new voters (among poor Southern whites primarily), but had negligible effects on presidential elections. With headquarters in Washington, D.C., it tried to influence national policy towards more TRADITIONAL Judeo-Christian values and conservative economics. Having achieved its goal of establishing the Religious Right in the public arena, its founders dissolved the Moral Majority in 1989. Its work is continued by many other conservative Christian policy organizations, like the Christian Coalition.

moral sense

The idea that humans have a "moral" sense (the physical senses of sight, hearing, taste, etc.) that naturally tells them what is good and how to do it. Associated with the SCOTTISH ENLIGHTENMENT thinkers (1740–90) Frances Hutcheson, Lord Kames, and Thomas Reid, this moral-sense philosophy affected American Thomas JEFFERSON's political theory. Generally with LIBERAL, optimistic tendencies, the idea that people had a good, benevolent, nature through this moral sense, led to a belief in the perfection of human society: political DEMOCRACY, legal and economic EQUALITY, and social JUSTICE. This positive view of human nature contrasted with the traditional Augustinian and Calvinist CHRISTIAN view of the human's innate sinful nature (redeemable only through Christ and good only by the Holy Spirit). By situating morality and ethics in a physical sense, these philosophers also tried to reconcile traditional grounds for justice with the new scientific materialism of their age. Now, good conduct didn't require great philosophy or religion (or grace), but simply the development and application of a natural human faculty that everyone possessed. Its implications were thus also EGALITARIAN and democratic. This view did, however, believe that some people were born with a keener moral sense than others (just as some have a better sense of hearing or smell), but even a "crippled" or deformed moral sense could be compensated for by training and cultivation. So even if a government would be best if governed by people of superior moral sense, those "disabled" in that faculty should be provided for by the society at large.

In some ways, this concept resembles ARISTOTLE's idea (in the *Politics*) of the human capacity for ethical judgment or knowledge of justice, the biblical idea of the knowledge of good and evil (Genesis 3:1–8), and St. Paul's view that everybody's conscience teaches them right and wrong (Romans 2:15). The moral sense merely places this moral capacity in a physical constitution rather than in reason or spirit.

More, Sir/St. Thomas (1478–1535) *English statesman, churchman, and political philosopher*

Most famous for his book UTOPIA, which continues the literature of ideal societies begun in PLATO's *Republic*, More represents the High MIDDLE AGES and RENAISSANCE in European political thought. He studied at Oxford and for the law at the Inns at Chancery. His brilliance led to a distinguished political career, culminating as lord chancellor of England under King HENRY VIII. Deeply religious, he wrote extensively on CHRISTIAN doctrine especially CATHOLIC/Protestant disputes. His home was an international center for the great thinkers of his age, including ERASMUS, Colet, and Groeyn. He refused to affirm the king's divorce and was executed for treason, making him an official martyr of the church. His resistance to civil authority on

religious grounds make him, like Dietrich BONHOEFFER later, a prominent figure in CHURCH-AND-STATE controversies.

More's principal work in political philosophy is the famous book *Utopia* (which means "no where")—a description of an ideal society and government. Like all utopian literature, More's book critiques present wrongs and social injustices of his time and prescribes ideal solutions. This medieval vision of the good Christian society is a mixture of traditional HIERARCHIES (in the family and state) and radical COMMUNISM (in the economy). This blending of conservative morality with SOCIALIST EQUALITY is sometimes compared to the Catholic monastery, where strict order and obedience mixes with FREEDOM and DEMOCRACY. That a religious community influences More's conception of the ideal state shows the depth of his faith and its relevance to his political thought. Also revealing his relating of religion and politics is the governing council of Utopia, which is made up of political and religious officials regulating every aspect of life for the common good. Rationality and intellectualism are valued by More but only if balanced by revelation (the Bible). The spiritual is always higher in importance, to More, than the worldly. He is particularly troubled by the widespread poverty in England, reflecting the rise of MODERN CAPITALISM and the decline of FEUDALISM, producing alarming numbers of paupers in the land. More's prescriptions of common property and laws against idleness seek to cure this economic ill in 16th-century England.

Thomas More is recognized as a great intellectual, churchman, and "Renaissance man," whose life and ideals changed history.

Further Readings
Fox, A. *Thomas More: History and Providence*. New Haven, Conn.: Yale University Press, 1982.
Guy, A. *The Public Career of Sir Thomas More*. New Haven, Conn.: Yale University Press, 1980.

multiculturalism

A movement and IDEOLOGY in American education and politics during the late 20th century. As opposed to a traditional view of United States culture as predominantly European, Judeo-CHRISTIAN, and Lockean LIBERAL, multiculturalism taught that the United States is a collection of equally valid cultures (African, Asian, Hindu, etc.) and that not to value all the same constitutes cultural IMPERIALISM. This ideological movement infused U.S. education (especially university education) and politics (especially the DEMOCRATIC PARTY) with alternative viewpoints (for example, African-American literature alongside Shakespeare; HOMOSEXUAL rights; New Age spirituality, etc.). Multicultural perspectives claim that non-Western philosophies have been underrepresented in U.S. education, economy, society, and government. Its political program, then, was to advance the "diversity" of non-Western, non-Christian, noncapitalist ideologies and persons.

Minimally, multiculturalism asserts the absolute EQUALITY of all cultures (rejecting the traditional view that Western civilization, Christianity, economics, and democracy are superior to African, Asian, Chinese, Islamic, etc. systems and assumptions). In its extreme form, multiculturalism claims that established Western (and U.S.) culture is bad—the source of all oppression, EXPLOITATION, war, racism, sexism, classism, and homophobia.

Conservatives often fault multicultural education, media, and politics for excessive EGALITARIANISM, destruction of valuable Western cultural traditions and standards, and deceived self-interest.

Muslim   See ISLAMIC.

N

National Socialism

The political movement and ideology of the German NAZI party led by Adolf HITLER from 1920–45. Like other FASCIST theories, national socialism asserted that a nation's salvation and prosperity required a national unity directed by a single-party, all powerful STATE led by a dynamic leader (Führer). The Hegelian idea of a universal will that is embodied in LAW contributed to this fascist vision. Besides this fascistic feature of Nazism (which it shared with Italian and Spanish fascism), German National Socialism added the racist idea that its Aryan race was by nature superior to all other peoples and was by destiny the "master race" of the world. This racial supremacy of Germany grew partly from NIETZSCHE's philosophy of a ruling culture.

Intellectually, this German fascism was less sophisticated than French fascist theory (Maurice Barrès or Charles Maurras) or Italian fascist philosophy (GENTILE). Only Alfred Rosenberg, in a book called *The Myth of the Twentieth Century,* and Hitler's *Mein Kampf* provide the theoretical basis for National Socialism, and they are incoherent and confused. German fascism is more a social and political phenomenon than a philosophical system. The success of the Nazi regime lay in its seeming to satisfy the conflicting needs of German society during the historical period between World War I and World War II (1918–39). Economic depression, the rise of COMMUNISM, destruction of traditional German culture, and the weakness of LIBERAL REPUBLICANISM all contributed to the appeal of the simple solutions offered by Hitler and the Nazis. By calling itself National "Socialism," this movement appealed to workers; its "nationalism" drew support from German conservatives, and its Aryan racism united the nation. Anti-Slavic and anti-Semitic features of Nazism provided convenient enemies on which to blame Germany's problems. Its international military aggressive followed Nazi Germany's view of its destiny to rule the world. The dictatorial leadership of Hitler and industrial power of Germany imposed National Socialism on several conquered nations (Poland, France, Austria), but it was not respected as a political theory. Since its defeat by its opponents in World War II (Britain, United States, Soviet Union), National Socialism has disappeared as an IDEOLOGY except for a few extreme RIGHT-wing groups.

Further Readings

Bullock, A. *Hitler: A Study in Tyranny.* New York: Harper & Row, 1962.
Nolte, E. *Three Faces of Fascism.* New York: Holt, Rinehart and Winston, 1965.

nationalism

An IDEOLOGY that places the nation at the center of importance and emphasizes people subordinating their other INTERESTS (personal, economic, class, religious) to the "common good" of the nation. This most extreme expression of nationalism occurred in German (NAZI) FASCISM (1920–45), in which all other considerations of German citizens were subordinated to the STATE and the leader (HITLER). Other fascist countries (Spain, Italy) and Soviet Russian COMMUNISM (under Joseph STALIN) exhibited extreme nationalism.

In nationalistic ideology, the individual's loyalty is to be first to his or her country and its interests, so friends, local community, culture, religion, and personal views are to be subjected to the national view of the state. Hence, PATRIOTISM is the premier social VIRTUE in nationalism.

During times of war or conflict between nations, nationalism naturally increases, even in culturally diverse countries such as Britain, the United States, and the Soviet Union. Milder forms of nationalism occur in countries by distinct regions or cultures, such as French Canada (Quebec), Ireland, Scotland, and Wales. These peaceful nationalistic movements within larger countries usually strive to gain greater political autonomy, influence, or recognition (as bilingualism in Canada—French and English—or Wales—English and Welsh). In the United States, several groups and regions (black or African American; Muslims; Hispanic or Spanish American in the Southwest; Jewish Americans) assert a form of separatist nationalism, but the DEMOCRATIC PLURALISM of the United States tends to subsume different cultures into a basically homogeneous nationality.

With the spread of global economics and international pacts and organizations, nationalism is declining in the 21st century.

Further Readings
Kohn, H. *The Idea of Nationalism.* New York: Macmillan, 1946.
Smith, A. D. *Theories of Nationalism.* New York: Harper & Row, 1971.

natural law

The idea or philosophy that there is an objective law and system in nature or the universe that prevails over individual human preference or social structures. Further, a natural law view asserts that if a person, society, or government does not conform to the laws of nature,

he or she—or they, if that be the case—will not function effectively and ultimately will be harmed and destroyed. Thus, natural law conceives of a given order of things that people should try to know and follow so that they will be prosperous and happy and enjoy JUSTICE in their lives and social relations. Political natural law theories say that states must adhere to this objective law to be just, stable, and healthy.

The earliest Western view of natural law occurs in the ancient Greek thinker ARISTOTLE with his TELEOLOGICAL philosophy. According to Aristotle, everything has a natural *telos*, or purpose, which its nature strives to attain or complete: An acorn, by nature, is made to become an oak tree; even if the acorn "wanted" to be a pine tree, its nature limits it to becoming an oak tree. Similarly, humans are made with certain capacities and limitations, and philosophy is devoted to learning that human nature so that people can be fulfilled in their proper place and end. Several surrounding social circumstances affect that purpose (family, economics, society, politics), so the government should arrange the environment to further that human development within the confines of natural law. Politics, for Aristotle, should follow nature.

ROMAN LAW as expressed in CICERO followed this natural law perspective, conceiving of a universally valid code that applied to all the different nations and cultures within the Roman Empire.

CHRISTIAN political thought (St. AUGUSTINE, St. Thomas AQUINAS) applies this natural-law view through the Bible and church teaching. In this, humans are made by God with a certain nature (in his own image, creative, with free will and reason, etc.). Human sin and pride rebels against God's order and law; people putting themselves in God's place leads to disorder and death. St. Thomas Aquinas provides the most elaborate depiction of Christian natural law in his *Summa Theologica.* He details three levels of law: divine, natural, and human. Divine or God's universal law encompasses everything. Natural law is that part of divine law that governs nature (the planets, animals, plants, humans). After Aristotle, St. Thomas Aquinas holds that each thing has a given goal or purpose that limits its possibilities. Sin and pride cause people to try to live outside their natural-law limits, but that leads to disaster. Humans, for example, are not made by nature to fly, so jumping off a building leads to injury and death. Any violation of natural law has serious negative consequences. So, a government, or human law, should conform to divine and natural law to have the best society. A political law or system that ignores natural law will not last long and will bring problems and suffering on its people. The way to know natural law, for Aquinas, is through reason, scripture, experience, and tradition. The church should advise the state on divine and natural law. This THOMIST natural-law philosophy still informs CATHOLIC Church social theory. For example, the Catholic opposition to easy divorce laws is that Christ and nature teach that the purpose of marriage is procreation (having children) and is to be lifelong; allowing frequent divorce in a society, then, according to the Catholic Church, violates natural law and leads to many social problems (juvenile delinquency, crime, homosexuality, alcoholism, suicide, etc.). Similarly, natural-law logic explains the Catholic Church's opposition to ABORTION. The end, or *telos*, of the fetus is to develop and be born. Interrupting that purpose violates natural law (the mother's affection for her child; the fetus development into human life, etc.) and leads to problems (guilt, the devaluing of human life, etc.). So, Thomist natural law places limits on what humans and societies should do. A system (idolatrous NAZI FASCISM) or practice (HOMOSEXUALITY) that disregards God's natural law will produce disastrous personal and political consequences, according to Catholic Church thought.

In the MODERN period, natural law theory is applied to international politics by Hugo GROTIUS and to market economics by Adam SMITH. Early NATURAL-RIGHTS liberal philosophy (in John LOCKE, Thomas JEFFERSON) is beholden to the natural-law school. The American DECLARATION OF INDEPENDENCE and James MADISON's U.S. CONSTITUTION reflect natural-law philosophy: that a God-given Nature system can be known through reason and that the governmental structure can be constructed to conform to it, producing an orderly, stable, and just state and society.

MEDIEVAL European society applied natural-law thought to every aspect of life: individual psychology, politics, and the universe. Shakespeare portrays the need for order in the individual (reason over passion), the society (good over evil), and cosmos ("God's in His heaven and all's right with the world"). A disordered person can throw off the whole polity and even the natural universe itself.

The rise of POSITIVISM, materialism, and ethical relativism in the 19th and 20th centuries reduces the prevalence of natural-law doctrine. Personal preference, imagination, popular opinion, and majoritarian politics challenge the idea that humans have given laws and limits. Technology and science claim to transcend and transform nature.

natural rights

The idea that humans have certain rights by nature that no government can legitimately violate or justly take away. These natural rights, in John LOCKE's phrase, include "Life, LIBERTY, and PROPERTY." The state in this LIBERAL theory is created to protect and preserve these INDIVIDUAL, natural rights (against criminal murder, theft, slavery, etc.).

The original concept of natural HUMAN RIGHTS to be protected by the government occurs in the ancient Roman Empire, in which Roman citizens enjoyed certain rights (especially to a fair trial and against cruel treatment) anywhere in the imperial realm (Israel, Germany, Britain, etc.).

Natural-rights philosophy became prominent in 17th-century British liberal political theory (Thomas HOBBES and John LOCKE) and 18th-century American democratic thought (Thomas JEFFERSON, James MADISON). For Hobbes, humans in their natural state (or STATE OF NATURE) have a right to everything each can get by physical power (including theft, murder, kidnapping). This absolute natural right of everyone to everything leads to competition and violence. The state is formed by human reason into a SOCIAL CONTRACT, which gives power to a sovereign ruler who protects citizen's lives. The only right retained in CIVIL SOCIETY for Hobbes is the right to life; the state controls everything else (property, communications, religion, economics). Locke's theory modifies the ABSOLUTIST state to a more limited state that protects the natural rights to life against murder of injury; LIBERTY (of movement, thought, expression, and religion); and PROPERTY (ownership, exchange, and investment). If the state violates these citizens' rights, the people have a "right to revolution" to change their government to one that protects their rights. Such natural-rights theory is encoded in several historical documents (for example, the English Bill of Rights of 1689; the French Declaration of the Rights of Man and Citizen of 1789; the American DECLARATION OF INDEPENDENCE, 1776, and CONSTITUTION's Bill of Rights, 1791; and the United Nations' Declaration of Human Rights, 1948).

Many applications and extensions of these human rights occur in contemporary Western society (women's rights; gay rights; children's rights; rights for the disabled; ANIMAL RIGHTS; and the right to life of the unborn against ABORTION). Most political issues in MODERN society are discussed in terms of someone's rights. The effect of this is to make government primarily interested in balancing the rights of conflicting individuals or groups, for example, the rights of children versus the rights of doctors or hospitals; the rights of minorities versus the rights of the majority. Usually, the state sides with those individuals or groups who are most vulnerable or weak (the aged, the unborn, minorities, the mentally disabled, etc.), who cannot defend their own rights. Society, then, tries to achieve JUSTICE by balancing the rights and INTERESTS of its various members. Often, as in the U.S. constitutional Bill of Rights (first ten amendments), this entails judicial procedures to ensure a fair hearing or trial (impartial judge and jury, aid of counsel, speedy and public trial, etc.). Human rights then is both a constant and an evolving concept.

Nazi

The National Socialist German Workers Party (1919–45) led by Adolf HITLER and establishing the FASCIST state in Germany. See NATIONAL SOCIALISM and FASCISM.

Further Reading
Bullock, A. *Hitler: A Study in Tyranny*. New York: Harper & Row, 1962.

neo-Platonism

A philosophy of IDEALISM that affected several political thinkers, notably J. J. ROUSSEAU, G. W. F. HEGEL, T. H. GREEN, FASCISM, COMMUNISM, and COMMUNITARIAN thought. Developed by the Roman philosopher Plotinus, after PLATO, this school of thought conceived of reality as a One, all-sufficient Unity from which all particulars emanate or come. The One or Universal produces the Divine Mind or Logos (Word), which contains all living individuals. The material world is a part of the World Soul. The goal of the separate individual is to become "one" with this unity, losing oneself in the infinite. Soon this philosophy, like Eastern mysticism (Chinese, Hindu) became involved in divination, spiritism, demonology, and astrology. In contemporary religions, it appears in the NEW AGE MOVEMENT. St. AUGUSTINE attempted to turn this philos-

ophy to CHRISTIANITY through the Holy Spirit, and St. Thomas AQUINAS identified this One with God and the Divine Mind with angels.

Politically, neo-Platonism often contributed to TOTALITARIAN regimes, which saw the STATE as the "One" to which all individuals and groups must be subordinated and subsumed. Fascism probably is the most clear expression of this, but Rousseau's GENERAL WILL, MARX's perfect communism and some contemporary U.S. communitarian thought flirts with it.

New Age Movement

A social and religious movement in the late 20th century, primarily in the United States. Drawing on Eastern mysticism (see HINDU POLITICAL THOUGHT), spiritism, and the occult, New Age philosophy emphasizes the unlimited powers of the individual's unlocked mind, astrology, communication or "channeling" with dead people, and individual self-realization. Politically, the INDIVIDUALISM and self-deification of New Age believers lends itself to LIBERTARIAN and ANARCHIST sympathies. Because a "new age" will soon usher in a world of peace and prosperity, political or ethical involvement is not essential. With a positive view of HUMAN NATURE shared with the ENLIGHTENMENT, New Age ideology rejects traditional CHRISTIAN views of human sin and the need for God (as found in St. AUGUSTINE, John CALVIN, and others who influenced the founding of America).

New Deal

A series of social programs developed by the Liberal DEMOCRATIC PARTY in the United States during the 1930s under the leadership of President Franklin ROOSEVELT. This was in response to the Great Depression, a period of economic stagnation, low production, and high unemployment in the industrial world from 1929 to World War II. The New Deal tried to remedy this economic crisis by regulating the economy from the central (federal) government in Washington, D.C., providing public-works employment and social welfare to the poor, and (public) borrowing and spending by the national government to stimulate the private, CAPITALIST economy. Federal agencies (BUREAUCRACY) increased tremendously with the "alphabet soup" of new government programs: the National Recovery Administration (NRA), the Agricultural Adjustment

Administration (AAA), the Civilian Conservation Corps (CCC), and so on. The CONSERVATIVE U.S. Supreme Court declared most of these New Deal programs unconstitutional as granting the federal government excessive power, violating PROPERTY and contract rights, and giving the executive branch too much AUTHORITY. U.S. conservatives (especially business) saw the liberal New Deal as quasi-SOCIALIST (state-owned and -planned economy). Radical LEFTISTS accused it of being FASCISM (state control of capitalist property). Most historians later saw it as a compromise solution, developing a mixed economy of capitalism with extensive government regulation for the common good. Relying on Keynesian economic theories, the New Deal did not completely end the economic Depression, but it addressed the most severe symptoms (starvation, homelessness), which probably prevented extreme political results (like NAZISM in Germany and COMMUNISM in Russia).

Debate over the wisdom and effectiveness of the New Deal liberalism continue, but most of its general features (such as Social Security) are widely accepted in the United States and other Western democracies.

New Left

As opposed to the "Old Left" (early 1900s MARXISTS, COMMUNISTS, and SOCIALISTS associated with orthodox Soviet thinkers), the "New Left" consisted most of intellectual Marxists and Liberals in the 1960s and 1970s. Like CRITICAL-THEORY figures Herbert MARCUSE and Max HORKHEIMER, most New Left thinkers focused less on economic issues (class struggle) and more on the cultural, social, and sexual aspects of CAPITALIST oppression. They greatly affected university academic life, the media, religion, and the arts in the United States and Western Europe. Though declining in influence since the CONSERVATIVE revival in the 1980s and 1990s, the New Left ideology persists in the "POLITICALLY CORRECT" movement, ENVIRONMENTALISM, and the liberal wing of the U.S. DEMOCRATIC PARTY. A continuing theme of the New Left was to attack most AUTHORITY (in schools, government, family, and business) as "domination" and to "liberate" all oppressed individuals and groups (the poor, minorities, workers, women, gays, lesbians, transsexuals, and animals). Members of the New Left universally opposed the Vietnam War (being actively involved in the peace movement), but they disagreed on positive social strategy (from WEL-FARE-STATE liberalism to socialism, communism, and ANARCHISM). From the height of its influence in U.S. politics (with the Democratic Party nomination of George McGovern), it has declined as both political parties have become more MODERATE.

Further Reading
Long, P. *The New Left.* Indianapolis: Bobbs-Merrill, 1969.

New Right

A political group and IDEOLOGY in the United States and Britain in the 1980s and 1990s, associated with President Ronald REAGAN in the United States and Prime Minister Margaret Thatcher in Great Britain. This "New Right" applies the ideals of the "Old Right" of the 19th century, LAISSEZ-FAIRE CONSERVATISM (free-market CAPITALISM, limited government regulation of business, lower taxes, increased military spending). Sometimes call neo-Conservatives (such as William BENNETT, William F. BUCKLEY), these New Right thinkers also advocate traditional morality, discipline, authority, and religion, linking them politically with the CHRISTIAN RIGHT (Marion "Pat" ROBERTSON). Besides being a prominent presence in the U.S. REPUBLICAN PARTY, the New Right exercises influence in various conservative institutes (such as the American Enterprise Institute) and conservative media (such as CBN, the *Washington Times,* and radio commentators Rush Limbaugh and Oliver North). Although partly responsible for the Conservative shift in national politics in the United States and Britain, the New Right has not been able to dominate the prevailing MODERATE politics of either political party.

Further Reading
Levita, R., ed. *The Ideology of the New Right.* Oxford, Eng.: Blackwell Publishers, 1986.

Newman, John Henry (Cardinal) (1801–1890)
British churchman and leader of the Oxford Movement

Raised in an EVANGELICAL environment associated with parliamentary DEMOCRACY (as in the PURITANS, Oliver CROMWELL), Newman became a great exponent for the Anglo CATHOLIC Oxford Movement (usually associated with European MONARCHY and FEUDALISM). This ecclesiastical/political transformation occurred over many years, but it greatly affected (and reflected) British and

U.S. conservatism in the 19th century. It was a logical consequence that Newman finally broke completely with the Protestant Anglican Church and became an official of the Roman Catholic HIERARCHY.

Educated at Trinity College, Oxford University, Newman remained at Oxford for much of his career (fellow of Oriel College, vicar of St. Mary's Cathedral). He tried to strike a "middle way" between dissenters and papists with an Anglican *via media* but soon drifted toward Catholicism. He is most famous for his inaugural lecture as Rector of Dublin University "The Idea of a University" (1852) which presents a CLASSICAL definition of a liberal arts education.

Niebuhr, Reinhold (1892–1971) *American political and religious philosopher*

Famous for his development of CHRISTIAN REALISM, Niebuhr applied the theology of St. AUGUSTINE to the 20th-century world. From the neo-orthodoxy perspective, he criticized the vain illusions of both COMMUNISM and ENLIGHTENMENT LIBERALISM to pretend to create JUSTICE and peace in this world. Like James MADISON, Niebuhr believed that the reality of human sin prevented people from ever being able to remove injustice, corruption, and oppression from politics. Human pride and self-deception is worst in utopian, IDEALISTIC, and "progressive" schemes such as SOCIALISM. Social reformers often are blind to their own selfishness and sinful pride, and they consequently turn out to be cruel rulers. The great challenge in the 20th century, for Niebuhr, was to improve society humbly without being seduced by the prideful illusions of grandeur that lead to TOTALITARIAN regimes (like FASCIST NAZI Germany, Soviet Communism, etc.).

Part of Niebuhr's Christian realism led him to oppose U.S. isolationism and PACIFISM in the 1930s that kept the United States out of World War II for that decade. He insisted that certain forms of evil were demonic (HITLER's Nazi government) and must be opposed militarily.

In his books, *Moral Man and Immoral Society* (1932) and *Humun Nature and Destiny* (1942), Niebuhr endorses the "tolerable justice" of American constitutional DEMOCRACY (CHECKS AND BALANCES) that divides and limits the power of interest groups and individuals.

Educated at Elmhurst College, Eden, and Yale Divinity Schools, Niebuhr taught ETHICS at Union Seminary in New York City. He admired Abraham LINCOLN for that president's application of religious knowledge to political and historical events. Niebuhr was active in Liberal DEMOCRATIC PARTY politics but warned continually of the temptations to self-righteous pride among U.S. liberals and reformers. He is considered one of the deepest thinkers in religion and politics in the 20th century.

Further Readings
Davis, H. R., and Good, R. C., eds. *Reinhold Niebuhr on Politics.* New York: Scribners, 1960.
Niebuhr,R. *Moral Man and Immoral Society.* New York: Scribners, 1932.

Nietzsche, Friedrich, Wilhelm (1844–1900) *German philosopher*

Nietzsche is one of the most compelling and controversial philosophers of the MODERN era, whose thought has had a profound effect on many POST-MODERN thinkers. Born in Saxony, Prussia, Nietzsche was raised in a devout Christian home. His father, a Lutheran minister, died when Nietzsche was five years old. Nietzsche attended the boarding school of Pforta where he studied religion, literature and classical languages, and philosophy. In 1864, Nietzsche attended the University of Bonn, and the next year, he transferred to the University of Leipzig, continuing his studies in classical philology. It was during his studies at the universities of Bonn and Leipzig that Nietzsche abandoned Christianity. Nietzsche was appointed to his only university post, as professor of classical philology at the University of Basel in Switzerland, at the age of 24, but he retired 10 years later due to ill health. For the next 10 years, Nietzsche wrote a large number of works, including *Beyond Good and Evil* (1886), *On the Genealogy of Morals* (1887), and *Thus Spake Zarathustra* (1883–85), until becoming mentally ill. Nietzsche's writings explore the place of moral and aesthetic value in human existence through a merciless critique of Judeo-Christianity and traditional metaphysics captured in the phrase "God is dead."

Nietzsche's philosophy is notoriously difficult and often misunderstood. With respect to questions of knowledge, Nietzsche believed that truths are the artificial results of creative acts of interpretation, and not natural essences or objective facts that exist apart from interpretation. Consequently, knowledge can never be impartial because it is always constructed from some particular point of view. Nevertheless, Nietzsche did not adhere to a simple relativism that all interpretations are equally good. Even though knowledge is the product of certain interpretations of reality, Nietzsche argued that some points of view or interpretations are more valuable than others. In particular, those interpretations that promote what Nietzsche called the will to power—the universal venting of life and the basic drive of individuals to control their own intentions and actions—have more value for human existence than interpretations that inhibit will to power. In Nietzsche's view, values reflect the different capabilities of individuals to exert their force or power toward some goal, expressed in different moral codes.

Nietzsche argued that Christian morality represents a "slave" or "herd" morality that is destroying the health and strength of humanity in general and of noble persons or "free spirits" in particular. Noble types exhibit a "master" morality that celebrates powerful, aristocratic individuals and the virtues of strength, courage, individuality, and risk-taking; slave morality, however, esteems the common person and the virtues of humility, meekness, self-denial, and prudence. Master morality is characterized by the act of self-affirmation, and slave morality is characterized by the act of other-negation, driven by resentment of the free and powerful. Parts of NAZI IDEOLOGY were thought to be influenced by the ideas of will to power and master morality. Historically, Nietzsche suggested, slave morality has become the dominant value system with the result that society now valorizes sameness and obedience and condemns difference and independence.

Nietzsche therefore believed that Christian morality takes on a secular form in the leveling ideologies of EGALITARIANISM and DEMOCRACY. He contended that the modern notions of equal worth and equal rights are signs of mass weakness, generated by fear of naturally superior individuals. Modern democratic societies, he believed, have developed out of the triumph of slave morality in its struggle against the master morality. According to Nietzsche's metaphysics, however, the struggle of the common person against the aristocratic person is also a struggle against life itself. For Nietzsche, inequality is an inherent phenomenon of life, and inequality should be allowed to thrive between humans because some are superior and others are inferior. In Nietzsche's view, the democratic denial of inequality has led to a progressive degeneration of human excellence. In response, Nietzsche recom-

mended the disciplined pursuit of an individual self-creation that transcended the norms of conventional morality.

Further Reading
Ansell-Pearson, K. *An Introduction to Nietzsche as a Political Thinker.* Cambridge, Eng.: Cambridge University Press, 1994.

Nixon, Richard Milhous (1913–1994)   *U.S. president and politician*

A CONSERVATIVE member of the REPUBLICAN PARTY. Nixon was known for his fervent antiCOMMUNISM in the 1950s. As U.S. president (1969–74), however, Nixon displayed MODERATE positions on economic and civil rights issues. He normalized diplomatic relations with (communist) China and reduced tensions with the SOVIET UNION.

Unfortunately, Nixon's long public career is primarily remembered for "Watergate"—an incident of political corruption and abuse of power that led to his resigning as president (the only presidential resigna-

Richard M. Nixon. (LIBRARY OF CONGRESS)

tion in U.S. history) rather than face impeachment. Nixon and Watergate became synonymous with *corruption* in American political and social life, so that even later scandals had the word *gate* attached to them (Post-Office-gate; Bill Clinton's "Bimbo-gate," etc.).

Nozick, Robert (1938–) *U.S. political philosopher, libertarian*

Best known for his popular book *Anarchy, State and Utopia* (1974), which presents a classic contemporary LIBERTARIAN theory, Nozick provides a philosophical argument for CONSERVATIVE, LAISSEZ-FAIRE, REPUBLICAN PARTY IDEOLOGY. His emphasis on INDIVIDUALISM, free-market CAPITALISM, low taxes and government regulations, and private FREEDOM make him a favorite among business interests. President Ronald REAGAN's policies reflected some of Nozick's ideals.

Nozick begins with ordinary LIBERAL assumptions about HUMAN NATURE, drawn from John LOCKE's NATURAL-RIGHTS philosophy. Individuals "have rights" by nature that no government can legitimately take away (life, liberty, and PROPERTY). This view leads to Nozick's theory of the minimalist state, which protects individual rights (through the police and judicial system) but otherwise leaves people alone to take care of themselves through private contracts. Most of life's activities (family, education, health care, housing, etc.) should be taken care of in the private economy, not by the government. Nozick is particularly adamant about the state not doing two things: (1) forcing some people (the wealthy) to help other people (the poor) through legal taxation and redistribution of property; and (2) having legal prohibitions on activities that only endanger those engaged in them (such as illegal drug use and prostitution)—so-called victimless crimes. These objections to the WELFARE STATE (with widespread social programs for the needy) and the moral government (with laws against sinful activities) show the ANARCHIST bent of Nozick's thought.

For him, the ideal society would leave people free to fend for themselves, sell their talents on the open marketplace, make private contracts with others, keep most of their income, and live with the consequences of their decisions. Everyone will function best in this environment, and the society will prosper. Like earlier SOCIAL DARWINISM, Nozick's libertarianism leaves the poor, disabled, and helpless to their own devices and any private charity they can get. In his famous "Wilt Chamberlain example," Nozick shows how money earned by one's sale of talent or goods is personal property that only unjustly is taxed to give to others more needy. This contrasts with John RAWLS's theory of justice, which places one's talents within social obligation.

But Nozick, who teaches philosophy at Harvard University, claims this utopia of a minimalist state allows for private charity and even SOCIALISM (in private organizations). He envisions a "smorgasbord" (or "food bar") of societies in the perfect country (some COMMUNIST, some religious, some laissez-faire, etc.), where each individual may choose the best one for them. Such relativistic anarchy ignores the unity of society for critics of Nozick, and the need for some shared values to prevent chaos and destruction. But besides the appeal of Nozick's theories to wealthy businesspeople, they provide a certain prophetic voice of contemporary America, which, through cable, television, private schools, and the Internet, increasingly has become a society of separate, isolated communities and alienated individuals.

Oakeshott, Michael (1901–1990) *British political philosopher*

Like Edmund BURKE, Oakeshott emphasizes the importance of TRADITIONAL culture and custom to politics. He rejects radical rationalist, or utopian, thought that prescribes reforms without taking into account past social practices and institutions. For this reason, he is considered CONSERVATIVE. In his book *On Human Conduct* (1975), Oakeshott maintains that political or civic philosophy involves analyzing the practices (prudential and moral) of a society, identifying the ideal character of a civilization, and integrating rules or procedures with ETHICAL standards. This implies that civil association is more than an economic association but includes a common commitment to a shared moral vision. A country (or REPUBLIC) can legitimately expect members to abide by the prevailing moral code, even if they can criticize the procedures for implementing and enforcing it. Aside from this public commonality exists private enterprise, or what John LOCKE termed *CIVIL SOCIETY*, which operates within the social norms. This reflects a kind of traditional modern conservative British thought.

Further Reading
Greenleaf, W. H. *Oakeshott's Philosophical Politics*. London: Longman's, 1966.

obligation

In political thought, obligation means a duty that an individual, group, or society has to another because of an agreement, COVENANT, or contract. So, in John LOCKE's theory of the SOCIAL CONTRACT, the citizens who form the government (to protect their RIGHTS) have an obligation to obey the laws. This is related to CONSENT, which implies that once a person enjoys the benefits of society (defense, protection of rights, peace, economy, education, etc.), he or she is obliged to obey the laws and support the government. Similar to "obedience," this idea goes back to the Judeo-CHRISTIAN religious tradition that enjoins people to acknowledge God as the giver and protector of life, obeying his COMMANDMENTS and serving his purposes. Earlier states (Greece, Rome, China) based political obligation on force, domination and absolutist power, but MODERN LIBERAL theory balances rights with obligations. NATURAL-LAW philosophy ties an individual's moral obligations to their objective condition and circumstances. So, for example, CATHOLIC social philosophy (St. AUGUSTINE) would say that the action of being involved in sexual relations carries the obligation to keep and raise any child produced by that activity. St. Thomas AQUINAS might say that the subjects' obedience to a ruler creates the king's obligation to rule in the common inter-

223

est. A condition or place in society brings responsibilities or obligations with it. FREEDOM is balanced by duty, responsibility, and obligation in much of Western political thought.

Further Readings
Flathman, R. *Political Obligation*. New York: Atheneum, 1972.
Green, T. H. *Lectures on the Principles of Political Obligation*. London: Longmans, 1882, 1966.

orthodoxy

Literally, "true doctrine." In political thought, the various theories or systems that claimed to be the one true interpretation or institution, for example, the Eastern Orthodox Church of Christianity (Greek Orthodox; Russian Orthodox) that split from the Western (CATHOLIC) Church and still claim to represent the one true faith. Consequently, the Orthodox churches often align themselves with the STATE, becoming the official government church, and persecute other CHRISTIAN churches (denying FREEDOM of religion or LIBERTY of conscience).

Another common reference for the term *orthodox* is *orthodox MARXISM*. This refers to the Russian or Soviet communist view of the ideas of Karl MARX, and the SOCIALIST system established in the SOVIET UNION (1917–87). So, *orthodox COMMUNISM* or *Soviet orthodoxy* means the emphasis in MARXISM-LENINISM on economic determinism and class conflict, violent revolution, the dictatorship of the proletariat, a bureaucratic central government, secret police, etc. Sometimes this is connected with the Soviet dictator Joseph STALIN or Stalinism. Later, Western Marxism (CRITICAL THEORY) rejected this authoritarian orthodox Marxism for more DEMOCRATIC socialism.

Owen, Robert (1771–1853) *British utopian socialist*

As a cotton-mill owner in New Lanark, England, Owen experimented with SOCIALIST community ideas.

He argued that social ills (ignorance, poverty, crime) were due to environmental factors (slums, overwork, lack of education) and could be cured through healthy DEMOCRATIC, EGALITARIAN communities. Through highly controlled education, economics, and politics, all social problems could be cured. Owen saw his planned socialist experiments as more rational than the prevailing Victorian English social, religious, and economic system. The three great barriers to progress for Owen were religion, marriage, and private PROPERTY. He attacked the church for promoting superstition and an unjust view of human nature (as sinful). Still, he saw his socialist communities as ushering in the "Second Coming of Christ," an early expression of SOCIAL-GOSPEL and LIBERATION-THEOLOGY views.

Unlike MARXIST communism, Owen preferred small agricultural communes, maintaining that a population of 1,000 to 2,000 people on 600 to 1,800 acres of land was ideal. He saw INDUSTRIALISM as increasing wealth but suspected that it would devalue work. Like French utopian socialist Charles FOURIER, he remained an agrarian thinker. Money also was suspect, as true socialism would involve exchange of goods and labor according to need. This positive view of human nature and economic development formed the basis of later sociology, but it remains contrary to free-market CAPITALIST ideas of individual self-interest, competition, and economic growth.

Owen started a utopian socialist community in the United States (New Harmony, Indiana) that was positively received by Thomas JEFFERSON but viewed with skepticism by James MADISON (because of his Calvinist Christian view of people's innate sinful selfish nature).

Although ridiculed by both radical communists and liberal CONSERVATIVES as impractical, Owen had a tremendous effect on progressive British politics (toward democracy, public education, trade unionism, health care, and economic EQUALITY). He is remembered as a kinder, gentler socialist than MARX, ENGELS, or LENIN.

Further Reading
Pollard, S., and Salt, J., eds. *Robert Owen—Prophet of the Poor.* Lewisburg, Pa.: Bucknell University Press, 1971.

P

pacifism

The belief that all war is wrong and that only peaceful means of resolving conflicts (rational discussion, mediation, prayer) are morally legitimate. Pacifists assert that participation in the military and war is wrong, even if their own country is threatened (i.e., self-defense) or if war is waged to protect innocent victims of aggression. Most pacifism is based in religious convictions, but some comes out of HUMANIST or economic considerations.

The origin of pacifism is CHRISTIANITY, especially the Judeo-Christian commandment against murder and Christ's injunction to "resist not evil." Early in church history, many Christians refused to serve in the imperial Roman armies, causing widespread persecution of Christians as "unpatriotic." The CATHOLIC teaching that God's family crosses national boundaries proscribed killing one's "brothers" in warfare. This pacifist Christianity eventually evolved into JUST-WAR DOCTRINE, allowing the faithful to engage in war to defend oneself, protect the innocent, and as a last resort (after negotiations). Many Christian groups still adhere to pacifist positions, however (notably, Quakers, Mennonites, and Jehovah's Witnesses), all of whom practice CONSCIENTIOUS OBJECTION by refusing to serve in the military. This is permitted in the United States, but several other countries jail pacifists for refusing military service.

During the Middle Ages, the code of chivalry and military honor discouraged pacifism, even during the Crusades. Some Renaissance thinkers, such as ERASMUS, criticized the barbaric side of war, attacking its MEDIEVAL glorification. ENLIGHTENMENT LIBERALISM believed that DEMOCRACY, human reason, and economic FREEDOM would eliminate war. After the Napoleonic Wars (1814), several peace treaties ensured European order until World War I. The 20th-century wars destroyed any illusions of human PROGRESS away from violence. Still, pacifist movements developed, especially against nuclear weapons and against the Vietnam War. Certain ideologies were inherently pacifist, at least in theory. MARXIST-LENINIST COMMUNISM opposed "CAPITALIST imperialist" wars, and some working class groups refused military service. ANARCHISM opposed most wars but not all violent revolution. Leo Tolstoy, Mohandas GANDHI, and Martin Luther KING, Jr., advocated nonviolent resistance to social injustice. Some pacifists now oppose nationalistic wars but accept military action by international organizations (such as the United Nations). Most pacifists believe that violence and war as means lead to destructive ends, and therefore military force is ineffective. Reinhold NIEBUHR disagreed, citing people's inherent evil and the inevitability of aggression.

Further Readings

Brock, P. *Twentieth Century Pacifism.* New York: Van Nostrand Reinhold, 1970.

Mayer, P., ed. *The Pacifist Conscience.* New York: Holt, Rinehart and Winston, 1966.

Paine, Thomas (1737–1809) *British/American political philosopher and revolutionary*

Best known for his political pamphlet "Common Sense," which argued for the cause of the American Revolution, Paine was a radical REPUBLICAN thinker who also wrote *Rights of Man* and *The Age of Reason,* for which he received worldwide fame. Born into a poor working-class family in Norfolk, England, Paine was raised in the moralistic Quaker faith. He immigrated to America after losing his job, wife, and social standing by working for labor causes. There, he immediately became active in American revolutionary causes, encouraging the colonists' resistance to Britain, working in General Washington's army, and writing a liberal state CONSTITUTION for Pennsylvania (which included universal SUFFRAGE, annual elections, representative government, and religious FREEDOM).

After the successful conclusion of the American Revolution, Paine traveled to Europe to help with the French Revolution (1789). He encouraged the French republic but was later imprisoned by the radical JACOBINS' "Reign of Terror," barely escaping being executed. In France, he wrote the book *Rights of Man,* assailing Edmund BURKE'S CONSERVATIVE criticism of the French Revolution. There, Paine also wrote *The Age of Reason,* attacking established religion and CHRISTIANITY (which even offended Thomas JEFFERSON and Benjamin FRANKLIN). His criticism of MONARCHY and aristocratic government (still prevalent in Europe and Britain) made him one of the most RADICAL democrats of his time. Without the subtlety and education of a Jefferson or MADISON, Paine's bluntness offended many middle-class people but appealed to the poor, common people.

Paine's political philosophy was basically the SOCIAL-CONTRACT, NATURAL-RIGHTS theories of John LOCKE: people have rights to Life, LIBERTY, and PROPERTY that governments are created, by CONSENT of the people, to protect; and if the state violates those natural rights, the people collectively can overthrow the government. From this MODERN, LIBERAL perspective, the

Thomas Paine. (NATIONAL ARCHIVES)

old MEDIEVAL politics of kings, hereditary noblemen, official state churches, fixed social classes, and human inequality were a fraud and a crime. Waste, war, corruption, and expense result from traditional HIERARCHICAL government, and only representative DEMOCRACY is just. This attack on the very foundations of British political culture caused Paine to be outlawed for seditious libel and forever banished from his homeland.

Paine further developed his radical political ideas in his book *Agrarian Justice,* which advanced almost SOCIALIST ideas. He advocates the WELFARE-STATE proposals of universal public education, poor relief, shelters for the indigent and infirm, maternity grants, and progressive income and inheritance taxes. Though most of these policies are now common in Western democracies, they were exceedingly radical in the 18th century. So, Paine can be seen as an exceptionally forward-looking thinker, seeing the need for a mixed private/public economy in Modern industrial societies. He even proposed giving a large sum of money to each citizen at age 21 (to set them up) and a pension to all people older than 50. The "social-welfare" programs were to be financed by the savings from eliminating the costly monarchy and ARISTOCRACY, along with taxes on the wealthy. Still, Paine adhered to Adam SMITH's free-market economic theories and belief that CAPITAL-IST commerce would reconcile social interests and create prosperity.

He extolled the new American republic but found when he returned to the United States in 1802 that his radical democratic and deistic ideas made him unpopular. The Conservative FEDERALISTS vilified him as a dangerous French radical and the growing EVANGELICAL Christian population resented his attacks on religion. Paine was granted a farm by the state of New York, honoring his service in the American Revolution, but he died poor, lonely, and isolated in 1809.

Further Readings

Foner, E. *Tom Paine and Revolutionary America*. Oxford, Eng.: Oxford University Press, 1976.
Williamson, A. *Thomas Paine: His Life, Work and Time*. New York: St. Martin's Press, 1973.

Pangle, Thomas (1944–) *North American political philosopher and academic*

A prominent political theorist of the Straussian school, Pangle adopts the Platonic concern for clarifying conventional notions of JUSTICE. His writing has as its unifying aim the clarification and defense of the original Socratic view of political philosophy: the conversation refutations that purify commonsense notions of justice and nobility, of self-knowledge and an inquiry into HUMAN NATURE as the highest and most fulfilling aspect of human existence. Pangle's scholarship on CLASSICAL political thought show how the Socratic arguments for the supremacy of intellectual virtues shape and enrich the CLASSICAL REPUBLICAN teachings on civic and moral virtues and the spiritual goals of true self-governance. His studies of MEDIEVAL and biblical thought revive the mutually challenging dialogue between the classical and Western spiritual notions of wisdom, virtue, and civic justice. Pangle's interpretations of the philosophical bases of the American founding, grounded in both John LOCKE and MONTESQUIEU, along with his analysis of NIETZSCHE, argue for the significance within modernity of a continued if dramatically eclipsed commitment to the life of understanding for its own sake, while diagnosing the effects on civic life and intellec-

tual pursuits of the contemporary diminution of moral and intellectual virtues in Modern republicanism. Pangle, thus, is a contemporary political philosopher of unusual depth and breadth, who has greatly influenced 20th-century academic political theory and social criticism.

Educated at Cornell University and the University of Chicago, Professor Pangle has taught at Yale, Dartmouth, Chicago, the University of Toronto, Canada, and the École des Hautes Études en Sciences Sociales, Paris. Winner of numerous academic awards (including a Guggenheim Fellowship), Pangle has lectured worldwide and is a fellow of the Royal Society of Canada. His books include *Montesquieu's Philosophy of Liberalism*; *The Laws of Plato*; *The Spirit of Modern Republicanism*; *The Ennobling of Democracy*; *The Learning of Liberty*; and *Justice Among Nations*. He has edited *The Roots of Political Philosophy*; *The Rebirth of Classical Political Rationalism*; *Political Philosophy and the Human Soul*, and the political theory section of the *Encyclopedia of Democracy*.

Pascal, Blaise (1623–1662) *French mathematician, social and religious philosopher*

Most famous for his (uncompleted) book *Pensées* ("*Reflections*")—a reasoned defense of the CHRISTIAN faith—Pascal combined an advanced scientific mind with a profound mysticism. Seen as a traditional religious response to the rise of MODERN HUMANIST thought (as in Francis BACON), Pascal's philosophy warns against the consequences of human life and society without a consciousness of the divine.

Politically, Pascal adopts the view of St. AUGUSTINE that governmental JUSTICE is always imperfect and that pursuit of worldly honor, prestige, and fame is vain and foolish. Still, people should obey the STATE as a necessary force to prevent ANARCHY and civil war. Any government that maintains order and a semblance of JUSTICE should be supported. Given human evil, no state can engender VIRTUE or goodness, and no secular community can produce real fellowship. Human envy and hatred of others prevents genuine society; only a spiritual fellowship has a chance of harmony. Pascal followed this philosophy by entering a Jansenist monastery at age 31, renouncing his social eminence as a scholar and international celebrity. Afterwards he defined all such efforts at worldly distinction (fame, money, notoriety) as vain attempts of individuals to divert their thoughts from death and the ultimate purpose of life. This attack on the rationalistic, scientific worldview and retreat to individual responsibility and knowledge of God reappears in religious EXISTENTIALISM (as in KIERKEGAARD). Pascal is also an early DIALECTICAL thinker, as when he shows that the Holy Spirit is both a convictor of sin and comforter of the sinner (and that without the former, pride would dominate, but without the latter, despair would ruin). He remains one of the most profound and fascinating thinkers in the Western TRADITION.

Further Reading
Mesnard, J. *Pascal: His Life and Works*. New York: Philosophical Library, 1952.

paternalism

Traditionally, paternalism means the rule (governance) and care of a father or fatherlike person or institution. In Western political thought, this appears in ARISTOTLE's ideal of a DEMOCRATIC POLIS of heads of households and, therefore, a "paternalistic" Greek culture generally. The Roman emperor assumes this paternal role, as does the CATHOLIC Church's pope in the MIDDLE AGES. Medieval European culture generally is paternalistic, or ruled by senior male figures (king, lord, GUILD master, priest, family father). The biblical basis of the patriarchal order is Adam's headship over Eve, Moses' fatherhood over the Hebrew people, and other kings and patriarchs of Israel. The authority of this paternalistic view of God (as "Father") then extends to religious and civil organizations (see St. Thomas AQUINAS). It conveys both a strict and a loving patriarch, requiring respect and obedience, but providing care and protection. This hierarchical view of society (see FILMER) is challenged by the EGALITARIAN MODERN DEMOCRATIC perspective of John LOCKE, MARXISM, and FEMINISM. In contemporary political thought, the concept of a superior male role is almost nonexistent.

Paternalism, then, in contemporary thought takes on the meaning of a secular state that treats citizens like children by enforcing laws that protect individuals from dangerous influences or themselves and provide for their economic, social, and even emotional needs. So, SOCIALISM is sometimes called paternalistic because it provides for the material needs of citizens "from cradle to grave." Social-welfare legislation (school lunches, social security, etc.) is sometimes considered paternalistic or the Father (or Mother) State—treating adults as helpless children. Laws protecting individuals from harmful substances (tobacco, drugs, alcohol) or "consumer safety laws" (auto seatbelts, regulation of food production, etc.) are sometimes criticized as paternalistic. Particularly CONSERVATIVE, LIBERTARIAN, and ANARCHIST thinkers (such as Robert NOZICK) resent government control of individual freedom and choice in the name of safety or morality. So, LEFTIST politics tend to be more favorably disposed to paternalism in government, while RIGHT-WING IDEOLOGY is often more critical of political paternalism.

Further Reading
Sartorius, R., ed. *Paternalism*. Minneapolis: University of Minnesota Press, 1983.

patriarchal/patriarchalism

The theory or doctrine that political AUTHORITY (such as that of a king) is premised in the role and power of the father in a traditional family structure. The philosophical basis of this is the Judeo-CHRISTIAN religion with its view of God as a "father"; the origin of humanity in a male person (Adam); the rule of God's people Israel in prominent men (Moses, Noah, King David, Jesus, Paul); and the early church rule by popes (*papa*) and bishops. Also, in the CLASSICAL tradition, ARISTOTLE's anthropological genesis of politics (in household, village, and POLIS) situates primary authority in the male husband/father, which then forms the all-male citizenry. In both of these traditions, the political rule of men follows a "natural" role and capacity (given by God or NATURAL LAW) and therefore is best. In the MIDDLE AGES, this produces a view of the realm (such as England) or the empire (under CHARLEMAGNE) as a family, with the king or emperor as the father of the whole country. This leads to a HIERARCHY in which all adult subjects are children and the government is a kind of parent. Like paternalism, this usually involved a strict ABSOLUTIST rule combined with a benevolent, protective fatherhood.

Sir Robert FILMER articulates this MEDIEVAL view of king-as-father at the close of the Middle Ages in his book *Patriarcha* (1680). The Modern, SOCIAL-CONTRACT LIBERALISM of John LOCKE challenged this patriarchic view with an image of all humans as equal and independent adults. This EGALITARIAN perspective (the equality of men and women) flows into the contemporary concept of the *patriarchal society* as male-dominated and oppressive. FEMINIST views of the inequality and EXPLOITATION of women derive from this antipatriarchal movement.

Further Reading
Sartorius, R., ed. *Paternalism*. Minneapolis: University of Minnesota Press, 1983.

patriotism

The love of country, and feelings and actions of loyalty, service, and pride in one's nation. From the Latin, *patria*, the word *patriotic* means identity with the fatherland. Related to NATIONALISM, patriotism is a sense of respect and duty to one's country. Famous or prominent national founders and leaders are considered patriots (such as George Washington and Paul Revere in America; Winston Churchill of Great Britain; MAO TSE-TUNG in China; Kemal ATATÜRK of Turkey, etc.). Patriotism is generally a popular, valued ideal, but it can be diminished by government abuse or public cynicism (such as the decline of patriotism in the United States during the 1960s because of the U.S. war policy in Vietnam). Patriotic sentiments tend to increase during times of national crisis, especially during periods of war when the nation is threatened by foreign aggression. Consequently, as MACHIAVELLI points out, political leaders (such as NAZI leader HITLER or Soviet dictator STALIN) used international conflict to increase public support for their governments.

All nations promote patriotism through public education, national celebrations (e.g., the Fourth of July or Independence Day in the United States), symbols (such as the flag), and remembrance of patriotic deeds and persons. Persecution of the early CHRISTIANS in the Roman Empire was partly because they regarded no earthly nation as their home but were loyal only to the Kingdom of God. This separation of religion and politics (see CHURCH AND STATE) is not present in those countries where nationality is tied to one religion (ISLAM for Arabs, Hinduism for India, ORTHODOXY for Russians, etc.), and belonging to that faith is part of patriotism. Religious liberty and freedom has diminished that necessity for having certain religious beliefs to be considered patriotic.

Famous statements about patriotism include U.S. President John F. KENNEDY's plea to "Ask not what your country can do for you—ask what you can do for your country" (a paraphrase of CICERO) and English critic Samuel Johnson's statement that "Patriotism is the last refuge of a scoundrel" (implying that false patriotism can be a self-interested trick). Excessive or mindless patriotism ("My Country—Right or Wrong") is called jingoism and is often associated with the proud, military aggression of FASCISM. This is sometimes contrasted with "true patriotism" in which love of country includes criticizing the government or political leaders when they are acting immorally or unjustly.

patronage

A political system or practice that involves employment given by a "patron," or sponsor. So, for example, government jobs (ambassadorships, judgeships) conferred by a person in authority (president, governor, mayor) rather than by popular election are "patronage appointments."

Patronage has been a feature of most states throughout history. The MEDIEVAL CATHOLIC Church was a patron of the arts—employing artists to decorate churches, and so on. The Roman EMPIRE granted most political jobs through royal patronage. In the Middle Ages, European monarchs had the power to grant titles of nobility, land, pensions, and honors to anyone. This reliance on patronage employment was seen as corrupt by the independent lords and citizens because it concentrated power in the central government and made most officials personally dependent on the king. By contrast, the CLASSICAL REPUBLICAN school of political theory argued for a popular election of officials, placing power in the people or decentralized regions and encouraging distribution of power and CHECKS AND BALANCES.

In Britain, the republican-versus-royal-patronage battle takes the form of shifting authority between king and Parliament (Lords and Commons). In America, the STATES-RIGHTS advocates (such as Thomas JEFFERSON) attacked the patronage of the federal government (as under Alexander HAMILTON). Propatronage sentiments arose in the presidential administration of Andrew JACKSON, where loyalty to and work for the DEMOCRATIC PARTY was rewarded with public employment. The abuse and undemocratic corruption of these Democratic Party "machines" caused civil-service reform in the United States that required qualified government personnel based on examinations and nonpartisan qualifications. The president of the United States still has control over thousands of government jobs and usually appoints political-party supporters (such as to ambassadorships), but most of the federal BUREAUCRACY is under the civil service system.

Patronage is still regarded as ineffective, corrupt, and unresponsive government employment, but its supporters consider it an appropriate reward for party or leader loyalty and friendship and a necessary ingredient in MODERN government.

Penn, William (1644–1718) *English Quaker, political and religious thinker, and founder of Pennsylvania*

Son of an English aristocrat, Penn was educated at Christ Church (college), Oxford, and studied law at Lincoln's Inn, London. At age 22, he became a Quaker CHRISTIAN, which, because of that sect's belief in religious FREEDOM, DEMOCRACY, and direct revelation from the Holy Spirit, caused him to be persecuted and imprisoned.

In 1680, the king of England paid a debt owed Penn's father in land in North America (now the state of Pennsylvania), giving Penn virtual control over the colony. He wrote a highly democratic CONSTITUTION for Pennsylvania, emphasizing religious LIBERTY and Christian morality. Quakers and other persecuted Protestants flocked to the colony from England and Europe. Philadelphia, the chief city in Pennsylvania, became a model Christian community, with clean, orderly, and prosperous streets and citizens. The REPUBLICAN political principles and religious FREEDOM of Pennsylvania became a model for other U.S. states and the U.S. Constitution. Voluntary liberty of conscience and democratic government was proven in Pennsylvania. Benjamin FRANKLIN grew up in Philadelphia, and the Pennsylvania system greatly impressed James MADISON. Most North American settlements had hostile relations with the Native Americans (Indians), but William Penn's just and peaceful policies resulted in good relations with the Pennsylvanian Native peoples.

Penn's main writing include *No Cross, No Crown* (1668)—on his religious beliefs—and *Essay Towards the Present and Future Peace of Europe* (1693)—on international politics.

philosopher-king

The term used by PLATO in his *Republic* to describe the ideal rulers. It conveys the combination of wisdom and power in government. This ideal of wise political leadership continues throughout Western political thought, including in Thomas JEFFERSON's conception of a natural ARISTOCRACY of wisdom and goodness in America.

Plato conceived of certain people being by nature (born) to be such wise and virtuous rulers. This natural capacity for knowledge and morals, however, required strict training and cultivation by the society's educational system. Intellectual discipline was especially important for the naturally gifted to develop into effective rulers, but once they were educated, these philosopher-kings (who could be either men or women) would foster the most just, peaceful, and virtuous society. Their unique VIRTUE was the knowledge of other peoples' virtues (the courage and honor of the military class, and the moderation of the business class). If such philosophers did not govern, some other class (soldiers or workers) would rule society, impose their own narrow virtues on the whole country, and cause injustice and national disaster.

Plato's CLASSICAL ideal of philosopher-kings is thought to have influenced the Hindu hierarchy in India; the ideal CHRISTIAN knight in the European MIDDLE AGES; and even MODERN ideas of superior leaders in DEMOCRACY. Its hereditary qualities make Plato's concept less compatible with EGALITARIAN ideology, but it continues to influence most political thought.

physiocracy

The physiocratic school of political economy was founded by François QUESNAY. His most prominent work *Tableau Économique* (*Economic Table*) was completed in 1758. The first English translation in 1766 described the field as:

> Political economy is the study of the natural laws governing the production and distribution of wealth. In their systematic analysis of the process and their emphasis on the ordre naturel, the physiocrats merit the distinction of being the founders of political economy. The Impot Unique remains to be implemented as does their legacy of free trade and free markets.

Because for Quesnay the basis of the social order lay in the economic order, an understanding of the laws and regularities governing economic life appeared to be of primary necessity if the sickness of society was to be cured. In short, by modifying economic realities, one could address social and political ills. Physiocrats assumed that the system of market exchange was subject to certain objective economic laws. Furthermore, these laws operated independently of human will.

These economic laws governed the shape of the economic order and therefore affirmed Quesnay's primary assumption, the shape and movement of the social order as a whole.

The first task for the physiocrats was to construct a theoretical model based on the objective economic laws that they would articulate. In so doing, they would explain the basis for economic activity and its impact on social and political order. In explaining their model, they chose to describe economic activity in circular terms. In this circle, production and consumption appeared as interdependent variables, whose interaction proceeded according to certain predetermined laws and could be replicated regardless of the economic period. Within this circle, the physiocrats then endeavored to discover some key variable movement that could be regarded as the basic factor, causing an expansion or a contraction of the circle. The variable that they identified was the capacity of agriculture to yield a profit. Anything that increased this net gain would lead to increased economic activity, and anything that reduced it would lead to economic contraction.

One influential physiocrat, the Marquis de Mirabeau, summed up the importance of the net gain or loss in the following terms:

> The whole moral and physical advantage of societies is . . . summed up in one point, an increase in the net product; all damage done to society is determined by this fact, a reduction in the net product. It is on the two scales of this balance that you can place and weigh laws, manners, customs, vices, and virtues.

As a result of this thinking, physiocrats encouraged, in almost myopic terms, policies supporting agricultural improvements. Their theoretical paradigm labeled as "moral" agricultural pursuits and as "immoral" all others. Agriculture was the supreme occupation, not only because it was morally and politically superior to others, not only because its produce was primary in the scale of wants and always in demand, but also because it alone yielded a profit. Indeed, for the physiocrat, being productive meant productive agricultural profit. Conversely, manufacture- and commerce-related activities were unproductive and sterile.

In the years to follow, physiocracy came under some significant criticism by such notable political economists as Karl MARX, David RICARDO, and Adam SMITH. Although they acknowledge physiocracy as an important contribution to political economy, they are quick to note that its dismissal of nonagricultural pursuits is a debilitating limitation of the paradigm.

Further Reading
Meek, Ronald L. *The Economics of Physiocracy.* Cambridge, Mass.: Harvard University Press, 1993.

Pilgrims

English Protestant CHRISTIANS who formed the first European settlement in North America in 1620. As followers of John CALVIN, they combined Reformed theology with DEMOCRATIC political governance, as reflected in their founding document, the MAYFLOWER COMPACT. The EQUALITY of saints (Christians), democratic church governance, the reality and persistence of human sin, reliance on the Bible for moral instruction, a strong work ethic, and a belief in the imminent return of Christ made PURITAN New England a pious, efficient culture. Emphasis on both political and religious LIBERTY contributed to the American emphasis on FREEDOM and INDIVIDUALISM. Resistance to a monarchical state and the Episcopal Church, the Pilgrims' theology logically led to the American Revolution and independence. Adhering to a COVENANT view of theology and politics, the Pilgrims affected much of later U.S. culture and society. Although PLURALISM weakened the Puritan ethic in the United States, their ideal of a holy "City on a Hill," or haven and lighthouse of a Christian commonwealth that would preserve and extend godly truth and civilization, soon became a kind of CIVIL RELIGION. "MANIFEST DESTINY" in the 19th-century United States and President Ronald REAGAN's CONSERVATIVE rhetoric about the U.S.'s "divine mission" to defeat COMMUNISM and to extend liberty around the world follows from the Pilgrim IDEOLOGY. A leading writer on Puritan political thought is John WINTHROP (1588–1649).

Plato (427–347 B.C.)   *Greek political philosopher, teacher of Aristotle*

One of the greatest CLASSICAL philosophers, Plato was from an aristocratic family in Athens. His "Dialogues" present much of SOCRATES' ideas, especially *The Apology* of Socrates' trial. It is assumed that Plato was a follower of Socrates and then developed Socratic philosophy in his great work of political theory, *The Republic.*

The Republic of Plato is the first systematic work of political theory in the Western world. It strives to give a definition of JUSTICE in the ideal state and society. Plato relates the order and goodness of the individual to that of the nation, claiming that society is just "the individual writ large." Plato's ideas have influenced much of subsequent political philosophy, especially the CHRISTIAN political thought of St. AUGUSTINE, the NEO-PLATOIST philosophers, and U.S. thinkers Leo STRAUSS, Allan Bloom, and Thomas PANGLE.

Plato begins by dividing human nature into three categories, or dispositions: (1) the philosophic (or intellectual); (2) the spirited (or military); and (3) the appetitive (or economic). Every individual has all three elements in him or her, but one disposition dominates the personality. The philosophic soul is characterized by learning and knowledge—a natural curiosity, a desire for truth, and a capacity to understand and communicate. A spirited person is interested in adventure and combat and has physical abilities to be a good athlete and warrior. The appetitive personality cares most about physical consumption (food, clothes, PROPERTY) and likes economic matters. For Plato, these natural predispositions in people render individuals inevitably unequal and form a natural class structure. The philosophic or wise should rule as PHILOSOPHER-KINGS; the aggressive, spirited people form a natural army or military class; and appetitive types belong in the economy (workers, managers, etc.). This sets up a HIERARCHY of citizens in society, which constitutes justice, for Plato. His classic definition of *social justice* as "giving each his or her due" follows from this theory. If everyone is in their proper place, utilizing their natural gifts and talents and cooperating with the others, a perfectly harmonious and just society exists. Such a just order requires strict STATE education—to identify the natural abilities of children on an individual basis and to train them for the common good (and for the individual's fulfillment and happiness). This means that each person is incapable of determining his or her abilities or desires; the public realm must do that. If a society neglects this categorizing of individuals and leaves it up to them, injustice and disorder will result. The state must cultivate these natural characteristics to develop the VIRTUE of each citizen and class. The Platonic notion of virtue comes from the Greek term *arête*, which means functional excellence or a thing working well according to its purpose. So the virtue of a knife is to cut well because that is its job; the virtue of the ruling class is wisdom and goodness because those are necessary qualities to effective governance. The virtue of the military, for Plato, is courage and honor because those are qualities necessary to effective military defense. The economic class's virtue is "moderation" because it controls the greed that is the besetting sin of business and that destabilizes the economy. Society must teach these virtues so that each member of the nation can function well and promote harmony and prosperity. A unique feature of the ruler's virtue is to be able to identify the virtue of others and to "put them in their place." The other classes of society (soldiers and workers) at best know their own virtues but cannot understand others' virtues, so military types want everyone in society to act like them, and business people want to run everything in society (schools, army, hospitals) along business lines.

To help people understand and accept this natural class order, Plato devises the "myth of the metals," which explains in a physiological way why people are different. According to this myth (taught to school children), the reason some people are born to rule is that they have gold in their bodies. The spirited military people are born with silver in their tissues, and the economic citizens have bronze inside them. This teaching reinforces the class system of Plato's ideal republic. For him, this "noble lie" is justified in making the hierarchy palatable to everyone. Plato sees injustice as any society that (1) does not identify and recognize the innate nature and talent of each citizen, (2) does not train and cultivate that nature through public education for the individual's fulfillment and common good, and (3) does not provide employment in that area for each qualified person (the philosophic in government, the spirited in military service, the appetitive in the economy). Most societies, in Plato's view, are practicing injustice by their haphazard educational, occupational, and economic systems. Crime and mental illness follow from such injustice.

Plato identifies various unjust regimes in his discussion of political change and revolution. He details in Book VIII of *The Republic* a certain logic of governmental change in a "degeneration of regimes." According to this theory of change, each kind of government is marked by a strength (virtue) and a weakness (vice), and each successive state satisfies the weakness of its predecessor. In the beginning, the ARISTOCRACY, whose virtue is wisdom, lacks honor and so is replaced by a timocracy, or military government (which has the virtue of honor but also has the vice of poverty). This, then, is overthrown by an oligarchy whose wealth corrects the poverty of timocratic government but brings the vice of greed. It is supplanted by a democracy whose creed of EQUALITY corrects the oligarchic greed but brings the disorder of ANARCHY and FREEDOM. Finally, the individual freedom and licentiousness of democracy brings forth the order of TYRANNY, which establishes peace through cruelty and oppression. The cycle of political change is logical and inevitable.

This explains the disdain Plato had for popular or democratic government, which continues in the Western tradition in monarchism, aristocracy, CONSERVATIVE thought, and FASCISM. For Plato, the average person is stupid and selfish, is concerned only for his or her own personal interest, and is envious of others. If the majority of these simpletons rule (as in a democracy), all standards and order will disappear. All authority will be questioned, and anarchy will ensue. Soon, subjects will disobey rulers, students will be disrespectful of their teachers, the young will revel against their elders, and children will resist their parents. Anarchy and instability constantly affects democracy. To be elected, candidates have to pander to the voters' interests and whims and so cannot have any principles. Democracy is doomed to failure and eventually leads to DICTATORSHIP. This is why Aristotle, the English CONSTITUTION, and the American Founders (e.g., James MADISON) developed a mixed republic (rather than a pure democracy) of kingship, aristocracy, and democracy. It also explains why later in his life, Plato (in his book *The Laws*) establishes rule by regulations rather than the character of the rulers and emphasizes the importance of a nation's religion for promoting morals.

Plato remains one of the major Western political thinkers in history: He affected much of the social philosophy that came after him.

Further Readings

Stalley, R. *An Introduction to Plato's Laws.* Oxford, Eng.: Blackwell, 1983.

pluralism

A political theory that sees society as made up of many (a "plurality") groups and INTERESTS, with the government balancing and moderating their influ-

ence. Growing out of the SOCIAL-CONTRACT theory of John LOCKE, pluralism is most deftly developed by American Founder James MADISON. According to Madison's theory in *THE FEDERALIST PAPERS*, a large REPUBLIC can better ensure individual and minority RIGHTS because it contains more groups that counteract each other, preventing any one group (economic, social, regional, religious) from dominating everyone else. Drawing from his Protestant CHRISTIANITY of John CALVIN, with its emphasis on human sin and selfishness, Madison constructs a U.S. CONSTITUTION with divided power, FEDERALISM, and CHECKS AND BALANCES to reflect the pluralism in his society. The idea is that a diversity of interests prevents TYRANNY, commends compromise, and preserves the individual rights to FREEDOM of speech, press, assembly, religion, and private PROPERTY. Governmental policy and LAW come out of the competition of various interest groups, encouraging organized participation in politics, lobbying, and so on.

This pluralist ideal has largely worked in the United States, where no single group or monopoly has been able to control the government completely for long periods of time.

The criticism of pluralistic politics has generally come from CONSERVATIVE thinkers (such as PLATO, Edmund BURKE, Alexis de TOCQUEVILLE, and Cardinal NEWMAN) who dislike the mediocrity and moral relativism of pluralism. In a purely pluralistic democracy, all interests and values are considered equal, leaving no absolute, objective standard for right and wrong, just and unjust. A transcendent ideal (in God, the Bible, the church, and so on), is necessary to measure different values and interests in society. The logical conclusion of pluralism, for these critics, is the cultural "diversity" in the United States that asserts ANIMAL RIGHTS, HOMOSEXUAL rights, and children's rights against more traditional hierarchies of moral and social systems.

Nevertheless, pluralism is expanding as the preferred social system in the world, as MODERN countries become more diverse in economics, religion, education, and ethnic background. The premier value of TOLERANCE of (if not acceptance or affirming of) difference follows the establishment of a pluralistic culture.

Political pluralism tends to accompany competitive, free market (CAPITALIST) economies, LIBERTY of belief (religion), and freedom of press. All of these features of pluralism are considered essential to Modern INDUSTRIALISM and democracy.

Further Readings

Dahl, R. *A Preface to Democratic Theory*. Chicago: University of Chicago Press, 1956.

Huntington, S. *The Promise of Disharmony*. Cambridge, Mass.: Belknap Press of Harvard University Press, 1981.

Pocock, J. G. A. (1924–) *British-U.S. political theorist and academic*

Pocock, who spent most of his academic career at Johns Hopkins University in Baltimore, Maryland, is the principal founder of the "CLASSICAL REPUBLICAN paradigm" in early American historical studies. In his book *The Machiavellian Moment* (1975), Pocock reinterpreted most of Western political philosophy through the civic republicanism of ARISTOTLE, CICERO, MACHIAVELLI, James HARRINGTON, and Thomas JEFFERSON. According to this theory, the dominant themes in Western political IDEOLOGY are: an economically independent, participatory-citizenry, small-scale (POLIS) DEMOCRACY, and civic or public VIRTUE (individual sacrifice to the common good). This REPUBLICAN ideal, then, continually resists ABSOLUTIST government (MONARCHY, TYRANNY, oligarchy), concentrated political and economic power (national banks, PATRONAGE), and military IMPERIALISM. All such "corruption" the republican tradition resists with appeals to the sturdy yeoman farmer, direct democracy, and a citizens' militia. In its MODERN manifestation, this takes the form of PURITAN simplicity and decentralized English virtuous, agrarian self-governance against the corrupt king, parliamentary ministry (political patronage), standing army, high taxes, Bank of England, stock companies, and royal EMPIRE. In America, this theory explains the colonial Revolution in terms of virtuous republican resistance to British imperial corruption. Jeffersonian democracy continues the republican ideal, while HAMILTON'S FEDERALISTS exhibit British corruption.

Pocock's comprehensive reinterpretation of the entire Western intellectual tradition offered an alternative to the prevailing British LIBERALISM of John LOCKE (explaining the American Revolution in terms of NATURAL RIGHTS) and the CHRISTIAN historiography of St. AUGUSTINE and Calvinism. Like most brilliant reassessments of an entire tradition, Pocock's theory is overdrawn in places (especially his writing out of Lockean SOCIAL-CONTRACT theory and his identification of Machiavelli as a classical thinker), but

it has illuminated an entire area of Western political thought (civic humanism or classical republicanism) that had not been adequately appreciated. His "civic republican paradigm" is probably the greatest discovery in historical scholarship in the 20th century.

polis

The small democratic community in ancient Greece (particularly Athens) that formed the CLASSICAL model for Western self-government. ARISTOTLE extols the wisdom, citizen participation, and public VIRTUE of this form of government, where every citizen knows every other citizen and shares in ruling. To Aristotle, the active involvement of each person in governing provided an education in civic duty and responsibility and developed the unique human *telos* or purpose in reasoned speech and ethical action. This idealized Greek "city-state" probably never performed as nobly as Aristotle conceived it, but it became the ideal of Western civilized DEMOCRACY in the Roman Republic, the early church government, MEDIEVAL CORPORATISM, and MODERN REPUBLICANISM. Thomas JEFFERSON applied this classical republicanism to the "ward republics" in Virginia: small self-governing communities or townships of a few thousand people. The "small town" ideal in America grows from this concept.

A negative consequence of this ideal polis, for large modern republics (according to MONTESQUIEU), is its limited population and geographic size. This required adapting the small democratic polis to a large country through republican FEDERALISM, as in America. But the ancient polis ideal—that real citizenship requires active participation and that weak or apathetic citizenship leads to TYRANNY—continues to exert a powerful influence in Western political theory (as, for example in the COMMUNITARIAN thought of Benjamin BARBER).

political science

The academic study of politics, especially in U.S. colleges and universities. The beginning of the "scientific" study of politics in the United States is usually dated at 1903 when the American Political Science Association was formed under the leadership of Professor Charles Merriam. Prior to this, the "politics" or "government" field had concentrated on the study of political history, LAW, political institutions, and POLITICAL THEORY. The rise of political science signified a BEHAVIORIST approach to studying politics, founded in the philosophical materialism of Thomas HOBBES. This perspective attempted to apply the methodology of empirical natural science to the study of society and politics. That scientific method emphasized observing material data, quantitative (mathematical) analysis of information, and compilation of facts. It claimed to be value-neutral, to *describe* phenomena simply (political systems, social change, governmental policy), without judging their goodness or morality. This separation of fact and value, or value-free politics, was later criticized as sterile and irrelevant to real political issues and problems.

Political science is taught as a major field in most U.S. colleges and universities. It contains several subfields that examine different aspects of politics: American politics, international politics, comparative politics, public law, political economy, and political theory. Graduates majoring in political science often pursue careers in law, government, or business. In the United States, political science is a popular major for university students who plan to attend law school.

Further Readings
Crick, B. *The American Science of Politics.* Westport, Conn.: Greenwood Press, 1959.
Somit, A., and Tanenhaus, J. *The Development of American Political Science.* Boston: Allyn & Bacon, 1967.

political theory

The academic study (in colleges and university) of the theories or philosophies of politics. As a branch (and foundation) of the academic field of POLITICAL SCIENCE, political theory tends to be a more abstract and general study of politics than the specific subfields of international politics, comparative politics, political economy, American politics, state and local politics, public law, and so on that study particular systems, institutions, and relations of politics.

Most political-theory study is historical, examining the great thinkers of the past (PLATO, ARISTOTLE, CICERO, St. AUGUSTINE, St. Thomas AQUINAS, MACHIAVELLI, John LOCKE, Karl MARX, etc.) and their ideals or concepts—JUSTICE, FREEDOM, DEMOCRACY, RIGHTS, LIBERTY, VIRTUE, and so on. More contemporary political theory applies these normative (or value-driven) concepts to current issues in present-day society. So, 20th-century political theorists Leo STRAUSS, John RAWLS, Robert NOZICK, Thomas PANGLE, Cary MCWILLIAMS, and Benjamin BARBER continue the CLASSICAL approach to political theory.

Political theory after the ancient Greek philosopher, SOCRATES, asks the perennial questions of HUMAN NATURE and politics: What is humanity? How should society and government be organized? What is justice? and so on. Although abstract and IDEALISTIC, this theoretical approach to politics informs and influences practical politics. Current world politics are arguably the result of past political theories (British LIBERALISM, MARXIST COMMUNISM, ISLAMIC thought, CATHOLIC CHRISTIAN political theory, Calvinism, etc.), so a premise of political theory is that ideas matter and affect the rest of life.

Further Readings
Sheldon, Garrett Ward. *The History of Political Theory.* New York: Peter Lang Publishing, 1988.
Miller, D., and Siedentop, L., eds. *The Nature of Political Theory.* Oxford, Eng.: Clarendon Press, 1983.
Strauss, L. *Natural Right and History.* Chicago: University of Chicago Press, 1953.

politically correct (p.c.)

Having the correct political or IDEOLOGICAL views and attitudes according to some party, group, or slant. Originally used in Stalinist Russia to infer adherence to the accepted COMMUNIST party line or position.

The term *politically correct* was revived in the United States in the 1990s to describe Liberal or LEFTIST attempts to express their political attitudes on society and education.

Polybius (approx. 200–118 B.C.) *Greek/Roman historian and political philosopher*

Known principally for his book *Histories,* Polybius provides a valuable history of the Roman Republic and EMPIRE, its political system and a theory of the life cycles of a state. Raised in the Achaean League of the southern Greek peninsula, Polybius served as a minor military and political official. When his nation opposed the Roman conquest of Macedonia, he was arrested and interned in Italy. There, his intellectual acumen won him favor with the ruling Roman elite. He further impressed his captors by writing an extensive and favorable history of the expansion of Rome from the taking of Sicily in 264 B.C. to the conquest of Carthage in 146 B.C. With his knowledge of ancient Greek, CLASSICAL philosophy (PLATO and ARISTOTLE), Polybius traced the ideas of government to the Roman state. He saw the government of Rome as a classic MIXED CONSTITUTION, blending MONARCHY, ARISTOCRACY, and DEMOCRACY. This balanced authority provided a premier system of CHECKS AND BALANCES and political stability for the Roman state. He also applied a Greek theory of natural life cycles of a government (birth, growth, maturity, decline, and death), or theory of revolution, to Rome. After Plato, he saw the corruption of the state in terms of a decline of public VIRTUE, and, like Aristotle, he saw this in terms of monarchy degenerating into tyranny, aristocracy declining into oligarchy, and democracy corrupted into ochlocracy (mob rule), followed by ANARCHY and a return to monarchy.

This Greco-Roman theory was widely read by MODERN Europeans and Americans (such as MONTESQUIEU and James MADISON) and informed their attempts to construct stable, just CONSTITUTIONS and governments.

Further Readings

Polybius. *The Histories,* W. R. Paton, transl., 6 vols. London: Heinemann, 1922–27.
Walbank, F. W. *Polybius.* Berkeley: University of California Press, 1972.

Popper, Karl (1902–1994)   *Political and scientific philosopher*

Born in Vienna, Austria, Popper emigrated to New Zealand and to London, England, when the NAZIS came to power in his native country. He taught scientific philosophy at the London School of Economics for most of his career.

Popper is most famous for his book *The Open Society and Its Enemies* (1945), which argues that political LIBERTY and DEMOCRACY are necessary to social and technological PROGRESS. An "open" society allows FREEDOM of thought, speech, press, and intellectual inquiry. This openness allows for new ideas and discoveries, advancing prosperity, happiness, and civilization. The "enemies" of such an open, free country are the various TOTALITARIAN systems (FASCISM, COMMUNISM) that control thought by some closed ideological doctrine (MARXISM, Nazism) and restrict individual freedom of thought and expression. Popper thus adheres to a basically British LIBERAL view of HUMAN NATURE and politics (as is John LOCKE and John Stuart MILL) and rejects philosophical ABSOLUTISM. He is especially critical of PLATO's political philosophy, claiming that the rulers in the Republic are a closed elite that restricts freedom. He also criticizes G. W. F. HEGEL and the DIALECTIC that leads to an Absolute Truth.

For Popper, the most important political question is not "How can we get the best rulers?" but "How can we prevent tyranny and correct errors quickly?" His liberalism follows the skeptical Calvinism of American Founder James MADISON and his CONSTITUTIONAL system of CHECKS AND BALANCES. Human pride and power are exceedingly dangerous and must not be allowed to dominate others. The STATE should protect individual liberty and EQUALITY and not engage in extensive social planning and reform. Ameliorating extreme misery and poverty is a valid function of the government; securing the greatest good possible (as in socialism) or trying to eliminate all social ills is not.

Popper also wrote against HISTORICISM—the philosophical view that believes that human history develops by scientific laws. Karl MARX's theory is the worst example of this historicist viewpoint—it takes problems or trends in CAPITALIST development and generalizes them across all history. This critique by communism effectively undercut its view of the inevitable emergence of socialism.

The Logic of Scientific Discovery (1959) and *The Poverty of Historicism* (1957) are Popper's other principal books. They are criticized by COMMUNITARIANS such as Benjamin BARBER for their absence of a sense of the human being as a social animal who needs community to develop fully.

Further Readings

Magee, B. *Popper.* London: Fontana, 1973.
Popper, K. R. *The Open Society and Its Enemies.* Princeton, N.J.: Princeton University Press, 1945.
———. *The Poverty of Historicism.* New York: Basic Books, 1957.

populism/populist

A political movement or IDEOLOGY that appeals to the common people against a minority ELITE; one who espouses the movement. In the United States in the late 1800s, populism occurred in the DEMOCRATIC PARTY under William Jennings Bryan. This came out of the concerns of poor farmers in the western United States who saw the national government controlled by an elite of intellectual, big-business "foreigners" and eastern banks. The populist program seeks to use the government to protect and advance the "democracy of the common man" against the craftiness of elites. This causes its image of ignorant "country bumpkins" reacting against MODERN technology, science, and economic progress. Consequently, populism is often portrayed by the media as unsophisticated and potentially FASCIST. Its appeal to religious FUNDAMENTALISM and its following of demagogue leadership further alienates many educated and urban people.

Populism has occurred in many cultures around the world, usually among rural populations. NAZI Germany appealed to the *Volk* (folk) or traditional German peasant mentality (simple morality, nationalistic pride, authoritarian attitudes); Russian populism in the 19th century extolled traditional peasant life; India under GANDHI emphasized ordinary Indian people. ISLAMIC fundamentalism in the Arab Middle Eastern countries has a strong populist sentiment (as in Iran) against Western and international, secular elites. Some CATHOLIC social thought (as in Poland) and the Green Party in Europe contain populist sentiments. When the U.S. Democratic Party claims to represent "the people" and accuses the REPUBLICAN Party of representing "the rich" or "business," it is drawing on populist ideas. President Ronald REAGAN's popularity was partly attributed to his populist appeal to average Americans.

As more citizens in Western nations become city dwellers and better educated, populism diminishes as a strong movement.

Further Readings
Godwyn, L. *Democratic Promise: The Populist Moment in American.* New York: Oxford University Press, 1976.
Ionescu, G., and Gellner, E. *Populism: Its Meanings and National Characteristics.* New York: Macmillan, 1969.

positivism/positivistic

The term is first used by COMTE to describe his theory that human society evolved through religious and metaphysical stages, culminating in a scientific stage. More generally, positivism refers to an assemblage of related ideas and doctrines that claim that (1) knowledge is obtained through sense experience; (2) knowledge of the natural world and of human behavior and society can be obtained through a single scientific methodology; and (3) any claim not based on sense experience and the methods of scientific inquiry is metaphysical nonsense.

The origin of the word *positivism* can be found in the writings of Francis BACON, the English philosopher and experimental scientist. Bacon (1561–1626) advocated the idea that sense experience is the foundation of knowledge, a new and radical idea at the time. Within the scholastic environment in which he set out these ideas, he described this source of knowledge as "positive" because it required no previous cause to explain it. We thus begin with sense experience and build knowledge from a natural, positive base.

Auguste COMTE coins the world *sociology* to describe his scientific approach to understanding how societies work and function and his normative account of how they should be structured and organized. He argues that there is a single methodology governing all inquiry of correlating observation-based facts and that this applies as equally to human society as it does in the area of astronomy, for example. He went on to argue that scientists should form a ruling class and that science itself should be the object of spiritual admiration. His ideas are set out in his *Course on the Positive Philosophy.* Although the particulars of Comte's theory are no longer well regarded, his determination to see society as falling within the scope of natural science and the baptizing of this position as positivist has had a great influence through to the present age.

Positivism is thus closely connected to the epistemological doctrine of empiricism and to the unified view of science, as well as to the sharp division between metaphysics and science. Most particularly, it is connected to the disposition to understand social phenomena by the methods of natural science.

Logical positivism was an early 20th-century philosophical movement that embraced these doctrines and that used the power of modern logic to articulate a specific form of empiricism and to reject, as literally meaningless, nonscientific, metaphysical theories. Logic positivism is associated with the Vienna Circle, a group of philosophers and logicians who met as a discussion group at the University of Vienna in the 1920s and 1930s. The leading members of this group were Moritz Schlick, Otto Neurath, Rudolp Carnap, and Friedrich Waismann. Others who attended some of the circle's discussions and were influenced by its philosophy were A. J. Ayer and Karl POPPER. The intellectual ancestor of the Vienna Circle was David HUME, who distinguished between two kinds of knowledge—knowledge based on sense experience and knowledge based on reason (as found, for example, in mathematics and formal logic). All other claims to knowledge that could not be traced to sense experience and that were not a claim of reason were, in Hume's word, "sophistry." Logical positivists set about defining the connection between sense data and propositions in strictly logical terms, and likewise defining the distinction between science and nonscience. This, they argued, was the only area in which philosophy had a genuine role. Naturally, within this schema, questions of morality and social justice could not be asked except in reductive terms. A. J. Ayer, for example, argued that moral language was merely the expression of emotions and not, properly speaking, propositional.

Positivism in its many forms has been widely criticized. Although it allies itself with the indubitable success of the natural sciences, its own claims about the nature of knowledge and society have been less persuasive.

The idea that human behavior and society can be explained in a reductive manner by employing the methods of the sciences (proceeding from sense experiences) has been systematically questioned. It has been argued that human behavior, originating in, for example, intentions and attitudes, cannot be captured by a description based on empirical data. In brief, the idea is that human actions are different in kind from physical events and so require a radically different method of investigation. In addition, the reduction and elimination of the normative dimension of human society, its morality and justice, leaves the crucial elements of society unexplained. Taken together, these criticisms deny the positivist's claim that there is a single scientific methodology based on empirical data.

Further criticism has been directed at the claim made by logical positivists that meaningful propositions can be distinguished from nonmeaningful propositions by a determination of their empirical or logical content. Work by contemporary philosophers such as W.V.O. Quine and Donald Davidson has undermined the possibility of making such determinations and has therefore called into question the central themes of the positivist's project.

The label *positivism* has also come to represent any theory that diminishes the humanity and agency of persons and that appeals to the authority of natural science.

Despite these many criticisms, positivism represents the ambition to bring within the single explanatory scheme of natural science both nature and society.

The possibility that we could understand ourselves as well as we now understand the natural world is intriguing to some, although frightening to others.

Further Readings

Ayer, A. J. *Logical Positivism*. New York: Free Press, 1966.
Comte, A. *The Positive Philosophy of August Comte*. New York: D. Appleton and Co., 1853.

post-Modernism

A philosophical and political school of thought that rejects the MODERN ENLIGHTENMENT LIBERAL view of reason, NATURAL RIGHTS, and order. Prominent in the late 20th century, post-Modernism is often associated with the writings of the French academic Michel FOUCAULT (1926–84).

Philosophically, post-Modernism declares the assumptions of modern science (of an orderly, rational universe, governed by LAWS that are known to humankind) inaccurate and distortive of reality. Both natural and social reality is irrational, unpredictable, and chaotic. There is no objective Truth but only relative, contingent knowledge. Similar to EXISTENTIALISM, this view encourages individual, subjective giving of meaning to life. Politically, it leads to a RADICAL INDIVIDUALISM (similar to LIBERTARIAN thought), moral relativism (similar to Thomas HOBBES's ethics), and antiauthority sentiments (such as ANARCHISM). This nihilism and vagueness made post-Modernist political theory less influential than other 20th-century political philosophies. By the 21st century, it, like COMMUNISM, FASCISM, and existentialism, had declined in significance.

power

A central concept in political thought, *power* comes from the Latin word *potentia*, meaning the capacity of one person affecting or controlling another person. This goes to the French term *pouvoir*, or the ability of influencing others. CICERO described political power in the Roman Empire as residing in the people but realized in the government. Other CLASSICAL Greek and CHRISTIAN thinkers discuss power less and VIRTUE and JUSTICE more. The MODERN period of Western political theory, beginning with RENAISSANCE Italian writer MACHIAVELLI, concentrates on power more extensively. The Prince, in Machiavellian theory, must be concerned primarily with getting and keeping power and with putting power above all other values (including goodness). Thomas HOBBES continues this emphasis on power, proclaiming it essential to the human purpose of avoiding pain and gaining pleasure. This materialistic view of power is continued in Karl MARX's theory of COMMUNISM, in which the whole history of politics is just an expression of the economic power of the ruling social class. This Marxist obsession with power informs much of 20th-century sociology, which sees all social relations in terms of who has more and less power, who controls whom, what groups are powerless, and how power can be redistributed. This LEFTIST attitude usually assigns power to the oppressors and lack of power to the oppressed. This view sees power as negative and destructive until the oppressed have it (and then it will be used positively and justly). American PLURALISM (as expressed by James MADISON), coming from a Calvinist view of human evil, seeks to divide and distribute political power because it will corrupt anyone who possesses it. In Lord ACTON's famous phrase, "Power corrupts, and absolute power corrupts absolutely." MEDIEVAL CATHOLIC political thought is less concerned about the misuse of power (in CHURCH AND STATE) and sees the possibility of really beneficial use of power and authority in the Christian king under the counsel of the church. POST-MODERNIST thinker Michel FOUCAULT emphasizes the informal influences of cultural power in Modern democratic society. Generally, in LIBERAL theory (John LOCKE), power is viewed with suspicion, as potentially tyrannical and abusive. But Modern politics remains obsessed and fascinated with power and the pursuit to define and acquire it.

Further Reading
Bell, R., Edwards, D. V., and Wagner, R. H., eds. *Political Power: A Reader in Theory and Research*. New York: Free Press, 1969.

pragmatism

Pragmatism holds that practice rather than cognition is the proper guide to understanding concepts such as meaning, truth, REASON, and values.

Charles Peirce's writings are the origin of pragmatism as an approach to philosophical and ethical issues. In the late 1800s, Peirce argued that the meaning of words should be determined by the practical consequences of their application and use. Thus, the practical effect of the use of a word, as measured by our experience of the world, determined its meaning. The full meaning of a word would be a catalogue of all its effects, and a word that produced no effects would be meaningless.

Peirce confined his use of the term *pragmatism* to his theory of meaning. However, others, most notably William James and John Dewey, adopted its use and applied it in a much broader context. In general, this trio of U.S. philosophers aimed to articulate a philosophical approach that was distinct from the then dominant European philosophical position of IDEALISM. James and Dewey applied the idea of pragmatism to the concept of truth. They argued that the truth of a proposition rested on the practical consequences of taking it to be true. The relevant consequences are those that make a difference to our experiences, our "actual lives." A true proposition is one that is useful or beneficial. This theory of truth was intended to oppose the correspondence-theory truth that held that the truth of a proposition is determined by a correspondence between its content and some state of affairs in the world. This latter theory of truth seemed to require an objective, or ideal, standpoint outside both proposition and world, and it was this sort of "absurdity" to which pragmatists objected.

Peirce argued that the determination of what is useful and beneficial is made by the objective standards determined by an ideal community of inquirers. James, however, argued that success and usefulness are determined by actual communities. James's subjectivist pragmatism was rejected by Peirce.

Pragmatism is now most closely associated in philosophy with its theory of truth. It was however quickly challenged, most notably by Bertrand Russell who argued that pragmatists gave no account of what truth is, only an account of what means we use for deciding which propositions are true. In other words, this is not a theory of truth but of justification (i.e., we are justified in taking "useful" beliefs to be true), but this says nothing about the concept itself and is compatible with a correspondence theory of truth. Moreover, Russell pointed out that useful beliefs could also be false and so undermined the conceptual connection pragmatists attempted to draw between usefulness and truth.

Although the specific account of truth pragmatists offered was not widely adopted, the general spirit of the pragmatists' approach to conceptual questions had a very large influence on the development of U.S. philosophy. Those most directly influenced include W. V. O. Quine, Hilary Putnam, and Richard Rorty.

Further Readings

Hauser, N., and Kloesel, C. *The Essential Peirce.* Bloomington: Indiana University Press, 1992.

James, W. *Pragmatism.* Cambridge, Mass.: Harvard University Press, 1981.

prayer in school

As a political issue in the United States, prayer in public (government) schools reflects the tensions of CHURCH AND STATE relations in the United States.

In 1962, the U.S. Supreme Court ruled in the case of *Engel v. Vitale* that in New York public schools, collective prayer led by a schoolteacher or an official violated the religious-liberty clause of the FIRST AMENDMENT of the U.S. CONSTITUTION. That amendment states, in part, that "Congress shall make no law respecting an establishment of religion . . ." The Supreme Court held that prayers led by state officials in a public building during regular school hours, in effect, "established" or supported a certain religion or church, violating freedom of religion.

EVANGELICAL CHRISTIANS (especially the CONSERVATIVE CHRISTIAN RIGHT) have resisted this ban on prayer in public schools, favoring a teacher-led Christian prayer. Attempts have been made (as those by the former MORAL MAJORITY) to pass a constitutional amendment allowing such prayer in public schools, but they have not succeeded. REPUBLICAN president Ronald REAGAN advocated such an amendment.

The conservative and FUNDAMENTALIST Christians who resist the ban on school prayer claim that the absence of such religious observances has caused moral decline in the United States and its schools and has contributed to school violence, sexual promiscuity, and a lack of discipline.

Although not altering the basic decision in *Engel v. Vitale*, the U.S. Supreme Court in recent years has modified the absolute prohibition on school prayer by allowing student-led religious groups to use school facilities for prayer before and after regular school hours and at school events outside the public school building. Of course, individual silent student prayer has not been banned by the Supreme Court, especially before and during tests.

Presbyterian

A MODERN form of church government (or "polity") that contrasts with the CATHOLIC HIERARCHY of priest, bishops, and the pope. Associated with the 16th-century Protestant REFORMATION, especially the churches led by John CALVIN, Presbyterian church governance establishes a REPUBLICAN system of rule in the CHRISTIAN church. Rather than church leaders chosen from above (pope or archbishop) for life, Presbyterians elect church leaders (presbyters, elders, deacons) from below (congregation) for limited terms. This DEMOCRATIC system of church governance grows out of the Protestant view of "the priesthood of all believers." It influenced not only church polity in England, Scotland, Switzerland, and Holland, but also state representative democracy (especially in the United States). The U.S. CONSTITUTION, with its system of elected government representatives, rotation of office, CHECKS AND BALANCES, and term limits, essentially replicates the Presbyterian polity. In the United States, Presbyterian churches are ruled by a hierarchical series of councils, beginning with the local church "session," regional "synods," and a national "general assembly." This model of government claims to be historical and apostolic, tracing its origins to the early church and the conciliar movement.

Historically, Presbyterianism accompanies Republican political movements (English PURITANS under Oliver CROMWELL, American Puritans in New England, HUGUENOTS in France) against existing monarchies (kings and popes).

press, free

Freedom of the press means that individuals can publish their writings without legal or political restrictions or censorship. The early classic expression for publishing liberty occurs in John MILTON's book *Areopagitica* (1644), which argued against English laws for licensing books. Milton attacked this legal requirement to obtain a government license before one could publish material as restrictive of new ideas and preventing healthy criticism of the STATE. This idea of a free press advancing knowledge and exposing public corruption formed the basis for American press freedom. In the Virginia Declaration of Rights and the U.S. CONSTITUTION (FIRST AMENDMENT) laws abridging the freedom of press are prohibited. Only publication of national or military secrets (which would endanger national security) is punished by law. Civil law courts can treat cases of personal injury by libelous publications (knowingly publishing false statements that harm a person's reputation or professional standing), but the U.S. Supreme Court gives wide latitude to the free press in regards to written attacks on public figures (politicians, celebrities) as necessary to DEMOCRATIC discussion and government. This followed the disastrous effects of the Alien and Sedition Acts under the presidential administration of John ADAMS (1797– 1801), which legally punished newspapers that criticized the government. The fear caused by this state censorship and the prospect of a TYRANNY, helped Adams's political opponents (Thomas JEFFERSON and James MADISON) to win the national elections in 1800. Since then, public repression of the free press has only taken informal means.

John Stuart MILL gives the classic MODERN arguments for freedom of the press in his essay *On Liberty*. Mill argues that even unpopular or obnoxious ideas should be freely expressed because (1) they may turn out to be true, or (2) even if they are wrong, their refutation by the correct views will strengthen the truth.

Contemporary communications technology (such as the Internet) has raised new questions of the freedom of the press. The increase of obscene and pornographic publications, causing addiction and crime, have raised issues of state restrictions on those publications. In general, the U.S. Supreme Court has protected the freedom of such obscene publications but has regulated them to prevent them from infecting children (minors). Several religious and CONSERVATIVE nations (ISLAMIC or CATHOLIC) restrict the publication of pornographic materials as corruptive of morals.

Because restrictions on freedom of the press are associated with closed tyrannical states (as NAZI Germany), most democratic countries are moving toward more publication liberty.

Price, Richard (1723–17 91)   *British moral and political philosopher*

As a RADICAL DEMOCRAT and a Unitarian, Price criticized Edmund BURKE's CONSERVATIVE politics in his book *Discourse on the Love of Our Country* (1789). He, like Thomas PAINE, was critical of the British MONARCHY and was in favor of the French and American revolutions. His ethics resembled those of Immanuel KANT, and his Unitarian religion that of Joseph PRIESTLY.

Priestley, Joseph (1733–1804)   *British scientist, theologian, and political philosopher*

Trained as a PRESBYTERIAN minister, Priestley left the church after denying the divinity of Christ and embraced Unitarian beliefs. He was considered a political RADICAL for his attacks on the British system of government (MONARCHY and ARISTOCRACY) and his endorsement of the French and American revolutions. His *Essay on the First Principles of Government* (1768) developed the earliest UTILITARIAN philosophy of JUSTICE as "the greatest good for the greatest number" (later developed by Jeremy BENTHAM). He was critical of Edmund BURKE's CONSERVATIVE theory, opposed the British Empire, and attacked religious orthodoxy. His radical ideas enraged public opinion, and after an angry mob burned down his house in England, he moved to Pennsylvania. He was friends with Thomas JEFFERSON.

Priestley's main successes came in his scientific investigations, where he made original discoveries in the areas of electricity and oxygen. A controversial character, he carried on fierce debates on politics, religion, economics, and chemistry. His deism was tolerated in William PENN's colony, but Priestley's anti-CHRISTIAN ideology made him suspect in EVANGELICAL America.

privacy

Primarily a MODERN, Western (American, British, and European) concept, *privacy* refers to the individual human being's autonomy, separateness, and inviolate RIGHTS. This includes LIBERTY of personal action and PROPERTY ownership and lifestyle and freedom from disturbance by unwanted noise, smells, sights, or other interferences. The emphasis on INDIVIDUALISM and biological autonomy make privacy as a social issue that is unknown in more collectivist cultures (ISLAMIC, Chinese, African, etc.), so privacy as a social category tends to arise with CAPITALISM, DEMOCRACY, and LIBERALISM.

In U.S. CONSTITUTIONAL LAW, privacy has been identified as a right that justifies the legal use of birth control and ABORTION, although the term *privacy* is not listed as a constitutional right. This interpretation of the U.S. Constitution has been challenged by CONSERVATIVE scholars who claim that no such "right to privacy" is in this founding document of the American republic and that the unborn's "right to life" is more important than any mere privacy right.

Much of contemporary expressions of individual privacy have to do with the invasion of one's "space" by computer technology. The right to have a private or secret identity, known only to the self, is potentially compromised by current information systems that gather data on individuals for business or marketing purposes. The commercial use of public information about a person (financial condition, health records, educational history, etc.) has led to "privacy legislation," or laws to protect individual privacy from use by unauthorized persons or organizations. Even giving out one's telephone number or e-mail address (without the person's consent) may be a violation of legally protected privacy.

In Modern mass society, where individual privacy is invaded by government, business, and social organizations, the issue of how individual space, peace, and solitude are preserved and protected will continue to be a major social problem. Hannah ARENDT in *The Human Condition* argued that Modern society destroys both private life and true public life.

Further Readings

Pennock, J. R., and Chapman, J. W., eds. *Nomos XIII: Privacy.* New York: Atherton Press, 1971.
Schoeman, F., ed. *Philosophical Dimensions of Privacy.* Cambridge, Eng.: Cambridge University Press, 1984.

progress/progressive

The idea that human life and society improves or "progresses" (morally, educationally, technologically, politically, economically) over time and through history. The view that humanity is improving as time goes on is prevalent in MODERN ENLIGHTENMENT LIBERALISM, which sees reason and CAPITALISM as continually improving the world. This IDEOLOGY of human progress continues in the HISTORICISM of HEGEL and Karl MARX (COMMUNISM). The DIALECTIC claims to explain this historical progress mechanism. Scientifically, Charles Darwin's theory of the evolution of species over time contributes to the Modern worldview of historical progress. SOCIAL DARWINISM applies this evolutionary perspective to society, seeing free-market competition as advancing economic and national (as well as individual and corporate) progress.

So, progressive politics tends to have an optimistic view of humans' ability to change and improve their collective lives. Like the Liberal U.S. DEMOCRATIC PARTY, such progressive philosophy believes in social reform and improvement (through legal, educational, welfare, and economic government policy). The NEW DEAL in the United States is an example of such progressive politics. As James Davison HUNTER shows in his book *Culture Wars,* this progressive outlook tends to dismiss older moral, religious, and cultural standards as old fashioned and out-of-date. Consequently, CONSERVATIVE social thought views progressive IDEOLOGY as destructive of traditional Judeo-CHRISTIAN values and the timeless truths of CLASSICAL philosophy (ARISTOTLE, St. Thomas AQUINAS, NATURAL LAW, etc.).

The idea of historical progression actually begins with the writings of St. AUGUSTINE, but this Christian thinker places progress within God's providence or divine plan for humanity. For him, historical progress occurs only within God's plan for human redemption through Christ, the fulfillment of human purpose through creation. The reality of human sin and helplessness means, for St. Augustine, that humankind cannot improve itself or the world through earthly reforms (educational, economic, political), but only by obedience to God's will and plan.

The United States is known for its faith in progress, primarily through technological and educational development. But the Western ideal of human progress has been shaken by the decline of moral progress, the enormous destruction of Modern warfare, and setbacks in medicine, poverty relief, and cultural civilization. Faith in human technical progress has been tempered by such disasters as the sinking of the *Titanic,* two world wars, failed space rockets, and computer viruses. Such humbling experiences partly explain the revival of traditional CONSERVATIVE religious and political doubts over the prospects of human progress. Optimistic opinions over human progress in these views may just be an expression of human pride and ignorance.

Further Readings

Bury, J. B. *The Idea of Progress.* London: Macmillan, 1920.
Tuveson, E. L. *Millennium and Utopia: A Study in the Background of the Idea of Progress.* Berkeley: University of California Press, 1964.

Prohibition

The social movement, primarily in the United States of America, to prohibit alcoholic beverages legally. The motive behind this social movement was the negative effects of alcohol on families, human health, work performance, incidence of violence, and crime prevention. Alcoholism ruined millions of lives and families in 19th-century America, and Prohibition, or the legal elimination of alcohol (beer, wine, gin, whiskey, etc.), was seen as the solution for this social problem. Most of the impetus for the Prohibition movement came from EVANGELICAL CHRISTIAN churches (BAPTIST, Methodist, etc.). Protestant America was shocked by the widespread alcoholism and drunkenness of new immigrants (Irish, Italian, Russian), many of whom were CATHOLIC. Prohibition, then, can be seen partly as a white Protestant reaction to non-northern-European cultural influences in the United States.

In 1917, Congress approved the Eighteenth Amendment to the CONSTITUTION, forbidding the manufacture, sale, or transportation of alcoholic beverages. It took effect in 1920 and was repealed by the Twenty-first Amendment in 1933. Prohibition had the unwelcome results of encouraging large criminal or mobster organizations that gained great wealth by illegally producing and distributing alcoholic beverages. In major cities, widespread violations of Prohibition laws made the legislation ineffective. Rural areas adapted to the measures more easily, and alcoholism did decline in the United States. Since the repeal of Prohibition, alcoholism, deaths by drunk drivers, and violent crime related to alcohol have increased. Attempts to curb the negative effects of alcohol (rather than the prohibition of alcohol) include increased penalties for alcohol-related traffic violations and job screening for drug and alcohol use.

The social benefits of Prohibition are still debated, but it remains an example of CHURCH-AND-STATE relations and problems.

property

In political thought, property is discussed in terms of what constitutes property (land, skills, money, jobs, industry, income, RIGHTS, etc.), whether it

Prohibition officers raiding the lunchroom of a Washington, D.C., establishment. (LIBRARY OF CONGRESS)

should be owned privately or by the community, and how the STATE should regulate, limit, or distribute property.

An early treatment of the subject of property occurs in PLATO's *Republic* where the "Guardians" or military are said to have no personal property but to possess things in common. This led to the criticism of Platonic philosophy that it advocated COMMUNISM. In fact, Plato simply affirms the common practice of governments providing for the material needs of soldiers (housing, clothing, food, etc.). Other classes in Plato's ideal Republic can own personal property.

ARISTOTLE advocates private-property ownership (against SOCIALISM) because it enhances the purpose of economics (sustaining human life and freeing citizens to serve in public life) by rewarding work, making society more orderly, and encouraging the VIRTUE of generosity. But an overconcern with money "enslaves" a person to one's lowest animal impulses, for Aristotle. Property is a "means" to a higher "end," for him—wealth is to be used to establish an independence that allows one to enter politics. This "gentleman's" attitude toward money and trade continues in Western political thought (James HARRINGTON, Edmund BURKE, etc.).

The early CHRISTIAN society diminished the absolute right to private property by "holding all things in common" (Acts 2:44); this did not mean formal state communism, but rather a sharing of goods according to need (those with more wealth giving to those in the church who had less) in obedience to God's prompting to charity. St. AUGUSTINE commends this practice.

St. Thomas AQUINAS combines Christian and Aristotelian philosophy in his discussion of property. He adopts Aristotle's arguments for the utility of private ownership (orderly society, incentives for work), but qualifies them with the biblical injunctions to see one's wealth as a blessing from God, to be used for God's purposes and within his limitations (helping the poor, charity, generosity), or "stewardship." Aquinas adopts the TELEOLOGICAL view that the divine-law purpose of material things is to support human life, so a person who is starving can take another's overabundance of bread, even if it violates human laws against theft.

Modern LIBERALISM (Thomas HOBBES and John LOCKE) emphasizes property in a CAPITALIST sense of labor and investment. Government's main duty is to protect the NATURAL RIGHTS to "Life, LIBERTY, and Property," in Locke's phrase. A state that unjustly violates the individual's right to property can be overthrown. John Stuart MILL extends this right to property to include intellectual ownership (of ideas, opinions, expression).

Karl MARX presents all of history in terms of property, work, and economic class conflict. Systems of property (and government) are determined by the level of technology existing in a given society. The means of economic production determines how property is owned and protected. MARXISM describes Western civilization in terms of primitive (tribal) communism, ancient (CLASSICAL) slave society, MEDIEVAL FEUDALISM, industrial capitalism, socialism, and COMMUNISM. Driven by advances in technology, Marxism argued that history inevitably led to a communist UTOPIA where production was so advanced that no one would have to work and that goods would be in abundance. This prediction did not come true in the communist countries (SOVIET UNION, China, Cuba). Contemporary discussion of property in political thought tends to be over the proper mix of private, free-enterprise property and public regulation of property and business. John RAWLS provides a theory of Liberal WELFARE-STATE economics where private property and enterprise are heavily regulated and taxed to provide public services and opportunities for the socially disadvantaged. Robert NOZICK gives a CONSERVATIVE, LIBERTARIAN theory of very limited state control of private property.

Generally, in the advanced Western democracies (Europe, the United States, Canada) a mixed economy of private capitalist enterprise and public social welfare produces the greatest prosperity and social JUSTICE. The LEFT, or the liberal DEMOCRATIC PARTY, in the United States tends to lean toward more government regulation and public services, while the RIGHT, or the conservative REPUBLICAN PARTY, favors more unrestricted private property and less governmental regulation of the economy.

The extremes of wealth and poverty in the world make property and economic development continuing issues in political thought.

Further Readings

Becker, Lawrence C. *Property Rights—Philosophic Foundations.* London: Routledge, 1977.
Reeve, A. *Property.* Amherst, Mass.: Prometheus Books, 1986.

Protagoras (490–415 B.C.) *classical Greek philosopher and sophist*

One of the earliest political thinkers in the Western world, Protagoras asserted that all adult male Greek citizens should participate in government. This formed the early basis for CLASSICAL DEMOCRACY. But he also held, as did ARISTOTLE later, that the capacity for self-rule had to be taught and developed. This especially required training in thought (reasoning) and speech (discussion). Because the sophists were teachers of rhetoric (public speaking), Protagoras advocated the schooling of young men in intellectual and DIALECTICAL subjects. This forms the early classical view that politics is primarily about thought and speech—rational discourse in the public arena. The ideal CITIZEN in this system is a well-educated, economically independent, ethical, and politically active person. This perspective is taken up by PLATO, Aristotle, and CICERO and forms the classical REPUBLICAN school of political thought. SOCRATES criticizes the formal and pretentious qualities of sophistic education but embraces the ideal of public service.

This classical view of politics continues through St. Thomas AQUINAS, James HARRINGTON, and Thomas JEFFERSON.

Protestant political thought

The ideas of politics or CHURCH AND STATE of the Protestant CHRISTIAN churches (such as HUGUENOT, PRESBYTERIAN, PURITAN, BAPTIST) after the writings of Martin LUTHER, John CALVIN, John WINTHROP, and others.

Protestant political theory can be contrasted with the views of religion and politics of both the CATHOLIC church and the Eastern Orthodox Christian churches. The differences in these perspectives tend to center around two issues: (1) the governing structure, or polity, of the church institution itself; and (2) the proper relationship between that church and the secular government, or STATE. In general, Protestant political thought has a DEMOCRATIC or REPUBLICAN system of church government (voluntary membership in congregations) and believes in the separation of church and state (as in the United States). By contrast, the Catholic Church has a monarchic and aristocratic view of church polity (AUTHORITY in the pope and bishops) and believes in a strong role for the church in state matters. The Eastern Orthodox churches (Greek, Russian, etc.) share the Catholic HIERARCHY of church structure and integrate the church even more directly in official state

structures. Consequently, Protestant political thought emphasizes religious LIBERTY and "FREEDOM of individual conscience" more than either Catholic or Orthodox churches. This may be seen as reflecting modern values of INDIVIDUALISM, CAPITALISM, and democracy.

Historically, the Protestant political thought of Luther and Calvin came out of a reformed theology that emphasized individual salvation thought faith in Christ (over a mediating role of priests and saints); a depreciation of elaborate church rituals and corrupt practices (such as selling God's indulgences); a belief in the EQUALITY of all Christians (as opposed to the clergy/laity distinction and hierarchy of church offices); and an emphasis on "preaching the Word" or teaching the Bible scriptures as the sole truth of God (contrasted with nonbiblical church tradition, the Aristotelian scholasticism of St. Thomas AQUINAS, and other pagan influences on church doctrine). This REFORMATION church rejected the Catholic, papal claim to universality, stating that the "united" Christian church was a spiritual fellowship of all who belong to Christ, and it advocated an EGALITARIAN notion of a church "priesthood of all believers," where no one Christian is superior to any other, in a worldly sense. This contributed to the ANTICLERICALISM of the Reformation and ENLIGHTENMENT periods. RADICAL "anabaptists" claimed that baptism should only be performed on adult believers, not infants. Such Protestantism led to a view of government as confined to "the Sword" or criminal justice, with the state having no jurisdiction over the church. The "free church," then, concentrated on winning souls, teaching the faith, and evangelizing the world according to Jesus' great commission.

PURITAN or Calvinist political thought (as in Oliver CROMWELL) saw a cooperative social rule of "godly ministers" (church) and "godly magistrates" (state). Such cooperation between Christian clergy and Christian statesman became the Protestant ideal (especially in Switzerland, Scotland, Holland, and the United States). This Protestant view of the proper relation between religion and politics survives in various EVANGELICAL churches, including the CHRISTIAN RIGHT in the contemporary United States.

Proudhon, Pierre-Joseph (1809–1865) *French anarchist*

Proudhon, born into a peasant family in Besançon, is generally regarded as the founder of modern ANAR-

CHISM, the theory that coercive government or the STATE should be abolished. Proudhon was for the most part self-educated, teaching himself Hebrew, Greek, and Latin, although he briefly attended the college in Besançon. Trained as a printer and compositor, Proudhon developed strong skills as a writer, which eventually enabled him to win a scholarship to study in Paris from the Besançon Academy in 1838. While working as a printer in Besançon, Proudhon met Charles FOURIER, whose ideas of utopian SOCIALISM were to influence Proudhon's political philosophy. In Paris, Proudhon devoted his time to studying and to writing his first significant book, *What Is Property?* (1840). In this work, Proudhon not only identified himself as an anarchist, but he also famously declared that "Property is theft!" By this, Proudhon meant that the institution of private PROPERTY under CAPITALISM allows the wealthy few to exploit the labor of the poor masses. In this way, property becomes treated as an exclusive privilege that can be used to engender widespread inequality.

Despite Proudhon's critique of property under the capitalist system, he was also critical of the doctrines of COMMUNISM. While capitalism destroys equality, communism, Proudhon argued, negates LIBERTY because communism advocates the need for a strong, centralized state and economy. In doing so, Proudhon suggested, it dismisses claims to individual liberty. In particular, a communist state would not recognize what Proudhon referred to as "possession," the right of a worker or group of workers to control the land and tools required for production. For Proudhon, it was most important to protect the individual's control over the means of production and thereby preserve the individual's independence or liberty.

In contrast to capitalism and communism, Proudhon articulated a theory of anarchism called mutualism. Proudhon's social theory is based on a model of decentralized FEDERALISM in which social organization would consist of a federal system of autonomous local communities and industrial associations bound by "a system of contracts" rather than by a "system of laws." The mutualist society envisioned by Proudhon would function through the formation of free contracts based on the recognition of mutual interests. This, Proudhon insisted, would maintain workers' autonomy and avoid the dangers of a rigid, bureaucratic AUTHORITY. To promote the development of mutualism, Proudhon maintained that working-class credit associations must be created worldwide that would help keep economic power in the hands of workers and foster liberation from control by the government. Proudhon unsuccessfully attempted to organize a "people's bank" following his election to the constituent assembly of the Second Republic in June 1848.

In 1849 Proudhon was imprisoned for criticizing the authoritarian tendencies of the new government, especially of Louis-Napoleon (Napoleon III). He spent his three-year prison term writing several books and expanding on his notion of a world federation that would replace the divisive nationalism of sovereign states. After being sentenced to prison again in 1858, Proudhon fled to Belgium, where he remained until 1862. He spent the final years of his life in Paris, completing his last works.

Further Reading

Woodcock, G. *Pierre-Joseph Proudhon: A Biography*. London: Routledge, 1956.

Pufendorf, Samuel (1632–1694)   *German philosopher and jurist*

Born in Saxony, Pufendorf was the son of a Lutheran pastor. He first studied theology at the University of Leipzig but soon became interested in philosophy, history, and jurisprudence. In 1656, Pufendorf went to the University of Jena where he continued his study of philosophy and law, especially the works of Hugo GROTIUS and Thomas HOBBES. He then acquired the position of tutor to the son of the Swedish ambassador in Denmark. However, because of a war between Sweden and Denmark, Pufendorf was arrested and imprisoned for six months. During his imprisonment, Pufendorf wrote his first book, *Elements of Universal Jurisprudence*, published in 1660. After returning to Germany, Pufendorf was appointed to the professorship in natural and international law at the University of Heidelberg, a position he held until 1668. He spent the next eight years as a professor at Lund in Sweden, where he completed his *On the Law of Nature and of Nations* (1672). This book was followed the next year by his *On the Duty of Man and Citizen*, a shorter and widely successful version of *On the Law of Nature and of Nations*, which was used as a standard textbook by students of NATURAL LAW throughout Europe and the American colonies. Pufendorf spent his final years as court historian to both the king of Stockholm (1677–88) and the elector of Brandenburg (1688–94).

Pufendorf based his political and legal theories on a conception of natural law. According to Pufendorf, there exists both divine law, created by God, and human law, created by governments. From a consideration of divine and human law, it is possible to discern a fundamental law of nature. To demonstrate the existence of natural laws, Pufendorf advanced an account of the STATE OF NATURE similar to the one provided by Hobbes. Pufendorf argued that human beings are characterized by weakness and self-interest, which contributes to our need to live in common to overcome our individual vulnerability. However, a common life can be preserved only when all persons maintain a sociable attitude toward one another. The fundamental law of nature, then, is to create a peaceful society for the purpose of self-preservation. This mandate has the status of natural law, Pufendorf believed, because it is part of the divine plan for how the physical and human worlds should operate. Consequently, the fundamental law of nature serves as the basis from which all other human laws regulating social conduct are derived.

Given the basic law of sociability, a number of moral duties follow, many of which are negative duties, such as not harming others; others are positive duties, such as treating others as equals. Pufendorf also believed that, because of our shared subjection to the law of nature, all individuals were entitled to RIGHTS of EQUALITY and FREEDOM. Moreover, just as God imposes obligations by legislating divine or natural laws, so too can humans impose obligations by legislating and enacting laws. For Pufendorf, civil government is formed to restrain people from harming others through a system of laws and punishments that govern human conduct. Established through a SOCIAL CONTRACT, the government is responsible for promoting safety by enforcing civil laws and securing human dignity by protecting natural rights. Pufendorf then elaborated theories of civil, constitutional, and international law based on his doctrine of natural law.

Further Reading
Krieger, L. *The Politics of Discretion: Pufendorf and the Acceptance of Natural Law.* Chicago: University of Chicago Press, 1965.

punishment

In political and legal philosophy, the concept of social punishment addresses the reasons, justifications, and practices of inflicting pain or deprivation on a person for some crime that he or she has committed. Two main rationale exist for carrying out punishments in society (such as imprisonment, monetary fines, execution, deportation, loss of civil rights, etc.). First, retribution is the just inflicting of pain or injury on someone who has harmed another. From the biblical standard "an eye for an eye, and a tooth for a tooth," retribution means state-inflicted hurt on a criminal, similar to that inflicted by the criminal on the victim (such as the death penalty for murderers). Immanuel KANT develops this theory of "punishment deserved" or justified social "punishment by desert," the criminal getting what he/she deserves. CHRISTIAN principles of mercy, forgiveness, and forbearance (not inflicting punishment even on those whom you have a right to harm) has mitigated the severity of such justifiable punishment but not eliminated social control of criminals altogether. So, for example, St. AUGUSTINE urges a Roman official to show leniency on some convicted murderers of some church priests, not because they have not sinned but because the church must show Christ's principles of mercy and forgiveness. This does not mean that the perpetrators should not be punished, only that it should be done in a way (such as prison terms) that encourages repentance and turning to God and a good, new life. Hence, the idea of a "penitentiary"—a place where criminals might be confined to (1) be unable to commit more crimes and (2) become penitent or sorry for their past sins, and reform.

The second view of punishment is UTILITARIAN, as in the criminal justice theory of Jeremy BENTHAM. This school of thought sees punishment as securing social peace and affording a deterrent to further crime. If a sure punishment for criminal activity exists, people will be less likely to commit crimes against others (theft, assault, murder, etc.). Debates continue over this "deterrent" theory of punishment. The MODERN liberal and Marxist sociological view is that social conditions (poverty, ignorance, ALIENATION, etc.) cause crime and that only improved economic and social environments will eliminate crime (see ROUSSEAU). CONSERVATIVE thought situates responsibility for criminal actions on the individual, regardless of social condition, and demands personal accountability for criminal behavior (see BURKE).

Contemporary penalogy and criminal justice policy reflects different views of social punishment. The rise of the prison population in America partly reflects a conservative shift toward retribution perspectives.

Puritan

The political thought and views of CHURCH AND STATE of the Puritans: English Calvinist CHRISTIANS especially prominent in the 1600s in England and America. Their identity as "Puritans" came from their Protestant urge to purify the corrupt Anglican and CATHOLIC churches and return to the simple, devout faith of the early Christian church. In theology, this meant a rejection of elaborate rituals and traditions and of highly intellectual doctrine (as in St. Thomas AQUINAS), and a reliance on DEMOCRATIC church governance and teaching from the Bible.

Politically, the Puritans adopted a COVENANT view of government, seeing humanity's relationship to God, the Christians' relationship to the church, and the citizens' relationship to the STATE in terms of covenant commitments and mutual promises. The New England MAYFLOWER COMPACT is an example of this political theory. In both Puritan England (under Oliver CROMWELL) and Puritan America (under John WINTHROP), this covenant view of politics meant that the individual Christian and the "Christian commonwealth" received great blessings (of LIBERTY and prosperity) from God and were responsible to God to use those blessings for God's glory by following his COMMANDMENTS and living godly lives.

Both church governance (in PRESBYTERIAN, Congregationalist, and BAPTIST churches) and state rule (Boston, London, New Haven) were operated on a REPUBLICAN model with EQUALITY among believers and representative, democratic institutions. An example of this Christian republic was the Massachusetts government that rested on cooperation of "godly ministers" and "godly magistrates." An effect of this ideology is seen in Winthrop's view of liberty and AUTHORITY. He divides liberty into (1) natural liberty (of self-interest of sinful human nature) and (2) moral liberty (to do good by those regenerated by Christ in whom the Holy Spirit acts). The state is to support only moral liberty, and its authority comes from God. CITIZENS may elect their rulers, but the magistrates then rule in the name of God and are accountable to Christ for their actions. Natural human liberty leads to selfishness and crime and should be suppressed by the state; the sinful human nature resists all authority; only the "new man in Christ" acknowledges the need for moral and political authority.

The Puritan ideals continue in U.S. EVANGELICAL Christianity, most notably in the CHRISTIAN churches' public opposition to legalized "sin" (ABORTION, pornography, HOMOSEXUALITY, gambling) and support of religious education, reverence, and prayer in school. As part of the United States's CIVIL RELIGION (as in Benjamin FRANKLIN), Puritanism emphasizes America's unique place in the world (a "City on a Hill") and its divine mission to preserve human liberty and dignity and to spread God's truth. Emphasizing the work ethic, honesty, sobriety, and reverence for the Lord, this Puritan ethic is still expressed by U.S. political leaders and movements (such as the CHRISTIAN RIGHT and the REPUBLICAN PARTY).

Quebec Act of 1774

Legislation by the British Parliament that granted religious toleration to the French CATHOLIC population in Canada. This act precipitated the American Revolution and an independent United States because the North American Protestant Christians (especially New England PURITANS) saw it as exemplifying British corruption, compromise, and TYRANNY. Fear that Britain would next impose the Anglican or Catholic system on the REPUBLICAN and free churches of America contributed greatly to the fervor for national independence. Along with other British imperial policies in the 1760s and 1770s (such as increased taxation without representation, military occupation, political usurpation), the Quebec Act symbolized the corruption and evil of the British Empire, from the American colonists' CLASSICAL REPUBLICAN perspective.

The act formally recognized the Catholic Church HIERARCHY and its legal right to collect tithes and educate priests, established French civil law, and extended Quebec's political jurisdiction into the territory between the Ohio and the Mississippi Rivers. This threatened the territorial integrity of the New England settlements, causing massive resistance among the British colonials to the empire. It may have been the decisive factor that pushed a majority of Americans to political independence and the Revolution of 1776 because it combined a political, religious, and economic threat to the North American English Colonists. See the DECLARATION OF INDEPENDENCE.

Quesnay, François (1694–1774)   *French economist and leader of the physiocrats*

François Quesnay was the founder and leader of the physiocratic school of economics who formulated an economic system that emphasized the importance of agriculture and land, as well as of free trade. Quesnay was the court physician for Louis XV and influenced not only French politics, but also the later work of economists such as Adam Smith.

Quesnay was born in Merey and studied medicine at Paris, served as a court physician, and eventually became the personal physician of Louis XV. Quesnay did not actually begin to study economics until his later years. In 1756, he wrote a series of articles for Diderot's *Encyclopédie*. Quesnay's essays included "Farmers" and "Grains," but his chief essay was the *Tableau Économique* (*Economic Table*), which was published in 1758 and translated into English in 1766. The *Economic Table* exerted a significant influence on the economic policies of the king and formed the basis for Quesnay's system of natural economic law. The *Tableau* used the example of an agricultural society to trace the flow of production within an economy. It also provided a precise chart with which to study the economy. The followers of Quesnay came to be known as the *économistes* or physiocrats. Quesnay's ideas ran counter to the prevailing economic theories of the day, which were based on mercantilism and which held that a nation's wealth was based on its accumulation of gold and silver. However, the physiocrats quickly became the dominant economic force within the French court, and Quesnay became the king's main economic advisor.

The French physician advocated that a nation's political economy should be developed as a hierarchy with natural production at its apex. He maintained that agriculture formed the main source of wealth for a nation. Agriculture was different than commerce or industry in that, Quesnay asserted, farming produced products and wealth while manufacturing merely transformed or distributed goods. As such, merchants and industry were neutral factors in a nation's economy and only exchanged wealth from one source to another. Hence, farmers were producers; industrial workers were engaged "sterile" pursuits. Quesnay named his system the *ordre naturel* (natural order).

A central component of Quesnay's economic system was the taxation of land as the sole means for revenue for a government. He believed that taxes on wealth or income inhibited economic performance. The physiocrats were also among the first to advocate free and open trade among nations. Their belief in laissez-faire had a major impact on Adam Smith: The Scottish economist met with Quesnay in 1764 and developed an intense fondness for the French physician.

Quesnay and his system did help inspire Smith's development of the rules of free-market capitalism, but it had limited actual practical value. By contending that laborers were engaged in a sterile occupation and thereby incapable of the production of wealth, Quesnay failed to account for the vast potential of industry to create wealth. Nonetheless, Quesnay's theories continued to exert an influence on economic thought and to underscore the political importance that Western European nations continue to place on agriculture.

Further Reading

Vaggi, G. *The Economics of François Quesnay*. Durham, N.C.: Duke University Press, 1987.

R

racism

The idea or attitude that the human species is separated into different races (European, African, Asian, etc.) and ethnic groups and that these ethnic or geographical differences affect intellectual and social differences. So, for example, white racism historically asserted that Africans' black skin also distinguished them in mental, moral, and cultural capacities. Often, this racist view ranked different groups in terms of superiority, so it identified certain races as "inferior" or deficient in some area (e.g., the stereotypes that black people are lazy or oversexed, that Chinese are mysterious and sneaky, etc.). Such racism is as old as humanity: Ancient tribes showed negative attitudes toward each other and attributed negative characteristics to them. Traditional Chinese culture regarded non-Chinese people as "barbarians"; CLASSICAL Greek culture (such as in ARISTOTLE) saw all non-Greeks as irrational; ancient Israelites, as God's "chosen people," looked down on non-Jews (or "Gentiles"); Muslims believe they are God's only true people.

Such racism changed only with the spread of Christianity, which claimed all people were God's children: In St. Paul's words (Galatians 3:26–28), "In Christ there is no Jew or Greek, slave or free, male or female; but all are one in Christ." This Christian ideal of the interrelationship of all people (or CATHOLIC universalism transcending nationality and ethnic identity) remains incomplete, even in the Christian world, when nationalist orthodox churches (Russian, Greek) and separate denominations (Catholic, Protestant) belie the unity of the faithful.

MODERN, ENLIGHTENMENT science advanced racist ideas through early anthropology and SOCIAL DARWINISM. Classifications by race and ethnicity were considered valid into the 20th century. The violent consequences of this in NAZI Germany where racist theories led to the near-extermination of the Jewish people showed the genocidal consequences of racism. Only in the United States of America, because of its racial, religious, and ethnic mix is racism clearly denounced; most countries and cultures in the world adhere to some form of racial prejudice or NATIONALISM. This renders international politics difficult, given the racist tendency to "dehumanize" other races, justifying warfare and inhumane treatment of foreign peoples. Various United Nations proclamations on HUMAN RIGHTS have advocated EQUALITY of races and cultures, but the human tendency to regard its own cultural identity as superior is stubborn and difficult to ameliorate. The rise of LIBERALISM, CAPITALISM, and DEMOCRACY has tended to break down many characteristics of racism because they emphasize the individual (his or her talents, abilities) over any group identity.

Further Readings

Biddiss, M.D. *Father of Racist Ideology: The Social and Political Thought of Count Gobineau*. New York: Weybright and Talley, 1970.
Mosse, G. L. "Toward the final solution." In *A History of European Racism*. New York: H. Fertig, 1978.

radical

A person, social movement, or IDEOLOGY that criticizes the existing social or political system and works to change it. This radical challenging of the status quo (current social or political structure) usually grows from an exposing of the problems or injustices of the existing order and proposes reforms or alternative systems that will improve the country or ruling institutions. In this sense, radicalism can come from many sources (religious, moral, economic, political) and can seek different results. SOCRATES challenges decadent Athens with an appeal to ethical and moral goodness; Savonarola attacks decadent Italian CATHOLIC society from a radical CHRISTIAN perspective; Karl MARX's communism levels an economic critique of CAPITALIST society and politics. MODERN radicalism usually is associated with the LEFT (LIBERALISM and SOCIALISM), but RIGHT-WING movements (such as FASCISM) can be equally radical, in the sense of dramatically changing the existing social order. However, like Jean-Jacques ROUSSEAU, radical thought believes in the human capacity to remake society and to make things better by human action. This optimism of the human ability to improve individuals and society is contrasted with CONSERVATIVE thought (as in St. AUGUSTINE, Edmund BURKE) with its view that human nature is constant and that social problems exist in all political systems (and, therefore, efforts must be made to conserve what is valuable in existing systems). Radicals tend to become conservative when they achieve power and to display the same intolerance to change that their opponents did before them (such as did Joseph STALIN).

Radical views tend to arise when the existing political order no longer functions effectively (as in prerevolutionary France and Russia), so periods of order and prosperity tend to discourage radicalism.

Further Reading

Lincoln, A. H. *Some Political and Social Ideas of English Dissent*. London: Octagon Books, 1938.

rational/rationalism/reason

The human capacity to think and decide according to knowledge, evidence, and understanding, which leads to intelligent and just conclusions. For the CLASSICAL Greek philosophers (PLATO and ARISTOTLE), this reasoning faculty (or "soul") is what made humans distinct and superior to other animals (or "beasts") and like the gods. The wisdom of Plato's PHILOSOPHER-KING and the "reasoned speech" of Aristotle's civilized ruler made rationality the center of good politics. Roman theory (CICERO) similarly values reason and LAW that emerges from rational deliberation. The Judeo-CHRISTIAN view that humankind is formed "in the image" of God is partly related to reason, thought, and speaking. St. AUGUSTINE's emphasis on human weakness and sin dilutes the efficacy of human reason (because it can be deceived), but St. Thomas AQUINAS places human reason as one source of the knowledge of the divine (and NATURAL LAW). The positive view of human reason's ability to know reality and improve society continues in the MODERN ENLIGHTENMENT and MARXISM. Thomas HOBBES identifies reason as the calculating function (tabulating pleasure and pain) that leads people out of the barbaric STATE OF NATURE and into civilized society and government. John LOCKE includes a moral dimension to human reason, which enjoins respecting others' RIGHTS. Karl MARX's "DIALECTICAL" reasoning supports the view that history is moving toward COMMUNISM.

The benefits, qualities, and limitations of human reason underlie much of Western political thought. Systems (spiritual, emotional, intuitive) that depreciate reason as a reliable source of knowledge tend to be less deliberative, procedural, and based on facts or evidence. When different societies (Eastern vs. Western; TOTALITARIAN vs. REPUBLICAN; etc.) subscribe to different systems or styles of reasoning, it can cause misunderstanding and confusion, making negotiations difficult. For example, the Soviet or Arab culture does not consider it rational to tell the truth to one's enemy while Americans view honesty as essential to rationality; conflict can result from these differing concepts of "reason." If Chinese culture teaches that all Western peoples are unintelligent barbarians, Western arguments for liberty may not be appreciated or accepted.

The complexity of definition of reason, then, makes the concept of little use unless it is carefully explained and thoroughly defined.

Further Readings

Copp, D., and Zimmerman, D., eds. *Morality, Reason and Truth: New Essays on the Foundations of Ethics.* Totowa, N.J.: Rowman & Allanheld, 1984.

Hollis, M., and Lukes, S., eds. *Rationality and Relativism.* Cambridge, Mass.: MIT Press, 1979.

Rauschenbusch, Walter (1861–1918)   *U.S. social gospel thinker and activist*

A leading figure in the SOCIAL GOSPEL MOVEMENT of the early 20th century in the United States, Rauschenbusch applied CHRISTIAN social ETHICS to problems of INDUSTRIALISM, poverty, unemployment, disease, and crime in the United States. As a BAPTIST minister, witnessing the horrible social conditions of the poor in New York City, Rauschenbusch sought to solve MODERN social problems with the teachings of Jesus (charity, love, peace), using the government to promote education, health care, poverty relief, and safe working conditions. This "social gospel" became part of the PROGRESSIVE-era DEMOCRATIC PARTY's social reforms and led to the liberal WELFARE STATE of the NEW DEAL.

This social gospel blending of religion and politics (like later LIBERATION THEOLOGY) believed that curing social ills would contribute to the establishment of the kingdom of God on earth. It tended to be optimistic about the human capacity to improve humanity and society by the right use of political power and also diminished the realism of St. AUGUSTINE and John CALVIN who saw the persistence of sin in all social reforms and systems.

Rauschenbusch blended an EVANGELICAL, practical faith with SOCIALISM in his main books, *Christianity and the Social Crisis* (1912) and *A Theology for the Social Gospel* (1917). His writings greatly influenced Christian and liberal social thinkers in 20th-century United States, including Charles SHELDON, Reinhold NIEBUHR, and civil-rights leader Martin Luther KING, Jr. His emphasis on the social responsibility of Christians grew out of his Protestant religious faith.

Rawls, John (1921–)   *U.S. political philosopher*

Most famous for his book *A Theory of Justice* (1971), John Rawls taught philosophy at Harvard University. His theory provides a philosophical basis and rationale for American Liberal WELFARE-STATE DEMOCRACY (or European SOCIAL DEMOCRACY). He claims that his work provides an alternative to UTILITARIAN philosophy, but it remains a more contemporary justification of LEFTIST political policy.

Rawls begins with a British, liberal (John LOCKE), SOCIAL-CONTRACT approach to the formation of government. He posits an "original position" (like the STATE OF NATURE) in which a RATIONAL individual finds himself or herself choosing the best form of STATE. An important feature of this theoretical position is the "veil of ignorance" over the individual, which prevents him or her from knowing where in the future society he or she will be placed (rich or poor, famous or obscure, secure or insecure, etc.). This lack of knowledge of what social advantages one might have in society makes a rational person choose a society where the least advantaged are better off than the least advantaged in any other society. In other words, if you should find yourself poor, sick, lowly, and without help, you would want a social system that takes care of such miserable people better than any other society. This may at first glance be COMMUNISM, but the general poverty of that system disqualifies it. The society that best takes care of the least advantaged (Rawls's "maximin strategy") is a mixed economy: free-enterprise CAPITALISM with extensive government regulation for the common good and with social-welfare Liberalism. This constitutes JUSTICE for Rawls. The free-market economy creates prosperity, rewards innovation, and provides material incentives to work, while the state welfare programs provide equal opportunity to succeed; aid to the poor, sick, and disabled; and overall social harmony.

Rawls bases this "justice as fairness" on two principles of justice: (1) that each individual has the right to the most extensive LIBERTY (of speech, religion, property, movement) compatible with the equal liberty of everyone else; and (2) that any inequality of wealth and position is arranged so that the result is a greater benefit to the least advantaged and that all high positions are DEMOCRATIC and open to all people through equal opportunity. For example, the government tax and economic regulation should ensure that great wealth is earned by legitimate means (inventing truly useful products, establishing more productive systems, etc., not financial manipulation or dishonest, fraudulent business practices); and that the fruits of those unequal benefits can be justly taxed to provide help to the poor and weak in society (through funding public education, public housing, health care, unemployment compensation, etc.). One side benefit of this social-welfare system for Rawls is that the wealthy can truly enjoy their riches (or high positions) without guilt because they have both "earned" them and have helped their weaker brethren. A CONSTITUTIONAL REPUBLIC, like the United States, that guarantees individual RIGHTS, combined with a liberal social-welfare state that redistributes wealth, is probably the best possible system, in Rawls's view.

Critics on the LEFT (SOCIALISM) of Rawls attack his acceptance of free-market capitalism and the need for material incentives. Critics on the CONSERVATIVE RIGHT (Robert NOZICK) fault him for giving the state too much power and for excessive taxation. But Rawls's *Theory of Justice* remains one of the most influential, original political theories of the 20th century and an exemplary philosophical treatment of the U.S. political/economic/social system.

John Rawls was educated at Princeton University.

Further Reading
Daniels, N., ed. *Reading Rawls*. Stanford, Calif.: Stanford University Press, 1975.

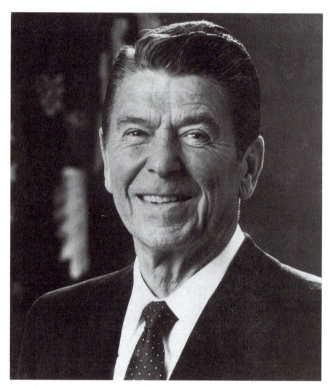

Ronald Reagan, 1981. (LIBRARY OF CONGRESS)

Reagan, Ronald (1911–) *U.S. politician, president of the United States, and Conservative Republican*

Reagan is noteworthy in political thought for his forceful advocacy of CONSERVATIVE REPUBLICAN PARTY politics and their implementation during his presidential terms (1980–88). His Conservative LAISSEZ-FAIRE policies of reducing government taxes and regulation of business came to be known as "Reaganomics." He combined this anti-Liberal WELFARE-STATE ideology with a fierce antiCOMMUNISM and resistance to the SOVIET UNION. Reagan's Conservative Republican policies in the United States in the 1980s led to widespread deregulation of business (communications, airlines, etc.) along free-market lines, reductions of federal income taxes, cuts in social-welfare programs, and increases in military spending. These programs led to an increased federal deficit, revived economic growth and prosperity, and contributed to the eventual defeat of the Soviet Union in the cold war and the decline of communism throughout the world. This, along with Reagan's win-

ning personality, made him one of the most popular presidents in Modern history.

Raised in Illinois, Ronald Reagan imbibed the traditional middle-class U.S. values of that time (EVANGELICAL Christianity, strong family loyalty, PATRIOTISM, and a belief in hard work). His mother was a devout Protestant CHRISTIAN, raising her children in the church with a deep religious faith. Ronald Reagan accepted this Evangelical Christianity early in life, and it influenced his attitudes toward politics throughout his political career. This explains the support he received from the CHRISTIAN RIGHT.

Reagan attended Eureka College and worked in radio, films, and television before entering politics in 1966. After serving two terms as governor of California, he campaigned for president, finally being elected in 1980.

The enormous impact of Reagan's presidency on both domestic U.S. and international politics led to a whole ideological branch of the U.S. Republican Party ("Reagan Republican"). This "Reaganesque" political philosophy combines moral and fiscal conservatism, uncompromising anticommunism, and fervent patriotism. Reagan's personality and politics were seen to reflect and reinforce basic U.S. cultural attitudes, CIVIL

RELIGION, and social values, explaining his popularity among even some traditional DEMOCRATIC PARTY supporters.

Further Reading

Shepherd, D., ed. *Ronald Reagan: In God I Trust*. Wheeling, Illinois: Tyndale House Publishers, 1984.

realism

Political realism is the recognition of evil and injustice in the nature of humanity, society, and government. A realist acknowledges the persistent selfishness and cruelty in human behavior and the use of political power to oppress and tyrannize others. Such realism is contrasted with political or psychological optimism, or IDEALISM (see ENLIGHTENMENT), which believes that people and states can be improved, civilized, and even perfected.

The realist political tradition emerges in several political IDEOLOGIES, mostly CONSERVATIVE. The CATHOLIC thinker St. AUGUSTINE draws his realistic assessment of human nature and politics from the biblical view of humanity as sinful and of society as full of conflict and strife. Only the grace of God through Christ can transform humans into kind, loving creatures through spiritual rebirth in Jesus. Even then, the world is dominated by evil, power struggles, crime, and war; Christians themselves are not totally immune from being deceived and led into wrong actions. This "CHRISTIAN realism" continues in the Protestant theology of John CALVIN, American Constitution Founder James MADISON, and, in the 20th century, Reinhold NIEBUHR.

Secular realism is expressed in the RENAISSANCE Italian thinker MACHIAVELLI. His assessment of human nature and society resembles Augustinian thought but without the hope of redemption in Christ. For Machiavelli, humans always desire everything (infinite wealth, power, prestige, honor) but are frustrated by not being able to get it, so they are mean and petty, ready to blame others for their difficulties, especially the government. Therefore, the STATE (or Prince) must know how to trick and control these ignorant, self-centered masses, using deceit, cunning, and fear. An immoral (or "prudent") leader is needed to fool people and to maintain order. It is believed that both Adolf HITLER and Joseph STALIN took lessons from Machiavellian realism.

In modern Conservative thought, Edmund BURKE displays realism in his suspicions of RADICAL social reformers' optimism. The idealism of Jean-Jacques ROUSSEAU's theories, implemented in the disastrous French Revolution of 1789, represent the dangers of not having an accurate, "realistic" conception of human nature. For Burke, humans require extensive cultivation and civilizing to make them even moderately good. This requires stable, traditional institutions (schools, family, church, property, government) to bring out the best in people and to suppress their natural evil impulses.

Such "RIGHT" political realism is rejected by the LEFTIST political theories that paint a more positive image of human nature: that humanity is naturally good and kind if only freed from authority and restraints (ANARCHISM) or given sufficient economic prosperity, education, and political power (SOCIALISM and COMMUNISM). This favorable view of humanity is shared by ARISTOTLE, Thomas JEFFERSON, and Karl MARX. Realism sees these views as naïve and self-righteous.

Reformation

The political thought of the Protestant Reformation in Europe in the 1500s. This view of proper CHURCH-AND-STATE relations broke with the CATHOLIC Church (St. Thomas AQUINAS) and was expressed by Martin LUTHER, John CALVIN, the French HUGUENOTS, and English PURITANS. In general, it emphasizes the EQUALITY of all believers, fosters a DEMOCRATIC or REPUBLICAN structure in the government and church, and advocates LIBERTY of individual conscience (freedom of religion). Emphasis on the scriptures (Bible) as the sole source of knowledge (vs. tradition, experience, or reason) and the spiritual unity of the churches characterized the Reformation and its political thought. Given the large number of churches that emerged during the Reformation (Lutheran, Reformed, BAPTIST, PRESBYTERIAN, etc.), it is not a single movement but a collection of movements that greatly changed MODERN Europe and America. See PROTESTANT POLITICAL THOUGHT.

Further Readings

Davies, R. E. *The Problem of Authority in the Continental Reformers*. London: Epworth Press, 1946.

Franklin, J. H. *Constitutionalism and Resistance in the Sixteenth Century*. New York: Pegasus, 1969.

Grimm, H. J. *The Reformation Era 1500–1650*, 2nd ed. New York: Macmillan, 1973.

Williams, G. H. *The Radical Reformation*. Philadelphia: Westminster Press, 1962.

reification

A concept in MARXIST, COMMUNIST, and CRITICAL THEORY philosophy that describes the reverse of the proper relationship of subject and object (or humans and things). In healthy, free humanity, humans properly control and order nature, society, and things, but with ALIENATION in society, this proper human dominance of the world is reversed, and things, commodities, economics come to control people. In CAPITALISM, this reification takes the form of the economic market (which should serve humankind) dominating and controlling humanity. MARXISM is confident that SOCIALISM will end this unnatural reversal of roles between humans and their environment, as people take over the processes of production, distribution, and life generally. The experience of communism in the SOVIET UNION and China did not confirm this optimistic perspective. Instead, as even such Marxist thinkers as Georg Lukács and Herbert MARCUSE showed, socialism imposed even more control over humans than did market capitalism.

The underlying assumption of the reification view is that humanity can and should control its own destiny, unencumbered by divine, natural, or social limitations. This proud perspective of human abilities is challenged by the REALISM of various thinkers (St. AUGUSTINE, Edmund BURKE, Reinhold NIEBUHR, etc.) and by NATURAL-LAW theory.

religion and politics   See CHURCH AND STATE.

Renaissance

Meaning the "rebirth" of CLASSICAL (Greek and Roman) HUMANISM in 13th- to 16th-century Italy, Renaissance political thought is seen as a rejection of MEDIEVAL CHRISTIAN conceptions (St. AUGUSTINE) of humanity and politics. Reviving the REPUBLICAN ideals of ARISTOTLE, PLATO, and CICERO, Renaissance philosophy focused on the REALISM of worldly politics (as opposed to religious or spiritual dimensions), humanity's social nature and reason, direct participation of all citizens in governance, and the separation of CHURCH AND STATE.

Growing partly from the new independence of several Italian city-states (such as Florence), the translation of Aristotle's *Politics* in the year 1260, the strength of trade GUILDS, and a discovery of Arabic astrology, Renaissance politics were known for their ruthlessness, cruelty, deceit, and violence (as expressed in MACHIAVELLI). Still, they led to the development of MODERN SOCIAL-CONTRACT theory (Thomas HOBBES) and, ultimately, LIBERALISM. With the rise of legalism, the RULE-OF-LAW doctrine, and prominence of lawyers in government, Renaissance political theory diminished the value of citizens' characters and personal ETHICS. Christian REFORMATION thought responded to this void by emphasizing the individual's responsibility to God and Christian vocation in public service (as described by John CALVIN).

An effect of Renaissance ideas on perception of history was the replacing of a providential view of time (moving toward the return of Christ by God's plan) with an ancient cyclical and Arabic astrological perspective (seeing history repeating itself and fortune-tellers' ability to predict the future).

A mixture of classical, Eastern, and civic HUMANIST ideology and Renaissance literature was essentially Modern and eclectic.

Further Readings

Cochrane, E., and Kirschner, J., eds. *The Renaissance*. Chicago: University of Chicago Press, 1986.
Skinner, Q. *The Foundations of Modern Political Thought*, vol. I. *The Renaissance*. Cambridge, Eng.: Cambridge University Press, 1979.

representation/representative

When a person or institution governs for another person or group, it is said that the first represents the second. Most common in a REPUBLIC, the people elect government representatives to express their INTERESTS and to rule the country accordingly. The details of *how* state officials are selected and in what manner they represent their constituents vary widely in different political theories and political systems.

CLASSICAL Greek political thought (ARISTOTLE) maintained that all CITIZENS should rule in some capacity and that the human need to rule could not be delegated to other representatives. This classical or "direct-DEMOCRACY" tradition continues in much of Western political theory (MONTESQUIEU, ROUSSEAU, BARBER) that denies the possibility of delegating the human political function or of having democracy in a large or populous country.

MEDIEVAL CATHOLIC theory (St. Thomas AQUINAS) is more positive about the possibility of rulers representing the nation's common interest; even MONARCHY, or the rule of one person, can represent all citizens' concerns and needs. In MODERN republican theory (as in that of British liberal John LOCKE and American James MADISON), a government can be truly representative if it has the mechanisms of regular elections, limited terms for state officials, and popular voting or SUFFRAGE. Most Modern INDUSTRIAL democracies are representative in that sense. The COMMUNIST theories of Karl MARX and V. I. LENIN assert that a revolutionary, working-class political party can represent the interests of the entire proletariat, or workers, through STATE-operated SOCIALISM.

In representative democracies, where public officials are elected periodically, the question of *how* representatives govern arises. Edmund BURKE argued that members of the British Parliament should be "trustee" representatives—exercising their own best judgment on policy issues, whether or not they agreed with the majority of the voters. A contrasting "delegate" view is that elected representatives should simply reflect the preferences of their constituents. The American model of representative democracy contains both the "trustee" role of elected officials, trusting their judgment and giving them considerable autonomy, and the "delegate" role, which expects government representatives to express generally the opinions of the voters.

Other informal groups and organizations can represent citizens' interests in government within modern PLURALISTIC democracies. Business and professional associations; women's groups, minority, and religious organizations; ENVIRONMENTAL groups and organizations representing certain age groups (such as the American Association of Retired Persons, or A.A.R.P.) all affect government policy through lobbying, legislative influence, and court cases. Pluralism allows a variety of means of influence or representation.

Further Readings

Birch, A. H. *Representation.* New York: Praeger, 1972.
Pitkin, H. F. *The Concept of Representation.* Berkeley: University of California Press, 1967.

republic

A system of government that involves the whole community (from the Latin, *res publica*) and rules for the common good. In MODERN times, a republic is often contrasted with MONARCHY on the one hand and with pure DEMOCRACY on the other. Most republics are REPRESENTATIVE democracies; that is, political leaders are elected or chosen by the majority of the people in the nation. In this sense, Thomas JEFFERSON is considered a typical republican thinker and the United States of America is a typical modern republic. The specific forms of representative government differ in various Modern republics, but they all share a rejection of MEDIEVAL kingship and ARISTOCRACY. For the historical origins of this ideal, see REPUBLICANISM.

republican/republicanism

A political philosophy or IDEOLOGY that emphasizes government for the common good, direct CITIZEN participation in governing, a sense of public VIRTUE (or personal sacrifice for the good of society), and preservation of the LIBERTY and legal RIGHTS of citizens.

The earliest form of this thought comes in the CLASSICAL republicanism of PLATO, ARISTOTLE, and CICERO. This ancient Greek and Roman republicanism specifically rejected the rule of one king, TYRANT, or emperor. Just laws and policies, as well as intelligent, virtuous citizens, required wide participation of the population in governing. Citizens must be qualified educationally, economically, and ethically to be responsible rulers who will establish and maintain JUSTICE. The view that concentrated political and economic POWER corrupts leaders; that wealth, luxury, moral decadence, and tyranny come together, commends a republic of simple, modest, hearty citizens who rule together for the common good. This links "republican virtue" to the middle-class farmers and artisans who have discipline, decency, and healthy instincts. A sturdy yeoman PATRIOTISM, military valor, and basic honesty combine to ward off political and financial intrigue, oppression, and perversion in the STATE. The decline of both the Greek and Roman republics into commercial empires that became political oligarchies and immoral societies confirms the republican fear of opulence and power.

After the largely monarchical MIDDLE AGES, republicanism revived in RENAISSANCE Italy and Protestant Europe. Again, the themes of simple, popular government by common people were seen as a virtuous alternative to a corrupt and decadent monarchy, court life, Catholicism, and tyranny. MARSILIUS OF PADUA asserted this republican ideal in terms of popular SOVEREIGNTY. CHRISTIAN thinkers Martin LUTHER and John CALVIN presented republican government as the appropriate CHURCH-AND-STATE structure for the Protestant "priesthood of all believers." John LOCKE portrayed Modern republics in terms of a SOCIAL CONTRACT of all individuals, delegating limited power to the state. James HARRINGTON applied classical republicanism to England through the virtuous yeoman farmer, the country gentry ruling England rather than the corrupt monarchy and administration in London. This portrayal of agrarian culture as naturally more virtuous and republican than city dwellers continues in the American version of republicanism (in Thomas JEFFERSON). French liberalism (as in Jean-Jacques ROUSSEAU) presents a more COMMUNITARIAN republicanism, explaining the TOTALITARIAN qualities of the French Revolution of 1789.

British liberalism lends itself to a more legalistic, mechanical republic in which CONSTITUTIONAL structures of CHECKS AND BALANCES, periodic elections, individual rights, and divided power ensures protection against concentrated power, tyranny, and oppression. James MADISON constructed the U.S. Constitution to prevent any person or group from gaining all power in the state. Thus, the mechanics of the state protect republican values, even if the citizens are not all virtuous.

PURITAN England, under Oliver CROMWELL, and Puritan America, under John WINTHROP, argued that a Christian commonwealth could embody the virtues of moral government and moral citizens.

The popularity of this republican ideal led it to be adopted as a title of some states that were not democratic, such as COMMUNIST China (the People's "Republic" of China); the SOVIET UNION (Union of Soviet Socialist "Republics"); Communist Eastern Germany (the Democratic "Republic" of Germany); and North Korea (the Democratic "Republic" of Korea). This use of the term *republic* by governments that were dictatorial led to confusion in those countries over what constituted republicanism.

Contemporary studies of republican government tend to concentrate on the structures and procedures of the state and the insurance of individual NATURAL RIGHTS, popular sovereignty, and economic liberty.

Further Readings

Pocock, J. G. A. *The Machiavellian Moment: Florentine Political Thought and the Atlantic Republican Tradition.* Princeton, N.J.: Princeton University Press, 1975.
Tocqueville, A. de. *Democracy in America,* G. Lawrence, transl., J. P. Mayer and M. Lerner, eds. Garden City, N.Y.: Anchor Books, 1968.

Republican Party

One of the two major political parties in the United States of America, the other being the DEMOCRATIC PARTY. In terms of political thought or IDEOLOGY, the U.S. Republican Party tends to be more CONSERVATIVE, favoring business, free-enterprise, CAPITALISM, limited federal government, lower taxes, and reduced WELFARE-STATE social programs. This RIGHT-WING political stance can be traced back to the FEDERALIST Party of early America and the Whig Party of the early 1800s.

Historically, the Republican Party dates from 1854, its first president being Abraham LINCOLN (elected in 1860). Lincoln's presidency was dominated by the American Civil War and the ABOLITION of black slavery. Through most of its history the Republican Party has advanced business interests and identified U.S. prosperity and FREEDOM with unrestricted capitalist economics, low taxes, tariffs to protect U.S. industry, and LAISSEZ-FAIRE government policies. Republican presidents Calvin Coolidge (1924–28), Herbert Hoover (1928–32), Dwight Eisenhower (1952–60), Richard NIXON (1968–74), and Ronald REAGAN (1980–88) all espoused these conservative, probusiness ideals.

Since the 1960s, the Republican Party has also represented conservative moral values ("family values," CHRISTIAN religious ethics, antiCOMMUNISM); the Democratic Party has been more PROGRESSIVE in its moral stance (FEMINISM, HOMOSEXUAL rights, pro-ABORTION rights, etc.). Thus, the Republican Party has endorsed the CHRISTIAN RIGHT's agenda against abortion, pornography, gay rights, and HUMANISM. This has led to the Republican Party as a symbol of traditional values or what James Hunter in his book, *Culture Wars,* calls "orthodox" morality. Consequently, the Republican Party tends to receive support from EVANGELICAL Christians, conservative CATHOLIC, traditional women.

As U.S. political parties seek to attract a majority of voters, each tries to appear MODERATE in its policy stances, but the Republican Party remains more conservative, probusiness, and traditional in moral values.

revolution

A sudden, often violent, changing of government, rulers, and often social, cultural, economic, and religious systems in a country. Example of major political revolutions include the English Glorious Revolution of 1688, the American Revolution of 1776, the French Revolution of 1789, the Russian (COMMUNIST) Revolution of October 1917, and the Chinese (Communist) revolution of 1949. Leading revolutionary leaders include Thomas JEFFERSON, Robespierre, Oliver CROMWELL, V.I. LENIN, and MAO TSE-TUNG.

Most revolutions include three components: (1) the collapse of the established system (through financial bankruptcy, defeat in war, loss of public confidence, ineffectiveness in governing); (2) a struggle for control of the state (by former rulers, new RADICALS, alternative groups using electoral machinery, military warfare, alignment with foreign nations); and (3) the establishment of new institutions of government, political parties, LAWS, ownership of PROPERTY, education, and customs. The forms and time of these revolutionary occurrences vary widely in history, making prediction of the outcomes of social revolutions extremely problematical.

The political theories of revolution attempt to explain the causes and effects of revolutions; whether revolutionary activity is good or evil; and if revolutions are necessary and inevitable.

PLATO describes revolutionary political change in Book VIII of *The Republic* as having an internal logic. Each system of government or regime has a certain VIRTUE or strength and a certain vice or weakness, and governments succeed others by satisfying the deficiency of the previous regime. So, for example, ARISTOCRACY has the virtue of wisdom but the vice of dishonor. The state that replaces it, timocracy (military government), has the virtue of honor, which addresses the weakness of aristocracy. But a military state has the vice of poverty, which causes it to be overthrown by an oligarchy, which has the virtue of wealth. Oligarchy's greed leads to inequality, which causes DEMOCRACY to replace it. Democracy has EQUALITY, but its FREEDOM causes chaos, leading to TYRANNY. So revolution, in Plato's view can be understood in terms of successive regimes that address the deficiencies of their predecessors.

ARISTOTLE sees more varied causes of social and political change, but the chief one is a ruler violating the principles of his or her own CONSTITUTION. Most common changes are not to different types of regimes, but are a corruption of the existing one. So kingship, the rule of one person for the common good, is corrupted to tyranny, the rule of one for the ruler's self-interest. Aristocracy, the government of a few for the common good, is corrupted by selfish rulers who become an oligarchy. Polity is the rule of the many (majority) for the good of the whole nation; its corrupt

form is democracy, or the majority ruling for its own interest.

Roman theories of revolutionary change (POLYBIUS) emphasize a natural cycle of a state's development (birth, growth, decay, death). It advises those practices that prolong the life of a REPUBLIC and keep it healthy (high moral standards, military virtue, the RULE OF LAW, financial frugality, a sense of public duty). CICERO expresses the Roman ideal in his image of the sturdy republican soldier-citizen: Luxury and moral decadence weaken this healthy republic, leading to economic, ethical, military, and political decline and destruction. The wealth and violence of the Roman Empire fulfilled this Ciceronian prophecy.

The CHRISTIAN era expressed a biblical and providential view of political change. St. AUGUSTINE sees the fall of the Roman Empire as God's wrath on the immorality and pride of imperial Rome. PURITAN notions of political COVENANT see stable government following from obedience to God's laws; personal sin and political corruption lead to social revolution.

John LOCKE's British LIBERALISM presents a SOCIAL-CONTRACT view of the state (a legitimate government preserving the NATURAL RIGHTS of the people) that allows for a "Right to Revolution" overthrowing a STATE that violates citizens' rights to life, LIBERTY, and property. This theory justified the American colonists revolution against the British Empire.

MARXISM views revolution as inevitable and reflecting natural, historical social PROGRESS. As economic technology advances beyond the control of the ruling ELITE, it empowers a rising social class to take over the government. Thus, for Karl MARX, the CAPITALIST class of INDUSTRIALISM grows more powerful than the landed aristocracy of FEUDALISM and eventually takes political power from the MEDIEVAL monarchs (in the English revolution of 1688, the French Revolution of 1789). When the workers gain sufficient might, they overthrow the capitalist, bourgeois republics and establish SOCIALISM under the "dictatorship of the proletariat." Thus, revolution is inevitable and good, for COMMUNIST thinkers.

Max WEBER portrayed political history as the tension between BUREAUCRATIC rationality, economic change, and charismatic leadership. As kings faltered through wars and economic crises, dynamic leaders arose, leading radical movements to overthrow them.

Edmund BURKE's traditional CONSERVATISM resisted sudden revolutionary change (especially in France), which he thought caused the destruction of much of the valuable past institutions, cultures, and habits. He saw the British and American revolutions as orderly, rational, and preserving historic liberty and RIGHTS. The U.S. Constitution attempted to institutionalize political change through periodic elections, Supreme Court interpretation, and the constitutional-amendment procedure.

Further Readings

Brinton, C. *The Anatomy of Revolution*. New York: Vintage Books, 1965.
Goldstone, J. A., ed. *Revolutions: Theoretical, Comparative, and Historical Studies*. San Diego, Calif.: Harcourt Brace Jovanovich, 1986.

Ricardo, David (1772–1823)   *Economist*

David Ricardo is associated with the classical school of economics along with such figures as Adam SMITH, Jeremy BENTHAM, James MILL, and John McCulloch. Aspects of his work were also important to SOCIALIST and COMMUNIST political theorists.

Ricardo along with Smith and others argued for open economic markets, minimum taxation, and the least possible government control and influence in economic affairs and relations. The thought here was that individuals left free to pursue their own economic interests would contribute through this activity to the general prosperity and well-being of the country. Ricardo's main contribution to this economic theory was his theory of rent and its associated theory of value.

Ricardo argued that the value of commodities was determined by the value of the labor required to produce them. Ricardo applied this idea, along with his commitments to LAISSEZ-FAIRE CAPITALISM, to the economic issues of his time, specifically to the role of precious metals in the national economy, the price of corn, and the role of rent on the productivity of agricultural lands. He addressed these concerns in a number of pamphlets published from 1809 onward. With the encouragement of his friend James Mill, he published a systematic account of his views in 1817 titled *Principles of Political Economy and Taxation*.

Ricardo's claim that labor is the source of value was taken up by thinkers such as MARX as a basis for attacking and criticizing capitalist economic and social arrangements. They argued that workers deserve the full value, or at least most of the value, of their labor.

Correspondingly, it was argued that capitalist profit is the theft of value from the worker who produces it.

Ricardo was born in England and was educated in both England and Holland, where his father was born. He left school at the age of 14 when he joined his father's business. Although he had no higher education, Ricardo was a very successful businessman and made his fortune early. In 1819, he became a member of Parliament for a very small Irish constituency. Because Ricardo had never been to Ireland, it is assumed he bought the seat, which he kept until his death at the age of 51.

Further Reading

Samuels, W. J. *The Classical Theory of Economic Policy*. Cleveland: World, 1966.

Richelieu, Armand-Jean du Plessis, Cardinal de (1585–1642)   *French politician and churchman*

An able CHURCH AND STATE administrator, Richelieu was consecrated bishop of Luçon, France, in 1606 and elected to national Estates-General assembly in 1614. King Louis XIII appointed him secretary of state in 1616. Later, as President of the Council of Ministers, he became the de facto ruler of France. During the CATHOLIC–Protestant wars, Richelieu at times tolerated, at other times attacked, the HUGUENOTS; supported German Protestant princes; and advocated church independence from Rome. He wrote on ABSOLUTISM similar to Jean BODIN. As an active late MEDIEVAL cardinal and statesman, he exemplified the European integration of religion and politics.

Right/Right-wing

In political IDEOLOGY, the Right is a CONSERVATIVE position associated in Britain and the United States with the probusiness, limited WELFARE-STATE views of the Conservative Party (United Kingdom) and REPUBLICAN PARTY (United States). Familiar leaders of these Right-wing attitudes and policies include Prime Minister Margaret Thatcher and President Ronald REAGAN. Rightist politics favor free-enterprise CAPITALISM, lower taxes, reduced social welfare programs, and individual FREEDOM. This is contrasted with the Liberal LEFT, which advocates increased welfare-state SOCIALISM, regulation of business, and social EQUALITY.

Right politics have tended to be very antiCOMMUNIST, while Leftists were more sympathetic to communism. Rightists tend to be pro-economic development, while Leftists are more pro-ENVIRONMENTALISM.

In the United States and Britain, the extreme Right tends to be LIBERTARIAN; in Europe, it has approached FASCISM. Both tend to be NATIONALISTIC, in favor of a strong military and defense spending. Other conservative Right-wing leaders and movements include William J. BUCKLEY, George F. WILL, Richard NIXON, the JOHN BIRCH SOCIETY, and the Liberty Fund.

During the 1980s and 1990s, a resurgence of Rightist conservatism in Great Britain and the United States reversed the 50-year dominance of Leftist (Labour Party and Liberal Democratic Party) politics in those countries.

rights

Benefits or possessions held by individuals or groups and granted by God, nature, custom, or society. For example, the individual NATURAL RIGHTS (described by John LOCKE) to "Life, LIBERTY and PROPERTY" form the basis of MODERN LIBERAL DEMOCRACY and CAPITALISM. Locke traces the origins of these rights to physical existence and self-preservation: Once a person is alive, created, he or she has the right to continue existence (until natural death occurs), or "Life," and to those things necessary to that continued existence ("Liberty and Property"). Liberalism extends these basic rights (by John Stuart MILL) to the social and intellectual rights (FREEDOM of speech, press, religion, assembly, fair trial, etc.). The U.S. CONSTITUTION's Bill of Rights expresses these British liberal rights.

From such MODERN individual rights come contemporary group rights (women's rights; HOMOSEXUAL rights; ANIMAL RIGHTS; HUMAN RIGHTS—see related articles).

CLASSICAL and Judeo-CHRISTIAN political theory hardly mentions "rights," emphasizing interrelated JUSTICE, public VIRTUE, obedience, and religious morality more than the INDIVIDUALISM of private rights. Like the concept of *freedom* or *liberty,* these ancient and Christian thinkers (see ARISTOTLE, St. AUGUSTINE) place indivi-dual rights within a context of community responsibility and conformance to God's will and COMMANDMENTS, and they regard the selfish assertion of rights as rebellion and sin. Similarly, various Modern nonliberal philosophies (MARXISM, COMMUNISM, SOCIALISM, FASCISM) disregard individual rights for their divisive effects on the society, the community, the nation, or the economy.

So the language of rights is primarily one of modern, individual self-assertion and not representative of the entire Western tradition. The main value of rights theory is the protection of individual belief and conscience (religious and political), expression (speech and press), and action against TYRANNICAL government or oppressive institutional invasion.

Further Readings

Dworkin, R. *Taking Rights Seriously,* rev. ed. Cambridge, Mass.: Harvard University Press, 1979.
Finnis, J. *Natural Law and Natural Rights.* Oxford, Eng.: Clarendon Press, 1980.

Robertson, Marion "Pat" (1930–   ) *U.S. conservative political and religious leader*

Founder of the Christian Broadcasting Network (CBN) and Regent University in Virginia Beach, Virginia, "Pat" Robertson is an outspoken CHRISTIAN CONSERVATIVE and leader of religious telecommunications worldwide. The son of a prominent U.S. senator, Robertson attended Yale Law School before entering the BAPTIST ministry. His Christian television network grew to a multimillion-dollar media empire that broadcasts EVANGELICAL teaching and programming from hundreds of television stations around the world.

Politically, Robertson advances the CHRISTIAN RIGHT agenda of opposition to liberal, HUMANIST, WELFARE-STATE, HOMOSEXUAL, and FEMINIST U.S. politics. This tended to align him with the conservative RIGHT WING of the REPUBLICAN PARTY and against the LEFTIST DEMOCRATIC PARTY.

In 1986, he announced he would become a Republican candidate for the presidency of the United States. After early successes, his campaign faltered under continuous attacks from the liberal media and the Democrats. Robertson's involvement in U.S. politics continued in his founding of the Christian Coalition, a national conservative religious political organization that encourages local chapters to oppose liberal educational, cultural, and governmental policies. He reflects a traditional COVENANT view of American religion and politics.

Further Readings
Harrell, D. E., Jr. *Pat Robertson*. San Francisco: Harper & Row, 1988.
Robertson, Pat. *Shout It From the Housetop*. Plainfield, N.J.: Bridge-Logos, 1972.

Roman law

The code of LAW developed in the Roman EMPIRE (roughly 500 B.C.–A.D. 500) and applied to Europe through Emperor JUSTINIAN I, GAIUS, and, later, CANON LAW.

Roman law grew out of unwritten customs over PROPERTY ownership, trade, family practices, and governance procedures. As the Roman Empire conquered vast areas of Europe, Asia, and the Middle East, this Roman law was applied to "foreign" peoples within the empire (Israel, Germany, Britain, etc.). CICERO stated that the universal law of Rome encoded the reason and wisdom of the greatest philosophers and could establish justice throughout the empire. Thus, any Roman official could maintain JUSTICE by applying Roman law, whether or not he was wise or just. This doctrine of the benefits of the "RULE OF LAW" flows into the Western legal TRADITION, ultimately including English common law and U.S. CONSTITUTIONAL law. James MADISON, then, relies on the legal mechanisms of the U.S. CONSTITUTION to preserve DEMOCRACY and to prevent TYRANNY (rather than relying on the virtuous character of the CITIZENS, as in ARISTOTLE).

Roman law protects the individual RIGHTS of Roman citizens, no matter where they are in the empire. So, for example, St. Paul (as described in the Bible, Acts 22) reminds a Roman military commander that he cannot whip a Roman citizen until the latter has been found guilty by a legal trial. Such universal Roman law allowed trade and commerce to spread safely across the empire and to be protected from local custom (and business practices) by Roman law and the Roman military. Such uniform law becomes necessary to all later commercial empires.

The texts of Roman law were developed by the jurist Julian under Emperor Hadrian (A.D. 117–138). These included written custom, actual cases, and judges' commentaries on those cases (developing "rules" or principles). So Roman law was always a mixture of traditional custom, rulers' decisions, and past practices (the origin of legal precedent—or judges' similar cases according to past decisions). This gave Western law its CONSERVATIVE quality, favored by Edmund BURKE.

With the decline of the Roman REPUBLIC (Senate) and rise of ABSOLUTIST authority of the emperor, Roman law assumed the nature of royal edicts or dictates. Such "orders" by one ruler eventually led to the CATHOLIC pope's use of encyclicals or authoritative statements from the Roman bishop in the MIDDLE AGES.

With the fall of the Roman Empire, the code of Roman law temporarily disintegrated as the customs of invading tribes supplanted Latin law. In the Orthodox Eastern Roman Empire (Constantinople), the traditional code continued, increasingly through the BYZANTINE BUREAUCRACY. In Western Europe, Roman law was finally revived in Italy during the 12th century. Fed by both Byzantine and ISLAMIC remnants of the Roman law, it was encapsulated in the HOLY ROMAN EMPIRE through church canon law.

Roman law demonstrates how a long and varied tradition can affect political thought.

Further Readings
Jolowicz, H. F., and Nicholas, B. *Historical Introduction to the Study of Roman Law,* 3rd ed. Cambridge, Eng.: Cambridge University Press, 1972.
Nicholas, B. *Introduction to Roman Law.* Oxford, Eng.: Oxford University Press, 1962.

Roman political thought

The political ideas of the ancient Roman Republic and Roman Empire (approximately 500 B.C. to A.D. 500). This thousand-year reign of Roman civilization contained a diverse set of political theories, but they are synthesized in the thought of the Roman lawyer and statesman CICERO. All of Roman philosophy shows the influence of CLASSICAL Greek thought (PLATO, ARISTOTLE, stoicism), but Rome adapted these ideas of human social nature and VIRTUE to the contingencies of a vast EMPIRE. The result was a sturdy, Roman imperial virtue—stoic, military, and honorable. The ideal citizen in Rome was the soldier-ruler whose patriotism and duty was sacrificed for the good of his country. A hearty, masculine virtue was characteristic of this Roman model. Such a strong patriotic ideal suited the growing empire that conquered the Western world with military discipline and toughness. Cicero lamented that this traditional Roman virtue was declining as the commercial wealth and power of the empire corrupted political leaders. Instead of self-sacrifice and duty, young people in Rome were interested only in money and pleasure. They were becoming soft and decadent, and this moral weakness was beginning to destroy the economic, political, and military foundations of the empire. Cicero warned that if Roman culture did not return to the integrity of its social and military virtue, it would be destroyed. Luxury, violence, sexual perversion, self-indulgence would weaken the country and would lead to its downfall. This Ciceronian prophecy largely came true, as the Roman Empire declined morally, politically, economically, and, finally, militarily. The peoples it had conquered ultimately conquered and destroyed it.

Another aspect of Roman political thought was the preeminence of ROMAN LAW. A vast empire could not be ruled by a small, participatory DEMOCRACY like the Greek POLIS. It required a uniform code of law over the many diverse cultures within the empire. With such a universal Roman law, officials could simply apply its precepts and keep the peace (*pax Romana*). This diminished the emphasis in Aristotle of developing the character of citizens; even mediocre officials could apply Roman statutes, as long as they could read Latin. This continued in the MEDIEVAL CATHOLIC Church tradition of CANON LAW, English common law, and American CONSTITUTIONAL law. In each case, the quality of the CITIZENS was less important than the quality of the laws. Cicero even claimed that reason and the best knowledge of philosophers was realized in Roman law.

These themes of Roman virtue and law were expressed in the histories written by SENECA and TACITUS and in the political writings of POLYBIUS, MARCUS AURELIUS, and Cato. In all cases, these reflected the classical Greek philosophers and, rather unoriginally, adapted them to Roman civilization. So, for example, Cicero endorses Aristotle's concept of a MIXED CONSTITUTION (blending MONARCHY, ARISTOCRACY, and democracy).

Roman political thought greatly affected later Western political theory, especially CLASSICAL REPUBLICANISM, the common-law tradition, constitutionalism, and the American Revolution and republic.

Further Readings
Beard, W. M., and Crawford, M. H. *Rome in the Late Republic.* Ithaca, N.Y.: Cornell University Press, 1985.
Syme, R. *Tacitus.* Oxford, Eng.: Oxford University Press, 1958.

Romanticism

A philosophical and literary movement in the 18th and 19th century (Europe) that emphasized the importance of art, nature, emotions, and childlike innocence in human life and society. In political theory, it is expressed in Jean-Jacques ROUSSEAU with a concern for human sentiment (as opposed to reason), COMMUNITARIAN politics (as opposed to Lockean contractual government and INDIVIDUALISM), and a belief in the basic goodness and innocence of people (as opposed to the REALISM of St. AUGUSTINE, MACHIAVELLI, and others). Romanticism is a reaction against the MODERN, scientific rationalism of 17th- and 18th-century ENLIGHTENMENT, which it regards as cold, calculating, and unfeeling. It embraces human emotions, spontaneous acts of love, crying in public, and the FREEDOM of the imagination (against the confining rules of science, CLASSICAL rationality, and capitalist PROGRESS). Consequently, romanticism is often identified with the "feminine"—soft, caring, spontaneous, emotional—while Modern, SOCIAL-CONTRACT LIBERALISM is portrayed as "masculine"—formal, legal, practical. Many of the English Romantic poets (Shelley, Keats) extol natural beauty, the countryside, and the virtues of women and children. Fantasy, folk art, peasants, and the mentally retarded are portrayed as innocent and virtuous, attaining a contentment and happiness lost to the calculating, mechanical Modern civilization. Rejection of technology and government as dehumanizing often accompanies Romantic political thought. In Germany, Friedrich Schliermacher and Friedrich Schlegel expressed Romantic, nostalgic ideals, as did COLERIDGE and CARLYLE in Great Britain, and THOREAU in the United States.

Partly looking to an ideal MEDIEVAL past (of simple, natural, rural life; uncomplicated HIERARCHICAL politics; and unquestioned religious faith), and partly encouraging a "liberated" future (of spontaneous feelings, emotions, and relationships), Romanticism contributed to the rise of NATIONALISM, FASCISM, AND ANARCHISM. Looking both to comfortable, quaint tradition and to a new world order of love, beauty, and harmony, Romantics embraced such diverse figures and movements as Napoleon, COMMUNISM, free love, HOMOSEXUALITY, Wagnerian opera, and peasant revolution. When these failed to produce the Romantic UTOPIA of peace and love, the blame was often assigned to brutal (masculine) authority, INDUSTRIALISM, commercial exploitation, and the oppressive family. Consequently, Romanticism was not a coherent political movement or ideology, but it affected several other social movements. Even WELFARE-STATE Liberalism and SOCIALISM contain Romantic elements, with sympathy for the poor and weak and a general PACIFISM. Up to the 1980s Romantic trends have appeared in the United States, such as the movement to rural communes in the 1960s, the hippie movement, the NEW AGE MOVEMENT, and strains of the anti-(Vietnam) War movement. Whenever an appeal is made to nonrational emotion, spontaneous feelings, caring, sharing, and abstract loving, a Romantic sentiment is expressed: The assumption that the coming-out of people's "inner" childlike natures will make the world a peaceful, happy place reflects a Romantic sensibility, and the view that humans are naturally good but are corrupted by society (education, PROPERTY, politics) corresponds to a Romantic perspective. The solution, then, is either to reject the Modern, rational, technological world or to reform it along Romantic lines. But no uniform Romantic political program exists (or could exist without violating natural, individual spontaneity), so Romanticism remains a minor tendency in various social movements and figures, rather than a systematic philosophy.

Further Readings

Halsted, J. B., ed. *Romanticism.* New York: Walker, 1969.
Reiss, H., ed. *The Political Thought of the German Romantics, 1793–1815.* Oxford, Eng.: Blackwell, 1955.

Roosevelt, Franklin Delano (1882–1945)
U.S. politician and president (1932–1945)

In AMERICAN POLITICAL THOUGHT, Roosevelt (FDR) represents the triumph of WELFARE-STATE Liberalism begun by Woodrow WILSON: the use of the central, federal government to regulate the economy, provide extensive social services (public employment, welfare, housing, retirement pensions, health care), and protect civil rights. Employing the economic theory of John Maynard KEYNES, Roosevelt used the federal government's borrowing and spending power to manage the economy during the Great Depression of the 1930s.

The philosophical rationale for FDR's DEMOCRATIC PARTY Liberalism (see the NEW DEAL) was that big government was needed to protect the people from big business. National state power could be used by ordinary people to force large corporations to serve the public interest, assist the poor and underprivileged, and preserve individual RIGHTS. Following on the PROGRESSIVE welfare politics of President Woodrow Wilson, Franklin Roosevelt saw a positive role for the federal government in promoting social EQUALITY and JUSTICE. The new Democratic Party coalition of the 1930s (Liberals, SOCIALISTS, labor unions, minorities, and Jewish Americans) reflected this LEFT slant of FDR's politics. As he stated in his campaign address of 1936: "Our job was to preserve the American ideal of economic as well as political democracy against the abuse of concentration of economic power. . . ." In this, he claimed to be in the democratic tradition of Thomas JEFFERSON, despite the weakening of STATES RIGHTS caused by his policies.

Democratic Party liberalism fundamentally changed the U.S. national government's role in the economy and individual citizens' lives. It dominated U.S. politics until the 1980s when President Ronald REAGAN's CONSERVATIVE policies challenged its premises and shifted more state programs to business or local governments. Roosevelt's Liberal welfare-state policies continue in the United States through federal aid to education, the arts, public housing, Social Security, and health care, but contemporary public perception by some of Liberal politics as causing high taxes, wasteful federal programs, economic inflation, and ineffective policy has diminished the prestige of Roosevelt's vision. Its "mixed economy" of private-enterprise CAPITALISM and public regulation, however, is now the pattern for Western democracies.

Rousseau, Jean-Jacques (1712–1778) *French political philosopher*

Considered both a FRENCH ENLIGHTENMENT and ROMANTIC thinker, Rousseau presented a distinctive French LIBERALISM, influencing the French Revolution of 1789, FASCISM, COMMUNISM, and COMMUNITARIAN thought.

Born in Geneva, Switzerland, he spent most of his life in Paris and wrote on education, music, and drama as well as politics. Raised in Protestant Christianity, he converted briefly to Catholicism and then to a deistic CIVIL RELIGION.

Rousseau modifies the stark INDIVIDUALISM of John LOCKE's liberalism by conceiving of HUMAN NATURE as both private and public, motivated by self-interest and social sympathy. Human empathy for others' suffering makes them altruistic and caring. In its natural, child-like innocence, humankind is sympathetic to others' needs and is kindly, but this natural goodness is soon corrupted, for Rousseau, by the vanity, pride, and competition of CIVIL SOCIETY. So, like the later sociology that he influenced, Rousseau sees humans' environment as molding their character. He elevates the primitive, tribal human (the "noble savage") as more decent, humane, and good than civilized, educated, and MODERN humanity. This begins the Romantic view of the virtuous innocence of simple, natural, rural peasants, children, women, and the simple minded: they are sweet and tender, while rational, economic, developed people are corrupt, cruel, and mean. This blaming of evil on social circumstances (as in later MARXISM) rather than innate human sin (as in CHRISTIANITY—St. AUGUSTINE or John CALVIN) leads to Rousseau's prescription for abolishing evil through social and political reform. Politics can establish morality.

The political system needed to reform society and human beings is based on a REPUBLICAN model of popular SOVEREIGNTY. Only "the people" generally can form just laws for the common good (contrary to St. Thomas AQUINAS). Rousseau's version of the SOCIAL CONTRACT differs widely from that of Thomas HOBBES or John Locke. He claims that every citizen must participate in governance and each must give up his or her RIGHTS to the whole community. Because individuals have the social community within them, obeying the STATE is really following one's own interest. In his famous remark, Rousseau asserts that "Liberty is obedience to laws one has prescribed to oneself." This forms Rousseau's ideal of law as the GENERAL WILL or common good. Through discussion, each individual (or group's) selfish particular will drop away and is subsumed with the shared common or general will of the whole community. Consensus and absolute oneness, or unity of thought, can be achieved in the virtuous republic. This assertion of social unity is disputed by the British liberalism of Hobbes, Locke, and J. S. MILL (who conceive of the private person as inviolable) by Christianity (except in the spiritual unity of the church), and Marxism (until pure communism). The assertion of a possibility of such social uniformity is blamed for TOTALITARIANISM (such as the SOVIET UNION) and fascism (as NAZI Germany). Once the general will is proclaimed by the community, any civil disobedience to it is considered treason, and the dissenter can justly be executed, for Rousseau. Such a justification for harsh penalties for disagreeing with the state led to the brutality of the mass executions during the French Revolution.

This ABSOLUTIST state premised on community unity has a civil religion to sustain it, in Rousseau's political theory. This civil religion reinforces the values and sanctity of the state; it teaches the virtues of social cooperation, PATRIOTISM, and sacrifice. The state becomes God. Rejecting traditional Christianity, Rousseau's government religion teaches that good CITIZENS go to heaven and bad citizens go to hell, that the social contract and the state are holy, and that all religions are tolerated that accept this dogma. This would exclude Judaism, Christianity, and ISLAM.

Rousseau's ideas of human EQUALITY, democracy, and FREEDOM greatly influenced Modern republican governments. Using the language of LIBERTY, RIGHTS, and morality, he infused it with very different meaning than either British-American liberalism (Locke, Jefferson, Madison) or Western Christianity (St. Thomas Aquinas, Martin LUTHER).

Rousseau lived a contentious and confused existence. Extolling domestic virtue, he nevertheless kept a mistress and put their 10 children into orphanages. Idolizing community and friendship, he remained alienated from most society and quarreled with many of his friends. Near the end of his life Rousseau suffered from paranoia and madness. He seemed to be tormented by demons and died lonely and insane.

His major books include *Discourses on the Arts and Sciences* and *On the Origin of Inequality, The Social Contract, Emile,* and *Confessions.*

Further Readings
Cranston, M. *Jean-Jacques: the Early Life and Work of Jean-Jacques Rousseau, 1712–1754.* New York: Norton, 1983.
Gilden, H. *Rousseau's Social Contract: The Design of the Argument.* Chicago: University of Chicago Press, 1983.

rule of law

A prominent concept in Western political thought, the rule of law implies government by written rules and statutes rather than the arbitrary or ABSOLUTIST "rule of man." ARISTOTLE argues that laws are written when people are most rational (in assemblies or legislatures) and so provide wiser governance than the direct rule of people who are susceptible to irrational passions, emotions, and demagoguery. This contrasts with PLATO's *Republic,* which relied on the character and VIRTUE of rulers (though he later modified this in his book *The Laws*). The Roman statesman CICERO maintained that all the reason and wisdom of the philosophers was encoded in ROMAN LAW. This enabled the Roman Empire to expand across the globe, ruling diverse populations with a uniform legal code applied by Roman officials. Such legalism continued in the West through CATHOLIC Church CANON LAW, English common law, and American CONSTITUTIONAL law. In each case, the rule of law diminishes the need for highly qualified, virtuous, or active CITIZENS because the mechanism of law can provide JUSTICE. The consequence of this, historically, may be the decline of citizen education and, finally, insufficient personnel to make or apply the law.

A primary motivation for the rule of law is as a limitation or check on absolutist power or TYRANNY. If even rulers are subject to the laws, excessive personal authority or DESPOTIC oppression is less likely to occur. According to this ideal, "no one is above the law," even kings, presidents, princes, or popes. The impeachment of a U.S. president is an example of this rule-of-law principle, in which a powerful ruler can be removed from power for breaking the law.

Another advantage to the rule of law is the EQUALITY of treatment of citizens by the state. *Equality before the law* implies that rules are upheld fairly, regardless of the person's wealth, social position, or fame. Without universal law, the concept of *equal justice* would be imperiled. Therefore the rule of law underlies MODERN DEMOCRATIC and REPUBLICAN government.

Further Readings

Jennings, I. *The Law and the Constitution*, 5th ed. London: University of London Press, 1959.
Lyons, D. *Ethics and the Rule of Law*. Cambridge, Eng.: Cambridge University Press, 1984.

Ruskin, John (1819–1900)   *Art critic and social reformer*

Ruskin was an art critic and historian who argued that the art of a society reflected its social conditions and that the nature of art provides a framework for assessing and reforming society.

Ruskin opposed the value of INDIVIDUALISM that accompanied the industrial revolution and the view of work as mere productivity. He connected the rise of CAPITALISM with a splintering of the organic "wholeness" of the universe, and he blamed capitalism for degrading the value of work so that workers, instead of being creative and fulfilling their natural purposes, were used as means and tools for making things.

The function of art for Ruskin is to unveil truth through beauty. Beauty meant two things; first, the external quality of an object or body and, second, a fulfillment of function, "more especially of the joyful and right exertion of perfect life in man." The former he called typical beauty and the latter he called vital beauty. The possibility of revealing truth through beauty depended not only on the wholeness of the artist in the act of creation, but also on the nature of the society in which the art is produced. A corrupt society is incapable of producing beauty, so a way of measuring the health of a society is to examine its art.

Ruskin contrasted wealth with what he called "illth." He rejected the capitalist notion of wealth as exclusively exchange value and instead argued that things had intrinsic value that was represented in their capacity to contribute to the perfect life. Such things were true wealth and contributed to the general design and organic whole of society.

Ruskin's criticisms of 19th-century capitalism were an important influence on English SOCIALIST movements, although his positive account of society as an organic whole is nostalgic, authoritarian, and antiLIBERAL.

Ruskin was born in London, England, and attended Oxford University.

Further Reading

Hobson, J. A. *John Ruskin Social Reformer*. Boston: Dana Estes and Company, 1898.

Russell, Bertrand (1872–1970)   *British philosopher and political activist*

Born into an aristocratic Liberal family, Russell advocated LEFTIST social programs (universal public education, welfare for the poor, women's rights, old-age pensions, etc.) but criticized MARXIST COMMUNISM as DESPOTIC and TYRANNICAL. Most of his political ACTIVISM centered around antiwar, PACIFISM movements. He found warfare irrational and nuclear warfare terrifying. He participated widely in antinuclear protest marches and urged the United States and the Soviet Union to limit nuclear weapons. He feared U.S. domination of the world as a new Roman Empire (*pax Americana*) for the benefit of U.S. CAPITALISM. Russell engaged in many protests against U.S. resistance to communism in Vietnam. He believed in the efficacy of CIVIL DISOBEDIENCE and urged critical attacks on all MODERN governments, which he claimed were run by the criminally insane.

Russell's utopian optimism held that human evil could be educated out of people by training children's "creative impulse" and encouraging a happy, constructive personality that is immune to aggression or selfishness. This was regarded as naïve and foolish by more realistic politicians of his day.

His opposition to all war led Russell to advocate pacifism toward NAZI Germany in the 1930s. The goal was always to preserve European civilization, art, and culture. In the 1920s, he endorsed GUILD SOCIALISM and attempted several experiment in communal living, all of which failed.

Bertrand Russell became a kind of popular joke. This view was expressed by John Maynard KEYNES as "He thinks the world is terrible because everyone is mad; happily the remedy is simple: They must all behave better."

Further Readings

Clark, R. *The Life of Bertrand Russell.* New York: Knopf, 1975.

Vellacott, J. *Bertrand Russell and the Pacifists in the First World War.* New York: St. Martin's Press, 1980.

S

Saint-Simon, Claude-Henri de Rouvroy, count de (1760–1825) *French political and economic thinker; founder of socialism*

One of the first philosophers of MODERN SOCIALISM, Saint-Simon was an aristocratic Frenchman influenced by ENLIGHTENMENT ideals of PROGRESS, EQUALITY, and DEMOCRACY.

Applying Modern scientific methods, Saint-Simon believed that history and technology advanced according to natural laws, inevitably leading to socialism. Like Karl MARX, he believed that humanity could know these historical laws and contribute to PROGRESSIVE change. All political and economic systems have an IDEOLOGY that supports them, and CAPITALIST INDUSTRIALISM needed a philosophy that reinforced it ("positive science"). The MEDIEVAL social system of FEUDALISM was maintained by CATHOLIC theology (St. Thomas AQUINAS) and monarchical political theory (DIVINE RIGHT OF KINGS), so Modern bourgeois society could be furthered by a progressive, evolutionary economic theory. His ideal society was to be run by "enlightened" scientists, engineers, artists, and entrepreneurs, creating a technologically advanced, prosperous nation.

At first, Saint Simon adopted the LIBERAL philosophy of John LOCKE, emphasizing individual RIGHTS, LIBERTY, and so on, but as he saw the impoverished working masses suffer ALIENATION and powerlessness, he moved toward more collectivist, socialist principles. He envisioned a society, like PLATO's *Republic,* of different classes performing various functions (agriculture, manufacturing, educators) but having equal worth and dignity within a harmonious whole. Some people (like PHILOSOPHER-KINGS) would be natural leaders, but they would serve their subordinates and the common good of the country.

His CHRISTIANITY introduced an ethical and religious dimension to Saint-Simon's socialist UTOPIA. The true teaching of Jesus Christ enjoined humility and equality, not the HIERARCHY and authority of the CATHOLIC Church of the Middle Ages. Caring for the poor and lowly, creating a just society of peace and harmony were truly Christian prospects, for him. By making his faith practical and economic, Saint-Simon foreshadowed the SOCIAL GOSPEL MOVEMENT and LIBERATION THEOLOGY.

With Charles FOURIER and Robert OWEN, Saint-Simon is considered one of the original socialist thinkers.

Further Readings
Ionescu, G., ed. *The Political Thought of Saint-Simon.* London: Oxford University Press, 1976.

Manuel, R. E. *The New World of Henri Saint-Simon.* Cambridge, Mass.: Harvard University Press, 1956.

Sanhedrin

The supreme council and high court of ancient Israel. Located in Jerusalem, this governing council handled religious issues for the entire Jewish world, collected taxes to support the Israeli state, and served as a civil court. It consisted of 71 members, dominated by the Jewish priestly class but included lawyers (Scribes) and Pharisees. Presided over by a high priest, the Sanhedrin enjoyed considerable governing authority even under Roman rule. It pronounced the death sentence on Jesus Christ but was not authorized to carry out executions. An example of representative government in religion and politics, this Jewish council was destroyed when the Roman Empire annihilated Jerusalem in A.D. 70, but some of its functions were continued by the dispersed Jews in Jamnia and Tiberias. Although the majority of Sanhedrin members condemned Christ and persecuted the early CHRISTIANS, the Bible records several councilmen supporting Jesus and the Apostles (Gamaliel, Acts 5; Joseph of Arimathaea, Matthew 27; Nicodemus, John, 3).

Sartre, Jean-Paul (1905–1980)   *French existentialist and Marxist philosopher*

Expressing his political thought in novels, plays, and essays as well as books of philosophy (*Being and Nothingness; Critique of Dialectical Reason*), Sartre presents a view of human life as meaningless, without objective (divine) order, and requiring the individual to take responsibility for one's existence. This EXISTENTIALIST perspective regards God, the church, transcendent religious faith, LAW, and organized social movements as cowardly escapes from individual FREEDOM (and making one's own reality). The separate person, for Sartre, must make his or her own reality, purpose, and morality. Ironically, this leads to a kind of INDIVIDUALISTIC nihilism, allowing any person to avoid responsibility if it conforms to some moral or religious system. So, for Sartre's "free" individual to be "authentic," he or she may love someone one day and abandon the loved one the next.

He combines this existentialist self with COMMUNISM by arguing that one can overcome this ALIENATION and meaninglessness by participating in revolutionary political activity, including VIOLENCE. Such RADICAL

French author and philosopher Jean-Paul Sartre. (LIBRARY OF CONGRESS)

political ACTIVISM is not carried on for the benefit of the poor and oppressed but for one's own fulfillment. Historically, Sartre represents that cultural and intellectual alienation and sense of futility common in LEFTIST European academics in the 20th century. He projects his own insignificance onto all humanity and society. A favorite among CRITICAL-THEORY MARXIST, Sartre, nevertheless, quarreled with other communists and POSTMODERN thinkers.

Further Readings
Aronson, B. *Jean-Paul Sartre: Philosophy in the World.* London: NLB, 1980.
Jameson, F. *Sartre after Sartre.* New Haven, Conn.: Yale University Press, 1985.

Savonarola, Girolamo (1452–1498)   *Italian political and religious reformer*

As a CATHOLIC monk of the Dominican order, Savonarola attacked the immoral society of Florence and corruption of the Roman church. With the support of French king Charles VIII, he established a theocratic REPUBLIC in Florence, instituting strict moral codes and virtuous government. His "Rule and Government of the City of Florence" detailed an ideal CHRISTIAN polity, similar to Geneva under John CALVIN. Applying religious standards to all manner of private and public conduct, his resembled the PURITAN political system of Oliver CROMWELL and New England. Causing widespread resentment among the worldly and sophisticated citizens of Florence, he was excommunicated by Pope Alexander VI. Refusing to recant, Savonarola called for the church council to diminish the authority of the papacy. He was imprisoned, tortured, and executed by hanging.

Savonarola's main writings (such as "The Triumph of the Cross") reflect traditional Catholic doctrine influenced by St. Thomas AQUINAS. With St. Francis of Assisi, he is recognized as a Christian reformer attempting to purge the church and the HOLY ROMAN EMPIRE of luxury, immorality, and corruption, thereby preventing the breach of the Protestant REFORMATION.

Schaeffer, Francis August (1912–1984) U.S. political and social critic

In his famous book, *The Rise and Decline of Western Thought and Culture* (1976), Schaeffer detailed the moral and political decline in Europe and the United States during MODERN times. From an EVANGELICAL CHRISTIAN perspective, he saw the rise of ENLIGHTENMENT relativism, HUMANISM, and INDIVIDUALISM as contributing to the social evils of the 20th century. This began, for Schaeffer, with the philosophy of G. W. F. HEGEL, which replaces Western notions of moral absolutes with DIALECTICAL relativity in ETHICS. This quickly led to the EXISTENTIALISM, ALIENATION, and moral decline of the West. A depreciation of the truths of the Bible, reason, and God's plan for humanity leads to escapist and immoral lifestyles (drug use, pornography, ABORTION, HOMOSEXUALITY). This social evil spread from Europe (especially Germany) to Great Britain to the United States. It often takes the form of alternative religions and the occult.

Thus, for Schaeffer, social, economic, and political problems cannot be separated from religious and spiritual matters. He advised a return to the strict CHRISTIAN doctrine of St. AUGUSTINE and John CALVIN, an Evangelical faith based on the inerrancy of the Bible, and a

CHURCH-AND-STATE position of publicly resisting contemporary social ills. Without a moral revival like the GREAT AWAKENING, the Western world will decline into chaos and AUTHORITARIAN government, he believed.

Born in Philadelphia, Pennsylvania, Schaeffer studied at a PRESBYTERIAN school (Westminster Theological Seminary) and was ordained a minister. In 1948, he moved to Switzerland and established an international conference center ("L'Abri") where visitors studied religion and Modern culture. This retreat center became world famous and, with Schaeffer's writings, greatly affected contemporary discussion of politics and society.

Schiller, Johann Christoph Friedrich von (1759–1805)   *Poet, dramatist, and philosopher*

Schiller's contribution to POLITICAL THEORY is closely connected to, and arises from, his theories on the nature of art, the understanding of beauty, and the aesthetic response.

Schiller's aesthetics is largely a critical response to KANT. Where Kant attempted to define beauty through a rationalist argument whereby agents adopt a disinterested stance toward the object that could then appear in its pure form, Schiller argues that the freedom that constitutes beauty is displayed and is present in the object itself. This was an attempt to discover an objective definition of *beauty*. An object that has "overcome" its purpose displays its freedom and thus its beauty.

The question of FREEDOM and its ethical and political consequences occupied an important part of Schiller's philosophy. He saw no fundamental division between freedom in its aesthetic sense as beauty and freedom in the ethical and political spheres. Schiller discusses political and ethical questions and their connection to aesthetics in *Letters on the Aesthetic Education of Man* published in 1795. Schiller's ideas are clearly a response to the political upheavals occasioned by the French Revolution. He rejects Kant's dualistic account of people as comprised of both reason and inclination in an antagonistic relation with each other. He thus rejects Kant's view that moral duty requires agents to disregard their inclination and attend only to their reason. Schiller argued for the intergradations of both inclination and reason into a balanced whole. Furthermore, Schiller identified a third impulse beyond reason and duty, one that he called the aesthetic impulse: It through art as a force of integration and balance that true humanity can emerge and undo the antagonisms that are the source of ethical and political disturbance.

Art offers an ideal of balance and integration most clearly expressed through play. Schiller's ideas here are an important precursor to MARXISTS and socialists in defining a form of ALIENATION brought about by a lack of wholeness and the distortion of humanity through division and antagonism.

Schiller was born in Marbach, Germany. He studied medicine and worked briefly as a doctor before devoting himself to writing. Schiller was an important poet, a dramatist, and a leading figure in the German Romantic movement. He was a professor at the University of Jena and died at the early age of 45.

Further Reading
Sharpe, L. *Friedrich Schiller: Drama, Thought and Politics.* Cambridge, Eng.: Cambridge University Press, 1991.

Schumpeter, Joseph Alois (1883–1950) *Economist*

Schumpeter was an economist whose ideas concerning the nature of CAPITALISM, the proper definition of democracy, and the possibility of SOCIALISM have been very influential.

Schumpeter's economic ideas are most clearly set out in his early book, *Theory of Economic Development,* first published in 1912 and translated into English in 1934. He offers a dynamic account of the nature of capitalism by which he meant that capitalism as an economic system is always changing, and he identified the source of this change in the entrepreneur: The entrepreneur innovates and thereby alters the course of the economy by encouraging others to follow. An entrepreneur innovates by bringing to the market new goods, new ways of producing existing goods, opening new markets, and so on. What is crucial here for Schumpeter is the idea that the social is not a slave to an economic base, as is the case, for example, with Marx.

Schumpeter's most well-known work is *Capitalism, Socialism and Democracy,* published in 1942. The three main topics discussed are MARX, Schumpeter's reluctantly held belief that socialism would replace capitalism, and, finally and probably most importantly, his redefinition of *democracy.* The critique of Marx is also

Schumpeter's acknowledgement of Marx's influence and "greatness." Schumpeter answers negatively the question of whether capitalism will survive. He argues, among other points, that capitalism's success undermines its capacity to innovate through entrepreneurs who are replaced by managers, concedes that a democratic socialism is possible and likely, and, finally, sets out a detailed criticism of the standard definition of *democracy* as rule by the people for the common good. He argues that there is no identifiable good that is common to all, and he denies that politicians are passive representatives of the people's will. Instead he claims that "the democratic method is that institutional arrangement for arriving at political decisions in which individuals acquire the power to decide by means of a competitive struggle for the people's vote." Democracy is thus the rule of the masses by an elite who acquire the right to rule by competing with each other for the votes of the people. This allegedly nonideological definition was seen as a productive way of analyzing and understanding the character of political power in democratic states.

Schumpeter was born in the Austro-Hungarian Empire and studied at the University of Vienna where he received a doctorate in 1906. He was a professor at the University of Graz. In 1919, he was briefly the finance minister but resumed his academic career and later moved to the United States, joining Harvard University where he remained until his death.

Further Reading
Harris, S. *Schumpeter: Social Scientist.* North Stratford, N.H.: Ayer Co. Publishing, 1951.

Scottish Enlightenment

A philosophic movement in Scotland from 1740 to 1790, including economic theory, political thought, and moral philosophy, represented in the writings of Adam SMITH, David HUME, Frances HUTCHESON, Lord Kames, and Thomas Reid. Besides its influence on MODERN British political theory, the Scots Enlightenment greatly affected the United States of America (as in Thomas JEFFERSON, James MADISON, and John WITHERSPOON).

Like the FRENCH ENLIGHTENMENT, this Scottish school of thought emphasized PROGRESS in society, politics, and ETHICS, but unlike the European intellectual movement, it did not divorce this from religion. Many of the leading Scots Enlightenment thinkers were

Protestant CHRISTIANS, adapting the faith to CAPITALISM, REPUBLICANISM, and science. The PRESBYTERIAN view of humanity and history informed much of the Scots Enlightenment, as it did AMERICAN POLITICAL THOUGHT. For example, Reid's commonsense theology, emphasizing the rational appreciation of scripture and human MORAL SENSE, showed that scientific materialism and DEMOCRACY are not incompatible with Christianity. In economics, Adam Smith showed that the INDIVIDUALISM and LIBERTY of Protestant Christianity could promote a work ethic and material prosperity; that poverty and misery were not divinely ordained, and free markets could promote economic progress; that wealth was not necessarily a sign of God's grace, but neither was economic privation and suffering; and that a self-disciplined moral individual could be religious, socially beneficial, and politically responsible, improving the country and humankind.

Politically, the Scots Enlightenment adapted the Calvinist COVENANT tradition with NATURAL LAW, SOCIAL-CONTRACT liberalism (John LOCKE) seeing the state as promoting HUMAN RIGHTS and private PROPERTY. Smith described the governments of different economic historic systems (hunting, pastoral, agricultural, commercial) and saw republicanism as serving both market and political liberty: Material progress need not lead to luxury and moral depravity (as in CLASSICAL REPUBLICANISM) if it is undergirded by a sound Christian culture. Hume saw society developing from the family, a need for national defense, and the security of property. Adam Fergerson believed that without a moral dimension to capitalism, specialization could lead to exploitation, and that classical VIRTUE was inculcated through a citizen militia.

Many of the ideas of the Scottish Enlightenment found their way into the American political system through the immigration of many Scots into North America in the 18th century and through the popularity of these Scots thinkers' writings.

Further Reading
Campbell, R. H., and Skinner, A. S., eds. *The Origins and Nature of the Scottish Enlightenment.* Amherst, Mass.: Prometheus Books, 1982.

Second Great Awakening

A religious revival in the United States of America from 1790 to 1860 that helped to spread a POPULIST, DEMOCRATIC culture across the American frontier. Like the GREAT AWAKENING, this CHRISTIAN revival was led by Protestant ministers speaking to large crowds of common people, often in rural areas or camp meetings. The social effect of this EVANGELICAL spread of Christianity was to reinforce the democratic, EGALITARIAN culture and politics of the United States through informal language and church schedules; ordinary, uneducated "lay" people (farmers, mechanics) becoming gospel preachers and ministers; and local communities building new churches across America. Although all Christian churches participated in this growth of religion in the 19th-century United States, the BAPTIST and Methodist denominations spread most rapidly. The use of traveling revivalist ministers, indigenous democratically run congregations, and simple biblical teaching allowed this Evangelical Christianity to move across the expanding Western frontier easily.

Millions of converts to Protestant Christianity resulted from the Second Great Awakening, exhibiting reformed morals, self-control, a reduction of alcoholism and crime, and increased family life and education. The religious revivals empowered young communities confidently to build schools, churches, hospitals, libraries, parks, and organized civil life. Historian Gordon Wood claims that this religious expression effectively "Christianized" the United States and made it the most evangelical nation on earth. Other political effects of this Second Great Awakening were the social reform movements around ABOLITIONISM, (ending slavery), PROHIBITION (outlawing alcoholic beverages), and eventually the SOCIAL GOSPEL MOVEMENT (helping the urban poor and workers in INDUSTRIALISM). So, as both a social and a spiritual movement, the Second Great Awakening changed the United States in significant ways.

Further Reading
Boles, J. B. *The Great Revival.* Lexington: University Press of Kentucky, 1972.

secularism

A philosophy or worldview that emphasizes worldly, human ("secular"), as opposed to spiritual or religious, perspectives in explaining society and politics. Often referred to as HUMANISM, a secular approach dismisses or ignores God, the divine, the supernatural, and other religious viewpoints when discussing or participating in politics. Examples of such secular thought include the RENAISSANCE thinker Niccolo

MACHIAVELLI; ENLIGHTENMENT thinker Jean-Jacques ROUSSEAU; COMMUNIST thinkers Karl MARX, Friedrich ENGELS, and V.I. LENIN; and contemporary COMMUNITARIAN Benjamin BARBER.

Often secular theorists draw from CLASSICAL political thought (PLATO, ARISTOTLE) and MODERN LEFTIST perspectives on HUMAN NATURE and politics. Emphasis is placed on *human* excellence, potential, fulfillment, "actualization," and so on, instead of the godly, providential, or spiritual dimensions of life. Often, reason and technology are extolled as the source of political and ethical excellence; this contrasted with the major Christian political theorists (St. AUGUSTINE, St. Thomas AQUINAS, John CALVIN) who start from a godly, Bible, church, spiritual perspective, depreciate the human capacity for goodness or social improvement, and advise humble appreciation of the REALISM of sin and of looking to God for guidance and help in the world.

Contemporary expressions of secularism occur in the mainstream liberal media, business, public education, and social organizations. Criticism of secularism comes primarily from the CHRISTIAN RIGHT, CATHOLIC, and other CONSERVATIVE religious groups and sections of the dominant political parties (REPUBLICAN and DEMOCRATIC). In CHURCH-AND-STATE matters, secularists demand a strict separation of religion and politics, keeping prayer and religious instruction out of government, public schools, and other common institutions. Sociologist James Davison HUNTER describes the differences in secular-sacred debates in his book, *Culture Wars.*

Much of the criticism of the West (and of the United States in particular) from the ISLAMIC world is that it is too secular.

Seneca, L. Annaeus (4 B.C.–A.D. 65) *Roman statesman and political philosopher*

Representing Roman CLASSICAL REPUBLICANISM, Seneca, like CICERO, emphasizes the importance of moral VIRTUE in rulers, the dangers of arbitrary AUTHORITARIAN governance (especially TYRANNY), and the need for wisdom and PATRIOTISM in a government. Because of his ridicule of autocratic, dictatorial emperors in the Roman Empire, Seneca became a favorite author of the MODERN LIBERAL philosophers (James HARRINGTON, John LOCKE) who similarly attacked MONARCHY.

Seneca worked as an advisor to the notorious Roman emperor Nero and wrote a satire on the deifica-tion (or godlike qualities) of his predecessor, Claudius (*Apocolocyntosis divi Claudi*). His other main political writing is *De clementia,* in which he advises rulers to show clemency (or mercy) to their political opponents. In all of these works, Seneca urges moderation, decency, and wisdom in rulers. Living during the most brutal, decadent period in Roman history, he, like Cicero, was trying to restore the virtue and nobility of the old Roman Republic. Unsuccessful, he was implicated in a plot to assassinate the insane emperor Nero and was compelled to commit suicide.

Further Reading
Griffin, M. T. *Seneca: A Philosopher in Politics.* Oxford, Eng.: Clarendon Press, 1976.

separation of powers

The doctrine in POLITICAL THEORY that the government should be divided into different branches serving distinct functions (such as legislative, executive, judicial). Traceable to ARISTOTLE's MIXED CONSTITUTION, the separation of powers doctrine underlies the structure of the U.S. CONSTITUTION and Madisonian American DEMOCRACY. Derived from the Protestant CHRISTIAN theology of John CALVIN, which fears the TYRANNICAL use of power by sinful people, this constitutional separation of powers limits the authority of any one person, group, class, or level of government, preventing political DESPOTISM and oppression. British LIBERAL philosopher John LOCKE and French thinker MONTESQUIEU detail the advantages of breaking up political power in the MODERN REPUBLIC. The American FEDERALISTS made this into a new "science of politics," establishing a system of CHECKS AND BALANCES to preserve individual RIGHTS and LIBERTY.

Specifically, the U.S. Constitution sets up three branches of government (executive, or president; legislative, or Congress; judicial, or the federal courts), conferring definite duties and powers on each. These governmental groups are considered equal and autonomous, none under the total control of any other (so the Congress does not chose the president or the courts the legislature). Each branch of government has a distinct function that the other branches are not to invade (so the Judicial branch should not legislate or execute laws; the Congress should not judge law). There is overlapping jurisdiction between the branches (the president appoints federal court judges and the Congress confirms those nominations; the president can veto congressional legislation, but Congress can impeach and remove the president); to ensure further limits on POWER. Terms and elections are staggered for various officials (executive, senators, representative), and the independence of the judiciary is guaranteed by life-tenure appointments, also distributing power to prevent tyranny or "one person rule."

Besides the United States, most other Modern, industrial republics in the world have instituted separation of powers in their governments. German federalism, French and Australian republics, and most of the newly formed Eastern European states establish separation of powers.

The benefit of this limitation of STATE power is obvious in securing FREEDOM, DEMOCRACY, and individual RIGHTS. Where Modern states have abolished such limitations on state or leader power (as in NAZI Germany or the SOVIET UNION), TYRANNY and oppression have usually resulted.

Given the proud, weak, and sinful nature of human beings (as St. AUGUSTINE argued), putting limits on their political power seems to be the wisest approach. As Lord ACTON said, "power corrupts [people], and absolute power corrupts absolutely," so it is best to place formal limits on anyone's power in government. The separation of powers seeks to do that through formal, institutional, and constitutional means.

settlement-house movement

A social movement in Great Britain and the United States begun during the late 1800s involving middle-class CHRISTIANS living among the poor in large cities. The most famous settlement house in America was Hull House in Chicago, led by Jane Addams. These houses, founded primarily by Protestant Christian women, provided a variety of services to the urban poor, including vocational counselors, social workers, teachers, kindergartens, youth clubs, and home-economics classes. As part of the SOCIAL GOSPEL MOVEMENT, the workers in these houses also pursued PROGRESSIVE social legislation (against child labor; for union organizations, prohibition, public housing, unemployment compensation, and women's suffrage).

Begun in England by an Anglican clergyman, the intention of the settlement-house movement was to have young, middle-class Christians live among (or "settle" with) the impoverished city residents of East London. Rev. Samuel Barnett established Toynbee Hall in 1884, encouraging Anglican university students to live there and serve the poor, as Christ did. Soon, U.S. reformers visited this center in London and transported the idea to New York City. By 1910, more than 400 such houses existed in the United States, and 46 in Britain. Usually led by single women from prosperous families, these settlement houses helped the poor INDUSTRIAL working class of the early 20th century. As social-welfare legislation and programs expanded in the United States and Britain, many of the functions of the settlement houses were taken over by the government.

Sheldon, Charles M. (1857–1946)   *U.S. religious and political reformer; writer*

As a representative of the SOCIAL GOSPEL MOVEMENT, Sheldon championed the application of CHRISTIAN principles to social problems. He fought for racial EQUALITY, social-welfare legislation, PROHIBITION, and ecumenism. From a traditional Protestant faith (John CALVIN) reflecting his PURITAN ancestry, Sheldon identified contemporary social injustice (poverty, alcoholism, family violence, EXPLOITATION) with human sin (greed, lust, selfishness) that required confession, repentance, and redemption through Christ. Once the person is cleansed and renewed through faith in Jesus Christ, that spiritual "rebirth" should be manifest in good works in society: helping the poor, the sick, and the downtrodden; Sheldon says that is a concern for "the least among us" as a natural effect of EVANGELICAL regeneration, after Jesus' words in Matthew 25:34–45. He criticized Christians who were complacent and self-concerned, especially wealthy and middle-class churchgoers who did not care for the poor.

Sheldon, a Congregational minister who was educated at Phillips Academy, Brown University, and Andover Seminary, became world famous with the publication of his Christian novel, *In His Steps* (1896). For several decades the best-selling book after the Bible, *In His Steps* detailed the experiences of a group of Christians who decided to live by asking "What would Jesus do?" whenever making a decision. Presenting a RADICAL Christian discipleship in business, government, LAW, the media, and education, this theme electrified the world. An estimated 30 million copies of this book were sold in 20 different languages. It sparked religious revivals in the United

States, the United Kingdom, and Europe. Because of a faulty copyright, Dr. Sheldon did not receive money from the sale of this book, but, periodically, the "What would Jesus do?" theme of the book revived in U.S. society, most recently in the "What Would Jesus Do" movement in the 1990s, partly due to an updating by Sheldon's great-grandson of *In His Steps,* under the title *What Would Jesus Do?*

As an example of CHURCH-AND-STATE relations in the United States, Charles Sheldon shows the continuing relevance of Protestant Christianity in U.S. politics. His other books include *The Crucifixion of Philip Strong* (1894), *Jesus is Here!* (1913), and *In His Steps, Today* (1921).

Further Readings

Miller, Timothy. *Following in His Steps.* Knoxville: University of Tennessee Press, 1987.
Sheldon, Charles M. *Charles M. Sheldon: His Life Story.* New York: George H. Doran Company, 1925.

Skinner, Quentin Robert Duthie (1940–)
British political philosopher and academic

Best known for his study of Western POLITICAL THEORY in terms of IDEOLOGY, Quentin Skinner (regius professor of modern history, Cambridge University) applies this approach in a much more sophisticated and effective way than the MARXIST method. As he described it in his first volume of *The Foundation of Modern Political Thought* (1978): "I have tried not to concentrate so exclusively on the leading theorists, and have focused instead on the more general social and intellectual matrix out of which their works arose." He sees that "political life itself sets the main problems for the political theorist," and an understanding of the social context of a thinker is as important as the intellectual environment of the thinker: "the context of earlier writings and inherited assumptions about political society." This balanced approach to historical ideologies contributed greatly to the scholarship of Western political thought.

Educated at Cambridge University, Q.R.D. Skinner has lectured at Oxford University, Princeton, Harvard, the University of Paris, Rutgers, and numerous other schools and institutes. A member of the British Academy Council, he has received several academic awards (notably the Wolfson Literary Prize) and has written or edited 18 books.

slavery

The social institution in which one human being owns another human being as private PROPERTY. Human slavery has existed in almost every country and culture in history and still exists in some African, Middle Eastern, and Asian nations. In the history of POLITICAL THEORY, slavery is discussed by ARISTOTLE, CHRISTIAN political thought, John LOCKE, Karl MARX, Thomas JEFFERSON, G. W. F. HEGEL, George FITZHUGH, and others.

CLASSICAL Greek political thought (Aristotilean) gives the ancient justification for slavery: In *The Politics,* Aristotle argues that some people (individuals or races) are by nature slaves because they cannot rule themselves (and therefore require masters). Because the ruling faculty is reason, those without rationality are the natural slaves of the reasonable. In fact, most slaves in ancient Greece and Rome were the result of military defeat (as in ancient Israel), so the more common reason for enslavement was military conquest (as by King David in the Old Testament or Jewish Bible). Christianity (as in the Epistles of St. Paul) accepted the institution of slavery but advised masters to be kind to their slaves as they themselves have a master in God, to whom they are accountable (Ephesians 6).

German philosopher Hegel writes of the famous "master-slave" DIALECTIC, in which slavery is largely a matter of recognition, the slave giving the master his identity, and therefore the ruler is actually dependent on the slave. MARXISM adapts the image of slavery to the enslaved working class under CAPITALISM ruled by an economic ruling class. That even formally free people in a DEMOCRACY can be slaves affects all MODERN sociological thought, beginning with Jean-Jacques ROUSSEAU. The radical, revolutionary character and rhetoric of various liberation movements is explained by this equating of any social or economic dependence with slavery, so slavery to men (FEMINISM), to imperialism (LENIN), to sin (St. AUGUSTINE), or to consumerism (ENVIRONMENTALISM) becomes a common metaphor in Western political thought.

American slavery of blacks (Africans) in the 18th and early 19th centuries gave rise to a distinctive political theory. Based on both racial and intellectual grounds, American enslavement of AFRICAN AMERICANS is most rationalized in the writings of southerner George Fitzhugh. Although most black slaves in the United States had been previously enslaved by other Africans in their native land, the principles of FREEDOM and RIGHTS in Jefferson's DECLARATION OF INDEPENDENCE made the institution untenable in America. The antislavery arguments made by Frederick DOUGLASS and Abraham LINCOLN made emancipation inevitable.

Smith, Adam (1723–1790) *British political, moral, and economic philosopher*

Most famous for his economic book *The Wealth of Nations* (1776) and its classical defense of free-market CAPITALISM, Adam Smith is equally important from a moral and ethical perspective as a representative of the SCOTTISH ENLIGHTENMENT.

From a Calvinist CHRISTIAN perspective, he viewed HUMAN NATURE as selfish, vain, and proud, yet capable of human sympathy to others' suffering. In his book *A Theory of Moral Sentiments* (1759), Smith elaborated on Francis HUTCHESON's idea of an innate MORAL SENSE in humans, which like the natural conscience described by St. Paul (Romans 2:15) leads people to do good, at least occasionally, but because sinful self-interest prevails most of the time, society cannot rely totally upon people's benevolent qualities. This leads to Smith's idea of using individual selfish behavior in the marketplace to serve the common good. In a competitive, free-market economy, one must work for others, produce high quality goods, and provide good service to prosper, so economic self-INTEREST can benefit everyone. The government, then, should ensure free markets and fair competition and allow the "invisible hand" of "natural LIBERTY and perfect JUSTICE" to prevail. This is not pure LAISSEZ-FAIRE freedom and noninterference with society, but the careful public supervision of private FREEDOM. A just state will not allow monopolies (or MERCANTILISM) or governmental privilege of any person or group; it will defend the EQUALITY and RIGHTS of all. Also, the state should provide those things (such as education) that the private economy cannot provide for the poor. A good government will see that the country is well defended from external enemies and secure from crime within. Justice for Smith, like John LOCKE, is the respecting of NATURAL RIGHTS to life, liberty, and private PROPERTY. Such a MODERN REPUBLIC and commercial economy is more just than MONARCHY and FEUDALISM.

Adam Smith was educated in Scotland (Glasgow) and at Balliol College, Oxford. He later taught ETHICS, jurisprudence (law), and politics at Glasgow University. He is considered a major Modern CONSERVATIVE advocate of capitalism, limited government, and traditional moral values.

Further Readings

Campbell, T. D. *Adam Smith's Science of Morals.* Totowa, N.J.: Rowman & Littlefield, 1971.
Winch, D. *Adam Smith's Politics.* Cambridge, Eng.: Cambridge University Press, 1978.

social contract

A major concept in MODERN political thought (HOBBES, LOCKE, ROUSSEAU) that says that the government of a state is the result of a social contract or an agreement of all the members to establish it. This means that the STATE's power and legitimate authority come from the people generally (rather than from God—DIVINE RIGHT OF KINGS—or a few people—ARISTOCRACY, oligarchy). Any state not based in such voluntary CONSENT of the governed is illegitimate, illegal, and a TYRANNY, according to this social-contract view. Primarily developed by British liberal thinkers Thomas Hobbes, John Locke, and John Stuart MILL, this social-contract theory underlies the U.S. CONSTITUTION and American DEMOCRACY. Thomas JEFFERSON's famous DECLARATION OF INDEPENDENCE and James MADISON's U.S. Constitution express the social-contract theory of U.S. government.

The reasons for "free" individuals in a STATE OF NATURE forming a social contract vary according to the thinkers describing it. For Hobbes, the threat of ANARCHY and violence lead reasonable people to form a state to protect their lives; for Locke, a rational people create a government to preserve their NATURAL RIGHTS (life, liberty, and PROPERTY) from criminal invasion. These purposes of "government by consent of the governed" then limit what the state can do. If the state violates citizens' rights, it breaks the contract. The people can replace it.

Social-contract theory emerges from the INDIVIDUALISM of Protestant CHRISTIANITY. The REFORMATION religion that believed in the individual's direct, personal relationship to God soon spread to political ideas of consensual government. So, John CALVIN and Martin LUTHER formed the theological basis of Modern REPUBLICANISM. Earlier thinkers hinted at this idea of representative government (CICERO, SENECA), but Modern social-contract theory did not appear until the end of the MIDDLE AGES (WILLIAM OF OCKHAM, Francisco SUAREZ, JOHN OF PARIS). Contemporary social-contract thinkers include John RAWLS and Robert NOZICK.

Now the accepted rationale for legitimate, democratic government, social-contract theory remains an unrealized ideal in many countries. Argument over how far the state can legislate after the initial contract forming it, whether or not people born "into" the society after the contract is constructed are bound by it, and how to amend the founding contract continue. Generally, procedures of LAW continue the original form of the state, and CITIZENS are expected to obey the government (tacit consent) or move to another country. Only extreme abuse of authority or individual rights justifies overthrowing the state and creating a new government.

Critics of social-contract views of politics fault its legalistic, amoral qualities (e.g., St. Thomas AQUINAS) or its business contract, capitalist features (e.g., Karl MARX). But the populism, democracy, and freedom afforded by a social-contract view of government explain its wide acceptance.

Further Reading
Barker, E. *The Social Contract*. London: Oxford University Press, 1946.

Social Darwinism/Darwinist

A social theory in the late 19th-century United States that applied the scientific evolutionary ideas of Charles Darwin to society and economics. Just as Darwin claimed that competition and adaptation to environment by animal species led to the "survival of the fittest" and the extinction of the weak, Social Darwinists insisted that individual social competition in CAPITALISM led to the success of the fittest and the defeat of the weak or lazy. Corresponding with a LAISSEZ-FAIRE business ETHIC, Social Darwinism justified the rich as "the good people" and the poor as "bad," lazy, or unproductive. This led to the CONSERVATIVE IDEOLOGY against social welfare (which would only reward and encourage laziness and inefficiency) that followed into RIGHT-WING REPUBLICAN PARTY policy (see Ronald REAGAN). A leading proponent of Social Darwinist thought was William Graham SUMNER, a Yale sociologist. He allowed for private charity to the poor but resisted public welfare as (1) unjust to the wealthy, who are taxed to support it, and (2) destructive to the poor, who will lose all incentive to work to improve their own lives. A contemporary thinker from this LIBERTARIAN perspective is Robert NOZICK.

With the rise of INDUSTRIALISM the Social-Darwinist perspective was increasingly discredited and eclipsed by the WELFARE-STATE liberalism of Franklin D. ROO-SEVELT, the NEW DEAL, and the PROGRESSIVE U.S. DEMOCRATIC PARTY.

social democracy

A SOCIALIST political movement and IDEOLOGY that rejected the RADICAL, revolutionary ideas of Karl MARX and held that socialism could be achieved democratically. In Europe, social democracy was led by the German Social Democratic Party and its chief theoretician, Edward Bernstein. Similar social-democratic movements existed in France, Italy, and with the FABIANS in Britain. All agreed that social and economic reform (benefiting the industrial working class) could be accomplished through standard political activity (elections, parties, rallies, etc.) rather than through armed, violent revolution (as in Russia). This reformist or revisionist approach to achieving COMMUNISM conflicted with classical MARXISM, which insisted that the state was a tool of the ruling CAPITALIST class and was unwilling to transfer power to its class enemies. Radical Marxists accused social democrats of compromising with the bourgeoisie oppressors and weakening the working-class movement. Russian communist V.I. LENIN especially attacked these reformist social democrats.

Social democracy uses the existing government to "legislate socialism" through laws favorable to labor unions, workers, public education, health care, and housing. In the United States, this stance is expressed in the far-LEFT of the DEMOCRATIC PARTY; in Great Britain, in the Labour Party. With the fall of orthodox communist regimes (such as the SOVIET UNION), the reform approach of the social democrats seems to have prevailed.

Further Readings
Bernstein, E. *Evolutionary Socialism 1898*. New York: Schocken Books, 1961.
Clarke, P. F. *Liberals and Social Democrats in Historical Perspective*. Cambridge, Eng.: Cambridge University Press, 1978.
Durbin, E. *The Politics of Democratic Socialism*. London: Routledge, 1940.

social ethics

The way in which political thinkers view and justify moral or ethical conduct or behavior in society; or what makes an individual and society "good." Various thinkers value different ideals of ETHICS. PLATO discussed social ethics in terms of fitting into one's place in the REPUBLIC, exercising the VIRTUES appropriate to one's innate talents, and contributing to the harmonious ordering of the whole society (or JUSTICE). ARISTOTLE viewed ethics in terms of the golden mean of moderation: A personal character always chooses the virtue between two vices (excess and deficiency); courage resides between cowardliness and recklessness. CICERO presented social ethics in terms of PATRIOTISM and obedience to ROMAN LAW. CHRISTIAN social ethics (St. AUGUSTINE, St. Thomas AQUINAS, John CALVIN, etc.) enjoin obedience to God and Christlikeness (the values of love, humility, forgiveness, patience, etc.). MODERN RENAISSANCE and ENLIGHTENMENT social ethics focus more on respecting rights of others (John LOCKE, Thomas HOBBES). COMMUNIST theory (Karl MARX, V.I. LENIN, Friedrich ENGELS) dismisses absolute ethics, claiming that morality is historically conditioned and relative; each economic system has its own ethics, and the only "true" good is violent revolution that overthrows CAPITALISM and establishes SOCIALISM. FASCIST theory (NAZI; Giovanni GENTILE) advocates obedience to the STATE and the leader as the highest social ethic.

In general, social ethical systems can be broken down into two schools of thought: positive and negative. Negative social ethics (as in the British LIBERALISM of John Locke) commend a standard of goodness by what one does not do (does not kill, steal, enslave, etc.). The Old Testament Ten COMMANDMENTS are primarily negative ethical statements. A good society in this view is one in which people respect others' individual rights, and otherwise leave others alone. Positive social ethics (as in CLASSICAL and Christian philosophy) emphasize doing positive good to others (training, love, charity, etc.); the good society is one full of concerned, caring people, not separate autonomous individuals. For example, on the issue of ABORTION or HOMOSEXUALITY, the negative social ethics would say those individuals involved have private RIGHTS that should be absolutely respected (pro-choice, pro-gay). The positive ethical system would say that the good society would seek what is best for the people involved, applying a transcendent standard (NATURAL LAW).

Social ethics are a part of every political system, though they are often assumed rather than explicitly understood. With the rise of CONSERVATIVE religious and moral character issues in the United States, examination of standards of social ethics increases. James Davi-

son HUNTER's book *Culture Wars* presents the major ethical approaches in the contemporary United States.

Social Gospel Movement

A PROGRESSIVE social movement primarily of Protestant CHRISTIANS in late 19th- and early 20th-century United States. In response to the urban poverty, alcoholism, and social conflict of early INDUSTRIALISM in the United States, the Social Gospel Movement applied Christian ETHICS of love, charity, peace, and justice to U.S. politics. Endorsement of Liberal social legislation (favoring labor unions, social welfare to the poor, PROHIBITION of liquor, and civil rights for AFRICAN AMERICANS) characterized this LEFTIST church movement. Leaders included Walter RAUSCHENBUSCH (whose book *Christianity and the Social Crisis* encapsulated its thought), Charles M. SHELDON (whose novel *In His Steps* expressed its ideal), and CATHOLIC cardinal James Gibbons (who supported the KNIGHTS OF LABOR). Organizations such as the Salvation Army and the Volunteers of America embodied Social Gospel ideals. In its most extreme form, the Social Gospel Movement endorsed a Christian SOCIALISM and the hope that the kingdom of God could be realized on earth through economic and political reform.

After World War I, the optimism of the Social Gospel Movement waned, but many of its programs were revived by the Liberal DEMOCRATIC PARTY of Franklin D. ROOSEVELT's NEW DEAL. Critics of the Social Gospel Movement arose from CONSERVATIVE churches and the Christian REALISM of Reinhold NIEBUHR's neo-ORTHODOXY. Nevertheless, the social conscience of the Liberal Protestant churches continued in the Methodist, Presbyterian, Episcopal, and United Church of Christ churches throughout the 20th century. LIBERATION THEOLOGY became the most RADICAL, MARXIST COMMUNIST form of this movement.

socialism/socialist

An economic and social system and IDEOLOGY that denies the absolute individual RIGHT to private PROPERTY ownership and insists that society as a whole (or its state) should control production and distribution of wealth. Often contrasted with CAPITALISM or a free-market economy, socialist theory developed in Europe during the 18th and 19th centuries in response to INDUSTRIALISM. Ranging from full-scale TOTALITARIAN-state control of every aspect of human life (as in the SOVIET UNION) to the milder governmental regulation of the economy in WELFARE-STATE legislation (as in Great Britain and Europe) Modern socialism has existed in some form since SAINT-SIMON and Karl MARX each wrote on the subject.

The general argument for economic socialism (or political control of property) is that material wealth is a social product and activity that involves the cooperation of the whole community rather than a private right of autonomous individuals. So, the control and benefits of that social economy should be by the society at large rather by than a few rich and powerful individuals or groups. From this logic, the state can be the instrument of the whole community to order all economic activity for the common good. Socialist thought tends to be EGALITARIAN, that is, to believe that each individual is equal to all the rest and is deserving of EQUALITY of treatment, opportunities, and benefits. So, for example, *socialized medicine* (as in Great Britain) means a health-care system in which everyone receives equal medical services, regardless of their income, status, age, and so on. Only human need and the resources available determine the receiving of medical treatment. The limits on that social benefit are made by overall social resources (number of doctors, prescriptions, hospitals, etc.) and overall social priorities (health care vis-à-vis education, housing, food, clothing, entertainment, and so on).

Socialist theories and systems vary widely over the extent of private property and trade allowed, the state management of the economy, and the community regulation of individual behavior (see COMMUNISM). PROUDHON advocated an agricultural commune style of society (like the contemporary Israeli kibbutz); MARXISM focused on advanced, mass industrial production; social democracy blends private entrepreneurship with state regulation for the economy and state ownership of key industries (e.g., steel, telecommunications, transportation, etc.). In all cases, socialism seeks to restrict the FREEDOM and LIBERTY of individuals and businesses for the purpose of benefiting the whole society (though Jean-Jacques ROUSSEAU's COMMUNITARIAN ideal claims to give everyone more liberty through such state control).

Socialist ideas appear throughout Western political thought and practice: PLATO's *Republic* advocated common property for the "guardian" (military) class; early CHRISTIANS (Acts 2) held "all things in common"; MEDIEVAL FEUDALISM involved considerable common or GUILD property. Qualifying these views were ARISTOTLE's critique of Plato (saying that private wealth was more efficient and contributed to the virtue of generosity); St. Thomas AQUINAS asserting that private property is allowable if existing within the bounds of Christian charity and NATURAL LAW; and John LOCKE's claim that individual ownership advances PROGRESS and prosperity.

Most of 19th- and 20th-century socialist ideas were attempts to ameliorate the harsh working conditions and poverty of the urban working class. A Christian socialist movement in Great Britain and the United States (e.g., Robert OWEN, Charles SHELDON) applied Christian ETHICS to capitalist economics. Most socialist movements were radically secular, however, and emphasized purely worldly notions of class EXPLOITATION and JUSTICE. Arguments that workers created most of the wealth in society and therefore deserved to receive most of it led to often violent rebellion and social REVOLUTION. The idea that capitalist "property is theft" inflamed workers' revolt and resentment. Led by dynamic figures such as V.I. Lenin, MAO TSE-TUNG, and Fidel Castro, RADICAL socialist principles were implemented in Russia, China, and Cuba. In each case, the promised prosperity, freedom, and elimination of ALIENATION failed to appear. Instead of a more productive, rational, and efficient economy, pure socialism's control from a central state created inefficient, wasteful, corrupt, and oppressive economics and politics. The REALISM that doubted humanity's ability to produce heaven on earth seemed to be confirmed by the failure of socialism and communism.

Still, socialist ideals continue to be developed through CRITICAL THEORY and the NEW LEFT, and MODERATE socialism exists in every industrialized Western democracy through governmental regulation of the economy, public services (education, housing, health care), and programs for the poor, aged, and infirm. Other social movements, such as ENVIRONMENTALISM, FEMINISM, and LIBERALISM, have meshed with socialist ideas.

The main premise of socialism is that people will work harder and be more creative, kind, and happy if all their basic material needs are taken care of by society. A popular phrase among socialists was that the state would paternalistically take care of its people "from cradle to grave." Critics of this socialist premise (St. AUGUSTINE, MACHIAVELLI, John CALVIN, Reinhold NIEBUHR) argue that such social welfare, absent of incentives and punishments, will just make people lazy and bored. With the collapse of the Soviet Union, the move of Communist China toward a market economy, and the impoverishment of Cuba, the contemporary world views socialism with less optimism than many did a hundred years ago.

Further Readings
Laidler, H. W. *History of Socialism.* New York: Crowell, 1948.
Landauer, C. *European Socialism: A History of Ideas and Movements.* Berkeley: University of California Press, 1959.

Socrates (469–399 B.C.) *classical Greek philosopher*

Often compared to Christ because he criticized the religious establishment, was executed by the STATE, but forgave his accusers, Socrates was a teacher of PLATO, influencing all CLASSICAL political thought.

Most famous for his dictum "Know Thyself" and "the unexamined life is not worth living," Socrates begins the Western philosophic tradition. His "Socratic method" of educating students by asking them questions continues in the Oxford tutorial system, the adversarial legal method, and the free press as a "Fourth Estate," critically examining the government.

Socrates wrote nothing himself, but his philosophical life and activity is written by various disciplines, especially in the *Dialogues* of Plato. The most biographical is *The Apology,* a description of Socrates' trial in Athens on charges of heresy and corrupting the young. In his defense ("apology"), Socrates provides logical refutation of both charges and reveals, through questioning, their true source in his challenging of the established authority in Greece. Most serious was his embarrassing of the proud, self-satisfied, prominent leaders of Athens, who only think they are wise, when in fact their pride and arrogance makes them foolish and ignorant. True wisdom, for Socrates, is a humble appreciation of one's own lack of knowledge. Such personal, intellectual humility fuels the search for knowledge and is the true "philosopher's" ("lover of wisdom") premier trait. Most prominent people are infected with the sin of pride and therefore are stupid. This attitude lands Socrates in court, in jail, and finally to being executed by the state. He insists that he is not being disrespectful to Athens's leaders or disloyal to his country; quite the contrary, Greece in its Golden Age has become so rich, proud, and decadent that it needs a patriotic "gadfly" to sting it and wake it up, according to Socrates. He did that to save his country.

The Platonic Dialogue *Crito* details Socrates' time, his obedience to the states' laws, his patriotism, and his love of country. He even refuses to escape and save his own life when the opportunity presents itself. Socrates insists that he is following a "higher law," God's command, when he criticizes the state.

Elsewhere, Socrates is recorded as critical of the Athenean democracy because the majority of people are selfish, proud, and ignorant. He faults the political leaders for pandering to the masses to be elected, rather than having any independent intelligence, judgment, or principles.

These Socratic views are developed by his greatest student, Plato, especially in *The Republic.* His concern for education leads to a Platonic state, ruled by a PHILOSOPHER-KING and preoccupied with educating the VIRTUES of all its CITIZENS. His plea that Athens treat his sons as he treated them and that then they will have "justice" (getting their "due") becomes the central theme of Plato's *Republic*—the definition of *justice* and how to achieve it.

Many subsequent philosophers claim Socrates as their inspiration and example, including John Stuart MILL, C. S. LEWIS, and Henry David THOREAU.

Further Reading
Kraut, R. *Socrates and the State.* Princeton, N.J.: Princeton University Press, 1984.

sovereignty

The ultimate political AUTHORITY or POWER in government. For example, DEMOCRATIC political thought says that "the people" are "the sovereign" because they possess ultimate, legitimate political authority. During the European MIDDLE AGES, the king was often referred to as the sovereign because a MONARCH had absolute political power. In SOCIAL-CONTRACT theory, because the individuals form the government, they have sovereignty.

In the history of political thought, the term *sovereignty* does not become prominent until the latter Middle Ages. St. Thomas AQUINAS, the leading medieval CATHOLIC theologian, places ultimate sovereignty in God through DIVINE LAW. The ruler's sovereignty (or human law) is dependent on that divine authority and must be exercised within the bounds of Christian truth for the common good, or justice. Frenchman Jean BODIN develops this notion of CHRISTIAN sovereignty into a doctrine of DIVINE RIGHT OF KINGS. British liberal theorist Thomas HOBBES also places sovereignty in a king or a single absolutist ruler but has his authority derive from a social contract among the common people. John LOCKE, similarly, situates sovereignty in free individuals in the STATE OF NATURE, possessing NATURAL RIGHTS to "Life, LIBERTY and PROPERTY" and setting up a state to protect those RIGHTS. So, sovereignty is delegated to the government by the people and is only legitimate if it is serving those CITIZENS' good. If the STATE offends those rights (by killing, robbing, or enslaving the people) the original sovereignty of the masses can be reclaimed and given to a new government (as Thomas JEFFERSON explains in the DECLARATION OF INDEPENDENCE for the United States). One of the key differences between Great Britain and the United States of America is their respective conceptions of sovereignty. For Britain, sovereignty resides in Parliament, or the institution of government; for the United States, sovereignty resides the "The People." In one, the state controls the people; in the other, the people control the state. Jean-Jacques ROUSSEAU, the MODERN French liberal, places sovereignty in the GENERAL WILL of the community that (unlike British/U.S. liberalism) can rule over individual rights. This image of a sovereign "will" over individual rights proceeds to the COMMUNIST and FASCIST ideas of sovereignty in a ruling class or unified state.

How *sovereignty* is defined, then, greatly affects how individual rights and the power of government are practiced.

Further Readings

Hinsley, F. H. *Sovereignty.* Cambridge, Eng.: Cambridge University Press, 1966.

Jouvenel, B. de. *Sovereignty.* Chicago: University of Chicago Press, 1957.

Soviet Union

The political thought of the Soviet Union (or USSR) was officially MARXISM-LENINISM, or orthodox COMMUNISM. It claimed a government ruled by the industrial working class (or proletariat). In MARXIST theory, this DICTATORSHIP of the proletariat is the appropriate government under socialism. Although claiming to rule for the people, the Soviet communist state under V.I. LENIN and Joseph STALIN came to be an oppressive monopolistic one-party dictatorship that employed terror, secret police, censorship, and IDEOLOGICAL indoctrination to maintain its rule. All aspects of economic,

My stroim kommunizm! (We are building Communism!), 1968, USSR. (LIBRARY OF CONGRESS)

social, educational, and family life were controlled by the central state. This TOTALITARIAN system restricted individual FREEDOM and RIGHTS to thought, movement, and PROPERTY. *Soviet communism* became synonymous with BUREAUCRATIC rule, inefficiency, oppression, and international aggression. By the mid-1980s, the Soviet economy was declining with decreased productivity, alcoholism and depression were rampant in Soviet society, and numerous dissidents criticized the Soviet system. President Gorbachev attempted DEMOCRATIC reforms in the 1980s that finally led to the dissolution of the Soviet Union, the establishment of independent regional REPUBLICS, and formal constitutional democracy and CAPITALISM. Full freedom, individual rights (for example to private property or religious belief), and representative government have not yet been realized in Russia.

Further Readings
Harding, N., ed. *Marxism in Russia: Key Documents, 1879–1906.* Cambridge, Eng.: Cambridge University Press, 1983.
Marcuse, H. *Soviet Marxism: A Critical Analysis.* New York: Columbia University Press, 1958.

Spencer, Herbert (1820–1903) *British philosopher and sociologist*

Adapting the scientific evolutionary ideas of Charles Darwin to politics, Spencer became a leading SOCIAL DARWINISM thinker in Britain. According to his view, social progress involves LAISSEZ-FAIRE competition, the success of the "superior," adaptable individuals, and the death of "inferior" (lazy, stupid) persons. Attempts to ameliorate this system of social "natural selection" (social welfare, public assistance to the poor, etc.) only disrupt the evolutionary process and protect idleness and incompetence from the consequences of their weakness, harming social PROGRESS. Like the American William Graham SUMNER, Spencer believed that social competition rewarded the smart and industrious and punished the foolish and lazy. Absolute economic freedom and a limited Lockean state foster the general good of the nation. This doctrine continues in the LIBERTARIAN thought of Robert NOZICK and other RIGHT-WING CONSERVATIVES. Its appeal to big business and successful corporations is obvious. Its ideological opponents on the LEFT included SOCIALISTS, COMMUNISTS, FABIANS, and SOCIAL DEMOCRATIC Liberals, all of whom saw a positive role for the state in mitigating the negative effects of early INDUSTRIALISM and capitalism (urban crowding, ill health, poverty, child labor, etc.).

Herbert Spencer was more of a popular writer than a scholarly philosopher. His education was largely technical, and he worked as a railroad engineer. He wrote for the *Economist* magazine, and his main book was entitled *Synthetic Philosophy* (published in multiple volumes from 1860 to 1896). His later years were plagued with illness and intellectual disputations.

Further Reading
Peel, J.D.Y. *Herbert Spencer.* New York: Basic Books, 1971.

Spinoza, Baruch (1632–1677) *Dutch moral and political philosopher*

A descendent of Spanish Jews who immigrated to the Netherlands, Spinoza combines the REALISM of MACHI-AVELLI, the SOCIAL-CONTRACT theory of Thomas HOBBES, and the sense of ALIENATION of his own people. With a pessimistic, materialistic view of HUMAN NATURE (people are governed by their irrational passions and emotions), Spinoza portrays society and politics as unhappy and tragic. Conflict is inevitable among individuals who only pursue their own self-INTEREST and are ignorant of true human happiness.

Like Hobbes, he takes a biological view of humanity, regards religion as a myth, and views government as, at best, only mildly corrupt. True JUSTICE is impossible, given human ignorance and selfishness. The majority of people are so stupid that it is unlikely that the few wise and good will rule, so improvement through politics is rare. DEMOCRACY is the best regime (balancing pluralistic interests) but requires a lengthy tradition of civic culture (FREEDOM; tolerance; a large, educated middle class). The STATE should be run as a MONARCHY or an ARISTOCRACY and prepare the people for self-government. Most countries in the world are not prepared for a REPUBLICAN form of government.

Spinoza reflects much of the MODERN, ENLIGHTENMENT liberalism of his time and expresses a secular republican ideology that was later developed by John LOCKE, David HUME, and Jean-Jacques ROUSSEAU.

Further Readings
Duff, R. A. *Spinoza's Political and Ethical Philosophy.* New York: Augustus M. Kelley, 1970.
McShea, R. J. *The Political Philosophy of Spinoza.* New York: Columbia University Press, 1968.

Stalin, Joseph (1879–1953) *Communist dictator of the Soviet Union*

Stalin or "Stalinist" represents the brutal TOTALITARIAN TYRANNY of COMMUNIST Russia. Ruling as an ABSOLUTIST tyrant over the USSR from 1929 to 1953, Stalin epitomized the oppressive, harsh society of communism. The total loss of personal FREEDOM, individual RIGHTS, and DEMOCRATIC government marked Stalinist Russia. Brutal DICTATORSHIP, state censorship, secret police, arbitrary arrests and executions, fear, and terror characterized Soviet life under Stalin. This closed, impoverished, paranoid, aggressive nation belied the liberation and prosperity promised by MARXIST theory: Instead of a heaven on earth, Soviet communism under Stalin displayed a hell-like existence.

In his political thought, Stalin claimed to follow Russian Marxist V.I. LENIN, working for the BOLSHEVIK Party's revolutionary overthrow of the czarist government. Once in power, Stalin asserted that the Communist Party was not just the leader of the working class but "the embodiment of unity of will," or the absolute political authority in the country (*The Foundations of Leninism*). This modified Lenin's more POPULIST "democratic centralism" to create a dictatorial Communist Party. As leader of that centralized party, Stalin became an absolute dictator in Russia. He led purges that tried and executed fellow communists who opposed him.

Stalin developed a theory of "socialism in one country" that claimed that the USSR could advance to communist perfection even if the other countries of the world remained CAPITALIST. This was contrary to the common Marxist view that many nations must have socialist revolutions for communism to exist in any one of them.

Stalin tried to advance the Soviet economy by rapid industrialization and forcible collectivization of agriculture (turning private farms into communes). Popular resistance (especially by peasants) to these measures led to the Stalinist state's murder of millions of its own citizens.

During World War II, Stalin first made a peace pact with Hitler's NAZI Germany and then, when Germany invaded Russia, with the Allies (Britain, United States). After the Allied victory, Stalin's Soviet troops retained control of the conquered Eastern European countries (Romania, Hungary, Czechoslovakia, Bulgaria, Poland, and East Germany). After Stalin's death, the Soviet government denounced his cruel and dictatorial rule.

state

The government system and structure of a given country or community. The formal, legal "state" in the United States of America is the federal or national government, outlined in the U.S. CONSTITUTION, and the regional and local governments, throughout the country. In a broader sense, a state is not just the formal governing apparatus, but the distinct society, culture, and economy of a given region and community that exists under a single governmental authority. So the "Russian state" or the "British state" includes more than the ruling institutions (Parliament, courts, etc.); it encompassed customs, historical traditions, the reli-

gion of the people, education, culture, economics, arts, and so on.

When most CLASSICAL thinkers discussed the state, they meant both the nonpolitical characteristics and the governing structures of a region. Theories of the state both described existing states and ideal political/social systems. So, PLATO's *Republic* describes an ideal society and government that partly reflects the Ancient Greek state of Athens. ARISTOTLE described 150 state constitutions of his time, including the Greek POLIS. CICERO describes the state in terms of the Roman REPUBLIC and Roman Empire. CHRISTIAN political theory (St. AUGUSTINE, St. Thomas AQUINAS) views all worldly states in relation to God's kingdom (The City of God, or divine law), as does ISLAMIC political thought. MODERN theory (MACHIAVELLI, Thomas HOBBES) tends to see the state purely in terms of POWER. Liberalism (John LOCKE, John Stuart MILL) emphasizes the limited quality of the state and its responsibility to preserve individual NATURAL RIGHTS (to "Life, LIBERTY, and PROPERTY"). MARXIST COMMUNIST theory reduces the state to an instrument of economic class rule (by the owners of property). ANARCHISM and LIBERTARIAN thought deny the LEGITIMACY of the state altogether, seeing the government as the source of all oppression and wanting to abolish it as quickly as possible. COMMUNITARIAN theory (Jean-Jacques ROUSSEAU, Benjamin BARBER) sees politics and the state as everything and the proper controller of all aspects of human life (economics, religion, family).

Discussions of the state in political thought invariably lead to issues of legitimacy (what makes a state just and legal), SOVEREIGNTY (how far does the authority of the state extend), LAW (the formal rules in a state), and HIERARCHY (the relationship of the government to the governed). In a sense, study of the state is the whole subject of POLITICAL THEORY. With the rise of TOTALITARIAN states (Soviet Communism, FASCISM) in the 20th century, concern for defining the proper role and limits of the state increased. With the globalization of the world's economy in the 21st century (the internet, world trade agreements, the European Community, etc.), the nation-state's power is being diminished when compared to this one-world system.

Further Readings
Bosanquet, B. *The Philosophical Theory of the State 1899.* New York: Macmillan, 1958.
Dyson, K. *The State Tradition in Western Europe.* New York: Oxford University Press, 1980.
Poggi, G. *The Development of the Modern State.* Stanford, Calif.: Stanford University Press, 1978.

state of nature

A concept developed by various European political thinkers (Thomas HOBBES, John LOCKE, Jean-Jacques ROUSSEAU) in the 17th and 18th centuries that portrays a pregovernment human society or "natural state" of humankind. It is another way to defining HUMAN NATURE, by saying what the earliest human society looked like before government, LAWS, and other social institutions existed. By defining the human in a "state of nature," these SOCIAL-CONTRACT thinkers formulated what people were originally like and what kind of state they developed and thereby define what a LEGITIMATE or proper government is, what its purposes and duties are, and how citizens are to relate to it.

In Thomas Hobbes's *Leviathan,* the state of nature is filled with separate, selfish individuals who are led by their private senses and desires to take whatever they want. In such a "natural" state, Hobbes's scientific, behaviorist approach sees humans as having RIGHTS to everything and total LIBERTY to do what they want (even kill each other). This leads to a society of fierce competition, VIOLENCE, and insecurity. So human reason, which calculates individual interest, leads these people to make a social contract to give up their POWER, rights, and liberty (to the state) to secure peace. Therefore, Hobbes's total freedom in the state of nature leads to an ABSOLUTIST government with tremendous authority to control individuals and regulate society.

John Locke conceives of the state of nature as a more orderly, peaceful society in which most people are rational and orderly, respecting the NATURAL RIGHTS of others (to "Life, Liberty, and Property") and pursuing their self-interest peacefully. If all humans had reason (or the law of nature) and self-control, no government would ever be needed. But Locke says that some people invade the rights of others (killing, stealing, kidnapping) and that it is inconvenient for victims to catch and punish those offenders, so the "good" people form a state to defend their rights and enforce the law.

Jean-Jacque Rousseau conceives of the state of nature in more still positive ways as a society of innocent, childlike creatures living in peace and harmony. Advanced civil society corrupts this ROMANTIC scene, requiring a political REPUBLIC to restore justice and right.

More recent uses of the state-of-natural theme occur in John RAWLS's "original position" in his book *A Theory of Justice* and in Robert NOZICK's argument for LIBERTARIAN society in *Anarchy, State and Utopia.*

Most political theorists do not think that the state of nature ever actually existed in the world. Political communities historically developed (as described by ARISTOTLE) through family, tribe, and villages, but the state-of-nature concept helped to formulate the origins of MODERN liberal government, INDIVIDUALISM, CAPITALISM, natural rights, and private property.

states rights

A doctrine or political stance in American history that places primary SOVEREIGNTY in the United States government in the individual states (Virginia, Massachusetts, North Carolina, etc.). Beginning with the ANTIFEDERALISTS, states-rights thinkers (such as Patrick HENRY, Thomas JEFFERSON) believed that the national (or federal) government derived its authority from the states that compacted to form the U.S. CONSTITUTION in 1789. According to this view, the central government could not impose any laws on the states that individual state governments did not approve, John C. CALHOUN and his theory that states could "nullify" federal laws that were displeasing to them expressed the extreme view of this states-rights doctrine. James MADISON expressed it in his Virginia resolutions that criticized the Alien and Sedition Acts of President John ADAMS's administration. Eventually, states-rights principles led to the American Civil War, as Southern states seceded from the Union to establish a confederacy based on states-rights principles. In the 20th century, states-rights attitudes were again expressed against the increasing federal-government power of the NEW DEAL.

Drawn from ideas in CLASSICAL REPUBLICANISM that encourage decentralized, small-scale DEMOCRACY, states-rights IDEOLOGY reflects sentiments that government closer to the people is more responsive and less corrupt.

Strauss, Leo (1899–1973) *German-born U.S. philosopher*

Generally regarded as one of the most important CONSERVATIVE political thinkers of the 20th century, Strauss was born in Kirchhain, Germany. After serving briefly in the German army, Strauss studied at the universities of Marburg, Frankfurt, Berlin, and Hamburg, where he received his doctorate in 1921. From 1925 to 1932, Strauss served as a research assistant at the Academy for Jewish Research in Berlin. As a student and researcher, he was attracted to the works of Friedrich NIETZSCHE and attended lectures by the phenomenologists Edmund Husserl and Martin HEIDEGGER. Strauss left Germany following the NAZI rise to power, spending two years in France and four years in England on a Rockefeller Foundation fellowship. In 1938, he immigrated to the United States and became a naturalized U.S. citizen in 1944. Between 1938 and 1973, Strauss taught political philosophy at several universities, although he spent most of his career at the University of Chicago (1949–68).

Strauss published a large number of scholarly books and articles. Most of his writings examined classical political philosophers and the issues raised by comparisons between the ancients and the moderns on topics such as DEMOCRACY, INDIVIDUALISM, religion, and JUSTICE. Strauss's work was motivated by what he considered to be the spiritual crisis of the modern age. For Strauss, MODERNITY is characterized by a conflict between the claims of reason and of revelation, a struggle between rationalistic science and religious wisdom. The result, he argued, was the prevalence of cultural nihilism in modern Western civilization, seen politically in the appearance of such oppressive systems as FASCISM and COMMUNISM. Strauss believed that modern thinkers and politicians had sought to break with the ideals and virtues of excellence espoused by the premoderns, especially the ancient Greeks. In place of the premodern virtues, modernity has substituted a notion of EGALITARIAN affluence that is to be fulfilled for everyone by means of the tools of science. Yet, even as the moderns have sought to liberate themselves from the orthodoxies of the past, they have enslaved themselves to the power of a science that seeks to dominate nature.

As Strauss portrayed it, there were several stages to this process of domination. First, modern political philosophy began to view society as a construct to be differentiated from the natural world, as Thomas HOBBES and John LOCKE argued in their SOCIAL-CONTRACT theories. Second, philosophers such as Jean-Jacques ROUSSEAU initiated the argument that human nature itself was malleable rather than fixed; this argument was taken further by Karl MARX, who emphasized the historical quality of human existence and, consequently, the potential that exists to transform both individuals and society. In the third stage, identified

with the philosophy of Nietzsche, this HISTORICISM culminated in a radical relativism of beliefs and values. Because what can be defined as the good, it was believed, was historically determined rather than eternal, those who can control social history can control knowledge and the path of civilization. The contemporary period, then, has become a power struggle between forces that seek to define *reality,* with technology and its consumption becoming ever more important than the demands of morality. Strauss's primary concern was that this situation would undermine modernity's greatest success, its commitment to democracy. For Strauss, this commitment must be supplemented by the virtues recognized by the premoderns as necessary for civic life.

Further Reading
Deutsch, K. L., and Nicgorski, W., eds. *Leo Strauss: Political Philosopher and Jewish Thinker.* Lanham, Md.: Rowman & Littlefield Publishing, 1994.

Suárez, Francisco (1548–1617)   *Spanish Catholic theologian and political philosopher*

A leading thinker of the CATHOLIC counterreformation against Protestant Christianity, Suárez addressed questions of NATURAL LAW, HUMAN RIGHTS, SOVEREIGNTY, MONARCHY, and INTERNATIONAL LAW. Drawing heavily from the political thought of St. Thomas AQUINAS, he developed an original political theory in the book *A Treatise on the Laws and God the Lawgiver* (1612), which still influences Catholic political thought in Europe and Latin America.

Suárez integrated MODERN individual-rights philosophy into the traditional Catholic natural-law worldview by subordinating private material rights to higher divine law and CHRISTIAN JUSTICE. Natural law is rational because it reflects God's reason, but its primary authority flows not from our human (rational) appreciation but from its origin in God's will, as lawgiver. Thus, natural rights (to FREEDOM, PROPERTY, etc.) must still be subordinated to God's natural and divine law, as explicated by the church.

Living during the expansion of the Spanish state and EMPIRE, Suárez applied this theory to international law and economic development, so although he saw war and SLAVERY as not part of God's will, they exist in the custom of countries and must be dealt with by Christian states.

Sovereignty, for Suárez, is the absolute power of the state (monarch) to make laws, in conformity with divine and natural law, for the common good. A sovereign is not subject to the law (as in Jean BODIN, he or she "is" the law); although the sovereign rules in the interest of the people and thereby with their CONSENT, the populace does not choose the rulers or have a right to overthrow them (unless the ruler is a Protestant or becomes a TYRANT who seeks to destroy the community). A nation, as a collective, has a natural right to defend itself against either foreign invaders or a tyrannical leader. On this basis, Suarez argued in *A Defence of the Catholic and Apostolic Faith against the Errors of the Anglican Sect* (1612) that the people of England should overthrow the Protestant King James I.

Suárez modifies the CONCILIARISM of WILLIAM OF OCKHAM, arguing for the supreme authority of the pope over church councils and secular kings and queens.

Suárez held the professorship of theology at the University of Coimbra in Spain. Most of his writing derives from his university lectures.

Further Reading
Wilenius, Reijo. *The Social and Political Theory of Francisco Suárez.* Helsinki: 1963.

suffrage

Voting and the right to vote or to participate in choosing governmental officials by election. Suffrage is considered a basic RIGHT of CITIZENSHIP in a DEMOCRACY or REPUBLIC.

During the MODERN period, the tendency has been to extend the suffrage to more people. In 18th-century Britain and the United States only adult, white males owning a certain amount of PROPERTY were allowed to vote. Gradually, the suffrage was extended to working and poor men, women, blacks, and younger people. In the United States, AFRICAN-AMERICAN ex-slaves were guaranteed the right to vote after the Civil War (1865), women gained the suffrage in 1920, and the voting age was reduced to 18 in 1971. The right to vote can be taken away because of insanity, being convicted of a felony, or being dishonorably discharged from the military.

In most REPUBLICAN countries, suffrage is not considered LEGITIMATE unless there is more than one candidate to choose from and the voting is done by secret ballot.

Sumner, William Graham (1840–1910)   *U.S. sociologist and political theorist*

A leading advocate of SOCIAL DARWINISM, Sumner was influenced by Herbert SPENCER. His ideas, especially in the book *What Social Classes Owe to Each Other* (1884), reflect a belief in INDIVIDUALISM, social competition, and CAPITALISM. The struggle for economic success (like the competition of species in Darwin's evolutionary theory) leads to the strong, intelligent, and hard-working getting ahead, while the weak, stupid, and lazy are defeated. This system in good, for Sumner, as it aids economic and social PROGRESS. He, therefore, opposes social-welfare programs as rewarding the "bad" (poor) people and harming the "good" (rich) people. He especially hates social reformers, who self-righteously claim to care about the poor and disadvantaged when their programs really indulge laziness, sin, and their own self-interest. "Certain ills," he wrote, "belong to the hardships of human life." Emphasizing individual FREEDOM, Sumner wrote, "A free man in a free democracy has no duty whatever toward other men of the same rank and standing, except respect, courtesy, and good will. . . . In a free state every man is held and expected to take care of himself and his family, to make no trouble for his neighbor, and to contribute his full share to public interests and common necessities."

Sumner's ideas accompanied LAISSEZ-FAIRE thought during early INDUSTRIALISM in the United States. He taught at Yale University and was an ordained priest in the Episcopal Church. His philosophy of limited government welfare programs, probusiness competition, and individual enterprise continues in CONSERVATIVE, REPUBLICAN PARTY IDEOLOGY.

Supreme Court, U.S.

The highest court of the judicial branch of the United States government established by Article III of the U.S. CONSTITUTION. Balancing the legislative (Congress) branch and the executive (President) branch of government, this reflects the CHECKS AND BALANCES in James MADISON's theory of FEDERALISM.

As the highest tribunal in the country, the U.S. Supreme Court has jurisdiction over legal cases affecting constitutional interpretation, federal laws, and relations between the national and state govern-

U.S. Supreme Court Building, Washington, D.C. (LIBRARY OF CONGRESS)

ments (and between states). As such, the Supreme Court is the ultimate "umpire" in U.S. politics, defining the limits and duties of public life. In the tradition of English common law, the Supreme Court decides cases based on "precedent," or past case decisions. Its primary function is to uphold the principles and RIGHTS in the Constitution. For example, because the FIRST AMENDMENT of the Constitution guarantees the individual right to FREEDOM of speech, if Congress or a state passes a law censoring free speech, the U.S. Supreme Court will declare that law "unconstitutional" and invalid. This practice is known as judicial review.

It is important in the Court's functioning and preservation of a constitutional REPUBLIC that this judiciary is independent from the other branches of government and public pressure, so lifetime appointments or "tenure" of the judges (or "justices") on the bench protect the Supreme Court from political influence and allow it to rule on the basis of law and tradition. This makes the U.S. Supreme Court a kind of unelected ARISTOCRACY, as in ARISTOTLE's notion of mixed government, to balance the "one" of the president and the "many" of the Congress.

Supreme Court judges are appointed by the United States president and approved by the U.S. Senate. Since 1869, the number of judges on the Supreme Court has been nine, making each justice an extremely powerful person in the United States.

Common constitutional issues dealt with by the U.S. Supreme Court include federalism, individual rights (freedom of speech, press, religion), police procedures in criminal investigation and trials, and governmental regulation of business. Some Supreme Court decisions (such as those related to ABORTION and PRAYER IN SCHOOL) are highly controversial.

The U.S. Supreme Court is one of the most respected institutions in the country, and its function is essential to the maintenance of the Republic.

Swift, Jonathan (1667–1745) *Irish political writer*

Active in British-government controversies of his day, Swift was at times a LIBERAL Whig, at other times a CONSERVATIVE Tory. His satirical writings ridicule the absurdities and abuses of state policy in the British Empire. Most famous of these is the book *Gulliver's Travels* (1726), which criticizes NATIONALISM, colonialism, Modern warfare, political pride, and hypocritical language. Even more devastating is his pamphlet *A Modest Proposal* (1729), which suggested eating the babies of the Irish poor (exposing the brutality of English rule "devouring" Ireland). The horror of this proposal was more shocking before the widespread practice of ABORTION. His *A Tale of a Tub* and *Mechanical Operation of the Spirit* (1701) satirized religious toleration and diversity.

Born in Dublin, Swift was educated at Trinity College and served as dean of St. Patrick's Cathedral.

Further Reading
Lick, F. P. *Swift's Tory Politics.* Newark: University of Delaware Press, 1983.

syndicalism

A SOCIALIST movement in early 20th-century France, Italy, and Spain. Derived from the MEDIEVAL GUILD system, syndicalist IDEOLOGY saw economic protest by labor unions (strikes, walkouts, etc.) as more effective challenges to the CAPITALIST system than MARXIST working-class REVOLUTION. Particularly, the general strike, in which all unions in a country stopped working, could bring down capitalist domination of workers or certain government policies. A violent proletarian revolution (like that of the COMMUNIST SOVIET UNION) would simply lead to many workers being killed, according to syndicalist thinker Fernand Pelloutier. Socialism could better be accomplished within economic organizations (labor unions such as the Industrial Workers of the World) than through political means (parliamentary elections, parties, change of government). In Italy, syndicalism was subsumed within FASCISM; in Spain, it was associated with ANARCHISM. The massive general strike in Great Britain in 1926 followed some syndicalist ideas, but the British socialist (and other dominant European LEFTIST movements) followed either Marxist or SOCIAL DEMOCRAT models.

Further Readings
Roberts, D. L. *The Syndicalist Tradition in Italian Fascism.* Chapel Hill: University of North Carolina Press, 1979.

Stearns, P. *Revolutionary Syndicalism and French Labor.* New Brunswick, N.J.: Rutgers University Press, 1971.

T

Tacitus, Cornelius (A.D. 55–117) Roman historian and statesman

In his Latin books *Germania* (on the German provinces of the Roman Empire) and *Histories* (on the Roman REPUBLIC from A.D. 68), Tacitus provides a critique of the decline of Roman morals and civilization much like that of his contemporary CICERO and, later, Edward GIBBON. He compares the simplicity and VIRTUE of the German people and the early republic with the increasing decadence, luxury, and immorality of the Roman state. DESPOTISM, moral depravity, and economic abundance seem to go together, for Tacitus. This makes his writings part of the CLASSICAL REPUBLICAN IDEOLOGY that is revived in Western political thought in James HARRINGTON, John MILTON, Thomas JEFFERSON, and others.

Tawney, Richard Henry (1880–1962) British economic historian

Richard Tawney was a CHRISTIAN SOCIALIST who wrote a number of influential works on economics and politics. Tawney served a long tenure as a professor at the London School of Economics. He was also prominent in the labor movement and in the leadership of the Worker's Educational Association (WEA).

Tawney was born in Calcutta, India, but educated at Rugby and Balliol College, Oxford, where he graduated with a degree in modern history. An early work, *The Agrarian Problem in the 16th Century* (1912), helped solidify his academic reputation. In the piece, Tawney examined the use of land in a society that was also undergoing a population explosion and rapid inflation, resulting from the impact of the increased availability of gold and silver. The work created a new field of research for social historians.

Throughout his life, Tawney was a vocal advocate for education. He taught classes for working-class students and served as a social worker at Toynbee Hall in London. An early supporter of labor rights and a Christian socialist, Tawney joined the WEA in 1905 and then became a member of the organization's executive board. He remained on the board until 1917 and, in 1920, was elected vice president of the WEA, a post he retained until 1928. He was subsequently elected president and served in that capacity from 1928 to 1944. Concurrently, Tawney began a long academic career by serving as a lecturer at Glasgow University. He joined the faculty of the London School of Economics in 1912 and went on to serve as the director of the Ratan Tata Foundation at the school.

While at the London School of Economics, Tawney published a number of influential works on the economy, including *The Acquisitive Society* (1920), *Religion and the Rise of Capitalism* (1926), and *Equality* (1931). Tawney often emphasized that acquisitiveness in a CAPITALIST society corrupted society because it provided an immoral motivating factor. In addition, Tawney believed that the inherent greed of capitalism deprived workers of the true value of their work. As such, workers lost any pride in their occupation because labor simply became a means to achieve material possessions.

In *Religion and the Rise of Capitalism,* Tawney examined the relationship between capitalism and CALVINISM. The socialist author sought to discredit the perceived positive benefits of the "Protestant work ethic" and present the flaws of capitalism, as well as the uneasy relationship between organized religion and commerce. He became a full professor in 1931 and taught in London until his retirement in 1949.

As an expert on early capitalism and a leading socialist economist, Tawney was an important advisor to the Labor Party and campaigned vigorously for a number of reforms, including the establishment of a minimum wage. In addition to economic and political policy, Tawney helped develop educational policy. His most prominent achievements centered around the lengthening of required public education and expanding workers' education. Some of his most famous later works dealt with education, including *Secondary Education for All* (1922) and *Education: The Socialist Policy* (1924). He also often gave speeches and addresses to the WEA and other labor organizations.

Further Reading
Wright, A. *R. H. Tawney.* Manchester, Eng.: Manchester University Press, 1987.

teleology/teleological

An approach in philosophy holding that everything has an internal goal, purpose, or "end" (Greek: *telos*) to which it naturally strives. ARISTOTLE originated the teleological view of nature and politics, later developed in NATURAL LAW philosophy (especially St. Thomas AQUINAS). In this perspective, everything in the universe is designed by God with a given purpose, which it strives to fulfill. A frequent example is the acorn,

whose *telos* is a fully grown, healthy oak tree. This development is internal but requires external conditions (proper sunlight, rain, soil, etc.). Humankinds' *telos,* for Aristotle, is becoming a fully developed, mature, rational, social human being. This is innate human nature in potential but requires a careful environment and education (in the family, the community, and politics). Human reason, speech, and morals are most developed, for Aristotle, in the POLIS, or small DEMOCRATIC community, in which all CITIZENS participate. This, along with the ideal of a public-spirited gentleman, forms the person's capacity for judgment, thought, deliberation, and governing. A society full of such excellent individuals creates a happy, just STATE. St. Thomas Aquinas simply imposes a Christian cosmology on Aristotle's teleology by making the human purpose to know and glorify God.

Such a teleological view believes that humans' capacities are given (not individually chosen) and that their fruition depends on definite objective criteria (not individual preferences). The training of the young becomes especially important in this natural-law perspective.

terrorism

Deliberate VIOLENCE against a government or social system that is designed to strike terror or fear in the citizenry or state leaders and to accomplish some political change. Examples might include Arab terrorists, who bomb government and military buildings in Israel or the United States to assert the political claims of Palestinians in the Middle East. Often, innocent civilians are the victims of terrorist attacks that are designed to frighten and demoralize an enemy. Other terrorist acts include taking people hostage, destroying public buildings, and assassinating governmental officials.

Terrorist actions are often conceived as part of a larger strategy for revolutionary overthrow of an existing regime. V. I. LENIN, leader of the Soviet COMMUNIST revolution, included terrorism with deception, bribery, propaganda, and armed uprising to weaken the czarist Russian state. Anarchists believe that a terrorist act can ignite a spontaneous rebellion against all authority.

In recent years, terrorist acts have occurred around the world by a variety of groups. In the United States, the worst terrorist violence was by an American espousing radical RIGHT-WING ideas who killed hundreds in a bombing of a federal building in Oklahoma. Most governments and societies reject terrorism as a legitimate means of political expression and change; often, it discredits the groups perpetuating the terrorism and reduces their effectiveness. Most groups that employ terrorism do so because they do not have sufficient power to affect society in a more productive manner.

Further Reading
Laqueur, W. *Terrorism*. Boston: Little, Brown, 1977.

theocracy

Literally "government of God" (Greek), *theocracy* was first mentioned by Jewish historian Flavius Josephus to denote God's rule over his people of Israel. Unlike other ancient civilizations, the Bible describes the Jews as having no earthly king, but the Lord Jehovah as its leader. Even after the Jews took kings (Saul, David), their God continued to rule them through divine messages and guidance (especially through the prophets, as Isaiah and Jeremiah).

Other CLASSICAL civilizations (Egypt, Rome, Tibet) had theocracies, but these relied on the human ruler being considered a god.

ISLAMIC political thought usually sees the Muslim state as a theocracy, the state either ruled directly by clerics (as in Iran) or under the religious law of the KORAN (Qur'an).

CHRISTIAN political thought occasionally conceives of the state as a theocracy, especially in Eastern Orthodox churches. Western Christianity (St. AUGUSTINE) typically separates the secular government from the church but admits of influence from the "higher law" of Christ on the state. MEDIEVAL CATHOLIC kingdoms saw greater theocratic qualities through the powerful influence of the popes, but St. Thomas AQUINAS advocates considerable autonomy for the human law of the STATE (so long as it does not directly contradict NATURAL LAW or divine law).

MODERN Protestant Christianity advances a stricter separation of CHURCH AND STATE (in REFORMATION thinker Martin LUTHER and BAPTISTS), but Calvinist churches (like the English PURITAN Oliver CROMWELL) conceive of closer integration of religion and politics. The United States of America was partially founded by English Puritans (such as John WINTHROP) who applied this Christian-commonwealth view.

In the Modern democratic world, a theocracy is often disparaged as harsh, intolerant, and overly CONSERVATIVE.

Thomism/Thomist

The development of St. Thomas AQUINAS's political thought from the time of his death to the present. Sometimes called neo-Thomism, this perspective applies the NATURAL LAW, CATHOLIC view of HUMAN NATURE, society, and politics to contemporary issues, especially the social challenges of MODERN INDUSTRIALISM. Thomist theory has often been the official IDEOLOGY of the Roman Catholic Church as expressed by the curia and the pope (including most recently Pope John Paul II). Although this traditional perspective has diminished somewhat in the church since the Second Vatican Council (1962–65), it remains a dominant force in Catholic doctrine and education.

Like St. Thomas Aquinas's integration of ARISTOTLE's philosophy with CHRISTIANITY, later Thomism views humanity in terms of its teleology or perfection as an intellectual and moral being. Politically, this relies on a society and a state that promotes the common good. Although private PROPERTY and CAPITALISM can contribute to society, they properly exist within social and political regulation and control, according to natural and divine law.

Thomism, especially since Pope Leo XIII's encyclical *Aeterni Patris* (1879) against Modernism, is an alternative social philosophy to LIBERALISM and COMMUNISM. Prominent advocates of this third way include Englishman G. K. Chesterton (1874–1936) and Frenchman Jacques Maritain (1882–1973). The latter's open Thomism was compatible with Liberal pluralistic DEMOCRATIC society but was still critical of capitalist INDIVIDUALISM. Conforming to LEFTIST attacks on EXPLOITATION and social ALIENATION but from a religious perspective, this recent Thomist thought underlies much of contemporary U.S. Catholic social philosophy, which combines economic and political Liberalism with moral and ethical conservatism.

Further Readings
Gilby, T. *Between Community and Society: A Philosophy and Theology of the State*. London: Longmans, 1953.
Welty, E. *A Handbook of Christian Social Ethics*, G. Kirstein, transl. New York: Freiburg Herder, 1960–64.

Thompson, Kenneth W. (1921–) *U.S. scholar; political philosopher of international politics*

A leading writer on the ETHICS and theories of international relations, Thompson's ideas reflect the Christian REALISM of Reinhold NIEBUHR and Hans Morgenthau. The reality of human sin and evil in power politics requires a thoughtful, careful approach to world affairs. Like Niebuhr and Morgenthau, Thompson applies these theological norms to political, governmental practice.

Educated at the University of Chicago, he served as a consultant in international relations to the Rockefeller Foundation, director of the Institute for the Study of World Politics, and head of the Miller Center of Public Affairs at the University of Virginia. Thompson held professorships in the government and religion departments at that university. The recipient of numerous awards and honorary degrees, his important books include *Christian Ethics and the Dilemmas of Foreign Policy* (1959), *The Moral Issue in Statecraft, Understanding World Politics* (1975).

Thoreau, Henry David (1817–1862)   *U.S. writer and social philosopher*

An eclectic thinker, Thoreau drew on several unorthodox philosophies, including Asian mysticism, the occult, Native American religions, and transcendentalism. He was hostile to CHRISTIANITY, U.S. DEMOCRACY, and CAPITALISM.

Thoreau is best known for his RADICAL INDIVIDUALISM and naturalism (ENVIRONMENTALISM). He withdrew from the staid New England society of his time (Concord, Massachusetts) and lived alone, sometimes in the wild (as during the two years he lived in the woods near Walden Pond). He presented this as a pristine independence from vain, hypocritical PURITAN society, but his fellows often saw it as a selfish, self-righteous display.

From his detached position, Thoreau judged and criticized U.S. society, especially the social ills of war, SLAVERY, and materialism. His ROMANTICISM about human innocence and nature led him to practice CIVIL DISOBEDIENCE, or protesting the STATE through nonviolent resistance (in his case, refusing to pay taxes). Seeing himself as a heroic, righteous individual, Thoreau represents a kind of 19th-century "New Age" philosopher. His attitude continues in many PACIFIST, environmentalist, and Liberal spiritist and naturalist movements in U.S. society. In particular, his writing on nature, especially *Walden; or, Life in the Woods* (1854), exerted a profound influence on the conservation movement that arose in the late 19th and early 20th centuries.

Further Reading
Harding, W., and Meyer, M. *The New Thoreau Handbook.* New York: New York University Press, 1980.

Tocqueville, Alexis de (1805–1859)   *French political historian and philosopher*

Best known for his massive study of 19th-century U.S. society, *Democracy in America* (1835), Tocqueville provides one of the most perceptive views of the political culture of the United States. DEMOCRATIC society, for him, is premised on the absolute EQUALITY of individuals. Each individual's opinion is equally valid in a democracy. No transcendent authority (God, church, leader, king) is truer or greater than even the poorest individual in democratic society. This means that the only overriding authority is a *majority* of those equal individuals. The consequence of this, for Tocqueville, is that true individual liberty tends to be stifled by the conformity of the tyranny of the majority. Social pressure rather than governmental power controls people in the United States; for example, a general CHRISTIAN morality exists in the United States, despite religious diversity.

The INDIVIDUALISM of this democracy leads to a culture of materialistic self-interest, egoism, private ambition, and competition. Envy and conflict pervade this middle-class democracy, where everyone is on his or her own and measured by his or her economic success. U.S. democratic culture is predominantly commercial, then, with constant business, selling, and moneymaking. Everyone is in trade; no one is secure.

A few institutions in the United States mitigate against this pervasive individualism, equality, and materialistic competition. The legal profession, because of its education, CONSERVATISM, and aristocratic qualities, checks the democratic EGALITARIANISM of U.S. culture. Also, participatory institutions (such as voluntary organizations and the jury system) break down the privatism of U.S. culture, providing civic education and public spiritedness. These check the democratic tendency to look to the central government for the majority opinion and social welfare.

Tocqueville's analysis of, and predictions for, U.S. democratic society have largely been confirmed in the 170 years since he wrote them, making *Democracy in America* a classic study. The preoccupation with private economic ambition, personal self-interest, and extension of equality continues to characterize U.S. culture. The drift of local, state, and parochial organizations toward the central government makes mass society and the TYRANNY of majority opinion ever more threatening to true individual LIBERTY. The mitigating influence of intermediate civic organizations (churches, clubs, etc.) that are independent of the federal government is less powerful than during Tocqueville's time. Fear over the loss of individual freedom is more pervasive in the United States than ever before.

Tocqueville saw the march of this democratic culture from the United States into Western Europe and the world, so its problems and benefits would soon infect the entire globe. His greatest hope for true individual rights was the existence of independent persons, families, and communities that are not controlled by mass opinion or the state. CONSTITUTIONAL guarantees of free association and belief would be the ultimate guardian of liberty.

Alexis de Tocqueville was from an aristocratic French family. He served in the French government in several capacities and wrote a history of prerevolutionary France (*The Ancient Regime,* 1856). Recognized throughout the world as a leading political intellectual, Tocqueville analyzed the MODERN democratic society with unusual acumen.

Further Readings
Lively, J. *The Social and Political Thought of Alexis de Tocqueville.* Oxford, Eng.: Clarendon Press, 1962.

Zetterbaum, M. *Tocqueville and the Problem of Democracy.* Stanford, Calif.: Stanford University Press, 1967.

toleration

A political concept that began with religious toleration in REFORMATION Europe. When nations had a single official church (for example, CATHOLIC in Spain or Anglican in England), other churches were persecuted (with fines, prison, etc.). These DISSENTing churches (e.g., PRESBYTERIAN, BAPTIST) eventually won legal toleration from the government, meaning that they were no longer persecuted or outlawed, though they usually did not receive full civil rights either. For example, in England, the Toleration Act allowed Baptists to worship freely, but legal marriages still had to be conducted in the official Church of England. John Locke's *Letter Concerning Toleration* (1689) gives a reasoned argument for religious toleration (that the state deals with external behavior of CITIZENS, not their internal thoughts or conscience). This argument goes into Thomas JEFFERSON's case for religious liberty. Since then, toleration has been applied to other dissenting IDEOLOGIES (e.g., COMMUNISM), lifestyles (e.g., HOMOSEXUALITY), and attitudes (e.g., RADICAL criticism of the

state). In all these cases, toleration does not mean acceptance or affirmation of the deviant behavior or belief but simply that legal penalties are no longer enforced. It means, as John Stuart MILL in *On Liberty* argued, that a person or society can tolerate unusual ideas or behavior (as long as they do not violate other RIGHTS), but they don't have to approve of them. James MADISON simply said that it shifts the means of persuasion from law to informal social action (reasoned discussion, prayer, etc.). In contemporary U.S. society, for example, it can mean that homosexuals are no longer arrested and imprisoned, but the majority of citizens do not accept homosexuality as normal. Atheists and communists may be left free to advocate their causes, but this does not give official governmental endorsement of their beliefs.

Toleration becomes a premier social value in Modern, ENLIGHTENMENT LIBERALISM where individual freedom and community diversity require it. Most traditional societies (ISLAMIC, Chinese) see no reason to endorse toleration until they wish to enter the worldwide community and economy, where it becomes necessary to function.

CONSERVATIVE religious groups (e.g., the CHRISTIAN RIGHT) often regard toleration as compromise with values they find repulsive (for example to tolerate ABORTION). In general, however, U.S. society has become increasingly tolerant of all manner of things, as Alexis de TOCQUEVILLE predicted. Radical LEFTIST thinkers (such as CRITICAL THEORY writer Herbert MARCUSE) or POLITICALLY CORRECT Liberals often oppose toleration as much as Conservatives but for different reasons.

Further Readings
Kamen, H. *The Rise of Toleration.* London: Weidenfeld & Nicolson, 1967.

King, P. *Toleration.* London: George Allen & Unwin, 1976.

Wolff, R. P., Marcuse, H., and Moore, B. *A Critique of Pure Tolerance.* Boston: Beacon Press, 1969.

totalitarian/totalitarianism

A governmental and social system in which the central STATE completely controls every aspect of life (economic, family, religious, educational, cultural, etc.). Examples of totalitarian countries include NAZI (FASCIST) Germany, Soviet (Stalinist) Russia (COMMUNISM), and Communist China. In each of these 20th-century regimes, the state controls the individual through total political regulation of the household, schooling, jobs, residence, and IDEOLOGY. The state imposes a single value system on every citizen (MARXISM-LENINISM, Fascism) and abolishes any independent groups, businesses, clubs, or associations. Everything in society is somehow tied to the state, and loyalty is enforced through domestic spies, secret police, torture, prison, and executions. Fear and desperation characterize totalitarian societies, and individual FREEDOM and free association are eliminated. It is contrasted with DEMOCRACY and CAPITALISM.

Leading writers on totalitarianism include Karl POPPER, Hannah ARENDT, and Jean-François Revel. Critics of totalitarian regimes tend to be CONSERVATIVE, LAISSEZ-FAIRE, and LIBERTARIAN thinkers. Liberal COMMUNITARIANS such as Benjamin BARBER tend to see discussions of totalitarianism as a simple expression of cold-war resistence to communism by the Western democracies.

In the 1980s, U.S. President Ronald REAGAN adopted Jeane Kirkpatrick's distinction between RIGHT-WING authoritarian governments and LEFT-WING totalitarian states. This allowed U.S. foreign policy to assist various conservative dictatorships (especially in Latin America) in opposing SOCIALIST regimes (such as Cuba and Nicaragua). The U.S. rationale for this was that Rightist states allowed a measure of autonomy and freedom (in business, religion, cultural and family life), while totalitarian states strictly controlled everything.

The strict regulation of individual and social life by totalitarian states bred despair and frustration in Nazi and Soviet countries. Widespread dissatisfaction, alcoholism, emigration, and lack of productivity led to the destruction of these totalitarian realms. Since the demise of fascism and Soviet communism, most of the world recognizes the danger of centralized, concentrated governmental power and seeks to preserve, by constitutional means, individual rights and freedom, LIBERTY of association, intermediate social groups, and private PROPERTY. But one effect of totalitarian rule has been to make the people living under it incapable of independence and self-government. The difficulty of the former Soviet countries' transition to democracy and their tendency to return to ABSOLUTIST politics show that the consequences of totalitarianism take a long time to overcome.

Further Readings

Arendt, H. *The Origins of Totalitarianism,* 2nd ed. New York: Meridian Books, 1958.
Revel, J.-F. *The Totalitarian Temptation.* Garden City, N.Y.: Doubleday, 1976.

tradition/traditional

The political, social, and religious values, practices, and institutions of the past. Concern with historical traditions and their value emerged in 18th-century political theory and is associated with such CONSERVATIVE thinkers as Edmund BURKE. It is partly a response to the MODERN destruction of MEDIEVAL culture (MONARCHY, FEUDALISM, HIERARCHY, CATHOLIC Christianity) by DEMOCRACY, CAPITALISM, INDUSTRIALISM, and Protestant Christianity. Traditional thinkers seek to justify and preserve the good and valuable qualities of the past Western civilization (classical education, art, music, manners, etc.). Traditionalism tends, therefore, to be aristocratic, antitechnology, and critical of innovation.

The rise of traditionalism is discussed in Burke (Britain versus the French Revolution); Karl MARX (feudalism versus capitalism); Max WEBER (rational versus traditional); and Alexis de TOCQUEVILLE (traditional versus democratic).

Although most conservative theorists have a nostalgic, ROMANTIC view of past traditions, Modern liberal and SOCIALIST thinkers regard history as PROGRESSIVE and, therefore, new things to be superior to traditions. Early Moderns (as in the ENLIGHTENMENT) had contempt and hatred of the past as oppressive, ignorant, and impoverished. Tradition, then, has been both praised and condemned in political thought; as a rallying point for NATIONALISM and PATRIOTISM, however, it has often been employed during times of crisis and war.

PLATO maintains (in *The Republic*) that a society must carefully preserve and transmit its best traditions through education. RENAISSANCE thinker MACHIAVELLI advises leaders to use and manipulate traditions to secure their power and position. Edmund Burke, the archetypical Modern British traditionalist, sees the preservation of the best in Western civilization as dependent on the respect given tradition (especially LAW, religion, the aristocracy, CLASSICAL learning, and property).

Contemporary democratic INDIVIDUALISM tends to wish to choose its traditions, which diminish their force, uniformity, and influence.

Trotsky, Leon (1879–1940) *Russian Marxist philosopher and revolutionary*

One of the leaders of the Soviet COMMUNIST Revolution of 1917, along with V.I. LENIN and Joseph STALIN, Trotsky is best known for his theory of uneven develop-

1792 cartoon shows a woman wearing a liberty cap, representing the genius of France, holding a cat-o'-nine tails in one hand, acting as the scourge of tyrants from many nations. (LIBRARY OF CONGRESS)

ment and permanent revolution. This allowed an economically underdeveloped country like Russia to have a SOCIALIST workers' revolution, even though advanced CAPITALISM had not occurred there. According to traditional MARXISM, a socialist revolution could not succeed in a society dominated by FEUDALISM. But Trotsky claimed that sufficient development had occurred in Russian urban areas (INDUSTRIALISM) to permit a Communist Party–led workers' revolution. This theory became an integral part of MARXISM-LENINISM and Lenin's theory of capitalist IMPERIALISM. However, Trotsky insisted that although a socialist revolution could start in a less-developed country like Russia, it would need the assistance of socialist revolutions in surrounding advanced countries (Germany, France, etc.) to succeed fully. When those other nations did not have workers' revolutions, Trotsky despaired over the prospect of communism in Russia. Contrary to this view, Stalin put forward the theory of socialism in one country, asserting that Soviet communism could exist

alone. Trotsky fell out of favor with Stalin and was exiled from the Soviet Union in 1929. From his exile in Mexico, Trotsky criticized the Soviet state under Stalin, denouncing it as "BUREAUCRATIC state capitalism" a betrayal of the workers' revolution, and a criminal DICTATORSHIP. He was assassinated, probably at Stalin's orders, in 1940.

Trotsky's ideas and criticism of Soviet communism created a branch of the Marxist socialist movement called Trotskyism. It favored a more DEMOCRATIC workers' government (without abandoning socialist revolution as had the SOCIAL DEMOCRATS) and believed in permanent or ongoing socialist reform. His conflict with other Marxist revolutionaries is an example of the complexity and quarrelsome quality of much of LEFTIST IDEOLOGY and ACTIVISM.

Further Readings

Day, R. *Leon Trotsky and the Politics of Economic Isolation.* Cambridge, Eng.: Cambridge University Press, 1973.

Knei-Paz, B. *The Social and Political Thought of Leon Trotsky.* Oxford, Eng.: Clarendon Press, 1978.

tyranny/tyrant/tyrannical

A government ruled by an individual with absolute POWER. A tyrannical ruler is often termed a *DESPOT* or a *DICTATOR.* These are negative terms, signifying not just the STATE run by one person (as in MONARCHY or kingdom), but also a cruel, evil governor.

CLASSICAL political thought describes tyranny as the worst form of government. PLATO warns that it can arise out of the disorder and ANARCHY of extreme DEMOCRACY and INDIVIDUALISM. The tyrant imposes order (like Adolf HITLER did) through brutal AUTHORITARIAN terror. ARISTOTLE describes the characteristics of a tyranny at some length in his book, *The Politics.* The tyrant keeps power by hurting his or her own country: killing intelligent people (who are seen as rivals), encouraging social conflict between races and classes (to "divide and conquer"), spying on citizens and arresting anyone critical of the government, discouraging learning and prosperity, and often starting wars with neighboring countries. So a tyrant serves selfish passions rather than the INTERESTS of the people or the common good. The tyrant's state is a "corrupt" form of monarchy, according to Aristotle.

MODERN, LIBERAL political theory (John LOCKE) emphasizes the popular resistance to tyrants, the lack of CONSENT in tyrannical government, and a right to revolution against them. The American DECLARATION OF INDEPENDENCE (by Thomas JEFFERSON) accuses British King George III of being a tyrant for violating the colonists' RIGHTS to life, LIBERTY, PROPERTY, and due process of law. Later liberation movements adopted this use of the term *tyrant,* and this has caused the casual employment of the term to be applied to any leader who uses power in a manner unpopular with some individual or group. Consequently, the meaning and significance of the concept of *tyranny* has been somewhat diminished in contemporary political language.

U

United States   See AMERICAN POLITICAL THOUGHT.

utilitarian/utilitarianism

An ethical and political perspective developed in the 19th century by British philosophers Jeremy BENTHAM, James MILL, and John Stuart MILL. Its name comes from the fact that it defines *goodness* by social utility, or usefulness. A social policy is good if it produces "the greatest happiness for the greatest number" of people. *Happiness* is defined by utilitarians in materialistic terms: economic or physical pleasure or avoidance of pain. This hedonistic conception of ethical goodness comes from the BEHAVIORIST theory of Thomas HOBBES. So, for example, a social (economic or political) policy or LAW that spreads goods to more people would be considered just, by utilitarian thinkers. A process like mass production of cars, which provides more cars for everybody, would be better than handcrafted automobiles (which may be better made but are accessible to fewer people). A socialized medicine policy that provided health care (even at a low level) to everyone would be better than highly refined or specialized care for a few.

The political effect of utilitarian ETHICS is obviously, then, DEMOCRATIC and EGALITARIAN. They were considered very RADICAL in 19th-century Britain, where morality was based more on the CHRISTIAN standards of God, the social good of the ARISTOCRACY, TRADITION, or some other high standard. Utilitarian thought logically leads to SOCIALISM, in which everyone is treated equally and in which the inclusive ethics of every personal preference is considered equally valid or moral. This absence of an objective moral standard above individual pleasure rejects NATURAL LAW philosophy and leads to ethical relativism.

Later utilitarian thought (John Stuart Mill), attempts to provide a quality standard of pleasure (over merely greater quantity) through higher intellectual and moral pleasures. Like Aristotle, Mill argued that true human pleasure and goodness did not come from just more and more goods but from higher intellectual and moral pursuits. This added a more noble, aristocratic dimension to utilitarian thought. As Mill put it: "It is better to be a human being dissatisfied than a pig satisfied; better to be Socrates dissatisfied than a fool satisfied." By this, he meant that social policy should cultivate citizens' higher faculties (knowledge, virtue, art, morals) rather than just providing more and more base consumer pleasures.

Utilitarian philosophy continues to be refined into the 20th century by R. M. Hare, Ronald Dworkin, and H. Sidgwick. John RAWLS provides a contemporary critique of utilitarian philosophy in his book *A Theory of Justice.*

Further Readings

Lyons, D. *Forms and Limits of Utilitarianism.* Oxford, Eng.: Clarendon Press, 1965.

Smart, J. J. C., and Williams, B., eds. *Utilitarianism: For and Against.* New York: Cambridge University Press, 1973.

utopia

An ideal society that does not currently exist. Literary depictions of utopia include PLATO's *Republic,* Sir Thomas MORE's *Utopia* (1516), and Edward BELLAMY's novel *Looking Backward* (1888). Utopian literature serves the purpose of criticizing contemporary political injustice and formulating a system of greater JUSTICE. This critical and constructive effect of utopian writing has led to many practical social reforms and more humane policies. Plato's *Republic* formulates the perfect state governed by wise PHILOSOPHER-KINGS; Francis BACON's *New Atlantis* presents an ideal government of scientists and engineers; Charles FOURIER offers a SOCIALIST utopian society.

The utopian urge flows from a dissatisfaction with existing society and the belief that humanity can create perfect social and political systems. CONSERVATIVE thinkers (St. AUGUSTINE, Edmund BURKE), who see evil as inevitable in HUMAN NATURE and unalterable by social change, are less likely to formulate ideal utopias.

The disastrous results of idealistic theories in the 20th century (COMMUNISM, FASCISM) have made utopias less popular and actually spawned a dysptopian literature, showing the tragedy of trying to create "heaven on earth," such as Huxley's *Brave New World* and George Orwell's *1984.* In these critiques of utopian thinking, the idealistic reformers produce the most cruel, TOTALITARIAN regimes (like the SOVIET UNION) where all FREEDOM and prosperity are lost in the TYRANNICAL enforcement of EQUALITY.

For CHRISTIAN political thought, only an internal, individual change or spiritual "new birth" can change society, not a reordering of social or economic institutions. U.S. writer Nathaniel Hawthorne parodied a New England utopian community in his novel BLYTHEDALE ROMANCE.

Despite the decline in utopian writing during the mid-20th century, IDEALISM arose again in the 1960s New LEFTIST movements, and communal utopias again flourished. Traditional MARXISM denounced such socialist utopias as idealistic and contrary to the objective laws of history.

Karl MANNHEIM described the sociology of utopian thinking in his book *Ideology and Utopia* (1929). Utopias tend to emerge in response to difficult or tragic social conditions and then inform political change and reform.

Further Readings

Manuel, F. E., and Manuel, F. P. *Utopian Thought in the Western World.* Cambridge, Mass.: Belknap Press, 1979.

Mannheim, K. *Ideology and Utopia,* L. Wirth and E. Shils, transl. New York: Harcourt, Brace & World, 1936.

V

Vico, Giambattista (1668–1744) *Italian political and legal philosopher*

An early LIBERAL political theorist, Vico develops a historical philosophy in which civil rights and LIBERTY emerge with human reason. Earlier human society reflects the family organization and ABSOLUTIST DESPOTISM of the father. As descendants inherit PROPERTY, they establish an ARISTOCRACY. Eventually, doubts about the semigodly status of these aristocratic rulers or heroes cause the majority of people to rebel, claiming rights themselves. This spreads the SOVEREIGNTY or governmental authority more democratically.

Vico fears that the individualistic self-INTEREST of popular government will lead to ANARCHY and chaos, as PLATO detailed in *The Republic*. This causes a recurrence of TYRANNY to impose social order. This HISTORICISM obviously influences the later DIALECTICAL theory of history found in HEGEL and CROCE.

Vico taught rhetoric at the University of Naples, Italy. His major books include *On the Ancient Wisdom of the Italians* (1710), *On the Coherence of the Jurist* (1721), and *The New Science* (1725, 1730, 1744).

Further Readings
Tagliacozzo, G., ed. *Vico: Past and Present*. Atlantic Highlands, N.J.: Humanities Press, 1981.

Tagliacozza, G., and Verene, D. P., eds. *Giambattista Vico's Science of Humanity*. Baltimore: Johns Hopkins University Press, 1976.

violence

The inflicting of physical harm, such as killing, injuring, terrorizing, and torturing living beings. Political violence takes the form of violent, armed warfare, revolution, rioting, assassination, executions, and torture.

The history of political thought displays several attitudes toward violence from total rejection of it (in PACIFISM) to acceptance and even encouragement of it (in MARXISM, COMMUNISM, ISLAM, and FASCISM) to acknowledgement of violence as a political reality but also an undesirable necessity to be minimized as much as possible (as in REALISM and JUST-WAR DOCTRINE).

The theories that favor violence give various reasons for this view. Marxism insists that political revolution is a historical necessity and that it ushers in a more economically advanced social system. Peaceful change is not possible for communists, so those social democrats who try to establish socialism by parliamentary means are just holding back PROGRESS. MARXISM-LENINISM also justifies violent revolution by the rationale that existing society already has so much violence in it (economic class warfare) that seizing the STATE violently is hardly increasing the total level of violence and may in fact be diminishing it. Fascism extols violence and war as bringing out heroism, bravery, self-sacrifice, and devotion to country (PATRIOTISM). NAZI Germany portrayed warfare as displaying the superiority of the master race. Algerian Marxist Frantz Fanon in the 1960s celebrated the anti-French violence of national liberation warfare as fulfilling and liberating of the human spirit. Islam sees a "holy war" against non-Muslims as serving God.

Objections to political violence argue that such harmful deeds dehumanize both the victims and the perpetrators of violent actions. Deliberately hurting others violates God's COMMANDMENTS against murder and creates further resentment and warfare. Moral and political change can be effected by peaceful means such as nonviolent CIVIL DISOBEDIENCE. Indian leader GANDHI and U.S. civil rights leader Martin Luther KING, Jr., employed peaceful resistance to change society. Based on the CHRISTIAN principle, "Do not return evil for evil, but overcome evil with good" (Matthew 5:39), this appeal to persuasion, reason, and prayer does not ignore injustice but avoids making it worse by resorting to violence. This pacifist perspective regards all harming of humans as making the situation worse and perpetuating injustice and pain.

The MODERATE approach to political violence admits that it is a part of the world but strives to minimize it through the RULE OF LAW, negotiations, and so on. If government is democratic by the CONSENT of the governed, violent revolt should be less likely. If trade agreements, treaties, and international organizations function properly, war should only be a "last resort" in defense against aggression. A violent revolution is only justified (in John LOCKE's theory) by absolute TYRANNY and government injustice. The state's violent apparatus-policy army should only be used against criminals who violate the RIGHTS of others.

Much of political thought addresses the subject of violence, and governments' attitudes toward violence explain much of their conduct.

virtue

Virtue is an important concept in many political theories, but it has several meanings: public and private, religious, social, and moral. In general, Western political thought conceives of *virtue* as the individual sacrifice of personal INTEREST or preference for the common good or some higher moral standard, so *virtue* serves as a value for promoting public JUSTICE, harmony, and goodness.

CLASSICAL political philosophy understood virtue in terms of human relationships: both functioning and just. The original Greek term for "virtue," *areté,* meant the qualities necessary for a thing to perform its function or duty. A good knife has the "virtue" of sharpness because its function is to cut. A bad knife (or a knife lacking virtue) is dull because it cannot perform its job well. So *virtue* in this sense means "competence."

PLATO applies this functional standard of virtue to individual CITIZENS in the state. He claims, in *The Republic,* that every society needs three classes of people: rulers, soldiers, and workers. Each group needs certain virtues to perform well. The virtue of rulers is wisdom, required to govern justly. The virtue of the military soldier is courage, needed to defend the country well. People working in the economy (production, sales, banking) need the virtue of moderation to do their work well. The STATE, for Plato, should recognize and train each person in his or her function and virtue to create justice. Virtue, then, serves the whole community, not just private desires.

ARISTOTLE adds *moral virtue* to Plato's scheme: a virtue governing all human relationships. The ideal of this virtue is the Golden Mean, or habitually choosing the right action between extremes. For example, in regard to humor, the Golden Mean is wit, or knowing when and how to be funny, between the deficiency of boorishness (never being funny) and the excess of buffoonery (being funny all the time). Such personal virtue makes for pleasant, ethical human relationships and social harmony. For Aristotle, the cultivation of such virtue required education in the family, the state, and friendship. Politically, such virtue helps the POLIS to operate smoothly.

Roman notions of virtue, as in CICERO, emphasize this public-spirited quality of classical thought. The main civic virtues of the Roman Empire were military honor and patriotic sacrifice to the realm. Inculcated by example and training, Roman virtue was exemplified in the noble soldier-statesman, like Julius CAESAR.

CHRISTIAN virtues focus on biblical moral conduct between the individual, God, and other people. St. AUGUSTINE, St. Thomas AQUINAS, and others wrote on the Christian virtues of prudence, temperance, fortitude, and justice (cardinal virtues) and faith, hope, and charity (theological virtues). For MEDIEVAL and

REFORMATION political thought, the education of these virtues in society by the church is essential to a just, peaceful country.

The revival of social concern for virtue in the latter 20th century (for example, by William BENNETT) draws from both classical and Christian notions of virtue and sees their restoration as necessary for overcoming social and personal problems.

Voltaire (François-Marie Arouet) (1694–1778)
French playwright, novelist, and philosopher

Voltaire was born in Paris into a prosperous middle-class family. He attended the Jesuit college of Louis le Grand, where he received an excellent classical education. Voltaire began to study law but soon abandoned it in favor of a literary career. Much of Voltaire's writings were satirical critiques of religion and injustice, and he frequently offended the French authorities, with the result that he was imprisoned and forced into exile several times during his life. After a brief period in prison following the publication of his epic poem *Le Henriade* (1723), Voltaire went to England in 1726. There, he spent nearly three years studying English literature, science, politics, and philosophy, especially the works of John LOCKE. Locke's influence on the development of Voltaire's philosophy was manifested in Voltaire's *Letters Concerning the English Nation,* published in 1733. In this book, Voltaire praised the cultural, economic, and political achievements of England, writing in favor of religious TOLERATION, the fair distribution of taxes, and equal legal status for noble and merchants. Viewed in France as an attack on the power of the church, the privileges of the aristocracy, and the despotism of the king, the *Letters* were condemned, and Voltaire was ordered arrested. He fled Paris and spent the next 15 years living with Mme. du Châtelet in a château at Cirey in Lorraine. He then wrote a number of tragedies for the stage and continued his study of science, publishing *Éléments de la philosophie de Newton* in 1738. In recognition of his outstanding contributions to scholarship, Voltaire was elected to the French Academy in 1746.

In addition to his support of political LIBERALISM and religious toleration, Voltaire addressed the moral problem of the existence of evil, most famously in his masterpiece *Candide* (1759). In this novel, Voltaire uses the character of Candide, a young disciple of Doctor Pangloss, to criticize the philosophical optimism of G. W. Leibniz, who had declared this to be the "best of all possible worlds." According to Leibniz, because this is the best possible world the presence of evil in it must be necessary, and any world with less evil than this one would actually be worse overall. In the novel, Candide saw and suffered such adversity and misfortune that he was unable to believe that this was the best of all possible worlds. Suggesting that Leibniz's idealism can offer little consolation to the suffering individual, Voltaire believed instead that positive action must be taken to limit the political and religious abuses found in society.

Voltaire argued that moral principles cannot be derived from abstract theological premises and that they have meaning only in relation to the satisfaction of social INTERESTS. He held that human beings are naturally endowed with a sense of JUSTICE and a sentiment of benevolence, which assist us in promoting the well-being of society against a variety of moral evils. As an example of Voltaire's own sense of justice, he worked diligently for the reform of the judicial system and condemned the courts and judges involved in several cases that resulted in the deaths of innocents, most notably that of the Protestant Jean Calas. He proposed that criminal laws be standardized and written, that judicial procedures be public, that torture be abolished, and that the accused be provided legal counsel and be judged by a jury of his or her peers. Voltaire's HUMANISM led him to suggest other sweeping social reforms, concerned mostly with the freedoms provided by liberal political and economic institutions, including the rights to own PROPERTY, to engage in commerce, and to express and publish one's opinions. Voltaire also became an advocate of the democratic changes that occurred in America, although he regarded the steady, peaceful progress of civilization to be preferable to sudden, violent revolutions.

Further Reading
Gay, P. *Voltaire's Politics: The Poet as Realist.* New Haven, Conn.: Yale University Press, 1988.

W

Ward, Nathaniel (1578–1652) *English/American jurist and clergyman*

A PURITAN minister and lawyer, Ward wrote the New England legal code that was adopted by the Massachusetts General Court in 1641. Entitled "The Body of Liberties," these Puritan civil LAWS were based on the Bible and English common law. This approach to a CHRISTIAN commonwealth formed the basis of law in early America for several generations and the Calvinist theory of CHURCH AND STATE relations to this day.

Ward was educated at Cambridge University and practiced law in London before immigrating to America. While visiting Heidelberg, Ward studied John CALVIN's theology and entered the ministry. He served as a pastor in Prussia, England, and America. His most famous book was the Puritan classic *The Simple Cobbler of Agawam* (1647).

Further Readings
Mather, Cotton. *Magnalia Christi Americana.* London: 1702.
Morison, S. E. *Builders of the Bay Colony.* Boston: Houghton Mifflin Co., 1930.

Weber, Max (1864–1920) *German sociologist and historian*

Best known for his study of modern BUREAUCRACY, Weber wrote extensively on the connections between economics, politics, and religion. In his famous book, *The Protestant Ethic and the Spirit of Capitalism,* Weber argued that the Calvinist view of work as a divine calling from God encouraged industry and frugality, savings and investment, leading to a CAPITALIST economy. The Protestant CHRISTIAN ETHIC of hard work ("as unto the Lord" [Colossians 3:23]), revealing (but not earning) the believer's salvation and election by God, combined with a simplicity of life, eschewing luxury, inevitably led to wealth and prosperity in Switzerland, Britain, and the Netherlands. This, combined with scientific reason, makes MODERN Western civilization more orderly and efficient. Organization and rationalization of the economy and government follow these developments.

For example, Weber shows that political leadership goes through a transformation from MEDIEVAL traditional rulership based on family, personal accomplishment and loyalty to impersonal offices, procedures, and rules. The standard for legitimate AUTHORITY changes from a leader with certain personal characteristics or pedigree to an official chosen for professional training and following specified procedures. This forms the basis of Modern bureaucratic states: impersonal rules, professionally trained officials, rational procedures. Although orderly and fair, Weber acknowledges the threat of bureaucracy to personal, humane governance.

Weber provided an alternative to the materialistic sociology of Karl MARX by seeing the interplay of culture, economics, politics, and religion, as opposed to MARXISM's emphasis on economic production. His method of objective study also led to the development of value-free social science.

Further Readings

Beetham, D. *Max Weber and the Theory of Modern Politics*, 2nd ed. London: George Allen & Unwin, 1985.
Roth, G., and Schluchter, W. *Max Weber's Vision of History*. Berkeley: University of California Press, 1979.

welfare state

The Liberal or LEFTIST policy of providing extensive social services (in public education, housing, health care, poverty relief, etc.) by the central government. As part of a mixed economy of CAPITALISM and SOCIALISM, a welfare state uses the state to redistribute some of the wealth generated by a market economy (through taxes) to provide goods and services to the poor, the elderly, the infirm, and the helpless. In Britain and the United States, this social-welfare policy expanded in the 1930s and 1940s (see NEW DEAL) under the influence of economist John Maynard KEYNES. Opposition to the welfare state comes from CONSERVATIVE and LIBERTARIAN thinkers and politicians (such as Robert NOZICK and Ronald REAGAN). Since the 1980s, the term *welfare state* has been used negatively to describe wasteful and fraudulent social-welfare programs that supposedly indulge the poor and lazy in society.

Still, such programs are widely accepted in most Western democracies and in Europe as SOCIAL DEMOCRACY.

Further Reading

Timms, N., ed. *Social Welfare: Why and How?* London: Routledge, 1980.

Whitefield, George (1715–1770)   *British minister*

An Anglican clergyman, Whitefield began the EVANGELICAL CHRISTIAN practice of itinerate teaching in large outdoor settings that transformed American political and religious culture prior to the American Revolution in 1776.

Whitefield traveled to the British North American colonies seven times between 1738 and 1770, holding religious revival meetings during the GREAT AWAKENING from Massachusetts to Georgia. Many times, he would preach to audiences of thousands in the open countryside. In Philadelphia, he spoke to a crowd of 20,000 people, including Benjamin FRANKLIN, who became a close friend of Whitefield's.

The political effects of Whitefield's evangelism were important in preparing the North American colonists for the Revolution, independence from the British Empire, and DEMOCRACY. His informal style outside the formal church establishment and his RADICAL Protestant message on the "New Birth in Christ" had the effect of encouraging INDIVIDUALISM, EQUALITY, and FREEDOM—qualities that quickly transformed American political and social culture. Giving an estimated 8,000 sermons to large audiences in America during the 1700s, Whitefield reached millions of ordinary citizens and became arguably the most famous person in 18th-century America. His FUNDAMENTALIST message unified often diverse regions (New England, Middle Atlantic, Southern), preparing them for unified action during the American Revolutionary War. He is a classic example of the integration of religion and politics, CHURCH AND STATE, in the United States of America.

Educated at Pembroke College, Oxford University, Whitefield was also famous in England and Scotland. He died in Newburyport, Massachusetts.

Further Readings

Dallimore, A. *George Whitefield*. Edinburgh, Scotland: Banner of Truth, 1980.
Henry, S. C. *George Whitefield*. New York: Abingdon Press, 1957.

Will, George F. (1941–)   *U.S. political writer and philosopher*

As the author of regular writings in popular American periodicals (newspapers and *Newsweek* magazine) George Will presents a CLASSICAL CONSERVATIVE perspective on contemporary United States politics. Like traditional British conservative Edmund BURKE, Will values tradition, order, ETHICS, and decorum. He strives to revive the best of the U.S. political and cultural past, including CLASSICAL REPUBLICANISM and Judeo-CHRISTIAN moral standards.

Besides current political analysis, Will has written several serious books of political philosophy, including *The Pursuit of Virtue* and *Statecraft and Soulcraft.* He received a Ph.D. in political philosophy at Princeton University. He is one of the few political commentators in the United States who brings a classical education to discussion of current events.

Further Readings

Will, George F. *The Pursuit of Virtue.* New York: Simon & Schuster, 1982.

Will, George F. *Statecraft and Soulcraft.* New York: Simon & Schuster, 1983.

William of Ockham (Occam) (1280–1349) *English cleric and political philosopher*

An early proponent of government by the CONSENT of the governed, SOCIAL CONTRACT, and separation of CHURCH AND STATE, Ockham criticized the MEDIEVAL CATHOLIC popes' encroachment on civil rule. Ockham was educated at Oxford University but spent much of his life in Bavaria. For Ockham, the STATE and the church are separate, autonomous, if related institutions. The state is primarily concerned with protecting citizens from criminals and foreign invaders; the church is to deal with spiritual matters (worship, religious teaching, etc.). The division of temporal government and church function was later adopted by Protestant Reformers John CALVIN and Martin LUTHER. Ockham sees all Christians as members of both church and state, espouses divine law, and firmly believes that Christ supervises both governmental and religious institutions.

Like John LOCKE later, Ockham sees both PROPERTY as a consequence of the fall of man from paradise and the state's duty to protect the NATURAL RIGHT to property ownership. He opposes any idea of COMMUNISM as inappropriate to either paradise (where Adam and Eve simply used nature) or the current world (where private ownership is necessary to social order). Also like Locke, Ockham perceives SOVEREIGNTY as originally in the government. Once that social contract is made, however, later generations must obey the state, and there is not a right to revolution except in cases of extreme criminality on the part of the rulers.

Ockham adopts St. Thomas AQUINAS's division of divine law, natural law, and positive law. His criticism

of the Roman See led to his censure by the pope and his defection to the court of Emperor Louis of the HOLY ROMAN EMPIRE, along with the minister general of the Order of St. Francis. His polemical writings greatly influenced later LIBERAL and REFORMATION political thought.

Further Reading

McGrade, A. S. *The Political Thought of William of Ockham.* London: Cambridge University Press, 1974.

Williams, Roger (1603–1683) *English/American minister and statesman*

Known chiefly for his advocacy of religious FREEDOM or LIBERTY, Williams was banished from PURITAN New England and established an independent colony (Providence, Rhode Island). Becoming a BAPTIST, he wrote on the separation of CHURCH AND STATE, toleration for Quakers and Jews in his new colony, and liberty of conscience. The freedom, INDIVIDUALISM, and fierce independence of Williams's creed became characteristic of the state of Rhode Island and soon of all America.

Williams, educated at Cambridge University, frequently traveled between America and England. His acquaintances included John MILTON and Oliver CROMWELL. In North America, he was known for his fair and just relations with the Native American tribes in his area; he learned their language and negotiated a peace treaty that ended the Pequot War. He was governor of Rhode Island from 1654 to 1657.

Further Readings

Brockunier, S. H. *Irrepressible Democrat: Roger Williams.* New York: Ronald Press, 1940.

Garrett, J. *Roger Williams: Witness Beyond Christendom.* London: Macmillan, 1970.

Wilson, Woodrow (1856–1924) *U.S. president, Progressive reformer, and peace advocate*

Wilson's political thought represents the Progressive Era of the DEMOCRATIC PARTY (1890s–1920s). These policies of New Freedom, as Wilson called them, were the beginning of Liberal federal social programs in the United States (regulation of business; support for labor unions; WELFARE-STATE benefits for the poor and disabled; safety, wage, and hour legislation for

Woodrow Wilson. (LIBRARY OF CONGRESS)

industrial workers; etc.). Wilson claimed that the emergence of large business corporations required the national government to control the economy for the benefit of common people. This LEFTIST IDEOLOGY was expanded by the Democratic Party during the 1930s NEW DEAL under President Franklin D. ROOSEVELT.

Wilson's Liberal social conscience came from his PRESBYTERIAN CHRISTIAN upbringing and the Calvinist theology that made politics a kind of ministry. His IDEALISM that Christian ethics should guide public policy also extended to his international peace efforts during World War I. Trying to negotiate a fair treaty between the Allies and Germany, President Wilson advocated the Fourteen Points of European peace. He believed that an international organization (the League of Nations—a predecessor to the United Nations) could prevent future wars. The U.S. CONGRESS however refused to ratify U.S. participation in the League of Nations, much to Wilson's disappointment.

Woodrow Wilson, a Virginian, was educated at Princeton and Johns Hopkins Universities and served as a college professor before entering politics (as governor of New Jersey and then president of the United States). His main book was *A History of the American People* (1902).

Further Readings
Blum, J. M. *Woodrow Wilson*. Boston: Little, Brown, 1956.
Grayson, C. T. *Woodrow Wilson*. New York: Holt, Rinehart and Winston, 1960.

Winthrop, John (1588–1649)   *English/American statesman*

As the first governor of Massachusetts (1630–49), Winthrop's political thought reflected the PURITAN views of government as commissioned by and accountable to God. As John CALVIN, he saw governors (or "magistrates") as serving a CHRISTIAN ministry as important as church ministers. Leaders may be elected democratically by the people, but they serve God first, not the popular or even majority interests. This perspective is shown in Winthrop's "Little Speech" of 1639, showing the COVENANT view of CHURCH AND STATE in Puritan New England. In it, he distinguishes two kinds of LIBERTY: natural and moral. Natural liberty, in this view, is people doing whatever they want (good or evil). Moral or "CIVIL" LIBERTY is that freedom to choose to do what is right ("the same kind of liberty where-with Christ hath made us free"). Natural liberty, for Winthrop, expresses humans' corrupt, sinful nature. Moral liberty reflects the regenerated Christian life. The state and law should represent only moral (or "federal") liberty—enjoining the Bible precepts of goodness, justice, and morality. Sinful humans resent and resist the moral law and the government authority that enforces it, but rulers must not submit to the sinful desires of natural humanity but uphold the high standards of Christian morality. Godly CITIZENs will gladly submit to the moral authority of the STATE, recognizing the Christian commonwealth as a gift and instrument of God.

Winthrop, in his book *The History of New England from 1630 to 1649*, sees America in terms of God's providence, a "City on a Hill" (like Jerusalem), and therefore protected by Christ but continually attacked and tempted by Satan. If Americans humbly and obediently serve God, repenting when they sin, the Almighty will protect and prosper them, but if they become proud, vain, sinful, and disdainful of God's LAWS, the Lord will punish them. This providential, covenant view of American politics leads to an American CIVIL RELIGION and is still expressed by the CHRISTIAN RIGHT.

Further Readings

Morgan, E. S. *The Puritan Dilemma*. Boston: Little, Brown, 1958.

Winthrop, John. *The History of New England from 1630 to 1649*. Boston: Little, Brown, 1853.

Witherspoon, John (1723–1794) *Early Scottish-American educational, religious, and political leader*

A PRESBYTERIAN minister from Scotland, Witherspoon became the president of Princeton University in 1768 and greatly influenced the IDEOLOGY of the American Revolution, the U.S. CONSTITUTION, and the early American REPUBLIC. He is credited with teaching students who went on to serve as president (James MADISON) and vice president (Aaron Burr), as well as 10 U.S. presidential cabinet officers, 60 members of the U.S. CONGRESS, 12 state governors, 30 judges, three justices of the U.S. Supreme Court, and numerous ministers, lawyers, and educators. As such, Witherspoon was one of the most influential men in America in the late 1700s.

Educated at the University of Edinburgh, Dr. Witherspoon adhered to a Calvinist theology that, after St. AUGUSTINE, emphasized human evil and sin. Only God's grace and forgiveness through Jesus Christ can produce any goodness in humanity. This perspective on HUMAN NATURE commends a political system of CHECKS AND BALANCES, which prohibits any group or person gaining all power and sinfully using it to oppress others. This view goes directly into Madison's *FEDERALIST PAPERS* and the constitutional division of power in FEDERALISM. Witherspoon wrote of humanity: "I am none of those who either deny or conceal the depravity of human nature til it is purified by the light of truth, and renewed by the Spirit of the living God." In similar language, James Madison (the Father of the Constitution) wrote: "As there is a degree of depravity in mankind which requires a certain degree of circumspection and distrust; so there are other qualities in human nature, which justify a certain portion of esteem and confidence." This leads Witherspoon to recommend a government of divided powers "so that one . . . may check the other. . . . They must be so balanced, that when everyone draws his own INTEREST or inclination there must be an even poise upon the whole." Madison presents this idea in terms of a federal system that pits "ambition against ambition." The U.S. Constitution takes Witherspoon's theology and puts it into a governing structure.

Witherspoon's main writings are his *Lectures on Moral Philosophy* (given at Princeton) that combine the NATURAL-RIGHTS theory of John LOCKE, the CLASSICAL REPUBLICANISM of ARISTOTLE, and the Protestant theology of John Calvin. He was a signer of the DECLARATION OF INDEPENDENCE and a member of the Continental Congress during the American Revolution, but his main political influence in early America came through his academic work at Princeton. John ADAMS described him as "a high Son of Liberty."

Further Reading

Morrison, Jeffrey. "John Witherspoon and The Public Interest of Religion." In *Journal of Church and State 41* (Summer 1999).

Wycliffe, John (1329–1384) *English philosopher and religious reformer*

Called the Morning Star of the Reformation, Wycliffe, though a MEDIEVAL thinker, propounded ideas that led to Protestant CHRISTIANITY, INDIVIDUALISM, and REPUBLICANISM in Britain and Europe.

Wycliffe's theology advocated "The Lordship of all Believers"; interpretation of the Bible by individual Christians; the primacy of scripture over church tradition; and the illegitimacy of papal authority. All of these principles and their EGALITARIAN, DEMOCRATIC implications were later adopted by the LOLLARDS, Martin LUTHER, and John CALVIN and, via J. Huss, throughout Western and Central Europe.

Wycliffe was denounced by Pope Gregory XI and the Council of Constance (1415), causing his writings to be burned and his bones dug up. He was educated at Oxford, becoming Master of Balliol College, Oxford, in 1360. Appointed warden of Canterbury Hall (now Christ Church, Oxford), he later served as a clergyman in Ludgershall and Lutterworth. The EVANGELICAL college at Oxford is named for him (Wycliffe Hall).

Further Readings

Lewis, J. *The History of the Life and Suffering of John Wycliffe*. London: For Robert Knaplock and Richard Wilkin, 1720, 1820.

Poole, R. L. *Wycliffe and the Movements for Reform*. New York: AMS Press, 1893.

Robson, J. A. *Wycliffe and the Oxford Schools*. Cambridge, Eng.: Cambridge University Press, 1961.

X

Xavier, Francis, St. (1506–1552) *Spanish Jesuit minister*

Born of an aristocratic family in Basque Spain, Xavier joined the Jesuits under the original founder of the religious order, IGNATIUS LOYOLA. He is primarily significant to political thought as a leading CATHOLIC missionary who brought Western CHRISTIANITY to Eastern countries (East Indies, Ceylon, and especially Japan). He employed the governmental power in Goa, India, to assist in proselytizing, showing a CHURCH-AND-STATE affinity with St. AUGUSTINE. Famous for his EVANGELICAL methods, Xavier is recorded to have had more than 700,000 conversions under his preaching. He left organized Christian communities in every area he visited. He is the patron saint of foreign missions.

Further Readings

Brodrick, S. J. *St. Francis Xavier.* New York: The Wicklow Press, 1952.

Stewart, E. A. *St. Francis Xavier.* London: Headley Bros. Ltd., 1917.

Young Hegelians

Followers of the German philosopher G.W.F. HEGEL, whose DIALECTIC greatly influenced Karl MARX, MARXISM, COMMUNISM, and FASCIST political thought. Principal Young Hegelians (divided into RADICAL "LEFT Hegelians" and CONSERVATIVE "RIGHT Hegelians") include Ludwig Feuerbach, Max Stirner, Moses Hess, and David Strauss. Most were academic philosophers, political ACTIVISTS, and RADICAL journalists; all were atheists, especially attacking CHRISTIANITY and the church. Their ideas led to secular HUMANIST socialism, Soviet IDEOLOGY, and NAZI FASCISM.

Feuerback's book *Thoughts on Death and Immortality* (1830) argued from the Hegelian dialectic that life after death is impossible, denying the spiritual survival of the individual. In his *Essence of Christianity* (1841), he denied the existence of God and claimed that all religious attributes of the divine (love, power, reason) were really human qualities projected onto an abstract ideal. Once God and religion were eliminated, the truly divine nature of humanity would emerge. Organized religion, then, caused human ALIENATION, for Feuerback. Strauss's book *The Life of Jesus* (1835) denounced the historical and spiritual teachings of Christianity, claiming that they were just myths made up by the early church. He denied that the Bible presented literal truth but only humanistic symbols. This view affected Liberal Christianity and contributed to the arguments for suppressing religion in the communist countries.

The Young Hegelians, whom Marx criticized for being too MODERATE, saw themselves as followers of the FRENCH ENLIGHTENMENT. They optimistically believed that humanity, through reason, DEMOCRACY, and technology, could create a perfect society based on secular science, education, and INDUSTRIALISM; human control of nature and economics would end the oppression of aristocratic government, FEUDALISM, and religious superstition. This attitude finds expression still in various LEFTIST ideology (CRITICAL THEORY).

Further Readings

McLellan, D. *The Young Hegelians and Karl Marx.* New York: Praeger, 1969.
Stepelevich, L. S., ed. *The Young Hegelians: An Anthology.* Cambridge, Eng.: Cambridge University Press, 1983.

Z

Zionism

Zionism is a Jewish IDEOLOGY dedicated to the formation of a Jewish homeland. Although Zionism for many focused on Palestine, there were numerous discussions about alternative locations for the Jewish STATE. Early Zionists considered land in Africa because it was perceived to be a faster route to the realization of Zionist goals. Britain, for example, offered the Zionists 15,500 kilometers in Uganda to form their state. However, with its central motivation coming from the Diaspora, which started with the Jewish exile to Babylon in the sixth century B.C., modern Zionists shared a feeling of being in exile from their true homeland near Jerusalem. The term *Zionism* comes from the hill, Zion, on which the temple of Jerusalem was situated. Ultimately, the realization of Zionist efforts centered around the creation of the state of Israel in 1948.

Within Zionism, there have been several divisions. Among these are secular and orthodox interpretations of the formation of a Jewish state. The division surrounds the argument made by orthodox Jewry that Israel could not be established without the return of the Messiah. More secular Jews rebutted this argument by claiming that the modern state of Israel was a necessary preparatory step for the coming of Messiah.

Political Zionism stressed the importance of political action and deemed the attainment of political RIGHTS in Palestine a prerequisite for the fulfillment of the Zionist enterprise. Political Zionism is linked to Theodore Herzl, the father of modern Zionism. Herzl considered the Jewish problem to be a political one that should be solved by overt political action in the international arena. His goal was to obtain an internationally accepted charter, granting the Jews SOVEREIGNTY over some portion of territory. In 1898, the Basle Program, as it came to be known, was formed, articulating Zionist aims to establish a secure haven, under public LAW, for the Jewish people in the land of Israel. Institutions such as the Zionist Organization, the Jewish National Fund, and the Jewish Colonial Trust were charged with carrying out the program.

Zionists efforts to reach Palestine were significantly encouraged by the Balfour Declaration of 1917. According to the document, the British government supported Jewish settlement in Palestine so long as the existing Arab population was not displaced. In the succeeding years, Jewish immigration to Palestine was modest. However, as the political climate deteriorated in Europe during the interwar years, increased numbers of Jews began to arrive in Palestine. Disturbances between Jews and Arabs in Palestine grew with the swelling numbers of Jewish arrivals. By the end of World War II, an exhausted Britain turned the question of Palestine over to the newly created United Nations. On May 14, 1948, Israel was created, and Zionist aspirations were realized.

In the following years after the creation of the Jewish state, Zionism's emphasis on creation was transformed to one of maintenance. Israeli practices of encouraging Jewish immigration while refusing Palestinian Arab civil rights and liberties led the United Nations in 1975 to declare in Resolution 3379 that Zionism, like South African apartheid, was racist. Modern Zionists have since shifted their efforts toward the realization of Greater Israel. Such a minority opinion among increasingly secular, democratic Israelis runs counter to the current Arab-Israeli peace process. Indeed, as a result of progress between Palestinians and Israelis, in 1991, the United Nations repealed Resolution 3379.

Further Reading
Herzl, Theodore. *The Jewish State.* New York: Herzel Press, 1989.

APPENDIX
CLASSIC BOOKS IN POLITICAL THOUGHT

Plato, *The Republic*

Aristotle, *The Politics*

Aristotle, *Nicomachean Ethics*

Cicero, *The Republic*

St. Augustine, *The City of God*

St. Thomas Aquinas, *Summa Theologica*

Machiavelli, *The Prince*

Thomas Hobbes, *Leviathan*

John Locke, *Second Treatise of Government*

Jean-Jacques Rousseau, *Social Contract*

Edmund Burke, *Reflections on the French Revolution*

John Stuart Mill, *On Liberty*

Karl Marx, *The Communist Manifesto*

V. I. Lenin, *Imperialism*

Sigmund Freud, *Civilization and its Discontents*

Giovanni Gentile, *Genesis and Structure of Society*

Hannah Arendt, *The Human Condition*

Alexis de Tocqueville, *Democracy in America*

Reinhold Niebuhr, *Moral Man and Immoral Society*

Robert Nozick, *Anarchy, State and Utopia*

John Rawls, *A Theory of Justice*

CHRONOLOGY OF POLITICAL THOUGHT AND EVENTS

2000-1400 B.C.E.	Patriarchal age of Judaism: Abraham, Isaac, Jacob, and Joseph.
1792 B.C.E.	Hammurabi's Code establishes law in Babylonia.
c. 1500	The Vedic Aryans invade India, introducing the formative beliefs of early Hinduism.
c. 1275	Possible date of the Exodus from Egypt.
594	Reforms of Solon in Athens curtail aristocratic rule.
586-539	Babylonian captivity of the Jews: main Old Testament books written in their present form.
551-479	The Chinese sage Confucius writes *The Analects*.
510	Establishment of the Roman Republic.
508	Cleisthenes introduces democratic reforms in Athens.
c. 500	Classical Age of Chinese philosophy or Age of a Hundred Philosophers. Six major schools exist, of which two are still popular: Confucianism, concerned with morality and good government, and Taoism, concerned with understanding *tao* (way or road) of nature and universe.
427	Birth of Greek philosopher Plato.
339	Socrates, about 70, is tried and executed.
384	Birth of Greek philosopher Aristotle.
c. 380	Greek philosopher Plato founds Academy in Athens.
372-289	Mencius develops Confucian political theory.
367	Aristotle joins Academy as student.
c.348	Plato dies.
336	Hellenistic Age begins in Greece.
334	Aristotle founds Lyceum in Athens.
322	Aristotle dies.
c. 200	Decline of Confucianism as Taoism and Buddhism flourish in politically disunited China.
200–118	Polybius, Greek/Roman historian, writes *The Histories*.
106	Cicero born.
51	Cicero publishes *de Republica*.
50	Beginning of the Roman Empire.
43	Cicero killed by soldiers.
c. 6	Birth of Jesus Christ.
c. 30 C.E.	Crucifixion of Jesus Christ.
46	Paul begins his missionary journeys to Asia Minor, Greece, and Rome.
64	The first persecution of Christians in Rome under Nero.
70–100	The Christian Gospels are written.
161–180	Marcus Aurelius writes the *Meditations*.

313	Constantine the Great's Edict of Milan, granting Christians toleration.
354	St. Augustine born.
386	St. Augustine converts to Christianity.
393	Christianity official religion in Roman Empire
395	St. Augustine becomes Bishop of Hippo, Milan.
426	St. Augustine writes *The City of God*.
430	St. Augustine dies.
433	Emperor Justinian institutes the Pandects.
622	Mohammed's flight from Mecca (*hegira*) begins the Muslim era.
800	Charlemagne crowned Emperor of the West.
	First printed book appears in China.
1141	Council of Basle collects the Corpus Iuris Canonici, or the Canon Law.
1154	Henry II establishes common law in Britain.
1159	John of Salisbury's *Polycraticus* is published.
1170	Sir Thomas Becket murdered in a cathedral.
1215	King John of England signs the Magna Carta, limiting royal power.
1232	The Inquisition is founded by the papacy to prosecute heretics.
c. 1260	Aristotle's *Politics* rediscovered in the West.
1267–73	St. Thomas Aquinas writes the *Summa theologica*.
c.1313	Dante writes the *De monarchia* (*On Monarchy*).
1324	Marsilius of Padua publishes *Defensor Pacis*.
1456	Guttenberg prints the Bible.
	Platonic Academy founded in Florence by Cosimo de' Medici.

1466	Erasmus born.
	Machiavelli born.
1483	Martin Luther born.
1503	Erasmus writes *Manual of the Christian Knight*.
1509	John Calvin born.
1513	Machiavelli writes both *The Prince* and *The Discourses*.
	Thomas More writes *Utopia*.
1515	Erasmus writes *The Education of a Christian Prince*.
1517	Martin Luther nails up his 95 theses at Wittenberg in Germany.
1520	Martin Luther publishes *On Christian Liberty*.
	Luther excommunicated as a heretic.
1527	Machiavelli dies at age 58.
1532	John Calvin begins Reformation in France.
	Ignatius of Loyola founds the Jesuits (Society of Jesus).
	Michel de Montaigne born.
	English king Henry VIII breaks with Roman Catholic Church.
	Thomas More executed.
	Erasmus dies.
1541	John Calvin introduces Reformation to Geneva, Switzerland.
1546	Martin Luther dies.
1554	Richard Hooker born.
	Scottish Theologian John Knox introduces Calvin's ideas to Scotland.
1564	John Calvin dies.
1576	Jean Bodin writes *The Six Books of a Commonweal*.
	Montaigne publishes first edition of the *Essays*.
1583	Hugo Grotius born.

1588	Thomas Hobbes born.
1598	James I's Trew Law of Free Monarchies. Claims sovereignty by divine right.
1600	Richard Hooker dies.
1601	First Christian missionaries (Jesuits) arrive in Peking (modern Beijing).
1605	Sir Francis Bacon publishes *The Advancement of Learning*.
1611	James Harrington born.
1612	Francisco Suarez writes *A Treatise on the Laws and God the Lawgiver*.
1620	Puritan American settlers sign the Mayflower Compact.
1625	Grotius' *De Jure Belli ac Pacis* published.
1627	Sir Francis Bacon's *The New Atlantis* is published.
1628	English Parliament draws up Petition of Rights requesting limits on monarch's power.
	John Locke born.
	Spinoza born.
	Pufendorf born.
1641	First law against cruelty to animals is passed by Christian Puritans in Massachusetts, North America.
1644	John Milton publishes *Aeropagitica*.
1645	Grotius dies.
1651	Thomas Hobbes publishes *Leviathan*.
1649	King Charles of England beheaded; England becomes republic.
1653	Oliver Cromwell established as Lord Protector of the Commonwealth.
1656	James Harrington publishes *The Commonwealth of Oceana*.
1658	Oliver Cromwell dies; his son Richard Cromwell established as Lord Protector of Commonwealth.
1660	Charles II restored to the English throne.
1666	John Bunyan publishes his autobiography *Grace Abounding to the Chief of All Sinners*.
1667	John Milton publishes *Paradise Lost*.
1673	Pufendorf's *On the Duty of Man and Citizen* published.
1675	Spinoza publishes the *Ethics*.
1677	James Harrington dies.
1679	Hobbes dies.
1680	Sir Robert Filmer publishes *The Patriarcha*.
1681	William Penn founds Pennsylvania.
1688	James II of England deposed in Glorius Revolution.
1689	English Bill of Rights gives political power to Parliament.
	John Locke publishes *Two Treatises of Government*.
1690	Locke publishes *Essay Concerning Human Understanding*.
1694	Voltaire born.
	Pufendorf dies.
1704	John Locke dies.
1705	Pierre Bayle completes the *Dictionnaire historique et critique* (*Historical and Critical Dictionary*).
1706	Benjamin Franklin born.
1711	David Hume born.
1712	Jean-Jacques Rousseau born.
1714	Bernard Mandeville publishes *Private Vices, Public Benefits*.
1723	Adam Smith born.
1724	Immanuel Kant born.
1729	Edmund Burke born.
1733	Voltaire publishes *Letters Concerning the English Nation*.
1737	Thomas Paine born.
1740	Hume publishes *Treatise of Human Nature*.

1743	Thomas Jefferson born.
1747	Voltaire publishes *Zadig*.
1748	Charles Montesquieu publishes *The Spirit of Laws*.
1750	Rousseau publishes the *Discourse on the Arts and Sciences*.
	Denis Diderot begins publication of his *Encyclopédie*.
1751	Hume publishes *An Enquiry Concerning the Principles of Morals*.
1752	Hume publishes *Political Discourses*.
1754	Rousseau publishes the *Discourse on the Origins of Inequality*.
1755	Alexander Hamilton born.
1758	Helvétius writes *Essays of the Mind*.
1759	Voltaire publishes *Candide*.
	Adam Smith publishes *The Theory of Moral Sentiments*.
1762	Rousseau publishes the *Social Contract* and *Emile*.
1764	Cesare Beccaria publishes *Dei delitti e delle pene* (*On Crimes and Punishment*).
1765–69	Sir William Blackstone publishes the *Commentaries on the Laws of England*.
1767	Andrew Jackson born.
1768	Joseph Priestly's *Essay on the First Principles of Government* published.
1770	Rousseau publishes the *Confessions*.
	Hegel born.
	Holbach writes *The System of Nature*.
1771	Robert Owen born.
1772	Keeping of slaves banned in Britain.
1774	Herder's *Another Philosophy of History and Humanity* is published.
1775	American Revolutionary War begins.
1776	Thomas Paine publishes *Common Sense*.
	The *Declaration of Independence*, written by Thomas Jefferson, is adopted by the American colonies.
	Adam Smith publishes *The Wealth of Nations*.
	David Hume dies.
1778	Rousseau dies.
1780	Kant publishes first edition of *Critique of Pure Reason*.
1781	Articles of Confederation ratified by U.S.
1787–88	The *Federalist Papers*, written by Alexander Hamilton, James Madison, and John Jay, are published in New York newspapers.
	John Adams publishes *Defence of the Constitutions of the Government of the United States*.
1788	U.S. states ratify Consitution.
1789	Mob storms Bastille, marking beginning of the French Revolution.
	Declaration of the Rights of Man and Citizen approved by the National Assembly in Paris.
	Jeremy Bentham publishes his *Introduction to the Principles of Morals and Legislation*.
1790	Kant publishes his *Critique of Pure Reason*.
	Benjamin Franklin dies.
	Burke publishes *Reflections on the Revolution in France*.
	Adam Smith dies.
1791	Paine publishes *Rights of Man*, Part I, in England.
	John Adams publishes *Discourses of Davila*.
1792	First French Republic established.
	Mary Wollstonecraft publishes *A Vindication of the Rights of Woman*.
1793	Paine, with Condorcet, Brissot, Sieyes, and others, drafts a proposed French constitution, which is not adopted.

King Louis XVI is guillotined; Reign of Terror begins in France.

Robespierre gains power.

William Godwin's *Enquiry Concerning Political Justice* published.

1794 Paine publishes *The Age of Reason*, Part I, written in prison.

Condorcet writes the *Sketch for a Historical Picture of the Progress of the Human Mind*.

France abolishes slavery in its colonies.

Robespierre executed.

1795 Paine publishes *Dissertation of the First Principles of Government* in Paris.

Schiller publishes the *Letters on the Aesthetic Education of Man*.

1796 Burke publishes *Letters on a Regicide Peace*.

Paine publishes *Age of Reason*, Part II.

1797 Burke dies.

1799 End of French Revolution.

1803 Thomas Malthus publishes *An Essay on the Principle of Population*.

1804 Kant dies.

1806 John Stuart Mill born.

1807 Hegel publishes *Phenomenology of Spirit*.

1808 Charles Fourier publishes *The Social Destiny of Man; or, Theory of the Four Movements*.

1812 Hegel publishes *Science of Logic*.

1816 American Colonization Society founded.

1817 Hegel publishes *Encyclopedia of the Social Sciences*.

David Ricardo's *Principles of Political Economy and Taxation* published.

1818 Marx born.

1819 de Maistre's *Du Pape* (*The Pope*) is published.

1820 James Mill publishes "Essay on Government."

1821 Hegel publishes *Philosophy of the Right*.

1825 Robert Owen establishes utopian community in the U.S.

1830 French choose Louis-Phillippe to rule as "citizen-king" following the July Revolution.

Samuel Taylor Coleridge publishes *The Constitution of Church and State*.

1831 Hegel dies.

1832 Jeremy Bentham dies.

1833 Great Britain abolishes slavery.

1837 Carlyle publishes *History of the French Revolution*.

1840 Pierre-Joseph Proudhon's *What is Property?* is published.

1844 Engels publishes *Conditions of the Working Class in England*.

Nietzsche born.

1845 Margaret Fuller publishes *Women in the Nineteenth Century*.

The term "Manifest Destiny" first appears in U.S. publications.

1846 Marx publishes *The German Ideology*.

1848 Revolutions sweep Europe.

Marx and Engels' *Communist Manifesto* first published in England.

J. S. Mill publishes *Principles of Political Economy*.

Henry Davis Thoreau publishes essay "Civil Disobedience."

1851 Auguste Comte publishes *Systeme de Politique Positive* (System of Positive Polity).

1854 Wilhelm von Humboldt's *The Sphere and Duties of Government* published.

1856 De Tocqueville publishes *L'Ancien Régime*.

Freud born.

1859	J. S. Mill publishes *Essay on Liberty*.
	Charles Darwin publishes *The Origin of Species*.
1861	American Civil War begins.
	Russia emanicipates its serfs.
1863	J. S. Mill publishes *Utilitarianism*.
	Abraham Lincoln's Emancipation Proclamation frees U.S. slaves.
1864	Ferdinand Lassalle is killed in a duel.
1865	Lincoln is assassinated.
1867	Marx publishes first volume of *Das Kapital*.
1869	Gandhi born.
	J. S. Mill publishes *The Subjection of Women*.
1870	Lenin born.
1872	Nietzsche publishes *The Birth of Tragedy*.
	Marx secures the explusion of Bakunin from the International Workingmen's Association.
1873	J. S. Mill dies.
1882	Bakunin publishes *God and the State*.
1883	Marx dies.
	Mussolini born.
	Keynes born.
1884	Engels publishes *The Origin of the Family, Private Property and the State*.
	William Graham Sumner's *What Social Classes Owe to Each Other* published.
1887	Theodor Herzl organizes the first Zionist World Congress.
1889	Edward Bellamy publishes *Looking Backward*.
1893	Emile Durkheim publishes *The Division of Labor in Society*.
1902	Kropotkin's *Mutual Aid* is published.
	Vladimir Lenin publishes *Chto Dielat?* (*What Is To Be Done?*) one of the primary works of Soviet communism.

1904	Leonard Hobhouse's *Democracy and Reaction* is published.
1910	Emma Goldman's *Anarchism and Other Essays* published.
1911	Robert Michels's *Zur Soziologie des Partweiwesens in der modernen Demokratie* (*Political Parties: A Sociological Study of the Oligarchical Tendencies of Modern Democracy*) published.
1912	Chinese Republic declared. Confucian-based imperial system ends.
	Walter Rauschenbusch publishes *Christianity and the Social Crisis*.
1916	Giovanni Gentile's *Teoria generale dello spirito come atto puro* (*The Theory of Mind as Pure Act*) is published.
1917	The Bolsheviks gain power in the Russian Revolution.
	U.S. Congress approves 18th Amendment, starting the Prohibition era.
	John Rawls's *A Theory for Justice* published.
1920	Richard Tawney's *The Acquisitive Society* is published.
	The Nineteenth Amendment, guaranteeing women's right to vote, becomes law in the United States.
	Max Weber publishes *The Protestant Ethic and the Spirit of Capitalism*.
1921	Nikolay Bukharin publishes *The Theory of Historical Materialism*.
	Antonio Gramsci helps found the Italian Communist Party.
1923	The Institute for Social Research, also known as the Frankfurt School, is founded as part of the University of Frankfurt.
1925	Scopes Trial takes place in Tenneessee, U.S.
	Hitler publishes *Mein Kampf*.
1927	John Dewey publishes *The Public and its Problems*.

Freud's *The Future of Illusion* is published.

Heidegger publishes *Being and Time*.

1929 Russian revolutionary leader Leon Trotsky exiled from the Soviet Union.

1930 Max Horkheimer becomes director at the Institute for Social Research.

Freud's *Civilization and its Discontents* is translated.

Gandhi leads the famous 200-mile march to the sea.

Trotsky publishes *The Permanent Revolution*.

1932 Niebuhr's *Moral Man and Immoral Society* published.

1933 Hitler and the Nazi Party come to power in Germany.

Heidegger is appointed rector of the University of Freiburg by the Nazi government.

The Institute of Social Research moves to the U.S. to escape the Nazis; many German-Jewish scholars are forced to flee Germany.

1934 Mao Tse-tung and the Chinese Red Army embark on the Long March.

1936 John Maynard Keynes's *The General Theory of Employment, Interest and Money* is printed.

1937 Bukharin is put on trial and executed by the Soviet Union.

1938 Benedetto Croce publishes *History as the Story of Liberty*.

1940 Leon Trotsky assassinated.

1942 Albert Camus publishes *The Stranger* and *The Myth of Sisyphus*.

Joseph Schumpeter's *Capitalism, Socialism and Democracy* published.

1943 Jean-Paul Sartre's *Being and Nothingness* is published.

1944 Friedrich von Hayek publishes *The Road to Serfdom*.

1945 Dietrich Bonhoeffer executed for his role in a plot to assassinate Hitler.

Karl Popper's *The Open Society and Its Enemies* published.

1947 India becomes an independent nation.

Horkheimer publishes *Eclipse of Reason* and *Dialectics of Enlightenment* (with Theodor Adorno).

1948 Ghandi is assassinated by a Hindu radical.

1949 Mao becomes chairman of the newly formed People's Republic of China.

Chinese Communist government condemns Confucianism and religions.

Martin Buber publishes *Paths in Utopia*.

Simone de Beauvoir publishes *The Second Sex*.

1950 The beginnings of the Red Scare and McCarthyism in the U.S.

1951 Hannah Arendt publishes *The Origins of Totalitarianism*.

1953 The Institute for Social Research moves back to Germany.

1954 The U.S. Supreme Court, in *Brown v. Board of Education*, declares segregation of schools to be unconstitutional.

Frantz Fanon publishes *The Wretched of the Earth*.

1957 Sir Isaiah Berlin writes "Two Concepts of Liberty."

1958 Arendt publishes *The Human Condition*.

Mao begins social programs in China known as the "Great Leap Forward."

1959 Ernst Bloch publishes *The Principle of Hope*.

John Birch Society is founded.

1961 Michel Foucault publishes *Madness and Civilization*.

1962 U.S. Supreme Court rules in *Engel v. Vitale* that school prayer violates the First Amendment.

1963   Martin Luther King, Jr., writes "Letters From a Birmingham Jail."

The March on Washington, a peaceful demonstration for civil rights, has over 200,000 participants.

1965   Louis Althusser publishes *For Marx.*

1966   The Cultural Revolution begins in China. Mao's "Little Red Book" is published.

Althusser publishes *Reading Capital.*

1968   Martin Luther King, Jr., is assassinated.

1969   The modern gay rights movement begins with the Stonewall riots.

Isaiah Berlin publishes *Four Essays on Liberty.*

Herbert Marcuse publishes *An Essay on Liberation.*

1972   U.S. Supreme Court rules that capital punishment is unconstitutional.

1973   U.S. Supreme Court legalizes abortion in *Roe v. Wade.*

Gustavo Gutiérrez's *A Theology of Liberation* is published.

1974   Robert Nozick's *Anarchy, State and Utopia* published.

U.S. President Richard Nixon resigns from office due to the Watergate scandal.

1975   Foucault publishes *Discipline and Punish.*

Michael Oakeshott's *On Human Conduct* published.

J. G. A. Pocock publishes *The Machiavellian Moment.*

1976   U.S. Supreme Court allows capital punishment to resume in certain states.

Francis Schaeffer's *The Rise and Decline of Western Thought and Culture* published.

1977   In China, Communist government opposition to Confucianism and religions ends.

1983   Jurgen Habermas's *Moral Consciousness and Communicative Action* is published.

1984   Benjamin Barber publishes *Strong Democracy.*

1989   The Berlin Wall is dismantled and the border between East and West Germany is opened.

1990   The Russian parliament votes to abolish the laws of the USSR, and the Russian Federation becomes a sovereign state.

Nelson Mandela is released after almost 26 years in prison.

1991   James Davison Hunter publishes *Culture Wars.*

South Africa ends apartheid.

1992   Francis Fukuyama publishes *The End of History and the Last Man.*

INDEX

Boldface page numbers indicate extensive treatment of a topic; *italic* page numbers denote illustrations.